*Recursive Methods
in Economic Dynamics*

Recursive Methods
in Economic Dynamics

NANCY L. STOKEY
AND
ROBERT E. LUCAS, JR.

with Edward C. Prescott

Harvard University Press

Cambridge, Massachusetts, and London, England

Library of Congress Cataloging-in-Publication Data

Stokey, Nancy L.
    Recursive methods in economic dynamics / Nancy L. Stokey and
Robert E. Lucas, Jr., with the collaboration of Edward C. Prescott.
        p.   cm.
    Bibliography: p.
    Includes index.
    ISBN 0-674-75096-9 (alk. paper)
    1. Economics, Mathematical. 2. Dynamic programming. I. Lucas,
Robert E.   II. Prescott, Edward C.   III. Title.
HB135.S7455   1989   88-37681
330'.01'51—dc19   CIP

To our parents

Preface

This book was motivated by our conviction that recursive methods should be part of every economist's set of analytical tools. Applications of these methods appear in almost every substantive area of economics—the theory of investment, the theory of the consumer, search theory, public finance, growth theory, and so on—but neither the methods nor the applications have ever been drawn together and presented in a systematic way. Our goal has been to do precisely this. We have attempted to develop the basic tools of recursive analysis in a systematic, rigorous way, while at the same time stressing the wide applicability of recursive methods and suggesting new areas where they might usefully be exploited.

Our first outlines for the book included a few chapters devoted to mathematical preliminaries, followed by numerous chapters treating the various substantive areas of economics to which recursive methods have been applied. We hoped to keep the technical material to a minimum, by simply citing the existing literature for most of the required mathematical results, and to focus on substantive issues. This plan failed rather quickly, as it soon became apparent that the reader would be required either to take most of the important results on faith or else to keep a dozen mathematics books close at hand and refer to them constantly. Neither approach seemed reasonable, and we were led to make major alterations in the overall structure of the book.

The methods became the organizing principle, and we began to focus on providing a fairly comprehensive, rigorous, and self-contained treatment of the tools and techniques used in recursive analysis. We then found it natural to group applications by the nature of the technical tools involved rather than by their economic substance. Thus Parts II–IV of the book deal with deterministic models, stochastic models, and equilibrium theory, respectively, with substantive applications appearing in all three places. Indeed, many of the applications appear more than once, with different aspects of the same problem treated as the appropriate tools are developed.

Once we had decided to write a book focused on analytical tools rather than on economic substance, the choice of technical level became more important than ever. We wanted the book to be rigorous enough to be useful to researchers and at the same time to be accessible to as wide an audience as possible. In pursuing these twin goals we have aimed for a rigorous and fairly general treatment of the analytical tools, but one that requires relatively little by way of mathematical background. The reader should have had a course in advanced calculus or real analysis and should be comfortable with delta-epsilon arguments. A little background in probability theory is also useful, although not at all essential. The other mathematical topics that arise—and there are a wide variety—are treated in a largely self-contained way.

The most difficult decision we faced was choosing the appropriate level at which to treat probability theory. Our first inclination was to restrict attention to discrete probabilities and continuous densities, but in the end we found that this approach caused more trouble than it saved. We were pleased to find that a relatively small investment in measure theory produced enormous returns. We provide a modest number of definitions and basic results from the abstract theory of measure and integration in Chapter 7, and then draw on them repeatedly in our treatment of stochastic models. The reader will find that this investment yields returns elsewhere as well: measure theory is rapidly becoming the standard language of the economics of uncertainty.

The term *recursive methods* is broad enough to include a variety of interesting topics that might have been included in the book but are not. There is a large literature on linear-quadratic formulations of dynamic problems that, except for examples discussed briefly in Chapters 4 and 9, we ignore. There is also a growing body of expertise on methods for the numerical solution of recursive models that we have not attempted to incorporate in this volume. Although a wide variety of dynamic games can be analyzed by recursive methods, our examples of equilibrium are almost exclusively competitive. We have included a large collection of applications, but we certainly have not exhausted the many applied literatures where recursive methods are being used. Yet these omissions are not, we feel, cause for apology. The book is long enough as it is, and we will certainly not be disappointed if one of the functions it serves is to stimulate the reader to a more serious exploration of some of these closely related areas.

We have tried to write this book in a way that will make it useful for several different types of readers. Those who are familiar with dynamic economic models and have specific questions in mind are invited simply to consult the table of contents and proceed to the particular topics that interest them. We have tried to make chapters and sections sufficiently self-contained so that the book can be used in this way. Primarily, however, the book is directed at the reader with little or no background in dynamic models. The manuscript has, at a variety of stages, been used for graduate-level courses at Chicago, Minnesota, Northwestern, and elsewhere, and we have been gratified with the response from students. The book is about the right length and level for a year-long course for second-year students but can easily be adapted for shorter courses as well. After the introductory material in Chapters 1 and 2, it is probably advisable to cover Chapter 3 in detail, skim Section 4.1, cover Section 4.2 in detail, and then choose a few applications from Chapter 5. For a one-quarter course, there are then several possibilities. One could skip to Chapters 15 and 16, and if time permits, go on to 17 and 18. Alternatively, with measure theory as a prerequisite, one could proceed to Section 8.1, then to Section 9.2, and then to applications from Chapter 10. Covering the required measure theory, Sections 7.0–7.5, takes about three weeks and could be done in a one-semester course.

A consequence of our decision to make the book technically self-contained is that completing it involved a much higher ratio of exposition to new results than any of us had anticipated. Ed Prescott found he did not wish to spend so much of his time away from the research frontier, and so proposed the reduced level of involvement reflected in the phrase "with the collaboration of." However, there is no part of the book that has not benefited from his ideas and contributions.

We are grateful also to many friends and colleagues for their comments and criticism. In particular we thank Andrew Caplin, V. V. Chari, Lars Hansen, Hugo Hopenhayn, Larry Jones, Lars Ljungquist, Rodolfo Manuelli, Masao Ogaki, José Victor Rios-Rull, and José Scheinkman for fruitful discussions. Arthur Kupferman read large portions of the manuscript at an early stage, and his detailed comments enhanced both the content and the style of the final product. We are also indebted to Ricard Torres, whose comments on the entire manuscript led to many improvements and, in several places, to major revisions along lines he proposed.

We owe special thanks to Michael Aronson, whose patience and enthusiasm have supported this project from its beginning—more years ago than any of us cares to remember. We are grateful too to Jodi Simpson, whose editing led to many refinements of style and logic; her skillful work is much valued. June Nason began typing our early drafts on an IBM Selectric and stayed to finish the job on a LaserJet printer. We appreciate her cheerful assistance, and the tact she showed by never asking how a job could remain urgent for six years. Finally, we would like to thank Mary Ellen Geer for helping us see the book through to its completion.

Contents

III   STOCHASTIC MODELS

IV COMPETITIVE EQUILIBRIUM

Symbols Used

$x \in X$	element
$A \subseteq B, A \subset B$	subset, strict subset
$A \supseteq B, A \supset B$	superset, strict superset
$\cup, \cap$	union, intersection
$\emptyset$	empty set
$A \backslash B$	difference, defined only if $A \supseteq B$
A^c	complement
$\mathring{A}, \overline{A}$	interior, closure
∂A	boundary
χ_A	indicator function
$X \times Y$	Cartesian product
$\mathbf{R}, \overline{\mathbf{R}}$	real numbers, extended real numbers
$\mathbf{R}^l$	l-dimensional Euclidean space
$\mathbf{R}^l_+, \mathbf{R}^l_{++}$	subspace of $\mathbf{R}^l$ containing nonnegative vectors, strictly positive vectors
$(a, b), [a, b]$	open interval, closed interval
$(a, b], [a, b)$	half-open intervals
$\mathscr{B}, \mathscr{B}^l$	Borel subsets of $\mathbf{R}$, of $\mathbf{R}^l$
$\mathscr{B}_X$	Borel subsets of X, defined for $X \in \mathscr{B}^l$
$\rho(x, y)$	distance
$\|x\|$	norm
$C(X)$	space of bounded continuous functions on X
f^+, f^-	positive and negative parts of the function f
$\{x_i\}_{i=1}^n$	finite sequence
$\{x_i\}_{i=1}^\infty$	infinite sequence

$x_i \to x$	converges
$x_i \uparrow x$	converges from below
$x_i \downarrow x$	converges from above
$(X, \mathscr{X})$	measurable space
$M(X, \mathscr{X})$	space of measurable real-valued functions on $(X, \mathscr{X})$
$M^+(X, \mathscr{X})$	subset of $M(X, \mathscr{X})$ containing nonnegative functions
$B(X, \mathscr{X})$	space of bounded measurable real-valued functions on $(X, \mathscr{X})$
$(X, \mathscr{X}, \mu)$	measure space
$L(X, \mathscr{X}, \mu)$	space of μ-integrable functions on $(X, \mathscr{X})$
$\Lambda(X, \mathscr{X})$	space of probability measures on $(X, \mathscr{X})$
μ-a.e.	except on a set A with $\mu(A) = 0$
$\mu \perp \lambda$	mutually singular
$\mu \ll \lambda$	absolutely continuous with respect to
$\lambda_n \to \lambda$	converges in the total variation norm
$\lambda_n \Rightarrow \lambda$	converges weakly
$\mathscr{A} \times \mathscr{B}$	product σ-algebra

PART I

The Recursive Approach

1 Introduction

Research in economic dynamics has undergone a remarkable transformation in recent decades. A generation ago, empirical researchers were typically obliged to add dynamic and stochastic elements as afterthoughts to predictions about behavior derived from static, deterministic economic models. Today, in every field of application, we have theories that deal explicitly with rational economic agents operating through time in stochastic environments. The idea of an economic equilibrium has undergone a similar evolution: it no longer carries the connotation of a system at rest. Powerful methods are now available for analyzing theoretical models with equilibrium outcomes described by the same kinds of complicated stochastic processes that we use to describe observed economic behavior.

These theoretical developments are based on a wide variety of results in economics, mathematics, and statistics: the contingent-claim view of economic equilibria introduced by Arrow (1953) and Debreu (1959), the economic applications of the calculus of variations pioneered long ago by Ramsey (1928) and Hotelling (1931), the theory of dynamic programming of Bellman (1957) and Blackwell (1965). Our goal in this book is to provide self-contained treatments of these theoretical ideas that form the basis of modern economic dynamics. Our approach is distinguished by its systematic use of recursive methods, methods that make it possible to treat a wide variety of dynamic economic problems—both deterministic and stochastic—from a fairly unified point of view.

To illustrate what we mean by a recursive approach to economic dynamics, we begin with a list of concrete examples, drawn from the much longer list of applications to be treated in detail in later chapters. These examples also serve to illustrate the kinds of substantive economic questions that can be studied by the analytical methods in this book.

First consider an economy that produces a single good that can be either consumed or invested. The quantity consumed yields immediate utility to the single decision-maker, a "social planner." The quantity invested augments the capital stock, thereby making increased production possible in the future. What is the consumption–investment policy that maximizes the sum of utilities over an infinite planning horizon?

Next consider an economy that is otherwise similar to the one just described, but that is subject to random shocks affecting the amount of output that can be produced with a given stock of capital. How should the consumption-investment decision be made if the objective is to maximize the expected sum of utilities?

Suppose a worker wishes to maximize the present value of his earnings. In any period he is presented with a wage offer at which he can work one unit of time or zero. If he works, he takes the earnings and retains the same job next period. If he does not work, he searches, an activity that yields him a new wage offer from a known probability distribution. What decision rule should he adopt if his goal is to maximize the expected present discounted value of his lifetime earnings?

A store manager has in stock a given number of items of a specific type. Demand is stochastic, so in any period he may either stock out and forgo the sales he would have made with a larger inventory or incur the costs of carrying over unsold items. At the beginning of each period he can place an order for more items. The cost of this action includes a fixed delivery charge plus a charge per item ordered. The order must be placed before the manager knows the current period demand. If his goal is to maximize the expected discounted present value of profits, when should he place an order; and when an order is placed, how large should it be?

An economy is endowed with a fixed number of productive assets that have exogenously given yields described by a stochastic process. These assets are privately owned, and claims to all of them are traded on a competitive equities market. How are the competitive equilibrium prices in this market related to consumer preferences over consumption of goods and to the current state of the yield process? How is the answer to this question altered if assets can be produced?

A monopolist faces a stochastically shifting demand curve for his product. His current production capacity is determined by his past investments, but he has the option to invest in additions to capacity, additions that will be available for production in the future. What investment strategy maximizes the expected discounted present value of profits? Alternatively, suppose there are many firms in this industry. In competitive equilibrium what are the investment strategies for all of these firms, and what do they imply for the behavior of industry production and prices?

These problems evidently have much in common. In each case a decision-maker—a social planner, a worker, a manager, an entire market, a firm, or collection of firms—must choose a sequence of actions through time. In the first example there is no uncertainty, so the entire sequence may as well be chosen at the outset. In the other five examples the environment is subject to unpredictable outside shocks, and it is clear that the best future actions depend on the magnitudes of these shocks. Consider how we might formulate each of these problems mathematically and what we might mean by a recursive approach to each.

The first example is the problem of optimal savings that Frank Ramsey formulated and solved in 1928. Ramsey viewed the problem as one of maximizing a function (total utility) of an infinity of variables (consumption and capital stock at each date) subject to the constraints imposed by the technology. He set up the problem in continuous time and applied the calculus of variations to obtain a very sharp characterization of the utility-maximizing dynamics: the capital stock should converge monotonically to the level that, if sustained, maximizes consumption per unit of time.

In the Ramsey problem the feature of the production possibility set that changes over time is the current stock of capital. This observation suggests that an alternative way to describe the optimal policy is in terms of a function that gives the society's optimal current investment as a function of its current capital stock; and, in fact, Ramsey's solution can be expressed in this way. Thus an alternative mathematical strategy is to seek the optimal savings function directly and then to use this function to compute the optimal sequence of investments from any initial stock. This way of looking at the problem—decide on the immediate action to take as a function of the current situation—is called a recursive formulation because it exploits the observation that a decision problem of the same general structure recurs each period.

Since Ramsey completely solved his problem using variational methods, this example is better suited to defining a recursive approach than to motivating it. Consider next the stochastic variation on this problem. In this case it obviously makes no sense to choose a deterministic plan of investments for all future dates: the best future choices will depend on how much output is available at the time, and that in turn will depend on as-yet-unrealized shocks to the productivity of capital. To carry out the analogue to Ramsey's strategy, one must follow the contingent-claim formulation introduced by Kenneth Arrow (1953) and Gerard Debreu (1959) and view an investment plan as a sequence of investments, each of which is made contingent on the history of shocks that have been realized up to the time the decision is actually implemented.

This contingent-claim formulation is an enormously useful point of view for many purposes (and is, indeed, essential to the analysis in parts of this book), but in the current context it leads to a maximization problem in a space that is much more difficult to work in than the space of sequences Ramsey used. Yet a recursive formulation of the stochastic Ramsey problem is hardly more complicated than the one for the deterministic case. With random shocks the current state of the system is described by two variables: capital and the current shock. We search, in this case, for a savings function that expresses the optimal investment decision as a function of these two variables only.

The optimal job-search problem can also be set up as one of choosing a sequence of contingent actions, but it is awkward to do so. In this problem the shocks the decision-maker observes depend on his actions: if he takes a job, he never learns what wage offers he would have received if he had kept looking. Formulated recursively, the problem becomes one of choosing a single number, the reservation wage. The worker should then accept any job offering a wage above this level and reject any offer below it. The inventory problem discussed next has a similar structure, although in this case two numbers must be chosen: the inventory level that triggers an order and the order size.

The asset-pricing example does not have a single decision-maker, as did the first four examples. The issue here is the determination of market equilibrium prices. We can, for this economy, calculate the Arrow-Debreu prices for dated claims to goods, contingent on the histories of shocks up to the date at which the exchange is to occur. Alternatively (and, one can show, equivalently), we can think of prices as being set in a sequence of spot equity markets. From this second, recursive viewpoint we seek an expression for equilibrium prices as functions of the system's state that is exactly analogous to expressing agents' decisions as functions of the state.

Our final example was a microeconomic problem involving investment in a single industry with given consumer demand behavior. When the industry is a monopoly, this problem has a single decision-maker and thus is similar in structure to the social planner's problem of choosing optimal savings in a stochastic economy. If the industry is competitive, we would like to solve simultaneously for equilibrium prices and investment levels, both as functions of the industry state. As Harold Hotelling conjectured in his 1931 paper on exhaustible resources, in this case the industry as a whole solves a consumer surplus maximization problem that has exactly the same mathematical structure as does the monopoly problem.

As we hope these examples illustrate, a great variety of economic and other decision problems are quite naturally cast in a recursive framework. A first purpose of this book, then, is to present in a unified way the theory of recursive decision-making—dynamic programming (in Richard Bellman's terminology)—and to illustrate the application of this theory to a wide variety of economic problems.

A second purpose is to show how the methods of dynamic programming can be combined with those of modern general equilibrium theory to yield tractable models of dynamic economic systems. This possibility is easiest to see when the system as a whole itself solves a maximum problem, and some of our applications take this form. We will also consider systems the behavior of which cannot be mimicked by any individual decision problem but to which recursive methods can still fruitfully be applied.

These examples give a sense of the kinds of economic issues we will address and of the general point of view from which we intend to study them. Because at this informal level it is not possible to discuss the technical questions such problems raise, we cannot at this juncture provide a useful overview of the remainder of the book. Accordingly, in the next chapter we study a concrete economic example that illustrates the range of analytical methods we will be dealing with. At that point we will be in a position to outline the rest of the book.

2   An Overview

In this chapter we preview the recursive methods of analysis to be developed in detail in the rest of the book. This material falls into three broad parts, and the remainder of the book is structured accordingly. Part II deals with methods for solving deterministic optimization problems, Part III with the extension of these methods to problems that include stochastic shocks, and Part IV with ways of using solutions of either type within a competitive equilibrium framework.

To make this preview as concrete as possible, we examine these three sets of issues by looking at a specific example, a one-sector model of economic growth. Our goal is not to provide a substantive treatment of growth theory but to illustrate the types of arguments and results that are developed in the later chapters of the book—arguments that can be applied to a wide variety of problems. A few of these problems were mentioned in Chapter 1, and many more will be discussed in detail in Chapters 5, 10, 13, 16, 17, and 18, all of which are devoted exclusively to substantive applications. With that said, in this chapter we focus exclusively on the example of economic growth.

In the next three sections we consider resource allocation in an economy composed of many identical, infinitely lived households. In each period t there is a single good, y_t, that is produced using two inputs: capital, k_t, in place at the beginning of the period, and labor, n_t. A production function relates output to inputs, $y_t = F(k_t, n_t)$. In each period current output must be divided between current consumption, c_t, and gross investment, i_t,

$$(1) \qquad c_t + i_t \leq y_t = F(k_t, n_t).$$

This consumption-savings decision is the only allocation decision the economy must make. Capital is assumed to depreciate at a constant rate

$0 < \delta < 1$, so capital is related to gross investment by

(2) $k_{t+1} = (1 - \delta)k_t + i_t.$

Labor is taken to be supplied inelastically, so $n_t = 1$, all t. Finally, preferences over consumption, common to all households, are taken to be of the form

(3) $\displaystyle\sum_{t=0}^{\infty} \beta^t U(c_t),$

where $0 < \beta < 1$ is a discount factor.

In Sections 2.1 and 2.2 we study the problem of optimal growth. Specifically, in Section 2.1 we examine the problem of maximizing (3) subject to (1) and (2), given an initial capital stock k_0. In Section 2.2 we modify this planning problem to include exogenous random shocks to the technology in (1), in this case taking the preferences of households over random consumption sequences to be the expected value of the function in (3). In Section 2.3 we return to the deterministic model. We begin by characterizing the paths for consumption and capital accumulation that would arise in a competitive market economy composed of many households, each with the preferences in (3), and many firms, each with the technology in (1) and (2). We then consider the relationship between the competitive equilibrium allocation and the solution to the planning problem found earlier. We conclude in Section 2.4 with a more detailed overview of the remainder of the book, discussing briefly the content of each of the later chapters.

2.1   A Deterministic Model of Optimal Growth

In this section we study the problem of optimal growth when there is no uncertainty. Assume that the production function is $y_t = F(k_t, n_t)$, where $F: \mathbf{R}_+^2 \to \mathbf{R}_+$ is continuously differentiable, strictly increasing, homogeneous of degree one, and strictly quasi-concave, with

$$F(0, n) = 0, \quad F_k(k, n) > 0, \quad F_n(k, n) > 0, \quad \text{all } k, n > 0;$$

$$\lim_{k \to 0} F_k(k, 1) = \infty, \quad \lim_{k \to \infty} F_k(k, 1) = 0.$$

Assume that the size of the population is constant over time and normalize the size of the available labor force to unity. Then actual labor
supply must satisfy

(1a) $0 \leq n_t \leq 1$,   all t.

Assume that capital decays at the fixed rate $0 < \delta \leq 1$. Then consumption c_t, gross investment $i_t = k_{t+1} - (1 - \delta)k_t$, and output $y_t =$
$F(k_t, n_t)$ must satisfy the feasibility constraint

(1b) $c_t + k_{t+1} - (1 - \delta)k_t \leq F(k_t, n_t)$,   all t.

Assume that all of the households in this economy have identical preferences over intertemporal consumption sequences. These common
preferences take the additively separable form

(2) $$u(c_0, c_1, \ldots) = \sum_{t=0}^{\infty} \beta^t U(c_t),$$

where the discount factor is $0 < \beta < 1$, and where the current-period
utility function $U: \mathbf{R}_+ \to \mathbf{R}$ is bounded, continuously differentiable,
strictly increasing, and strictly concave, with $\lim_{c \to 0} U'(c) = \infty$. Households do not value leisure.

Now consider the problem faced by a benevolent social planner, one
whose objective is to maximize (2) by choosing sequences $\{(c_t, k_{t+1}, n_t)\}_{t=0}^{\infty}$,
subject to the feasibility constraints in (1), given $k_0 > 0$. Two features of
any optimum are apparent. First, it is clear that output will not be
wasted. That is, (1b) will hold with equality for all t, and we can use it to
eliminate c_t from (2). Second, since leisure is not valued and the marginal
product of labor is always positive, it is clear that an optimum requires
$n_t = 1$, all t. Hence k_t and y_t represent both capital and output per
worker and capital and output in total. It is therefore convenient to
define $f(k) = F(k, 1) + (1 - \delta)k$ to be the total supply of goods available
per worker, including undepreciated capital, when beginning-of-period
capital is k.

Exercise 2.1   Show that the assumptions on F above imply that
$f: \mathbf{R}_+ \to \mathbf{R}_+$ is continuously differentiable, strictly increasing, and strictly

concave, with

$$f(0) = 0, \quad f'(k) > 0, \quad \lim_{k \to 0} f'(k) = \infty, \quad \lim_{k \to \infty} f'(k) = 1 - \delta.$$

The planning problem can then be written as

(3) $$\max_{\{k_{t+1}\}_{t=0}^{\infty}} \sum_{t=0}^{\infty} \beta^t U[f(k_t) - k_{t+1}]$$

(4) $$\text{s.t.} \quad 0 \le k_{t+1} \le f(k_t), \quad t = 0, \ldots;$$

$$k_0 > 0 \quad \text{given.}$$

Although ultimately we are interested in the case where the planning horizon is infinite, it is instructive to begin with the (much easier!) problem of a finite horizon. If the horizon in (3) were a finite value T instead of infinity, then (3)–(4) would be an entirely standard concave programming problem. With a finite horizon, the set of sequences $\{k_{t+1}\}_{t=0}^{T}$ satisfying (4) is a closed, bounded, and convex subset of $\mathbf{R}^{T+1}$, and the objective function (3) is continuous and strictly concave. Hence there is exactly one solution, and it is completely characterized by the Kuhn-Tucker conditions.

To obtain these conditions note that since $f(0) = 0$ and $U'(0) = \infty$, it is clear that the inequality constraints in (4) do not bind except for k_{T+1}, and it is also clear that $k_{T+1} = 0$. Hence the solution satisfies the first-order and boundary conditions

(5) $$\beta f'(k_t) U'[f(k_t) - k_{t+1}] = U'[f(k_{t-1}) - k_t], \quad t = 1, 2, \ldots, T;$$

(6) $$k_{T+1} = 0, \quad k_0 > 0 \quad \text{given.}$$

Equation (5) is a second-order difference equation in k_t; hence it has a two-parameter family of solutions. The unique optimum for the maximization problem of interest is the one solution in this family that in addition satisfies the two boundary conditions in (6). The following exercise illustrates how (5)–(6) can be used to solve for the optimum in a particular example.

Exercise 2.2   Let $f(k) = k^\alpha$, $0 < \alpha < 1$, and let $U(c) = \ln(c)$. (No, this does not fit all of the assumptions we placed on f and U above, but go ahead anyway.)

a.   Write (5) for this case and use the change of variable $z_t = k_t/k_{t-1}^\alpha$ to convert the result into a first-order difference equation in z_t. Plot z_{t+1} against z_t and plot the 45° line on the same diagram.

b.   The boundary condition (6) implies that $z_{T+1} = 0$. Using this condition, show that the unique solution is

$$z_t = \alpha\beta \, \frac{1 - (\alpha\beta)^{T-t+1}}{1 - (\alpha\beta)^{T-t+2}}, \quad t = 1, 2, \ldots, T + 1.$$

c.   Check that the path for capital

$$(7) \qquad k_{t+1} = \alpha\beta \, \frac{1 - (\alpha\beta)^{T-t}}{1 - (\alpha\beta)^{T-t+1}} \, k_t^\alpha, \quad t = 0, 1, \ldots, T,$$

given k_0, satisfies (5)–(6).

Now consider the infinite-horizon version of the planning problem in Exercise 2.2. Note that if T is large, then the coefficient of k_t^α in (7) is essentially constant at $\alpha\beta$ for a very long time. For the solution to the infinite-horizon problem, can we not simply take the limit of the solutions in (7) as T approaches infinity? After all, we are discussing households that discount the future at a geometric rate! Taking the limit in (7), we find that

$$(8) \qquad k_{t+1} = \alpha\beta k_t^\alpha, \quad t = 0, 1, \ldots .$$

In fact, this conjecture is correct: the limit of the solutions for the finite-horizon problems is the unique solution to the infinite-horizon problem. This is true both for the parametric example in Exercise 2.2 and for the more generally posed problem. But proving it involves establishing the legitimacy of interchanging the operators "max" and "$\lim_{T\to\infty}$"; and doing this is more challenging than one might guess.

Instead we will pursue a different approach. Equation (8) suggests another conjecture: that for the infinite-horizon problem in (3)–(4), for any U and f, the solution takes the form

$$(9) \qquad k_{t+1} = g(k_t), \quad t = 0, 1, \ldots ,$$

where $g: \mathbf{R}_+ \rightarrow \mathbf{R}_+$ is a fixed savings function. Our intuition suggests that this must be so: since the planning problem takes the same form every period, with only the beginning-of-period capital stock changing from one period to the next, what else but k_t could influence the choice of k_{t+1} and c_t? Unfortunately, Exercise 2.2 does not offer any help in pursuing this conjecture. The change of variable exploited there is obviously specific to the particular functional forms assumed, and a glance at (5) confirms that no similar method is generally applicable.

The strategy we *will* use to pursue this idea involves ignoring (5) and (6) altogether and starting afresh. Although we stated this problem as one of choosing infinite sequences $\{(c_t, k_{t+1})\}_{t=0}^{\infty}$ for consumption and capital, the problem that in fact faces the planner in period $t = 0$ is that of choosing today's consumption, c_0, and tomorrow's beginning-of-period capital, k_1, and nothing else. The rest can wait until tomorrow. If we knew the planner's preferences over these two goods, we could simply maximize the appropriate function of (c_0, k_1) over the opportunity set defined by (1b), given k_0. But what are the planner's preferences over current consumption and next period's capital?

Suppose that (3)–(4) had already been solved for all possible values of k_0. Then we could define a function $v: \mathbf{R}_+ \rightarrow \mathbf{R}$ by taking $v(k_0)$ to be the value of the maximized objective function (3), for each $k_0 \geq 0$. A function of this sort is called a *value function*. With v so defined, $v(k_1)$ would give the value of the utility from period 1 on that could be obtained with a beginning-of-period capital stock k_1, and $\beta v(k_1)$ would be the value of this utility discounted back to period 0. Then in terms of this value function v, the planner's problem in period 0 would be

(10)
$$\max_{c_0, k_1} [U(c_0) + \beta v(k_1)]$$

s.t. $\quad c_0 + k_1 \leq f(k_0),$

$\quad c_0, k_1 \geq 0, \quad k_0 > 0 \quad$ given.

If the function v were known, we could use (10) to define a function $g:$ $\mathbf{R}_+ \rightarrow \mathbf{R}_+$ as follows: for each $k_0 \geq 0$, let $k_1 = g(k_0)$ and $c_0 = f(k_0) - g(k_0)$ be the values that attain the maximum in (10). With g so defined, (9) would completely describe the dynamics of capital accumulation from any given initial stock k_0.

We do not at this point "know" v, but we have defined it as the maximized objective function for the problem in (3)–(4). Thus, if solving (10) provides the solution for that problem, then $v(k_0)$ must be the maximized objective function for (10) as well. That is, v must satisfy

$$v(k_0) = \max_{0 \le k_1 \le f(k_0)} \{U[f(k_0) - k_1] + \beta v(k_1)\},$$

where, as before, we have used the fact that goods will not be wasted.

Notice that when the problem is looked at in this recursive way, the time subscripts have become a nuisance: we do not care what the date is. We can rewrite the problem facing a planner with current capital stock k as

(11) $$v(k) = \max_{0 \le y \le f(k)} \{U[f(k) - y] + \beta v(y)\}.$$

This one equation in the unknown function v is called a *functional equation,* and we will see later that it is a very tractable mathematical object. The study of dynamic optimization problems through the analysis of such functional equations is called *dynamic programming.*

If we knew that the function v was differentiable and that the maximizing value of y—call it $g(k)$—was interior, then the first-order and envelope conditions for (11) would be

$$U'[f(k) - g(k)] = \beta v'[g(k)], \quad \text{and}$$

$$v'(k) = f'(k)U'[f(k) - g(k)],$$

respectively. The first of these conditions equates the marginal utility of consuming current output to the marginal utility of allocating it to capital and enjoying augmented consumption next period. The second condition states that the marginal value of current capital, in terms of total discounted utility, is given by the marginal utility of using the capital in current production and allocating its return to current consumption.

Exercise 2.3 We conjectured that the path for capital given by (8) was optimal for the infinite-horizon planning problem, for the functional forms of Exercise 2.2.

a. Use this conjecture to calculate v by evaluating (2) along the consumption path associated with the path for capital given by (8).

b. Verify that this function v satisfies (11).

Suppose we have established the existence of an optimal savings policy g, either by analyzing conditions (5)–(6) or by analyzing the functional equation (11). What can we do with this information? For the particular parametric example in Exercises 2.2 and 2.3, we can solve for g with pencil-and-paper methods. We can then use the resulting difference equation (8) to compute the optimal sequence of capital stocks $\{k_t\}$. This example is a carefully chosen exception: for most other parametric examples, it is not possible to obtain an explicit analytical solution for the savings function g. In such cases a numerical approach can be used to compute explicit solutions. When all parameters are specified numerically, it is possible to use an algorithm based on (11) to obtain an approximation to g. Then $\{k_t\}$ can be computed using (9), given any initial value k_0.

In addition, there are often qualitative features of the savings function g, and hence of the capital paths generated by (9), that hold under a very wide range of assumptions on f and U. Specifically, we can use either (5)–(6) or the first-order and envelope conditions for (11), together with assumptions on U and f, to characterize the optimal savings function g. We can then, in turn, use the properties of g so established to characterize solutions $\{k_t\}$ to (9). The following exercise illustrates the second of these steps.

Exercise 2.4   a. Let f be as specified in Exercise 2.1, and suppose that the optimal savings function g is characterized by a constant savings rate, $g(k) = sf(k)$, all k, where $s > 0$. Plot g, and on the same diagram plot the 45° line. The points at which $g(k) = k$ are called the *stationary solutions, steady states, rest points,* or *fixed points* of g. Prove that there is exactly one positive stationary point k^*.

   b. Use the diagram to show that if $k_0 > 0$, then the sequence $\{k_t\}$ given by (9) converges to k^* as $t \to \infty$. That is, let $\{k_t\}_{t=0}^{\infty}$ be a sequence satisfying (9), given some $k_0 \geq 0$. Prove that $\lim_{t \to \infty} k_t = k^*$, for any $k_0 > 0$. Show that this convergence is monotonic. Can it occur in a finite number of periods?

This exercise contains most of the information that can be established about the qualitative behavior of a sequence generated by a deterministic dynamic model. The stationary points have been located and characterized, their stability properties established, and the motion of the system has been described qualitatively for all possible initial positions. We take this example as a kind of image of what one might hope to establish for more complicated models, or as a source of reasonable conjectures. (Information about the rate of convergence to the steady state k^*, for k_t near k^*, can be obtained by taking a linear approximation to g in a neighborhood of k^*. Alternatively, numerical simulations can be used to study the rate of convergence over any range of interest.)

From the discussion above, we conclude that a fruitful way of analyzing a stationary, infinite-horizon optimization problem like the one in (3)–(4) is by examining the associated functional equation (11) for this example—and the difference equation (9) involving the associated policy function. Several steps are involved in carrying out this analysis.

First we need to be sure that the solution(s) to a problem posed in terms of infinite sequences are also the solution(s) to the related functional equation. That is, we need to show that by using the functional equation we have not changed the problem. Then we must develop tools for studying equations like (11). We must establish the existence and uniqueness of a value function v satisfying the functional equation and, where possible, to develop qualitative properties of v. We also need to establish properties of the associated policy function g. Finally we must show how qualitative properties of g are translated into properties of the sequences generated by g.

Since a wide variety of problems from very different substantive areas of economics all have this same mathematical structure, we want to develop these results in a way that is widely applicable. Doing this is the task of Part II.

2.2 A Stochastic Model of Optimal Growth

The deterministic model of optimal growth discussed above has a variety of stochastic counterparts, corresponding to different assumptions about the nature of the uncertainty. In this section we consider a model in which the uncertainty affects the technology only, and does so in a specific way.

Assume that output is given by $y_t = z_t f(k_t)$ where $\{z_t\}$ is a sequence of independently and identically distributed (i.i.d.) random variables, and f is defined as it was in the last section. The shocks may be thought of as arising from crop failures, technological breakthroughs, and so on. The feasibility constraints for the economy are then

(1) $k_{t+1} + c_t \leq z_t f(k_t)$, $c_t, k_{t+1} \geq 0$,   all t, all $\{z_t\}$.

Assume that the households in this economy rank stochastic consumption sequences according to the expected utility they deliver, where their underlying (common) utility function takes the same additively separable form as before:

(2) $E[u(c_0, c_1, \ldots)] = E\left[\sum_{t=0}^{\infty} \beta^t U(c_t)\right].$

Here $E(\cdot)$ denotes expected value with respect to the probability distribution of the random variables $\{c_t\}_{t=0}^{\infty}$.

Now consider the problem facing a benevolent social planner in this stochastic environment. As before, his objective is to maximize the objective function in (2) subject to the constraints in (1). Before proceeding, we need to be clear about the timing of information, actions, and decisions, about the objects of choice for the planner, and about the distribution of the random variables $\{c_t\}_{t=0}^{\infty}$.

Assume that the timing of information and actions in each period is as follows. At the beginning of period t the current value z_t of the exogenous shock is realized. Thus, the pair (k_t, z_t), and hence the value of total output $z_t f(k_t)$, are known when consumption c_t takes place and end-of-period capital k_{t+1} is accumulated. The pair (k_t, z_t) is called the *state* of the economy at date t.

As we did in the deterministic case, we can think of the planner in period 0 as choosing, in addition to the pair (c_0, k_1), an infinite sequence $\{(c_t, k_{t+1})\}_{t=1}^{\infty}$ describing all future consumption and capital pairs. In the stochastic case, however, this is not a sequence of numbers but a sequence of *contingency plans*, one for each period. Specifically, consumption c_t and end-of-period capital k_{t+1} in each period $t = 1, 2, \ldots$ are contingent on the realizations of the shocks $z_1, z_2, \ldots, z_t$. This sequence of realizations is information that is available when the decision is being carried out but is unknown in period 0 when the decision is being made.

Technically, then, the planner chooses among sequences of functions, where the tth function in the sequence has as its arguments the history $(z_1, \ldots, z_t)$ of shocks realized between the time the plan is drawn up and the time the decision is carried out. The feasible set for the planner is the set of pairs (c_0, k_1) and sequences of functions $\{[c_t(\cdot), k_{t+1}(\cdot)]\}_{t=1}^{\infty}$ that satisfy (1) for all periods and all realizations of the shocks.

For any element of this set of feasible contingency plans, the exogenously given probability distribution of the shocks determines the distribution of future consumptions, so the expectation in (2) is well defined. The next exercise indicates the issues involved when one views the problem directly as one of choosing a sequence of contingency plans.

Exercise 2.5   Consider the finite-horizon version of the planning problem, with the objective function in (2), the constraints in (1), and the horizon T. Assume that the shocks $\{z_t\}_{t=0}^{T}$ take on only the finite list of values $a_1, \ldots, a_n$; and assume that the probabilities of these outcomes are $\pi_1, \ldots, \pi_n$ respectively in each period. State the first-order conditions for this problem. (This is mainly bookkeeping, but working out the details is instructive. Begin by making a list of *all* decision variables. In what Euclidean space does the planner's feasible set lie?)

This is one way of setting out the problem of optimal growth under uncertainty. There is another way, the analogue of the recursive formulation for the deterministic case. Here we let $v(k, z)$ be the value of the maximized objective (2) when the initial state is (k, z). Then a choice (c, y) of current consumption c and end-of-period capital y yields current utility $U(c)$ and implies that the system next period will be in the state (y, z'), where z' will be chosen by "nature" according to the fixed distribution governing the exogenous shocks. The maximum expected utility that can be obtained from this position is $v(y, z')$; so its discounted value as viewed in the current period, with z' unknown, is $\beta E[v(y, z')]$. These considerations motivate the functional equation

$$(3) \qquad v(k, z) = \max_{0 \le y \le f(k)} \{U[zf(k) - y] + \beta E[v(y, z')]\}.$$

The study of (3) yields the optimal choice of capital $y^* = g(k, z)$ as a function of the state (k, z) at the time the decision is taken. From this recursive point of view, then, the stochastic optimal growth problem is formally very similar to the deterministic one.

The methods used to characterize the optimal policy in the stochastic case are completely analogous to those used for the deterministic case. If we assume differentiability and an interior optimum, the first-order condition for (3) is

$$U'[zf(k) - g(k, z)] = \beta E\{v_1[g(k, z), z']\}.$$

This condition implicitly defines a policy function g that has as its arguments the two state variables k and z. Then the optimal capital path is given by the stochastic difference equation

(4) $k_{t+1} = g(k_t, z_t),$

where $\{z_t\}$ is an i.i.d. sequence of random shocks. The following exercise looks at (3)–(4) for the special case of log utility and Cobb-Douglas technology studied in the last section.

Exercise 2.6 Let $U(c) = \ln(c)$ and $f(k) = k^\alpha$, $0 < \alpha < 1$, as we did in Exercises 2.2–2.4. Conjecture that an optimal policy is, as before,

(5) $k_{t+1} = \alpha\beta z_t k_t^\alpha,$ all t, all $\{z_t\}$.

Calculate the value of the objective function (2) under this policy, given $k_0 = k$ and $z_0 = z$, and call this value $v(k, z)$. Verify that the function v so defined satisfies (3).

Working out the dynamics of the state variable k_t that are implied by the policy function g is quite different in the stochastic case. Equation (4) and its specialization (5) are called (first-order) *stochastic difference equations,* and the random variables $\{k_t\}$ generated by such equations are called a (first-order) *Markov process.* It is useful to recall the results obtained for the deterministic difference equation in Exercise 2.4 and to think about possible analogues for the stochastic case. Clearly, the sequence $\{k_t\}$ described by (5) is not going to converge to any single value in the presence of the recurring shocks z_t. Can anything be said about its behavior?

Taking logs in (5), we obtain

$$\ln(k_{t+1}) = \ln(\alpha\beta) + \alpha \ln(k_t) + \ln(z_t).$$

Since the shocks $\{z_t\}$ are i.i.d. random variables, so are the logs $\{\ln(z_t)\}$. Now suppose that the latter are normally distributed, with common mean μ and variance σ^2.

Exercise 2.7   Given k_0, $\{\ln(k_t)\}_{t=1}^{\infty}$ is a sequence of normally distributed random variables with means $\{\mu_t\}_{t=1}^{\infty}$ and variances $\{\sigma_t^2\}_{t=1}^{\infty}$. Find these means and variances and calculate their limiting values as $t \to \infty$.

In this example, then, the sequence of probability distributions for the random variables $\{k_t\}$ converges as t increases without bound. Moreover, the combination of linearity and normality permits explicit pencil-and-paper calculation of the distributions of all the k_t's. This type of calculation is not possible in general, but convergence of the sequence of distribution functions for the k_t's to a limiting distribution can be verified under much broader assumptions. The basic idea is as follows.

Let the sequence $\{k_t\}$ be described by (5) but drop the assumption that the z_t's are log-normally distributed. Instead let G be the (common) cumulative distribution function for the z_t's. Then given the initial capital stock $k_0 > 0$, next period's stock k_1 is a random variable whose cumulative distribution function—call it ψ_1—is determined by G. In particular, for any $a > 0$,

$$\psi_1(a) = \Pr\{k_1 \le a\} = \Pr\{\alpha\beta z_0 k_0^{\alpha} \le a\}$$

$$= \Pr\{z_0 \le a/\alpha\beta k_0^{\alpha}\} = G(a/\alpha\beta k_0^{\alpha}).$$

Thus k_0 and G determine the distribution function ψ_1 of k_1.

Since the same logic holds for any successive pair of periods, we can define the function

$$(6) \qquad H(a, b) = \Pr\{k_{t+1} \le a | k_t = b\} = G(a/\alpha\beta b^{\alpha}), \quad \text{all } a, b > 0.$$

H is called a *transition function*. With H so defined, the sequence of distribution functions $\{\psi_t\}_{t=1}^{\infty}$ for the k_t's is given inductively by

$$(7) \qquad \psi_{t+1}(a) = \Pr\{k_{t+1} \le a\} = \int H(a, b)d\psi_t(b), \quad t = 0, 1, \ldots,$$

where the distribution ψ_0 is simply a mass point at the given initial value k_0.

More generally, given a stochastic difference equation of the form in (4) and given a distribution function G for the exogenous shocks, we can define a transition function H as we did in (6). Then for any initial value $k_0 > 0$, the sequence $\{\psi_t\}$ of distribution functions for the k_t's is given by (7). Exercise 2.7 suggests that if g and G are in some suitable families, then H is such that this sequence converges (in some sense) to a limiting distribution function ψ satisfying

$$(8) \qquad \psi(k') = \int H(k', k) \, d\psi(k).$$

A distribution function ψ satisfying (8) is called an *invariant distribution* for the transition function H. The idea is that if the distribution ψ gives a probabilistic description of the capital stock k_t in any period t, then ψ also describes the distribution of the capital stock in periods $t + 1, t + 2, \ldots$. An invariant distribution is thus a stochastic analogue to a stationary point of a deterministic system.

Now suppose that g and G are given and that the associated transition function H has a unique stationary distribution ψ. Suppose further that for any $k_0 > 0$, the sequence $\{\psi_t\}$ defined by (7) converges to ψ. Let ϕ be a continuous function and consider the sample average $(1/T)\Sigma_{t=1}^{T}\phi(k_t)$ for this function, along some sample path. One might expect that this sample average is, for long time horizons, approximately equal to the mathematical expectation of ϕ taken with respect to the limiting distribution ψ. That is, one might expect that

$$(9) \qquad \lim_{T \to \infty} \frac{1}{T} \sum_{t=1}^{T} \phi(k_t) = \int \phi(k) d\psi(k),$$

at least along most sample paths. A statement of this sort is called a *law of large numbers*. Later we will specify precisely what is meant by "most sample paths" and will develop conditions under which (9) holds.

When (9) does hold, we can calculate the sample average on the left in (9) from observed time series, calculate the integral on the right in (9) from the theory, and use a comparison of the two as a test of the theory. The first calculation is easy. Much of this book is concerned with methods for carrying out the second.

As the discussion above suggests, the techniques of dynamic programming are, if anything, even more useful for analyzing stochastic models than they are for looking at deterministic problems. Exercise 2.5 illustrates the complexity of looking at stochastic, dynamic problems in terms of sequences, even when the horizon is finite. On the other hand, we will see later that functional equations like (3) are no more difficult to handle than their deterministic counterparts. The main ingredients are a convenient language for talking about distributions for stochastic shocks and a few basic results about expectation operators like the one in (3).

The solution to a functional equation like (3) involves an optimal policy function g like the one in (4), and hence we are interested in studying the properties of time series produced by systems like (4). This analysis is significantly harder than the analysis of solutions to deterministic difference equations, but it is not unmanageable. Clearly a stability theory for stochastic systems requires several things. First we must define precisely what convergence means for a sequence of distribution functions. Then we need to develop sufficient conditions on transition functions, like the function H above, to ensure that H has a unique invariant distribution and that the sequence of distribution functions given by (7) converges, in the desired sense, to that invariant distribution. Finally, to connect the theory to observed behavior, we must develop conditions under which a law of large numbers holds.

The reader should not be surprised that carrying out this agenda requires laying some preliminary groundwork. Some definitions, notation, and basic results from modern probability theory are needed, as well as some basic information about Markov processes. This preliminary material, as well as the analysis of stochastic recursive models, is the content of Part III.

2.3 Competitive Equilibrium Growth

In the last two sections we were concerned exclusively with the allocation problem faced by a hypothetical social planner. In this section we show that the solutions to planning problems of this type can, under appropriate conditions, be interpreted as predictions about the behavior of market economies. The argument establishing this is based, of course, on the classical connection between competitive equilibria and Pareto optima. These connections hold under fairly broad assumptions, and in later chapters we will establish them in a very general setting. At that time we will also show that in situations where the connection between competitive equilibria and Pareto optima breaks down, as it does in the presence of taxes or other distortions, the study of competitive equilibria can be carried out by a direct analysis of the appropriate first-order conditions.

Recall that in the models discussed above there were many identical households, and we took the (common) preferences of these households to be the preferences attributed to the social planner. In addition, there were many identical firms, all with the same constant-returns-to-scale technology, so the technology available to the economy was the same as that available to each firm. Thus, the planning problems considered in Sections 2.1 and 2.2 were Pareto problems for economies with many agents. That is, they can be viewed as problems of maximizing a weighted average of households' utilities, specialized to a case where all households had identical tastes and were given equal weight, and hence received identical allocations. Thus the solutions to planning problems of the type we considered were Pareto-optimal allocations. In this section we show that these allocations are exactly the ones that correspond to competitive equilibria. For simplicity we restrict attention here to the case of certainty and of a finite time horizon.

Suppose that we have solved the finite-horizon optimal growth problem of Section 2.1 and that $\{(c_t^*, k_{t+1}^*)\}_{t=0}^T$ is the solution. Our goal is to find prices that support these quantities as a competitive equilibrium. However, we must first specify the ownership rights of households and firms, as well as the structure of markets. It is crucial to be specific on these matters.

Assume that households own all factors of production and all shares in firms and that these endowments are equally distributed across households. Each period households sell factor services to firms and buy the goods produced by firms, consuming some and accumulating the rest as capital. Assume that firms own nothing; they simply hire capital and labor on a rental basis to produce output each period, sell the output produced back to households, and return any profits that result to shareholders. Finally, assume that all transactions take place in a single once-and-for-all market that meets in period 0. All trading takes place at that time, so all prices and quantities are determined simultaneously. No further trades are negotiated later. After this market has closed, in periods $t = 0, 1, \ldots, T$, agents simply deliver the quantities of factors and goods they have contracted to sell and receive those they have contracted to buy.

Assume that the convention for prices in this one big market is as follows. Let p_t be the price of a unit of output delivered in period t, for $t = 0, 1, \ldots, T$, expressed in abstract units-of-account. Let w_t be the price of a unit of labor delivered in period t, expressed in units of goods in period t, so that w_t is the real wage. Similarly let r_t be the real rental price of capital in period t.

Given the prices $\{(p_t, r_t, w_t)\}_{t=0}^{T}$, the problem faced by the representative firm is to choose input demands and output supplies $\{(k_t, n_t, y_t)\}_{t=0}^{T}$ that maximize net discounted profits. Thus its decision problem is

$$(1) \qquad \max \pi = \sum_{t=0}^{T} p_t[y_t - r_t k_t - w_t n_t]$$

$$(2) \qquad \text{s.t.} \quad y_t \leq F(k_t, n_t), \quad t = 0, 1, \ldots, T.$$

Given the same price sequence, the typical household must choose demand for consumption and investment, and supplies of current capital and labor, $\{(c_t, i_t, x_{t+1}, k_t, n_t)\}_{t=0}^{T}$, given initial capital holdings x_0. In making these choices the household faces several constraints. First, the total value of goods purchased cannot exceed the total value of wages plus rental income plus profits the household receives. Second, the household's holdings of real capital in each period $t + 1$ are equal to its holdings in period t, net of depreciation, plus any new investment. Third, the quantity of each factor supplied by the household in each period must be nonnegative but cannot exceed the quantity available to it in that period. Finally, consumption and capital holdings must be nonnegative. Thus its decision problem is

$$(3) \qquad \max \sum_{t=0}^{T} \beta^t U(c_t)$$

$$(4) \qquad \text{s.t.} \quad \sum_{t=0}^{T} p_t[c_t + i_t] \leq \sum_{t=0}^{T} p_t[r_t k_t + w_t n_t] + \pi;$$

$$(5) \qquad x_{t+1} = (1 - \delta)x_t + i_t, \quad t = 0, 1, \ldots, T, \text{ given } x_0;$$

$$(6) \qquad 0 \leq n_t \leq 1, 0 \leq k_t \leq x_t, \quad t = 0, 1, \ldots, T;$$

$$(7) \qquad c_t \geq 0, x_{t+1} \geq 0, \quad t = 0, 1, \ldots, T.$$

Note that capital stocks owned, x_{t+1}, and capital supplied to firms, k_{t+1}, are required to be nonnegative. However, gross investment, i_t, may be negative. This assumption is the one that was made, implicitly, in Section 2.1.

A competitive equilibrium is a set of prices $\{(p_t, r_t, w_t)\}_{t=0}^{T}$, an allocation $\{(k_t^d, n_t^d, y_t)\}_{t=0}^{T}$ for the typical firm, and an allocation $\{(c_t, i_t, x_{t+1}, k_t^s, n_t^s)\}_{t=0}^{T}$ for the typical household, such that

a. $\{(k_t^d, n_t^d, y_t)\}$ solves (1)–(2) at the stated prices;

b. $\{(c_t, i_t, x_{t+1}, k_t^s, n_t^s)\}$ solves (3)–(7) at the stated prices;

c. all markets clear: $k_t^d = k_t^s$, $n_t^d = n_t^s$, $c_t + i_t = y_t$, all t.

To find a competitive equilibrium, we begin by conjecturing that it has certain features. Later we will verify that these conjectures are correct. First, since the representative household's preferences are strictly monotone, we conjecture that goods prices are strictly positive for each period: $p_t > 0$, all t. Also, since both factors have strictly positive marginal products, we conjecture that both factor prices are strictly positive for all periods: $w_t > 0$ and $r_t > 0$, all t. Finally, since in equilibrium markets clear, we let $k_t = k_t^s = k_t^d$ and $n_t = n_t^s = n_t^d$, all t, denote the quantities of capital and labor traded.

Now consider the typical firm. If the price of goods is strictly positive in each period, then the firm supplies to the market all of the output that it produces each period. That is, (2) holds with equality, for all t. Also, note that since the firm simply rents capital and hires labor for each period, its problem is equivalent to a series of one-period maximization problems. Hence its input demands solve

(8) $\qquad \max_{k_t, n_t} p_t[F(k_t, n_t) - r_t k_t - w_t n_t], \quad t = 0, 1, \ldots, T.$

It then follows that (real) factor prices must be equal to marginal products:

(9) $\qquad r_t = F_k(k_t, n_t), \quad t = 0, 1, \ldots, T;$

(10) $\qquad w_t = F_n(k_t, n_t), \quad t = 0, 1, \ldots, T.$

Since F is homogeneous of degree one, when we substitute from (9) and (10) into (8), we find that $\pi = 0$. Note, too, that $k_{T+1} = 0$.

Next consider the typical household. Since supplying available factors causes no disutility to the household, in every period it supplies all that is available. That is, $n_t = 1$ and $k_t = x_t$, all t. Using these facts and substituting from (5) to eliminate i_t, we can write the household's problem as

$$(11) \qquad \max \sum_{t=0}^{T} \beta^t U(c_t)$$

$$(12) \qquad \text{s.t.} \ \sum_{t=0}^{T} p_t[c_t + k_{t+1} - (r_t + 1 - \delta)k_t - w_t] \leq 0,$$

$$(13) \qquad c_t \geq 0, \, k_{t+1} \geq 0, \quad t = 0, 1, \ldots, T;$$

$$\text{given } k_0 = x_0.$$

Since $\lim_{c \to 0} U'(c) = \infty$, the nonnegativity constraints on the c_t's in (13) are never binding. Hence the first-order conditions for the household are

$$(14) \qquad \beta^t U'(c_t) - \lambda p_t = 0,$$

$$(15) \qquad \lambda[(r_{t+1} + 1 - \delta)p_{t+1} - p_t] \leq 0,$$

$$\text{with equality if } k_{t+1} > 0, \quad t = 0, 1, \ldots, T;$$

where λ is the multiplier associated with the budget constraint (12).

Therefore a competitive equilibrium is characterized by quantities and prices $\{(c_t^e, k_{t+1}^e, p_t^e, r_t^e, w_t^e)\}_{t=0}^{T}$, with all goods and factor prices strictly positive, such that $\{(k_t^e, n_t = 1)\}_{t=0}^{T}$ solves (8) at the given prices, $\{(c_t^e, k_{t+1}^e)\}_{t=0}^{T}$ solves (11)–(13) at the given prices, $k_0 = x_0$, $k_{T+1} = 0$, and in addition

$$(16) \qquad F(k_t^e, 1) = c_t^e + k_{t+1}^e - (1 - \delta)k_t^e, \quad \text{all } t.$$

Now that we have defined and partially characterized a competitive equilibrium for the economy of Section 2.1, we can be more specific about the connections between equilibrium and optimal allocations that we referred to earlier. First note that if $\{(c_t^e, k_{t+1}^e, p_t^e, w_t^e, r_t^e)\}_{t=0}^{T}$ is an equilibrium, then $\{(c_t^e, k_{t+1}^e)\}_{t=0}^{T}$ is a solution to the planning problem discussed in Section 2.1. To prove this we need only show that $\{(c_t^e, k_{t+1}^e)\}$ is Pareto optimal. Suppose to the contrary that $\{(c_t', k_{t+1}')\}$ is a feasible allocation and that $\{c'_t\}$ yields higher total utility in the objective function (11). Then this allocation must violate (12), or the household would have chosen it. But if (12) is violated, then (16) implies that

$$\pi' = \sum_{t=0}^{T} p^e_t[F(k'_t, 1) - r^e_t k'_t - w^e_t] > 0 = \pi^e,$$

contradicting the hypothesis that $\{(k^e_t, n_t = 1)\}_{t=0}^T$ was a profit-maximizing choice of inputs. This result is a version of the first fundamental theorem of welfare economics.

Conversely, suppose that $\{(c^*_t, k^*_{t+1})\}_{t=0}^T$ is a solution to the planner's problem in Section 2.1. Then $\{k^*_{t+1}\}_{t=0}^T$ is the unique sequence satisfying the first-order and boundary conditions

(17) $\quad \beta f'(k^*_t)U'[f(k^*_t) - k^*_{t+1}] = U'[f(k^*_{t-1}) - k^*_t], \quad t = 1, 2, \ldots, T;$

(18) $\quad k^*_{T+1} = 0, \, k^*_0 = x_0;$

and $\{c^*_t\}$ is given by

(19) $\quad c^*_t = f(k^*_t) - k^*_{t+1}, \quad t = 0, 1, \ldots, T;$

where the function $f(k) = F(k, 1) + (1 - \delta)k$ is as defined in Section 2.1. To construct a competitive equilibrium with these quantities, we must find supporting prices $\{(p^*_t, r^*_t, w^*_t)\}_{t=0}^T$.

To do this, note that (9) and (15) together suggest that goods prices must satisfy

(20) $\quad p^*_t = p^*_{t-1}/f'(k^*_t), \quad t = 1, 2, \ldots, T;$

where $p_0 > 0$ is arbitrary, and (9) and (10) imply that real wage and rental rates must satisfy

(21) $\quad r^*_t = f'(k^*_t) - (1 - \delta), \quad t = 1, 2, \ldots, T;$

(22) $\quad w^*_t = f(k^*_t) - k^*_t f'(k^*_t), \quad t = 1, 2, \ldots, T.$

It is not difficult to verify that these prices together with the quantities in (17)–(19) constitute a competitive equilibrium, and we leave the proof as an exercise. This result is a version of the second fundamental theorem of welfare economics.

Exercise 2.8   Show that at the prices given in (20)–(22), the allocation $\{(c_t^*, k_{t+1}^*)\}_{t=0}^T$ defined in (17)–(19) is utility maximizing for the household [solves (11)–(13)]; that the allocation $\{(k_t^*, n_t^* = 1)\}_{t=0}^T$ is profit maximizing for the firm [solves (8)]; and that $\{(c_t^*, k_{t+1}^*)\}_{t=0}^T$ satisfies (16).

We also leave it as an exercise to show that the same quantities and prices constitute a competitive equilibrium if firms instead of households are the owners of capital.

Exercise 2.9   Suppose that households are prohibited from owning capital directly. Instead, firms own all of the initial capital stock k_0 and also make all future investments in capital. Households own all shares in firms, and returns to the latter now include returns to capital. Modify the statements of the firm's and the household's problems to fit these arrangements and show that the quantities in (17)–(19) together with the prices in (20)–(22) still constitute a competitive equilibrium.

We have interpreted these equilibrium prices and quantities as being determined in a single market-clearing operation. But there is another way to think of an economy as arriving at the quantities and prices calculated above. Suppose that the agents meet in a market at the beginning of every period, not just in period 0. In the market held in period t, agents trade current-period labor, rental services of existing capital, and final output. In addition, one security is traded: a claim to one unit of final output in the subsequent period. In each period, factor and bond prices are expressed in terms of current-period goods.

Notice that with a sequence of markets the household must form expectations about future prices in order to arrive at its decisions in the market in period t. In particular, its expectations about future consumption goods prices and future rental rates on capital affect its current consumption-savings decision. Thus some assumption is needed about how these expectations are formed. Suppose, for example, that the household has perfect foresight about all future prices. (This assumption is the specialization for a deterministic context of the more general notion of rational expectations.) Although we do not carry out the proof here, it is not hard to show that, under the assumption of perfect foresight, this set of markets is equivalent to the one above in the sense that the competitive equilibrium allocation is the same for the two settings, and the prices are closely related.

Exercise 2.10 Suppose that the market structure is as described above. Modify the statements of the firm's and the household's problems to fit these arrangements. Show that under perfect foresight the quantities in (17)–(19), the factor prices in (21)–(22), and the bond prices

$$q_t = \beta U'(c_{t+1}^*)/U'(c_t^*) = 1/f'(k_{t+1}^*), \quad t = 0, 1, \ldots, T - 1;$$

constitute a competitive equilibrium.

(In fact, for the representative household economy here, the sequential market structure can be even further simplified by eliminating securities markets. Since the net supply of such securities is zero, in equilibrium each household has a net demand of zero for each of the securities. Hence, if these markets are simply shut down, the remaining prices and the real allocation are unaltered. This conclusion does *not* hold, however, in an economy with heterogeneous households.)

We have, then, two examples of market economies: one with complete markets in the Arrow-Debreu sense, the other with markets limited to spot transactions in factors of production, goods, and one-period securities. Both economies reproduce the optimal path of capital accumulation discussed in Section 2.1, provided agents in the sequence economy have perfect foresight about future prices.

There is yet a third way in which the solution to the optimal growth model of Section 2.1 can be interpreted as a competitive equilibrium, one that is closely related to the dynamic programming approach of Section 2.1 and to the sequence of markets interpretation of equilibrium above. The general idea is to characterize equilibrium prices as functions of the single state variable k, the economy-wide capital stock, and to view individual households as dynamic programmers.

To develop this idea, first note that since firms in the sequence economy solve the sequence of one-period problems in (8), factor prices can be expressed as functions of the state:

(23) $R(k) = F_k(k, 1)$ and $\omega(k) = F_n(k, 1)$,   all $k > 0$.

At these prices, which in each period are taken by the firms as fixed numbers, the quantities $(k, 1)$ are profit maximizing and lead to zero profits.

Next we must develop a dynamic program representing the decision problem faced by a typical household. To do so we need a notation that distinguishes between the economy-wide capital stock, k, over which the household has no control, and its own capital stock, K, over which it has complete control. Looking ahead, we know that in equilibrium it must be the case that $K = k$, but it is important to keep in mind that the representative household does not behave as it does out of a sense of social responsibility: it must be induced by prices to do so.

Let the individual household's state variable be the pair (K, k), let $V(K, k)$ denote its optimum value function, and suppose that it expects the economy-wide capital stock next period to be $k' = h(k)$. Then the household's decision problem is represented by the functional equation

(24) $$V(K, k) = \max_{C, Y} \{U(C) + \beta V[Y, h(k)]\}$$

$$\text{s.t.} \quad C + [Y - (1 - \delta)K] \leq KR(k) + \omega(k).$$

Let $H(K, k)$ be the optimal policy function for this problem.

Under the assumption of perfect foresight, the fact that all households are identical implies that in equilibrium it must be the case that $h(k) = H(k, k)$. Thus we define a recursive competitive equilibrium to be a value function $V: \mathbf{R}_+^2 \to \mathbf{R}$, a policy function $H: \mathbf{R}_+^2 \to \mathbf{R}_+$ for the representative household, an economy-wide law of motion $h: \mathbf{R}_+ \to \mathbf{R}_+$ for capital, and factor price functions $R: \mathbf{R}_+ \to \mathbf{R}_+$ and $\omega: \mathbf{R}_+ \to \mathbf{R}_+$, such that V satisfies (24), given h; H is the optimal policy function for (24); $H(k, k) = h(k)$, all k; and R and ω satisfy (23).

From this recursive point of view, the statement that competitive equilibrium allocations are Pareto optimal means that if (V, H, h, R, ω) is an equilibrium, then the function $v(k) = V(k, k)$ is the value function for the planner's problem, and $g = h$ is the planner's optimal policy function. Conversely, the fact that Pareto-optimal allocations can be supported as competitive equilibria means the following. If v is the value function for the planner's problem and g is the planner's optimal policy function, then the value and policy function for the individual household, the pair (V, H) satisfying (24), have the property that $V(k, k) = v(k)$ and $H(k, k) = g(k)$, all k.

The sense in which these statements are economically reasonable conjectures can be spelled out by a comparison of the first-order and envelope conditions for the two dynamic programs. For the planner's problem these are

(25) $U'[f(k) - g(k)] = \beta v'[g(k)];$

(26) $v'(k) = U'[f(k) - g(k)]f'(k).$

For the household's problem, the analogous conditions are

$$U'[f(k) + f'(k)(K - k) - H(K, k)] = \beta V_1[H(K, k), h(k)] \quad \text{and}$$

$$V_1(K, k) = U'[f(k) + f'(k)(K - k) - H(K, k)]f'(k).$$

In equilibrium, $K = k$; since $H(k, k) = h(k)$, these conditions can then be
written as

(27) $U'[f(k) - h(k)] = \beta V_1[h(k), h(k)] \quad \text{and}$

(28) $V_1(k, k) = U'[f(k) - h(k)]f'(k).$

Thus, if $v'(k) = V_1(k, k)$, then the equilibrium conditions (27)–(28) match
the conditions (25)–(26) for the planner's problem.

We will repeatedly exploit these classic connections between competitive equilibria and Pareto optima as a device for proving the existence of
equilibria in market economies and for characterizing them. That is, we
will solve planning problems, not for the normative purpose of prescrib-
ing outcomes, but for the positive purpose of predicting market outcomes from a given set of preferences and technology.

This device is useful in situations where the two fundamental theorems of welfare economics apply, but these theorems fail in the presence
of increasing returns to scale, externalities, distorting taxes, and so on.
Suppose that we want to consider the competitive equilibrium in an
economy in which there is, say, a flat-rate tax on labor income. We know
that in the presence of such a tax the competitive equilibrium allocation
is not, in general, Pareto optimal. That is, in general we cannot describe
the competitive equilibrium of such an economy by describing an associated social planning problem.

In such cases, establishing the existence and qualitative properties of a competitive equilibrium requires looking directly at the equilibrium conditions. In the recursive context above this approach means that we must establish the existence of functions (V, H, h) such that V and H are the value and policy functions for the household's dynamic programming problem, given the economy-wide law of motion h for the state variable; and $H(k, k) = h(k)$, all k. These considerations lead us to look directly at the analogues of (27)–(28). Establishing the existence of a competitive equilibrium involves establishing directly the existence of functions $\phi(k) = V_1(k, k)$ and $h(k)$ satisfying those equations. Given h, the functions V and H can then be found by solving (24).

In this section, we have illustrated that the methods for studying recursive optimization problems developed in Parts II and III can be used in two ways in the analysis of competitive equilibria. In situations where the connections between competitive equilibria and Pareto optima hold, equilibria can be studied by analyzing the associated Pareto problem. In situations where those connections fail, the methods of dynamic programming can still be used to study the problems facing individual agents in the economy. However, new arguments are needed to establish the existence of equilibria. These two approaches to the study of competitive equilibria are the subject of Part IV.

2.4   Conclusions and Plans

We began this chapter with a deterministic model of optimal growth and then explored a number of variations on it. In the course of the discussion, we have raised a wide variety of substantive and technical issues, passing over questions in both categories lightly with promises of better treatments to come. It is time to spell out these promises in more detail. We will do this by describing briefly the plan for the rest of the book.

Deterministic systems like those discussed in Section 2.1 are the subject of Part II (Chapters 3–6). Chapter 3 contains some preliminary mathematical material needed to study functional equations like those discussed earlier. This background allows us to develop the needed results for deterministic models and also lays the foundation for the study of stochastic problems.

Chapter 4 then deals with dynamic programming in a deterministic context. The optimal growth model of Section 2.1 is a typical example and illustrates the necessary ingredients of such a treatment. First we must show that for stationary, infinite-horizon optimization problems like the social planner's problem, the problem stated as one of choosing an optimal sequence of decisions is equivalent (in some sense) to the problem stated in the form of a functional equation. With this established, we can then study functional equations for bounded, constant-returns-to-scale, and unbounded problems.

In Chapter 5 we turn to substantive economic models that are amenable to analysis using these tools. These applications, which are drawn from a variety of substantive areas of economics, are intended to give some idea of the broad applicability of these methods.

Chapter 6 treats methods for characterizing the behavior of deterministic, recursive systems over time: the theory of stability for autonomous difference equations. We first review results on global stability and then treat local stability. We conclude with several economic applications of these methods and with some examples that illustrate the types of behavior possible in unstable systems.

Stochastic systems, like those we saw in Section 2.2, are treated in Part III (Chapters 7–14). In generalizing the analysis of Chapters 4–6 to include stochastic shocks, a variety of approaches are possible. We have chosen to take a modern attack, one that allows us to deal with very general classes of stochastic shocks when looking at dynamic programming problems, and that yields additional benefits later when we study the stochastic counterpart of stability theory. To take this approach, we must first develop some of the basic tools of the theory of measure and integration.

This background is presented in Chapters 7 and 8. Chapter 7 is a self-contained treatment of the definitions and results from measure theory that are needed in later chapters; and Chapter 8 contains an introduction to Markov processes, the natural generalization of the stochastic difference equations discussed above.

With these mathematical preliminaries in place, Chapter 9 deals with stochastic dynamic programming, paralleling Chapter 4 as closely as possible. The rewards from Chapters 7 and 8 are apparent here (we hope!). With the appropriate notation and results in hand, the arguments used in Chapter 9 to study stochastic models are fairly simple extensions of those in Chapter 4.

Chapter 10 then provides a variety of economic applications, drawn from a number of different substantive areas. Some of these are stochastic analogues to models discussed in Chapter 5; others are entirely new.

Chapters 11 and 12 survey results on convergence, in various senses, for Markov processes: extensions of the ideas sketched in Section 2.2 to a much wider variety of problems. This material is the body of theory suited to characterizing the dynamics for state variables generated by optimal policy functions for stochastic dynamic programs. Substantive economic applications of these methods are discussed in Chapter 13. Some of these applications are continuations of those discussed in Chapter 10, others are new. Chapter 14 provides a law of large numbers for Markov processes.

The use of recursive systems within a general equilibrium framework, as illustrated in Section 2.3 above, is the subject of Part IV (Chapters 15–18). Chapter 15 returns at a more abstract level to the connections between Pareto-optimal and competitive equilibrium allocations. In particular, we there review the two fundamental theorems of welfare economics in a way that applies to the kinds of infinite dimensional commodity spaces that arise in dynamic applications. We also treat the issue of constructing prices for problems involving infinite time horizons and/or uncertainty. Chapter 16 then contains a number of applications, designed to illustrate how a variety of planning problems can be interpreted as market equilibria.

When a market equilibrium is also the solution to a benevolent social planner's problem, this fact vastly simplifies the analysis. However, there are many market situations of great interest—situations in which markets are subject to distortions due to taxes, external effects, or various kinds of market imperfections—that cannot be analyzed in this way. In many such cases it is still possible to construct recursive equilibria directly, using the line of argument discussed briefly in Section 2.3. Chapter 17 presents several mathematical results, fixed-point theorems, that have proved useful in such cases, and illustrates their application. In Chapter 18 we conclude with further illustrations of these methods.

2.5 Bibliographic Notes

Modern growth theory began with Frank Ramsey's (1928) classic paper and then lay dormant for almost 30 years. (Although a substantial body of literature on growth developed during the 1930s and 1940s, this work is quite different from the neoclassical theory of growth both in motivation and in terms of the specific models used: its goal was to show that high, persistent rates of unemployment are a necessary feature of long-run growth, and the models used generally featured fixed-proportions technologies.) The field was reawakened by the work of Solow (1956) and Swan (1956) and has been active ever since. The work by Solow and Swan, and much that followed immediately, relied on the assumption that households save a fixed proportion of their income. These models were meant to be descriptive rather than prescriptive, and no attempt was made to model households' preferences and expectations.

Households' preferences finally reentered the discussion when economists looked at the issue of growth from a normative point of view. The deterministic theory of optimal growth, of which the one-sector model discussed in Section 2.1 is the simplest case, was developed independently and simultaneously by Cass (1965) and Koopmans (1965). A stochastic model that incorporated shocks to production, like the one discussed in Section 2.2, was first studied by Brock and Mirman (1972) and by Mirman and Zilcha (1975).

The first modern treatment of the connections between Pareto optima and competitive equilibria was provided by Arrow (1951) for the case where the commodity space is a finite-dimensional Euclidean space. This treatment applies, for example, to the finite-horizon optimal growth problem discussed in Section 2.3. Debreu (1954) showed that the same line of argument holds in certain infinite-dimensional spaces, and his is the treatment that we will need later to deal with infinite-horizon models.

The interpretation of a competitive equilibrium in terms of a sequence of markets can also be made for stochastic models. To make this interpretation, it must be assumed that agents have *rational expectations* in the sense of Muth (1961). See Radner (1972) for a pioneering general equilibrium application of this idea.

PART II

Deterministic Models

3 Mathematical Preliminaries

In Chapter 2 the optimal growth problem

$$\max_{\{(c_t, k_{t+1})\}_{t=0}^{\infty}} \sum_{t=0}^{\infty} \beta^t U(c_t)$$

$$\text{s.t.} \quad c_t + k_{t+1} \leq f(k_t),$$

$$c_t, k_{t+1} \geq 0, \quad t = 0, 1, \ldots,$$

$$\text{given } k_0,$$

was seen to lead to the functional equation

(1) $$v(k) = \max_{c,y} [U(c) + \beta v(y)]$$

$$\text{s.t.} \quad c + y \leq f(k),$$

$$c, y \geq 0.$$

The purpose of this chapter and the next is to show precisely the relationship between these two problems and others like them and to develop the mathematical methods that have proved useful in studying the latter. In Section 2.1 we argued in an informal way that the solutions to the two problems should be closely connected, and this argument will be made rigorous later. In the rest of this introduction we consider alternative methods for finding solutions to (1), outline the one to be pursued, and describe the mathematical issues it raises. In the remaining sections of the chapter we deal with these issues in turn. We draw upon this material extensively in Chapter 4, where functional equations like (1) are analyzed.

In (1) the functions U and f are given—they take specific forms known to us—and the value function v is unknown. Our task is to prove the existence and uniqueness of a function v satisfying (1) and to deduce its properties, given those of U and f. The classical (nineteenth-century) approach to this problem was the *method of successive approximations,* and it works in the following very commonsensical way. Begin by taking an initial guess that a specific function, call it v_0, satisfies (1). Then define a new function, v_1, by

(2) $$v_1(k) = \max_{0 \leq y \leq f(k)} \{U[f(k) - y] + \beta v_0(y)\}.$$

If it should happen that $v_1(k) = v_0(k)$, for all $k \geq 0$, then clearly v_0 is a solution to (1). Lucky guessing (cf. Exercise 2.3) is one way to establish the existence of a function satisfying (1), but it is notoriously unreliable. The method of successive approximations proceeds in a more systematic way.

Suppose, as is usually the case, that $v_1 \neq v_0$. Then use v_1 as a new guess and define the sequence of functions $\{v_n\}$ recursively by

(3) $$v_{n+1}(k) = \max_{0 \leq y \leq f(k)} \{U[f(k) - y] + \beta v_n(y)\}, \quad n = 0, 1, 2, \ldots.$$

The hope behind this iterative process is that as n increases, the successive approximations v_n get closer to a function v that actually satisfies (1). That is, the hope is that the limit of the sequence $\{v_n\}$ is a solution v. Moreover, if it can be shown that $\lim_{n \to \infty} v_n$ is the same for any initial guess v_0, then it will follow that this limit is the only function satisfying (1). (Why?)

Is there any reason to hope for success in this analytical strategy? Recall that our reason for being interested in (1) is to use it to locate the optimal capital accumulation policy for a one-sector economy. Suppose we begin by choosing any feasible capital accumulation policy, that is, any function g_0 satisfying $0 \leq g_0(k) \leq f(k)$, all $k \geq 0$. [An example is the policy of saving a constant fraction of income: $g_0(k) = \theta f(k)$, where $0 < \theta < 1$.] The lifetime utility yielded by this policy, as a function of the initial capital stock k_0, is

$$w_0(k_0) = \sum_{t=0}^{\infty} \beta^t U[f(k_t) - g_0(k_t)],$$

where

$$k_{t+1} = g_0(k_t), \quad t = 0, 1, 2, \ldots.$$

The following exercise develops a result about (g_0, w_0) that is used later.

Exercise 3.1 Show that

$$w_0(k) = U[f(k) - g_0(k)] + \beta w_0[g_0(k)], \quad \text{all } k \geq 0.$$

If the utility from the policy g_0 is used as the initial guess for a value function—that is, if $v_0 = w_0$—then (2) is the problem facing a planner who can choose capital accumulation optimally for one period but must follow the policy g_0 in all subsequent periods. Thus $v_1(k)$ is the level of lifetime utility attained, and the maximizing value of y—call it $g_1(k)$—is the optimal level for end-of-period capital. Both v_1 and g_1 are functions of beginning-of-period capital k.

Notice that since $g_0(k)$ is a feasible choice in the first period, the planner will do no worse than he would by following the policy g_0 from the beginning, and in general he will be able to do better. That is, for any feasible policy g_0 and associated initial value function v_0,

$$(4) \qquad v_1(k) = \max_{0 \leq y \leq f(k)} \{U[f(k) - y] + \beta v_0(y)\}$$

$$\geq \{U[f(k) - g_0(k)] + \beta v_0[g_0(k)]\}$$

$$= v_0(k),$$

where the last line follows from Exercise 3.1.

Now suppose the planner has the option of choosing capital accumulation optimally for two periods but must follow the policy g_0 thereafter. If y is his choice for end-of-period capital in the first period, then from the second period on the best he can do is to choose $g_1(y)$ for end-of-period capital and enjoy total utility $v_1(y)$. His problem in the first period is thus $\max[U(c) + \beta v_1(y)]$, subject to the constraints in (1). The maximized value of this objective function was defined, in (3), as $v_2(k)$. Hence it follows from (4) that

$$v_2(k) = \max_{0 \le y \le f(k)} \{U[f(k) - y] + \beta v_1(y)\}$$

$$\ge \max_{0 \le y \le f(k)} \{U[f(k) - y] + \beta v_0(y)\}$$

$$= v_1(k).$$

Continuing in this way, one establishes by induction that $v_{n+1}(k) \ge v_n(k)$, all k, $n = 0, 1, 2, \ldots$. The successive approximations defined in (3) are improvements, reflecting the fact that planning flexibility over longer and longer finite horizons offers new options without taking any other options away. Consequently it seems reasonable to suppose that the sequence of functions $\{v_n\}$ defined in (3) might converge to a solution v to (1). That is, the method of successive approximations seems to be a reasonable way to locate and characterize solutions.

This method can be described in a somewhat different and much more convenient language. As we showed in the discussion above, for any function $w: \mathbf{R}_+ \to \mathbf{R}$, we can define a new function—call it $Tw: \mathbf{R}_+ \to \mathbf{R}$—by

(5) $$(Tw)(k) = \max_{0 \le y \le f(k)} \{U[f(k) - y] + \beta w(y)\}.$$

When we use this notation, the method of successive approximations amounts to choosing a function v_0 and studying the sequence $\{v_n\}$ defined by $v_{n+1} = Tv_n$, $n = 0, 1, 2, \ldots$. The goal then is to show that this sequence converges and that the limit function v satisfies (1). Alternatively, we can simply view the operator T as a mapping from some set C of functions into itself: $T: C \to C$. In this notation solving (1) is equivalent to locating a *fixed point* of the mapping T, that is, a function $v \in C$ satisfying $v = Tv$, and the method of successive approximations is viewed as a way to construct this fixed point.

To study operators T like the one defined in (5), we need to draw on several basic mathematical results. To show that T maps an appropriate space C of functions into itself, we must decide what spaces of functions are suitable for carrying out our analysis. In general we want to limit attention to continuous functions. This choice raises the issue of whether, given a continuous function w, the function Tw defined by (5) is also continuous. Finally, we need a fixed-point theorem that applies to operators like T on the space C we have selected. The rest of the chapter deals with these issues.

In Section 3.1 we review the basic facts about metric spaces and normed vector spaces and define the space C that will be used repeatedly later. In Section 3.2 we prove the Contraction Mapping Theorem, a fixed-point theorem of vast usefulness. In Section 3.3 we review the main facts we will need about functions, like Tw above, that are defined by maximization problems.

3.1 Metric Spaces and Normed Vector Spaces

The preceding section motivates the study of certain functional equations as a means of finding solutions to problems posed in terms of infinite sequences. To pursue the study of these problems, as we will in Chapter 4, we need to talk about infinite sequences $\{x_t\}_{t=0}^{\infty}$ of states, about candidates for the value function v, and about the convergence of sequences of various sorts. To do this, we will find it convenient to think of both infinite sequences and certain classes of functions as elements of infinite-dimensional normed vector spaces. Accordingly, we begin here with the definitions of vector spaces, metric spaces, and normed vector spaces. We then discuss the notions of convergence and Cauchy convergence, and define the notion of completeness for a metric space. Theorem 3.1 then establishes that the space of bounded, continuous, real-valued functions on a set $X \subseteq \mathbf{R}^l$ is complete.

We begin with the definition of a vector space.

DEFINITION *A **(real) vector space** X is a set of elements (vectors) together with two operations, addition and scalar multiplication. For any two vectors $x, y \in X$, addition gives a vector $x + y \in X$; and for any vector $x \in X$ and any real number $\alpha \in \mathbf{R}$, scalar multiplication gives a vector $\alpha x \in X$. These operations obey the usual algebraic laws; that is, for all $x, y, z \in X$, and $\alpha, \beta \in \mathbf{R}$:*

a. $x + y = y + x$;

b. $(x + y) + z = x + (y + z)$;

c. $\alpha(x + y) = \alpha x + \alpha y$;

d. $(\alpha + \beta)x = \alpha x + \beta x$; *and*

e. $(\alpha\beta)x = \alpha(\beta x)$.

Moreover, there is a zero vector $\theta \in X$ *that has the following properties:*

f. $x + \theta = x$; *and*

g. $0x = \theta$.

Finally,

h. $1x = x$.

The adjective "real" simply indicates that scalar multiplication is defined taking the real numbers, not elements of the complex plane or some other set, as scalars. All of the vector spaces used in this book are real, and the adjective will not be repeated. Important features of a vector space are that it has a "zero" element and that it is closed under addition and scalar multiplication. Vector spaces are also called *linear spaces*.

Exercise 3.2   Show that the following are vector spaces:

a. any finite-dimensional Euclidean space $\mathbf{R}^l$;

b. the set $X = \{x \in \mathbf{R}^2 : x = \alpha z,$ some $\alpha \in \mathbf{R}\}$, where $z \in \mathbf{R}^2$;

c. the set X consisting of all infinite sequences $(x_0, x_1, x_2, \ldots)$, where $x_i \in \mathbf{R}$, all i;

d. the set of all continuous functions on the interval $[a, b]$.

   Show that the following are not vector spaces:

e. the unit circle in $\mathbf{R}^2$;

f. the set of all integers, $I = \{\ldots, -1, 0, +1, \ldots\}$;

g. the set of all nonnegative functions on $[a, b]$.

To discuss convergence in a vector space or in any other space, we need to have the notion of distance. The notion of distance in Euclidean space is generalized in the abstract notion of a *metric*, a function defined on any two elements in a set the value of which has an interpretation as the distance between them.

DEFINITION   *A **metric space** is a set* S, *together with a metric (distance function)* $\rho: S \times S \to \mathbf{R}$, *such that for all* $x, y, z \in S$:

a. $\rho(x, y) \geq 0$, *with equality if and only if* $x = y$;

b. $\rho(x, y) = \rho(y, x)$; *and*

c. $\rho(x, z) \leq \rho(x, y) + \rho(y, z)$.

The definition of a metric thus abstracts the four basic properties of Euclidean distance: the distance between distinct points is strictly positive; the distance from a point to itself is zero; distance is symmetric; and the triangle inequality holds.

Exercise 3.3 Show that the following are metric spaces.
a. Let S be the set of integers, with $\rho(x, y) = |x - y|$.
b. Let S be the set of integers, with $\rho(x, y) = 0$ if $x = y$, 1 if $x \neq y$.
c. Let S be the set of all continuous, strictly increasing functions on $[a, b]$, with $\rho(x, y) = \max_{a \leq t \leq b} |x(t) - y(t)|$.
d. Let S be the set of all continuous, strictly increasing functions on $[a, b]$, with $\rho(x, y) = \int_a^b |x(t) - y(t)| dt$.
e. Let S be the set of all rational numbers, with $\rho(x, y) = |x - y|$.
f. Let $S = \mathbf{R}$, with $\rho(x, y) = f(|x - y|)$, where $f : \mathbf{R}_+ \to \mathbf{R}_+$ is continuous, strictly increasing, and strictly concave, with $f(0) = 0$.

For vector spaces, metrics are usually defined in such a way that the distance between any two points is equal to the distance of their difference from the zero point. That is, since for any points x and y in a vector space S, the point $x - y$ is also in S, the metric on a vector space is usually defined in such a way that $\rho(x, y) = \rho(x - y, \theta)$. To define such a metric, we need the concept of a norm.

DEFINITION *A **normed vector space** is a vector space S, together with a norm $\|\cdot\| : S \to \mathbf{R}$, such that for all $x, y \in S$ and $\alpha \in \mathbf{R}$:*
 a. $\|x\| \geq 0$, with equality if and only if $x = \theta$;
 b. $\|\alpha x\| = |\alpha| \cdot \|x\|$; and
 c. $\|x + y\| \leq \|x\| + \|y\|$ (the triangle inequality).

Exercise 3.4 Show that the following are normed vector spaces.
a. Let $S = \mathbf{R}^l$, with $\|x\| = [\Sigma_{i=1}^l x_i^2]^{1/2}$ (Euclidean space).
b. Let $S = \mathbf{R}^l$, with $\|x\| = \max_i |x_i|$.
c. Let $S = \mathbf{R}^l$, with $\|x\| = \Sigma_{i=1}^l |x_i|$.
d. Let S be the set of all bounded infinite sequences $(x_1, x_2, \ldots)$, $x_k \in \mathbf{R}$, all k, with $\|x\| = \sup_k |x_k|$. (This space is called l_∞.)
e. Let S be the set of all continuous functions on $[a, b]$, with $\|x\| = \sup_{a \leq t \leq b} |x(t)|$. (This space is called $C[a, b]$.)
f. Let S be the set of all continuous functions on $[a, b]$, with $\|x\| = \int_a^b |x(t)| dt$.

It is standard to view any normed vector space $(S, \|\cdot\|)$ as a metric space, where the metric is taken to be $\rho(x, y) = \|x - y\|$, all $x, y \in S$.

The notion of convergence of a sequence of real numbers carries over without change to any metric space.

DEFINITION   *A sequence $\{x_n\}_{n=0}^{\infty}$ in S **converges** to $x \in S$, if for each $\varepsilon > 0$, there exists N_ε such that*

(1) $\rho(x_n, x) < \varepsilon,$ all $n \geq N_\varepsilon.$

Thus a sequence $\{x_n\}$ in a metric space (S, ρ) converges to $x \in S$ if and only if the sequence of distances $\{\rho(x_n, x)\}$, a sequence in $\mathbf{R}_+$, converges to zero. In this case we write $x_n \rightarrow x$.

Verifying convergence directly involves having a "candidate" for the limit point x so that the inequality (1) can be checked. When a candidate is not immediately available, the following alternative criterion is often useful.

DEFINITION   *A sequence $\{x_n\}_{n=0}^{\infty}$ in S is a **Cauchy sequence** (satisfies the **Cauchy criterion**) if for each $\varepsilon > 0$, there exists N_ε such that*

(2) $\rho(x_n, x_m) < \varepsilon,$ all $n, m \geq N_\varepsilon.$

Thus a sequence is Cauchy if the points get closer and closer to each other. The following exercise illustrates some basic facts about convergence and the Cauchy criterion.

Exercise 3.5   a. Show that if $x_n \rightarrow x$ and $x_n \rightarrow y$, then $x = y$. That is, if $\{x_n\}$ has a limit, then that limit is unique.

b. Show that if a sequence $\{x_n\}$ is convergent, then it satisfies the Cauchy criterion.

c. Show that if a sequence $\{x_n\}$ satisfies the Cauchy criterion, then it is bounded.

d. Show that $x_n \rightarrow x$ if and only if every subsequence of $\{x_n\}$ converges to x.

The advantage of the Cauchy criterion is that, in contrast to (1), (2) can be checked with knowledge of $\{x_n\}$ only. For the Cauchy criterion to be useful, however, we must work with spaces where it implies the existence of a limit point.

DEFINITION *A metric space (S, ρ) is* **complete** *if every Cauchy sequence in S converges to an element in S.*

In complete metric spaces, then, verifying that a sequence satisfies the Cauchy criterion is a way of verifying the existence of a limit point in S.

Verifying the completeness of particular spaces can take some work. We take as given the following

FACT *The set of real numbers* **R** *with the metric ρ(x, y) = |x − y| is a complete metric space.*

Exercise 3.6 a. Show that the metric spaces in Exercises 3.3a,b and 3.4a–e are complete and that those in Exercises 3.3c–e and 3.4f are not. Show that the space in 3.3c is complete if "strictly increasing" is replaced with "nondecreasing."

b. Show that if $(S, ρ)$ is a complete metric space and S' is a closed subset of S, then $(S', ρ)$ is a complete metric space.

A complete normed vector space is called a **Banach space.**

The next example is no more difficult than some of those in Exercise 3.6, but since it is important in what follows and illustrates clearly each of the steps involved in verifying completeness, we present the proof here.

THEOREM 3.1 *Let $X \subseteq \mathbf{R}^l$, and let $C(X)$ be the set of bounded continuous functions $f: X \to \mathbf{R}$ with the sup norm, $\|f\| = \sup_{x \in X} |f(x)|$. Then $C(X)$ is a complete normed vector space. (Note that if X is compact then every continuous function is bounded. Otherwise the restriction to bounded functions must be added.)*

Proof. That $C(X)$ is a normed vector space follows from Exercise 3.4e. Hence it suffices to show that if $\{f_n\}$ is a Cauchy sequence, there exists $f \in C(X)$ such that

for any $\varepsilon > 0$ there exists N_ε such that $\|f_n - f\| \leq \varepsilon$, all $n \geq N_\varepsilon$.

Three steps are involved: to find a "candidate" function f; to show that $\{f_n\}$ converges to f in the sup norm; and to show that $f \in C(X)$ (that f is bounded and continuous). Each step involves its own entirely distinct logic.

Fix $x \in X$; then the sequence of real numbers $\{f_n(x)\}$ satisfies

$$|f_n(x) - f_m(x)| \leq \sup_{y \in X} |f_n(y) - f_m(y)| = \|f_n - f_m\|.$$

Therefore it satisfies the Cauchy criterion; and by the completeness of the real numbers, it converges to a limit point—call it $f(x)$. The limiting values define a function $f : X \to \mathbf{R}$ that we take to be our candidate.

Next we must show that $\|f_n - f\| \to 0$ as $n \to \infty$. Let $\varepsilon > 0$ be given and choose N_ε so that $n, m \geq N_\varepsilon$ implies $\|f_n - f_m\| \leq \varepsilon/2$. Since $\{f_n\}$ satisfies the Cauchy criterion, this can be done. Now for any fixed $x \in X$ and all $m \geq n \geq N_\varepsilon$,

$$|f_n(x) - f(x)| \leq |f_n(x) - f_m(x)| + |f_m(x) - f(x)|$$

$$\leq \|f_n - f_m\| + |f_m(x) - f(x)|$$

$$\leq \varepsilon/2 + |f_m(x) - f(x)|.$$

Since $\{f_m(x)\}$ converges to $f(x)$, we can choose m separately for each fixed $x \in X$ so that $|f_m(x) - f(x)| \leq \varepsilon/2$. Since the choice of x was arbitrary, it follows that $\|f_n - f\| \leq \varepsilon$, all $n \geq N_\varepsilon$. Since $\varepsilon > 0$ was arbitrary, the desired result then follows.

Finally, we must show that f is bounded and continuous. Boundedness is obvious. To prove that f is continuous, we must show that for every $\varepsilon > 0$ and every $x \in X$, there exists $\delta > 0$ such that

$$|f(x) - f(y)| < \varepsilon \quad \text{if} \quad \|x - y\|_E < \delta,$$

where $\|\cdot\|_E$ is the Euclidean norm on $\mathbf{R}^l$. Let ε and x be given. Choose k so that $\|f - f_k\| < \varepsilon/3$; since $f_n \to f$ (in the sup norm), such a choice is possible. Then choose δ so that

$$\|x - y\|_E < \delta \quad \text{implies} \quad |f_k(x) - f_k(y)| < \varepsilon/3.$$

Since f_k is continuous, such a choice is possible. Then

$$|f(x) - f(y)| \leq |f(x) - f_k(x)| + |f_k(x) - f_k(y)| + |f_k(y) - f(y)|$$

$$\leq 2\|f - f_k\| + |f_k(x) - f_k(y)|$$

$$< \varepsilon. \quad \blacksquare$$

Although we have organized these component arguments into a theorem about a function space, each should be familiar to students of calculus. Convergence in the sup norm is simply uniform convergence. The proof above is then just an amalgam of the standard proofs that a sequence of functions that satisfies the Cauchy criterion uniformly converges uniformly and that uniform convergence "preserves continuity."

Exercise 3.7   a. Let $C^1[a, b]$ be the set of all continuously differentiable functions on $[a, b] = X \subset \mathbf{R}$, with the norm $\|f\| = \sup_{x \in X}\{|f(x)| + |f'(x)|\}$. Show that $C^1[a, b]$ is a Banach space. [*Hint.* Notice that

$$\sup_{x \in X}|f(x)| + \sup_{x \in X}|f'(x)| \geq \|f\| \geq \max\{\sup_{x \in X}|f(x)|, \sup_{x \in X}|f'(x)|\}.]$$

b. Show that this set of functions with the norm $\|f\| = \sup_{x \in X}|f(x)|$ is not complete. That is, give an example of a sequence of functions that is Cauchy in the given norm that does not converge to a function in the set. Is this sequence Cauchy in the norm of part (a)?

c. Let $C^k[a, b]$ be the set of all k times continuously differentiable functions on $[a, b] = X \subset \mathbf{R}$, with the norm $\|f\| = \sum_{i=0}^{k} \alpha_i \max_{x \in X}|f^i(x)|$, where $f^i = d^i f(x)/dx^i$. Show that this space is complete if and only if $\alpha_i > 0, i = 0, 1, \ldots, k$.

3.2   The Contraction Mapping Theorem

In this section we prove two main results. The first is the Contraction Mapping Theorem, an extremely simple and powerful fixed point theorem. The second is a set of sufficient conditions, due to Blackwell, for establishing that certain operators are contraction mappings. The latter are useful in a wide variety of economic applications and will be drawn upon extensively in the next chapter.

We begin with the following definition.

DEFINITION   *Let (S, ρ) be a metric space and $T: S \to S$ be a function mapping S into itself. T is a **contraction mapping** (with **modulus** β) if for some $\beta \in (0, 1)$, $\rho(Tx, Ty) \le \beta\rho(x, y)$, for all $x, y \in S$.*

Perhaps the most familiar examples of contraction mappings are those on a closed interval $S = [a, b]$, with $\rho(x, y) = |x - y|$. Then $T: S \to S$ is a contraction if for some $\beta \in (0, 1)$.

$$\frac{|Tx - Ty|}{|x - y|} \le \beta < 1, \quad \text{all } x, y \in S \text{ with } x \ne y.$$

That is, T is a contraction mapping if it is a function with slope uniformly less than one in absolute value.

Exercise 3.8   Show that if T is a contraction on S, then T is uniformly continuous on S.

The **fixed points** of T, the elements of S satisfying $Tx = x$, are the intersections of Tx with the 45° line, as shown in Figure 3.1. Hence it is clear that any contraction on this space has a unique fixed point. This conclusion is much more general.

THEOREM 3.2 (*Contraction Mapping Theorem*)   *If (S, ρ) is a complete metric space and $T: S \to S$ is a contraction mapping with modulus β, then*
   a. T has exactly one fixed point v in S, and
   b. for any $v_0 \in S$, $\rho(T^n v_0, v) \le \beta^n \rho(v_0, v)$, $n = 0, 1, 2, \dots$.

Proof. To prove (a), we must find a candidate for v, show that it satisfies $Tv = v$, and show that no other element $\hat{v} \in S$ does.

Define the iterates of T, the mappings $\{T^n\}$, by $T^0 x = x$, and $T^n x = T(T^{n-1}x)$, $n = 1, 2, \dots$. Choose $v_0 \in S$, and define $\{v_n\}_{n=0}^{\infty}$ by $v_{n+1} = Tv_n$, so that $v_n = T^n v_0$. By the contraction property of T,

$$\rho(v_2, v_1) = \rho(Tv_1, Tv_0) \le \beta\rho(v_1, v_0).$$

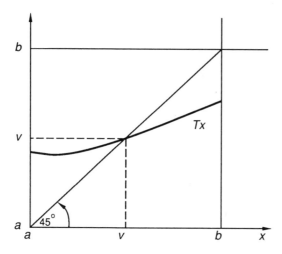

Figure 3.1

Continuing by induction, we get

(1) $\rho(v_{n+1}, v_n) \le \beta^n \rho(v_1, v_0), \quad n = 1, 2, \ldots.$

Hence, for any $m > n$,

$$\rho(v_m, v_n) \le \rho(v_m, v_{m-1}) + \cdots + \rho(v_{n+2}, v_{n+1}) + \rho(v_{n+1}, v_n)$$

$$\le [\beta^{m-1} + \cdots + \beta^{n+1} + \beta^n] \rho(v_1, v_0)$$

$$= \beta^n [\beta^{m-n-1} + \cdots + \beta + 1 \, \rho(v_1, v_0)$$

(2) $$\le \frac{\beta^n}{1 - \beta} \rho(v_1, v_0),$$

where the first line uses the triangle inequality and the second follows from (1). It is clear from (2) that $\{v_n\}$ is a Cauchy sequence. Since S is complete, it follows that $v_n \to v \in S$.

To show that $Tv = v$, note that for all n and all $v_0 \in S$,

$$\rho(Tv, v) \le \rho(Tv, T^n v_0) + \rho(T^n v_0, v)$$

$$\le \beta \rho(v, T^{n-1} v_0) + \rho(T^n v_0, v).$$

We have demonstrated that both terms in the last expression converge to zero as $n \to \infty$; hence $\rho(Tv, v) = 0$, or $Tv = v$.

Finally, we must show that there is no other function $\hat{v} \in S$ satisfying $T\hat{v} = \hat{v}$. Suppose to the contrary that $\hat{v} \neq v$ is another solution. Then

$$0 < a = \rho(\hat{v}, v) = \rho(T\hat{v}, Tv) \leq \beta\rho(\hat{v}, v) = \beta a,$$

which cannot hold, since $\beta < 1$. This proves part (a).

To prove part (b), observe that for any $n \geq 1$

$$\rho(T^n v_0, v) = \rho[T(T^{n-1}v_0), Tv] \leq \beta\rho(T^{n-1}v_0, v),$$

so that (b) follows by induction. ∎

Recall from Exercise 3.6b that if (S, ρ) is a complete metric space and S' is a closed subset of S, then (S', ρ) is also a complete metric space. Now suppose that $T: S \to S$ is a contraction mapping, and suppose further that T maps S' into itself, $T(S') \subseteq S'$ (where $T(S')$ denotes the image of S' under T). Then T is also a contraction mapping on S'. Hence the unique fixed point of T on S lies in S'. This observation is often useful for establishing qualitative properties of a fixed point. Specifically, in some situations we will want to apply the Contraction Mapping Theorem twice: once on a large space to establish uniqueness, and again on a smaller space to characterize the fixed point more precisely.

The following corollary formalizes this argument.

COROLLARY 1 *Let (S, ρ) be a complete metric space, and let $T: S \to S$ be a contraction mapping with fixed point $v \in S$. If S' is a closed subset of S and $T(S') \subseteq S'$, then $v \in S'$. If in addition $T(S') \subseteq S'' \subseteq S'$, then $v \in S''$.*

Proof. Choose $v_0 \in S'$, and note that $\{T^n v_0\}$ is a sequence in S' converging to v. Since S' is closed, it follows that $v \in S'$. If in addition $T(S') \subseteq S''$, then it follows that $v = Tv \in S''$. ∎

Part (b) of the Contraction Mapping Theorem bounds the distance $\rho(T^n v_0, v)$ between the nth approximation and the fixed point in terms of the distance $\rho(v_0, v)$ between the initial approximation and the fixed point. However, if v is not known (as is the case if one is computing v), then neither is the magnitude of the bound. Exercise 3.9 gives a computationally useful inequality.

Exercise 3.9 Let (S, ρ), T, and v be as given above, let β be the modulus of T, and let $v_0 \in S$. Show that

$$\rho(T^n v_0, v) \le \frac{1}{1 - \beta} \rho(T^n v_0, T^{n+1} v_0).$$

The following result is a useful generalization of the Contraction Mapping Theorem.

COROLLARY 2 (*N-Stage Contraction Theorem*) *Let (S, ρ) be a complete metric space, let $T: S \to S$, and suppose that for some integer N, $T^N: S \to S$ is a contraction mapping with modulus β. Then*
  a. *T has exactly one fixed point in S, and*
  b. *for any $v_0 \in S$, $\rho(T^{kN} v_0, v) \le \beta^k \rho(v_0, v)$, $k = 0, 1, 2, \ldots$.*

Proof. We will show that the unique fixed point v of T^N is also the unique fixed point of T. We have

$$\rho(Tv, v) = \rho[T(T^N v), T^N v] = \rho[T^N(Tv), T^N v] \le \beta \rho(Tv, v).$$

Since $\beta \in (0, 1)$, this implies that $\rho(Tv, v) = 0$, so v is a fixed point of T. To establish uniqueness, note that any fixed point of T is also a fixed point of T^N. Part (b) is established using the same argument as in the proof of Theorem 3.2. ∎

The next exercise shows how the Contraction Mapping Theorem is used to prove existence and uniqueness of a solution to a differential equation.

Exercise 3.10 Consider the differential equation and boundary condition $dx(s)/ds = f[x(s)]$, all $s \ge 0$, with $x(0) = c \in \mathbf{R}$. Assume that $f: \mathbf{R} \to \mathbf{R}$ is continuous, and for some $B > 0$ satisfies the Lipschitz condition $|f(a) - f(b)| \le B|a - b|$, all $a, b \in \mathbf{R}$. For any $t > 0$, consider $C[0, t]$, the space of bounded continuous functions on $[0, t]$, with the sup norm. Recall from Theorem 3.1 that this space is complete.
  a. Show that the operator T defined by

$$(Tv)(s) = c + \int_0^s f[v(z)] dz, \quad 0 \le s \le t,$$

maps $C[0, t]$ into itself. That is, show that if v is bounded and continuous on $[0, t]$, then so is Tv.

   b. Show that for some $\tau > 0$, T is a contraction on $C[0, \tau]$.

   c. Show that the unique fixed point of T on $C[0, \tau]$ is a differentiable function, and hence that it is the unique solution on $[0, \tau]$ to the given differential equation.

   Another useful route to verifying that certain operators are contractions is due to Blackwell.

THEOREM 3.3 (*Blackwell's sufficient conditions for a contraction*) Let $X \subseteq \mathbf{R}^l$, and let $B(X)$ be a space of bounded functions $f: X \to \mathbf{R}$, with the sup norm. Let $T: B(X) \to B(X)$ be an operator satisfying
   a. (*monotonicity*) $f, g \in B(X)$ and $f(x) \leq g(x)$, for all $x \in X$, implies $(Tf)(x) \leq (Tg)(x)$, for all $x \in X$;
   b. (*discounting*) there exists some $\beta \in (0, 1)$ such that

$$[T(f + a)](x) \leq (Tf)(x) + \beta a, \quad \text{all } f \in B(X), a \geq 0, x \in X.$$

[*Here* $(f + a)(x)$ *is the function defined by* $(f + a)(x) = f(x) + a$.] *Then T is a contraction with modulus* β.

   Proof. If $f(x) \leq g(x)$ for all $x \in X$, we write $f \leq g$. For any $f, g \in B(X)$, $f \leq g + \|f - g\|$. Then properties (a) and (b) imply that

$$Tf \leq T(g + \|f - g\|) \leq Tg + \beta\|f - g\|.$$

Reversing the roles of f and g gives by the same logic

$$Tg \leq Tf + \beta\|f - g\|.$$

Combining these two inequalities, we find that $\|Tf - Tg\| \leq \beta\|f - g\|$, as was to be shown. ∎

   In many economic applications the two hypotheses of Blackwell's theorem can be verified at a glance. For example, in the one-sector optimal growth problem, an operator T was defined by

$$(Tv)(k) = \max_{0 \leq y \leq f(k)} \{U[f(k) - y] + \beta v(y)\}.$$

If $v(y) \leq w(y)$ for all values of y, then the objective function for which Tw is the maximized value is uniformly higher than the function for which Tv is the maximized value; so the monotonicity hypothesis (a) is obvious. The discounting hypothesis (b) is equally easy, since

$$T(v + a)(k) = \max_{0 \leq y \leq f(k)} \{U[f(k) - y] + \beta[v(y) + a]\}$$

$$= \max_{0 \leq y \leq f(k)} \{U[f(k) - y] + \beta v(y)\} + \beta a$$

$$= (Tv)(k) + \beta a.$$

Blackwell's result will play a key role in our analysis of dynamic programs.

3.3 The Theorem of the Maximum

We will want to apply the Contraction Mapping Theorem to analyze dynamic programming problems that are much more general than the examples that have been discussed to this point. If x is the beginning-of-period state variable, an element of $X \subseteq \mathbf{R}^l$, and $y \in X$ is the end-of-period state to be chosen, we would like to let the current period return $F(x, y)$ and the set of feasible y values, given x, be specified as generally as possible. On the other hand, we want the operator T defined by

$$(Tv)(x) = \sup_y [F(x, y) + \beta v(y)]$$

s.t. y feasible given x,

to take the space $C(X)$ of bounded continuous functions of the state into itself. We would also like to be able to characterize the set of maximizing values of y, given x.

To describe the feasible set, we use the idea of a **correspondence** from a set X into a set Y: a relation that assigns a set $\Gamma(x) \subseteq Y$ to each $x \in X$. In the case of interest here, $Y = X$. Hence we seek restrictions on the correspondence $\Gamma: X \to X$ describing the feasibility constraints and on the return function F, which together ensure that if $v \in C(X)$ and $(Tv)(x) =$

$\sup_{y \in \Gamma(x)}[F(x, y) + \beta v(y)]$ then $Tv \in C(X)$. Moreover, we wish to determine the implied properties of the correspondence $G(x)$ containing the maximizing values of y for each x. The main result in this section is the Theorem of the Maximum, which accomplishes both tasks.

Let $X \subseteq \mathbf{R}^l$; let $Y \subseteq \mathbf{R}^m$; let $f: X \times Y \rightarrow \mathbf{R}$ be a (single-valued) function; and let $\Gamma: X \rightarrow Y$ be a (nonempty, possibly multivalued) correspondence. Our interest is in problems of the form $\sup_{y \in \Gamma(x)} f(x, y)$. If for each x, $f(x, \cdot)$ is continuous in y and the set $\Gamma(x)$ is nonempty and compact, then for each x the maximum is attained. In this case the function

(1) $$h(x) = \max_{y \in \Gamma(x)} f(x, y)$$

is well defined, as is the nonempty set

(2) $$G(x) = \{y \in \Gamma(x): f(x, y) = h(x)\}$$

of y values that attain the maximum. In this section further restrictions on f and Γ will be added, to ensure that the function h and the set G vary in a continuous way with x.

There are several notions of continuity for correspondences, and each can be characterized in a variety of ways. For our purposes it is convenient to use definitions stated in terms of sequences.

DEFINITION *A correspondence $\Gamma: X \rightarrow Y$ is **lower hemi-continuous** (l.h.c.) at x if $\Gamma(x)$ is nonempty and if, for every $y \in \Gamma(x)$ and every sequence $x_n \rightarrow x$, there exists $N \geq 1$ and a sequence $\{y_n\}_{n=N}^{\infty}$ such that $y_n \rightarrow y$ and $y_n \in \Gamma(x_n)$, all $n \geq N$. [If $\Gamma(x')$ is nonempty for all $x' \in X$, then it is always possible to take $N = 1$.]*

DEFINITION *A compact-valued correspondence $\Gamma: X \rightarrow Y$ is **upper hemi-continuous** (u.h.c.) at x if $\Gamma(x)$ is nonempty and if, for every sequence $x_n \rightarrow x$ and every sequence $\{y_n\}$ such that $y_n \in \Gamma(x_n)$, all n, there exists a convergent subsequence of $\{y_n\}$ whose limit point y is in $\Gamma(x)$.*

Figure 3.2 displays a correspondence that is l.h.c. but not u.h.c. at x_1; is u.h.c. but not l.h.c. at x_2; and is both u.h.c. and l.h.c. at all other points. Note that our definition of u.h.c. applies only to correspondences that are compact-valued. Since all of the correspondences we will be dealing

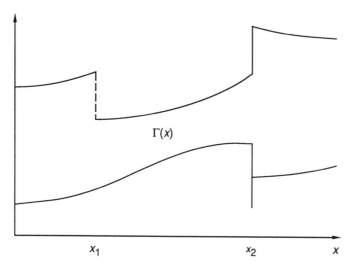

$\Gamma(x)$

x_1

x_2

x

Figure 3.2

with satisfy this requirement, the restriction will not be binding. (A definition of u.h.c. for all correspondences is available, but it is stated in terms of images of open sets. For our purposes this definition is much less convenient, and its wider scope is never useful.)

DEFINITION *A correspondence* $\Gamma: X \to Y$ *is* **continuous** *at* $x \in X$ *if it is both u.h.c. and l.h.c. at x.*

A correspondence $\Gamma: X \to Y$ is called l.h.c., u.h.c., or continuous if it has that property at every point $x \in X$. The following exercises highlight some important facts about upper and lower hemi-continuity. Note that if $\Gamma: X \to Y$, then for any set $\hat{X} \subset X$, we define

$$\Gamma(\hat{X}) = \{y \in Y: y \in \Gamma(x), \text{ for some } x \in \hat{X}\}.$$

Exercise 3.11 a. Show that if Γ is single-valued and u.h.c., then it is continuous.

b. Let $\Gamma: \mathbf{R}^k \to \mathbf{R}^{l+m}$, and define $\phi: \mathbf{R}^k \to \mathbf{R}^l$ by

$$\phi(x) = \{y_1 \in \mathbf{R}^l: (y_1, y_2) \in \Gamma(x) \text{ for some } y_2 \in \mathbf{R}^m\}.$$

Show that if Γ is compact-valued and u.h.c., then so is ϕ.

c. Let $\phi: X \rightarrow Y$ and $\psi: X \rightarrow Y$ be compact-valued and u.h.c., and define $\Gamma = \phi \cup \psi$ by

$$\Gamma(x) = \{y \in Y: y \in \phi(x) \cup \psi(x)\}, \quad \text{all } x \in X.$$

Show that Γ is compact-valued and u.h.c.

d. Let $\phi: X \rightarrow Y$ and $\psi: X \rightarrow Y$ be compact-valued and u.h.c., and suppose that

$$\Gamma(x) = \{y \in Y: y \in \phi(x) \cap \psi(x)\} \neq \emptyset, \quad \text{all } x \in X.$$

Show that Γ is compact-valued and u.h.c.

e. Show that if $\phi: X \rightarrow Y$ and $\psi: Y \rightarrow Z$ are compact-valued and u.h.c., then the correspondence $\psi \circ \phi = \Gamma: X \rightarrow Z$ defined by

$$\Gamma(x) = \{z \in Z: z \in \psi(y), \text{ for some } y \in \phi(x)\}$$

is also compact-valued and u.h.c.

f. Let $\Gamma_i: X \rightarrow Y_i$, $i = 1, \ldots, k$, be compact-valued and u.h.c. Show that $\Gamma: X \rightarrow Y = Y_1 \times \ldots \times Y_k$ defined by

$$\Gamma(x) = \{y \in Y: y = (y_1, \ldots, y_k), \text{ where } y_i \in \Gamma_i(x), i = 1, \ldots, k\},$$

is also compact-valued and u.h.c.

g. Show that if $\Gamma: X \rightarrow Y$ is compact-valued and u.h.c., then for any compact set $K \subseteq X$, the set $\Gamma(K) \subseteq Y$ is also compact. [*Hint.* To show that $\Gamma(K)$ is bounded, suppose the contrary. Let $\{y_n\}$ be a divergent sequence in $\Gamma(K)$, and choose $\{x_n\}$ such that $y_n \in \Gamma(x_n)$, all n.]

Exercise 3.12   a. Show that if Γ is single-valued and l.h.c., then it is continuous.

b. Let $\Gamma: \mathbf{R}^k \rightarrow \mathbf{R}^{l+m}$, and define $\phi: \mathbf{R}^k \rightarrow \mathbf{R}^l$ by

$$\phi(x) = \{y_1 \in \mathbf{R}^l: (y_1, y_2) \in \Gamma(x), \text{ for some } y_2 \in \mathbf{R}^m\}.$$

Show that if Γ is l.h.c., then so is ϕ.

c. Let $\phi: X \rightarrow Y$ and $\psi: X \rightarrow Y$ be l.h.c., and define $\Gamma = \phi \cup \psi$ by

$$\Gamma(x) = \{y \in Y: y \in \phi(x) \cup \psi(x)\}, \quad \text{all } x \in X.$$

Show that Γ is l.h.c.

d. Let $\phi: X \to Y$ and $\psi: X \to Y$ be l.h.c., and suppose that

$$\Gamma(x) = \{y \in Y: y \in \phi(x) \cap \psi(x)\} \neq \emptyset, \quad \text{all } x \in X.$$

Show by example that Γ need not be l.h.c. Show that if ϕ and ψ are both convex-valued, and if int $\phi(x) \cap$ int $\psi(x) \neq \emptyset$, then Γ is l.h.c. at x.

e. Show that if $\phi: X \to Y$ and $\psi: Y \to Z$ are l.h.c., then the correspondence $\psi \circ \phi = \Gamma: X \to Z$ defined by

$$\Gamma(x) = \{z \in Z: z \in \psi(y), \text{ for some } y \in \phi(x)\}$$

is also l.h.c.

f. Let $\Gamma_i: X \to Y_i, i = 1, \ldots, k$, be l.h.c. Show that $\Gamma: X \to Y = Y_1 \times \ldots \times Y_k$ defined by

$$\Gamma(x) = \{y \in Y: y = (y_1, \ldots, y_k), \text{ where } y_i \in \Gamma_i(x), i = 1, \ldots, k\}$$

is l.h.c.

The next two exercises show some of the relationships between constraints stated in terms of inequalities involving continuous functions and those stated in terms of continuous correspondences. These relationships are extremely important for many problems in economics, where constraints are often stated in terms of production functions, budget constraints, and so on.

Exercise 3.13 a. Let $\Gamma: \mathbf{R}_+ \to \mathbf{R}_+$ be defined by $\Gamma(x) = [0, x]$. Show that Γ is continuous.

b. Let $f: \mathbf{R}_+^l \to \mathbf{R}_+$ be a continuous function, and define the correspondence $\Gamma: \mathbf{R}_+^l \to \mathbf{R}_+$ by $\Gamma(x) = [0, f(x)]$. Show that Γ is continuous.

c. Let $f_i: \mathbf{R}_+^l \times \mathbf{R}^m \to \mathbf{R}_{++}, i = 1, \ldots, l$, be continuous functions. Define $\Gamma: \mathbf{R}_+^l \times \mathbf{R}^m \to \mathbf{R}_+^l$ by

$$\Gamma(x, z) = \left\{y \in \mathbf{R}_+^l: 0 \leq y_i \leq f_i(x^i, z), i = 1, \ldots, l; \text{ and } \sum_{i=1}^{l} x^i \leq x\right\}.$$

Show that Γ is continuous.

Exercise ***3.14*** a. Let $H(x, y): \mathbf{R}_+^l \times \mathbf{R}_+^m \to \mathbf{R}$ be continuous, strictly increasing in its first l arguments, strictly decreasing in its last m arguments, with $H(0, 0) = 0$. Define $\Gamma: \mathbf{R}^l \to \mathbf{R}^m$ by $\Gamma(x) = \{y \in \mathbf{R}^m: H(x, y) \geq 0\}$. Show that if $\Gamma(x)$ is compact-valued, then Γ is continuous at x.

b. Let $H(x, y): \mathbf{R}^l \times \mathbf{R}^m \to \mathbf{R}$ be continuous and concave, and define Γ as in part (a). Show that if $\Gamma(x)$ is compact-valued and there exists some $\hat{y} \in \Gamma(x)$ such that $H(x, \hat{y}) > 0$, then Γ is continuous at x.

c. Define $H: \mathbf{R} \times \mathbf{R} \to \mathbf{R}$ by $H(x, y) = 1 - \max\{|x|, |y|\}$, and define $\Gamma(x)$ as in part (a). Where does Γ fail to be l.h.c.?

When trying to establish properties of a correspondence $\Gamma: X \to Y$, it is sometimes useful to deal with its **graph,** the set

$$A = \{(x, y) \in X \times Y: y \in \Gamma(x)\}.$$

The next two results provide conditions on A that are sufficient to ensure the upper and lower hemi-continuity respectively of Γ.

THEOREM 3.4 *Let $\Gamma: X \to Y$ be a nonempty-valued correspondence, and let A be the graph of Γ. Suppose that A is closed, and that for any bounded set $\hat{X} \subseteq X$, the set $\Gamma(\hat{X})$ is bounded. Then Γ is compact-valued and u.h.c.*

Proof. For each $x \in X$, $\Gamma(x)$ is closed (since A is closed) and is bounded (by hypothesis). Hence Γ is compact-valued.

Let $\hat{x} \in X$, and let $\{x_n\} \subseteq X$ with $x_n \to \hat{x}$. Since Γ is nonempty-valued, we can choose $y_n \in \Gamma(x_n)$, all n. Since $x_n \to \hat{x}$, there is a bounded set $\hat{X} \subset X$ containing $\{x_n\}$ and $\hat{x}$. Then by hypothesis $\Gamma(\hat{X})$ is bounded. Hence $\{y_n\} \subset \Gamma(\hat{X})$ has a convergent subsequence, call it $\{y_{n_k}\}$; let $\hat{y}$ be the limit point of this subsequence. Then $\{(x_{n_k}, y_{n_k})\}$ is a sequence in A converging to $(\hat{x}, \hat{y})$; since A is closed, it follows that $(\hat{x}, \hat{y}) \in A$. Hence $\hat{y} \in \Gamma(\hat{x})$, so Γ is u.h.c. at $\hat{x}$. Since $\hat{x}$ was arbitrary, this establishes the desired result. ∎

To see why the hypothesis of boundedness is required in Theorem 3.4, consider the correspondence $\Gamma: \mathbf{R}_+ \to \mathbf{R}_+$ defined by

$$\Gamma(0) = 0, \quad \text{and} \quad \Gamma(x) = \{0, 1/x\}, \quad \text{all } x > 0.$$

The graph of Γ is closed, but Γ is not u.h.c. at $x = 0$.

The next exercise is a kind of converse to Theorem 3.4.

Exercise 3.15 Let $\Gamma: X \to Y$ be a compact-valued u.h.c. correspondence with graph A. Show that if X is compact then A is compact.

The next theorem deals with lower hemi-continuity. For any $x \in \mathbf{R}^l$ and any $\varepsilon > 0$, let $B(x, \varepsilon)$ denote the closed ball of radius ε about x: $B(x, \varepsilon) = \{x' \in X: \|x - x'\| \leq \varepsilon\}$.

THEOREM 3.5 *Let $\Gamma: X \to Y$ be a nonempty-valued correspondence, and let A be the graph of Γ. Suppose that A is convex; that for any bounded set $\hat{X} \subseteq X$, there is a bounded set $\hat{Y} \subseteq Y$ such that $\Gamma(x) \cap \hat{Y} \neq \emptyset$, all $x \in \hat{X}$; and that for every $x \in X$, there exists some $\varepsilon > 0$ such that the set $B(x, \varepsilon) \cap X$ is closed and convex. Then Γ is l.h.c.*

Proof. Choose $\hat{x} \in X$; $\hat{y} \in \Gamma(\hat{x})$; and $\{x_n\} \subset X$ with $x_n \to \hat{x}$. Choose $\varepsilon > 0$ such that the set $\hat{X} = B(\hat{x}, \varepsilon) \cap X$ is closed and convex. Note that for some $N \geq 1$, $x_n \in \hat{X}$, all $n \geq N$; without loss of generality we take $N = 1$.

Let D denote the boundary of the set $\hat{X}$. Every point x_n has at least one representation as a convex combination of $\hat{x}$ and a point in D. For each n, choose $\alpha_n \in [0, 1]$ and $d_n \in D$ such that

$$x_n = \alpha_n d_n + (1 - \alpha_n)\hat{x}.$$

Since D is a bounded set and $x_n \to \hat{x}$, it follows that $\alpha_n \to 0$. Choose $\hat{Y}$ such that $\Gamma(x) \cap \hat{Y} \neq \emptyset$, all $x \in \hat{X}$. Then for each n, choose $\hat{y}_n \in \Gamma(d_n) \cap \hat{Y}$, and define

$$y_n = \alpha_n \hat{y}_n + (1 - \alpha_n)\hat{y}, \quad \text{all } n.$$

Since $(d_n, \hat{y}_n) \in A$, all n, $(\hat{x}, \hat{y}) \in A$, and A is convex, it follows that $(x_n, y_n) \in A$, all n. Moreover, since $\alpha_n \to 0$ and all of the $\hat{y}_n$'s lie in the bounded set $\hat{Y}$, it follows that $y_n \to \hat{y}$. Hence $\{(x_n, y_n)\}$ lies in A and converges to $(\hat{x}, \hat{y})$, as was to be shown. ∎

We are now ready to answer the questions we posed at the beginning of this section: Under what conditions do the function $h(x)$ defined by the maximization problem in (1) and the associated set of maximizing y values $G(x)$ defined in (2) vary continuously with x? An answer is provided in the following theorem, which will repeatedly be applied later.

THEOREM 3.6 (*Theorem of the Maximum*) Let $X \subseteq \mathbf{R}^l$ and $Y \subseteq \mathbf{R}^m$, let $f: X \times Y \to \mathbf{R}$ be a continuous function, and let $\Gamma: X \to Y$ be a compact-valued and continuous correspondence. Then the function $h: X \to \mathbf{R}$ defined in (1) is continuous, and the correspondence $G: X \to Y$ defined in (2) is nonempty, compact-valued, and u.h.c.

Proof. Fix $x \in X$. The set $\Gamma(x)$ is nonempty and compact, and $f(x, \cdot)$ is continuous; hence the maximum in (1) is attained, and the set $G(x)$ of maximizers is nonempty. Moreover, since $G(x) \subseteq \Gamma(x)$ and $\Gamma(x)$ is compact, it follows that $G(x)$ is bounded. Suppose $y_n \to y$, and $y_n \in G(x)$, all n. Since $\Gamma(x)$ is closed, $y \in \Gamma(x)$. Also, since $h(x) = f(x, y_n)$, all n, and f is continuous, it follows that $f(x, y) = h(x)$. Hence $y \in G(x)$; so $G(x)$ is closed. Thus $G(x)$ is nonempty and compact, for each x.

Next we will show that $G(x)$ is u.h.c. Fix x, and let $\{x_n\}$ be any sequence converging to x. Choose $y_n \in G(x_n)$, all n. Since Γ is u.h.c., there exists a subsequence $\{y_{n_k}\}$ converging to $y \in \Gamma(x)$. Let $z \in \Gamma(x)$. Since Γ is l.h.c., there exists a sequence $z_{n_k} \to z$, with $z_{n_k} \in \Gamma(x_{n_k})$, all k. Since $f(x_{n_k}, y_{n_k}) \geq f(x_{n_k}, z_{n_k})$, all k, and f is continuous, it follows that $f(x, y) \geq f(x, z)$. Since this holds for any $z \in \Gamma(x)$, it follows that $y \in G(x)$. Hence G is u.h.c.

Finally, we will show that h is continuous. Fix x, and let $\{x_n\}$ be any sequence converging to x. Choose $y_n \in G(x_n)$, all n. Let $\bar{h} = \lim \sup h(x_n)$ and $\underline{h} = \lim \inf h(x_n)$. Then there exists a subsequence $\{x_{n_k}\}$ such that $\bar{h} = \lim f(x_{n_k}, y_{n_k})$. But since G is u.h.c., there exists a subsequence of $\{y_{n_k}\}$, call it $\{y_j'\}$, converging to $y \in G(x)$. Hence $\bar{h} = \lim f(x_j, y_j') = f(x, y) = h(x)$. An analogous argument establishes that $h(x) = \underline{h}$. Hence $\{h(x_n)\}$ converges, and its limit is $h(x)$. ∎

The following exercise illustrates through concrete examples what this theorem does and does not say.

Exercise 3.16 a. Let $X = \mathbf{R}$, and let $\Gamma(x) = Y = [-1, +1]$, all $x \in X$. Define $f: X \times Y \to \mathbf{R}$ by $f(x, y) = xy^2$. Graph $G(x)$; show that $G(x)$ is u.h.c. but not l.h.c. at $x = 0$.

b. Let $x = \mathbf{R}$, and let $\Gamma(x) = [0, 4]$, all $x \in X$. Define

$$f(x, y) = \max\{2 - (y - 1)^2, x + 1 - (y - 2)^2\}.$$

Graph $G(x)$ and show that it is u.h.c. Exactly where does it fail to be l.h.c.?

c. Let $X = \mathbf{R}_+$, $\Gamma(x) = \{y \in \mathbf{R}: -x \le y \le x\}$, and $f(x, y) = \cos(y)$. Graph $G(x)$ and show that it is u.h.c. Exactly where does it fail to be l.h.c.?

Suppose that in addition to the hypotheses of the Theorem of the Maximum the correspondence Γ is convex-valued and the function f is strictly concave in y. Then G is single-valued, and by Exercise 3.11a it is a continuous function—call it g. The next two results establish properties of g. Lemma 3.7 shows that if $f(x, y)$ is close to the maximized value $f[x, g(x)]$, then y is close to $g(x)$. Theorem 3.8 draws on this result to show that if $\{f_n\}$ is a sequence of continuous functions, each strictly concave in y, converging uniformly to f, then the sequence of maximizing functions $\{g_n\}$ converges pointwise to g. The latter convergence is uniform if X is compact.

LEMMA 3.7 *Let $X \subseteq \mathbf{R}^l$ and $Y \subseteq \mathbf{R}^m$. Assume that the correspondence $\Gamma: X \to Y$ is nonempty, compact- and convex-valued, and continuous, and let A be the graph of Γ. Assume that the function $f: A \to \mathbf{R}$ is continuous and that $f(x, \cdot)$ is strictly concave, for each $x \in X$. Define the function $g: X \to Y$ by*

$$g(x) = \operatorname*{argmax}_{y \in \Gamma(x)} f(x, y).$$

Then for each $\varepsilon > 0$ and $x \in X$, there exists $\delta_x > 0$ such that

$$y \in \Gamma(x) \text{ and } |f[x, g(x)] - f(x, y)| < \delta_x \text{ implies } \|g(x) - y\| < \varepsilon.$$

If X is compact, then $\delta > 0$ can be chosen independently of x.

Proof. Note that under the stated assumptions g is a well-defined, continuous (single-valued) function. We first prove the claim for the case where X is compact. Note that in this case A is a compact set by Exercise 3.15. For each $\varepsilon > 0$, define

$$A_\varepsilon = \{(x, y) \in A: \|g(x) - y\| \ge \varepsilon\}.$$

If $A_\varepsilon = \emptyset$, all $\varepsilon > 0$, then Γ is single-valued and the result is trivial. Otherwise there exists $\hat\varepsilon > 0$ sufficiently small such that for all $0 < \varepsilon < \hat\varepsilon$, the set A_ε is nonempty and compact. For any such ε, let

$$\delta = \min_{(x,y) \in A_\varepsilon} |f[x, g(x)] - f(x, y)|.$$

Since the function being minimized is continuous and A_ε is compact, the minimum is attained. Moreover, since $[x, g(x)] \notin A_\varepsilon$, all $x \in X$, it follows that $\delta > 0$. Then

$$y \in \Gamma(x) \text{ and } \|g(x) - y\| \geq \varepsilon \text{ implies } |f[x, g(x)] - f(x, y)| \geq \delta,$$

as was to be shown.

If X is not compact, the argument above can be applied separately for each fixed $x \in X$. ∎

THEOREM 3.8 *Let X, Y, Γ, and A be as defined in Lemma 3.7. Let $\{f_n\}$ be a sequence of continuous (real-valued) functions on A; assume that for each n and each $x \in X$, $f_n(x, \cdot)$ is strictly concave in its second argument. Assume that f has the same properties and that $f_n \to f$ uniformly (in the sup norm). Define the functions g_n and g by*

$$g_n(x) = \operatorname*{argmax}_{y \in \Gamma(x)} f_n(x, y), \quad n = 1, 2, \ldots, \text{ and}$$

$$g(x) = \operatorname*{argmax}_{y \in \Gamma(x)} f(x, y).$$

Then $g_n \to g$ pointwise. If X is compact, $g_n \to g$ uniformly.

Proof. First note that since $g_n(x)$ is the unique maximizer of $f_n(x, \cdot)$ on $\Gamma(x)$, and $g(x)$ is the unique maximizer of $f(x, \cdot)$ on $\Gamma(x)$, it follows that

$$0 \leq f[x, g(x)] - f[x, g_n(x)]$$

$$\leq f[x, g(x)] - f_n[x, g(x)] + f_n[x, g_n(x)] - f[x, g_n(x)]$$

$$\leq 2\|f - f_n\|, \quad \text{all } x \in X.$$

Since $f_n \to f$ uniformly, it follows immediately that for any $\delta > 0$, there exists $M_\delta \geq 1$ such that

(3) $$0 \leq f[x, g(x)] - f[x, g_n(x)] \leq 2\|f - f_n\| < \delta,$$

all $x \in X$, all $n \geq M_\delta$.

To show that $g_n \to g$ pointwise, we must establish that for each $\varepsilon > 0$ and $x \in X$, there exists $N_x \geq 1$ such that

(4) $\|g(x) - g_n(x)\| < \varepsilon$,   all $n \geq N_x$.

By Lemma 3.7, it suffices to show that for any $\delta_x > 0$ and $x \in X$ there exists $N_x \geq 1$ such that

(5) $|f[x, g(x)] - f[x, g_n(x)]| < \delta_x$,   all $n \geq N_x$.

From (3), it follows that any $N_x \geq M_{\delta_x}$ has the required property.

Suppose X is compact. To establish that $g_n \to g$ uniformly, we must show that for each $\varepsilon > 0$ there exists $N \geq 1$ such that (4) holds for all $x \in X$. By Lemma 3.7, it suffices to show that for any $\delta > 0$, there exists $N \geq 1$, such that (5) holds for all $x \in X$. From (3) it follows that any $N \geq M_\delta$ has the required property. ∎

3.4   Bibliographic Notes

For a more detailed discussion of metric spaces, see Kolmogorov and Fomin (1970, chap. 2) or Royden (1968, chap. 7). Good discussions of normed vector spaces can be found in Kolmogorov and Fomin (1970, chap. 4) and Luenberger (1969, chap. 2), both of which also treat the Contraction Mapping Theorem. Blackwell's sufficient condition is Theorem 5 in Blackwell (1965). The Theorem of the Maximum dates from Berge (1963, chap. 6), and can also be found in Hildenbrand (1974, pt. I.B). Both of these also contain excellent treatments of upper and lower hemi-continuity.

4   Dynamic Programming under Certainty

Posed in terms of infinite sequences, the problems we are interested in are of the form

(SP) $\displaystyle\sup_{\{x_{t+1}\}_{t=0}^{\infty}} \sum_{t=0}^{\infty} \beta^t F(x_t, x_{t+1})$

   s.t. $x_{t+1} \in \Gamma(x_t), \quad t = 0, 1, 2, \ldots,$

   $x_0 \in X$ given.

Corresponding to any such problem, we have a functional equation of the form

(FE) $v(x) = \displaystyle\sup_{y \in \Gamma(x)} [F(x, y) + \beta v(y)], \quad \text{all } x \in X.$

In this chapter we establish the relationship between solutions to these two problems and develop methods for analyzing the latter.

   Exercise 4.1   a. Show that the one-sector growth model discussed at the beginning of Chapter 3 can be expressed as in (SP).
   b. Show that the many-sector growth model

   $\displaystyle\sup_{\{(c_t, k_{t+1})\}_{t=0}^{\infty}} \sum_{t=0}^{\infty} \beta^t U(c_t)$

   s.t. $(k_{t+1} + c_t, k_t) \in Y, \quad t = 0, 1, 2, \ldots,$

   given $k_0 \in \mathbf{R}_+^l,$

where $Y \subseteq \mathbf{R}_+^{2l}$ is a fixed production set, can also be written this way.

As we hinted in the last chapter and will show in this one, some very powerful—and relatively simple—mathematical tools can be used to study the functional equation (FE). To take advantage of these, however, we must show that solutions to (FE) correspond to solutions to the sequence problem (SP). In Section 4.1 we rigorously establish the connections between solutions to these two problems, connections that Richard Bellman called the *Principle of Optimality*. Section 4.2 then develops the main results of the chapter: existence, uniqueness, and characterization theorems for solutions to (FE) under the assumption that the return function F is bounded. The case where F displays constant returns to scale is treated in Section 4.3, and the case where F is an arbitrary unbounded return function in Section 4.4. Section 4.5 treats the relationship between the dynamic programming approach to optimization over time and the classical (variational) approach. Section 4.6 contains references for further discussion of some of the mathematical and economic ideas. In Chapter 5 we illustrate how the methods developed in Sections 4.2–4.4 can be applied to a wide variety of economic problems.

4.1 The Principle of Optimality

In this section we study the relationship between solutions to the problems (SP) and (FE). (Note that "sup" has been used instead of "max" in both, so that we can ignore—for the moment—the question of whether the optimum is attained.) The general idea, of course, is that the solution v to (FE), evaluated at x_0, gives the value of the supremum in (SP) when the initial state is x_0 and that a sequence $\{x_{t+1}\}_{t=0}^{\infty}$ attains the supremum in (SP) if and only if it satisfies

$$(1) \qquad v(x_t) = F(x_t, x_{t+1}) + \beta v(x_{t+1}), \quad t = 0, 1, 2, \ldots.$$

Richard Bellman called these ideas the Principle of Optimality. Intuitive as it is, the Principle requires proof. Spelling out precisely the conditions under which it holds is our task in this section.

The main results are Theorem 4.2, establishing that the supremum function v^* for the sequence problem (SP) satisfies the functional equation (FE), and Theorem 4.3, establishing a partial converse. The "partial" nature of the converse arises from the fact that a boundedness condition must be imposed. Theorems 4.4 and 4.5 then deal with the characterization of optimal policies. Theorem 4.4 shows that if $\{x_{t+1}\}_{t=0}^{\infty}$ is a sequence attaining the supremum in (SP), then it satisfies (1) for $v = v^*$. Conversely, Theorem 4.5 establishes that any sequence $\{x_{t+1}\}_{t=0}^{\infty}$ that satisfies (1) for $v = v^*$, and also satisfies a boundedness condition, attains the supremum in (SP). The four theorems taken together thus establish conditions under which solutions to (SP) and to (FE) coincide exactly, and optimal policies are those that satisfy (1).

To begin we must establish some notation. Let X be the set of possible values for the state variable x. In this section we will not need to impose any restrictions on the set X. It may be a subset of a Euclidean space, a set of functions, a set of probability distributions, or any other set. Let $\Gamma: X \to X$ be the correspondence describing the feasibility constraints. That is, for each $x \in X$, $\Gamma(x)$ is the set of feasible values for the state variable next period if the current state is x. Let A be the graph of Γ:

$$A = \{(x, y) \in X \times X : y \in \Gamma(x)\}.$$

Let the real-valued function $F: A \to \mathbf{R}$ be the one-period return function, and let $\beta \geq 0$ be the (stationary) discount factor. Thus the "givens" for the problem are X, Γ, F, and β.

First we must establish conditions under which the problem (SP) is well defined. That is, we must find conditions under which the feasible set is nonempty and the objective function is well defined for every point in the feasible set.

Call any sequence $\{x_t\}_{t=0}^{\infty}$ in X a *plan*. Given $x_0 \in X$, let

$$\Pi(x_0) = \{\{x_t\}_{t=0}^{\infty} : x_{t+1} \in \Gamma(x_t), \quad t = 0, 1, \ldots\}$$

be the set of plans that are *feasible from* x_0. That is, $\Pi(x_0)$ is the set of all sequences $\{x_t\}$ satisfying the constraints in (SP). Let $\underset{\sim}{x} = (x_0, x_1, \ldots)$ denote a typical element of $\Pi(x_0)$. The following assumption ensures that $\Pi(x_0)$ is nonempty, for all $x_0 \in X$.

ASSUMPTION 4.1 $\Gamma(x)$ *is nonempty, for all $x \in X$.*

The only additional restriction on X, Γ, F, and β we will need in this section is a requirement that all feasible plans can be evaluated using the objective function F and the discount rate β.

ASSUMPTION 4.2   *For all $x_0 \in X$ and $\underset{\sim}{x} \in \Pi(x_0)$, $\lim_{n \to \infty} \sum_{t=0}^{n} \beta^t F(x_t, x_{t+1})$ exists (although it may be plus or minus infinity).*

There are a variety of ways of ensuring that Assumption 4.2 holds. Clearly it is satisfied if the function F is bounded and $0 < \beta < 1$. Alternatively, for any $(x, y) \in A$, let

$$F^+(x, y) = \max\{0, F(x, y)\} \quad \text{and} \quad F^-(x, y) = \max\{0, -F(x, y)\}.$$

Then Assumption 4.2 holds if for each $x_0 \in X$ and $\underline{x} \in \Pi(x_0)$, either

$$\lim_{n \to \infty} \sum_{t=0}^{n} \beta^t F^+(x_t, x_{t+1}) < +\infty, \quad \text{or}$$

$$\lim_{n \to \infty} \sum_{t=0}^{n} \beta^t F^-(x_t, x_{t+1}) < +\infty, \quad \text{or both.}$$

Thus a sufficient condition for Assumptions 4.1–4.2 is that F be bounded above or below and $0 < \beta < 1$. Another sufficient condition is that for each $x_0 \in X$ and $\underline{x} \in \Pi(x_0)$, there exist $\theta \in (0, \beta^{-1})$ and $0 < c < \infty$ such that

$$F(x_t, x_{t+1}) \leq c\theta^t, \quad \text{all } t.$$

The following exercise provides a way of verifying that the latter holds.

Exercise 4.2 a. Show that Assumption 4.2 is satisfied if $X = \mathbf{R}_+^l$; $0 < \beta < 1$; there exists $0 < \theta < 1/\beta$ such that $y \in \Gamma(x)$ implies $\|y\| \leq \theta\|x\|$; $F(0, 0) = 0$; F is increasing in its first l arguments and decreasing in its last l arguments; F is concave in its first l arguments; and $0 \in \Gamma(x)$, all x.

b. Show that Assumption 4.2 is satisfied if $X = \mathbf{R}_+^l$; $0 < \beta < 1$; there exists $0 < \theta < 1/\beta$ such that $y \in \Gamma(x)$ implies $F(y, 0) \leq \theta F(x, 0)$; F is increasing in its first l arguments and decreasing in its last l arguments; and $0 \in \Gamma(x)$, all x.

For each $n = 0, 1, \ldots,$ define $u_n \colon \Pi(x_0) \to \mathbf{R}$ by

$$u_n(\underline{x}) = \sum_{t=0}^{n} \beta^t F(x_t, x_{t+1}).$$

Then $u_n(\underline{x})$ is the partial sum of the (discounted) returns in periods 0 through n from the feasible plan $\underset{\sim}{x}$. Under Assumption 4.2 we can also define $u: \Pi(x_0) \to \overline{\mathbf{R}}$ by

$$u(\underset{\sim}{x}) = \lim_{n \to \infty} u_n(\underset{\sim}{x}),$$

where $\overline{\mathbf{R}} = \mathbf{R} \cup \{+\infty, -\infty\}$ is the set of extended real numbers. Thus $u(\underset{\sim}{x})$ is the (infinite) sum of discounted returns from the feasible sequence $\underset{\sim}{x}$.

If Assumptions 4.1 and 4.2 both hold, then the set of feasible plans $\Pi(x_0)$ is nonempty for each $x_0 \in X$, and the objective function in (SP) is well defined for every plan $\underset{\sim}{x} \in \Pi(x_0)$. We can then define the *supremum function* $v^*: X \to \overline{\mathbf{R}}$ by

$$v^*(x_0) = \sup_{\underset{\sim}{x} \in \Pi(x_0)} u(\underset{\sim}{x}).$$

Thus $v^*(x_0)$ is the supremum in (SP). Note that it follows by definition that v^* is the unique function satisfying the following three conditions:
  a. if $|v^*(x_0)| < \infty$, then

(2) $v^*(x_0) \geq u(\underset{\sim}{x}), \quad$ all $\underset{\sim}{x} \in \Pi(x_0)$;

and for any $\varepsilon > 0$,

(3) $v^*(x_0) \leq u(\underset{\sim}{x}) + \varepsilon, \quad$ some $\underset{\sim}{x} \in \Pi(x_0)$;

  b. if $v^*(x_0) = +\infty$, then there exists a sequence $\{\underset{\sim}{x}^k\}$ in $\Pi(x_0)$ such that $\lim_{k \to \infty} u(\underset{\sim}{x}^k) = +\infty$; and
  c. if $v^*(x_0) = -\infty$, then $u(\underset{\sim}{x}) = -\infty$, for all $\underset{\sim}{x} \in \Pi(x_0)$.
Our interest is in the connections between the supremum function v^* and solutions v to the functional equation (FE). In interpreting the next results, it is important to remember that v^* is always uniquely defined (provided Assumptions 4.1–4.2 hold), whereas (FE) may—for all we know so far—have zero, one, or many solutions.

We will say that v^* satisfies the functional equation if three conditions hold:
  a. If $|v^*(x_0)| < \infty$, then

(4) $v^*(x_0) \geq F(x_0, y) + \beta v^*(y), \quad$ all $y \in \Gamma(x_0)$,

and for any $\varepsilon > 0$,

(5) $v^*(x_0) \leq F(x_0, y) + \beta v^*(y) + \varepsilon,$ some $y \in \Gamma(x_0)$;

b. if $v^*(x_0) = +\infty$, then there exists a sequence $\{y^k\}$ in $\Gamma(x_0)$ such that

(6) $\lim_{k \to \infty} [F(x_0, y^k) + \beta v^*(y^k)] = +\infty$;

c. if $v^*(x_0) = -\infty$, then

(7) $F(x_0, y) + \beta v^*(y) = -\infty,$ all $y \in \Gamma(x_0)$.

Before we prove that the supremum function v^* satisfies the functional equation, it is useful to establish a preliminary result.

LEMMA 4.1   *Let X, Γ, F, and β satisfy Assumption 4.2. Then for any $x_0 \in X$ and any $(x_0, x_1, \ldots) = \underline{x} \in \Pi(x_0)$,*

$$u(\underline{x}) = F(x_0, x_1) + \beta u(\underline{x}'),$$

where $\underline{x}' = (x_1, x_2, \ldots)$.

Proof. Under Assumption 4.2, for any $x_0 \in X$ and any $\underline{x} \in \Pi(x_0)$,

$$u(\underline{x}) = \lim_{n \to \infty} \sum_{t=0}^{n} \beta^t F(x_t, x_{t+1})$$

$$= F(x_0, x_1) + \beta \lim_{n \to \infty} \sum_{t=0}^{n} \beta^t F(x_{t+1}, x_{t+2})$$

$$= F(x_0, x_1) + \beta u(\underline{x}'). \quad \blacksquare$$

THEOREM 4.2   *Let X, Γ, F, and β satisfy Assumptions 4.1–4.2. Then the function v^* satisfies (FE).*

Proof. If $\beta = 0$, the result is trivial. Suppose that $\beta > 0$, and choose $x_0 \in X$.

Suppose $v^*(x_0)$ is finite. Then (2) and (3) hold, and it is sufficient to show that this implies (4) and (5) hold. To establish (4), let $x_1 \in \Gamma(x_0)$ and $\varepsilon > 0$ be given. Then by (3) there exists $\underline{x}' = (x_1, x_2, \ldots) \in \Pi(x_1)$ such that $u(\underline{x}') \geq v^*(x_1) - \varepsilon$. Note, too, that $\underline{x} = (x_0, x_1, x_2, \ldots) \in \Pi(x_0)$. Hence it follows from (2) and Lemma 4.1 that

$$v^*(x_0) \geq u(\underline{x}) = F(x_0, x_1) + \beta u(\underline{x}') \geq F(x_0, x_1) + \beta v^*(x_1) - \beta \varepsilon.$$

Since $\varepsilon > 0$ was arbitrary, (4) follows.

To establish (5), choose $x_0 \in X$ and $\varepsilon > 0$. From (3) and Lemma 4.1, it follows that one can choose $\underline{x} = (x_0, x_1, \ldots) \in \Pi(x_0)$, so that

$$v^*(x_0) \leq u(\underline{x}) + \varepsilon = F(x_0, x_1) + \beta u(\underline{x}') + \varepsilon,$$

where $\underline{x}' = (x_1, x_2, \ldots)$. It then follows from (2) that

$$v^*(x_0) \leq F(x_0, x_1) + \beta v^*(x_1) + \varepsilon.$$

Since $x_1 \in \Gamma(x_0)$, this establishes (5).

If $v^*(x_0) = +\infty$, then there exists a sequence $\{\underline{x}^k\}$ in $\Pi(x_0)$ such that $\lim_{k \to \infty} u(\underline{x}^k) = +\infty$. Since $x_1^k \in \Gamma(x_0)$, all k, and

$$u(\underline{x}^k) = F(x_0, x_1^k) + \beta u(\underline{x}'^k) \leq F(x_0, x_1^k) + \beta v^*(x_1^k), \quad \text{all } k,$$

it follows that (6) holds for the sequence $\{y^k = x_1^k\}$ in $\Gamma(x_0)$.

If $v^*(x_0) = -\infty$, then

$$u(\underline{x}) = F(x_0, x_1) + \beta u(\underline{x}') = -\infty, \quad \text{all } (x_0, x_1, x_2, \ldots) = \underline{x} \in \Pi(x_0),$$

where $\underline{x}' = (x_1, x_2, \ldots)$. Since F is real-valued (it does *not* take on the values $-\infty$ or $+\infty$), it follows that

$$u(\underline{x}') = -\infty, \quad \text{all } x_1 \in \Gamma(x_0), \text{ all } \underline{x}' \in \Pi(x_1).$$

Hence $v^*(x_1) = -\infty$, all $x_1 \in \Gamma(x_0)$. Since F is real-valued and $\beta > 0$, (7) follows immediately. ∎

The next theorem provides a partial converse to Theorem 4.2. It shows that v^* is the only solution to the functional equation that satisfies a certain boundedness condition.

THEOREM 4.3 *Let X, Γ, F, and β satisfy Assumptions 4.1–4.2. If v is a solution to (FE) and satisfies*

(8) $\lim_{n \to \infty} \beta^n v(x_n) = 0$,   all $(x_0, x_1, \ldots) \in \Pi(x_0)$, all $x_0 \in X$,

then $v = v^*$.

Proof. If $v(x_0)$ is finite, then (4) and (5) hold, and it suffices to show that this implies (2) and (3) hold. Now (4) implies that for all $\underline{x} \in \Pi(x_0)$,

$$v(x_0) \geq F(x_0, x_1) + \beta v(x_1)$$

$$\geq F(x_0, x_1) + \beta F(x_1, x_2) + \beta^2 v(x_2)$$

$$\vdots$$

$$\geq u_n(\underline{x}) + \beta^{n+1} v(x_{n+1}), \quad n = 1, 2, \ldots.$$

Taking the limit as $n \to \infty$ and using (8), we find that (2) holds.

Next, fix $\varepsilon > 0$ and choose $\{\delta_t\}_{t=1}^{\infty}$ in $\mathbf{R}_+$ such that $\Sigma_{t=1}^{\infty} \beta^{t-1} \delta_t \leq \varepsilon/2$. Since (5) holds, we can choose $x_1 \in \Gamma(x_0)$, $x_2 \in \Gamma(x_1)$, $\ldots$ so that

$$v(x_t) \leq F(x_t, x_{t+1}) + \beta v(x_{t+1}) + \delta_{t+1}, \quad t = 0, 1, \ldots.$$

Then $\underline{x} = (x_0, x_1, \ldots) \in \Pi(x_0)$, and

$$v(x_0) \leq \sum_{t=0}^{n} \beta^t F(x_t, x_{t+1}) + \beta^{n+1} v(x_{n+1}) + (\delta_1 + \ldots + \beta^n \delta_{n+1})$$

$$\leq u_n(\underline{x}) + \beta^{n+1} v(x_{n+1}) + \varepsilon/2, \quad n = 1, 2, \ldots.$$

Hence (8) implies that for all n sufficiently large, $v(x_0) \leq u_n(\underline{x}) + \varepsilon$. Since $\varepsilon > 0$ was arbitrary, it follows that (3) holds.

If (8) holds, then (7) implies that v cannot take the value $-\infty$. If $v(x_0) = +\infty$, choose $n \geq 0$ and $(x_0, x_1, \ldots, x_n)$ such that $x_t \in \Gamma(x_{t-1})$ and $v(x_t) = +\infty$ for $t = 0, 1, \ldots, n$, and $v(x_{n+1}) < +\infty$ for all $x_{n+1} \in \Gamma(x_n)$. Clearly (8) implies that n is finite. Fix any $A > 0$. Since $v(x_n) = +\infty$, (6) implies that we can choose $x_{n+1}^A \in \Gamma(x_n)$ such that

$$F(x_n, x_{n+1}^A) + \beta v(x_{n+1}^A) \geq \beta^{-n}\left[A + 1 - \sum_{t=0}^{n-1} \beta^t F(x_t, x_{t+1})\right].$$

Then choose $x_{n+1}^A \in \Pi(x_{n+1}^A)$ such that $u(x_{n+1}^A) \geq v(x_{n+1}^A) - \beta^{-(n+1)}$. Since $v(x_{n+1}^A)$ is finite, the argument above shows that this is possible. Then $x^A = (x_0, x_1, \ldots, x_n, x_{n+1}^A) \in \Pi(x_0)$, and

$$u(x^A) = \sum_{t=0}^{n-1} \beta^t F(x_t, x_{t+1}) + \beta^n F(x_n, x_{n+1}^A) + \beta^{n+1} u(x_{n+1}^A) \geq A.$$

Since $A > 0$ was arbitrary, it follows that $v^*(x_0) = +\infty$. ∎

It is an immediate consequence of Theorem 4.3 that the functional equation (FE) has at most one solution satisfying (8).

In summary, we have established two main results about solutions to (FE). Theorem 4.2 shows that v^* satisfies (FE). The functional equation may have other solutions as well, but Theorem 4.3 shows that these extraneous solutions always violate (8). Hence a solution to (FE) that satisfies (8) is v^*. The following example is a case where (FE) has an extraneous solution in addition to v^*.

Consider a consumer whose objective function is simply discounted consumption. The consumer has initial wealth $x_0 \in X = \mathbf{R}$, and he can borrow or lend at the interest rate $\beta^{-1} - 1$, where $\beta \in (0, 1)$. There are no constraints on borrowing, so his problem is simply

$$\max_{\{(c_t, x_{t+1})\}_{t=0}^{\infty}} \sum_{t=0}^{\infty} \beta^t c_t$$

$$\text{s.t.} \quad 0 \leq c_t \leq x_t - \beta x_{t+1}, \quad t = 0, 1, \ldots,$$

$$x_0 \text{ given.}$$

Since consumption is unbounded, the supremum function is obviously $v^*(x) = +\infty$, all x. Now consider the recursive formulation of this problem. The return function is $F(x, y) = x - \beta y$, and the correspondence describing the feasible set is $\Gamma(x) = (-\infty, \beta^{-1}x]$; so the functional equation is

$$v(x) = \sup_{y \leq \beta^{-1}x} [x - \beta y + \beta v(y)].$$

The function $v^*(x) = +\infty$ satisfies this equation, as Theorem 4.2 implies, but the function $v(x) = x$ does, too. But since the sequence $x_t = \beta^{-t}x_0$, $t = 0, 1, \ldots$, is in $\Pi(x_0)$, (8) does not hold and Theorem 4.3 does not apply.

The next exercise gives two variations on Theorem 4.3 that are sometimes useful when (8) does not hold.

Exercise 4.3 Let X, Γ, F, and β satisfy Assumptions 4.1–4.2. Let v be a solution to (FE) with

$$\limsup_{n \to \infty} \beta^n v(x_n) \le 0, \quad \text{all } x_0 \in X, \text{ all } (x_0, x_1, \ldots) \in \Pi(x_0),$$

a. Show that $v \le v^*$.

b. Suppose in addition that for each $x_0 \in X$ and $\underset{\sim}{x} \in \Pi(x_0)$, there exists $\underset{\sim}{x}' = (x_0, x_1', x_2', \ldots) \in \Pi(x_0)$ such that $\lim_{n \to \infty} \beta^n v(x_n') = 0$ and $u(\underset{\sim}{x}') \ge u(\underset{\sim}{x})$. Show that $v = v^*$.

Our next task is to characterize feasible plans that attain the optimum, if any do. Call a feasible plan $\underset{\sim}{x} \in \Pi(x_0)$ an *optimal plan from* x_0 if it attains the supremum in (SP), that is, if $u(\underset{\sim}{x}) = v^*(x_0)$. The next two theorems deal with the relationship between optimal plans and those that satisfy the policy equation (1) for $v = v^*$. The next theorem shows that optimal plans satisfy (1).

THEOREM 4.4 *Let X, Γ, F, and β satisfy Assumption 4.1–4.2. Let $\underset{\sim}{x}^* \in \Pi(x_0)$ be a feasible plan that attains the supremum in (SP) for initial state x_0. Then*

$$(9) \qquad v^*(x_t^*) = F(x_t^*, x_{t+1}^*) + \beta v^*(x_{t+1}^*), \quad t = 0, 1, 2, \ldots.$$

Proof. Since $\underset{\sim}{x}^*$ attains the supremum,

$$(10) \qquad v^*(x_0^*) = u(\underset{\sim}{x}^*) = F(x_0, x_1^*) + \beta u(\underset{\sim}{x}^{*\prime})$$

$$\ge u(\underset{\sim}{x}) = F(x_0, x_1) + \beta u(\underset{\sim}{x}'), \quad \text{all } \underset{\sim}{x} \in \Pi(x_0).$$

In particular, the inequality holds for all plans with $x_1 = x_1^*$. Since $(x_1^*, x_2, x_3, \ldots) \in \Pi(x_1^*)$ implies that $(x_0, x_1^*, x_2, x_3, \ldots) \in \Pi(x_0)$, it follows that

$$u(\underset{\sim}{x}^{*\prime}) \ge u(\underset{\sim}{x}'), \quad \text{all } \underset{\sim}{x} \in \Pi(x_1^*).$$

Hence $u(\underset{\sim}{x}^{*\prime}) = v(x_1^*)$. Substituting this into (10) gives (9) for $t = 0$. Continuing by induction establishes (9) for all t. ∎

The next theorem provides a partial converse to Theorem 4.4. It shows that any sequence satisfying (9) and a boundedness condition is an optimal plan.

THEOREM 4.5 *Let X, Γ, F, and β satisfy Assumptions 4.1–4.2. Let $\underline{x}^* \in \Pi(x_0)$ be a feasible plan from x_0 satisfying (9), and with*

$$(11) \qquad \limsup_{t \to \infty} \beta^t v^*(x_t^*) \le 0.$$

Then $\underline{x}^*$ attains the supremum in (SP) for initial state x_0.

Proof. Suppose that $\underline{x}^* \in \Pi(x_0)$ satisfies (9) and (11). Then it follows by an induction on (9) that

$$v^*(x_0) = u_n(\underline{x}^*) + \beta^{n+1} v^*(x_{n+1}^*), \quad n = 1, 2, \ldots .$$

Then using (11), we find that $v^*(x_0) \le u(\underline{x}^*)$. Since $\underline{x}^* \in \Pi(x_0)$, the reverse inequality holds, establishing the result. ∎

The consumption example used after Theorem 4.3 can be modified to illustrate why (11) is needed. Let preferences be as specified before, so that $c_t = x_t - \beta x_{t+1} = F(x_t, x_{t+1})$, all t. However, let us prohibit indebtedness by requiring $x_t \ge 0$, all t. Then in sequence form the problem is

$$\max_{\{x_{t+1}\}_{t=0}^{\infty}} \sum_{t=0}^{\infty} \beta^t(x_t - \beta x_{t+1})$$

$$\text{s.t. } 0 \le x_{t+1} \le \beta^{-1} x_t, \quad t = 0, 1, \ldots,$$

$$x_0 \text{ given.}$$

If we cancel all of the offsetting terms in the objective function, it follows immediately that the supremum function is $v^*(x_0) = x_0$, all $x_0 \ge 0$. It is also clear that v^* satisfies the functional equation

$$v^*(x) = \max_{y \in [0, \beta^{-1}x]} [(x - \beta y) + \beta v^*(y)], \quad \text{all } x,$$

as Theorem 4.2 implies.

Now consider plans that attain the optimum. Given any $x_0 \geq 0$, the set of feasible plans $\Pi(x_0)$ consists of the sequences

$$(x_0, 0, 0, 0, \ldots), (x_0, \beta^{-1}x_0, 0, 0, \ldots),$$

$$(x_0, \beta^{-1}x_0, \beta^{-2}x_0, 0, \ldots), \text{ etc.,}$$

and all convex combinations thereof. Hence every feasible plan satisfies (9). It is straightforward to verify that, as Theorem 4.5 implies, any plan that satisfies (11) as well yields utility $v^*(x_0) = x_0$. (Essentially, it does not matter when consumption occurs as long as it occurs in finite time.) On the other hand, the feasible plan $x_t = \beta^{-t}x_0$, $t = 0, 1, \ldots$, (in each period invest everything and consume nothing) yields discounted utility of zero, for all $x \geq 0$. For $x > 0$, however, it violates (11), so Theorem 4.5 does not apply.

We will call any nonempty correspondence $G: X \to X$, with $G(x) \subseteq \Gamma(x)$, all $x \in X$, a *policy correspondence*, since the set $G(x)$ is a feasible set of actions if the state is x. If G is single-valued, we will call it a *policy function* and denote it by a lowercase g. If a sequence $\underline{x} = (x_0, x_1, \ldots)$ satisfies $x_{t+1} \in G(x_t)$, $t = 0, 1, 2, \ldots$, we will say that $\underline{x}$ is *generated from x_0 by G*. Finally, we will define the *optimal policy correspondence G^** by

$$G^*(x) = \{y \in \Gamma(x): v^*(x) = F(x, y) + \beta v^*(y)\}.$$

Then Theorem 4.4 shows that every optimal plan $\{x_t^*\}$ is generated from G^*, and Theorem 4.5 shows that any plan $\{x_t^*\}$ generated from G^*—if, in addition, it satisfies (11)—is an optimal plan.

4.2 Bounded Returns

In this section we study functional equations of the form

$$(1) \qquad v(x) = \max_{y \in \Gamma(x)} [F(x, y) + \beta v(y)],$$

under the assumption that the function F is bounded and the discount factor β is strictly less than one.

As above, let X be the set of possible values for the state variable; let $\Gamma: X \to X$ be the correspondence describing the feasibility constraints; let

$A = \{(x, y) \in X \times X: y \in \Gamma(x)\}$ be the graph of Γ; let $F: A \to \mathbf{R}$ be the return function; and let $\beta \geq 0$ be the discount factor. Throughout this section, we will impose the following two assumptions on X, Γ, F, and β.

ASSUMPTION 4.3 *X is a convex subset of $\mathbf{R}^l$, and the correspondence Γ: $X \to X$ is nonempty, compact-valued, and continuous.*

ASSUMPTION 4.4 *The function $F: A \to \mathbf{R}$ is bounded and continuous, and $0 < \beta < 1$.*

It is clear that under Assumptions 4.3–4.4, Assumptions 4.1–4.2 hold, so the sequence problem corresponding to (1) is well defined. Moreover, Theorems 4.2–4.5 imply that under these assumptions solutions to (1) coincide exactly—in terms of both values and optimal plans—to solutions of the sequence problem.

The requirement that X be a subset of a finite-dimensional Euclidean space could be relaxed in much of what follows, but at the expense of a substantial additional investment in terminology and notation. (Recall that the definitions of u.h.c. and l.h.c. provided in Chapter 3 applied only to correspondences from one Euclidean space to another.) However, most of the arguments in this section apply much more broadly. Also note that the assumption that X is convex is not needed for Theorems 4.6 and 4.7.

If B is a bound for $|F(x, y)|$, then the supremum function v^* satisfies $|v^*(x)| \leq B/(1 - \beta)$, all $x \in X$. In this case it is natural to seek solutions to (1) in the space $C(X)$ of bounded continuous functions $f: X \to \mathbf{R}$, with the sup norm: $\|f\| = \sup_{x \in X}|f(x)|$. Clearly, any solution to (1) in $C(X)$ satisfies the hypothesis of Theorem 4.3 and hence is the supremum function. Moreover, given a solution $v \in C(X)$ to (1), we can define the policy correspondence $G: X \to X$ by

(2) $G(x) = \{y \in \Gamma(x): v(x) = F(x, y) + \beta v(y)\},$

and Theorems 4.4 and 4.5 imply that for any $x_0 \in X$, a sequence $\{x_t^*\}$ attains the supremum in the sequence problem if and only if it is generated by G.

The rest of the section proceeds as follows. Define the operator T on $C(X)$ by

(3) $(Tf)(x) = \max_{y \in \Gamma(x)}[F(x, y) + \beta f(y)],$

so (1) becomes $v = Tv$. First, if we use only the boundedness and continuity restrictions in Assumptions 4.3 and 4.4, Theorem 4.6 establishes that $T: C(X) \to C(X)$, that T has a unique fixed point in $C(X)$, and that the policy correspondence G defined in (2) is nonempty and u.h.c. Theorem 4.7 establishes that under additional monotonicity restrictions on F and Γ, v is strictly increasing. Theorem 4.8 establishes that under additional concavity restrictions on F and convexity restrictions on Γ, v is strictly concave and G is a continuous (single-valued) function. Theorem 4.9 shows that if $\{v_n\}$ is a sequence of approximations defined by $v_n = T^n v_0$, with v_0 appropriately chosen, then the sequence of associated policy functions $\{g_n\}$ converges uniformly to the optimal policy function g given by (2). Finally, Theorem 4.11 establishes that if F is continuously differentiable, then v is, too.

THEOREM 4.6 *Let X, Γ, F, and β satisfy Assumptions 4.3 and 4.4, and let $C(X)$ be the space of bounded continuous functions $f: X \to \mathbf{R}$, with the sup norm. Then the operator T maps $C(X)$ into itself, $T: C(X) \to C(X)$; T has a unique fixed point $v \in C(X)$; and for all $v_0 \in C(X)$,*

$$(4) \qquad \|T^n v_0 - v\| \le \beta^n \|v_0 - v\|, \quad n = 0, 1, 2, \dots.$$

Moreover, given v, the optimal policy correspondence $G: X \to X$ defined by (2) is compact-valued and u.h.c.

Proof. Under Assumptions 4.3 and 4.4, for each $f \in C(X)$ and $x \in X$, the problem in (3) is to maximize the continuous function $[F(x, \cdot) + \beta f(\cdot)]$ over the compact set $\Gamma(x)$. Hence the maximum is attained. Since both F and f are bounded, clearly Tf is also bounded; and since F and f are continuous, and Γ is compact-valued and continuous, it follows from the Theorem of the Maximum (Theorem 3.6) that Tf is continuous. Hence $T: C(X) \to C(X)$.

It is then immediate that T satisfies the hypotheses of Blackwell's sufficient conditions for a contraction (Theorem 3.3). Since $C(X)$ is a Banach space (Theorem 3.1), it then follows from the Contraction Mapping Theorem (Theorem 3.2), that T has a unique fixed point $v \in C(X)$, and (4) holds. The stated properties of G then follow from the Theorem of the Maximum, applied to (1). ∎

It follows immediately from Theorem 4.3 that under the hypotheses of Theorem 4.6, the unique bounded continuous function v satisfying

(1) is the supremum function for the associated sequence problem. That is, Theorems 4.3 and 4.6 together establish that under Assumptions 4.3–4.4 the supremum function is bounded and continuous. Moreover, it then follows from Theorems 4.5 and 4.6 that there exists at least one optimal plan: any plan generated by the (nonempty) correspondence G is optimal.

To characterize v and G more sharply, we need more information about F and Γ. The next two results show how Corollary 1 to the Contraction Mapping Theorem can be used to obtain more precise characterizations of v and G.

ASSUMPTION 4.5   *For each y, $F(\cdot, y)$ is strictly increasing in each of its first l arguments.*

ASSUMPTION 4.6   *Γ is monotone in the sense that $x \le x'$ implies $\Gamma(x) \subseteq \Gamma(x')$.*

THEOREM 4.7   *Let X, Γ, F, and β satisfy Assumptions 4.3–4.6, and let v be the unique solution to (1). Then v is strictly increasing.*

Proof. Let $C'(X) \subset C(X)$ be the set of bounded, continuous, nondecreasing functions on X, and let $C''(X) \subset C'(X)$ be the set of strictly increasing functions. Since $C'(X)$ is a closed subset of the complete metric space $C(X)$, by Theorem 4.6 and Corollary 1 to the Contraction Mapping Theorem (Theorem 3.2), it is sufficient to show that $T[C'(X)] \subseteq C''(X)$. Assumptions 4.5 and 4.6 ensure that this is so. ∎

ASSUMPTION 4.7   *F is strictly concave; that is,*

$$F[\theta(x, y) + (1 - \theta)(x', y')] \ge \theta F(x, y) + (1 - \theta)F(x', y'),$$

$$\text{all } (x, y), (x', y') \in A, \quad \text{and all } \theta \in (0, 1),$$

and the inequality is strict if $x \ne x'$.

ASSUMPTION 4.8   *Γ is convex in the sense that for any $0 \le \theta \le 1$, and $x, x' \in X$,*

$$y \in \Gamma(x) \quad \text{and} \quad y' \in \Gamma(x') \quad \text{implies}$$

$$\theta y + (1 - \theta)y' \in \Gamma[\theta x + (1 - \theta)x'].$$

Assumption 4.8 implies that for each $x \in X$, the set $\Gamma(x)$ is convex and there are no "increasing returns." Note that since X is convex, Assumption 4.8 is equivalent to assuming that the graph of Γ (the set A) is convex.

THEOREM 4.8 *Let X, Γ, F, and β satisfy Assumptions 4.3–4.4 and 4.7– 4.8; let v satisfy (1); and let G satisfy (2). Then v is strictly concave and G is a continuous, single-valued function.*

Proof. Let $C'(X) \subset C(X)$ be the set of bounded, continuous, weakly concave functions on X, and let $C''(X) \subset C'(X)$ be the set of strictly concave functions. Since $C'(X)$ is a closed subset of the complete metric space $C(X)$, by Theorem 4.6 and Corollary 1 to the Contraction Mapping Theorem (Theorem 3.2), it is sufficient to show that $T[C'(X)] \subseteq C''(X)$.

To verify that this is so, let $f \in C'(X)$ and let

$$x_0 \neq x_1, \quad \theta \in (0, 1), \quad \text{and} \quad x_\theta = \theta x_0 + (1 - \theta)x_1.$$

Let $y_i \in \Gamma(x_i)$ attain $(Tf)(x_i)$, for $i = 0, 1$. Then by Assumption 4.8, $y_\theta = \theta y_0 + (1 - \theta)y_1 \in \Gamma(x_\theta)$. It follows that

$$(Tf)(x_\theta) \geq F(x_\theta, y_\theta) + \beta f(y_\theta)$$

$$> \theta[F(x_0, y_0) + \beta f(y_0)] + (1 - \theta)[F(x_1, y_1) + \beta f(y_1)]$$

$$= \theta(Tf)(x_0) + (1 - \theta)(Tf)(x_1),$$

where the first line uses (3) and the fact that $y_\theta \in \Gamma(x_\theta)$; the second uses the hypothesis that f is concave and the concavity restriction on F in Assumption 4.7; and the last follows from the way y_0 and y_1 were selected. Since x_0 and x_1 were arbitrary, it follows that Tf is strictly concave, and since f was arbitrary, that $T[C'(X)] \subseteq C''(X)$.

Hence the unique fixed point v is strictly concave. Since F is also concave (Assumption 4.7) and, for each $x \in X$, $\Gamma(x)$ is convex (Assumption 4.8), it follows that the maximum in (3) is attained at a unique y value. Hence G is a single-valued function. The continuity of G then follows from the fact that it is u.h.c. (Exercise 3.11). ∎

Theorems 4.7 and 4.8 characterize the value function by using the fact that the operator T preserves certain properties. Thus if v_0 has property

P and if *P* is preserved by *T*, then we can conclude that each function in the sequence $\{T^n v_0\}$ has property *P*. Then, if *P* is preserved under uniform convergence, we can conclude that *v* also has property *P*. The same general idea can be used to establish facts about the policy function *g*, but we need to establish the sense in which the approximate policy functions—the functions g_n that attain $T^n v_0$—converge to *g*. The next result draws on Theorem 3.8 to address this issue.

THEOREM 4.9 (*Convergence of the policy functions*)   *Let X, Γ, F, and β satisfy Assumptions 4.3–4.4 and 4.7–4.8, and let v and g satisfy (1) and (2). Let C'(X) be the set of bounded, continuous, concave functions f: X → **R**, and let $v_0 \in C'(X)$. Let $\{(v_n, g_n)\}$ be defined by*

$$v_{n+1} = Tv_n, \quad n = 0, 1, 2, \ldots, \quad \text{and}$$

$$g_n(x) = \operatorname*{argmax}_{y \in \Gamma(x)} [F(x, y) + \beta v_n(y)], \quad n = 0, 1, 2, \ldots.$$

Then $g_n \to g$ pointwise. If X is compact, then the convergence is uniform.

Proof. Let $C''(X) \subset C'(X)$ be the set of strictly concave functions $f: X \to \mathbf{R}$. As shown in Theorem 4.8, $v \in C''(X)$. Moreover, as shown in the proof of that theorem, $T[C'(X)] \subseteq C''(X)$. Since $v_0 \in C'(X)$, it then follows that every function v_n, $n = 1, 2, \ldots$, is strictly concave. Define the functions $\{f_n\}$ and f by

$$f_n(x, y) = F(x, y) + \beta v_n(y), \quad n = 1, 2, \ldots, \quad \text{and}$$

$$f(x, y) = F(x, y) + \beta v(y).$$

Since *F* satisfies Assumption 4.7, it follows that each function f_n, $n = 1$, $2, \ldots$, is strictly concave, as is *f*. Hence Theorem 3.8 applies and the desired results are proved. ∎

The next exercise deals with the case where the state space *X* is finite or countable, as it is in computational applications.

Exercise 4.4   Let $X = \{x_1, x_2, \ldots\}$ be a finite or countable set; let the correspondence $\Gamma: X \to X$ be nonempty and finite-valued; let $A =$

$\{(x, y) \in X \times X: y \in \Gamma(x)\}$; let $F: A \to \mathbf{R}$ be a bounded function; and let $0 < \beta < 1$. Let $B(X)$ be the set of bounded functions $f: X \to \mathbf{R}$, with the sup norm. Define the operator T by (3).

a. Show that $T: B(X) \to B(X)$; that T has a unique fixed point $v \in B(X)$; that (4) holds for all $v_0 \in B(X)$; and that the optimal policy correspondence $G: X \to X$ defined by (2) is nonempty.

Let H be the set of functions $h: X \to X$ such that $h(x) \in \Gamma(x)$, all $x \in X$. For any $h \in H$, define the operator T_h on $B(X)$ by $(T_h f)(x) = F[x, h(x)] + \beta f[h(x)]$.

b. Show that for any $h \in H$, $T_h: B(X) \to B(X)$, and T_h has a unique fixed point $w \in B(X)$.

Let $h_0 \in H$ be given, and consider the following algorithm. Given h_n, let w_n be the unique fixed point of T_{h_n}. Given w_n, choose h_{n+1} so that $h_{n+1}(x) \in \mathrm{argmax}_{y \in \Gamma(x)} [F(x, y) + \beta w_n(y)]$.

c. Show that the sequence of functions $\{w_n\}$ converges to v, the unique fixed point of T. [*Hint.* Show that $w_0 \le T w_0 \le w_1 \le T w_1 \le \dots$.]

An algorithm based on Exercise 4.4 involves applying the operators T_{h_n}—operators that require no maximization—repeatedly and applying T only infrequently. Since maximization is usually the expensive step in these computations, the savings can be considerable.

Once the existence of a unique solution $v \in C(X)$ to the functional equation (1) has been established, we would like to treat the maximum problem in that equation as an ordinary programming problem and use the standard methods of calculus to characterize the policy function g. For example, consider the functional equation for the one-sector growth model:

$$v(x) = \max_{0 \le y \le f(x)} \{U[f(x) - y] + \beta v(y)\}.$$

If we knew that v was differentiable (and that the solution to the maximum problem in (1) was always interior), then the policy function g would be given implicitly by the first-order condition

(5) $U'[f(x) - g(x)] - \beta v'[g(x)] = 0$.

Moreover, if we knew that v was twice differentiable, the monotonicity of g could be established by differentiating (5) with respect to x and examining the resulting expression for g'. However, the legitimacy of these methods depends upon the differentiability of the functions U, f, v, and g. We are free to make whatever differentiability assumptions we choose for U and f, but the properties of v and g must be established. We turn next to what is known about this issue.

It has been shown by Benveniste and Scheinkman (1979) that under fairly general conditions the value function v is *once* differentiable. That is, (5) is valid under quite broad conditions. However, known conditions ensuring that v is *twice* differentiable (and hence that g is once differentiable) are extremely strong (see Araujo and Scheinkman 1981). Thus differentiating (5) is seldom useful as a way of establishing properties of g. However, in cases where g is monotone, it is usually possible to establish that fact by a direct argument involving a first-order condition like (5).

We begin with the theorem proved by Benveniste and Scheinkman.

THEOREM 4.10 (*Benveniste and Scheinkman*)   *Let $X \subseteq \mathbf{R}^l$ be a convex set, let $V: X \to \mathbf{R}$ be concave, let $x_0 \in int\ X$, and let D be a neighborhood of x_0. If there is a concave, differentiable function $W: D \to \mathbf{R}$, with $W(x_0) = V(x_0)$ and with $W(x) \leq V(x)$ for all $x \in D$, then V is differentiable at x_0, and*

$$V_i(x_0) = W_i(x_0), \quad i = 1, 2, \ldots, l.$$

Proof. Any subgradient p of V at x_0 must satisfy

$$p \cdot (x - x_0) \geq V(x) - V(x_0) \geq W(x) - W(x_0), \quad \text{all } x \in D,$$

where the first inequality uses the definition of a subgradient and the second uses the fact that $W(x) \leq V(x)$, with equality at x_0. Since W is differentiable at x_0, p is unique, and any concave function with a unique subgradient at an interior point x_0 is differentiable at x_0 (cf. Rockafellar 1970, Theorem 25.1, p. 242). ∎

Figure 4.1 illustrates the idea behind this result.

Applying this result to dynamic programs is straightforward, given the following additional restriction.

ASSUMPTION 4.9   *F is continuously differentiable on the interior of A.*

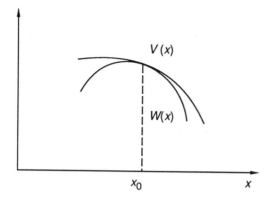

Figure 4.1

THEOREM 4.11 (*Differentiability of the value function*)   *Let X, Γ, F, and β satisfy Assumptions 4.3–4.4 and 4.7–4.9, and let v and g satisfy (1) and (2). If $x_0 \in int\ X$ and $g(x_0) \in int\ \Gamma(x_0)$, then v is continuously differentiable at x_0, with derivatives given by*

$$v_i(x_0) = F_i[x_0, g(x_0)], \quad i = 1, 2, \ldots, l.$$

Proof. Since $g(x_0) \in int\ \Gamma(x_0)$ and Γ is continuous, it follows that $g(x_0) \in int\ \Gamma(x)$, for all x in some neighborhood D of x_0. Define W on D by

$$W(x) = F[x, g(x_0)] + \beta v[g(x_0)].$$

Since F is concave (Assumption 4.7) and differentiable (Assumption 4.9), it follows that W is concave and differentiable. Moreover, since $g(x_0) \in \Gamma(x)$ for all $x \in D$, it follows that

$$W(x) \le \max_{y \in \Gamma(x)} [F(x, y) + \beta v(y)] = v(x), \quad \text{all } x \in D,$$

with equality at x_0. Hence v and W satisfy the hypotheses of Theorem 4.10, and the desired results follow immediately. ∎

Note that the proof requires only that F be differentiable in its first l arguments.

With differentiability of the value function established, it is often straightforward to show that the optimal policy function g is monotone, and to bound its slope.

Exercise 4.5   Consider the first-order condition (5). Assume that U, f, and v are strictly increasing, strictly concave, and once continuously differentiable, and that $0 < g(x) < f(x)$, all x. Use (5) to show that g is strictly increasing and has slope less than the slope of f. That is,

$$0 < g(x') - g(x) < f(x') - f(x), \quad \text{if } x' > x.$$

[*Hint.* Refer to Figure 4.2.]

In specific applications it is often possible to obtain much sharper characterizations of v or of G or of both than those provided by the theorems above. It is useful to keep in mind that once the existence and uniqueness of the solution to (1) has been established, the right side of that equation can be treated as an ordinary maximization problem. Thus whatever tools can be brought to bear on that problem should be exploited. But such arguments usually rely on properties of F or of Γ or of both that are specific to the application at hand. The problems in Chapter 5 provide a variety of illustrations of specific arguments of this type.

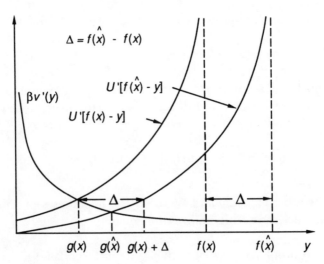

Figure 4.2

It should also be emphasized that even in cases that do not quite fit the assumptions of this section, arguments similar to the ones above can often be used. In this sense the results above should be viewed as suggestive, not (by any means) definitive. Sections 5.12 and 5.15 illustrate this point, as do many other applications in the literature. One particularly good illustration is the case of dynamic programming problems that exhibit constant returns to scale, to which we turn next.

4.3   Constant Returns to Scale

We sometimes wish to work with return functions F that are unbounded. For example, in the one-sector model of optimal growth, any utility function of the form $U(c) = (c^{1-\sigma} - 1)/(1 - \sigma)$, $\sigma \geq 1$, together with any technology of the form $f(k) = k^\alpha$, $0 < \alpha \leq 1$, leads to an unbounded return function. In this case and others like it, Assumption 4.4 is violated if X is taken to be all of $\mathbf{R}^l_+$. There are several ways to deal with problems of this type.

In some cases it is natural to restrict the state space to be a compact set $X \subset \mathbf{R}^l_+$. If Γ is compact-valued and continuous and if F is continuous, then with this restriction on X imposed, F is bounded on the compact set A. In these cases the arguments in Section 4.2 can be applied directly. Thus a judicious choice of the state space is very often all that is needed to apply those arguments to problems in which utility functions, profit functions, and so on, are unbounded. Illustrations of this method are given in Sections 5.1 and 5.9.

However, there are also many interesting cases where the state space cannot be so restricted. For example, no model of capital accumulation in which the technology permits sustained growth can be treated in this way. In this section and the next, we describe two ways in which the arguments in Section 4.2 can be adapted to models with unbounded returns.

This section deals with systems in which the return function and feasibility constraints both display constant returns to scale, and the constraints have the further property that feasible sequences $\{x_t\}$ cannot grow "too fast." First we show that Theorems 4.2–4.5 hold for problems of this type, so solutions to the functional equation correspond exactly to solutions of the original problem posed in terms of sequences, in terms of both values and policies. Theorems 4.12 and 4.13 then establish that the functional equation has a unique solution, and that this solution and the associated policy correspondence are homogeneous of degree one.

Throughout this section we let X be a *convex cone* in $\mathbf{R}^l$. That is, $X \subseteq \mathbf{R}^l$ is a convex set with the property that $x \in X$ implies $\alpha x \in X$, for any $\alpha \geq 0$. For example, $\mathbf{R}^l$ and $\mathbf{R}^l_+$ are both convex cones. In place of Assumptions 4.3 and 4.4, we will use the following restrictions. As in Section 4.2, let A denote the graph of Γ.

ASSUMPTION 4.10 $X \subseteq \mathbf{R}^l$ *is a convex cone. The correspondence* Γ: $X \to X$ *is nonempty, compact-valued, and continuous, and for any* $x \in X$,

$$y \in \Gamma(x) \text{ implies } \lambda y \in \Gamma(\lambda x), \quad \text{all } \lambda \geq 0.$$

That is, the graph of Γ *is a cone. In addition, for some* $\alpha \in (0, \beta^{-1})$,

$$\|y\|_E \leq \alpha \|x\|_E, \quad \text{all } x \in X \text{ and } y \in \Gamma(x),$$

(where $\|\cdot\|_E$ *denotes the Euclidean norm on* $\mathbf{R}^l$*).*

ASSUMPTION 4.11 $\beta \in (0, 1)$; *and* $F: A \to \mathbf{R}$ *is continuous and homogeneous of degree one, and for some* $0 < B < \infty$,

$$|F(x, y)| \leq B(\|x\|_E + \|y\|_E), \quad \text{all } (x, y) \in A.$$

Assumption 4.10 says that the correspondence Γ describing the feasibility constraints shows constant returns to scale, and it bounds the rate of growth of $\{\|x_t\|_E\}$ for feasible sequences $\{x_t\}$ by β^{-1}. Assumption 4.11 says that the return function F displays constant returns to scale, and it imposes a uniform bound on the ratio of F to the norm of its arguments.

Under Assumptions 4.10–4.11 we have the following results.

Exercise 4.6 Show that under Assumptions 4.10–4.11,
a. $\|x_t\|_E \leq \alpha^t \|x_0\|_E$, $t = 1, 2, \ldots$, all $x_0 \in X$, all $\{x_t\} \in \Pi(x_0)$;
b. Assumptions 4.1–4.2 hold; and
c. the supremum function $v^*: X \to \mathbf{R}$ defined in Section 4.1 is homogeneous of degree one, and for some $0 < c < \infty$, satisfies $|v^*(x)| \leq c\|x\|_E$, all $x \in X$.

Part (b) of this exercise establishes that under Assumptions 4.10–4.11, Theorems 4.2 and 4.4 hold. That is, the supremum function v^* satisfies the functional equation, and every optimal sequence $\{x_t^*\}$ (if any exist) is generated from the policy correspondence G associated with v^*. Moreover, v^* has the properties established in part (c) of the exercise.

Our next task is to choose an appropriate space of functions within which to look for solutions to the functional equation and then to define an appropriate operator on that space. In view of the results in Exercise 4.6c, it is natural to seek solutions to the functional equation within the space of functions $f: X \to \mathbf{R}$ that are continuous and homogeneous of degree one, and bounded in the sense that $|f(x)|/\|x\|_E < +\infty$, all $x \in X$. To capture the latter fact, it is useful to use the norm

$$(1) \qquad \|f\| = \max_{\substack{\|x\|_E=1 \\ x \in X}} |f(x)|.$$

Let $H(X)$ be the space of functions $f: X \to \mathbf{R}$ that are continuous and homogeneous of degree one, and bounded in the norm in (1). Define the operator T on $H(X)$ by

$$(2) \qquad (Tf)(x) = \sup_{y \in \Gamma(x)} [F(x, y) + \beta f(y)].$$

Exercise 4.7   a. Show that $H(X)$, with the norm in (1), is a complete normed vector space.

b. Show that under Assumptions 4.10 and 4.11, $T: H(X) \to H(X)$.

It follows directly from Exercise 4.6a that for any $f \in H(X)$,

$$|f(x_t)| \le \|x_t\|_E \|f\| \le \alpha^t \|x_0\|_E \|f\|, \quad \text{all } x_0 \in X, \quad \text{all } \{x_t\} \in \Pi(x_0).$$

Since $\alpha\beta < 1$, it then follows that the hypotheses of Theorems 4.3 and 4.5 hold. Therefore v^* is the only solution in $H(X)$ to the functional equation, and every sequence $\{x_t^*\}$ generated by the associated policy correspondence G is optimal. Thus the Principle of Optimality applies to this type of constant-returns-to-scale problem.

The contraction property of the operator T can be verified by using a modification of Blackwell's sufficient conditions for a contraction (Theorem 3.3). For any function f that is homogeneous of degree one and for any $a \in \mathbf{R}$, we will in this context define the function $f + a$ by

$$(f + a)(x) = f(x) + a\|x\|,$$

(where here and below we drop the subscript E). It is immediate that $f + a$ is also homogeneous of degree one.

THEOREM 4.12 *Let $X \subseteq \mathbf{R}^l$ be a convex cone, and let $H(X)$ be as above, with the norm in (1). Let $T: H(X) \rightarrow H(X)$ satisfy*

a. *(monotonicity) $f, g \in H$ and $f \leq g$ implies $Tf \leq Tg$;*

b. *(discounting) there exists $\gamma \in (0, 1)$ such that for all $f \in H$ and all $a \geq 0$,*
$T(f + a) \leq Tf + \gamma a$.
Then T is a contraction with modulus γ.

Proof. By homogeneity of degree one,

$$f(x) = \|x\| f(x/\|x\|), \quad \text{all } f \in H, \quad \text{all } x \neq 0.$$

Choose any $f, g \in H(X)$. Then

$$f(x) = g(x) + [f(x) - g(x)]$$

$$= g(x) + \|x\|[f(x/\|x\|) - g(x/\|x\|)]$$

$$\leq g(x) + \|x\| \|f - g\|, \quad \text{all } x \neq 0.$$

That is, $f \leq g + \|f - g\|$. Hence monotonicity and discounting respectively imply that

$$Tf \leq T(g + \|f - g\|) \leq Tg + \gamma\|f - g\|.$$

Reversing the roles of f and g and combining the two results, we find that $\|Tf - Tg\| \leq \gamma\|f - g\|$, as was to be shown. ∎

Our next result uses this theorem to establish that the operator T defined in (2) is a contraction with modulus $\alpha\beta$.

THEOREM 4.13 *Let X, Γ, F, and β satisfy Assumptions 4.10 and 4.11, and let $H(X)$ be as above. Then the operator T defined in (2) has a unique fixed point $v \in H(X)$. In addition*

$$(3) \qquad \|T^n v_0 - v\| \leq (\alpha\beta)^n \|v_0 - v\|, \quad n = 0, 1, 2, \ldots, \quad \text{all } v_0 \in H(X);$$

and the associated policy correspondence $G: X \rightarrow X$ is compact-valued and u.h.c. Moreover, G is homogeneous of degree one: for any $x \in X$,

$$y \in G(x) \text{ implies } \lambda y \in G(\lambda x), \text{ all } \lambda \geq 0.$$

Proof. As shown in Exercise 4.7, $H(X)$ is a complete metric space and $T: H(X) \rightarrow H(X)$. Clearly T satisfies the monotonicity condition of Theorem 4.12. Choose $f \in H(X)$ and $a > 0$. Then

$$T(f + a)(x) = \sup_{y \in \Gamma(x)} [F(x, y) + \beta(f + a)(y)]$$

$$= \sup_{y \in \Gamma(x)} [F(x, y) + \beta f(y) + \beta a \|y\|]$$

$$\leq \sup_{y \in \Gamma(x)} [F(x, y) + \beta f(y)] + \beta a \alpha \|x\|$$

$$= (Tf)(x) + \alpha \beta a \|x\|,$$

where the third line uses Assumption 4.10. Since $x \in X$ was arbitrary, it follows that $T(f + a) \leq Tf + \alpha\beta a$. Hence T satisfies the discounting condition, and, by Theorem 4.12, T is a contraction of modulus $\alpha\beta$. It then follows from the Contraction Mapping Theorem (Theorem 3.2) that T has a unique fixed point $v \in H(X)$ and that (3) holds.

That G is u.h.c. and compact-valued then follows from the Theorem of the Maximum (Theorem 3.6). Finally, suppose that $y \in G(x)$. Then $y \in \Gamma(x)$ and $v(x) = F(x, y) + \beta v(y)$. It then follows from Assumption 4.10 that $\lambda y \in \Gamma(\lambda x)$ and from the homogeneity of F and v that $v(\lambda x) = F(\lambda x, \lambda y) + \beta v(\lambda y)$. Hence $\lambda y \in G(\lambda x)$. ∎

Exercise 4.8 Call a function $f: X \rightarrow \mathbf{R}$ *quasi-concave* if $x \neq x'$, $f(x) \geq f(x')$ and $\theta \in (0, 1)$ implies $f[\theta x + (1 - \theta)x'] \geq f(x')$. Call f *strictly quasi-concave* if the last inequality is strict.

a. Show that if $X \subseteq \mathbf{R}_+^l$ is a convex cone and $f: X \rightarrow \mathbf{R}$ is homogeneous of degree one and quasi-concave, then f is concave.

b. Assume in part (a) that f is strictly quasi-concave. Show that if $x, x' \in X$ and $x \neq \alpha x'$, for any $\alpha \in \mathbf{R}$, then

$$f(\theta x + (1 - \theta)x') > \theta f(x) + (1 - \theta)f(x'), \text{ all } \theta \in (0, 1).$$

c. Under what conditions is the fixed point v of the operator T defined in (2) strictly quasi-concave? [*Hint.* Look at the proof of Theorem 4.8 and apply parts (a) and (b) of this exercise.]

d. Under what conditions is v differentiable?

4.4   Unbounded Returns

In this section we present a theorem that is useful when Assumptions 4.1–4.2 hold, so that the supremum function v^* satisfies the functional equation (Theorem 4.2), but the boundedness hypothesis needed for Theorem 4.3 does not hold. In such cases the functional equation may have other solutions as well. The main result of this section is Theorem 4.14, which gives sufficient conditions for a solution to the functional equation to be the supremum function v^*. We then show how this result can be applied to two economic models with specific functional forms. The first is a one-sector model of optimal growth with a logarithmic utility function and a Cobb-Douglas production function; the second is an investment model with a quadratic objective function and linear constraints.

The proof of Theorem 4.14 exploits only the monotonicity of the operator T, defined on the set of *all* functions $f: X \rightarrow \mathbf{R}$, by

$$(Tf)(x) = \sup_{y \in \Gamma(x)} [F(x, y) + \beta f(y)].$$

The idea behind the proof is to start with a function $\hat{v}$ that is an upper bound for v^* and then to apply the operator T to $\hat{v}$, iterating down to a fixed point.

THEOREM 4.14   *Let X, Γ, F, and β satisfy Assumptions 4.1–4.2, and let Π, u, and v^* be defined as they were in Section 4.1. Suppose there is a function $\hat{v}$: $X \rightarrow \mathbf{R}$ such that*

(1) $T\hat{v} \leq \hat{v}$;

(2) $\lim\limits_{n\to\infty} \beta^n \hat{v}(x_n) \leq 0,$ all $x_0 \in X$, all $\underline{x} \in \Pi(x_0)$;

(3) $u(\underline{x}) \leq \hat{v}(x_0),$ all $x_0 \in X$, all $\underline{x} \in \Pi(x_0)$;

If the function $v: X \to \overline{\mathbf{R}}$ defined by

$$v(x) = \lim\limits_{n\to\infty}(T^n \hat{v})(x)$$

is a fixed point of T, then $v = v^*$.

Proof. First we will show that v is well defined and that $v \leq v^*$. Since the operator T is monotone, (1) implies that $T^{n+1}\hat{v} \leq T^n\hat{v}$, all n. Hence for each $x \in X$, $\{(T^n\hat{v})(x)\}$ is a decreasing sequence. If the sequence converges, then $v(x)$ is the limiting value; if the sequence diverges, then $v(x) = -\infty$. Thus v is well defined and $v \leq \hat{v}$. It then follows from (2) that v satisfies the hypotheses in Exercise 4.3. Hence $v \leq v^*$.

Next we will show that $v \geq v^*$. Since Assumptions 4.1–4.2 hold, Theorem 4.2 implies that $v^* = Tv^*$. Moreover, (3) implies that $v^* \leq \hat{v}$. Hence by the monotonicity of T, $v^* = Tv^* \leq T\hat{v}$, continuing by induction, $v^* \leq T^n\hat{v}$, all n, establishing the desired result.   ∎

This theorem is particularly useful in the study of the unit elasticity and linear-quadratic models described above. For these cases it is easy to guess at a solution to the functional equation (cf. Exercise 2.3); Theorem 4.14 then ensures that this guess does indeed provide a solution to the problem at hand. Moreover, as will be seen below, in these examples the value function and policy function have convenient closed forms that involve only a finite number of parameters. This fact makes these two parametric structures especially useful for constructing examples, for computational purposes, and for econometric estimation.

We will apply Theorem 4.14 first to the unit elastic form of the one-sector optimal growth model:

$$\max_{\{k_{t+1}\}_{t=0}^{\infty}} \sum_{t=0}^{\infty} \beta^t \ln(k_t^\alpha - k_{t+1})$$

$$\text{s.t.} \quad 0 \leq k_{t+1} \leq k_t^\alpha, \quad t = 0, 1, 2, \ldots,$$

where $\alpha, \beta \in (0, 1)$, and the set X is the open interval $(0, \infty)$. The return function is unbounded above and below on this interval. (Note that even if we were to restrict attention to the set $X' = (0, 1]$ of maintainable capital stocks, the return would be unbounded below.)

Since $\Gamma(k) = (0, k^\alpha) \neq \emptyset$, clearly Assumption 4.1 holds for all $k \in X$. To apply Theorem 4.14 to this problem we must also show that Assumption 4.2 holds. To do this note that the technology constraint implies that $\ln(k_{t+1}) \leq \alpha \ln(k_t)$, all t. Given k_0, it then follows that any feasible path $\{k_t\} \in \Pi(k_0)$ satisfies

$$\ln(k_t) \leq \alpha^t \ln(k_0), \quad \text{all } t.$$

Hence for any k_0 and any feasible path $\{k_t\} \in \Pi(k_0)$, the sequence of one-period returns satisfies

(4) $F(k_t, k_{t+1}) \leq F(k_t, 0) = \ln(k_t^\alpha) = \alpha \ln(k_t) \leq \alpha^{t+1} \ln(k_0), \quad \text{all } t.$

Therefore

$$\lim_{n \to \infty} \sum_{t=0}^{n} \beta^t F^+(k_t, k_{t+1}) \leq \lim_{n \to \infty} \sum_{t=0}^{n} (\beta \alpha)^t \alpha |\ln(k_0)| = \alpha |\ln(k_0)| / (1 - \alpha\beta),$$

$$\text{all } \{k_t\} \in \Pi(k_0), \quad \text{all } k_0 > 0,$$

where F^+ is as defined in Section 4.1. Hence Assumption 4.2 holds.

Next we need a function $\hat{v}$ that is an upper bound for the supremum function v^*. Since (4) implies that

$$v^*(k) \leq \alpha \ln(k) / (1 - \alpha\beta), \quad \text{all } k > 0,$$

we may take $\hat{v}(k) = \alpha \ln(k) / (1 - \alpha\beta)$. With $\hat{v}$ so defined, clearly (1)–(3) hold. Moreover, with T defined by

$$(Tf)(k) = \sup_{0 \leq y \leq k^\alpha} [\ln(k^\alpha - y) + \beta f(y)],$$

we can verify by direct calculation that

$$(T^n \hat{v})(k) = \frac{1 - \beta^n}{1 - \beta} \left[\ln(1 - \alpha\beta) + \frac{\alpha\beta}{1 - \alpha\beta} \ln(\alpha\beta) \right]$$

$$+ \frac{\alpha}{1 - \alpha\beta} \ln(k), \quad n = 1, 2, \ldots.$$

This sequence converges to

$$v(k) = \frac{1}{1 - \beta} \left[\ln(1 - \alpha\beta) + \frac{\alpha\beta}{1 - \alpha\beta} \ln(\alpha\beta) \right] + \frac{\alpha}{1 - \alpha\beta} \ln(k).$$

Recall from Exercise 2.3 that this function v is a fixed point of T. Hence by Theorem 4.14, $v = v^*$. Moreover, since Theorem 4.5 applies, the associated policy function, the constant saving rate policy $g(k) = \alpha\beta k^\alpha$, generates the optimal sequence of capital stocks.

Theorem 4.14 is also applicable to problems with quadratic return functions. There is an extensive literature on such problems, but a simple economic example suffices to illustrate the main ideas. Let $X = \mathbf{R}$, and let $\Gamma(x) = \mathbf{R}$, all $x \in \mathbf{R}$. Consider the return function

(5) $$F(x, y) = ax - \frac{1}{2} bx^2 - \frac{1}{2} c(y - x)^2, \quad a, b, c > 0.$$

Think of the term $ax - bx^2/2$ as describing a firm's net revenue when its capital stock is x, and the term $c(y - x)^2/2$ as the cost of changing the capital stock from x to y. Then, given a constant interest rate $r > 0$, the problem facing the firm is

$$\max_{\{x_{t+1}\}_{t=0}^\infty} \sum_{t=0}^\infty \delta^t \left[ax_t - \frac{1}{2} bx_t^2 - \frac{1}{2} c(x_{t+1} - x_t)^2 \right],$$

where $\delta = 1/(1 + r)$.

To apply Theorem 4.14 to this problem, first note that the return function F in (5) is bounded above by $a^2/2b$. Hence the function $\hat{v}$ defined by $\hat{v}(x) = a^2/2b(1 - \delta)$, all $x \in \mathbf{R}$, satisfied (1)–(3). Moreover, it follows by induction that the functions $T^n\hat{v}$ take the form:

$$(T^n\hat{v})(x) = \alpha_n x - \frac{1}{2}\beta_n x^2 + \gamma_n,$$

where the coefficients of these quadratic functions are given recursively by $\alpha_0 = \beta_0 = 0$, $\gamma_0 = a^2/2b(1 - \delta)$, and

(6) $$\beta_{n+1} = b + \frac{\delta\beta_n c}{\delta\beta_n + c},$$

(7) $$\alpha_{n+1} = a + \frac{\delta\alpha_n c}{\delta\beta_n + c},$$

(8) $$\gamma_{n+1} = \delta\gamma_n + \frac{1}{2}\frac{(\delta\alpha_n)^2}{\delta\beta_n + c}, \quad n = 0, 1, \ldots.$$

It is a simple exercise to verify from (6) that $\beta_n \to \beta$, where $b < \beta < b + c$, and then from (7) and (8) that $\alpha_n \to \alpha$ and $\gamma_n \to \gamma$. The limit function $v(x) = \alpha x - \beta x^2/2 + \gamma$ clearly satisfies the functional equation, and hence Theorem 4.14 implies that it is the supremum function v^*. The associated policy function is $g(x) = (\delta\alpha + cx)/(\delta\beta + c)$, and it follows from Theorem 4.5 that any sequence $\{x_t\}$ generated from it is optimal.

In this particular example, it would make economic sense to restrict $\{x_t\}$ to the interval $X' = [0, a/b]$, since negative capital has no interpretation and accumulating more capital than a/b is costly and *decreases* revenues. F is bounded on $X' \times X'$, so with this restriction the theory of Section 4.2 would apply. But the computational advantage of quadratic returns stems from the fact that marginal returns are linear in the state variable(s). Thus if all maxima are described by first-order conditions, the optimal policy function is also linear in the state variable(s). Hence the convenience of the quadratic form is realized only if maxima are attained at interior points of the feasible set. Setting $X = \mathbf{R}$ and $\Gamma(x) = \mathbf{R}$, all $x \in X$, ensures that this is the case. After obtaining a solution, we can always check to see if it satisfies economically reasonable restrictions. [Note that in the example above, if x_0 is in the interval $[0, a/b]$, then the optimal sequence $x_{t+1} = g(x_t)$, $t = 0, 1, \ldots$, remains in this interval for all t.]

Theorem 4.14 is also useful in dealing with many-dimensional quadratic problems. An upper bound $\hat{v}$ satisfying (1)–(3) is easy to calculate,
since any concave quadratic is bounded above. The iterates $T^n\hat{v}$ are
readily computed, since they are defined by a finite number of parameters. If the sequence converges, Theorem 4.14 implies that the limit
function is the supremum function and Theorem 4.5 implies that the
linear policy that attains it is optimal. If the problem is strictly concave,
there are no other optimal policies.

4.5 Euler Equations

There is a classical (eighteenth-century) mode of attack on the sequence
problem

(SP) $\quad \sup_{\{x_{t+1}\}_{t=0}^{\infty}} \sum_{t=0}^{\infty} \beta^t F(x_t, x_{t+1})$

$\quad$ s.t. $\quad x_{t+1} \in \Gamma(x_t), \quad t = 0, 1, 2, \ldots,$

$\quad x_0 \in X$ given,

that involves treating it as straightforward programming problem in the
decision variables $\{x_{t+1}\}_{t=0}^{\infty}$. Necessary conditions for an optimal program
can be developed from the observation that if $\{x_{t+1}^*\}_{t=0}^{\infty}$ solves the problem
(SP), given x_0, then for $t = 0, 1, \ldots, x_{t+1}^*$ must solve

(1) $\quad \max_{y} [F(x_t^*, y) + \beta F(y, x_{t+2}^*)]$

$\quad$ s.t. $\quad y \in \Gamma(x_t^*)$ and $x_{t+2}^* \in \Gamma(y).$

That is, a feasible variation on the sequence $\{x_{t+1}^*\}$ at one date t cannot
lead to an improvement on an optimal policy. (A derivation of necessary
conditions by this kind of argument is called a *variational* approach. In
the present context the conditions so derived are called Euler equations,
since Euler first obtained them from the continuous-time analogue to
this problem.)

Let Assumptions 4.3–4.5, 4.7, and 4.9 hold; let F_x denote the l-vector consisting of the partial derivatives $(F_1, \ldots, F_l)$ of F with respect to its first l arguments, and F_y denote the vector $(F_{l+1}, \ldots, F_{2l})$. Since F is continuously differentiable and strictly concave, if x^*_{t+1} is in the interior of the set $\Gamma(x^*_t)$ for all t, the first-order conditions for (1) are

$$(2) \qquad 0 = F_y(x^*_t, x^*_{t+1}) + \beta F_x(x^*_{t+1}, x^*_{t+2}), \quad t = 0, 1, 2, \ldots.$$

This is a system of l second-order difference equations in the vector x_t of state variables. With the l-vector x_0 given, its solutions form an l-parameter family, and l additional boundary conditions are needed to single out the one solution that is in fact optimal.

These additional boundary conditions are supplied by the *transversality condition*

$$(3) \qquad \lim_{t \to \infty} \beta^t F_x(x^*_t, x^*_{t+1}) \cdot x^*_t = 0.$$

This condition has the following interpretation. Since the vector of derivatives F_x is the vector of marginal returns from increases in the current state variables, the inner product $F_x \cdot x$ is a kind of total value in period t of the vector of state variables. For example, in the many-sector growth model, F_x is the vector of capital goods prices. In this case (3) requires that the present discounted value of the capital stock in period t, evaluated using period t market prices, tends to zero as t tends to infinity. Whether or not one finds these market interpretations helpful, we have the following result.

THEOREM 4.15 (*Sufficiency of the Euler and transversality conditions*) Let $X \subset \mathbf{R}^l_+$, and let F satisfy Assumptions 4.3–4.5, 4.7, and 4.9. Then the sequence $\{x^*_{t+1}\}^\infty_{t=0}$, with $x^*_{t+1} \in int \, \Gamma(x^*_t)$, $t = 0, 1, \ldots$, is optimal for the problem (SP), given x_0, if it satisfies (2) and (3).

Proof. Let x_0 be given; let $\{x^*_t\} \in \Pi(x_0)$ satisfy (2) and (3); and let $\{x_t\} \in \Pi(x_0)$ be any feasible sequence. It is sufficient to show that the difference, call it D, between the objective function in (SP) evaluated at $\{x^*_t\}$ and at $\{x_t\}$ is nonnegative.

Since F is continuous, concave, and differentiable (Assumptions 4.4, 4.7, and 4.9),

$$D = \lim_{T \to \infty} \sum_{t=0}^{T} \beta^t [F(x_t^*, x_{t+1}^*) - F(x_t, x_{t+1})]$$

$$\geq \lim_{T \to \infty} \sum_{t=0}^{T} \beta^t [F_x(x_t^*, x_{t+1}^*) \cdot (x_t^* - x_t) + F_y(x_t^*, x_{t+1}^*) \cdot (x_{t+1}^* - x_{t+1})].$$

Since $x_0^* - x_0 = 0$, rearranging terms gives

$$D \geq \lim_{T \to \infty} \left\{ \sum_{t=0}^{T-1} \beta^t [F_y(x_t^*, x_{t+1}^*) + \beta F_x(x_{t+1}^*, x_{t+2}^*)] \cdot (x_{t+1}^* - x_{t+1}) \right.$$

$$\left. + \beta^T F_y(x_T^*, x_{T+1}^*) \cdot (x_{T+1}^* - x_{T+1}) \right\}.$$

Since $\{x_t^*\}$ satisfies (2), the terms in the summation are all zero. Therefore, substituting from (2) into the last term as well and then using (3) gives

$$D \geq - \lim_{T \to \infty} \beta^T F_x(x_T^*, x_{T+1}^*) \cdot (x_T^* - x_T)$$

$$\geq - \lim_{T \to \infty} \beta^T F_x(x_T^*, x_{T+1}^*) \cdot x_T^*,$$

where the last line uses the fact that $F_x \geq 0$ (Assumption 4.5) and $x_t \geq 0$, all t. It then follows from (3) that $D \geq 0$, establishing the desired result. ∎

(Note that Theorem 4.15 does not require any restrictions on Γ or β, because the theorem applies only if a sequence satisfying (2) and (3) has already been found. Restrictions on Γ and β are needed to ensure that such a sequence can be located.)

Exercise 4.9 a. Use Theorem 4.15 to obtain an alternative proof that the policy function $g(k) = \alpha\beta k^\alpha$ is optimal for the unit-elastic optimal growth model of Section 4.4.

b. Use Theorem 4.15 to obtain an alternative proof that the policy function $g(x) = (\delta\alpha + cx)/(\delta\beta + c)$ is optimal for the quadratic investment model of Section 4.4.

The Euler equations can also be derived directly from the functional equation

(FE) $v(x) = \max_{y \in \Gamma(x)} [F(x, y) + \beta v(y)].$

Suppose the value function v is differentiable; suppose, as above, that the right side of (FE) is always attained in the interior of $\Gamma(x)$; and let $v'(y)$ denote the vector $[v_1(y), \ldots, v_l(y)]$ of partial derivatives of v. Then the first-order conditions for the maximum problem (FE) are

(4) $0 = F_y[x, g(x)] + \beta v'[g(x)].$

The envelope condition for this same maximum problem is

(5) $v'(x) = F_x[x, g(x)].$

Now set $x = x_t$ and $g(x) = g(x_t) = x_{t+1}$ in (4) to get

$0 = F_y(x_t, x_{t+1}) + \beta v'(x_{t+1}),$

and set $x = x_{t+1}$ and $g(x) = g(x_{t+1}) = x_{t+2}$ in (5) to get

$v'(x_{t+1}) = F_x(x_{t+1}, x_{t+2}).$

Eliminating $v'(x_{t+1})$ between these two equations then gives the Euler equations (2).

Implicitly, (4) is a system of l first-order difference equations in x_t, and the l initial values x_0 are sufficient to select a unique solution. No boundary conditions are missing from the problem, viewed in this way. Using (5) to eliminate $v'[g(x)]$ from (4) reproduces the Euler equation (2), but this step also discards useful information, so it is not surprising that many sequences $\{x_t\}$ satisfy (2) but not (4).

4.6 Bibliographic Notes

The terms *dynamic programming* and *Principle of Optimality* were introduced by Richard Bellman. Bellman's (1957) monograph is still useful and entertaining reading, full of ideas, applications, and problems from operations research and economics. There are also a number of more recent treatments of dynamic programming. Denardo (1967), Bertsekas (1976), and Harris (1987) are three that provide much material complementary to ours. See Sargent (1987) and Manuelli and Sargent (1987) for an alternative discussion of some of the material here and for many applications of these methods to macroeconomic problems.

An existence theorem for a problem very close to the one in Section 4.1 was proved by Karlin (1955). Our treatment is adapted from Blackwell (1965) and Strauch (1966), whose approaches carry over to—indeed, were designed for—stochastic problems as well, and hence will serve us again in Chapter 9.

Two recent papers discuss issues related to the material in Section 4.2. Blume, Easley, and O'Hara (1982) studied the differentiability of the approximations $v_n = T^n v_0$, $n = 0, 1, \dots$, and the associated approximations g_n to the optimal policy function. Their Theorem 2.2, specialized to the deterministic case, provides conditions under which each function v_n is p times differentiable and each g_n is $(p - 1)$ times differentiable. In conjunction with Theorems 4.6 and 4.9, these facts can be useful in establishing properties of the limiting functions v and g.

Easley and Spulber (1981) studied the properties of rolling plans, policies for an infinite-horizon setting that are generated by solving, in each period t, a problem with finite horizon of $t + T$. They showed that for T sufficiently large, the plans so generated and the associated discounted returns are arbitrarily close to those generated by the optimal policy function.

Pablo Werning provided a most helpful counterexample to a claim about differentiability that appeared in class notes of Lucas, which were a predecessor to parts of Section 4.2.

Our treatment of the constant-returns-to-scale case discussed in Section 4.3 is based on Song (1986).

Our treatment of the unbounded-returns case in Section 4.4 draws on Prescott (1975) and Hansen (1985). Theorem 4.14 is adapted from

Strauch (1966), where a more complete treatment of the unbounded-loss case can be found.

Our proofs of the necessity of the Euler equations and the sufficiency of the transversality conditions are standard. The necessity of the transversality condition is a difficult issue, and resolving it involves conditions beyond those imposed here. Peleg and Ryder (1972) and Weitzman (1973) both dealt with this issue. See Ekeland and Scheinkman (1986) for an excellent recent treatment.

For deterministic problems there is a close connection between maximization problems formulated in discrete time and those formulated in continuous time. (Indeed, the term *Euler equation* is traditionally used for necessary conditions for continuous-time problems, but it has become standard in economics to use it for the discrete-time analogues of these conditions.) In most cases the adaptation from one setting to the other is straightforward, and in fact many of the applications we discuss in Chapter 5 were originally formulated and studied in continuous time. There are many good texts discussing the mathematical techniques used for such problems, the calculus of variations, and the closely related *Maximum Principle* of Pontryagin et al. (1962). Arrow and Kurz (1970) and Kamien and Schwartz (1981) are excellent examples.

5 Applications of Dynamic Programming under Certainty

This chapter contains some economic problems that illustrate how the methods developed in the last chapter can be applied. Some of the problems are straightforward exercises and can be solved as presented. Others are more open-ended, and in these cases specific results can be obtained only if additional assumptions are imposed. The problems are not ordered in terms of difficulty.

5.1 The One-Sector Model of Optimal Growth

In Chapter 2 we introduced the problem of optimal growth in a one-good economy:

$$(1) \qquad \max_{\{x_{t+1}\}_{t=0}^{\infty}} \sum_{t=0}^{\infty} \beta^t U[f(x_t) - x_{t+1}],$$

$$\text{s.t.} \quad 0 \le x_{t+1} \le f(x_t), \quad t = 0, 1, \ldots,$$

$$\text{given } x_0 \ge 0.$$

This problem is defined by the parameter β, the functions $U: \mathbf{R}_+ \to \mathbf{R}$ and $f: \mathbf{R}_+ \to \mathbf{R}_+$, and the initial capital stock x_0. The assumptions we will use for preferences are

(U1) $0 < \beta < 1;$
(U2) U is continuous;
(U3) U is strictly increasing;
(U4) U is strictly concave;
(U5) U is continuously differentiable.

For the technology we assume that

(T1) *f is continuous;*
(T2) $f(0) = 0$, *and for some* $\bar{x} > 0 : x \leq f(x) \leq \bar{x}$, *all* $0 \leq x \leq \bar{x}$, *and*
     $f(x) < x$, *all* $x > \bar{x}$;
(T3) *f is strictly increasing;*
(T4) *f is (weakly) concave;*
(T5) *f is continuously differentiable.*

Note that $[0, \bar{x}]$ is the set of maintainable capital stocks; let $X = [0, \bar{x}]$. Note, too, that (U3) and (T3) justify the assumption, implicit in (1), that free disposal is never used.

Corresponding to the problem in (1), we have the functional equation

$$(2) \qquad v(x) = \max_{0 \leq y \leq f(x)} \{U[f(x) - y] + \beta v(y)\}.$$

Exercise 5.1   a. Show that under (U1)–(U3) and (T1)–(T3), the hypotheses of Theorems 4.2–4.5 are satisfied.

     b. Show that under (U1)–(U3) and (T1)–(T3), the hypotheses of Theorems 4.6 and 4.7 are satisfied.

From part (a) we conclude that solutions to (1) and (2) coincide exactly. From part (b) we conclude that there exists a unique bounded continuous function v satisfying (2) and that the optimal policy correspondence G is nonempty and u.h.c. Hence a maximizing sequence for (1) exists, for each $x_0 \in X$, and $v(x_0)$ gives the present discounted value of total utility from an optimal sequence. We also conclude that the function v is strictly increasing.

A sharper characterization of v and G requires additional structure.

Exercise 5.1   c. Show that under (U1)–(U4) and (T1)–(T4), the hypotheses of Theorem 4.8 are satisfied.

From part (c) we conclude that under the additional restrictions, v is strictly concave, and the optimal policy correspondence G is single-valued and continuous.

Finally, consider the issue of differentiability.

Exercise 5.1   d. Assume that (U1)–(U5) and (T1)–(T5) hold, and let $G = g$. Show that if $g(x) \in (0, f(x))$, then v is differentiable at x and $v'(x) = U'[f(x) - g(x)]f'(x)$. Provide restrictions on U or f or both that, in addition to the assumptions above, guarantee that $0 < g(x) < f(x)$, all $0 < x \leq \bar{x}$. What can be said about the differentiability of v at x when these assumptions fail? What can be said when $g(x) = 0$ or $g(x) = f(x)$?

e. To emphasize their dependence on the discount factor β, write the value and policy functions as $v(x, \beta)$ and $g(x, \beta)$. Show that $g(x, \beta)$ is increasing in β.

5.2   A "Cake-Eating" Problem

Consider the model in Section 5.1, with preferences satisfying (U1)–(U5) and with the technology $f(k) = k$, all $k \in \mathbf{R}_+$.

Exercise 5.2   a. Show that f satisfies (T1) and (T3)–(T5) and that any $\bar{x} > 0$ can be used to define X.

b. For $U(c) = \ln(c)$, find the value function v and the policy function g explicitly.

c. What can be said about v and g in general?

5.3   Optimal Growth with Linear Utility

Consider the model in Section 5.1, with a technology f satisfying assumptions (T1)–(T5), with β satisfying (U1), and with $U(c) = c$, all $c \in \mathbf{R}_+$.

Exercise 5.3   a. Indicate which results from Exercise 5.1 hold under these assumptions and which do not.

b. Define $k^* = \max_{k \geq 0} [\beta f(k) - k]$. Show that for some $\varepsilon > 0$, $|k - k^*| < \varepsilon$ implies $v(k) = f(k) - k^* + \beta[f(k^*) - k^*]/(1 - \beta)$.

c. Characterize the optimal policy as fully as possible.

5.4   Growth with Technical Progress

The model presented in Section 5.1 can be viewed as describing an economy in which the size of the population, the (inelastic) supply of labor per capita, and the technology are all constant over time. In this problem we will retain the first two of these assumptions, but drop the third. Instead, assume that technological change increases the supply of effective labor units each period by the factor $(1 + \lambda) > 1$. Suppose in addition that the production function $F(K, L)$, which has capital and effective labor units as arguments, shows constant returns to scale, and assume that capital depreciates at the rate $\delta > 0$. Finally, suppose that the preferences of the representative consumer over consumption C are of the form $U(C) = C^{\gamma}/\gamma$, where $\gamma < 1$. [For $\gamma = 0$, this utility function is interpreted as $U(C) = \ln(C)$.] Then letting I denote gross investment, we can write the optimal growth problem as

$$\max_{\{(C_t, I_t, K_{t+1})\}_{t=0}^{\infty}} \sum_{t=0}^{\infty} \beta^t C_t^{\gamma}/\gamma$$

s.t. $C_t + I_t \leq F(K_t, L_t),$ all t;

$L_{t+1} = (1 + \lambda)L_t,$ all t;

$K_{t+1} = (1 - \delta)K_t + I_t,$ all t;

$K_0, L_0 > 0$ given.

It is easiest to analyze this problem by renormalizing all variables by the factor $(1 + \lambda)^t$. Without loss of generality, we may choose units of labor so that $L_0 = 1$. Then define

$$k_t = (1 + \lambda)^{-t}K_t; \quad c_t = (1 + \lambda)^{-t}C_t; \quad i_t = (1 + \lambda)^{-t}I_t, \quad \text{all } t.$$

In addition define the function $f: \mathbf{R}_+ \to \mathbf{R}_+$ by $f(k) = F(k, 1)$. Note that if F is strictly increasing, strictly concave, and continuously differentiable, then f also has these properties.

Using these definitions, we can write the optimal growth problem as

$$\max_{\{(c_t, i_t, k_{t+1})\}_{t=0}^{\infty}} \sum_{t=0}^{\infty} [\beta(1 + \lambda)^{\gamma}]^t c_t^{\gamma}/\gamma$$

s.t. $c_t + i_t \leq f(k_t),$ all t;

$k_{t+1} = [(1 - \delta)k_t + i_t]/(1 + \lambda),$ all t;

$k_0 > 0$ given.

Exercise 5.4 Write the functional equation for the renormalized problem and show that, if $\beta(1 + \lambda)^\gamma < 1$, the analysis of Section 5.1 goes through without change.

5.5 A Tree-Cutting Problem

Consider a tree whose growth is described by the function h. That is, if k_t is the size of the tree in period t, then $k_{t+1} = h(k_t)$, $t = 0, 1, \ldots$. Assume that the price of wood p, and the interest rate r, are both constant over time; let $p = 1$ and $\beta = 1/(1 + r)$. Assume that it is costless to cut down the tree.

Exercise 5.5 a. If the tree cannot be replanted, present value maximization leads to the functional equation $v(k) = \max \{k, \beta v[h(k)]\}$. Under what assumptions about h is there a simple rule describing when the tree ought to be cut down and sold?

b. Suppose that when the tree is cut down, another can be planted in its place. When this tree is cut down another can be planted, and so on. Assume that the cost of replanting, $c \geq 0$, is constant over time. Under what assumptions about h and c is there a simple rule describing when trees should be harvested?

5.6 Learning by Doing

Consider a monopolist producing a new product; we are interested in the case where the production function for the product displays learning by doing. Specifically, suppose that the unit cost of production within each period t is a constant, c_t, but that unit cost falls over time as a function of cumulative experience. Let q_t denote production and Q_t denote cumulative experience at the beginning of period t:

$$Q_0 = 0 \quad \text{and} \quad Q_{t+1} = Q_t + q_t, \quad t = 0, 1, \ldots .$$

Let $\gamma: \mathbf{R}_+ \to \mathbf{R}_+$ be the function relating unit cost to cumulative experience, $c_t = \gamma(Q_t)$. Assume that γ is strictly decreasing, strictly convex, and continuously differentiable, with

$$\gamma(0) = \bar{c} < \infty \quad \text{and} \quad \lim_{Q \to \infty} \gamma(Q) = \underline{c} \geq 0.$$

Assume that there is a stationary inverse demand function $\phi: \mathbf{R}_+ \to \mathbf{R}_+$, so that price in period t is given by $p_t = \phi(q_t)$. Assume that ϕ is strictly decreasing and continuously differentiable, with a strictly decreasing marginal revenue function $\phi(q) + q\phi'(q)$, and with

$$\phi(0) > \bar{c}; \quad \text{and} \quad \phi(\bar{q}) = \underline{c}, \quad \text{for some } \bar{q} < +\infty.$$

Thus demand is positive at the price $\bar{c}$ and is bounded at the price $\underline{c}$. Assume that the interest rate $r > 0$ is constant over time, and let $\beta = 1/(1 + r)$.

Consider first a profit-maximizing monopolist. The monopolist's problem is

$$\max_{\{Q_{t+1}\}_{t=0}^{\infty}} \sum_{t=0}^{\infty} \beta^t (Q_{t+1} - Q_t)[\phi(Q_{t+1} - Q_t) - \gamma(Q_t)],$$

$$\text{s.t.} \quad Q_t \leq Q_{t+1}, \quad \text{all } t;$$

given Q_0. The associated functional equation is

$$v(Q) = \max_{y \geq Q} \{(y - Q)[\phi(y - Q) - \gamma(Q)] + \beta v(y)\}.$$

Exercise 5.6   a. Show that there exists a unique bounded continuous function v satisfying the functional equation. Show that Assumptions 4.6 and 4.7 do not hold, so Theorems 4.7 and 4.8 do not apply. Supply another argument to show that v is strictly increasing. Show that any output level that is optimal exceeds the level that maximizes current-period profit. That is, $y^* \in G(Q)$ implies

$$y^* > \operatorname*{argmax}_{y \geq Q} (y - Q)[\phi(y - Q) - \gamma(Q)].$$

Next consider the problem facing a surplus-maximizing social planner. Define consumers' surplus $S(q)$ by

$$S(q) = \int_0^q \phi(z)dz.$$

Exercise 5.6 b. Show that S is strictly increasing, strictly concave, and continuously differentiable. Consider the functional equation

$$w(Q) = \max_{y \geq Q} [S(y - Q) - (y - Q)\gamma(Q) + \beta w(y)].$$

Show that there exists a unique bounded continuous function w satisfying the functional equation. Show that $w \leq S(\bar{q})/(1 - \beta)$ and that w is strictly increasing. Show that any output level that is optimal exceeds the level that maximizes current surplus. That is, if $\hat{y}$ is optimal, then $\hat{y} > \operatorname{argmax}_{y \geq Q}[S(y - Q) - (y - Q)\gamma(Q)]$.

c. Finally, suppose that the new good is produced by a competitive industry. Assume that the unit cost in period t is $c_t = \gamma(Q_t)$ for each firm, where Q_t is cumulative production for the entire industry. That is, there are complete spillovers in learning among firms. Describe the competitive equilibrium paths for production, price, and unit cost. Show that the competitive equilibrium displays too little production, compared with the efficient path described in part (b).

d. How can the analysis above be modified to describe the extraction of a nonrenewable resource? Assume that the unit cost of extraction in any period is a strictly increasing, strictly convex function of the stock remaining in the ground.

5.7 Human Capital Accumulation

Consider an individual just entering the labor force. His earnings in a given period t are the product of three factors: the number of hours he works, h_t; the level of his skill or human capital, k_t; and the wage rate per hour of effective labor, w_t. For simplicity, assume that the wage is constant over time and normalize it to be unity, $w_t = 1$, all t. Assume too that the interest rate is constant, $r_t = r > 0$, all t, and let $\beta = 1/(1 + r)$ be the discount factor. The worker retires after N periods; hence the present value of his total lifetime earnings is $\sum_{t=1}^{N} \beta^t h_t k_t$.

Assume that the worker can accumulate human capital in any period only by reducing the number of hours he works. Specifically, the number of hours h_t he has available for work in period t is a decreasing function of the ratio of end-of-period to beginning-of-period human capital: $h_t = \phi(k_{t+1}/k_t)$. Assume that ϕ is strictly decreasing, strictly concave, and continuously differentiable, with $\phi(1 - \delta) = 1$ for some $\delta \in (0, 1)$, and $\phi(1 + \lambda) = 0$ for some $\lambda > 0$. That is, human capital depreciates at the rate δ if all time is devoted to work ($h_t = 1$) and can grow at most at the rate λ if no time is devoted to work ($h_t = 0$).

The worker's problem, given his initial skill level $k_1 > 0$, is

(1)
$$\max_{\{k_{t+1}\}_{t=1}^{N}} \sum_{t=1}^{N} \beta^t k_t \phi(k_{t+1}/k_t),$$

$$\text{s.t.} \quad (1 - \delta)k_t \leq k_{t+1} \leq (1 + \lambda)k_t, \quad \text{all } t;$$

$$k_1 > 0 \text{ given.}$$

Let C be the space of bounded continuous functions $f: \mathbf{R}_+ \to \mathbf{R}_+$, and consider the operator T on C defined by

$$(Tf)(k) = \max_{(1-\delta)k \leq y \leq (1+\lambda)k} [k\phi(y/k) + \beta f(y)].$$

For this problem, the function $v_0(k) = 0$, all $k \geq 0$, describes the value of the worker's total future discounted earnings, given that his human capital is k and that he has no periods left in which to work (that is, has just retired). The function $v_1 = Tv_0$ describes the value of his total future earnings, given his human capital k and given that he has one period left in which to work; and so on, for v_n, $n = 0, 1, \ldots, N$. The function $v_N = T^N v_0$ is the maximum value in (1) of presented discounted earnings attainable by a worker just entering the labor force. In this problem, the fixed point of T would be the value function for a worker who continues working forever. Thus the "approximations" $T^n v_0$ are of more economic interest than the function they approximate.

Exercise 5.7   a. Prove by induction that $(T^n v_0)(k) = a_n k$, all n, and find a_{n+1} as a function of a_n, $n \geq 0$. Show that $a_1 = 1$ and that $a_{n+1} > a_n$, all n. Under what condition on the pair (r, λ) is the sequence $\{a_n\}$ bounded as $n \to \infty$?

   b. Characterize as fully as possible the optimal sequence of human capital levels $\{k_t\}$, and the age-earnings profile, $\{k_t \phi(k_{t+1}/k_t)\}$.

5.8 Growth with Human Capital

The description of human capital accumulation presented in the previous section can also be incorporated into a model of optimal growth.
Let the division of time and the law of motion for human capital be as
described there; but replace the constant wage rate with an aggregate
production function; and let the objective be to maximize total discounted utility of consumption rather than total discounted earnings.
Assume that human capital is the only input into production, and that
the production function f is strictly increasing, strictly concave, and continuously differentiable, with

$$f(0) = 0, \quad \lim_{L \to 0} f'(L) = +\infty, \quad \text{and} \quad \lim_{L \to \infty} f'(L) = 0.$$

Let U denote the preferences of the representative consumer; assume
that U is strictly increasing, strictly concave, and continuously differentiable, with

$$\lim_{c \to 0} U'(c) = +\infty, \quad \text{and} \quad \lim_{c \to \infty} U'(c) = 0.$$

Then the optimal growth problem can be written as

$$\max_{\{k_{t+1}\}_{t=0}^{\infty}} \sum_{t=0}^{\infty} \beta^t U(f[k_t \phi(k_{t+1}/k_t)]),$$

$$\text{s.t.} \quad (1 - \delta)k_t \leq k_{t+1} \leq (1 + \lambda)k_t, \quad \text{all } t;$$

$$k_0 > 0 \text{ given.}$$

The associated functional equation is

$$v(k) = \max_{(1-\delta)k \leq y \leq (1+\lambda)k} \{U(f[k\phi(y/k)]) + \beta v(y)\}.$$

Exercise 5.8   a. Assume that $\beta(1 + \lambda) < 1$. Show that there
exists a unique continuous function v satisfying the functional equation.

b. Suppose that the technology and preferences have the specific functional forms $f(L) = L^\alpha$, $\alpha \in (0, 1)$, and $U(c) = c^\sigma/\sigma$, $\sigma < 1$. Show that in this case v has the form $v(k) = Ak^{\alpha\sigma}$, where A has the same sign as σ. Show that the optimal policy is a constant growth rate for human capital: $g(k) = \theta k$, for some $\theta > 0$.

5.9   Investment with Convex Costs

A firm has the production technology $z = f(k)$, where physical capital, $k \in \mathbf{R}_+$, is the single input, and $z \in \mathbf{R}_+$ is output. Assume that f is continuously differentiable, strictly increasing, and strictly concave, and that

$$f(0) = 0, \quad \lim_{k \to 0} f'(k) = +\infty, \quad \text{and} \quad \lim_{k \to \infty} f'(k) = 0.$$

Assume that p the price of output, q the price of capital, and r the interest rate are constant over time, and let $\beta = 1/(1 + r)$.

Assume that capital must be purchased one period in advance and depreciates at the rate $\delta \in (0, 1)$. Then the firm's problem, given k_0, is

$$\max_{\{k_{t+1}\}_{t=0}^\infty} \sum_{t=0}^\infty \beta^t \{p \cdot f(k_t) - q \cdot [k_{t+1} - (1 - \delta)k_t]\}.$$

Consider the related functional equation

$$v(k) = \max_y \{p \cdot f(k) - q \cdot [y - (1 - \delta)k] + \beta v(y)\}.$$

Exercise 5.9   a. Find the exact solutions for v and for the policy function g, and interpret the economics of the results. What is the economic interpretation of the absence of a nonnegativity constraint on gross investment? How must the analysis of this problem be altered if there are lower and upper bounds on gross investment? That is, how does the solution change if the constraints $(1 - \delta)k_t \le k_{t+1} \le (1 - \delta)k_t + a$, $t = 0, 1, \ldots$, for some $a > 0$ are added to the firm's problem?

b. Suppose instead that the total cost of investment is a convex function c of the level of gross investment, where $c: \mathbf{R} \to \mathbf{R}_+$ is strictly increasing, strictly convex, and differentiable, with $c(0) = 0$. Then the firm's problem is

$$\max_{\{k_{t+1}\}_{t=0}^{\infty}} \sum_{t=0}^{\infty} \beta^t\{p \cdot f(k_t) - c[k_{t+1} - (1 - \delta)k_t]\}.$$

Formulate the functional equation for this problem, and characterize the solution v and the policy function g as fully as possible. Derive the Euler equations and compare them with the Euler equations in part (a).

c. Suppose that in addition to capital there is a variable input, labor. Let $F(k, l)$ be the production function, and let $w > 0$ be the wage rate. Consider the firm's "short-run" problem: Let $\Pi(k) = \max_{l \geq 0} \{pF(k, l) - wl\}$. Under what conditions on F are Π and the "short-run" labor demand function $l = \phi(k)$ well defined? Under what conditions does Π have the properties ascribed to f in parts (a) and (b)?

5.10 Investment with Constant Returns

Suppose that we modify the model in Section 5.9 so that output z depends negatively on end-of-period capital y, due to internal technological "adjustment costs." That is, let $z = F(k, y)$ where $F: \mathbf{R}_+ \times \mathbf{R}_+ \to \mathbf{R}_+$. Let F be continuously differentiable, increasing in k, and decreasing in y. Assume that F exhibits constant returns:

$$F(\lambda k, \lambda y) = \lambda F(k, y), \quad \text{all } \lambda > 0;$$

and that F is strictly quasi-concave:

if $(k', y') \neq \lambda(k, y)$, $F(k', y') \geq F(k, y)$, and $\theta \in (0, 1)$,

then $F(k^\theta, y^\theta) > F(k, y)$,

where $(k^\theta, y^\theta) = \theta(k, y) + (1 - \theta)(k', y')$.

Also assume that the marginal adjustment cost becomes arbitrarily high as the rate of growth of capital approaches $\alpha > 0$. That is,

$$\text{for some } \alpha > 0, \quad \lim_{y \to (1+\alpha)k} F_y(k, y) \to -\infty.$$

Let $\delta \in (0, 1)$ be the depreciation rate and $q > 0$ the price of capital. Define

$$v^*(k_0) = \max_{\{k_{t+1}\}_{t=0}^{\infty}} \sum_{t=0}^{\infty} \beta^t \{ p \cdot F(k_t, k_{t+1}) - q \cdot [k_{t+1} - (1 - \delta)k_t] \},$$

$$\text{s.t.} \quad (1 - \delta)k_t \leq k_{t+1} \leq (1 + \alpha)k_t, \text{ all } t;$$

$$k_0 > 0 \text{ given.}$$

Exercise 5.10   a. Show that v^* is homogeneous of degree one.

Consider the corresponding functional equation:

$$v(k) = \max_{(1-\delta)k \leq y \leq (1+\alpha)k} \{ p \cdot F(k, y) - q \cdot [y - (1 - \delta)k] + \beta v(y) \}.$$

Exercise 5.10   b. Show that any function v satisfying the functional equation is also homogeneous of degree one.

   c. Characterize as fully as possible solutions to the functional equation and the corresponding policy correspondence. What needs to be assumed about α and β? What is the relationship between solutions to the functional equation and solutions to the sequence problem?

5.11   Recursive Preferences

Let L be the space of sequences $c = (c_0, c_1, \ldots)$, with $c_t \in \mathbf{R}_+^l$, $t = 0, 1, \ldots$, that are bounded in the norm

$$\|c\|_L = \sup_t \|c_t\|_E,$$

where $\|\cdot\|_E$ is the Euclidean norm on $\mathbf{R}^l$. For any $c = (c_0, c_1, \ldots) \in L$, define

$$_1c = (c_1, c_2, \ldots) \in L,$$

$$c^n = (c_0, \ldots, c_n, 0, 0, \ldots) \in L.$$

We have so far been dealing with preferences $u\colon L \to \mathbf{R}$ of the form $u(c) = \Sigma_{t=0}^\infty \beta^t U(c_t)$, where $\beta \in (0, 1)$ and $U\colon \mathbf{R}_+ \to \mathbf{R}$ is bounded and continuous.

Exercise 5.11 a. Show that any function $u\colon L \to \mathbf{R}$ of this form is bounded and is continuous in the norm $\|\cdot\|_L$.

Let S be the vector space of all bounded continuous functions $u\colon L \to \mathbf{R}$, with the norm $\|u\| = \sup_{c \in L} |u(c)|$.

Exercise 5.11 b. Show that S is complete. Is it true that $\lim_{n \to \infty} |u(c) - u(c^n)| = 0$, all $u \in S$?

For any $\beta \in (0, 1)$ and $U\colon \mathbf{R}_+^l \to \mathbf{R}$, we can define an operator $T\colon S \to S$ by $(Tu)(c) = U(c_0) + \beta u(_1c)$.

Exercise 5.11 c. Show that the function $\hat{u} \in S$ defined by

$$\hat{u}(c) = \Sigma_{t=0}^\infty \beta^t U(c_t) \text{ is the unique fixed point of } T.$$

A much larger class of utility functions on L can be defined in an analogous way. Let $W\colon \mathbf{R}_+^l \times \mathbf{R}_+ \to \mathbf{R}_+$ be a continuous function with the following properties:

(W1) $W(0, 0) = 0$;
(W2) *for any $z \in \mathbf{R}_+$, $W(\cdot, z)\colon \mathbf{R}_+^l \to \mathbf{R}_+$ is bounded; and*
(W3) *for some $\beta \in (0, 1)$,*

$$|W(x, z) - W(x, z')| \le \beta|z - z'|, \quad \text{all } x \in \mathbf{R}_+^l \text{ and } z, z' \in \mathbf{R}_+.$$

We will call a function W with these properties an *aggregator function*. $W(x, z)$ is interpreted as the utility enjoyed from now on if $x \in \mathbf{R}_+^l$ is consumed today and if consumption from tomorrow on yields $z \in \mathbf{R}_+$ utils as of tomorrow. Two additional properties of W will be useful.

(W4) *W is increasing;*
(W5) *W is concave.*

Exercise 5.11   d. Let W satisfy (W1)–(W3), and define the operator T_W: $S \to S$ by $(T_W u)(c) = W[c_0, u(_1c)]$. Show that T_W has a unique fixed point $u_W \in S$ and that

$$|u_W(c) - u_W(c^n)| \leq \beta^n \|u_W\|, \quad \text{all } c \in L.$$

Show that if (W4) holds then u_W is increasing; show that if (W5) holds then u_W is concave.

e. Assume that W is continuously differentiable. Obtain an expression for the marginal rate of substitution between c_{it} and $c_{j,t+k}$, all i, j, t, k.

5.12   Theory of the Consumer with Recursive Preferences

Consider an infinitely lived consumer with preferences given by $u \in S$, where $u(c) = W[c_0, u(_1c)]$, all $c \in L$, and W is an aggregator function as defined in Section 5.11. The problem facing this consumer is

$$(1) \qquad \max_{c \in L} \; u(c) \qquad \text{s.t.} \; \sum_{t=0}^{\infty} R^t(p \cdot c_t) \leq A,$$

where $p \in \mathbf{R}_{++}^l$ is a constant vector of spot prices; $R = 1/(1 + r)$, where $r > 0$ is a constant rate of interest; and A is his initial wealth. The functional equation for this problem is

$$(2) \qquad v(A) = \max_{C \in \Gamma(A)} W(C, v[R^{-1}(A - p \cdot C)]),$$

where $\Gamma(A) = \{C \in \mathbf{R}_+^l : p \cdot C \leq A\}$.

Exercise 5.12   a. Modify Theorems 4.2–4.5 to relate (1) and (2).

b. Show that (2) has a unique bounded continuous solution v and that the consumer demand function $C = \phi(p, A)$ is well defined, continuous, and homogeneous of degree zero in (p, A).

c. Under what conditions is v continuously differentiable? Assuming these conditions hold, state and interpret the first-order conditions for the problem (2).

d. Let $h: \mathbf{R}_+ \to \mathbf{R}_+$ be a bounded, continuously differentiable, strictly increasing function, with $h(0) = 0$. Define $\tilde{W}(C, a) = h(W[C, h^{-1}(a)])$. Show that the demand functions from (2) implied by $\tilde{W}$ coincide with those for W. Is $\tilde{W}$ necessarily an aggregator function as defined in Section 5.11, provided W is?

5.13   A Pareto Problem with Recursive Preferences

Consider a two-person pure exchange economy in which both agents have preferences of the type described in Section 5.11. Assume that there is a single consumption good available each period. Hence the commodity space is the space of all bounded sequences $\underline{c} = (c_0, c_1, \ldots)$, with $c_t \in \mathbf{R}$, all t. Feasible consumption sequences for either agent are sequences c with $c_t \geq 0$, all t. The two agents are characterized by aggregator functions $W_i: \mathbf{R}_+ \times \mathbf{R}_+ \to \mathbf{R}_+$, $i = 1, 2$; let u_i, $i = 1, 2$, be the corresponding preferences over feasible consumption sequences.

The economy has an endowment of one unit of consumption good each period. Therefore, in any period t, if agent 1 gets c_t, agent 2 gets $1 - c_t$; let $\Pi = \{\underline{c} = \{c_t\}: 0 \leq c_t \leq 1,$ all $t\}$ be the space of feasible allocations for agent 1. Let $\underline{1}$ denote the sequence $(1, 1, 1, \ldots)$ and $\underline{0} = (0, 0, 0, \ldots)$, and let $I_i = [u_i(\underline{0}), u_i(\underline{1})]$, $i = 1, 2$, be the sets of possible utilities for the two agents.

Let S be the space of continuous functions $f: I_2 \to I_1$, with the sup norm. Consider the operator T defined by

$$(Tf)(x) = \max_{\substack{c \in [0,1] \\ y \in I_2}} W_1[c, f(y)],$$

$$\text{s.t.}\quad W_2(1 - c, y) \geq x.$$

Exercise 5.13 a. Show that $T: S \to S$ and that T is a contraction.

b. What is the relationship between the unique fixed point v of T and the function v^* defined on I_2 by

$$v^*(x) = \sup_{c \in \Pi} u_1(\underline{c})$$

s.t. $u_2(\underline{1} - \underline{c}) \geq x$?

5.14 An (s, S) Inventory Problem

Consider a manager who can sell up to one unit of a certain product each period, at a price p. If he has $x \geq 0$ units in stock, he can sell $\min\{x, 1\}$ units. He can also order any amount y of new goods, to be delivered at the beginning of next period, at a cost $c_0 + c_1 y$, paid now. His discount factor is $\beta = 1/(1 + r)$, where $r > 0$ is the interest rate. His objective is to choose an ordering policy that maximizes the present value of revenues less costs.

Assume that $\beta p > c_1$ (otherwise, no orders are ever placed); that $c_1 > 0$ (otherwise, an "infinite" order is placed); and that $c_0 > 0$ (otherwise, it is optimal to order one unit each period). The fixed cost c_0 gives this problem a structure very different from those we have studied earlier.

The value function v for this problem must satisfy the functional equation

$$(1) \quad v(x) = \begin{cases} px + \max\left\{\beta v(0), \sup_{y>0}[-c_0 - c_1 y + \beta v(y)]\right\}, & x \in [0, 1], \\ p + \max\left\{\beta v(x - 1), \sup_{y>0}[-c_0 - c_1 y + \beta v(x - 1 + y)]\right\}, \\ \qquad\qquad\qquad\qquad\qquad\qquad\qquad\qquad x \in (1, +\infty). \end{cases}$$

Let C be the space of bounded continuous functions on $\mathbf{R}_+$. We seek a solution to (1) in C.

Exercise 5.14 a. Show that (1) has a unique solution $v \in C$, that

$0 \le v(x) \le p/(1 - \beta)$, and that an optimal ordering policy exists. Is this policy unique?

The right side of (1) defines a contraction operator $T: C \to C$. One way to calculate a fixed point would be to begin with an initial guess v_0 and calculate Tv_0, T^2v_0, and so on. But in this case, it is more fruitful to conjecture the optimal policy directly, calculate the value function w associated with this conjectured policy, and then verify that w satisfies (1).

We will begin with the case in which the initial inventories are zero: Suppose that $x = 0$ in period $t = 0$. Consider actions of the following form: Order n units immediately, and then sell these units at the rate of one per period over the next n periods. Let r_n denote the net present value of this action:

$$r_n = -c_0 - c_1 n + (\beta + \beta^2 + \cdots + \beta^n)p$$

$$= -c_0 - c_1 n + \beta \frac{1 - \beta^n}{1 - \beta} p, \quad n = 1, 2, \ldots.$$

Then consider the policy that consists of repeating this action whenever the stock is at one unit, that is, at $t = n, 2n, \ldots$ Call the value of pursuing this policy Y_n; then

$$Y_n = r_n(1 + \beta^n + \beta^{2n} + \ldots) = \frac{r_n}{1 - \beta^n}$$

$$= -\frac{c_0 + c_1 n}{1 - \beta^n} + \frac{\beta}{1 - \beta} p, \quad n = 1, 2, \ldots.$$

For completeness, define r_0 and Y_0 to be zero, the value of not placing an order.

Exercise 5.14 b. Characterize Y_n as a function of n. Show that there is some finite integer $N \ge 1$ such that $Y_N \ge Y_n$, $n = 1, 2, \ldots$. How does N vary with the discount factor β, the level of fixed costs c_0, and the price p?

If $Y_N < 0$, it is better never to order (and thus to earn $Y_0 = 0$ profits) than to follow any of the policies above with $n \ge 1$. For given parameter values, it is easy to check whether this is the case. In what follows, assume $Y_N > 0$.

We conjecture that $w(0) = Y_N$ is the value of an optimal policy when $x = 0$. We further conjecture that for $x \in [0, 1]$ the optimal policy is to sell the existing stock at p, and order N units for delivery tomorrow. The value of doing this is

(2) $w(x) = px + Y_N, \quad x \in [0, 1]$.

If $x \in (1, 2]$, there are two sensible options: sell one unit immediately and place an order for $N - (x - 1)$ units; or, sell one unit immediately and order nothing. The first is preferred if x is near 1, the second if x is near 2. Let $x = 1 + A$ be the point of indifference; then

(3) $w(x) = \begin{cases} p + c_1(x - 1) + Y_N, & x \in (1, 1 + A), \\ p + \beta w(x - 1), & x \in [1 + A, 2]. \end{cases}$

Since A is the point of indifference, it must satisfy

$$p + c_1 A + Y_N = p + \beta w(A),$$

and since $A \in [0, 1]$, (2) holds at $x = A$. Combining these facts gives

(4) $A = \dfrac{(1 - \beta)Y_N}{\beta p - c_1}.$

Exercise 5.14   c. Show that $0 < A < 1$.

If $x \in (2, +\infty)$, our conjectured policy is simply to sell one unit per period out of inventories until the remaining stock falls into the interval $(1, 2]$, and from that point on to pursue the policy indicated above. Hence

(5) $w(x) = p + \beta w(x - 1), \quad x \in (2, +\infty)$.

We can tabulate the function $w(x)$ defined recursively by (2), (3), and (5) as follows. For any $x > 1$, define $v(x)$ to be the largest integer not exceeding x; then define $\alpha(x) = x - v(x) \in [0, 1)$. Then

$$(6) \quad w(x) = \begin{cases} px + Y_N, & 0 \le x \le 1, \\[2ex] p\dfrac{1 - \beta^{v(x)}}{1 - \beta} + \beta^{v(x)-1}[c_1\alpha(x) + Y_N], & x > 1 \text{ and } \alpha(x) \in [0, A), \\[2ex] p\dfrac{1 - \beta^{v(x)}}{1 - \beta} + \beta^{v(x)}[p\alpha(x) + Y_N], & x > 1 \text{ and } \alpha(x) \in [A, 1), \end{cases}$$

where A is given in (4).

Exercise 5.14 d. Verify (6) by solving the difference equation in (2), (3), and (5). Show that w is bounded, continuous, and piecewise linear. At what points is it differentiable, and what are its derivatives at these points?

It remains to be shown that w as defined in (6) satisfies the functional equation (1). It is useful first to establish three preliminary results.

Exercise 5.14 e. Let $I = \{1, 2, \ldots\}$. Show that for all $z \ge 0$,

$$\sup_{y>0} \left[-c_0 - c_1 y + \beta w(z + y) \right]$$

$$= \max\{-c_0 + \beta w(z), \max_{\substack{n>z \\ n \in I}} \left[-c_0 - c_1(n - z) + \beta w(n) \right]\}.$$

That is, either the supremum on the left is not attained, or it is attained where $z + y$ is an integer value. [*Hint*. Use the results in part (d).]

Exercise 5.14 f. Show that for all $z \ge 0$,

$$\sup_{y>0}[-c_0 - c_1 y + \beta w(z + y)]$$

$$= \max\{-c_0 + \beta w(z), c_1 z + \max_{\substack{n>z \\ n \in I}} [r_n + \beta^n Y_N]\}.$$

g. Show that $\max_{n \ge 1, n \in I}(r_n + \beta^n Y_N) = Y_N$.

In view of these three results, verifying that w satisfies (1) is equivalent to verifying that w is a fixed point of the operator T defined by

$$(Tf)(x) = \begin{cases} px + \max\{\beta f(0), Y_N\}, & x \in [0, 1), \\[2ex] p + \max\{\beta f(x - 1), c_1(x - 1) + Y_N\}, & x \in [1, 2), \\[2ex] p + \max\{\beta f(x - 1), c_1(x - 1) + \max_{\substack{n > x-1 \\ n \in I}} (r_n + \beta^n Y_N)\}, \\[2ex] \qquad\qquad\qquad\qquad\qquad\qquad\qquad\qquad x \in [2, \infty). \end{cases}$$

Exercise 5.14   h. Show that $(Tw)(x) = w(x)$ on each of the intervals $[0, 1)$, $[1, 1 + A)$, $[1 + A, 2)$, and $[2, +\infty)$. [*Hint.* For $x \in [1, 2)$, use (4). For $x \in [2, +\infty)$, define $\nu(x)$ and $\alpha(x)$ as we did above, and consider separately the cases $\alpha \in [0, A)$ and $\alpha \in [A, 1)$.]

It is customary for problems of this classic type to define $s = 1 + A$ and $S = N$, and to refer to the solution we have constructed as an "(s, S) policy." The optimal policy is, when inventories fall below s, order enough to bring them up to S. An algorithm for calculating s and S, like the one we have provided, is a complete description of the optimal policy.

5.15   The Inventory Problem in Continuous Time

One of the features that made Exercise 5.14 so difficult is its discrete time character. Sometimes it is much simpler to formulate a problem in continuous time. To do this for the inventory problem, let demand be a flow of α units of goods per unit time, and let the interest rate be $r > 0$. The decision facing a manager with initial stock $A \geq 0$ at date $t = 0$ is to choose the date $\tau \geq 0$ when he will next place an order, and the size y of the order. Then the functional equation is

$$v(A) = \max \left\{ \int_0^{A/\alpha} e^{-rt} \alpha p \, dt, \right.$$

$$\left. \sup_{\substack{\tau \geq 0 \\ y > 0}} \left[\int_0^\tau e^{-rt} pz(t) \, dt + e^{-r\tau} [v(x(\tau) + y) - c_0 - c_1 y] \right] \right\},$$

where

$$z(t) = \begin{cases} \alpha & \text{if } x(t) > 0 \\ 0 & \text{if } x(t) = 0, \end{cases}$$

and

$$\frac{dx(t)}{dt} = -z(t), \quad x(0) = A.$$

Define

$$Y^* = \max \left\{ 0, \sup_{\tau > 0} \left[(1 + e^{-r\tau} + e^{-2r\tau} + \ldots) \right. \right.$$

$$\left. \left. \times \int_0^\tau e^{-rt} \alpha p \, dt - c_0 - c_1 \alpha \tau \right] \right\}.$$

Exercise 5.15   a. Show that Y^* is well defined and finite.

If $Y^* = 0$, let $\tau^* = 0$. Otherwise define τ^* to be the value that attains the supremum.

Exercise 5.15   b. Show that the function

$$w(A) = \int_0^{A/\alpha} e^{-rt} \alpha p \, dt + e^{-rA/\alpha} Y^*$$

satisfies the functional equation. Show that if initial stocks are A, then the unique optimal policy is to place an order for $\alpha \tau^*$ units of goods after A/α units of time have elapsed.

5.16   A Seller with Unknown Demand

Consider a seller with no costs of production, facing a continuum of buyers who all have the same reservation price R. This price is not known to the seller; he knows only that R was drawn from a uniform distribution on the interval $[0, 1)$, and his only method for acquiring additional information about R is by experimentation.

Specifically, in each period he can announce a price P. If $P \leq R$, then all consumers buy the product, and the seller learns that $R \geq P$. If $P > R$, then no consumer buys the product, and the seller learns that $R < P$. In either case, the seller narrows down the interval on which the reservation price lies, and Bayes's rule implies that the seller has posterior beliefs that are uniform on the new interval.

Suppose that the seller knows that the reservation price lies on the interval $[A, B) \subseteq [0, 1)$. If he charges a price $P \leq A$, then with probability one all consumers buy the product and the seller gets no new information. Clearly he never chooses a price less than A. If he chooses a price $P \geq B$, then with probability one he sells nothing and gains no new information. Clearly he never sets a price greater than B.

If he sets a price $P \in (A, B)$, then the probability that $R \geq P$ is $(B - P)/(B - A)$; this is the probability that consumers buy the product and his posterior beliefs are a uniform distribution on $[P, B)$. Conversely, with probability $(P - A)/(B - A)$, he sells nothing and his posterior beliefs are a uniform distribution on $[A, P)$.

Let $v(A, B)$ denote the expected discounted profits of the seller when he knows that the reservation price is uniformly distributed on $[A, B) \subseteq [0, 1)$. Then v must satisfy the functional equation

$$v(A, B) = \sup_{P \in [A,B]} \left\{ \frac{B - P}{B - A} P + \beta \left[\frac{P - A}{B - A} v(A, P) + \frac{B - P}{B - A} v(P, B) \right] \right\}.$$

This functional equation does not quite fit the framework developed in Section 4.2, since the planner cannot choose next period's state. Rather, he can only choose an action, the price; next period's state is then a random function of the price. However, the arguments used in Section 4.2 can be modified to fit this case.

Let $D = \{(x, y) \in [0, 1]^2 : x \leq y\}$. Let C be the space of bounded continuous functions $f: D \to \mathbf{R}$, with the sup norm. Define the operator T on C by:

$$(Tf)(A, B) = \sup_{P \in [A,B]} \left\{ \frac{B - P}{B - A} P + \beta \left[\frac{P - A}{B - A} f(A, P) + \frac{B - P}{B - A} f(P, B) \right] \right\}.$$

Exercise 5.16   a. Show that $T: C \to C$, and that T satisfies Black-well's sufficient conditions for a contraction. Hence T has a unique fixed point $v \in C$. Use Corollary 1 to the Contraction Mapping Theorem to show that v is homogeneous of degree one.

Since v is homogeneous of degree one, there exists a bounded continuous function $w: [0, 1] \to \mathbf{R}_+$ such that

$$v(A, B) = Bw(A/B), \quad \text{all } 0 \le A \le B \le 1.$$

Define $a = A/B$ and $p = P/B$. It then follows that $v(A, P) = Pw(A/P) = Bpw(a/p)$, and $v(P, B) = Bw(p)$. Substituting these expressions into the functional equation above and dividing through by B, we find that w satisfies

$$w(a) = \sup_{p \in [a,1]} \left\{ \frac{1-p}{1-a} p + \beta \left[\frac{p-a}{1-a} pw \left(\frac{a}{p}\right) + \frac{1-p}{1-a} w(p) \right] \right\}.$$

Exercise 5.16   b. Show that w is strictly increasing and weakly convex, with $w(1) = 1/(1 - \beta)$. [*Hint.* What operator is w a fixed point of?] What properties does this imply for v?

It is reasonable to conjecture that, if the interval $[A, B]$ is sufficiently small, then it is optimal to set the price equal to A; that is, it is optimal simply to set the highest price for which it is known with certainty that consumers will buy. If this policy is adopted, the seller does not gain any new information. Hence he will face exactly the same problem next period and will set a price of A. To show that this is the case, it is convenient to work with the transformed problem.

In terms of the transformed problem, the conjecture above is that the optimal policy function g corresponding to w has the following form: there exists some $\hat{a}$ such that $g(a) = a$, all $a \in [\hat{a}, 1]$. Note that, if this conjecture is correct, then $w(a) = a/(1 - \beta)$, all $a \in [\hat{a}, 1]$.

Exercise 5.16   c. Use the functional equation for w to verify that this conjecture is correct and to show that $\hat{a} = 1/(2 - \beta)$.

5.17   A Consumption-Savings Problem

Consider a consumer with preferences

$$u(c) = \sum_{t=0}^{\infty} \beta^t U(c_t)$$

over infinite consumption sequences $c = (c_0, c_1, \ldots)$, where $U: \mathbf{R}_+ \to \mathbf{R}$ is continuously differentiable, strictly increasing, and strictly concave, and where $0 < \beta < 1$. The function U need not be bounded.

The consumer has a constant income $I > 0$ each period, and in addition has initial wealth $x_0 \geq 0$ in period 0. The consumer can save, but he cannot borrow. The interest rate r is constant over time, and the interest factor $R = (1 + r)$ satisfies $0 < R < 1/\beta$.

Exercise 5.17 a. State the consumer's problem in sequence form, and state the corresponding functional equation. Show that the supremum function $v^*: \mathbf{R}_+ \to \mathbf{R}$ for the sequence problem is well defined and that it satisfies the functional equation. Show that for any fixed $x_0 \geq 0$, if the plan $\underline{x}^* \in \Pi(x_0)$ attains the supremum for the sequence problem, then it satisfies

$$v^*(x_t^*) = U(I + x_t^* - x_{t+1}^*/R) + \beta v^*(x_{t+1}^*), \quad t = 0, 1, \ldots.$$

For this problem, we can construct both v^* and the associated optimal policy function g^* by conjecturing the form of the solution and then establishing that the conjecture is correct. Specifically, we will construct a function $v: \mathbf{R}_+ \to \mathbf{R}$ that satisfies

$$(1) \qquad v(x) = \sup_{0 \leq y \leq (I+x)R} [U(I + x - y/R) + \beta v(y)],$$

and establish that $v = v^*$. We will also show that the policy function g associated with v generates all of the optimal plans for the problem in part (a).

Since $R\beta < 1$ and $I > 0$, we conjecture that the consumer exhausts his initial wealth in finite time and then simply consumes his income $I > 0$ in every period thereafter. To check whether this conjecture is correct, construct $g: \mathbf{R}_+ \to \mathbf{R}$ and $v: \mathbf{R}_+ \to \mathbf{R}$ as follows.

We conjecture that for initial wealth in some interval $[0, m_1]$, the consumer's optimal policy is to consume his current income $I > 0$ plus his entire initial wealth $x > 0$ in the initial period (saving nothing), and in every subsequent period to consume his income $I > 0$. Define m_1 by

$$U'(I + m_1) = R\beta U'(I).$$

Then let

$$g(x) = 0, \quad x \in [0, m_1];$$

$$v(x) = U(I + x) + \beta U(I)/(1 - \beta), \quad x \in [0, m_1].$$

Exercise 5.17 b. Show that $m_1 > 0$ is well defined. Show that v is continuous, strictly increasing, and strictly concave. Show that v is continuously differentiable on $[0, m_1)$, with

$$v'(x) = U'(I + x), \quad x \in [0, m_1).$$

Next we conjecture that for initial wealth in some interval $(m_1, m_2]$, the consumer's optimal plan is to consume part of his wealth in period 0 and to save the quantity $y/R \in [0, m_1]$. Then from period $t = 1$ on, he follows the plan described in part (b). Define $h: (0, m_1) \to \mathbf{R}_+$ by

$$(2) \qquad U'[I + h(y) - y/R] = R\beta v'(y).$$

We conjecture that $h(y)$ is the level of initial wealth that induces the consumer to save y/R and thus begin the subsequent period with initial wealth of y.

Exercise 5.17 c. Show that h is continuous and strictly increasing, with $\lim_{y \downarrow 0} h(y) = m_1$.

Define $m_2 = \lim_{y \to m_1} h(y)$, and let

$$(3) \qquad g(x) = h^{-1}(x), \quad x \in (m_1, m_2],$$

$$(4) \qquad v(x) = U[I + x - g(x)/R] + \beta v[g(x)], \quad x \in (m_1, m_2].$$

Exercise 5.17   d. Show that $m_2 > m_1$. Show that g is continuous and strictly increasing on $(m_1, m_2]$. Show that g is continuous at the point $x = m_1$. Show that v is continuous, strictly increasing, and strictly concave on $(m_1, m_2]$. Show that v is continuously differentiable on (m_1, m_2), with

(5) $v'(x) = U'[I + x - g(x)/R], \quad x \in (m_1, m_2)$.

e. Show that v and v' are both continuous at the point m_1.

Continue by induction. Given v on $(m_{n-1}, m_n]$, define $h: (m_{n-1}, m_n] \to \mathbf{R}_+$ by (2) and let $m_{n+1} = h(m_n)$. Then define g and v on $(m_n, m_{n+1}]$ by (3)–(4).

Exercise 5.17   f. Show that the properties of h, g, v, and v' described in parts (c)–(e) hold on all of $\mathbf{R}_+$.

g. Show that v satisfies the functional equation (1). Show that $v = v^*$, where v^* is the supremum function for the sequence problem in part (a). [*Hint.* Show that

$$x_n \le R^n(x_0 + W), \quad \text{all } n, \text{ all } \underset{\sim}{x} \in \Pi(x_0), \text{ all } x_0 \ge 0,$$

where $W = RI/(R - 1)$ is the discounted value of the consumer's income stream in period 0.]

h. Show that for any initial wealth $x_0 > 0$, the sequence $x_{t+1} = g(x_t)$, $t = 0, 1, \ldots$, is the unique optimal plan for the sequence problem in part (a). Show that

$$0 \le g(x') - g(x) < x' - x, \quad \text{all } 0 \le x < x',$$

with equality only if $g(x) = g(x') = 0$.

5.18   Bibliographic Notes

The models in Sections 5.1, 5.3, 5.4, and 5.8 are all samples from the enormous literature on the theory of growth developed largely in the 1960s. Most of this literature is carried out in continuous time, but it is easily restated in discrete time; and in no case discussed here is any change in substance involved in the translation. Burmeister and Dobell (1970) is the best single reference to this body of theory.

Ramsey (1928) solved a version of the one-sector problem in Section 5.1, but with a discount factor equal to one. Since the objective function for this problem does not, in general, converge, he studied the problem

$$\min_{\{x_{t+1}\}_{t=0}^{\infty}} \sum_{t=0}^{\infty} \{U[f(x^*) - x^*] - U[f(x_t) - x_{t+1}]\},$$

where x^* is the capital stock that maximizes $f(x) - x$. This objective is bounded above by zero. The undiscounted problem clearly cannot be studied using the methods of Section 4.2, but try the theory of Sections 4.4 and 4.5.

The model of optimal growth with discounting in Section 5.1 was first studied by Cass (1965) and Koopmans (1965). The type of exogenous technological change treated in Section 5.4 was first studied in Solow (1956), in the context of a nonoptimizing model of growth.

Solutions of the type found in Section 5.3 are called *bang-bang* solutions. A two-sector model of this type that is a little more interesting is studied in Uzawa (1964).

The tree-cutting, or wine-aging, or cattle-fattening problem in Section 5.5 comes up in many different economic settings. See Brock, Rothschild, and Stiglitz (1989) for a continuous-time analysis that is both simpler and more complete than is possible with our formulation here.

The problem of a monopolist with a learning-by-doing technology in Section 5.6 was studied by Clarke, Darrough, and Heineke (1982). Parts (b) and (c) of this problem are from Stokey (1986).

The formulation of the individual human capital accumulation problem in Section 5.7 is taken from Rosen (1976). Earlier dynamic analyses of this decision problem can be found in Becker (1962) and Ben-Porath (1967). The model in Section 5.8 uses the human capital accumulation technology introduced by Rosen to obtain an aggregate growth model, a simplification of models described in Uzawa (1965) and in Lucas (1988).

Sections 5.9 and 5.10 provide samplings from the microeconomic literature on the investment decision of a single firm. Part (a) of Exercise 5.9 is a discrete-time version of Jorgenson (1963). Part (b) is from the model discussed in Eisner and Strotz (1963), later elaborated with variations in Lucas (1967a), Gould (1968), and Treadway (1969). Mortensen (1973) provides the definitive treatment of the many-capital-goods version of this model. The model in Section 5.10 is a constant-returns version of the one in Lucas (1967b). Note that the term *constant returns* is ambiguous in a dynamic context: Gould (1968) uses it in a way different from that used in Section 5.10, and Kydland and Prescott (1982) use it in still a third way.

The recursive preferences analyzed in Section 5.11 were first studied in Koopmans (1960). The analysis by Koopmans, Diamond, and Williamson (1964) is a useful sequel. Uzawa (1968) proposes a continuous-time version of recursive preferences, which is generalized in Epstein (1987).

Sections 5.11–5.13 are taken directly from Lucas and Stokey (1984). It is clear from Denardo (1967) that dynamic programming methods can be applied with recursive preferences that have a contraction property. Early applications of this idea to economics are Beals and Koopmans (1969), Iwai (1972), and Boyer (1975).

The (s, S) models in Sections 5.14 and 5.15 are adapted from Scarf (1959), although the specific results here are new. The (much harder) stochastic version of this problem is a classic, popularly thought to be thoroughly understood. In fact, results have been obtained only for special cases. For examples, see Arrow, Karlin, and Scarf (1958).

Section 5.16 is taken from Aghion, Bolton, and Jullien (1988).

See Rebelo (1987) or Jones and Manuelli (1987) for analyses of models similar to the one in Section 5.17, but with interest rates exceeding $1/\beta - 1$.

6   *Deterministic Dynamics*

In Chapter 4 we established that problems of the form

(SP) $\max\limits_{\{x_{t+1}\}_{t=0}^{\infty}} \sum\limits_{t=0}^{\infty} \beta^t F(x_t, x_{t+1}),$

s.t. $x_{t+1} \in \Gamma(x_t), \quad t = 0, 1, \ldots,$

given x_0, could be analyzed by studying the related functional equation

(FE) $v(x) = \max\limits_{y \in \Gamma(x)} [F(x, y) + \beta v(y)].$

[Recall that $X \subseteq \mathbf{R}^l$ is the state space; $\Gamma: X \to X$ is a nonempty correspondence describing the feasibility constraints; $A = \{(x, y) \in X \times X : y \in \Gamma(x)\}$ is the graph of Γ; $F: A \to \mathbf{R}$ is the one-period return function; and $\beta \in (0, 1)$ is the discount factor.] Under Assumptions 4.3–4.4 and 4.7–4.9, there is a unique bounded continuous function v satisfying (FE) (Theorem 4.6); v is strictly concave, and the associated optimal policy function g defined by

$$v(x) = F[x, g(x)] + \beta v[g(x)]$$

is single-valued and continuous (Theorem 4.8); and given x_0, the sequence $\{x_t\}$ defined by $x_{t+1} = g(x_t)$, $t = 0, 1, \ldots$, is the unique solution to (SP) (Theorems 4.4 and 4.5). If, in addition, Assumption 4.9 holds, then v is once differentiable at each point x for which $g(x) \in \text{int } \Gamma(x)$ (Theorem 4.11).

Suppose that Assumptions 4.3–4.4 and 4.7–4.9 hold and that the solution is everywhere interior. In this case the first-order and envelope conditions from (FE)

(1) $0 = F_y[x, g(x)] + \beta v'[g(x)],$

(2) $v'(x) = F_x[x, g(x)],$

provide further information on g. Equivalently, under these assumptions any sequence $\{x_t\}_{t=0}^{\infty}$ that satisfies the Euler equations and transversality condition

(3) $0 = F_y(x_t, x_{t+1}) + \beta F_x(x_{t+1}, x_{t+2}), \quad t = 0, 1, 2, \ldots,$

(4) $0 = \lim_{t \to \infty} \beta^t F_x(x_t, x_{t+1}) \cdot x_t,$

is the unique solution to (SP), given x_0 (Theorem 4.15). This chapter is concerned with methods for using (1)–(4) to characterize the behavior of solutions to (SP), either directly or by characterizing the function g.

In a numerical sense the problem (SP) has already been solved in Chapter 4. Given (X, Γ, A, F, β), the functions v and g can be calculated, and the solution, given by $x_{t+1} = g(x_t), t = 0, 1, \ldots$, computed from any initial state x_0. But this approach requires a particular specification of the constraints, return function, and discount factor, and gives no information about how the solution would be altered if these were changed. It is often possible, however, to establish qualitative facts about solution paths for fairly wide classes of return functions, discount factors, and so on. There is no single procedure for obtaining such characterizations, and sometimes an ad hoc approach to (1)–(2) or (3)–(4) is best. Still, there are two standard lines of attack that are widely applicable, and we discuss them here.

In Section 6.1, we first discuss two examples, designed to illustrate that the properties of solution paths may be very simple or quite complicated. Theorem 6.1 then shows that any function g in a very large class is the optimal policy function for some dynamic program and hence that the range of possible dynamics for solutions to (SP) is very broad. This theorem indicates in advance that properties like stability are simply not in the cards as general features of solutions to problems like (SP). On the contrary, solutions to problems of the form (SP) may cycle, explode, or display "chaotic" behavior.

We do not attempt to review all of these possibilities here; the literature is vast and Section 6.6 contains suggestions for further reading. Instead, in the remainder of the chapter we confine our attention to a review of two general methods that are often useful for establishing the global or local stability of solutions to (SP). We do this because in most cases a large part of the positive content of dynamic economic models consists of their predictions about steady-state behavior. The stability of the steady state is thus a crucial issue.

There are two relatively simple general methods for deciding whether a particular system is stable. The first, known as the method of Liapounov, relies on information about the function g and is used for establishing global stability; it is discussed in Section 6.2. The second approach is based on linear approximations to the Euler equations. Thus a review of the theory of linear difference equations and linear approximations to nonlinear systems is presented in Section 6.3; and in Section 6.4 we draw upon this material to build a theory of local stability for solutions to (SP). Section 6.5 contains several applications of these methods to particular economic models, and Section 6.6 contains suggested references for further reading.

6.1 One-Dimensional Examples

We begin with two simple examples. The first illustrates one-dimensional arguments that can be used to establish existence and uniqueness of a stationary point and monotone convergence to it from any initial state. The second, a variation of the first, illustrates that fairly innocuous-looking assumptions can lead to very complicated dynamics. Finally, Theorem 6.1 establishes that the range of possible behavior of difference equations arising as solutions to dynamic programs is extremely broad.

Recall that the one-sector model of optimal growth leads to the functional equation

$$(1) \qquad v(k) = \max_{0 \le y \le f(k)} \{U[f(k) - y] + \beta v(y)\},$$

where $f: \mathbf{R}_+ \to \mathbf{R}_+$ and $U: \mathbf{R}_+ \to \mathbf{R}$ are continuous functions, and $\beta \in (0, 1)$. Assume that both f and U are strictly increasing, strictly concave, and continuously differentiable, with

$$f(0) = 0, \quad \lim_{k \to 0} f'(k) = +\infty,$$

$$\lim_{k \to \infty} f'(k) = 0, \quad \text{and} \quad \lim_{c \to 0} U'(c) = +\infty.$$

These assumptions on f imply that there exists a unique positive value, call it $\bar{k}$, such that $f(\bar{k}) = \bar{k}$; this is the maximum maintainable capital stock. That is, for $k_t > \bar{k}$, $k_{t+1} \leq f(k_t) < k_t$, so the capital stock must fall. Hence we can restrict attention to the interval $[0, \bar{k}]$. Since f and U are both continuous, they are then bounded on the relevant ranges.

The theorems of Section 4.2 then establish (cf. Exercise 5.1) that (1) has a unique bounded continuous solution v on $[0, \bar{k}]$; that v is strictly increasing and strictly concave; that for each $k \in [0, \bar{k}]$, the maximum in (1) is attained at a unique value $g(k)$; that g is continuous; and that given $k_0 \in [0, \bar{k}]$, the sequence $\{k_t\}$ defined by $k_{t+1} = g(k_t)$, $t = 0, 1, 2, \ldots$, uniquely solves the originally posed problem. Our goal here is to characterize g as sharply as possible, in order to learn how optimal $\{k_t\}$ sequences behave.

Consider first *stationary points* of g. For this model, there is a trivial stationary point at zero: $g(0) = 0$. This stationary point corresponds to the fact that if the economy starts with no capital, $k_0 = 0$, then it can never produce any output, $f(0) = 0$; so the capital stock and total output are zero in every subsequent period as well.

To find other stationary points, consider the first-order and envelope conditions for (1); these are, respectively,

(2) $U'[f(k) - g(k)] = \beta v'[g(k)],$

(3) $v'(k) = U'[f(k) - g(k)]f'(k).$

Exercise 6.1   a. Show that the assumptions above on f and U ensure that for any $k \in (0, \bar{k}]$, the solution to the maximization problem in (1) is at an interior value for y, so that v is continuously differentiable on $(0, \bar{k}]$, and (2) and (3) hold for all $k \in (0, \bar{k}]$.

b. Using (2), show that g is strictly increasing.

Combining (2) and (3) to eliminate v' and using the fact that $g(k) = k$ at any stationary point, we find that a necessary condition for a stationary point is $1 = \beta f'(k)$. Under the stated assumptions on f, there exists a unique positive solution to this equation, $k* = f'^{-1}(1/\beta)$. This solution is our only candidate for a positive stationary point. To decide whether it is in fact a stationary point, more information is needed.

From the fact that v is strictly concave, we know that

(4) $\{v'(k) - v'[g(k)]\}[k - g(k)] \leq 0,$ all $k \in (0, \bar{k}],$

with equality if and only if $g(k) = k$. Now substitute from (3) for $v'(k)$ and from (2) for $v'[g(k)]$ and use the fact that $U'(c) > 0$ to conclude that

(5) $[f'(k) - 1/\beta][k - g(k)] \leq 0,$ all $k \in (0, \bar{k}],$

with equality if and only if $g(k) = k$. Since the left side of (5) evaluated at $k*$ is zero, it follows that $g(k*) = k*$, so $k*$ is indeed a stationary point.

Condition (5) also tells us a great deal about the dynamics of the system away from the stationary points. Since there are no positive stationary points other than $k*$, it follows that (5) holds with strict inequality for $k \neq k*$ and $k > 0$. Moreover, since f is concave, it follows that $f'(k) \gtrless$

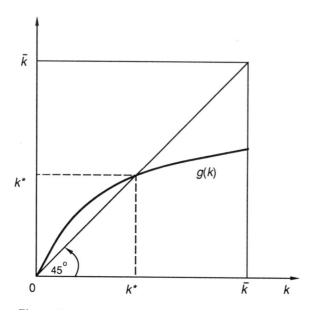

Figure 6.1

$1/\beta$ as $k \lesseqgtr k^*$. It then follows that $k \lesseqgtr g(k)$ as $k \lesseqgtr k^*$. Hence g is as shown in Figure 6.1. More formally, we have established the following global stability result.

PROPOSITION *Let f, U, and β satisfy the assumptions above, and let g be the policy function for (1). Then g has two stationary points, at $k = 0$ and $k^* = f'^{-1}(1/\beta)$, and for any $k_0 \in (0, \bar{k}]$, the sequence $\{k_t\}_{t=0}^{\infty}$ defined by $k_{t+1} = g(k_t)$ converges monotonically to k^*.*

In this example we have placed only very standard restrictions on the preferences and technology and have concluded that the system is globally stable and converges monotonically to the interior steady state. These conclusions are specific to the example; they are not general features of solutions to dynamic programs, even one-dimensional problems. A modified version of the example above illustrates some additional possibilities.

Let the preferences of the consumer be as specified before but modify the technology as follows: Endow the consumer with one unit of labor each period (which does not enter his utility function); and let there be two producible goods, capital and consumption goods. Assume that consumption goods are produced using both capital and labor, but that capital goods are produced using labor only. In particular, assume that

$$c_t = n_t f(k_t/n_t) \quad \text{and} \quad k_{t+1} = 1 - n_t,$$

where $0 \leq n_t \leq 1$ denotes labor used to produce consumption goods. Note that the capital stock must lie on the interval $[0, 1]$. Assume that f satisfies the same restrictions as imposed in the example above, so that f and U are bounded on the relevant ranges. In addition, assume that $\lim_{n \to 0} nf(k/n) = 0$, all $k \in [0, 1]$.

Using the technology constraints to eliminate c_t and n_t, we obtain the functional equation

$$(6) \qquad v(k) = \max_{y \in [0,1]} \left\{ U\left[(1 - y)f\left(\frac{k}{1 - y}\right) \right] + \beta v(y) \right\}.$$

By the same arguments cited above, v is strictly increasing and strictly concave, and the policy function $g: [0, 1] \to [0, 1]$ is well defined and continuous.

To locate stationary points, we proceed as before. First note that $k = 0$ is no longer a stationary point, since capital goods can be produced using labor alone, and it is desirable to do so. Next, consider the first-order and envelope conditions:

$$(7) \qquad U'\left([1 - g(k)]f\left[\frac{k}{1 - g(k)}\right]\right)$$

$$\times \left\{ f\left[\frac{k}{1 - g(k)}\right] - \frac{k}{1 - g(k)} f'\left[\frac{k}{1 - g(k)}\right] \right\} = \beta v'[g(k)],$$

$$(8) \qquad v'(k) = U'\left([1 - g(k)]f\left[\frac{k}{1 - g(k)}\right]\right) f'\left[\frac{k}{1 - g(k)}\right].$$

The assumptions on f and U ensure that for $k \in (0, 1]$, the maximum in (6) is always attained at an interior point, so that (7) and (8) hold. Therefore, setting $g(k) = k$ and eliminating v', we find that a necessary condition for a stationary point is

$$(9) \qquad f\left(\frac{k}{1 - k}\right) - \left(\frac{k}{1 - k} + \beta\right) f'\left(\frac{k}{1 - k}\right) = 0.$$

Under the stated assumptions on f, (9) has exactly one solution—call it k^*; and this solution lies on the open interval $(0, 1)$. Also, as before, since v is strictly concave, (4) holds; and substituting from (7) and (8), we find that

$$\left\{ \left[\beta + \frac{k}{1 - g(k)}\right] f'\left[\frac{k}{1 - g(k)}\right] - f\left[\frac{k}{1 - g(k)}\right] \right\} [k - g(k)] \leq 0,$$

all $k \in [0, 1]$,

with equality if and only if $g(k) = k$. Hence by the same argument as used above, k^* is indeed a stationary point.

The analysis thus far parallels the one-sector example. In this case, however, it does not follow from (7), as it did from (2), that g is increasing. In fact, it is clear from (6) and the assumptions on f that if the capital stock is zero, $k = 0$, then all labor is devoted to the production of capital, $g(0) = 1$. Hence g cannot be increasing near the origin.

Exercise 6.2   Let $U(c) = c^\alpha$, $0 < \alpha < 1$, and $f(z) = z^\theta$, $0 < \theta < 1$. Use (7) to show that g is strictly decreasing on $[0, 1]$, as shown in Figure 6.2.

Hence for the preferences and technology in this exercise, the system oscillates: $k_{t+1} \gtrless k^*$ as $k_t \lessgtr k^*$. Whether the system is stable or explosive thus depends on the slope of g. The first problem in Section 6.5 pursues the possibilities of this simple example more fully.

This example raises the question: Does the fact that it is a policy function imply restrictions on g? The answer is "no": Boldrin and Montrucchio (1986) have shown that it is possible to obtain any smooth policy function g from a dynamic program satisfying Assumptions 4.3–4.4 and 4.7–4.9. We cite their main result.

THEOREM 6.1 (*Boldrin and Montrucchio*)   *Let X be a compact set in* **R***, and let $g: X \to X$ be any twice continuously differentiable function. Let $\Gamma(x) = X$, all $x \in X$. Then there exists a return function F and a discount factor β such that (X, Γ, F, β) satisfies Assumptions 4.3–4.4 and 4.7–4.9, and g is the optimal policy function for the corresponding dynamic program.*

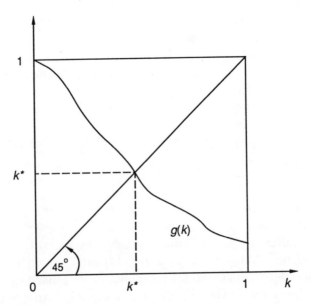

Figure 6.2

In short any sufficiently smooth, first-order, autonomous difference equation can be thought of as describing optimal behavior through time.

A first-order difference equation, in turn, has a much wider range of possible dynamics than one might imagine. The following exercise illustrates some of the possibilities.

Exercise 6.3 Consider the difference equation

$$x_{t+1} = g(x_t) = 4x_t - 4x_t^2.$$

a. Show that $g: [0, 1] \to [0, 1]$; graph g on this interval; and find all stationary points.

Next consider the behavior of the sequence $\{x_t\}$, starting from different initial values x_0. The graph of g shows x_{t+1} as a function of x_t, and intersections of g with the 45° line are stationary points, that is, one-cycles. Similarly, the graph of g^2 shows x_{t+2} as a function of x_t, and *its* intersections with the 45° line correspond to one-cycles and two-cycles, and so on.

b. Compute $g^2(x)$ for $x = 0, \frac{1}{4}, \frac{1}{2}, \frac{3}{4}$, and 1, and sketch g^2. Show that there is a two-cycle. Sketch g^3 and show that there is a three-cycle.

What types of behavior are possible for difference equations of the form $x_{t+1} = g(x_t)$, where g is continuous? As the exercise above suggests, solutions can cycle at fixed periods of any length; they can also behave in "chaotic" ways that resemble stochastic systems. There is a large body of theory directed at characterizing the possible types of behavior and relating them to properties of g. Reviewing this literature would lead us too far astray, however. Instead, in the rest of this chapter we impose stronger assumptions than those used in Chapter 4 and discuss methods for establishing global or local stability under those stronger restrictions.

6.2 Global Stability: Liapounov Functions

In this section we examine what is known as the Liapounov method for establishing the global or local stability of stationary points.

As noted at the beginning of the chapter, necessary conditions for an interior solution to the sequence problem (SP) defined there are the Euler equations

(1) $0 = F_y[x_t, x_{t+1}] + \beta F_x[x_{t+1}, x_{t+2}], \quad t = 0, 1, \ldots.$

Hence if $\bar{x} \in$ int $\Gamma(\bar{x})$, a necessary condition for $\bar{x}$ to be a stationary point is $0 = F_y(\bar{x}, \bar{x}) + \beta F_x(\bar{x}, \bar{x})$. If F is concave, this condition is also sufficient. This is about all that can be said at a general level about locating stationary points; those that occur at boundaries (like the point $k = 0$ in the first example of Section 6.1) must be located by arguments specific to the problem. In the rest of this section, we look at a method for establishing the global or local stability of stationary points of either sort.

Let $g: X \to X$ be a continuous function, and for any $x_0 \in X$, consider the sequence $\{x_t\}$ defined by

(2) $x_{t+1} = g(x_t), \quad t = 0, 1, \ldots.$

Let $\bar{x} \in X$ denote a fixed point of g.

DEFINITION   *The point $\bar{x}$ is* **globally stable** *if for all $x_0 \in X$ and $\{x_t\}_{t=0}^{\infty}$ satisfying (2), $\lim_{t \to \infty} x_t = \bar{x}$.*

We are concerned with conditions on g that imply the global stability of a given stationary point. Clearly, if there are two or more stationary points in X, neither can be globally stable, so resolving the question of global stability presupposes that there is a unique fixed point of g in X. Since we have no general way of resolving the latter question, we know we cannot have a general theory of stability. But the results developed below are sometimes helpful.

We follow the approach, due to Liapounov, of seeking a "hill" in X that solutions to (2) are always climbing, a hill with only the stationary point $\bar{x}$ at the top. If any such hill can be found (and there is no way other than unsystematic ingenuity to find them), then $\bar{x}$ is globally stable. More formally, we have the following result.

LEMMA 6.2   *Let $X \subset \mathbf{R}^l$ be compact, and let $g: X \to X$ be continuous with $g(\bar{x}) = \bar{x}$ for some $\bar{x} \in X$. Suppose there exists a continuous function $L: X \to \mathbf{R}$ that satisfies*

   a. $L(x) \le 0$,   with equality if and only if $x = \bar{x}$,
   b. $L[g(x)] \ge L(x)$,   with equality if and only if $x = \bar{x}$.

Then $\bar{x}$ is a globally stable solution to (2). (*Here the function L, called a **Liapounov function**, describes a hill whose highest elevation, occurring at $\bar{x}$, is zero.*)

Proof. Let $x_0 \in X$ be given, and let $\{x_t\}$ be the corresponding solution to (2). It follows from hypotheses (a) and (b) that the sequence $\{L(x_t)\}$ is nondecreasing and bounded and so has a limit; call it L^0. Moreover, since X is compact, $\{x_t\}$ has a convergent subsequence $\{x_{t_j}\}$; let x^0 be its limit point. Then since L is continuous, $L(x^0) = L^0$. The rest of the proof consists of showing that $x^0 = \bar{x}$ and that $x_t \to \bar{x}$.

First we will show that $x^0 = \bar{x}$. For any j,

$$L[g(x^0)] - L(x^0)$$

$$= \{L[g(x^0)] - L[g(x_{t_j})]\} + \{L[g(x_{t_j})] - L(x^0)\}.$$

Since $x_{t_j} \to x^0$ and L and g are continuous, the first term on the right side tends to zero as $j \to \infty$. Since $L[g(x_{t_j})] \to L^0 = L(x^0)$, the second tends to zero as well. Hence $L[g(x^0)] = L(x^0)$, and it follows from hypothesis (b) that $x^0 = \bar{x}$.

To show that the sequence $\{x_t\}$ (not just a subsequence) converges to $\bar{x}$, suppose the contrary. Then a second subsequence $\{x_{t_j}'\}$ and a number $\varepsilon > 0$ can be chosen such that $\|x_{t_j}' - \bar{x}\| \geq \varepsilon$, all j. Since the set $\{x \in X: \|x - \bar{x}\| \geq \varepsilon\}$ is compact, $\{x_{t_j}'\}$ has a convergent subsequence. By the argument above this subsequence must also converge to $\bar{x}$, a contradiction. ∎

This lemma can also be used to establish local stability in a neighborhood of a nonunique stationary point $\bar{x}$, by restricting attention to a compact set $\tilde{X}$ that contains $\bar{x}$ but contains no other stationary points. This is often useful if there is an irritating stationary point like $x = 0$. For example, if $\bar{x}$ is a stationary point and if a continuous function L: $X \to \mathbf{R}$ satisfying (b) can be found, we can restrict attention to the compact set defined by $\tilde{X} = \{x \in X: L(x) \geq c\}$, for some $c < 0$. Condition (b) guarantees that $g: \tilde{X} \to \tilde{X}$. Hence if L satisfies (a) on $\tilde{X}$, it is a Liapounov function on $\tilde{X}$.

As we have warned, Liapounov functions can be hard to come by, and one is not permitted to begin a stability argument by saying, "Assume we have a Liapounov function." For difference equations that arise from dynamic programs, the following choice works for the undiscounted problem and is suggestive for some discounted problems as well.

Consider a dynamic program defined by (X, Γ, A, F, β) satisfying Assumptions 4.3–4.4 and 4.7–4.9. Let (v, g) be the value and policy functions for the associated functional equation, and assume that $g(x) \in \text{int } \Gamma(x)$, all $x \in X$. Let $\bar{x} \in X$ be a fixed point of g, and define $L: X \to X$ by

$$L(x) = (x - \bar{x}) \cdot [v'(x) - v'(\bar{x})],$$

where $v'(x)$ is the vector $[v_1(x), \ldots, v_l(x)]$ of partial derivatives of v. Proofs based on this specification of L are often called "value loss" arguments. (Why?) Since v is strictly concave, L satisfies condition (a) of Lemma 6.2. If L also satisfies (b), it is a Liapounov function and the global stability on X of $\bar{x}$ is established. We know from the second example in Section 6.1 that (b) does not hold, in general, for L so specified, but it is instructive to proceed anyway.

Our interest is in $L[g(x)] - L(x)$. The return function F is strictly concave, so for all $(x, y), (x', y') \in A$,

(3) $(x - x') \cdot [F_x(x, y) - F_x(x', y')]$

$\quad\quad + (y - y') \cdot [F_y(x, y) - F_y(x', y')] \leq 0,$

with equality if and only if $(x, y) = (x', y')$. We also know that the first-order and envelope conditions hold:

(4) $F_y[x, g(x)] = -\beta v'[g(x)], \quad \text{all } x \in X,$

(5) $F_x[x, g(x)] = v'(x), \quad \text{all } x \in X.$

At any stationary point $\bar{x}$, (4) and (5) imply

(6) $v'(\bar{x}) = F_x(\bar{x}, \bar{x}) = -F_y(\bar{x}, \bar{x})/\beta.$

These are the facts we have to work with.

Now setting $y = g(x)$ and $x' = y' = \bar{x}$ and substituting from (4)–(6) into (3), we find that

(7) $(x - \bar{x})[v'(x) - v'(\bar{x})] - \beta[g(x) - \bar{x}]\{v'[g(x)] - v'(\bar{x})\} \leq 0,$

with equality if and only if $[x, g(x)] = (\bar{x}, \bar{x})$. But this in turn implies that $L[g(x)] \geq L(x)/\beta$. Hence if $\beta = 1, L$ is a Liapounov function. Our analysis in Chapter 4 did not cover the undiscounted case $\beta = 1$, but the Euler equations (1) continue to define a dynamic system in this case. When $\beta = 1$, the necessary condition for a stationary point, $F_y(\bar{x}, \bar{x}) + F_x(\bar{x}, \bar{x}) = 0$, is also a sufficient condition for $\bar{x}$ to maximize the strictly concave function $F(x, x)$ over $x \in X$. Hence there can be at most one stationary point in this case. Then (7) together with Lemma 6.2 implies that if such a stationary point exists, it is globally stable.

For the discounted case, $\beta < 1$, the best we can do is to go over the derivation of (7), to see whether there are possibilities for strengthening the inequality. Equations (4)–(6) do not offer any such opportunities, but (3) does. Since it is the "β" in (7) that needs to be offset, evidently a sufficient condition for $L[g(x)] \geq L(x)$, all x, is that

(8) $\qquad \beta(x - \bar{x}) \cdot [F_x(x, y) - F_x(\bar{x}, \bar{x})]$

$\qquad\qquad + (y - \bar{x}) \cdot [F_y(x, y) - F_y(\bar{x}, \bar{x})] \leq 0, \quad \text{all } (x, y) \in A.$

This condition has the important virtue that it can be checked using the return function only, without calculating v or g. The following exercise provides an example.

Exercise 6.4   Let $X = \mathbf{R}$ and suppose that F is a strictly concave quadratic function, with derivatives

$\qquad F_x(x, y) = a + b(x - \bar{x}) + c(y - \bar{x}), \quad \text{and}$

$\qquad F_y(x, y) = -\beta a + c(x - \bar{x}) + d(y - \bar{x}),$

where $b < 0$, $d < 0$, and $bd - c^2 > 0$. Then $\bar{x}$ is the unique stationary point. Show that a sufficient condition for (8) is $bd - (1 + \beta)^2 c^2/4 \geq 0$.

6.3   Linear Systems and Linear Approximations

There is a well-developed stability theory for systems of linear difference equations, systems of the form

(1) $\qquad x_{t+1} = a_0 + Ax_t, \quad t = 0, 1, \ldots,$

where $x_t \in \mathbf{R}^n$, and where the n-vector a_0 and the $n \times n$ matrix A are constant. If in (FE) the return function F is quadratic and $\Gamma(x) = \mathbf{R}^n$, all x, then the optimal policy function g is linear and direct use can be made of this theory. This was illustrated in Section 4.4 for the case $n = 1$. Even when g is not linear, it is often useful to study a suitable linear approximation to the dynamic system described by g. In this section we review the theory of linear systems and linear approximations; and in Section 6.4 we show how this theory can be used to study systems arising from dynamic programming problems.

Consider the system in (1). Assume that the matrix $I - A$ is nonsingular, so that $\bar{x} = (I - A)^{-1}a_0$ is the unique stationary point and the deviations $z_t = x_t - \bar{x}$ satisfy

$$(2) \qquad z_{t+1} = Az_t, \quad t = 0, 1, \ldots.$$

The solution to (2) is obviously $z_t = A^t z_0$, but this is not very informative unless we can characterize the behavior of the sequence $\{A^t\}$.

To do this we use the fact that any square matrix A can be written as

$$(3) \qquad A = B^{-1}\Lambda B,$$

where B is nonsingular and Λ is a Jordan matrix. A Jordan matrix, in turn, is a block-diagonal matrix

$$(4) \qquad \Lambda = \begin{bmatrix} \Lambda_1 & 0 & \cdots & 0 \\ 0 & \Lambda_2 & \cdots & 0 \\ \vdots & \vdots & \ddots & \vdots \\ 0 & 0 & \cdots & \Lambda_k \end{bmatrix},$$

where each block has the form

$$\Lambda_i = \begin{bmatrix} \lambda_i & 1 & 0 & \cdots & 0 & 0 \\ 0 & \lambda_i & 1 & \cdots & 0 & 0 \\ 0 & 0 & \lambda_i & \cdots & 0 & 0 \\ \vdots & \vdots & \vdots & \ddots & \vdots & \vdots \\ 0 & 0 & 0 & \cdots & \lambda_i & 1 \\ 0 & 0 & 0 & \cdots & 0 & \lambda_i \end{bmatrix}$$

The numbers λ_i—in general, complex—on the diagonal of the ith block are all the same, the entries immediately above the diagonal are ones, and all other entries are zeros. The numbers $\lambda_1, \ldots, \lambda_k$ are the distinct characteristic roots of A: the solutions to $\det(A - \lambda I) = 0$. This equation is called the *characteristic equation* of A or of (1), and the expression $\det(A - \lambda I)$ is called the *characteristic polynomial*. Thus if A has n distinct characteristic roots, its Jordan matrix Λ is diagonal.

The point of writing A as in (3) becomes clear if we use the matrix B to define the new variable

$$(5) \qquad w_t = Bz_t = B(x_t - \bar{x}), \quad t = 0, 1, \ldots.$$

Then using (2) and (3), we find that $w_{t+1} = \Lambda w_t$, so

$$(6) \qquad w_t = \Lambda^t w_0, \quad t = 1, 2, \ldots.$$

This result represents progress, because powers of Jordan matrices are easy to calculate. If Λ is as shown in (4), then

$$(7) \qquad \Lambda^t = \begin{bmatrix} \Lambda_1^t & 0 & \cdots & 0 \\ 0 & \Lambda_2^t & \cdots & 0 \\ \vdots & \vdots & \ddots & \vdots \\ 0 & 0 & \cdots & \Lambda_k^t \end{bmatrix}, \quad t = 1, 2, \ldots,$$

where each block has the form

$$(8) \qquad \Lambda_i^t = \begin{bmatrix} \lambda_i^t & t\lambda_i^{t-1} & \frac{t(t-1)}{2}\lambda_i^{t-2} & \cdots & \\ 0 & \lambda_i^t & t\lambda_i^{t-1} & & \cdots \\ \vdots & \vdots & \vdots & \ddots & \vdots \\ 0 & 0 & 0 & \cdots & \lambda_i^t \end{bmatrix}.$$

Each row of Λ_i^t contains zeros to the left of the diagonal, and the first terms in the expansion of $(\lambda_i + 1)^t$ on and to the right of the diagonal. Using (5)–(8), we can summarize what is known about the stability properties of (1) in two theorems.

THEOREM 6.3 *Let a_0 be an n-vector and let A be an $n \times n$ matrix. Suppose the matrix $I - A$ is nonsingular, and let $\bar{x} = (I - A)^{-1}a_0$. Then $\lim_{t\to\infty} x_t = \bar{x}$ for every sequence $\{x_t\}$ satisfying (1), if and only if the characteristic roots of A are all less than one in absolute value.*

Proof. Let B be a nonsingular matrix and Λ a Jordan matrix satisfying (3). Let $\{x_t\}$ be any sequence satisfying (1), and let $\{w_t\}$ be defined by (5). Clearly $x_t \to \bar{x}$ if and only if $w_t \to 0$. It is immediate from (6)–(8) that $w_t \to 0$ if the characteristic roots of A—the diagonal elements of Λ—are all less than one in absolute value. It is also evident that this condition is necessary if the convergence is to take place for every choice of w_0, and hence for every x_0. ∎

In addition, (5) and (6) give us the solution for x_t in a usable form:

$$(9) \qquad x_t = \bar{x} + B^{-1}\Lambda^t B(x_0 - \bar{x}).$$

If some of the characteristic roots of A have absolute value greater than or equal to one, (9) still holds, of course, and whether or not a particular sequence $\{x_t\}$ converges to $\bar{x}$ depends on the initial value x_0. However, the set of x_0 values for which (1) is stable can be characterized very sharply in terms of the matrices Λ and B.

THEOREM 6.4 *Let a_0 be an n-vector and let A be an $n \times n$ matrix. Suppose the matrix $I - A$ is nonsingular, and let $\bar{x} = (I - A)^{-1}a_0$. Let B be a nonsingular matrix and Λ a Jordan matrix satisfying (3), and suppose that the first m diagonal elements of Λ are less than one in absolute value, and the last $n - m$ are equal to or greater than one. Let $\{x_t\}$ be a sequence satisfying (1). Then $\lim_{t\to\infty} x_t = \bar{x}$ if and only if x_0 satisfies*

$$(10) \qquad x_0 = \bar{x} + B^{-1}w_0, \quad \text{where } w_{0i} = 0, \quad i = m + 1, \ldots, n.$$

Proof. Let m be the number of characteristic roots of A, including repetitions, that are less than one in absolute value. Then the matrices Λ and B in (3) can be chosen so that the first m diagonal elements of Λ are less than one in absolute value, and the last $n - m$ are equal to or greater than one. (In general, both groups contain repeated roots.)

Let $\{x_t\}$ be any sequence satisfying (1), and let $\{w_t\}$ be defined by (5). Clearly $x_t \to \bar{x}$ if and only if $w_t \to 0$. It is immediate from (6)–(8) that

$\lim_{t\to\infty} w_t = 0$ if and only if the last $n - m$ coordinates of w_0 are all zero. It then follows from (5) that the initial values x_0 that are consistent with stability are those that satisfy (10). ■

Note that the initial values x_0 for which the system is stable—that is, satisfying (10)—form an m-dimensional subspace of $\mathbf{R}^n$; this subspace is called the *stable manifold* of (1). Note, too, that for initial values in this subspace, it is clear from (7)–(9) that the speed of convergence to the stationary point $\bar{x}$ is determined by the value of the largest characteristic root that is less than one in absolute value.

Theorems 6.3 and 6.4 both have counterparts as local results for nonlinear systems, and it is these counterparts that have the widest applicability in economics. Let $X \subseteq \mathbf{R}^n$, let $h: X \to X$, and consider the difference equation

$$(11) \qquad x_{t+1} = h(x_t), \quad t = 0, 1, \ldots .$$

Let $\bar{x}$ be a stationary point of h. The general idea is to find a linear approximation to h at $\bar{x}$ and hope that, if x_0 is sufficiently close to $\bar{x}$, the solution to the linear system is a good approximation to the solution to (11). Common sense suggests that this idea will work for stable systems, since for these, if x_0 is close to $\bar{x}$, then so are all the terms in the sequence $\{x_t\}$. Hence the approximation remains good as $t \to \infty$. Here we simply state the main results, the counterparts to Theorems 6.3 and 6.4, respectively. (See Scheinkman 1973 for a full treatment.)

THEOREM 6.5 *Let $\bar{x}$ be a stationary point of (11) and suppose that h is continuously differentiable in a neighborhood N of $\bar{x}$. Let $A = [h_j^i(\bar{x})]$ be the $n \times n$ (Jacobian) matrix of first derivatives of $h = (h^1, \ldots, h^n)$, evaluated at $\bar{x}$, and assume that $I - A$ is nonsingular. Then if the n characteristic roots of A are all less than one in absolute value, there is a neighborhood $U \subseteq N$ such that if $\{x_t\}$ is a solution to (11) with $x_0 \in U$, then $\lim_{t\to\infty} x_t = \bar{x}$.*

THEOREM 6.6 *Let the hypotheses of Theorem 6.5 hold, but assume that A has m roots that are less than one in absolute value and $n - m$ roots that are equal to or greater than one. Then there is a neighborhood $U \subseteq N$, and a continuously differentiable function $\phi: U \to \mathbf{R}^{n-m}$ for which the matrix $[\phi_j^i(\bar{x})]$ has rank $n - m$, such that if $\{x_t\}$ is a solution to (11) with $x_0 \in U$ and $\phi(x_0) = 0$, then $\lim_{t\to\infty} x_t = \bar{x}$.*

Like its counterpart in the linear case, the set of x values satisfying $\phi(x) = 0$ is called the *stable manifold* of the system (11). Since $\phi(x) = 0$ is a system of $n - m$ equations in n unknowns, one may think of solving it for the last $n - m$ coordinates $(x_{0,m+1}, \ldots, x_{0n})$, given values $(x_{01}, \ldots, x_{0m})$ for the first m coordinates. Constructing a solution in this fashion is possible if (and only if) the $(n - m) \times (n - m)$ matrix

$$
\begin{bmatrix}
\phi^1_{m+1}(\bar{x}) & \cdots & \phi^1_n(\bar{x}) \\
\vdots & \ddots & \vdots \\
\phi^{n-m}_{m+1}(\bar{x}) & \cdots & \phi^{n-m}_n(\bar{x})
\end{bmatrix}
$$

is nonsingular.

6.4 Euler Equations

To apply the stability theory of the last section to the problem of characterizing solutions to dynamic programs, it would seem natural to use a linear approximation to the optimal policy function g. But, in general, we do not have enough information to do this. In particular, we do not typically know that g is differentiable. The strategy that does work is to use instead a linear approximation to the Euler equations.

Let (X, Γ, A, F, β) satisfy Assumptions 4.3–4.4 and 4.7–4.9. Recall from Theorem 4.15 that sufficient conditions for an interior solution to the problem (SP) are then the Euler equations and transversality condition:

(1a) $0 = F_y(x_t, x_{t+1}) + \beta F_x(x_{t+1}, x_{t+2}), \quad t = 0, 1, 2, \ldots,$

(1b) $0 = \lim_{t \to \infty} \beta^t F_x(x_t, x_{t+1}) \cdot x_t.$

Moreover, under these assumptions, the optimal solution is unique. Thus, our study of local stability in this section involves establishing additional conditions on F and β under which the following holds.

Condition 6.1 There exists a point $\bar{x} \in X$ and a neighborhood U of $\bar{x}$, such that for every $x_0 \in U$, there exists a sequence $\{x_t\}_{t=0}^{\infty}$ satisfying (1a) and with $x_t \rightarrow \bar{x}$.

Since convergence to $\bar{x}$ clearly implies (1b), any such sequence is the unique optimal solution starting from x_0.

To pursue this strategy, we will consider first the case when F is quadratic, so that the Euler equations are linear and Theorem 6.4 can be applied. Results for this case are summarized in Theorem 6.8, which gives sufficient conditions for the global stability of linear–quadratic systems. Then we will examine how Theorem 6.6 can be applied to a much wider class of return functions. Results for this more general case are summarized in Theorem 6.9, which gives sufficient conditions for the local stability, in the neighborhood of a stationary point, of a nonlinear system.

If F is quadratic, its first derivatives are linear; hence they can be written in the form

$$F_x(x, y) = \bar{F}_x + F_{xx}x + F_{xy}y, \quad \text{and}$$

$$F_y(x, y) = \bar{F}_y + F'_{xy}x + F_{yy}y,$$

where the l-vectors $\bar{F}_x, \bar{F}_y$, and the $l \times l$ matrices $F_{xx}, F_{xy} (= F'_{yx}), F_{yy}$ are all constants. In this notation, the Euler equations (1a) are

(2) $\qquad 0 = \bar{F}_y + \beta\bar{F}_x + F'_{xy}x_t + (F_{yy} + \beta F_{xx})x_{t+1} + \beta F_{xy}x_{t+2}.$

Assume that the matrix $(F'_{xy} + F_{yy} + \beta F_{xx} + \beta F_{xy})$ is nonsingular, so that (2) has a unique stationary point,

$$\bar{x} = -(F'_{xy} + F_{yy} + \beta F_{xx} + \beta F_{xy})^{-1}(\bar{F}_y + \beta\bar{F}_x),$$

and let $z_t = x_t - \bar{x}$. Assume, too, that F_{xy} is nonsingular. (These assumptions may not be easy to verify in particular applications.) Then (2) can be written

(3) $\qquad 0 = \beta^{-1}F_{xy}^{-1}F'_{xy}z_t + \beta^{-1}F_{xy}^{-1}(F_{yy} + \beta F_{xx})z_{t+1} + z_{t+2}.$

Equation (3) is a second-order linear system in z_t, and we have a theory of first-order linear systems. It is convenient, therefore, to define Z_t to be the "stacked" vector with $Z_t' = (z_{t+1}', z_t') \in \mathbf{R}^{2l}$, and to write (3) as

$$
(4) \qquad \begin{bmatrix} z_{t+2} \\ z_{t+1} \end{bmatrix} = Z_{t+1} = AZ_t = \begin{bmatrix} J & K \\ I & 0 \end{bmatrix} \begin{bmatrix} z_{t+1} \\ z_t \end{bmatrix},
$$

where A is a $2l \times 2l$ matrix, and where $J = -\beta^{-1}F_{xy}^{-1}(F_{yy} + \beta F_{xx})$, $K = -\beta^{-1}F_{xy}^{-1}F_{xy}'$, I and 0 are $l \times l$ matrices.

Exercise 6.5 Show that if F_{xy} and $(F_{xy}' + F_{yy} + \beta F_{xx} + \beta F_{xy})$ are nonsingular, then A and $(I - A)$ are also nonsingular.

Everything hinges, then, on the $2l$ characteristic roots of the matrix A. They are characterized in the following lemma.

LEMMA 6.7 *Assume that F_{xy} and $(F_{xy}' + F_{yy} + \beta F_{xx} + \beta F_{xy})$ are nonsingular, and let the matrix A be as defined in (4). Then, if λ is a characteristic root of A, so is $(\beta\lambda)^{-1}$.*

Proof. If λ is a root of A, then the matrix $A - \lambda I$ is singular. That is, for some stacked vector $x \neq 0$, with $x' = (x_1', x_2') \in \mathbf{R}^{2l}$,

$$
\begin{bmatrix} J - \lambda I & K \\ I & -\lambda I \end{bmatrix} \begin{bmatrix} x_1 \\ x_2 \end{bmatrix} = \begin{bmatrix} 0 \\ 0 \end{bmatrix}.
$$

Hence, x_1 and x_2 must satisfy

$$
(J - \lambda I)x_1 + Kx_2 = 0 \quad \text{and} \quad x_1 - \lambda x_2 = 0.
$$

Since A is nonsingular, the root λ cannot be 0. Since $x \neq 0$, the second of these equations then implies that $x_1 \neq 0$ and $x_2 \neq 0$. Then substituting from the second equation into the first, we find that

$$
(K + \lambda J - \lambda^2 I)x_2 = 0.
$$

Since $x_2 \neq 0$, this implies that λ is a characteristic root of A if and only if $K + \lambda J - \lambda^2 I$ is singular, or

$$0 = \det(K + \lambda J - \lambda^2 I)$$

$$= \det[-\beta^{-1}F_{xy}^{-1}F_{xy}' - \lambda\beta^{-1}F_{xy}^{-1}(F_{yy} + \beta F_{xx}) - \lambda^2 I].$$

Since F_{xy} is nonsingular, this is equivalent to

(5) $\qquad 0 = \det[\beta^{-1}F_{xy}' + \lambda\beta^{-1}(F_{yy} + \beta F_{xx}) + \lambda^2 F_{xy}].$

Summing up the argument to this point, we have shown that λ is a characteristic root of A if and only if (5) holds.

Now suppose λ satisfies (5); then it is sufficient to show that (5) also holds for $\hat{\lambda} = (\lambda\beta)^{-1}$. Substituting $\hat{\lambda}$ into (5), we obtain

$$\det[\beta^{-1}F_{xy}' + \hat{\lambda}\beta^{-1}(F_{yy} + \beta F_{xx}) + \hat{\lambda}^2 F_{xy}]$$

$$= \det[\beta^{-1}F_{xy}' + \lambda^{-1}\beta^{-2}(F_{yy} + \beta F_{xx}) + \lambda^{-2}\beta^{-2}F_{xy}]$$

$$= (\lambda^{-2}\beta^{-1})^l \det[\lambda^2 F_{xy}' + \lambda\beta^{-1}(F_{yy} + \beta F_{xx}) + \beta^{-1}F_{xy}].$$

Since $F_{yy} + \beta F_{xx}$ is symmetric, the matrix in brackets is just the transpose of the one in (5). Hence its determinant is zero if and only if (5) holds. ∎

Thus the $2l$ roots of A come in almost-reciprocal pairs: if λ_i is a root, so is $(\beta\lambda_i)^{-1}$. This fact implies that l roots are greater than or equal to $\beta^{-1/2} > 1$ in absolute value, and l are smaller. That is, no more than l roots are smaller than one in absolute value. The following theorem shows that if exactly l roots are smaller, then the linear–quadratic model is globally stable.

THEOREM 6.8 *Let $F : \mathbf{R}^{2l} \to \mathbf{R}$ be a strictly concave, quadratic function; let $\Gamma(x) = \mathbf{R}^l$, all $x \in \mathbf{R}^l$; and let $0 < \beta < 1$. Assume that the matrices $(F_{xy}' + F_{yy} + \beta F_{xx} + \beta F_{xy})$ and F_{xy} are nonsingular, and let $\bar{x}$ be the unique stationary point. Assume that the matrix A defined in (4) has l characteristic roots less than one in absolute value. Then for every $x_0 \in \mathbf{R}^l$, there exists a unique solution $\{x_t\}$ to the problem (SP). This sequence satisfies (2) and has $\lim_{t \to \infty} x_t = \bar{x}$.*

Proof. Fix x_0. Then any sequence satisfying (2) and (1b) is a solution to (SP). Since F is strictly concave, there is at most one such sequence. Hence it suffices to establish existence.

Let B be a nonsingular matrix and Λ a Jordan matrix, each composed of $l \times l$ blocks, such that

$$(6) \qquad \begin{bmatrix} J & K \\ I & 0 \end{bmatrix} = A = B^{-1}\Lambda B = \begin{bmatrix} B_{11} & B_{12} \\ B_{21} & B_{22} \end{bmatrix}^{-1} \begin{bmatrix} \Lambda_1 & 0 \\ 0 & \Lambda_2 \end{bmatrix} \begin{bmatrix} B_{11} & B_{12} \\ B_{21} & B_{22} \end{bmatrix},$$

where Λ_1 has diagonal elements less than one in absolute value. First we will show that given $(x_1, x_0) \in \mathbf{R}^{2l}$, the unique sequence $\{x_t\}$ satisfying (2) has $x_t \to \bar{x}$ if and only if

$$(7) \qquad B_{21}(x_1 - \bar{x}) + B_{22}(x_0 - \bar{x}) = 0.$$

Then we will show that for any $x_0 \in \mathbf{R}^l$, there exists a value x_1 satisfying this restriction.

Suppose that $\{x_t\}$ satisfies (2); let $z_t = x_t - \bar{x}$, and let

$$Z_t = \begin{bmatrix} z_{t+1} \\ z_t \end{bmatrix}, \quad t = 0, 1, \dots.$$

Then $\{Z_t\}$ satisfies (4), and $x_t \to \bar{x}$ if and only if $Z_t' \to (0, 0)$. Applying Theorem 6.4 to the system $Z_{t+1} = AZ_t$, we find that $Z_t' \to (0, 0)$ if and only if $Z_0 = B^{-1}W_0$, for some $W_0' = (w_1, w_0)$ with $w_0 = 0$. This condition, in turn, holds if and only if the pair (z_1, z_0) satisfies

$$\begin{bmatrix} B_{11} & B_{12} \\ B_{21} & B_{22} \end{bmatrix} \begin{bmatrix} z_1 \\ z_0 \end{bmatrix} = \begin{bmatrix} w_1 \\ 0 \end{bmatrix},$$

that is, if and only if $B_{21}z_1 + B_{22}z_0 = 0$. This condition, in turn, holds if and only if (7) holds.

Next we wish to show that if $x_0 \in \mathbf{R}^l$ is given, then x_1 can be chosen to satisfy (7). Clearly it suffices to show that B_{21} is nonsingular. Suppose, to the contrary, that B_{21} were singular; then $B_{21}\hat{z} = 0$ for some $\hat{z} \neq 0$. Now let $x_0 = \bar{x}$. Clearly (7) would hold for $x_1 = \bar{x}$ and also for $x_1 = \bar{x} + \hat{z} \neq \bar{x}$. That is, there would then be *two* sequences starting at $x_0 = \bar{x}$, each converging to $\bar{x}$, satisfying (2). This conclusion would contradict the fact that given x_0, there is at most one sequence satisfying (2) and (1b). ∎

Notice that $g(x) = \bar{x} - B_{21}^{-1}B_{22}(x - \bar{x})$ is the policy function for this linear–quadratic dynamic program. Also, recall from the discussion in Section 6.3 that the value of the largest characteristic root that is less than one in absolute value determines the speed of convergence to the stationary state.

Next we will show how Theorem 6.6 can be applied to establish an analogous local stability result for nonlinear systems.

THEOREM 6.9 *Let $(X, \Lambda, A, F, \beta)$ satisfy Assumptions 4.3–4.4 and 4.7– 4.9, and let $\bar{x}$ be an interior stationary point of (1). Assume that F is twice continuously differentiable in a neighborhood N of $(\bar{x}, \bar{x})$; let F_{xx}, F_{xy}, and F_{yy} denote the matrices of second derivatives of F, evaluated at $(\bar{x}, \bar{x})$; and assume that the matrices $(F'_{xy} + F_{yy} + \beta F_{xx} + \beta F_{xy})$ and F_{xy} are nonsingular. Define the matrix A as in (4); and assume that A has l characteristic roots less than one in absolute value. Then for any x_0 sufficiently close to $\bar{x}$, the unique solution $\{x_t\}$ to (SP) satisfies $\lim_{t \to \infty} x_t = \bar{x}$.*

Proof. Existence and uniqueness of a solution follow from Theorems 4.4–4.8. Hence it suffices to establish that the solution converges to $\bar{x}$, for any x_0 in some neighborhood U of $\bar{x}$.

Since F_{xy} is nonsingular, the implicit function theorem ensures that there exists a neighborhood $N' \subseteq N$ of $(\bar{x}, \bar{x})$, and a continuously differentiable function h defined on N' and satisfying

$$0 = F_y(x, y) + \beta F_x[y, h(y, x)],$$

$$0 = F_{yy}(x, y) + \beta F_{xx}[y, h(y, x)] + \beta F_{xy}[y, h(y, x)]h_1(y, x),$$

$$0 = F_{xy}(x, y) + \beta F_{xy}[y, h(y, x)]h_2(y, x), \quad \text{all } (x, y) \in N'.$$

Let $Z'_t = (x_{t+1}, x_t)$, and consider the "stacked" system

$$(8) \qquad \begin{bmatrix} x_{t+2} \\ x_{t+1} \end{bmatrix} = Z_{t+1} = H(Z_t) = \begin{bmatrix} h(x_{t+1}, x_t) \\ x_{t+1} \end{bmatrix}.$$

If $\{Z_t\}$ is a solution to (8), then it follows from the definition of h that the corresponding sequence $\{x_t\}$ satisfies (1a). Moreover, if $Z'_t \to (\bar{x}, \bar{x})$, then $x_t \to \bar{x}$.

Note that the matrix A is the Jacobian of H:

$$[H^i_j(\bar{x}, \bar{x})] = \begin{bmatrix} h_1 & h_2 \\ I & 0 \end{bmatrix} = \begin{bmatrix} J & K \\ I & 0 \end{bmatrix} = A,$$

where the $l \times l$ matrices J and K are defined as before in terms of F_{xx}, F_{xy}, F_{yy}, and β. As shown in Exercise 6.5, under the stated assumptions $I - A$ is nonsingular. Hence the difference equation $Z_{t+1} = H(Z_t)$ satisfies the hypotheses of Theorem 6.6. It then follows that there exists a neighborhood $U \subseteq N'$, and a continuously differentiable function $\phi: U \to \mathbf{R}^l$, such that if $\{Z_t\}$ is a solution to $Z_{t+1} = H(Z_t)$ with $Z_0 \in U$ and $\phi(Z_0) = 0$, then $\lim_{t \to \infty} Z_t = (\bar{x}, \bar{x})$. Moreover, the matrix $[\phi^i_j(\bar{x}, \bar{x})]$ has rank l.

Finally, we must show that given any x_0 sufficiently close to $\bar{x}$, there exists x_1 such that $(x_1, x_0) \in U$ and $\phi(x_1, x_0) = 0$. By the Implicit Function Theorem, this is true if the $l \times l$ matrix, call it B, consisting of the first l columns of $[\phi^i_j(\bar{x}, \bar{x})]$ has full rank. The argument that this is so is analogous to the last step in the proof of Theorem 6.8. For $x_0 = \bar{x}$, the only solution to (8) is $x_t = \bar{x}$, all t. That is, $\phi(x_1, \bar{x}) = 0$ if and only if $x_1 = \bar{x}$. Hence B has full rank. ∎

Note that Theorem 6.9 implies that the policy function g must satisfy $\phi[g(x), x] = 0$, all $x \in U$. It follows that g is continuously differentiable at $\bar{x}$, with derivatives given by $g'(\bar{x}) = -\phi_1^{-1}(\bar{x}, \bar{x})\phi_2(\bar{x}, \bar{x})$.

For a simple illustration of the application of Theorem 6.9, consider again the optimal growth model of Section 6.1. The return function for this example is $F(x, y) = U[f(x) - y]$, so the Euler equation is

$$0 = -U'[f(k_t) - k_{t+1}] + \beta f'(k_{t+1})U'[f(k_{t+1}) - k_{t+2}].$$

Solving for an interior steady state, we find, as before, that the only one is the unique value k^* satisfying $\beta f'(k^*) = 1$. Taking a second-order approximation around k^*, we find that

$$0 = -\beta^{-1}U'' \cdot (k_t - k^*) + [(1 + \beta^{-1})U'' + \beta f''U']$$

$$\cdot (k_{t+1} - k^*) - U'' \cdot (k_{t+2} - k^*),$$

where U', U'' are evaluated at $[f(k^*) - k^*]$, and f', f'' at k^*, and where $f'(k^*) = 1/\beta$. Note that since U' is positive and U'' and f'' negative, the 1×1 matrices $F_{yy} + (1 + \beta)F_{xy} + \beta F_{xx} = \beta U'f''$ and $F_{xy} = -\beta^{-1}U''$ are nonsingular (nonzero).

Hence, writing the linear approximation in the form given in (4), we obtain

$$\begin{bmatrix} z_{t+2} \\ z_{t+1} \end{bmatrix} = A \begin{bmatrix} z_{t+1} \\ z_t \end{bmatrix} = \begin{bmatrix} 1 + \beta^{-1} + \dfrac{f''/f'}{U''/U'} & -\beta^{-1} \\ 1 & 0 \end{bmatrix} \begin{bmatrix} z_{t+1} \\ z_t \end{bmatrix}.$$

The characteristic polynomial for A is then

$$\lambda^2 - \left[1 + \beta^{-1} + \frac{f''/f'}{U''/U'} \right] \lambda + \beta^{-1} = 0.$$

The roots of this equation are indicated in Figure 6.3. Clearly, both are real: one is positive and less than one, and the other exceeds β^{-1}. Let λ_1 denote the smaller of these two roots.

Using the fact, from (6), that $BA = B\Lambda$, we find the diagonalizing matrix B to be

$$B = \begin{bmatrix} b_{11} & -\lambda_1 b_{11} \\ -\lambda_1^{-1} b_{22} & b_{22} \end{bmatrix},$$

where b_{11} and b_{22} can be any nonzero values. Hence the derivatives of the stable manifold at the steady state are

$$\phi_1(k^*, k^*) = -\lambda_1^{-1} b_{22} \quad \text{and}$$

$$\phi_2(k^*, k^*) = b_{22}.$$

The derivative of the policy function at k^* is then

$$g'(k^*) = -\phi_2(k^*, k^*)/\phi_1(k^*, k^*) = \lambda_1.$$

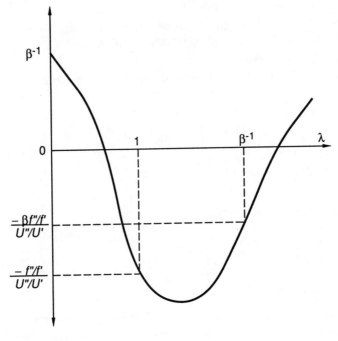

Figure 6.3

In a neighborhood of the stationary point k^*, then, optimal paths for capital behave approximately as $k_{t+1} = k^* + \lambda_1(k_t - k^*)$. Since $0 < \lambda_1 < 1$, this solution conforms with the conclusion reached in Section 6.1. It also gives information on the speed of convergence, which evidently increases as $(f''/f')/(U''/U')$ increases. Curvature in the technology speeds up convergence; curvature in preferences retards it. This conclusion is also consistent with the results for the limiting case of linear utility in Section 5.3.

Exercise 6.6 For the one state variable dynamic program, where F satisfies Assumptions 4.3–4.4 and 4.7–4.9, and is twice differentiable, show that

a. both roots of A are real,
b. both roots are positive if $F_{xy} > 0$, and
c. both roots are negative if $F_{xy} < 0$.

6.5 Applications

A Cyclical Example

Consider again the model in Exercise 6.2. The functional equation is

$$v(k) = \max_{0 \le y \le 1} [k^{\alpha\theta}(1 - y)^{\alpha(1-\theta)} + \beta v(y)],$$

where $0 < \alpha < 1$ and $0 < \theta < 1$.

Exercise 6.7 a. Verify that for any $k_0 \in [0, 1]$, there is a unique optimal capital sequence $\{k_t\}$. That is, verify that this problem satisfies Assumptions 4.3–4.4 and 4.7–4.9. Find the Euler equation.

b. Show that the unique stationary point is $k^* = \beta\theta/(1 - \theta + \beta\theta)$.

c. Expand the Euler equation around the point $k = k^*$ to obtain the linear approximation

$$(k_{t+2} - k^*) + B(k_{t+1} - k^*) + \beta^{-1}(k_t - k^*) = 0,$$

where

$$B = \frac{1 - \alpha(1 - \theta)}{\alpha(1 - \theta)} + \frac{1 - \alpha\theta}{\alpha\theta\beta}.$$

Show that both of the characteristic roots λ_1 and λ_2 of this equation are real, that $\lambda_2 = (\beta\lambda_1)^{-1}$, and that $\lambda_1 + \lambda_2 = -B$, so that both roots are negative. Under what conditions on α, θ, and β is the stationary point k^* locally stable?

The remainder of this problem considers the behavior of solutions for the parameter values $\beta = 0.1$, $\alpha = 0.8$, and $\theta = 0.75$.

Exercise 6.7 d. Conclude from your answers to (b) and (c) that for this case $k^* = 0.23$ and k^* is unstable.

Define a *two-cycle* to be a sequence $\{k_t\}$ of the form

$$k_t = \begin{cases} x & \text{if } t \text{ is odd} \\ y & \text{if } t \text{ is even,} \end{cases}$$

for any two numbers $x, y \in [0, 1]$, $x \ne y$.

Exercise 6.7   e. Show that the two-cycle (x, y) is optimal for $k_0 = x$ if and only if (x, y) satisfies

$$0 = F_y(x, y) + \beta F_x(y, x) \quad \text{and}$$

$$0 = F_y(y, x) + \beta F_x(x, y).$$

Exercise 6.7   f. Verify that for the parameter values given above, $(0.29, 0.18)$ is an optimal two-cycle.

g. Determine the local stability of the two-cycle $(0.29, 0.18)$. [*Hint.* Use the Euler equation to define the "stacked" system

$$K_{t/2+1} = \begin{bmatrix} k_{t+3} \\ k_{t+2} \end{bmatrix} = H \begin{bmatrix} k_{t+1} \\ k_t \end{bmatrix} = H(K_{t/2}),$$

where t is even. Take a linear approximation to this system around the stationary point $\bar{K} = (0.29, 0.18)$, and determine whether one of the characteristic roots is less than one in absolute value.]

A Firm with Adjustment Costs

Consider the dynamics of capital accumulation for the firm with convex adjustment costs introduced in Section 5.9. There is one capital good, k, and $f(k)$ is the firm's net operating profit (sales less payments for labor and materials) when its capital stock is k. Assume that f is strictly increasing, strictly concave, and twice continuously differentiable, with $f(0) = 0$, $\lim_{k \to 0} f'(k) = +\infty$, and $\lim_{k \to \infty} f'(k) = 0$.

Capital depreciates at the constant rate $\delta \in (0, 1)$ per period, and in any period the total cost of investment is a function c of the level of gross investment. That is, $c[k_{t+1} - (1 - \delta)k_t]$ is the total cost of investment if this period's capital is k_t and next period's is k_{t+1}. Assume that c is strictly increasing, strictly convex, and twice continuously differentiable, with $c(0) = 0$.

The firm's objective is to maximize the sum of net receipts, discounted at the constant rate r; so its functional equation is

$$v(k) = \max_y \left\{ f(k) - c[y - (1 - \delta)k] + \frac{1}{1 + r} v(y) \right\}.$$

Exercise 6.8 a. Characterize the stationary capital stock(s) $\bar{k}$ for this firm.

b. Use the method of Section 6.1 to study the global stability of $\bar{k}$.

c. Use the method of Section 6.4 to study the local stability of $\bar{k}$.

A Constant-Returns-to-Scale Industry

Consider a publicly owned firm whose output q_t in period t depends on its beginning-of-period capital stock x_t and its end-of-period capital stock x_{t+1}. In particular, suppose that its technology is homogeneous of degree one: $q_t = x_t \phi(x_{t+1}/x_t)$. Assume that $\phi: [0, \alpha] \to \mathbf{R}_+$ for some $1 < \alpha < \infty$, and that ϕ is strictly decreasing, strictly concave, and twice continuously differentiable, with

$$\phi(0) > 0, \qquad \phi(\alpha) = 0, \qquad \lim_{u \to \alpha} \phi'(u) = -\infty.$$

Assume that capital depreciates at the constant rate $\delta \in (0, 1)$ per period and that in any period new capital goods can be purchased at the constant price $\theta > 0$.

Let $S(q)$ be a measure of the benefits that accrue to society if the firm produces the quantity q. Assume that $S: \mathbf{R}_+ \to \mathbf{R}_+$ is bounded, strictly increasing, strictly concave, and twice continuously differentiable. Assume that society discounts benefits by the constant factor $\beta \in (0, 1)$ per period.

Consider the problem of maximizing net consumer surplus:

$$\max_{\{x_t\}_{t=1}^{\infty}} \sum_{t=0}^{\infty} \beta^t \left\{ S\left[x_t \phi\left(\frac{x_{t+1}}{x_t}\right)\right] - \theta[x_{t+1} - (1 - \delta)x_t] \right\}.$$

The functional equation for this problem can be written as

$$v(x) = \max_{y \in [0, \alpha x]} \{S[x\phi(y/x)] - \theta[y - (1 - \delta)x] + \beta v(y)\},$$

or

$$v(x) = \max_{u \in [0, \alpha]} \{S[x\phi(u)] - \theta x[u - (1 - \delta)] + \beta v(xu)\}.$$

Exercise 6.9 a. Prove that the functional equation has a unique continuous bounded solution v; that v is strictly increasing and strictly concave; that the optimal policy function g is continuous and single-valued; and that v is once differentiable, with

$$v'(x) = S'[x\phi(u)][\phi(u) - u\phi'(u)] + \theta(1 - \delta),$$

where $u = g(x)/x$.

b. Use the envelope condition above to prove that g is increasing.

c. Write the Euler equation, and prove that there is a unique, positive stationary point $\bar{x} > 0$.

d. Prove that the Euler equation is locally stable in a neighborhood of $\bar{x}$.

e. Use (b)–(d) to prove that if $x_0 > 0$, the solution to $x_{t+1} = g(x_t)$ converges monotonically to $\bar{x}$.

(In Section 16.4 we show that a solution to this problem is also a *rational expectations* or *perfect foresight* equilibrium for an industry with many firms, each with the constant returns technology above, and for which S is the integral under the market demand curve.)

A Consumer with Recursive Preferences

Consider a specialization of the consumer of Section 5.12, whose preferences over sequences of a single consumption good are given implicitly by an aggregator function $W: \mathbf{R}_+ \times \mathbf{R} \to \mathbf{R}$. He has wealth x, which he divides into savings $y \in [0, x]$ and current consumption, $x - y$. There is a fixed interest factor $R = 1/(1 + r)$; so if he saves y, his wealth next period is $R^{-1}y$. His functional equation is therefore

$$v(x) = \max_{0 \le y \le x} W[x - y, v(R^{-1}y)].$$

Maintain the assumptions of Section 5.11, so that the value function v has the properties derived in Exercise 5.12, and so that there is a unique optimal savings policy $y = g(x)$. This question is concerned with characterizing g and the wealth sequence $\{x_t\}$ defined by $x_{t+1} = R^{-1}g(x_t)$.

A useful general strategy is to begin by seeking restrictions on W that guarantee uniqueness of a stationary point. Sufficient conditions for this are often sufficient for local and even global stability as well.

If x is a stationary wealth level, then clearly $\bar{x} = R^{-1}g(\bar{x})$ and the associated consumption is $\bar{x} - g(\bar{x}) = \bar{x}(1 - R)$.

Exercise 6.10   a. Show that $\bar{x}$ is a stationary wealth level if and only if for some $\bar{z} \in \mathbf{R}$, $(\bar{x}, \bar{z})$ satisfy the two equations

$$R = W_2[\bar{x}(1 - R), \bar{z}] \quad \text{and} \quad \bar{z} = W[\bar{x}(1 - R), \bar{z}].$$

b. Provide sufficient conditions on W to guarantee existence and uniqueness of a solution $(\bar{x}, \bar{z})$ to this pair of equations.

c. What can be said about stationary points if W is additively separable, that is, if $W(x, v) = U(x) + \beta v$? Characterize all optimal wealth sequences under this assumption.

d. Derive the Euler equation for the consumer whose preferences are not additively separable.

e. Provide sufficient conditions on W to guarantee that a stationary solution, if it exists, is locally stable.

f. Can you prove global stability under the same restrictions found in (e)?

6.6   Bibliographic Notes

The stability proof for the one-sector growth model in Section 4.1 is due to Sangmoon Hahm. Earlier proofs of the same result, in continuous time, can be found in Cass (1965) and Koopmans (1965).

Theorem 6.1 is from Boldrin and Montrucchio (1986). See Boldrin and Montrucchio (1984) for a useful introduction to the literature on the possible pathologies of optimal growth paths.

Burmeister (1980, chap. 4) gives a useful discussion of sufficient conditions for the uniqueness of stationary points in models with many capital goods. See also Brock (1973) and Brock and Burmeister (1976).

The term *value loss*, as applied in Section 6.2, dates from Radner (1961). McKenzie (1987) provides an invaluable survey of the stability theory for both undiscounted and discounted problems that stemmed from this work. For global stability theory applied to the discounted problem, see especially Brock and Scheinkman (1976), Cass and Shell (1976), Rockafellar (1976), and Scheinkman (1976). Kurz (1968) and Sutherland (1970) provided early counterexamples to any general global stability result for multisector growth models.

The basic source for the stability theory of both linear and nonlinear differential equation systems is Coddington and Levinson (1955). Pontryagin (1962) is a very readable introduction to this topic. For a rigorous adaptation of this theory to the study of autonomous difference equation systems, see Scheinkman (1973). Our treatment in Section 6.3 draws heavily on this source.

Lemma 6.7 is due to Levhari and Liviatan (1972).

PART III

Stochastic Models

7   *Measure Theory and Integration*

Most of the results in Chapter 4 carry over almost without change to situations in which the return function is subject to stochastic shocks and the objective is to maximize the expected value of discounted returns. But to show that this is so, it is convenient to draw upon some of the terminology and results from modern probability theory and from the theory of Markov processes. The required material is set out in this chapter and the next. The following example illustrates the advantages of a modern approach.

Consider the stochastic growth model described in Chapter 2. Output $f(x)z$ is determined by the size of the capital stock, x, and a stochastic technology shock, z, where the latter is assumed to be independently and identically distributed over time. Hence the functional equation for optimal growth is

$$(1) \qquad v(x, z) = \max_{0 \le y \le f(x)z} \{U[f(x)z - y] + \beta E[v(y, z')]\},$$

where y is end-of-period capital and z' is next period's shock, and z' is unknown at the time y is chosen. To study this equation we need to spell out what is meant by the expression $E(\cdot)$.

One way to do this is to assume that z takes on values in a finite or countably infinite set, $z \in Z = \{z_1, z_2, \ldots, z_i, \ldots\}$, and that probabilities $(\pi_1, \pi_2, \ldots, \pi_i, \ldots)$ are assigned to these possibilities. Since the π_i's are probabilities, we require that

$$\pi_i \ge 0, \quad i = 1, 2, \ldots, \quad \text{and} \quad \sum_{i=1}^{\infty} \pi_i = 1.$$

In this case (1) can be written as

$$v(x, z) = \max_{0 \le y \le f(x)z} \left\{ U[f(x)z - y] + \beta \sum_{i=1}^{\infty} v(y, z_i)\pi_i \right\}.$$

It is a simple exercise to extend the analysis of Chapter 4 to include equations like this one.

Alternatively, one might wish to carry out the study of (1) under the hypothesis that z takes on values in an interval, $z \in Z = [a, b]$, and that probabilities are assigned to subsets by using a continuous density function $\pi(z)$. Then for any interval $[c, d] \subseteq [a, b]$, for example,

$$\Pr\{z \in [c, d]\} = \int_c^d \pi(z) \, dz,$$

and the probability interpretation requires that

$$\pi(z) \ge 0, \quad \text{all } z \in [a, b], \quad \text{and} \quad \int_a^b \pi(z) \, dz = 1.$$

In this case (1) can be written as

$$v(x, z) = \max_{0 \le y \le f(x)z} \left\{ U[f(x)z - y] + \beta \int_a^b v(y, z')\pi(z') \, dz' \right\}.$$

Again, the analysis of Chapter 4 can be extended to include functional equations like this one.

Both these formulations, discrete and continuous, arise in many economic applications, and it is an obvious—if unfortunate—fact that neither is a special case of the other. In addition, it is easy to think of economic problems that mix discrete and continuous elements. For example, in inventory problems the probability distribution over the stock is often described by a continuous density over strictly positive values, together with a positive probability on the value zero. In this chapter we show that these discrete, continuous, and mixed cases—and more complicated possibilities as well—can all be treated in a unified way.

Our concern in the rest of this chapter is to develop a framework for dealing with probability measures on a state space, where an element in the state space may include a description of exogenous random shocks (like the technology shocks z in the growth example above), or a description of endogenous state variables (like the capital stock x above), or both. At this point, though, we do not need to distinguish among these cases: we simply denote the state space by S and note that, to develop the mathematical tools we need, the elements in the set S can be anything.

In later chapters the state spaces we deal with are often finite or countably infinite sets, like the set $Z = \{z_1, z_2, \ldots\}$ in the first example above, or uncountable subsets of $\mathbf{R}^l$, like the interval $[a, b]$ in the second example. The approach to be developed here, which is based on measure theory, applies much more broadly, however; and no gain in simplicity would result if we were to restrict discussion to these particular cases. Accordingly, the next sections develop, at a general level and in a self-contained way, as much of the theory of measure and integration as is needed to streamline later discussions. It is not a complete treatment of the subject, as this would lead us too far afield. (Many excellent texts are available; for example, see Bartle 1966 or Royden 1968.) But before proceeding, in the remainder of this section we outline the main concepts in the context of a discrete state space.

If the state space is finite or countably infinite, $S = \{s_1, s_2, \ldots\}$, a probability distribution is an assignment of numbers $(\pi_1, \pi_2, \ldots)$ to the points $(s_1, s_2, \ldots)$, with $\pi_i \geq 0$, all i, and $\Sigma_i \pi_i = 1$. The interpretation is that π_i is the probability that s_i occurs, $\pi_i = \Pr\{s = s_i\}$. Such an assignment of probabilities to the *elements* of S leads to a natural assignment of probabilities to *subsets* of S. For any set $A \subseteq S$, let $I_A = \{i: s_i \in A\}$ be the set of indices of elements in A. Then define the function μ by

$$\mu(A) = \sum_{i \in I_A} \pi_i = \Pr\{s \in A\}, \quad \text{each } A \subseteq S.$$

The function μ is an example of a measure. Note that the domain of μ is a family of subsets and that this family includes the empty set $\emptyset$ and the set S itself. Note, too, that μ has the following properties: $\mu(A) \geq 0$, all $A \subseteq S$; $\mu(\emptyset) = 0$; $\mu(S) = 1$; and for any collection $A_1, A_2, \ldots$ of pairwise disjoint subsets, $\mu(\cup_i A_i) = \Sigma_i \mu(A_i)$. Finally, note that for any real-valued function f on S, the expected value of f (with respect to the probability measure μ) is $E(f) = \Sigma_i f(s_i)\mu(s_i)$.

If the set S is uncountable—for example, if S is an interval—it is not possible to define a function (measure) on the class of *all* subsets of S that has the obvious adding-up property for unions of disjoint sets: something must be dropped. It is more important to maintain the adding-up property, and hence we must limit the assignment of probabilities to a smaller family of subsets.

The rest of this chapter is organized as follows. Section 7.1 deals with the issue of what families are suitable to serve as the domain of a measure, a discussion that leads to the definition of a measurable space. Measures, including probability measures as a special case, are defined in Section 7.2, and we will see that certain measures capture the notions of length in $\mathbf{R}^1$, area in $\mathbf{R}^2$, and so forth. (Clearly these are not probability measures, since they do not assign the value one to the whole space.) We will also see that any measure defined on an appropriate small class of sets can be extended to a useful large class. The next two sections deal with defining the expected value operator $E(\cdot)$. In the example above, $E(f)$ can be defined for any real-valued function f. But if S is an uncountable set, expected values cannot be defined for arbitrary functions. A suitable class of functions—measurable functions—is introduced in Section 7.3, and in Section 7.4 we develop the theory of integration, of which expectation operators are a special case. Section 7.5 deals with product spaces; Section 7.6 contains a proof of the Monotone Class Lemma; and Section 7.7 deals with conditional expectation.

For the reader who is anxious to get on with the analysis of stochastic functional equations, only Sections 7.1–7.4 and the first part of Section 7.5 are needed. With that material in hand, the reader can, with no loss in continuity, proceed directly to Chapter 8 and beyond.

7.1 Measurable Spaces

Given a set S, we may ask: On what collection $\mathcal{S}$ of subsets of S are measures, including probability measures, to be defined? To deal with this question, it is useful to have a terminology for discussing certain families of subsets. We define first a *sigma-algebra* (σ-algebra) of sets.

DEFINITION *Let S be a set and let $\mathcal{S}$ be a family of subsets of S. $\mathcal{S}$ is called a σ-algebra if*
  a. $\emptyset, S \in \mathcal{S}$;
  b. $A \in \mathcal{S}$ implies $A^c = S \backslash A \in \mathcal{S}$; and
  c. $A_n \in \mathcal{S}$, $n = 1, 2, \ldots$, implies $\bigcup_{n=1}^{\infty} A_n \in \mathcal{S}$.

Thus, a σ-algebra is closed under complementation and countable union. [Since $\cap_{n=1}^{\infty} A_n = (\cup_{n=1}^{\infty} A_n^c)^c$, *it is also closed under countable intersection.] A pair* (S, 𝒮), *where S is a set and 𝒮 is a σ-algebra of its subsets is called a* **measurable space.** *Any set A* ∈ 𝒮 *is called an* **𝒮-measurable set,** *or—if 𝒮 is understood— simply a* **measurable set.**

For a trivial example of a measurable space, let S be any set and let 𝒮 consist of the two sets S and ∅. At the opposite extreme, let S be any set and let 𝒮 be the collection of all subsets of S. This σ-algebra is routinely used if S is a finite or countable set, as it was in the first example in the introduction.

If S is an uncountable set, like the interval $[a, b]$ in the continuous example in the introduction, the collection of all subsets of S is still a well-defined σ-algebra. However, a look ahead to our ultimate goal shows that it is not possible to let 𝒮 be the set of all subsets and then to define, in an internally consistent way, measures that capture our ideas of probability, length, area, and so on. The σ-algebra of all subsets is too big a class to be useful when S is uncountable. For these cases, however, it is possible to build up a useful class 𝒮 starting from sets that we obviously want to be able to deal with.

To do this, note that for any set S and any collection 𝒜 of subsets of S, we can consider the σ-algebras containing 𝒜. There is at least one: the family of all subsets of S. Moreover, as the following exercise shows, the intersection of all the σ-algebras containing 𝒜 is itself a σ-algebra containing 𝒜. It is the smallest one, and it is called the *σ-algebra generated by* 𝒜.

Exercise 7.1 Prove that for any set S and any collection 𝒜 of its subsets, the intersection of all the σ-algebras containing 𝒜 is a σ-algebra containing 𝒜.

An important example of a σ-algebra generated in this way is the following one for $\mathbf{R}^1$. Let 𝒜 be the collection of all open intervals, that is, all sets of the form $(-\infty, b)$, (a, b), $(a, +\infty)$, and $(-\infty, +\infty)$. Note that every σ-algebra containing 𝒜 must also contain all of the closed intervals. (Why?) The smallest σ-algebra containing all of the open sets is a class that is used in many applications. It is called the **Borel algebra** for $\mathbf{R}^1$ and is denoted by $\mathcal{B}^1$; any set in $\mathcal{B}^1$ is called a **Borel set.**

Exercise 7.2 Show that $\mathscr{B}^1$ is also the σ-algebra generated by all the closed intervals; or by all the half-open intervals $(a, b]$; or by all the half-rays $(a, +\infty) = \{x \in \mathbf{R}: x > a\}$.

For higher dimensional Euclidean spaces or for any other metric space (S, ρ), the Borel algebra is defined in an analogous way: it is always the smallest σ-algebra containing the open balls, that is, containing all sets of the form $A = \{s \in S: \rho(s, s_0) < \delta\}$, where $s_0 \in S$ and $\delta > 0$. For $S = \mathbf{R}^l$ with the Euclidean metric, the Borel algebra is denoted by $\mathscr{B}^l$. One can show that $\mathscr{B}^l$ is also the σ-algebra generated by the open rectangles, sets of the form $A = \{x \in \mathbf{R}^l: x_i \in (a_i, b_i), i = 1, \ldots, n\}$; or (as it was in Exercise 7.2) by the closed or half-open rectangles.

We often want to take S to be a Borel set in a Euclidean space, like the interval $[a, b] \subset \mathbf{R}^1$ in the continuous example in the introduction. In these cases we want to let $\mathscr{S}$ be the appropriate restriction of the Borel sets. Thus, for any Borel set S in $\mathbf{R}^l$, we define $\mathscr{B}_S = \{A \in \mathscr{B}^l: A \subseteq S\}$ to be the Borel sets that are subsets of S.

Exercise 7.3 Show that if $S \in \mathscr{B}^l$, then $\mathscr{B}_S$ is a σ-algebra.

7.2 Measures

Given a measurable space $(S, \mathscr{S})$, we consider next the problem of assigning values with the interpretation of size or probability—in a consistent way—to all of the sets in $\mathscr{S}$. The definition of a measure spells out what we mean by consistency.

DEFINITION Let $(S, \mathscr{S})$ be a measurable space. A **measure** is an extended real-valued function $\mu: \mathscr{S} \to \overline{\mathbf{R}}$ such that
  a. $\mu(\emptyset) = 0$;
  b. $\mu(A) \geq 0$, all $A \in \mathscr{S}$;
  c. if $\{A_n\}_{n=1}^{\infty}$ is a countable, disjoint sequence of subsets in $\mathscr{S}$, then $\mu(\cup_{n=1}^{\infty} A_n) = \Sigma_{n=1}^{\infty} \mu(A_n)$.

Thus a measure is nonnegative, assigns zero to the null set, and is *countably additive*. If $\mu(S) < \infty$, then μ is *finite*.

DEFINITION A **measure space** *is a triple* $(S, \mathcal{S}, \mu)$, *where* S *is a set*, $\mathcal{S}$ *is a* σ-*algebra of its subsets, and* μ *is a measure defined on* $\mathcal{S}$.

Given a measure space $(S, \mathcal{S}, \mu)$, we say that a proposition holds **μ-almost everywhere (μ-a.e.)** if there exists a set $A \in \mathcal{S}$ with $\mu(A) = 0$ such that the proposition holds on the complement of A. If the measure μ is understood, then we say simply that the proposition holds **almost everywhere (a.e.)**. For example, given a measure space $(S, \mathcal{S}, \mu)$, two functions f and g on S are equal almost everywhere ($f = g$, a.e.) if $f(s) = g(s)$ for $s \in A^c$, where $A \in \mathcal{S}$ and $\mu(A) = 0$. Or, a sequence $\{f_n\}$ of functions on S converges a.e. to a function f if there exists $A \in \mathcal{S}$ with $\mu(A) = 0$ such that $\lim_{n \to \infty} f_n(s) = f(s)$, all $s \in A^c$.

If $\mu(S) = 1$, then μ is a **probability measure** and $(S, \mathcal{S}, \mu)$ is called a **probability space**. In this case any measurable set $A \in \mathcal{S}$ is called an **event**, and $\mu(A)$ is called the **probability of the event** A. For a probability space, the phrase **almost surely (a.s.)** is used interchangeably with *almost everywhere*.

One example of a probability space is provided in the introduction. There, $S = \{s_1, s_2, \ldots\}$ is a finite or countable set; $\mathcal{S}$ is the σ-algebra consisting of all its subsets; and μ is defined by using the probabilities $\pi_1, \pi_2, \ldots$ of the individual elements of S. Hence $(S, \mathcal{S}, \mu)$ is a probability space.

Does the second example in the introduction provide another? For the set $S = [a, b]$, we would like to take the σ-algebra to be the Borel subsets of S, $\mathcal{S} = \mathcal{B}_S$. For open, half-open, and closed intervals, we can take the measure μ to be given by

$$(1) \qquad \mu([c, d]) = \mu([c, d)) = \mu((c, d]) = \mu((c, d)) = \int_c^d \pi(s) \, ds,$$

all $a \le c \le d \le b$,

where π satisfies $\int_a^b \pi(s) \, ds = 1$. Clearly μ is well defined for these sets. Moreover, it is clear that we can then extend the definition of μ in (1) to complements and to finite unions and intersections of intervals. However, we have no way—yet—of being sure that this measure can be extended in a consistent way to *all* of the Borel subsets of $[a, b]$. We will return to this example later.

The next exercise demonstrates two useful ways to construct measures. The following one develops an important property of measures.

Exercise 7.4   Let $(S, \mathscr{S})$ be a measurable space; let μ_1, μ_2 be measures on it.
a. Show that $\lambda: \mathscr{S} \to \overline{\mathbf{R}}$, defined by $\lambda(A) = \mu_1(A) + \mu_2(A)$, is a measure on $(S, \mathscr{S})$.
b. Let $B \in \mathscr{S}$. Show that $\lambda: \mathscr{S} \to \overline{\mathbf{R}}$ defined by $\lambda(A) = \mu_1(A \cap B)$ is a measure on $(S, \mathscr{S})$.

Exercise 7.5   Let $(S, \mathscr{S}, \mu)$ be a measure space, with $A, B \in \mathscr{S}$. Show that if $A \subseteq B$, then $\mu(A) \leq \mu(B)$, and if in addition $\mu(A) < \infty$, then $\mu(B \backslash A) = \mu(B) - \mu(A)$.

The next theorem provides a result that will be used later in establishing a basic property of integrals; it is also a good illustration of the implications of countable additivity.

THEOREM 7.1   *Let $(S, \mathscr{S}, \mu)$ be a measure space.*
  a. If $\{A_n\}_{n=1}^\infty$ is an increasing sequence in $\mathscr{S}$, that is, if $A_n \subseteq A_{n+1}$, all n, then $\mu(\cup_{n=1}^\infty A_n) = lim_{n \to \infty} \mu(A_n)$.
  b. If $\{B_n\}_{n=1}^\infty$ is a decreasing sequence in $\mathscr{S}$, that is, if $B_{n+1} \subseteq B_n$, all n, and if $\mu(B_m) < \infty$ for some m, then $\mu(\cap_{n=1}^\infty B_n) = lim_{n \to \infty} \mu(B_n)$.

Proof. a. If $\mu(A_n) = \infty$ for any n, then the result is trivial. Suppose $\mu(A_n) < \infty$, all n. Let $A_0 = \emptyset$. Then $\{(A_n \backslash A_{n-1})\}$ is a sequence of disjoint sets in $\mathscr{S}$, and $\cup_{n=1}^\infty A_n = \cup_{n=1}^\infty (A_n \backslash A_{n-1})$. Then using the result of Exercise 7.5, we find that

$$\mu \left(\bigcup_{n=1}^\infty A_n \right) = \mu \left[\bigcup_{n=1}^\infty (A_n \backslash A_{n-1}) \right] = \sum_{n=1}^\infty \mu(A_n \backslash A_{n-1})$$

$$= \lim_{N \to \infty} \sum_{n=1}^N \mu(A_n \backslash A_{n-1})$$

$$= \lim_{N \to \infty} \sum_{n=1}^N [\mu(A_n) - \mu(A_{n-1})] = \lim_{N \to \infty} \mu(A_N),$$

proving the first claim.

b. Without loss of generality, assume that $\mu(B_1) < \infty$. Then it is sufficient to show that

$$\mu(B_1) - \mu\left(\bigcap_{n=1}^{\infty} B_n\right) = \mu(B_1) - \lim_{n\to\infty} \mu(B_n),$$

or, with the result of Exercise 7.5 applied to each side, that

$$\mu\left(B_1 \setminus \bigcap_{n=1}^{\infty} B_n\right) = \lim_{n\to\infty} [\mu(B_1) - \mu(B_n)] = \lim_{n\to\infty} \mu(B_1 \setminus B_n).$$

$\{B_1 \setminus B_n\}$ is an increasing sequence in $\mathcal{S}$, and $\bigcup_{n=1}^{\infty}(B_1 \setminus B_n) = B_1 \setminus \bigcap_{n=1}^{\infty} B_n$. Therefore, applying the first result yields

$$\mu\left(B_1 \setminus \bigcap_{n=1}^{\infty} B_n\right) = \mu\left[\bigcup_{n=1}^{\infty}(B_1 \setminus B_n)\right] = \lim_{n\to\infty} \mu(B_1 \setminus B_n),$$

as was to be shown. ∎

In (1) we used a density function π on an interval $[a, b]$ to define a measure on subintervals of $[a, b]$, but we did not establish that the domain of this measure could be extended to all the Borel subsets of $[a, b]$. We can now return, but in a more abstract way, to the question of the *extension* of measures defined on a small family of sets to measures defined on an appropriate σ-algebra. We first define a useful small family of sets, an algebra; then define a measure on such a family; and finally present an extension theorem.

DEFINITION *Let S be a set, and let $\mathcal{A}$ be a family of its subsets. Then $\mathcal{A}$ is called an **algebra** if*
   a. $\emptyset, S \in \mathcal{A}$;
   b. $A \in \mathcal{A}$ implies $A^c = S \setminus A \in \mathcal{A}$; and
   c. $A_1, A_2, \ldots, A_n \in \mathcal{A}$ implies $\bigcup_{i=1}^{n} A_i \in \mathcal{A}$.

Thus an algebra is closed under complementation and *finite* union. Clearly, then, an algebra is in an important sense smaller than a σ-algebra.

Exercise 7.6   a. Let $S = \mathbf{R}$, and let $\mathcal{A}$ be the family of all complements and finite unions of sets of the form $(-\infty, b]$, $(a, b]$, $(a, +\infty)$, $(-\infty, +\infty)$. Show that $\mathcal{A}$ is an algebra. [*Hint*. Show that every set in $\mathcal{A}$ can be written as the union of a finite number of disjoint, half-open intervals.]

b. Show that the Borel algebra is the smallest σ-algebra containing $\mathcal{A}$.

The definition of a measure on an algebra is very close to the one for a σ-algebra, but there is one important difference.

DEFINITION *Let S be a set, and let $\mathcal{A}$ be an algebra of its subsets. Then a* **measure** *on $\mathcal{A}$ is a real-valued function μ satisfying*

  a. $\mu(\emptyset) = 0$;

  b. $\mu(A) \geq 0$, all $A \in \mathcal{A}$; and

  c. if $\{A_i\}_{i=1}^{\infty}$ is any disjoint sequence of sets in $\mathcal{A}$ with $\cup_{i=1}^{\infty} A_i \in \mathcal{A}$, then $\mu(\cup_{i=1}^{\infty} A_i) = \Sigma_{i=1}^{\infty} \mu(A_i)$.

The crucial difference between this definition and the one for measures on σ-algebras is that the measure of a countable union of disjoint sets is defined for an algebra only if that countable union is contained in the algebra. Clearly this restriction makes it easier to define a measure on an algebra—especially if the algebra has been chosen (with malice aforethought) to exclude awkward infinite unions.

Exercise 7.7   a. Let $S = \mathbf{R}$, and let $\mathcal{A}$ be as defined in Exercise 7.6. Show that length is a measure on $\mathcal{A}$, where by length we mean the function μ defined by

  1. $\mu(\emptyset) = 0$;

  2. $\mu((a, b]) = b - a$;

  3. $\mu((-\infty, b]) = \mu((a, +\infty)) = \mu((-\infty, +\infty)) = +\infty$;

  4. $\mu(\cup_{i=1}^{n}(a_i, b_i]) = \Sigma_{i=1}^{n}(b_i - a_i)$ if the intervals are disjoint.

b. Let $S = (a, b] \subset \mathbf{R}$, and let $\mathcal{A}$ be the algebra of subsets of S consisting of all finite unions and complements of half-open intervals $(c, d]$, $a \leq c \leq d \leq b$. Show that (1) can be used to define a measure μ on $\mathcal{A}$, and that $\mu(S) = 1$.

Defining measures on algebras rather than σ-algebras is clearly more convenient. On the other hand, we generally find it most convenient to *work* with a σ-algebra. The next two theorems show that we can have the best of both worlds.

THEOREM 7.2 (*Caratheodory Extension Theorem*) *Let S be a set, $\mathcal{A}$ an algebra of its subsets, and μ a measure on $\mathcal{A}$. Let $\mathcal{S}$ be the smallest σ-algebra containing $\mathcal{A}$. Then there exists a measure μ^* on $\mathcal{S}$ such that $\mu(A) = \mu^*(A)$, all $A \in \mathcal{A}$.*

This theorem leaves open the possibility that there may be more than one extension of μ to all of $\mathcal{S}$. To rule out this possibility, we need the following definition.

DEFINITION *Let S be a set, $\mathcal{A}$ an algebra of subsets of S, and μ a measure on $\mathcal{A}$. If there is a countable sequence of sets $\{A_i\}_{i=1}^{\infty}$ in $\mathcal{A}$ with $\mu(A_i) < \infty$, all i, and $S = \cup_{i=1}^{\infty} A_i$, then μ is $\boldsymbol{\sigma}$-finite.*

Clearly, any probability measure is σ-finite. The next theorem shows that the extension of a σ-finite measure is unique.

THEOREM 7.3 (*Hahn Extension Theorem*) *Let S, $\mathcal{A}$, μ, and $\mathcal{S}$ be as specified in Theorem 7.2. If μ is σ-finite, then the extension μ^* to $\mathcal{S}$ is unique.*

We omit the proofs of Theorems 7.2 and 7.3; they are not particularly difficult, but they do require a substantial additional investment in terminology and are available in any standard text on measure theory. Instead, we will focus on applications of the theorems.

Let $\mathcal{A}$ be the algebra of subsets of **R** defined in Exercise 7.6. Let μ be the measure on $\mathcal{A}$, namely, length, defined in Exercise 7.7a; and note that since **R** is the union of a countable set of intervals of length one, this measure is σ-finite. Hence by Theorems 7.2 and 7.3, μ has a unique extension to the smallest σ-algebra containing $\mathcal{A}$, the Borel sets. Thus length defines a unique measure on the Borel sets.

The argument is exactly analogous in higher dimensional Euclidean spaces. In Section 7.1 we observed that the Borel sets in $\mathbf{R}^l$ are generated by the half-open rectangles, that is, sets of the form $\{x \in \mathbf{R}^l: a < x \leq b\}$, where $a, b \in \mathbf{R}^l$ and $a \leq b$. Hence, if a measure can be defined on the algebra consisting of all complements and finite unions of these rectangles, it can be extended in a unique way to the Borel sets. In this way, area can be defined on $\mathcal{B}^2$, volume on $\mathcal{B}^3$, and so on.

Theorems 7.2 and 7.3 can be used in exactly the same way to generate probability measures. Let S, $\mathcal{A}$, and μ be as given in Exercise 7.7b. Then Theorems 7.2 and 7.3 imply that the measure μ on $\mathcal{A}$ has a unique extension to the Borel subsets of $[a, b]$. That is, (1) does indeed define a measure on the Borel sets of $[a, b]$. In higher dimensional Euclidean spaces the argument is analogous: begin with the algebra $\mathcal{A}$ consisting of complements and finite unions of half-open rectangles. For any measure defined on $\mathcal{A}$, for example by a density, there exists an extension to all of the Borel sets.

These are the basic facts about measures that will be used in the rest of this chapter and those that follow. Before proceeding, however, it is useful to state one additional definition.

Given a measure space $(S, \mathcal{S}, \mu)$, one would think that if $A \in \mathcal{S}$ has measure zero, then $B \subset A$ would, too. B may not be in $\mathcal{S}$, however, and hence $\mu(B)$ may be undefined. This gap is filled by the idea of the completion of a measure space.

Let $(S, \mathcal{S}, \mu)$ be a measure space. Let $A \in \mathcal{S}$ be any set with measure zero, and let C be any subset of A. Let $\mathcal{C}$ be the family of all such sets. That is,

$$\mathcal{C} = \{C \subset S : C \subseteq A \text{ for some } A \in \mathcal{S} \text{ with } \mu(A) = 0\}.$$

Now consider starting with any set $B \in \mathcal{S}$, and then adding and subtracting from it sets in $\mathcal{C}$. The **completion** of $\mathcal{S}$ is the family $\mathcal{S}'$ of sets constructed in this way. That is,

$$\mathcal{S}' = \{B' \subseteq S : B' = (B \cup C_1)\backslash C_2, \ B \in \mathcal{S}, \ C_1, C_2 \in \mathcal{C}\}.$$

That is, $\mathcal{S}'$ consists of all the subsets of S that differ from a set in $\mathcal{S}$ by a subset of a set of μ-measure zero. If $\mathcal{S}'$ is the completion of $\mathcal{S}$, a measure μ on $(S, \mathcal{S})$ can be extended to $(S, \mathcal{S}')$ in the obvious way: let $\mu(B') = \mu(B)$ for any set B' in $\mathcal{S}'$ that differs from $B \in \mathcal{S}$ by a subset of a set in $\mathcal{S}$ of measure zero.

Exercise 7.8   Let $(S, \mathcal{S}, \mu)$ be a measure space, and let $\mathcal{S}'$ be the completion of $\mathcal{S}$. Show that $\mathcal{S}'$ is a σ-algebra.

For any Euclidean space $\mathbf{R}^l$, the completion of the Borel sets is a family called the **Lebesgue measurable** sets, and the extension to this family of the measure corresponding to length, area, and so on is called **Lebesgue measure**. When restricted to the Borel sets it is called either Lebesgue measure or **Borel measure**. We will use the latter term. Both the Borel sets and the Lebesgue sets are commonly used in $\mathbf{R}^l$, and when a set in $\mathbf{R}^l$

is referred to as *measurable,* without reference to a particular σ-algebra, either may be intended (or it may be that it does not matter which is used).

The Caratheodory Extension Theorem can in fact be proved for *completions* of measures.

THEOREM 7.2′ (*Caratheodory Extension Theorem*) *Let S be a set, $\mathcal{A}$ an algebra of its subsets, and μ a measure on $\mathcal{A}$. Let $\mathcal{S}$ be the completion of the smallest σ-algebra containing $\mathcal{A}$. Then there exists a measure μ^* on $\mathcal{S}$, such that $\mu(A) = \mu^*(A)$, all $A \in \mathcal{A}$.*

Note that the Hahn Extension Theorem still implies that if μ is σ-finite, then μ^* is unique.

7.3 Measurable Functions

In the two examples in the introduction, we were interested in defining probability measures on the state space S so that we could talk sensibly about expressions like $E(f)$, the expected value of a real-valued function f defined on S. We need to ask, then, for which functions can expressions like $E(f)$ be reasonably interpreted. As with the assignment of measures to sets, the class of *all* functions $f: S \to \mathbf{R}$ is too large to work with, but we want as large a class as we can usefully manipulate. It is as follows.

DEFINITION *Given a measurable space $(S, \mathcal{S})$, a real-valued function $f: S \to \mathbf{R}$ is **measurable with respect to $\mathcal{S}$ (or $\mathcal{S}$-measurable)** if*

(1) $\{s \in S: f(s) \le a\} \in \mathcal{S}$,   all $a \in \mathbf{R}$.

If the σ-algebra $\mathcal{S}$ is understood, such a function is just called ***measurable***. If the space in question is a probability space, f is called a ***random variable***. Finally, note that the measurability criterion is exactly the same for extended real-valued functions: if $f: S \to \overline{\mathbf{R}}$, then f is measurable if (1) holds.

Exercise 7.9 a. Show that there are four equivalent ways to define measurable functions: using "$\le$", "$\ge$", "$<$", or "$>$" in (1).

b. Show that any of these implies that (1) holds with "=" in place of "≤". Give an example where the reverse implication does *not* hold.

c. Show that if $f: S \to \overline{\mathbf{R}}$ is measurable, then the sets $A = \{s \in S: f(s) = +\infty\}$ and $B = \{s \in S: f(s) = -\infty\}$ belong to $\mathscr{S}$.

Depending on the measurable space of interest, it may be easy, hard, or impossible to construct a nonmeasurable function. For example, if $S = \{0, 1\}$, then $\mathscr{S} = \{\emptyset, S, \{0\}, \{1\}\}$ and $\hat{\mathscr{S}} = \{\emptyset, S\}$ are both σ-algebras. Clearly, all functions on S are $\mathscr{S}$-measurable, but only the constant functions are $\hat{\mathscr{S}}$-measurable. For our purposes later, finite-dimensional Euclidean spaces with their Borel σ-algebras are particularly important. To give an example of a function $f: \mathbf{R}^l \to \mathbf{R}$ that is not Borel measurable, we would need an example of a set in $\mathbf{R}^l$ that is not Borel measurable. Such sets exist (see Royden 1968, pp. 63–64, for an example in $\mathbf{R}^1$), and hence there exist functions that are not Borel measurable (for example, any function that takes the value one on a set that is not Borel measurable and zero elsewhere). One does not run across such functions very often in economics, but clearly we would like to have sufficient conditions for ensuring that functions of interest are measurable. Sometimes, as in the next exercise, measurability can be verified directly.

Exercise 7.10 a. Show that any monotone or continuous function $f: \mathbf{R} \to \mathbf{R}$ is measurable with respect to the Borel sets.

b. Let $S = \{s_1, s_2, \ldots\}$ be a countable set, and let $\mathscr{S}$ be the *complete σ-algebra* for S. That is, $\mathscr{S}$ contains all subsets of S. Show that all functions $f: S \to \mathbf{R}$ are $\mathscr{S}$-measurable.

In other cases the measurability of a function is established by showing that it is the limit of a sequence of "simpler" functions. The next results pursue this idea.

Let $(S, \mathscr{S})$ be a measurable space, and consider first the indicator functions, functions $\chi_A: S \to \mathbf{R}$ of the form

$$\chi_A(s) = \begin{cases} 1 & \text{if } s \in A \\ 0 & \text{if } s \notin A. \end{cases}$$

Obviously these functions are $\mathscr{S}$-measurable if and only if $A \in \mathscr{S}$.

Next, consider functions that are finite weighted sums of indicator functions:

$$(2) \qquad \phi(s) = \sum_{i=1}^{n} a_i \chi_{A_i}(s),$$

where $\{A_i\}_{i=1}^{n}$ is a sequence of subsets of S, and $\{a_i\}_{i=1}^{n}$ is a sequence of real numbers. Functions like this, which take on only a finite number of values, are called *simple functions*. If the sets $\{A_i\}$ form a partition of S (that is, if $(A_i \cap A_j) = \emptyset$, all $i \neq j$, and $\cup_{i=1}^{n} A_i = S$), and if all of the values a_i are distinct, then (2) is the *standard representation* of the function.

Exercise 7.11 Show that if (2) is the standard representation of ϕ, then ϕ is measurable if and only if $A_i \in \mathscr{S}$, $i = 1, \ldots, n$.

The next two theorems show that the set of all measurable functions consists exactly of those that are pointwise limits of measurable simple functions. The first shows that any function f that is the pointwise limit of a sequence $\{f_n\}$ of measurable functions is itself measurable. The proof is a good illustration of the kind of argument often used to establish measurability. The second shows that any measurable function f can be expressed as the pointwise limit of a sequence $\{\phi_n\}$ of measurable simple functions; that if f is nonnegative, the sequence can be chosen to be strictly increasing; and that if f is bounded, the sequence can be chosen to converge uniformly.

THEOREM 7.4 (*Pointwise convergence preserves measurability*) Let $(S, \mathscr{S})$ be a measurable space, and let $\{f_n\}$ be a sequence of $\mathscr{S}$-measurable functions converging pointwise to f:

$$(3) \qquad \lim_{n \to \infty} f_n(s) = f(s), \quad \text{all } s \in S.$$

Then f is also $\mathscr{S}$-measurable.

Proof. We want to show that for any $a \in \mathbf{R}$,

$$(4) \qquad A = \{s \in S : f(s) \leq a\} \in \mathscr{S}.$$

Fix $a \in \mathbf{R}$, and for $k = 1, 2, \ldots$ and $n = 1, 2, \ldots$, let

$$A_{nk} = \{s \in S : f_n(s) \leq a + 1/k\}.$$

Since f_n is $\mathcal{S}$-measurable, $A_{nk} \in \mathcal{S}$, all n, k. Then, since $\mathcal{S}$ is closed under countable union and intersection, it follows that $B_{Nk} = \cap_{n=N}^{\infty} A_{nk} \in \mathcal{S}$, all N, k; so that $B_k = \cup_{N=1}^{\infty} B_{Nk} \in \mathcal{S}$, all k; and finally, that $B = \cap_{k=1}^{\infty} B_k \in \mathcal{S}$. Hence it is sufficient to show that $A = B$, where A is as defined in (4).

First we will show that $A \subseteq B$. Suppose that $s \in A$. Then $f(s) \leq a$, and for each $k = 1, 2, \ldots$, it follows from (3) that for some N_k,

$$n \geq N_k \;\Rightarrow\; f_n(s) \leq a + 1/k \;\Rightarrow\; s \in A_{nk}.$$

Hence for each k, we have $s \in B_{Nk}$, all $N \geq N_k$, so $s \in B_k$ and hence $s \in B$. Therefore $A \subseteq B$.

Next we will show that $B \subseteq A$. Suppose that $s \in B$. Then $s \in B_k$, for each k. Hence for each k, $s \in B_{N_k k}$ for some N_k. Hence for each k,

$$n \geq N_k \;\Rightarrow\; s \in A_{nk} \;\Rightarrow\; f_n(s) \leq a + 1/k.$$

Since $f_n(s) \to f(s)$, it follows that $f(s) \leq a$, so that $s \in A$. Hence $B \subseteq A$. ∎

Using this theorem, we can construct a class of measurable functions by taking the class of measurable simple functions and then closing this set under pointwise convergence. The next result shows that this set contains all the measurable functions.

THEOREM 7.5 (*Approximation of measurable functions by simple functions*) *Let $(S, \mathcal{S})$ be a measurable space. If $f : S \to \mathbf{R}$ is $\mathcal{S}$-measurable, then there is a sequence of measurable simple functions $\{\phi_n\}$, such that $\phi_n \to f$ pointwise. If $0 \leq f$, then the sequence can be chosen so that*

$$(5) \qquad 0 \leq \phi_n \leq \phi_{n+1} \leq f, \quad \text{all } n.$$

If f is bounded, then the sequence can be chosen so that $\phi_n \to f$ uniformly.

Proof. Suppose that $f \geq 0$. For $n = 1, 2, \ldots$, partition the interval $[0, n)$ into intervals of length 2^{-n}. Since f is measurable,

$$A_{kn} = \{s \in S : (k - 1)2^{-n} \leq f(s) < k2^{-n}\} \in \mathcal{S},$$

$$k = 1, 2, \ldots, n2^n; \; n = 1, 2, \ldots.$$

Define the simple functions ϕ_n by

$$\phi_n(s) = \sum_{k=1}^{n2^n} (k - 1)2^{-n}\chi_{A_{kn}}(s), \quad n = 1, 2, \ldots,$$

where $\chi_{A_{kn}}$ is the indicator function for A_{kn}. Since $A_{kn} \in \mathcal{S}$, all k, n, each function ϕ_n is $\mathcal{S}$-measurable. Clearly, too, (5) holds. Moreover, for any $s \in S$, there exists $N(s)$ such that

$$|\phi_n(s) - f(s)| \leq 2^{-n}, \quad \text{all } n \geq N(s).$$

Hence $\phi_n \to f$. If f is bounded, then N in the last step can be chosen independently of s, so the convergence is uniform.

To extend the result to all real-valued functions, simply apply the argument above separately to f^+ and f^-. ∎

The theorem is still valid if f is an extended real-valued function. To see this, consider the case where f is nonnegative. Define $C_n = \{s \in S : f(s) \geq n\}$, $n = 1, 2, \ldots$, and let

$$\phi_n(s) = \sum_{k=1}^{n2^n} (k - 1)2^{-n}\chi_{A_{kn}}(s) + n\chi_{C_n}, \quad n = 1, 2, \ldots.$$

Clearly each ϕ_n is a simple function, $\phi_n \to f$ pointwise, and (5) holds.

These two theorems show that a function is measurable if and only if it is the pointwise limit of a sequence of measurable simple functions. Finding such an approximation is a standard way to prove that a function is measurable.

Exercise 7.12   Let $(S, \mathcal{S})$ be a measurable space.

a. Show that if f and g are $\mathcal{S}$-measurable functions on S and $c \in \mathbf{R}$, then the functions $f + g$, fg, $|f|$, and cf are $\mathcal{S}$-measurable.

b. For any sequence $\{f_n\}$ of real-valued functions on S, define the function $g = \lim \inf f_n$ by

$$g(s) = \lim \inf f_n(s), \quad \text{all } s \in S.$$

Define the functions $\lim \sup f_n$, $\inf f_n$, and $\sup f_n$ similarly. Show that if $\{f_n\}$ is a sequence of $\mathcal{S}$-measurable functions, then $\inf f_n$, $\sup f_n$, $\lim \inf f_n$, and $\lim \sup f_n$ are all $\mathcal{S}$-measurable.

Exercise 7.13   a. Show that the continuous functions on $\mathbf{R}^l$ are $\mathcal{B}^l$-measurable.

b. Define the *Baire functions* on $\mathbf{R}^l$ to be the continuous functions, functions that are the pointwise limits of sequences of continuous functions, functions that are pointwise limits of sequences of these functions, and so on. Show that the Baire functions on $\mathbf{R}^l$ are exactly the Borel-measurable functions.

Exercise 7.14   Let $(S, \mathcal{S})$ be a measurable space, and let $f: S \rightarrow \mathbf{R}$ be an $\mathcal{S}$-measurable function. Show that the inverse image of every Borel set in $\mathbf{R}$ is in $\mathcal{S}$. That is,

$$\{x \in S: f(x) \in A\} \in \mathcal{S}, \quad \text{all } A \in \mathcal{B}.$$

[*Hint.* First show that the inverse image of every open set in $\mathbf{R}$ belongs to $\mathcal{S}$. Then show that the class of sets in $\mathbf{R}$ whose inverse image belongs to $\mathcal{S}$ is a σ-algebra.]

The last exercise can be used to establish the very useful fact that compositions of Borel measurable functions are Borel measurable. That is, if $f: \mathbf{R} \rightarrow \mathbf{R}$ and $g: \mathbf{R} \rightarrow \mathbf{R}$ are both Borel measurable, then the function $h: \mathbf{R} \rightarrow \mathbf{R}$ defined by $h(x) = g[f(x)]$ is also Borel measurable. To see this, recall that h is Borel measurable if (1) holds. Thus it is sufficient to show that for any Borel set A, the inverse image $h^{-1}(A) = f^{-1}[g^{-1}(A)]$ is a Borel set. It follows immediately from Exercise 7.14 that this is so.

The same is *not* true if Lebesgue measure is used. That is, if f and g are Lebesgue measurable functions, then h need *not* be Lebesgue measurable. To see this, note that if f and g are Lebesgue measurable, then Exercise 7.14 implies that for any Borel set A, the inverse images $f^{-1}(A)$ and $g^{-1}(A)$ are Lebesgue sets. Now let $A = (-\infty, a]$, and consider the inverse image $h^{-1}(A) = f^{-1}[g^{-1}(A)]$. The set $B = g^{-1}(A)$ is a Lebesgue set but need *not* be a Borel set. Thus $f^{-1}(B)$ need not be a Lebesgue set, and h need not be Lebesgue measurable. For this reason, we will always want to use the Borel sets rather than the Lebesgue sets as our σ-algebra when dealing with a Euclidean space.

Finally, we can extend the definition of measurability to functions from any measurable space into any other measurable space.

DEFINITION *Let $(S, \mathcal{S})$ and $(T, \mathcal{T})$ be measurable spaces. Then the function $f: S \to T$ is **measurable** if the inverse image of every measurable set is measurable, that is, if $\{s \in S: f(s) \in A\} \in \mathcal{S}$, all $A \in \mathcal{T}$.*

That is, $f: S \to T$ is measurable if the pre-image of each measurable set is measurable. Thus, as Exercise 7.14 shows, our earlier definition was a specialization of this one in which $(T, \mathcal{T}) = (\mathbf{R}^1, \mathcal{B}^1)$. An immediate consequence of this definition is that compositions of measurable functions are measurable. That is, if $(S, \mathcal{S})$, $(T, \mathcal{T})$, and $(U, \mathcal{U})$ are measurable spaces, and $f: S \to T$ and $g: T \to U$ are measurable functions, then $h: S \to U$ defined by $h(s) = g[f(s)]$ is a measurable function. (But, as shown above, if the spaces involved are Euclidean spaces, this conclusion must be interpreted carefully.)

Exercise 7.15 Show that a function $f: \mathbf{R}^l \to \mathbf{R}^m$, where

$$f(x_1, \ldots, x_l) = [f_1(x_1, \ldots, x_l), \ldots, f_m(x_1, \ldots, x_l)],$$

is measurable if and only if each of the functions $f_i: \mathbf{R}^l \to \mathbf{R}^1$, $i = 1, \ldots, m$, is $\mathcal{B}^l$-measurable.

Finally, the following definition and theorem are needed in Section 9.1, where the Principle of Optimality for stochastic systems is treated. Although the theorem is very easy to state, the proof is quite difficult, and we omit it.

DEFINITION *Let $(S, \mathcal{S})$ and $(T, \mathcal{T})$ be measurable spaces, and let Γ be a correspondence of S into T. Then the function $h: S \to T$ is a **measurable selection from Γ** if h is measurable and $h(s) \in \Gamma(s)$, all $s \in S$.*

THEOREM 7.6 (*Measurable Selection Theorem*)   *Let $S \subseteq \mathbf{R}^l$ and $T \subseteq \mathbf{R}^m$ be Borel sets, with their Borel subsets $\mathcal{S}$ and $\mathcal{T}$. Let $\Gamma : S \to T$ be a (nonempty) compact-valued and u.h.c. correspondence. Then there exists a measurable selection from Γ.*

(For a proof, see Hildenbrand 1974, Proposition 1 on p. 22 and Lemma 1 on p. 55.)

7.4   Integration

We began this chapter by noting that the task of incorporating stochastic elements into our theory would be simplified if we had a unified way of dealing with the expected value $E[v(y, z')]$ that appeared in the examples in the introduction. We have seen how to define a probability space $(Z, \mathfrak{L}, \mu)$ for the random shocks, and the reader has probably guessed, correctly, that the function v will be required to be $\mathfrak{L}$-measurable. In this section we combine these two pieces—measure spaces and measurable functions—to develop the theory of integration. The integral developed here (called the Lebesgue integral if we are dealing with Euclidean space and Lebesgue measure) is more general than the Riemann integral and includes it, as well as operations like $\Sigma_i \pi_i f(s_i)$ involving discrete probabilities, as special cases.

The difference between the two is illustrated by the following example. Consider a function $f : [a, b] \to \mathbf{R}_+$. To compute the Riemann integral, we consider the sum $\Sigma_{i=1}^n y_i(a_i - a_{i-1})$, where $a = a_0 \le a_1 \le \ldots \le a_n = b$, so that $(a_i - a_{i-1})$ is the length of the ith interval. Suppose, in addition, that $y_i \le f(x), x \in [a_{i-1}, a_i]$, all i. Then the sum above is the area under a step function that is less than f. The supremum over all such step functions is called the *lower Riemann integral*. Similarly, using $y_i \ge f(x), x \in [a_{i-1}, a_i]$, all i, gives a step function greater than f. The infimum of the sum over all such step functions is the *upper Riemann integral*. If the two coincide, the function f is called *Riemann integrable*, and the common value is the *Riemann integral* $\int_a^b f(x)\, dx$. The important point is that the approximations are made by taking successively finer grids on the x-axis, that is, by choosing a_i's that are closer together.

The Lebesgue integral of f on $[a, b]$ is defined in terms of $\Sigma_{i=1}^{n} y_i \lambda(A_i)$, where $0 = y_1 \leq \ldots \leq y_n$, $A_i = \{x: y_i \leq f(x) < y_{i+1}\}$, and $\lambda(A_i)$ is the Lebesgue measure of the set A_i. The Lebesgue integral is defined by taking y_i's that are closer together, that is, by taking successively finer grids on the y-axis.

Exercise 7.16   Let $f: [0, 1] \to [0, 1]$ be defined by

$$f(x) = \begin{cases} 1 & \text{if } x \text{ is rational} \\ 0 & \text{if } x \text{ is irrational.} \end{cases}$$

Show, by calculating the upper and lower Riemann integrals of f, that the Riemann integral does not exist.

Of course, the Lebesgue and Riemann integrals coincide when the latter exists. The advantage of the Lebesgue integral is that it is defined for a broader class of functions and thus allows more limiting operations. Moreover, Lebesgue's theory of integration can be extended to real-valued functions on *any* measure space $(S, \mathcal{S}, \mu)$. For example, if μ is a probability measure, $\int_S f(s)\mu(ds)$ is the **expected value** of the random variable f with respect to the distribution μ.

Throughout this section we take $(S, \mathcal{S}, \mu)$ to be a fixed measure space, and *measurable* always means $\mathcal{S}$-measurable. Let $M(S, \mathcal{S})$ be the space of measurable, extended real-valued functions on S, and let $M^+(S, \mathcal{S})$ be the subset consisting of nonnegative functions. Note, however, that simple functions take values in $\mathbf{R}$ rather than $\overline{\mathbf{R}}$.

We begin with the definition of the integral of a nonnegative, measurable, simple function.

DEFINITION   *Let $\phi \in M^+(S, \mathcal{S})$ be a measurable simple function, with the standard representation $\phi(s) = \Sigma_{i=1}^{n} a_i \chi_{A_i}(s)$. Then the **integral of ϕ with respect to μ** is*

$$\int_S \phi(s)\mu(ds) = \sum_{i=1}^{n} a_i \mu(A_i).$$

The following exercise establishes the linearity of the integral for simple functions.

Exercise 7.17   Show that if $\phi, \psi \in M^+(S, \mathcal{S})$ are simple functions and $c \geq 0$, then

$$\int (\phi + \psi)\, d\mu = \int \phi\, d\mu + \int \psi\, d\mu, \quad \text{and} \int c\phi\, d\mu = c \int \phi\, d\mu.$$

The definition of the integral can be extended from simple functions to all of $M^+(S, \mathcal{S})$ as follows.

DEFINITION   *For $f \in M^+(S, \mathcal{S})$, the **integral of f with respect to μ** is*

$$\int_S f(s)\mu(ds) = \sup \int_S \phi(s)\mu(ds),$$

*where the supremum is over all simple functions ϕ in $M^+(S, S)$ with $0 \leq \phi \leq f$. If $A \in \mathcal{S}$, then the **integral of f over A with respect to μ** is*

$$\int_A f(s)\mu(ds) = \int_S f(s)\chi_A(s)\mu(ds).$$

When there is no possibility for confusion, we denote the integrals above by the more concise $\int f\, d\mu$ and $\int_A f\, d\mu$. Note that these integrals may be infinite.

We know from Theorem 7.5 that any function $f \in M^+(S, \mathcal{S})$ can be expressed as the limit of an increasing sequence $\{\phi_n\}$ of simple functions in $M^+(S, \mathcal{S})$. Thus it might seem more natural to define the integral $\int f\, d\mu$ as the limit of the sequence $\{\int \phi_n\, d\mu\}$. But defining the integral in this way would leave open the possibility that the limit might depend on the particular sequence $\{\phi_n\}$ chosen. The next main result, the Monotone Convergence Theorem, shows that the limiting value is unique. To prepare the way, we need the following result, which shows that a simple function on a measure space can be used to define a new measure on the space.

LEMMA 7.7   *If $\phi \in M^+(S, \mathcal{S})$ is a simple function, and $\lambda: \mathcal{S} \to \mathbf{R}$ is defined by $\lambda(A) = \int_A \phi\, d\mu$, all $A \in \mathcal{S}$, then λ is a measure on $\mathcal{S}$.*

Proof. Let $\phi = \Sigma_{i=1}^{n} a_i \chi_{B_i}$ be the standard representation for ϕ. Then for each $A \in \mathscr{S}$, we have

$$\lambda(A) = \int_A \phi \, d\mu = \int \phi \chi_A \, d\mu = \int \left[\sum_{i=1}^{n} a_i \chi_{B_i} \right] \chi_A \, d\mu$$

$$= \int \left[\sum_{i=1}^{n} a_i \chi_{(A \cap B_i)} \right] d\mu = \sum_{i=1}^{n} a_i \left[\int \chi_{(A \cap B_i)} \, d\mu \right]$$

(1)
$$= \sum_{i=1}^{n} a_i \mu(A \cap B_i),$$

where the next-to-last step uses Exercise 7.17. Since $B_i \in \mathscr{S}$, each i, it follows from Exercise 7.4b that each mapping $\lambda_i(A) = \mu(A \cap B_i)$ is a measure. Hence $\lambda: \mathscr{S} \to \mathbf{R}_+$ defined by (1) is a linear combination of measures and therefore by Exercise 7.4a is itself a measure. ∎

Exercise 7.18   a. Show that if $f, g \in M^+(S, \mathscr{S})$ and $f \le g$, then $\int f \, d\mu \le \int g \, d\mu$.
   b. Show that if $f \in M^+(S, \mathscr{S})$, and $A, B \in \mathscr{S}$ with $A \subseteq B$, then $\int_A f \, d\mu \le \int_B f \, d\mu$.

We are now ready to prove a result we will draw upon many times.

THEOREM 7.8 (*Monotone Convergence Theorem*)   *If $\{f_n\}$ is a monotone increasing sequence of functions in $M^+(S, \mathscr{S})$ converging pointwise to f then*

$$\int f \, d\mu = \lim_{n \to \infty} \int f_n \, d\mu.$$

Proof. Since f is the limit of a sequence of measurable functions, it is measurable (Theorem 7.4), and since the sequence is monotone, it follows directly from Exercise 7.18a that $\int f_n \, d\mu \le \int f \, d\mu$, $n = 1, 2, \dots$. Hence

$$\lim_{n \to \infty} \int f_n \, d\mu \le \int f \, d\mu.$$

To establish the reverse inequality, we will show that

$$(2) \qquad \int f \, d\mu = \sup_{\phi} \int \phi \, d\mu \leq \lim_{n \to \infty} \int f_n \, d\mu,$$

where the sup is over nonnegative, measurable, simple functions satisfying $0 \leq \phi \leq f$.

Let $\phi \in M^+(S, \mathcal{S})$ be any simple function with $0 \leq \phi \leq f$; from Lemma 7.7 it follows that we can define a measure λ on $\mathcal{S}$ by $\lambda(A) = \int_A \phi \, d\mu$, all $A \in \mathcal{S}$. Then choose $0 < \alpha < 1$ and define the sets A_n by

$$A_n = \{s \in S: \alpha\phi(s) \leq f_n(s)\}, \quad n = 1, 2, \ldots.$$

By Exercise 7.18,

$$(3) \qquad \int_{A_n} \alpha\phi \, d\mu \leq \int_{A_n} f_n \, d\mu \leq \int f_n \, d\mu.$$

Since $\{f_n\}$ is an increasing sequence of functions, $\{A_n\}$ is a monotone increasing sequence of sets. Moreover, since $\phi \leq f$ and $\alpha < 1$, $\alpha\phi(s) < f(s)$, all $s \in S$. Since $f_n \to f$, it then follows that $\cup_{n=1}^{\infty} A_n = S$. Hence

$$(4) \qquad \lim_{n \to \infty} \int_{A_n} \phi \, d\mu = \lim_{n \to \infty} \lambda(A_n) = \lambda\left(\bigcup_{n=1}^{\infty} A_n\right) = \lambda(S) = \int \phi \, d\mu,$$

where the second equality uses Theorem 7.1. Then taking the limit in (3) as $n \to \infty$ and using (4), we obtain

$$\alpha \int \phi \, d\mu \leq \lim_{n \to \infty} \int f_n \, d\mu.$$

Since $0 < \alpha < 1$ and $0 \leq \phi \leq f$ were arbitrary, this implies that (2) holds. ∎

Exercise 7.19 Show by example that the proof fails if we take $\alpha = 1$.

The next two exercises, extensions of Exercise 7.17 and Lemma 7.7, respectively, establish the linearity of the integral for all functions in

$M^+(S, \mathcal{S})$ and establish that any function in $M^+(S, \mathcal{S})$ can be used to define a measure. Exercise 7.22 then provides a very useful sufficient condition for interchanging the order of summation and integration.

Exercise 7.20 a. Show that if $f, g \in M^+(S, \mathcal{S})$ and $c \geq 0$, then

$$\int (f + g)\, d\mu = \int f\, d\mu + \int g\, d\mu \quad \text{and} \quad \int cf\, d\mu = c \int f\, d\mu.$$

[*Hint.* Use Theorem 7.5, Exercise 7.17, and the Monotone Convergence Theorem.]

b. Let $f \in M^+(S, \mathcal{S})$ be an extended real-valued function, and let $A \in \mathcal{S}$, with $\mu(A) = 0$. Show that $\int_A f\, d\mu = 0$. [*Hint.* Use the sequence of approximating simple functions defined in the discussion following Theorem 7.5 and apply the Monotone Convergence Theorem.]

c. Let $f \in M^+(S, \mathcal{S})$ be an extended real-valued function, and suppose that $\int_S f\, d\mu < \infty$. Let $A = \{s \in S : f(s) = +\infty\}$. Show that $\mu(A) = 0$.

Exercise 7.21 Show that if $f \in M^+(S, \mathcal{S})$, then $\lambda \colon \mathcal{S} \to \mathbf{R}_+$ defined by $\lambda(A) = \int_A f\, d\mu$, all $A \in \mathcal{S}$, is a measure on $(S, \mathcal{S})$. [*Hint.* Let $\{A_i\}$ be a disjoint sequence of sets in $\mathcal{S}$, with union A, and let $f_n = \sum_{i=1}^{n} f \chi_{A_i}$. Then use Exercise 7.20 and the Monotone Convergence Theorem.]

Exercise 7.22 Let $\{g_i\}$ be a sequence of functions in $M^+(S, \mathcal{S})$. Show that

$$\int \left(\sum_{i=1}^{\infty} g_i \right) d\mu = \sum_{i=1}^{\infty} \int g_i\, d\mu.$$

[*Hint.* Define $f_n = \sum_{i=1}^{n} g_i$, $n = 1, 2, \ldots$, and $f = \sum_{i=1}^{\infty} g_i$; then use Exercise 7.20 and the Monotone Convergence Theorem.]

The next result, an extremely useful application of the Monotone Convergence Theorem, is drawn upon in the proof of the Lebesgue Dominated Convergence Theorem, another useful limit theorem for integrals.

LEMMA 7.9 (*Fatou's Lemma*)   If $\{f_n\}$ is a sequence of functions in $M^+(S, \mathscr{S})$, then

$$\int (\lim \inf f_n) \, d\mu \le \lim \inf \int f_n \, d\mu.$$

Proof.   Let $g_m = \inf\{f_m, f_{m+1}, \ldots\}$, so that $g_m \le f_n$, for $m \le n$. Then

$$\int g_m \, d\mu \le \int f_n \, d\mu, \quad \text{all } m \le n,$$

so that

$$\int g_m \, d\mu \le \lim \inf \int f_n \, d\mu, \quad \text{all } m.$$

The sequence $\{g_m\}$ is increasing and converges to $\lim \inf f_n$, so by the Monotone Convergence Theorem,

$$\int (\lim \inf f_n) \, d\mu = \lim \int g_m \, d\mu \le \lim \inf \int f_n \, d\mu. \quad \blacksquare$$

Exercise 7.23   Give an example of a sequence $\{f_n\}$ in $M^+(S, \mathscr{S})$ with

$$\int (\lim \inf f_n) \, d\mu \ne \lim \inf \int f_n \, d\mu.$$

Exercise 7.24   a. Show that for $f \in M^+(S, \mathscr{S}), f(s) = 0$, μ-a.e. if and only if $\int f \, d\mu = 0$.
   b. Show that the Monotone Convergence Theorem holds if $f_n \to f$ a.e.

Thus far we have dealt only with nonnegative functions and have allowed the integral of a function to be $+\infty$. In dealing with functions that take on both positive and negative values, it is convenient and customary to require the values of the functions and integrals to be finite. To define the integral of an arbitrary function, we begin by defining the positive and negative parts of a function, f^+ and f^- by

$$f^+(s) = \begin{cases} f(s) & \text{if } f(s) \geq 0 \\ 0 & \text{if } f(s) < 0 \end{cases}$$

and

$$f^-(s) = \begin{cases} -f(s) & \text{if } f(s) \leq 0 \\ 0 & \text{if } f(s) > 0. \end{cases}$$

Thus, if f is measurable, f^+ and f^- are both in $M^+(S, \mathscr{S})$, and $f = f^+ - f^-$. We then have the following definition of the integral of f.

DEFINITION *Let $(S, \mathscr{S}, \mu)$ be a measure space, and let f be a measurable, real-valued function on S. If f^+ and f^- both have finite integrals with respect to μ, then f is* **integrable** *and the* **integral of f with respect to μ** *is*

$$\int f \, d\mu = \int f^+ \, d\mu - \int f^- \, d\mu.$$

If $A \in \mathscr{S}$, the **integral of f over A with respect to μ** *is*

$$\int_A f \, d\mu = \int_A f^+ \, d\mu - \int_A f^- \, d\mu.$$

If either the positive or negative part of f has an infinite integral, we simply say that f is not integrable (or not integrable over A). In this way we avoid dealing with expressions like $+\infty$ and $-\infty$.

Recall that if $(S, \mathscr{S}, \mu)$ is a probability space and f is a measurable function, then f is called a random variable. If, in addition, f is integrable, then the integral of f with respect to μ is called the *expected value* of f and is denoted by $E(f) = \int f \, d\mu$.

Let $L(S, \mathscr{S}, \mu)$ denote the set of all $\mathscr{S}$-measurable, real-valued functions on S that are integrable with respect to μ. The next exercises demonstrate some methods for determining whether a function is integrable.

Exercise 7.25   Let $(S, \mathcal{S}, \mu)$ be a measure space. Show that if f is a bounded, measurable, real-valued function on S, and $\mu(S) < \infty$, then f is μ-integrable.

Thus a bounded random variable has a well-defined expected value.

Exercise 7.26   Let $(S, \mathcal{S}, \mu)$ be a measure space, and let f and g be real-valued functions on S.

a. Show that f is μ-integrable if and only if $|f|$ is μ-integrable and that, in this case, $|\int f \, d\mu| \leq \int |f| \, d\mu$.

b. Show that if f is $\mathcal{S}$-measurable, g is μ-integrable, and $|f| \leq |g|$, then f is μ-integrable and $\int |f| \, d\mu \leq \int |g| \, d\mu$.

c. Show that if f and g are μ-integrable and $\alpha \in \mathbf{R}$, then αf and $f + g$ are μ-integrable, and

$$\int \alpha f \, d\mu = \alpha \int f \, d\mu, \quad \text{and} \quad \int (f + g) \, d\mu = \int f \, d\mu + \int g \, d\mu.$$

The next result is an extremely widely applicable limit theorem for integrals.

THEOREM 7.10 (*Lebesgue Dominated Convergence Theorem*)   Let $(S, \mathcal{S}, \mu)$ be a measure space, and let $\{f_n\}$ be a sequence of integrable functions that converges almost everywhere to a measurable function f. If there exists an integrable function g such that $|f_n| \leq g$, all n, then f is integrable and

$$\int f \, d\mu = \lim \int f_n \, d\mu.$$

Proof.   Without loss of generality, assume that $\{f_n\}$ converges to f on all of S. Then as shown in Exercise 7.26b, f is integrable, and since $g + f_n \geq 0$,

$$\int g \, d\mu + \int f \, d\mu = \int (f + g) \, d\mu = \int \liminf (g + f_n) \, d\mu$$

$$\leq \liminf \int (g + f_n) \, d\mu = \liminf \left(\int g \, d\mu + \int f_n \, d\mu \right)$$

$$= \int g \, d\mu + \liminf \int f_n \, d\mu,$$

where the inequality follows from Fatou's Lemma. Hence

$$\int f \, d\mu \leq \liminf \int f_n \, d\mu.$$

Since $g - f_n \geq 0$, another application of Fatou's Lemma gives

$$\int g \, d\mu - \int f \, d\mu = \int (g - f) \, d\mu = \int \liminf (g - f_n) \, d\mu$$

$$\leq \liminf \int (g - f_n) \, d\mu = \liminf \left(\int g \, d\mu - \int f_n \, d\mu \right)$$

$$= \int g \, d\mu - \limsup \int f_n \, d\mu.$$

Hence

$$\limsup \int f_n \, d\mu \leq \int f \, d\mu.$$

Combining the two results gives the desired conclusion. ∎

Notice that if the functions $\{f_n\}$ are uniformly bounded and μ is a finite measure, then the Lebesgue Dominated Convergence Theorem applies trivially: simply take g to be the constant function equal to the uniform bound on the f_n's. We will make extensive use of this fact later, since we will often be dealing with bounded functions.

In Exercise 7.21 we saw that a measure λ on $(S, \mathscr{S})$ could be obtained by integrating a function $f \in M^+(S, \mathscr{S})$ with respect to a measure μ. The next two results pursue the converse. To state them we need the following definitions.

DEFINITIONS *Let λ and μ be finite measures on $(S, \mathscr{S})$. If for every $A \in \mathscr{S}$, $\mu(A) = 0$ implies $\lambda(A) = 0$, then λ is **absolutely continuous** with respect to μ, written $\lambda \ll \mu$. If there is a set $A \in \mathscr{S}$ such that $\lambda(B) = \lambda(A \cap B)$, all $B \in \mathscr{S}$, then λ is **concentrated on** A. If there are disjoint sets $A, B \in \mathscr{S}$ such that λ is concentrated on A and μ is concentrated on B, then λ and μ are **mutually singular**, written $\lambda \perp \mu$.*

It is clear that if λ is obtained by integrating $f \in M^+(S, \mathcal{S})$ with respect to a measure μ, then λ is absolutely continuous with respect to μ. The Radon-Nikodym Theorem proves the converse: that *every* measure λ that is absolutely continuous with respect to μ can be obtained as such an integral. It also establishes that the function to be integrated is, in a certain sense, unique. This theorem is extremely useful and very easy to state. However, the proof of existence is rather difficult, and we omit it. (See Bartle 1966, pp. 85–87, or Royden 1968, pp. 238–240.)

THEOREM 7.11 (*Radon-Nikodym Theorem*)   *Let λ and μ be σ-finite positive measures on $(S, \mathcal{S})$, with $\lambda \ll \mu$. Then there is an integrable function h such that*

$$\lambda(A) = \int_A h(s)\mu(ds), \quad \text{all } A \in \mathcal{S}.$$

The function is unique in the sense that if g also has this property, then $g = h$, μ-a.e.

    Proof of uniqueness.   Let $(S, \mathcal{S})$, λ, and μ be given. Suppose that there are two measurable functions g and h such that

(5) $$\int_A g \, d\mu = \lambda(A) = \int_A h \, d\mu, \quad \text{all } A \in \mathcal{S}.$$

Since both g and h are measurable, so is the function $g - h$. Hence the set

$$X = \{s \in S : g(s) - h(s) > 0\}$$

is in $\mathcal{S}$, and it follows from (5) that for $A = X$,

$$\int_X (g - h) \, d\mu = \int_X g \, d\mu - \int_X h \, d\mu = 0.$$

Hence by Exercise 7.24a, $\mu(X) = 0$. Reversing the roles of g and h and repeating the argument, we then find that $g = h$, μ-a.e. ∎

The function h satisfying (5) is called the *Radon-Nikodym derivative* of λ with respect to μ, written $d\lambda/d\mu$.

    Our next result draws on this theorem to show that any two measures can be uniquely represented as the sums of "common" and mutually singular parts.

L E M M A 7.12 *Let λ_1 and λ_2 be finite measures on $(S, \mathcal{S})$. Then there is a triple of measures γ, α_1, and α_2 such that $\lambda_i = \gamma + \alpha_i$, $i = 1, 2$, and $\alpha_1 \perp \alpha_2$.*

Proof. Let $\mu = \lambda_1 + \lambda_2$. Then μ is a finite measure on $(S, \mathcal{S})$, and λ_1 and λ_2 are both absolutely continuous with respect to μ. Hence by the Radon-Nikodym Theorem, there exist nonnegative, integrable functions h_1 and h_2 such that

$$\lambda_i(A) = \int_A h_i(s)\mu(ds), \quad \text{all } A \in \mathcal{S}, \quad i = 1, 2.$$

Define the function h by $h(s) = \min\{h_1(s), h_2(s)\}$, all $s \in S$, and note that h is nonnegative and integrable. Hence we can define the measures γ, α_1, and α_2 by

$$\gamma(A) = \int_A h(s)\mu(ds), \quad \text{all } A \in \mathcal{S}, \quad \text{and}$$

$$\alpha_i(A) = \int_A [h_i(s) - h(s)]\mu(ds), \quad \text{all } A \in \mathcal{S}, i = 1, 2.$$

Define $B = \{s \in S: h_1 > h\}$ and $C = \{s \in S: h_2 > h\}$. Clearly B and C are disjoint and lie in $\mathcal{S}$, with α_1 concentrated on B and α_2 on C, so that $\alpha_1 \perp \alpha_2$. ∎

7.5 Product Spaces

In this section we define product spaces, show how measures can be defined on such spaces, and develop a basic property of sets and functions in such spaces.

Let $(X, \mathcal{X})$ and $(Y, \mathcal{Y})$ be measurable spaces, and let Z be the Cartesian product of X and Y:

$$Z = X \times Y = \{z = (x, y): x \in X, y \in Y\}.$$

To define a σ-algebra of subsets of Z that is a natural product of $\mathcal{X}$ and $\mathcal{Y}$, we first define an algebra of subsets of Z in terms of $\mathcal{X}$ and $\mathcal{Y}$.

D E F I N I T I O N *A set $C = A \times B \subseteq Z$ is a **measurable rectangle** if $A \in \mathcal{X}$ and $B \in \mathcal{Y}$.*

Let $\mathscr{C}$ be the set of all measurable rectangles, and let $\mathscr{E}$ be the set of all finite unions of measurable rectangles.

Exercise 7.27 Show that $\mathscr{E}$ is an algebra and that every set in $\mathscr{E}$ can be written as the finite union of *disjoint* measurable rectangles.

Let $\mathscr{Z} = \mathscr{X} \times \mathscr{Y}$ be the σ-algebra generated by $\mathscr{E}$. The measurable space $(Z, \mathscr{Z})$ is called the **product space**. The next exercise establishes an important fact about the Borel σ-algebras.

Exercise 7.28 Show that $\mathscr{B}^{k+l} = \mathscr{B}^k \times \mathscr{B}^l$, all $k, l \geq 1$, where $\mathscr{B}^n$ denotes the Borel sets in $\mathbf{R}^n$.

The next result provides an extremely useful tool for defining measures on product spaces, one that is used extensively in the next section.

THEOREM 7.13 *Let $(X, \mathscr{X})$, $(Y, \mathscr{Y})$, $\mathscr{C}$, and $\mathscr{E}$ be as specified above. Let μ: $\mathscr{C} \to \mathbf{R}_+$ have the following properties:*

a. $\mu(\emptyset) = 0$; and

b. if $\{C_i\} = \{(A_i \times B_i)\}_{i=1}^{\infty}$ is a sequence of disjoint sets in $\mathscr{C}$ and $\cup_{i=1}^{\infty} C_i$ is in $\mathscr{C}$, then $\mu(\cup_{i=1}^{\infty} C_i) = \Sigma_{i=1}^{\infty} \mu(C_i)$.

Then there is a measure on $\mathscr{E}$ that coincides with μ on $\mathscr{C}$.

Proof. Let μ: $\mathscr{C} \to \mathbf{R}_+$ satisfying (a) and (b) be given. It was shown in Exercise 7.27 that any set in $\mathscr{E}$ can be written as the finite union of disjoint sets in $\mathscr{C}$. Suppose that $E \in \mathscr{E}$, and that $\cup_{i=1}^{I} C_i = E = \cup_{j=1}^{J} D_j$ are two such ways of writing E. We will show that $\Sigma_i \mu(C_i) = \Sigma_j \mu(D_j)$, and define $\mu(E)$ to be their common value.

Since each C_i and each D_j is a rectangle, so is each set $E_{ij} = C_i \cap D_j$. Moreover, the E_{ij}'s are all disjoint, and

$$\bigcup_{j=1}^{J} E_{ij} = C_i, \quad \text{all } i, \quad \text{and} \quad \bigcup_{i=1}^{I} E_{ij} = D_j, \quad \text{all } j.$$

Hence by property (b) above,

$$\sum_{j=1}^{J} \mu(E_{ij}) = \mu\left(\bigcup_{j=1}^{J} E_{ij}\right) = \mu(C_i), \quad \text{all } i; \quad \text{and}$$

$$\sum_{i=1}^{I} \mu(E_{ij}) = \mu\left(\bigcup_{i=1}^{I} E_{ij}\right) = \mu(D_j), \quad \text{all } j.$$

Hence

$$\sum_{i=1}^{I} \mu(C_i) = \sum_{i=1}^{I} \sum_{j=1}^{J} \mu(E_{ij}) = \sum_{j=1}^{J} \mu(D_j).$$

This proves that μ is well defined on $\mathscr{E}$. Properties (a) and (b) ensure that μ is a measure. ∎

It follows immediately from Theorem 7.13, together with the Caratheodory and Hahn Extension Theorems (Theorems 7.2 and 7.3), that to define a measure on a product space, it is sufficient to find a function μ defined on the measurable rectangles that satisfies (a) and (b) of Theorem 7.13.

The result in Theorem 7.13 can be extended in the obvious way to any space that is the product of a finite number of measurable spaces. Since this is the version that we will need later, we state the required result here.

Let $(X_k, \mathscr{X}_k)$, $k = 1, \ldots, n$, be measurable spaces, and let $Z = X_1 \times \ldots \times X_n$ be the Cartesian product of the X_k's. Call a set $C \subseteq Z$ a measurable rectangle if

$$C = A_1 \times \ldots \times A_n, \quad \text{where } A_k \in \mathscr{X}_k, \, k = 1, \ldots, n.$$

As above, let $\mathscr{C}$ be the family of all measurable rectangles, let $\mathscr{E}$ be the algebra consisting of all finite unions of measurable rectangles, and let $\mathscr{X}$ be the σ-algebra generated by $\mathscr{C}$ or by $\mathscr{E}$. We leave it as an exercise to show that the obvious analogue of Theorem 7.13 holds.

Exercise 7.29 Let $\mu: \mathscr{C} \to \mathbf{R}_+$ have the following properties:
a. $\mu(\emptyset) = 0$; and
b. if $\{C_i\} = \{(A_{1i} \times \ldots \times A_{ni})\}_{i=1}^{\infty}$ is a sequence of disjoint sets in $\mathscr{C}$ and $\cup_{i=1}^{\infty} C_i$ is in $\mathscr{C}$, then $\mu(\cup_{i=1}^{\infty} C_i) = \sum_{i=1}^{\infty} \mu(C_i)$.
Show that μ can be extended to a measure on $\mathscr{X}$.

Our final result is a very basic and very appealing property of sets and functions in product spaces. Before stating it, we need the following definitions. Let $(X, \mathscr{X})$ and $(Y, \mathscr{Y})$ be measurable spaces, and let $(Z, \mathscr{X})$ be the product space.

DEFINITION   *Let $E \subseteq Z$ and $x \in X$. Then the **x-section of E** is the set (in Y) $E_x = \{y \in Y : (x, y) \in E\}$. The y-section of E, (a set in X) denoted E_y is defined similarly.*

DEFINITION   *Let $f: Z \to \mathbf{R}$ and let $x \in X$. Then the **x-section of f** is the function $f_x: Y \to \mathbf{R}$ defined by $f_x(y) = f(x, y)$. The y-section of f, $f_y: X \to \mathbf{R}$ is defined similarly.*

Thus the x-section of a set E in $X \times Y$ is simply the cross section of E at the chosen x value, and a y-section of E is a cross section at the chosen y value. An x-section of a real-valued function f on $X \times Y$ is found by fixing x at the chosen value and viewing f as a function of y only. Similarly, a y-section of f is found by fixing y and viewing f as a function of x only. The next theorem shows that every section of a measurable set is measurable, as is every section of a measurable function.

THEOREM 7.14   *Let $(X, \mathscr{X})$ and $(Y, \mathscr{Y})$ be measurable spaces, and let $(Z, \mathscr{Z})$ be the product space. If the set E in Z is $\mathscr{Z}$-measurable, then every section of E is measurable; and if the function $f: Z \to \mathbf{R}$ is $\mathscr{Z}$-measurable, then every section of f is measurable.*

Proof.   Let $\mathscr{E}$ be the class of sets in $\mathscr{Z}$ with measurable x-sections. We will show that $\mathscr{E}$ contains the measurable rectangles and is a σ-algebra.

Let E be a measurable rectangle: $E = A \times B$, where $A \in \mathscr{X}$ and $B \in \mathscr{Y}$. Let $x \in X$; then

$$E_x = \begin{cases} B & \text{if } x \in A \\ \emptyset & \text{if } x \notin A. \end{cases}$$

Since B, $\emptyset \in \mathscr{Y}$, each set E_x is measurable. Hence $\mathscr{E}$ contains the measurable rectangles.

Suppose that $E \in \mathscr{E}$. Then $(E^c)_x = (E_x)^c$, and the latter is in $\mathscr{Y}$. Hence $\mathscr{E}$ is closed under complementation. Finally, let $\{E_n\}$ be a countable sequence in $\mathscr{E}$. Then $(\bigcup_{n=1}^{\infty} E_n)_x = \bigcup_{n=1}^{\infty} E_{nx}$. Since each set E_{nx} is in $\mathscr{Y}$ and $\mathscr{Y}$ is a σ-algebra, their union is also in $\mathscr{Y}$. Hence $\mathscr{E}$ is closed under countable union.

Let $f: Z \to \mathbf{R}$ be a measurable function, and let $x \in X$ and $\alpha \in \mathbf{R}$. Then the set $\{y \in Y : f_x(y) > \alpha\}$ is simply the x-section of the set $\{(x, y) \in X \times Y :$

$f(x, y) > \alpha\}$. Hence the desired conclusion follows immediately from the result above. ∎

It follows immediately from Theorem 7.14, together with Exercise 7.28, that if the Borel σ-algebras are used in Euclidean space, then sections of measurable sets and measurable functions are measurable. This is a fact that we will use extensively later. Notice that this is *not* true if the Lebesgue sets are used instead of the Borel sets.

Exercise 7.30 Show that $\mathcal{L}^2$ is *not* equal to $\mathcal{L}^1 \times \mathcal{L}^1$, where $\mathcal{L}^l$ denotes the Lebesgue measurable sets in $\mathbf{R}^l$. [*Hint.* Construct a set in $\mathbf{R}^2$ that is $\mathcal{L}^2$-measurable but has a section that is not $\mathcal{L}^1$-measurable.]

The next exercise establishes that compositions of functions in product spaces are measurable.

Exercise 7.31 Let $(S, \mathcal{S})$, $(W, \mathcal{W})$, $(X, \mathcal{X})$, $(Y, \mathcal{Y})$, and $(Z, \mathcal{Z})$ be measurable spaces. Let $f: W \to Y$ and $g: X \to Z$ and $h: Y \times Z \to S$ be measurable functions. Show that $\phi: W \times X \to S$ defined by $\phi(w, x) = h[f(w), g(x)]$ is measurable.

7.6 The Monotone Class Lemma

Many situations arise in which we want to establish that some property P holds for all sets in a certain σ-algebra $\mathcal{S}$. If $\mathcal{S}$ is the σ-algebra generated by a family $\mathcal{A}$ of sets, one way to do this is to show that
  a. P holds for every set in $\mathcal{A}$, and
  b. the family of sets for which P holds is a σ-algebra.
This is the method that was used above in the proof of Theorem 7.14. This line of reasoning is often useful, but in some cases (b) is difficult to establish directly. In this section we show that the same conclusion can be established by strengthening (a) and weakening (b).

To begin, we need the following definition.

DEFINITION *A **monotone class** is a nonempty collection $\mathcal{M}$ of sets such that $\mathcal{M}$ contains*
  a. *the union of every nested increasing sequence $A_1 \subseteq A_2 \subseteq \ldots$ of sets in $\mathcal{M}$;*
  b. *the intersection of every nested decreasing sequence $A_1 \supseteq A_2 \supseteq \ldots$ of sets in $\mathcal{M}$.*

We then have the following facts.

1. Every σ-algebra is a monotone class.
2. If $\mathcal{A}$ is a nonempty collection of subsets of S, then there is a smallest monotone class containing $\mathcal{A}$. This is called the monotone class *generated by* $\mathcal{A}$.
3. If $\mathcal{A}$ is a nonempty collection of subsets of S, then the σ-algebra generated by $\mathcal{A}$ contains the monotone class generated by $\mathcal{A}$.
4. If a monotone class is an algebra, then it is a σ-algebra.

Fact (1) is obvious. To prove (2), use an argument like the one in Exercise 7.1 for the smallest σ-algebra containing $\mathcal{A}$. To prove (3), note that every σ-algebra containing $\mathcal{A}$ is a monotone class containing $\mathcal{A}$. A trivial example where the monotone class generated by $\mathcal{A}$ is strictly smaller than the σ-algebra generated by $\mathcal{A}$ is

$$S = \{0, 1\}, \quad \mathcal{A} = \{\{0\}\}, \quad \mathcal{M} = \{\{0\}\}, \quad \mathcal{S} = \{\emptyset, \{0\}, \{1\}, \{0, 1\}\}.$$

To prove (4), note that if $\mathcal{M}$ is an algebra, then it is closed under complementation and finite union. Hence, given any sequence of sets $\{A_i\}_{i=1}^{\infty}$ in $\mathcal{A}$, we can construct the increasing sequence $\{B_i\}_{i=1}^{\infty}$ defined by

$$B_1 = A_1, \quad B_i = B_{i-1} \cup A_i, \quad i = 2, 3, \ldots .$$

Then $\bigcup_{i=1}^{\infty} A_i = \bigcup_{i=1}^{\infty} B_i$, and the latter is in $\mathcal{M}$. Hence $\mathcal{M}$ is closed under countable union.

The following lemma establishes an extremely useful fact about monotone classes generated by algebras.

LEMMA 7.15 *(Monotone Class Lemma)*   *Let S be a set and let $\mathcal{A}$ be an algebra of subsets of S. Then the monotone class $\mathcal{M}$ generated by $\mathcal{A}$ is the same as the σ-algebra $\mathcal{S}$ generated by $\mathcal{A}$.*

Proof. From fact (3) above, we have $\mathcal{M} \subseteq \mathcal{S}$. Hence by (4) it suffices to show that $\mathcal{M}$ is an algebra.

Since $\mathcal{A}$ is an algebra and $\mathcal{A} \subseteq \mathcal{M}$, it follows that $\emptyset, S \in \mathcal{M}$. Hence it suffices to show that $\mathcal{M}$ is closed under complementation and finite intersection. For each $A \in \mathcal{M}$, define

$$\mathcal{M}(A) = \{B \in \mathcal{M} : A \cap B, A \cap B^c \text{ and } A^c \cap B \in \mathcal{M}\}.$$

Now suppose that $\mathcal{M}(A) = \mathcal{M}$, for all $A \in \mathcal{M}$. Then $A, B \in \mathcal{M}$ implies $(A \cap B) \in \mathcal{M}$; and since $S \in \mathcal{M}$, it follows that $A \in \mathcal{M}$ implies $A^c \in \mathcal{M}$. That is, $\mathcal{M}$ is closed under complementation and finite intersection. Hence it suffices to show that $\mathcal{M}(A) = \mathcal{M}$, all $A \in \mathcal{M}$.

First we will show that each $\mathcal{M}(A)$ is a monotone class. To see this, fix A and suppose that $\{B_i\}$ is an increasing sequence in $\mathcal{M}(A)$. Then the sequences $\{A \cap B_i\}$, $\{A \cap B_i^c\}$, and $\{A^c \cap B_i\}$ are all in $\mathcal{M}$. But each of these sequences is monotone. Therefore, since $\mathcal{M}$ is a monotone class,

$$\bigcup_{i=1}^{\infty} (A \cap B_i) = A \cap \left(\bigcup_{i=1}^{\infty} B_i \right),$$

$$\bigcap_{i=1}^{\infty} (A \cap B_i^c) = A \cap \left(\bigcup_{i=1}^{\infty} B_i \right)^c, \quad \text{and}$$

$$\bigcup_{i=1}^{\infty} (A^c \cap B_i) = A^c \cap \left(\bigcup_{i=1}^{\infty} B_i \right)$$

are all in $\mathcal{M}$. Hence $(\bigcup_{i=1}^{\infty} B_i)$ is in $\mathcal{M}(A)$. A similar argument holds if $\{B_i\}$ is a decreasing sequence. Hence $\mathcal{M}(A)$ is a monotone class.

Next note that since $\mathcal{A}$ is an algebra and $\mathcal{A} \subseteq \mathcal{M}$, it follows that $\mathcal{A} \subseteq \mathcal{M}(A)$, all $A \in \mathcal{A}$. Then, since each $\mathcal{M}(A)$ is a monotone class and $\mathcal{M}$ is the *smallest* monotone class containing $\mathcal{A}$, it follows that $\mathcal{M}(A) = \mathcal{M}$, all $A \in \mathcal{A}$. Finally, since $B \in \mathcal{M}(A)$ implies $A \in \mathcal{M}(B)$, all $A, B \in \mathcal{M}$, it follows that $\mathcal{A} \subseteq \mathcal{M}(B)$, all $B \in \mathcal{M}$. Hence $\mathcal{M}(B) = \mathcal{M}$, all $B \in \mathcal{M}$, as was to be shown. ■

A very useful result follows immediately from the Monotone Class Lemma. Let $\mathcal{A}$ be an algebra of sets, let $\mathcal{S}$ be the σ-algebra generated by $\mathcal{A}$, and P be some property of sets. Then to establish that P holds for all sets in $\mathcal{S}$, it suffices to show that

a. P holds for all sets in the algebra $\mathcal{A}$; and

b. the family of sets for which P holds is a monotone class.

It is often easier to prove that the family of sets for which a property holds is a monotone class than it is to prove that the family is a σ-algebra.

We will often want to use this type of argument to show that a property P holds for all sets in a product σ-algebra $\mathcal{X} \times \mathcal{Y}$. Therefore, by

Exercise 7.27 and the Monotone Class Lemma, it will suffice to show that

    a. P holds for all finite unions of disjoint measurable rectangles, and

    b. the family of sets $\mathscr{C}$ for which P holds is a monotone class.

7.7 Conditional Expectation

Let $(\Omega, \mathscr{F}, \mu)$ be a probability space, and let A be any measurable set with $\mu(A) > 0$. Then for any measurable set B, it is standard usage to call $\mu(B \cap A)/\mu(A)$ the **conditional probability** of the event B given A, and to use $\Pr(B|A)$ or $\mu_A(B)$ to denote this value. Note that it follows immediately from Exercise 7.4 that $\mu_A: \mathscr{F} \to [0, 1]$ is itself a probability measure on $(\Omega, \mathscr{F})$. Then, for any measurable, real-valued function f, it is standard to call $\int f \, d\mu_A$ the **conditional expectation** of f given A and to use $E(f|A)$ to denote this value.

These definitions are fine as far as they go, but they do not cover all situations of interest. For example, let $(\Omega, \mathscr{F})$ be the unit square $[0, 1]^2$, with the Borel sets, and let μ be the probability measure corresponding to the uniform density on the square. That is, $\mu(B) = \lambda^2(B)$, all $B \in \mathscr{F}$, where λ^2 denotes Borel measure on $\mathbf{R}^2$. Now choose any $a \in [0, 1]$, and let $A = \{(x, y) \in \Omega: x = a\}$. Thus, the set A is simply a vertical "slice" from the square. Consider the problem of defining conditional probabilities and conditional expectations given A. Since $\mu(A) = 0$, the formulas above are of no use; in fact, they suggest that conditional probabilities and conditional expectations are undefined.

Common sense says, however, that they ought to be defined as follows. For any $B \in \mathscr{F}$, let $\mu_A(B) = \lambda^1(A \cap B)$, where λ^1 denotes Borel measure on $\mathbf{R}^1$. That is, μ_A should be the probability measure corresponding to the uniform density on the set A. Conditional expectations given A can then be defined exactly as before.

In both of these examples we have shown how to calculate a number that can be interpreted as the conditional expectation of a fixed function f given the occurrence of a fixed event $A \in \mathscr{F}$. As we have seen, a number can be calculated in each case, but the procedure is different for the two. Moreover, there are other cases of interest that cannot be dealt with by either of these procedures.

An alternative strategy is needed, one that is less direct but has the virtue of applying to all situations. This method proceeds by defining the conditional expectation of a given function $f: \Omega \to \mathbf{R}$ as itself a function, call it g, which also maps Ω to $\mathbf{R}$. This function is constructed so that for sets $A \in \mathscr{F}$ of interest, $g(\omega)$ is constant on A, and the value $g(\omega)$, $\omega \in A$, is interpreted as $E(f|A)$. Clearly, the construction of the function g requires choosing a suitable family $\{A_\eta\}$ of sets in $\mathscr{F}$.

The rest of this section is organized as follows. First we look more carefully at situations like the first example above and show how the function g is defined. We then derive an important property of the pair (f, g) and show that this property can be used to define the function g in situations where the direct strategy fails. Finally, we verify that the conditional expectation of f, given A, can be found by evaluating g at any point $\omega \in A$; and that the conditional probability of any event B, given A, can be found by taking f to be the indicator function χ_B.

Let $(\Omega, \mathscr{F}, \mu)$ be a fixed probability space. Call a family of subsets $\{A_\eta\}_{\eta \in H}$ of Ω a *measurable partition* (of Ω) if the following three conditions hold:

$$A_\eta \in \mathscr{F}, \text{ all } \eta \in H; \quad \bigcup_{\eta \in H} A_\eta = \Omega; \quad A_\eta \cap A_{\eta'} = \emptyset, \text{ all } \eta \neq \eta'.$$

Thus each partition element must be a measurable set; their union must be the entire space Ω; and they must be pairwise disjoint. We call a measurable partition *countable* if the index set H is countable.

Given $(\Omega, \mathscr{F}, \mu)$, let $\{A_i\}_{i=1}^\infty$ be any countable, measurable partition of Ω, with $\mu(A_i) > 0$, all i. Then as noted above, for each set A_i we can define the conditional probability of any event by

$$\Pr(B|A_i) = \mu_{A_i}(B) = \mu(B \cap A_i)/\mu(A_i), \quad \text{all } B \in \mathscr{F},$$

and the conditional expectation of any integrable function f by

(1) $\qquad E(f|A_i) = \int f \, d\mu_{A_i}, \quad \text{all } f \in L(\Omega, \mathscr{F}, \mu).$

Notice that it follows directly from these two definitions that

(2) $\qquad E(f|A_i)\mu(A_i) = \int_{A_i} f \, d\mu, \quad \text{all } f \in L(\Omega, \mathscr{F}, \mu).$

Next, let $\mathcal{A}$ be the σ-algebra generated by the family of sets $\{A_i\}$, and note that $\mathcal{A} \subseteq \mathcal{F}$. Define the function $E(f|\mathcal{A}): \Omega \to \mathbf{R}$ by

(3) $E(f|\mathcal{A})(\omega) = E(f|A_i), \quad \text{all } \omega \in A_i, \text{ all } A_i.$

Thus $E(f|\mathcal{A})$ is an $\mathcal{A}$-measurable function that takes the constant value $E(f|A_i)$ on each set A_i. Note carefully the distinction between $E(f|A_i)$ and $E(f|\mathcal{A})$. For any fixed function f, the former is simply a real number, for each A_i, whereas the latter is a *function* mapping Ω to $\mathbf{R}$. In what follows it is useful to rewrite (3) as

(4) $E(f|\mathcal{A})(\omega) = \sum_{j=1}^{\infty} E(f|A_j)\chi_{A_j}(\omega), \quad \text{all } \omega \in \Omega.$

What properties does the function $E(f|\mathcal{A})$ have? Let C be any set in $\mathcal{A}$. Since $\{A_i\}$ is a countable partition of Ω, there is a countable set $J \subseteq \{1, 2, \ldots\}$ such that $C = \bigcup_{j \in J} A_j$, and

(5) $\mu(A_j \cap C) = \begin{cases} \mu(A_j) & \text{if } j \in J \\ 0 & \text{if } j \notin J. \end{cases}$

Integrating $E(f|\mathcal{A})$ over the set C and using this fact, we find that

$$\int_C E(f|\mathcal{A})(\omega)\,d\mu = \int_C \left[\sum_{j=1}^{\infty} E(f|A_j)\chi_{A_j}(\omega) \right] d\mu$$

$$= \sum_{j=1}^{\infty} \left[E(f|A_j) \int_C \chi_{A_j}(\omega)\,d\mu \right]$$

$$= \sum_{j=1}^{\infty} [E(f|A_j)\mu(A_j \cap C)]$$

$$= \sum_{j \in J} E(f|A_j)\mu(A_j)$$

$$= \sum_{j \in J} \int_{A_j} f(\omega)\,d\mu$$

$$= \int_C f(\omega)\,d\mu,$$

where the first line uses (4); the second uses the Lebesgue Dominated Convergence Theorem; the third uses a basic fact about integrals of indicator functions; the fourth uses (5); the fifth uses (2); and the last uses the fact that $C = \cup_{j \in J} A_j$. This establishes that over any set $C \in \mathcal{A}$, the integrals of the $\mathcal{F}$-measurable function f and of the $\mathcal{A}$-measurable function $E(f|\mathcal{A})$ are equal.

To extend the concept of conditional expectation to σ-algebras not generated by a countable partition, we will use this last property to develop a method for defining a function $E(f|\mathcal{A})$, given any integrable function f and any σ-algebra $\mathcal{A} \subset \mathcal{F}$.

DEFINITION *Let $(\Omega, \mathcal{F}, \mu)$ be a probability space; let $\mathcal{A} \subset \mathcal{F}$ be a σ-algebra; and let $f: \Omega \to \mathbf{R}$ be an integrable function. Then the **conditional expectation of f relative to** $\mathcal{A}$ is an $\mathcal{A}$-measurable function $E(f|\mathcal{A}): \Omega \to \mathbf{R}$ such that*

(6)
$$\int_C E(f|\mathcal{A})(\omega)\mu\,(d\omega) = \int_C f(\omega)\mu\,(d\omega), \quad \text{all } C \in \mathcal{A}.$$

The following theorem shows that an $\mathcal{A}$-measurable function $E(f|\mathcal{A})$ satisfying (6) always exists and that it is unique in an appropriate sense.

THEOREM 7.16 *Let $(\Omega, \mathcal{F}, \mu)$ be a probability space; let $\mathcal{A} \subset \mathcal{F}$ be a σ-algebra; and let $f: \Omega \to \mathbf{R}$ be an integrable function. Then there exists an $\mathcal{A}$-measurable function $E(f|\mathcal{A})$ satisfying (6). This function is unique in the sense that if g also satisfies (6), then $E(f|\mathcal{A}) = g$, a.e.*

Proof. Consider first the case where $f \geq 0$. Define the set function $\nu: \mathcal{A} \to \mathbf{R}$ by

$$\nu(C) = \int_C f(\omega)\,d\mu, \quad \text{all } C \in \mathcal{A}.$$

Since f is integrable, $\int |f|\,d\mu < \infty$, so that ν is finite-valued. Clearly ν is also countably additive, and hence it is a measure on $\mathcal{A}$. Moreover, $\mu(C) = 0$ implies that $\nu(C) = 0$, so ν is absolutely continuous with respect to μ. Hence by the Radon-Nikodym Theorem (Theorem 7.11), there exists an $\mathcal{A}$-measurable function $E(f|\mathcal{A})$, unique in the sense claimed, such that

$$\nu(C) = \int_C E(f|\mathcal{A})(\omega)\,d\mu, \quad \text{all } C \in \mathcal{A}.$$

If f takes on both positive and negative values, apply the argument above separately to f^+ and f^-, and let $E(f|\mathcal{A}) = E(f^+|\mathcal{A}) - E(f^-|\mathcal{A})$.   ∎

Theorem 7.16 can be used as follows. Suppose that we are interested in calculating conditional expectations and probabilities, given events A_η, $\eta \in H$, where the family of sets $\{A_\eta\}_{\eta \in H}$ is a measurable partition of Ω. Let $\mathcal{A}$ be the σ-algebra generated by the family $\{A_\eta\}$. Given any integrable function f, define $E(f|\mathcal{A})$ by Theorem 7.16. Notice that the requirement that $E(f|\mathcal{A})$ be $\mathcal{A}$-measurable implies that $E(f|\mathcal{A})$ is constant on each of the sets A_η in the partition. (Why?) Hence for any partition element A_η, and any $\hat{\omega} \in A_\eta$,

$$(7) \qquad \int_{A_\eta} f(\omega) \, d\mu = \int_{A_\eta} E(f|\mathcal{A})(\omega) \, d\mu = E(f|\mathcal{A})(\hat{\omega})\mu(A_\eta).$$

Notice that if $\mu(A_\eta) > 0$, then

$$E(f|\mathcal{A})(\hat{\omega}) = \frac{1}{\mu(A_\eta)} \int_{A_\eta} f \, d\mu, \quad \text{all } \hat{\omega} \in A_\eta.$$

Hence for any set A_η of positive measure,

$$E(f|A_\eta) = E(f|\mathcal{A})(\hat{\omega}), \quad \text{all } \hat{\omega} \in A_\eta,$$

where $E(f|\mathcal{A})$ is defined by (6) and $E(f|A_\eta)$ is defined by (1) if we set $A_i = A_\eta$. That is, our formal definition of conditional expectation coincides with our intuitive notion whenever the latter is well defined.

Similarly, to obtain the conditional probability $\Pr(B|A_\eta)$ of any event $B \in \mathcal{F}$, simply take f to be the indicator function of B, χ_B. Then (7) implies that

$$E(\chi_B|\mathcal{A})(\hat{\omega})\mu(A_\eta) = \int_{A_\eta} \chi_B \, d\mu = \mu(B \cap A_\eta),$$

$$\text{all } \hat{\omega} \in A_\eta, \text{ all } \eta \in H.$$

If $\mu(A_\eta) > 0$, then

$$E(\chi_B|\mathcal{A})(\hat{\omega}) = \mu(B \cap A_\eta)/\mu(A_\eta), \quad \text{all } \hat{\omega} \in A_\eta.$$

That is, for any set B of positive measure, $E(\chi_B|\mathcal{A})$ as defined by Theorem 7.16 coincides with our earlier definition of conditional probability. Therefore we define $\Pr(B|A_\eta)$ for all sets A_η by

(8) $\Pr(B|A_\eta) = E(\chi_B|\mathcal{A})(\hat{\omega})$,   all $\hat{\omega} \in A_\eta$, all $\eta \in H$.

Exercise 7.32   Let $(\Omega, \mathcal{F}, \mu)$ be given, and let $\{A_i\}_{i=1}^\infty$ be a countable, measurable partition of Ω. Define the index set $J \subseteq \{1, 2, \ldots\}$ so that

$$\mu(A_i) > 0, \text{ all } i \in J; \quad \mu(A_i) = 0, \text{ all } i \in J^c.$$

Let $\mathcal{A}$ be the σ-algebra generated by $\{A_i\}$.

a. Let f be an integrable function on Ω. Describe explicitly the equivalence class of functions $E(f|\mathcal{A})$. On what set(s) A_i, if any, can functions in this equivalence class differ?

b. Let $B \in \mathcal{F}$ be any event. Describe explicitly the equivalence class of functions $E(\chi_B|\mathcal{A})$. On what set(s) A_i, if any, does $\Pr(B|A_i)$ as defined in (8) differ for different members of this equivalence class?

Exercise 7.33   Let $(\Omega, \mathcal{F})$ be the unit square $[0, 1]^2$, with its Borel subsets, and let μ be a probability measure on $(\Omega, \mathcal{F})$ defined by a continuous density. That is, there exists a continuous function $p: \Omega \to \mathbf{R}$ such that

$$\mu(B) = \int_B p(\omega) \, d\lambda, \quad \text{all } B \in \mathcal{F},$$

where λ denotes Borel measure on $\mathbf{R}^2$. Let $\{A_\eta\}_{\eta \in H}$ be the following family of subsets of Ω:

$$A_\eta = \{(x, y) \in \Omega: x \le \eta\}, \quad \eta \in [0, 1] = H.$$

Let $\mathcal{A}$ be the σ-algebra generated by the family $\{A_\eta\}$.

a. Let f be an integrable function on Ω. Describe explicitly the equivalence class of functions $E(f|\mathcal{A})$.

b. Let $B \in \mathcal{F}$ be any event. Describe explicitly the equivalence class of functions $E(\chi_B|\mathcal{A})$.

We have defined conditional expectation relative to a σ-algebra $\mathcal{A} \subset \mathcal{F}$. It is easy enough to relate this definition to the more familiar idea of the expectation of one random variable conditional on another. Let f and g be two random variables on $(\Omega, \mathcal{F})$. Let $\mathcal{G}$ be the σ-algebra generated by the sets of the form $\{\omega \in \Omega: g(\omega) \le \alpha\}$, $\alpha \in \mathbf{R}$. (We call $\mathcal{G}$ the σ-algebra *generated by* the random variable g.) Then $\mathcal{G} \subseteq \mathcal{F}$ and the function $E(f|\mathcal{G})$ is well defined by (6). We will write $E(f|\mathcal{G})$ and $E(f|g)$ interchangeably.

Finally, it is convenient to develop here a property of conditional expectations that we will use later. Let $(\Omega, \mathcal{F}, \mu)$ be a given; let $\mathcal{A}_1 \subseteq \mathcal{A}_2 \subseteq \mathcal{F}$ be two σ-algebras, one contained in the other; and let $f: \Omega \to \mathbf{R}$ be any integrable function. Then $E(f|\mathcal{A}_1)$ and $E(f|\mathcal{A}_2)$ are $\mathcal{A}_1$-measurable and $\mathcal{A}_2$-measurable functions respectively on Ω. Moreover, (6) implies that

$$(9) \qquad \int_C E(f|\mathcal{A}_i)(\omega)\, d\mu = \int_C f(\omega)\, d\mu, \quad \text{all } C \in \mathcal{A}_i,\, i = 1, 2.$$

Now consider the $\mathcal{A}_2$-measurable function $E(f|\mathcal{A}_2): \Omega \to \mathbf{R}$. The conditional expectation of this function, given $\mathcal{A}_1$, is the $\mathcal{A}_1$-measurable function $E[E(f|\mathcal{A}_2)|\mathcal{A}_1]$. We then have

$$\int_C E[E(f|\mathcal{A}_2)|\mathcal{A}_1]\, d\mu = \int_C E(f|\mathcal{A}_2)(\omega)\, d\mu$$

$$= \int_C f(\omega)\, d\mu$$

$$= \int_C E(f|\mathcal{A}_1)(\omega)\, d\mu, \quad \text{all } C \in \mathcal{A}_1,$$

where the first line uses (6); the second uses (9) and the fact that $\mathcal{A}_1 \subseteq \mathcal{A}_2$; and the last uses (9) again. This fact is referred to as the *law of the iterated expectation*. Stated a little differently, it says that if $\mathcal{A}_1 \subseteq \mathcal{A}_2$, then

$$\int_C E[f - E(f|\mathcal{A}_2)|\mathcal{A}_1]\, d\mu = 0, \quad \text{all } C \in \mathcal{A}_1.$$

7.8 Bibliographic Notes

There are many good texts on measure theory. Bartle (1966) and Royden (1968) are excellent introductory texts; Halmos (1974) is perhaps the most complete treatment of the subject. The material here follows Bartle most closely.

Chung (1974) is an excellent introduction to probability theory that uses a measure-theoretic approach throughout. Our treatment of conditional expectation in Section 7.7 is based on his Section 9.1. Neveu (1965), Breiman (1968), and Shiryayev (1984) are also good introductory treatments. Loève (1977), which is very complete, is extremely useful as a reference.

8 *Markov Processes*

In this chapter we draw on the language and results of the last to develop a suitable method for incorporating exogenous stochastic shocks into dynamic programs. To preserve the recursive structure of such models, clearly we must require that the exogenous shocks have a recursive structure as well. Shocks that have this structure, in an appropriate sense, are called Markov processes; in this chapter we define Markov processes and discuss some of their basic properties.

In the introduction to Chapter 7 we presented two ways of incorporating stochastic shocks into a functional equation, according to whether the space of possible values for the exogenous shocks was a discrete set or an interval in $\mathbf{R}^1$. We can now write both of these in a unified way. Let $(Z, \mathscr{Z})$ be a measurable space; let λ be a probability measure on $(Z, \mathscr{Z})$; and as in the discussion of functional equations under certainty, let X be a subset of a Euclidean space. Then we can consider the functional equation

$$(1) \qquad v(x, z) = \sup_{y \in \Gamma(x,z)} \left[F(x, y, z) + \beta \int_Z v(y, z') \lambda(dz') \right].$$

Here x is the current value of the endogenous state variable, z is the current value of the exogenous shock, y is the value of the endogenous state variable next period, and z' is the (currently unknown) value of next period's shock. The interpretation of (1) is that the current shock z is known at the time y is chosen, and that z may affect the current-period return, or the set of y values available for next period, or both. This equation includes as special cases both of those described in the introduction to Chapter 7, as well as other cases, and it is fine as far as it goes.

For our purposes, however, it does not go quite far enough. With the specification in (1), the exogenous shocks are assumed to be drawn from the same fixed distribution λ each period. That is, (1) excludes the possibility of period-to-period dependence (serial correlation) in the values of the shocks. Since many types of shocks (for example, temperature or rainfall) display such patterns, this is a serious drawback. To allow for such dependence, we must allow the current value of the shock to affect the probability measure over the shock next period. Thus, we are led to consider functional equations of the form

$$
(2) \qquad v(x, z) = \sup_{y \in \Gamma(x,z)} \left[F(x, y, z) + \beta \int_Z v(y, z') Q(z, dz') \right],
$$

where for each $z \in Z$, $Q(z, \cdot)$ is a probability measure on $\mathfrak{L}$.

With the specification in (2), the current value of the exogenous shock determines which probability measure is relevant for next period's shock. [Note that the example in (1) is a special case of (2) in which Q does not depend on its first argument.] Functions Q with the appropriate features are called transition functions, and we begin in Section 8.1 below by defining transition functions and developing several of their properties.

To state the sequence problem corresponding to (2) requires having a notation for sequences of shocks. In Section 8.2 we define the spaces in which such sequences lie and show how a transition function can be used to define probability measures over those spaces. We also provide formal definitions of the terms *stochastic process* and *Markov process* and show that a transition function as defined in Section 8.1 defines a Markov process. In Section 8.3 we develop a result that is useful in evaluating expectations of functions of Markovian shocks. This material is drawn upon in Section 9.1, where we develop the connections between solutions to functional equations like (2) and solutions to the corresponding sequence problems (the Principle of Optimality for stochastic dynamic programs).

Finally, in Section 8.4 we illustrate a standard line of argument used to prove that a function has the properties required of a transition function. To do this we prove that a transition function can be defined from a first-order stochastic difference equation. A similar argument is developed in Section 9.6, where we show that the solution to a functional equation like (1) or (2) defines a transition function on the space $(S, \mathcal{S}) = (X \times Z, \mathcal{X} \times \mathcal{L})$, the state space for the system. Thus, even if the exoge-

nous shocks are independently drawn in each period, as in (1), the
motion over time of the state variable $s = (x, z)$ is described by a Markov
process. This fact in turn motivates the study of convergence results for
Markov processes in Chapters 11 and 12, the stochastic analogue of the
stability theory in Chapter 6.

Although the material in Section 8.1 is needed before proceeding to
Chapters 9–13, the material in Sections 8.2–8.4 is not, and the reader
who is anxious to get on with the analysis of stochastic functional equations is invited to skip them. There is no loss in continuity in proceeding
directly from Section 8.1 to Section 9.2 (the analysis of stochastic functional equations) and then to Chapters 10–13 (economic applications of
stochastic dynamic programming, convergence results for Markov processes, and applications of the convergence results).

8.1   Transition Functions

In this section we define precisely the family of functions Q that can be
used to incorporate stochastic shocks into a functional equation, and we
develop some of their basic properties.

We begin with the following definition.

DEFINITION   *Let $(Z, \mathcal{Z})$ be a measurable space. A **transition function** is a
function $Q: Z \times \mathcal{Z} \to [0, 1]$ such that*

a. for each $z \in Z$, $Q(z, \cdot)$ is a probability measure on $(Z, \mathcal{Z})$; and

b. for each $A \in \mathcal{Z}$, $Q(\cdot, A)$ is a $\mathcal{Z}$-measurable function.

The interpretation is that $Q(a, A)$ is the probability that the next period's
shock lies in the set A, given that the current shock is a. That is

$$Q(a, A) = \Pr\{\tilde{z}_{t+1} \in A | \tilde{z}_t = a\},$$

where $\tilde{z}_t$ denotes the (random) state in period t. (The precise meaning of
this notation will be made clear in Section 8.2.)

(Notice that with Q as specified here, the probability measure over the
shock in any period can depend only upon the value of the shock in one
previous period. In some applications one might want to allow dependence on several lagged values. It is shown in Exercise 8.11 that, by
expanding the state space appropriately, any such system can be mod-
eled with only one lag.)

Associated with any transition function Q on a measurable space $(Z, \mathfrak{Z})$ are two operators, both of which are used repeatedly later. The first is an operator on $\mathfrak{Z}$-measurable functions; the other is an operator on probability measures on $(Z, \mathfrak{Z})$. We turn next to defining these operators and establishing their properties.

For any $\mathfrak{Z}$-measurable function f, define Tf by

$$(1) \qquad (Tf)(z) = \int f(z')Q(z, dz'), \quad \text{all } z \in Z.$$

Since for each $z \in Z$, $Q(z, \cdot)$ is a probability measure, it follows that Tf is well defined if f is either nonnegative or bounded. We interpret $(Tf)(z)$ as the expected value of the function f next period, given that the current state is z.

For any probability measure λ on $(Z, \mathfrak{Z})$, define $T^*\lambda$ by

$$(2) \qquad (T^*\lambda)(A) = \int Q(z, A)\lambda(dz), \quad \text{all } A \in \mathfrak{Z}.$$

Since for each $A \in \mathfrak{Z}$, $Q(\cdot, A)$ is bounded and $\mathfrak{Z}$-measurable, it follows that $T^*\lambda$ is well defined. We interpret $(T^*\lambda)(A)$ as the probability that the state next period lies in the set A, if the current state is drawn according to the probability measure λ. That is, $T^*\lambda$ is the probability measure over the state next period if λ is the probability measure over the current state.

Recall that for any measurable space $(Z, \mathfrak{Z})$, $M^+(Z, \mathfrak{Z})$ is the space of nonnegative, $\mathfrak{Z}$-measurable, extended real-valued functions; and $B(Z, \mathfrak{Z})$ is the space of bounded, $\mathfrak{Z}$-measurable, real-valued functions. In addition, define $\Lambda(Z, \mathfrak{Z})$ to be the space of probability measures on $(Z, \mathfrak{Z})$. The next two theorems deal with the properties of T viewed as an operator on $M^+(Z, \mathfrak{Z})$ or $B(Z, \mathfrak{Z})$, and of T^* viewed as an operator on $\Lambda(Z, \mathfrak{Z})$. The proofs of both theorems make use of the Monotone Convergence Theorem (Theorem 7.8).

THEOREM 8.1 *The operator T defined in (1) maps the space of nonnegative, $\mathfrak{Z}$-measurable, extended real-valued functions into itself; that is, $T: M^+(Z, \mathfrak{Z}) \to M^+(Z, \mathfrak{Z})$.*

Proof. Choose $f \in M^+(Z, \mathfrak{Z})$. Since f is nonnegative and measurable, Tf is well defined, although it may take on the value $+\infty$.

To see that Tf is measurable, first consider any indicator function for a measurable set: $f = \chi_A$, where $A \in \mathfrak{L}$. Then

$$(T\chi_A)(z) = \int_Z \chi_A(z')Q(z, dz') = \int_A Q(z, dz') = Q(z, A), \quad \text{all } z \in Z.$$

Hence by property (b) in the definition of a transition function, $T\chi_A$ is a measurable function.

Next consider any nonnegative simple function $\phi \in M^+(Z, \mathfrak{L})$, and let $\phi = \sum_{i=1}^n a_i \chi_{A_i}$ be its standard representation. Then

$$(T\phi)(z) = \int \phi(z')Q(z, dz')$$

$$= \int \left[\sum_{i=1}^n a_i \chi_{A_i}(z') \right] Q(z, dz')$$

$$= \sum_{i=1}^n a_i \left[\int \chi_{A_i}(z')Q(z, dz') \right]$$

$$= \sum_{i=1}^n a_i(T\chi_{A_i})(z), \quad \text{all } z \in Z.$$

Since each function $T\chi_{A_i}$ is $\mathfrak{L}$-measurable, it follows from Exercise 7.12 that $T\phi$ is also $\mathfrak{L}$-measurable.

Finally, let $f \in M^+(Z, \mathfrak{L})$. Then by Theorem 7.5 there exists an increasing sequence of simple functions $\{\phi_n\}$ in $M^+(Z, \mathfrak{L})$ converging pointwise to f. Hence

$$(Tf)(z) = \int f(z')Q(z, dz')$$

$$= \lim_{n \to \infty} \int \phi_n(z')Q(z, dz')$$

$$= \lim_{n \to \infty} (T\phi_n)(z), \quad \text{all } z \in Z,$$

where the second line uses the Monotone Convergence Theorem.

Hence the sequence of measurable functions $\{T\phi_n\}$ converges pointwise to Tf, so that by Theorem 7.4, Tf is measurable. ∎

COROLLARY *The operator T defined in (1) maps the space of bounded $\mathfrak{L}$-measurable functions into itself; that is, $T: B(Z, \mathfrak{L}) \to B(Z, \mathfrak{L})$.*

Proof. Since for each $z \in Z$, $Q(z, \cdot)$ is a probability measure, it is clear that $0 \le f \le m$ implies that $0 \le Tf \le m$. Choose $f \in B(Z, \mathfrak{L})$; apply the argument above to f^+ and f^-; and note that since Tf^+ and Tf^- are bounded, $Tf = Tf^+ - Tf^-$. ∎

The proof of Theorem 8.1 shows why property (b) in the definition of a transition function is needed. The following exercise establishes the linearity of the operator T.

> **Exercise 8.1** Let $f, g \in B(Z, \mathfrak{L})$ and $\alpha, \beta \in \mathbf{R}$. Show that $T(\alpha f + \beta g) = \alpha Tf + \beta Tg$.

We turn next to the operator T^*.

THEOREM 8.2 *The operator T^* defined in (2) maps the space of probability measures on $(Z, \mathfrak{L})$ into itself; that is, $T^*: \Lambda(Z, \mathfrak{L}) \to \Lambda(Z, \mathfrak{L})$.*

Proof. Choose $\lambda \in \Lambda(Z, \mathfrak{L})$. Since $Q \ge 0$, it is clear that $T^*\lambda \ge 0$. Also, since $Q(z, \emptyset) = 0$ and $Q(z, Z) = 1$, all $z \in Z$, it follows that $(T^*\lambda)(\emptyset) = 0$ and $(T^*\lambda)(Z) = 1$. Hence it suffices to show that $T^*\lambda$ is countably additive. Let $\{A_i\}$ be a disjoint sequence in $\mathfrak{L}$, with $A = \cup_{i=1}^{\infty}A_i$. Then

$$\sum_{i=1}^{\infty} (T^*\lambda)(A_i) = \sum_{i=1}^{\infty}\left[\int Q(z, A_i)\lambda(dz)\right]$$

$$= \int \left[\sum_{i=1}^{\infty} Q(z, A_i)\right] \lambda(dz)$$

$$= \int Q(z, A)\lambda(dz)$$

$$= (T^*\lambda)(A),$$

where the second line follows from the Monotone Convergence Theorem (cf. Exercise 7.22), and the third uses the fact that for each $z \in Z$, $Q(z, \cdot)$ is a probability measure [property (a) in the definition of a transition function]. ∎

The following exercise establishes the linearity of T^*.

Exercise 8.2 Let λ, $\mu \in \Lambda(Z, \mathfrak{L})$, and $\alpha \in (0, 1)$. Show that $T^*[\alpha\lambda + (1 - \alpha)\mu] = \alpha T^*\lambda + (1 - \alpha)T^*\mu$.

The operator T is called the *Markov operator* associated with Q, and T^* is called the *adjoint* of T. The following theorem shows the intimate connections between these two operators.

THEOREM 8.3 *Let Q be a transition function on the measurable space $(Z, \mathfrak{L})$, and let the operators T and T^* be defined by (1) and (2). Then for any function $f \in M^+(Z, \mathfrak{L})$,*

$$(3) \qquad \int (Tf)(z)\lambda(dz) = \int f(z')(T^*\lambda)(dz'), \quad \text{all } \lambda \in \Lambda(Z, \mathfrak{L}).$$

Proof. We will prove the result in three steps, showing in turn that (3) holds for all indicator functions of measurable sets, all measurable simple functions, and all nonnegative measurable functions.

First, let $A \in \mathfrak{L}$ be any measurable set, and let χ_A be the indicator function for A. Then as shown in the proof of Theorem 8.1, $(T\chi_A)(z) = Q(z, A)$, all $z \in Z$. Hence for any $\lambda \in \Lambda(Z, \mathfrak{L})$,

$$\int (T\chi_A)(z)\lambda(dz) = \int Q(z, A)\lambda(dz) = (T^*\lambda)(A)$$

$$= \int \chi_A(z')(T^*\lambda)(dz').$$

Hence (3) holds if f is the indicator function of a measurable set.

Next, let ϕ be any nonnegative measurable simple function, and let

$\phi = \Sigma_{i=1}^{n} \alpha_i \chi_{A_i}$ be its standard representation. Then

$$\int (T\phi)(z)\lambda(dz) = \int \left\{ \left[T \left(\sum_{i=1}^{n} \alpha_i \chi_{A_i} \right) \right](z) \right\} \lambda(dz)$$

$$= \int \left[\sum_{i=1}^{n} \alpha_i (T\chi_{A_i})(z) \right] \lambda(dz)$$

$$= \sum_{i=1}^{n} \alpha_i \left[\int (T\chi_{A_i})(z)\lambda(dz) \right]$$

$$= \sum_{i=1}^{n} \alpha_i \left[\int \chi_{A_i}(z')(T^*\lambda)(dz') \right]$$

$$= \int \left[\sum_{i=1}^{n} \alpha_i \chi_{A_i}(z') \right] (T^*\lambda)(dz')$$

$$= \int \phi(z')(T^*\lambda)(dz'), \quad \text{all } \lambda \in \Lambda(Z, \mathfrak{X});$$

where the first and last lines use the definition of ϕ, the second uses Exercise 8.1, the third and fifth use Exercise 7.17, and the fourth uses the fact that (3) holds for characteristic functions. Hence (3) holds for all measurable simple functions.

Finally, choose $f \in M^+(Z, \mathfrak{X})$. Then by Theorem 7.5, there exists an increasing sequence of measurable simple functions $\{\phi_n\}$ in $M^+(Z, \mathfrak{X})$ converging pointwise to f. And, as shown above, for any $\lambda \in \Lambda(Z, \mathfrak{X})$,

$$(4) \qquad \int (T\phi_n)(z)\lambda(dz) = \int \phi_n(z')(T^*\lambda)(dz'), \quad n = 1, 2, \ldots.$$

The rest of the proof consists of two applications of the Monotone Convergence Theorem (Theorem 7.8) to develop expressions for the limits on each side of (4) as $n \to \infty$.

As shown in the proof of Theorem 8.1, the sequence of functions $\{T\phi_n\}$ is increasing and converges pointwise to Tf. Hence by Theorem

7.4, Tf is measurable, and by the Monotone Convergence Theorem

$$\lim_{n\to\infty} \int (T\phi_n)(z)\lambda(dz) = \int (Tf)(z)\lambda(dz).$$

Similarly, since the sequence $\{\phi_n\}$ is increasing and converges pointwise to the measurable function f, by the Monotone Convergence Theorem

$$\lim_{n\to\infty} \int \phi_n(z')(T^*\lambda)(dz') = \int f(z')(T^*\lambda)(dz').$$

Taking the limit in (4) as $n \to \infty$ and substituting from these two results, we conclude that (3) holds for all $f \in M^+(Z, \mathfrak{Z})$. ∎

COROLLARY *Let Q be a transition function on the measurable space $(Z, \mathfrak{Z})$, and let the operators T and T^* be defined by (1) and (2). Then (3) holds for any function $f \in B(Z, \mathfrak{Z})$.*

Theorem 8.3 and its corollary show that both of the integrals in (3) express the expected value of the function f next period, if λ is the probability measure over the current state. We may write

$$\iint f(z')Q(z, dz')\lambda(dz)$$

for either expression, since we have established that the order in which the integrations are carried out does not matter.

In view of the close relationship between T and T^*, the following notation is sometimes convenient. Define $\langle \cdot, \cdot \rangle: B(Z, \mathfrak{Z}) \times \Lambda(Z, \mathfrak{Z}) \to \mathbf{R}$ by

$$\langle f, \lambda \rangle = \int f(z)\lambda(dz), \quad \text{all } f \in B(Z, \mathfrak{Z}), \text{ all } \lambda \in \Lambda(Z, \mathfrak{Z}).$$

Since f is bounded and λ is finite, the integral is also bounded. The next exercise shows that $\langle \cdot, \cdot \rangle$ is linear in each of its arguments. (Clearly, an analogous argument holds if $M^+(Z, \mathfrak{Z})$ is used.)

Exercise 8.3 Show that for any $a, b \in \mathbf{R}$; $\alpha \in [0, 1]$; $f, g \in B(Z, \mathfrak{Z})$; and $\lambda, \mu \in \Lambda(Z, \mathfrak{Z})$,
   a. $\langle af + bg, \lambda \rangle = a\langle f, \lambda \rangle + b\langle g, \lambda \rangle$; and
   b. $\langle f, \alpha\lambda + (1 - \alpha)\mu \rangle = \alpha\langle f, \lambda \rangle + (1 - \alpha)\langle f, \mu \rangle$.

In this notation (3) can be written as

$$\langle Tf, \lambda \rangle = \langle f, T^*\lambda \rangle, \quad \text{all } f \in B(Z, \mathcal{Z}), \text{ all } \lambda \in \Lambda(Z, \mathcal{Z}).$$

Thus, $\langle Tf, \lambda \rangle$ and $\langle f, T^*\lambda \rangle$ are both expressions for the expected value of the function f next period, if λ is the probability measure over the current state.

We are also interested in the iterates of a transition function and its associated operators. Given any transition function Q, we can define n-step transitions by

$$Q^1(z, A) = Q(z, A),$$

$$Q^{n+1}(z, A) = \int Q^n(z', A)Q(z, dz'), \quad n = 1, 2, \ldots.$$

If a sequence of shocks in successive periods is generated from Q, then $Q^n(z, A)$ is the probability of going from the point z to the set A in exactly n periods. The following exercise establishes several important properties of Q^n.

Exercise 8.4 a. Show that the functions Q^n, $n = 2, 3, \ldots$, are transition functions.

b. Let T^n and T^{*n} be the operators corresponding to the transition functions Q^n, $n = 1, 2, \ldots$. Show that

$$T^{(n+m)}f = (T^n)(T^m f), \quad \text{all } f \in B(Z, \mathcal{Z}), \ m, n = 1, 2, \ldots, \quad \text{and}$$

$$T^{*(n+m)}\lambda = (T^{*n})(T^{*m}\lambda), \quad \text{all } \lambda \in \Lambda(Z, \mathcal{Z}), \ m, n = 1, 2, \ldots.$$

It follows from this exercise that given any initial probability measure λ_0 on $(Z, \mathcal{Z})$, we can define a sequence of probability measures $\{\lambda_n\}$ by

$$\lambda_n = T^*\lambda_{n-1} = T^{*n}\lambda_0, \quad n = 1, 2, \ldots.$$

The interpretation is that if λ_0 is the probability measure over the state in period 0, then λ_n is the probability measure over the state in period n. In Chapters 11 and 12 we will be interested in finding conditions on T^* (or, equivalently, on Q) that ensure that the sequence $\{\lambda_n\}$ converges, in some sense, to a limiting measure λ.

Theorem 8.1 shows that any transition function defines a Markov operator $T: B(Z, \mathfrak{X}) \to B(Z, \mathfrak{X})$. The following two definitions describe stronger properties that we sometimes want to impose on T. Each requires additional structure on the space $(Z, \mathfrak{X})$.

If (Z, ρ) is a metric space and $\mathfrak{X}$ is the σ-algebra generated by the open sets, we are often primarily interested in the functions on Z that are continuous (with respect to the metric ρ). The space $C(Z)$ of bounded continuous functions is a subset of the space $B(Z, \mathfrak{X})$, and we often want to require that T map the space $C(Z)$ into itself.

DEFINITION *A transition function Q on $(Z, \mathfrak{X})$ has the **Feller property** if the associated operator T maps the space of bounded continuous functions on Z into itself; that is, if $T: C(Z) \to C(Z)$.*

(Markov operators that have the Feller property are also said to be *stable*.)

If Z is a subset of a finite-dimensional Euclidean space, we are sometimes particularly interested in monotone functions on Z. In such cases we often want to require that T map the space of monotone functions into itself.

DEFINITION *A transition function Q on $(Z, \mathfrak{X})$ is **monotone** if the associated operator T has the property that for every nondecreasing function $f: Z \to \mathbf{R}$, the function Tf is also nondecreasing.*

Although we make use of both properties in Chapter 9, a fuller discussion of them is deferred to Section 12.4. At that point we will be in a better position to characterize both in terms of properties of Q, and at that point both will be at the center of the analysis.

8.2   Probability Measures on Spaces of Sequences

Given a transition function Q on a measurable space $(Z, \mathfrak{X})$, a point $z \in Z$, and a set $A \in \mathfrak{X}$, we have interpreted $Q(z, A)$ as the probability that next period's shock lies in the set A, given that the current shock is z. In this section we look at partial (finite) histories of shocks, $z^t = (z_1, \ldots, z_t)$, $t = 1, 2, \ldots$, and at complete (infinite) histories, $z^\infty = (z_1, z_2, \ldots)$. We define the spaces in which such histories lie and show how, given an initial value

z_0, the transition function Q can be used to define probability measures on these spaces. To conclude, we give formal definitions of a stochastic process and a Markov process and show that what we have done is to construct a Markov process. This material is drawn upon in Section 9.1, where the Principle of Optimality for stochastic dynamic programs is discussed, and in Chapter 14, where the strong law of large numbers for Markov processes is developed. For the other parts of Chapter 9 and for all of Chapters 10–13, the definitions and results in the last section are sufficient.

Let $(Z, \mathscr{L})$ be a measurable space, and for any finite $t = 1, 2, \ldots,$ let

$$(Z^t, \mathscr{L}^t) = (Z \times \ldots \times Z, \mathscr{L} \times \ldots \times \mathscr{L}), \quad (t \text{ times})$$

denote the product space (cf. Section 7.5). Let Q be a transition function on $(Z, \mathscr{L})$, and let $z_0 \in Z$ be given. Then we can define probability measures $\mu^t(z_0, \cdot): \mathscr{L}^t \to [0, 1]$, $t = 1, 2, \ldots,$ on these spaces as follows.

Recall from Exercise 7.29 that it is sufficient to define $\mu^t(z_0, \cdot)$ on the measurable rectangles in $\mathscr{L}^t$ and to establish that it satisfies the two conditions stated there. For any rectangle $B = A_1 \times \ldots \times A_t \in \mathscr{L}^t$, let

$$\mu^t(z_0, B) = \int_{A_1} \ldots \int_{A_{t-1}} \int_{A_t} Q(z_{t-1}, dz_t) Q(z_{t-2}, dz_{t-1}) \ldots Q(z_0, dz_1).$$

Exercise 8.5 Show that $\mu^t(z_0, \cdot)$ satisfies the hypotheses of Exercise 7.29 and that $\mu^t(z_0, Z^t) = 1$.

It follows immediately from the Caratheodory and Hahn Extension Theorems (Theorems 7.2 and 7.3) that $\mu^t(z_0, \cdot)$ has a unique extension to a probability measure on all of $\mathscr{L}^t$.

This approach can also be used to define probabilities over infinite sequences $z^\infty = (z_1, z_2, \ldots)$. To do this we start with the infinite product space $Z^\infty = Z \times Z \times \ldots$. We must then do two things: find a suitable σ-algebra $\mathscr{L}^\infty$ of the subsets of Z^∞; and for each $z_0 \in Z$, define a probability measure $\mu^\infty(z_0, \cdot)$ on this σ-algebra.

Call a subset B of Z^∞ a *finite measurable rectangle* if it is of the form

(1) $\qquad B = A_1 \times A_2 \times \ldots \times A_T \times Z \times Z \times \ldots,$

$\qquad$ where $A_t \in \mathscr{L}, t = 1, \ldots, T < \infty.$

Let $\mathcal{C}$ be the family of all finite measurable rectangles, and let $\mathcal{A}^{\infty}$ be the family consisting of all finite unions of sets in $\mathcal{C}$. Note that $\mathcal{A}^{\infty}$ is closed under complementation: if B is as in (1), then

$$B^c = \bigcup_{t=1}^{T} Z \times Z \times \ldots \times Z \times A_t^c \times Z \times \ldots ,$$

which is a finite union of finite measurable rectangles. Hence $\mathcal{A}^{\infty}$ is an algebra. Let $\mathcal{L}^{\infty}$ be the σ-algebra generated by $\mathcal{A}^{\infty}$.

With $\mathcal{C}$, $\mathcal{A}^{\infty}$, and $\mathcal{L}^{\infty}$ so defined and given any $z_0 \in Z$, the probability measure $\mu^{\infty}(z_0, \cdot)$ on $\mathcal{L}^{\infty}$ is defined using exactly the same argument that we used for the finite product spaces. First $\mu^{\infty}(z_0, \cdot)$ is defined on $\mathcal{C}$; then it is extended to $\mathcal{A}^{\infty}$; and finally it is extended to $\mathcal{L}^{\infty}$.

Given the transition function Q and given any $z_0 \in Z$, define the set function $\mu^{\infty}(z_0, \cdot)$ on $\mathcal{C}$ as follows. If B is as in (1), let

$$\mu^{\infty}(z_0, B) = \mu^{\infty}(z_0, A_1 \times \ldots \times A_T \times Z \times Z \times \ldots)$$

$$= \int_{A_1} \ldots \int_{A_T} Q(z_{T-1}, dz_T) \ldots Q(z_0, dz_1).$$

Clearly $\mu^{\infty}(z_0, \cdot)$ is well defined and nonnegative, with $\mu^{\infty}(z_0, \emptyset) = 0$ and $\mu^{\infty}(z_0, Z^{\infty}) = 1$. It is also clear that if B and C are disjoint sets in $\mathcal{C}$, with $(B \cup C) \in \mathcal{C}$, then $\mu(z_0, B) + \mu(z_0, C) = \mu(z_0, B \cup C)$. That is, μ is finitely additive. It only remains to be shown that additivity also holds for all *countable* unions of disjoint sets: that if $\{B_i\}_{i=1}^{\infty}$ is a sequence of disjoint sets in $\mathcal{C}$, then

$$\mu^{\infty}(z_0, B) = \mu^{\infty}\left(z_0, \bigcup_{i=1}^{\infty} B_i\right) = \sum_{i=1}^{\infty} \mu^{\infty}(z_0, B_i).$$

The proof of countable additivity is more difficult than it was in the case of a finite product space, and we omit it. (See Shiryayev 1984, pp. 247–249, for a proof.) With this fact established, however, it follows that $\mu^{\infty}(z_0, \cdot)$ satisfies the hypotheses of Exercise 7.29 and hence has a unique extension to $\mathcal{A}^{\infty}$. By the Caratheodory and Hahn Extension Theorems it then follows that $\mu^{\infty}(z_0, \cdot)$ has a unique extension to $\mathcal{L}^{\infty}$.

Clearly, the arguments above could also be used to define measures $\mu^t(\lambda_0, \cdot)$, $t = 1, 2, \ldots$, and $\mu^\infty(\lambda_0, \cdot)$, given an initial probability measure λ_0 on $(Z, \mathcal{Z})$, rather than an initial state z_0.

With these probability spaces defined, we are in a position to define formally a general stochastic process and a Markov process and to demonstrate that the argument above can be used to construct a Markov process. Let $(\Omega, \mathcal{F}, P)$ be a fixed probability space.

DEFINITION *A **stochastic process** on $(\Omega, \mathcal{F}, P)$ is an increasing sequence of σ-algebras $\mathcal{F}_1 \subseteq \mathcal{F}_2 \subseteq \mathcal{F}_3 \subseteq \ldots \subseteq \mathcal{F}$; a measurable space $(Z, \mathcal{Z})$; and a sequence of functions $\sigma_t: \Omega \to Z$, $t = 1, 2, \ldots$, such that each σ_t is $\mathcal{F}_t$-measurable.*

The most common case is where $Z = \mathbf{R}$. In this case, for each fixed t, the function σ_t is simply a random variable on $(\Omega, \mathcal{F}, P)$. Alternatively, for each fixed $\omega \in \Omega$, the sequence of real numbers $\{\sigma_t(\omega)\}_{t=1}^\infty$ is called a *sample path* of the stochastic process.

Given a stochastic process, we can use the measure P to define the following finite-dimensional probability measures:

$$P_{t+1,\ldots,t+n}(C) = P(\{\omega \in \Omega: [\sigma_{t+1}(\omega), \ldots, \sigma_{t+n}(\omega)] \in C\}),$$

$$t = 0, 1, 2, \ldots; \; n = 1, 2, \ldots; \text{ all } C \in \mathcal{Z}^n.$$

A stochastic process is said to be *stationary* if the probabilities $P_{t+1,\ldots,t+n}(C)$ are independent of t, for all n and all $C \in \mathcal{Z}^n$. Similarly, let $P_{t+1,\ldots,t+n}(C \,|\, a_{t-s}, \ldots, a_{t-1}, a_t)$ denote the conditional probability of the event $\{\omega \in \Omega: [\sigma_{t+1}(\omega), \ldots, \sigma_{t+n}(\omega)] \in C\}$, given that the event $\{\omega \in \Omega: \sigma_\tau(\omega) = a_\tau, \tau = t - s, \ldots, t - 1, t\}$ occurs. We then have the following definition.

DEFINITION *A (**first-order**) **Markov process** is a stochastic process with the property that*

(2) $\qquad P_{t+1,\ldots,t+n}(C \,|\, a_{t-s}, \ldots, a_{t-1}, a_t) = P_{t+1,\ldots,t+n}(C \,|\, a_t),$

$$t = 2, 3, \ldots; \; n = 1, 2, \ldots; \; s = 1, 2, \ldots, t - 1; \; C \in \mathcal{Z}^n.$$

That is, a Markov process has the property that given the current realization $\sigma_t(\omega) = a_t$, future realizations are independent of the past. If the (conditional) probabilities $P_{t+1}(A|a)$ are independent of t for all $a \in Z$ and $A \in \mathfrak{L}$, a Markov process is said to have **stationary transitions.** Note the difference between a stationary Markov process (that is, a Markov process that is a stationary stochastic process) and a Markov process with stationary transitions: they are not the same. (For example, see Exercise 8.6.)

To relate the construction above to the definition of a Markov process, let Q be a transition function on a measurable space $(Z, \mathfrak{L})$, fix $z_0 \in Z$, and let $(\Omega, \mathfrak{F}, P) = [Z^\infty, \mathfrak{L}^\infty, \mu^\infty(z_0, \cdot)]$. Then define the following family of σ-algebras. For each $T = 1, 2, \ldots$, let $\mathcal{A}^T$ be the collection of all sets B of the form in (1), and let $\mathfrak{F}_T$ be the smallest σ-algebra containing $\mathcal{A}^T$. Note that these form an increasing sequence of σ-algebras, each one of which is contained in $\mathfrak{F}$; that is, $\mathfrak{F}_1 \subset \mathfrak{F}_2 \subset \ldots \subset \mathfrak{F}$. Then define the sequence of functions $\tilde{z}_t : \Omega \to Z$ by

$$\tilde{z}_t(\omega) = \tilde{z}_t(a_1, a_2, \ldots) = a_t, \quad t = 1, 2, \ldots.$$

Since each function $\tilde{z}_t$ is $\mathfrak{F}_t$-measurable, we have constructed a stochastic process.

Exercise 8.6   a. Show that the stochastic process with $(\Omega, \mathfrak{F}, P) = [Z^\infty, \mathfrak{L}^\infty, \mu^\infty(z_0, \cdot)]$ and with $\{(\tilde{z}_t, \mathfrak{F}_t)\}_{t=1}^\infty$ as defined above is a Markov process; that is, show that it satisfies (2).

b. Show that the Markov process in (a) has stationary transitions; that is, show that

$$P_{t+1}(C|a_{t-s}, \ldots, a_{t-1}, a_t) = P_{t+1}(C|a_t) = Q(a_t, C),$$

$$\text{all } t = 2, 3, \ldots; s = 1, 2, \ldots, t - 1; C \in \mathfrak{L}.$$

c. Suppose there is a probability measure λ on $(Z, \mathfrak{L})$ such that $Q(a, A) = \lambda(A)$, all $a \in Z$, all $A \in \mathfrak{L}$. Show that the Markov process defined in (a) is stationary.

The next exercise illustrates these ideas with a concrete example.

Exercise 8.7   Consider an infinite sequence of coin tosses, with possible outcomes heads or tails on each trial. Let $Z = \{H, T\}$; let $\mathfrak{L} =$

$\{\emptyset, Z, \{H\}, \{T\}\}$; and let $Q(a, \{b\}) = 1/2$, for $a, b \in \{H, T\}$. Let $(\Omega, \mathcal{F}, P)$ be constructed as above.

a. Describe in detail the σ-algebras $\mathcal{F}_1, \mathcal{F}_2, \ldots$

b. Let $\sigma_t(\omega) = 1$ if ω has H in the tth place, and zero otherwise. Show that $\{(\sigma_t, \mathcal{F}_t)\}_{t=1}^{\infty}$ is a stochastic process on $(\Omega, \mathcal{F}, P)$.

c. Let $g_t(\omega) = \Sigma_{s=1}^{t} \sigma_s(\omega)$, where the σ_s's are as defined in part (b). Show that $\{(g_t, \mathcal{F}_t)\}_{t=1}^{\infty}$ is a stochastic process on $(\Omega, \mathcal{F}, P)$.

Clearly there is, for each t, a very intimate relationship between the σ-algebras $\mathcal{F}_t$ and $\mathcal{L}^t$. (Note that $\mathcal{F}_t$ is a family of sets in $\Omega = Z^{\infty}$, while $\mathcal{L}^t$ is a family of sets in Z^t.) Specifically, given any $\mathcal{L}^t$-measurable function $f: Z^t \to \mathbf{R}$, we can define the function $\hat{f}: \Omega \to \mathbf{R}$ by $\hat{f}(z_1, z_2, \ldots, z_t, z_{t+1}, \ldots) = f(z_1, \ldots, z_t)$. Clearly $\hat{f}$ is $\mathcal{F}_t$-measurable, and hence $\mathcal{F}$-measurable. Conversely, given any $\mathcal{F}_t$-measurable function $\hat{f}$ on Ω, for some finite t, there is a corresponding $\mathcal{L}^t$-measurable function f on Z^t. In this sense, the family of $\mathcal{F}$-measurable functions contains all the $\mathcal{L}^t$-measurable functions, for all finite t.

8.3 Iterated Integrals

Expected values with respect to the measures $\mu^t(z_0, \cdot)$ constructed on $(Z^t, \mathcal{L}^t)$ in the last section are defined in the obvious way. Let $z^t = (z_1, \ldots, z_t)$ denote an element of Z^t, $t = 1, 2, \ldots$. Then for any function F that is $\mu^t(z_0, \cdot)$-integrable,

$$E(F|z_0) = \int_{Z^t} F(z^t)\mu^t(z_0, dz^t).$$

Our task in this section is to show that this integral can also be expressed, in a variety of ways, as an iterated integral. Specifically, we will need the following results in Section 9.1.

Let $t \in \{2, 3, \ldots\}$; let $F: Z^t \to \overline{\mathbf{R}}$ be a $\mathcal{L}^t$-measurable function; and suppose that F is $\mu^t(z_0, \cdot)$-integrable. Let $F(z^{t-1}, \cdot): Z \to \overline{\mathbf{R}}$ denote the z^{t-1}-section of F. We want to show that

(1a) $\displaystyle \int_{Z^t} F(z^t)\mu^t(z_0, dz^t)$

$$= \int_{Z^{t-1}} \left[\int_Z F(z^{t-1}, z_t)Q(z_{t-1}, dz_t) \right] \mu^{t-1}(z_0, dz^{t-1}).$$

That is, we are interested in proving that the expected value of F [the integral on the left in (1a)] is equal to the expected value of the conditional expected value given z^{t-1} [the double integral on the right in (1a)]. Similarly, let $F(z_1, \cdot)$ denote the z_1-section of F. We also want to show that

(1b) $\displaystyle \int_{Z^t} F(z^t)\mu^t(z_0, dz^t)$

$$= \int_Z \left[\int_{Z^{t-1}} F(z_1, z_2^t)\mu^{t-1}(z_1, dz_2^t) \right] Q(z_0, dz_1).$$

Clearly there are many ways of breaking up the integral on the left sides of (1a) and (1b). Thus it is useful to take a slightly more abstract approach and to establish (1a) and (1b) as by-products of a much more general result. This approach also has the advantage of simplifying much of the notation. We begin with the following definition.

DEFINITION Let $(X, \mathcal{X})$ and $(Y, \mathcal{Y})$ be measurable spaces. A **stochastic kernel** on $\{X, \mathcal{Y}\}$ is a function $P: X \times \mathcal{Y} \to [0, 1]$ such that
  a. for each $a \in X$, $P(a, \cdot)$ is a probability measure on $(Y, \mathcal{Y})$; and
  b. for each $B \in \mathcal{Y}$, $P(\cdot, B)$ is an $\mathcal{X}$-measurable function.

The interpretation is that $P(a, B)$ is the probability that $y \in B$ given that $x = a$. Clearly a transition function is simply a stochastic kernel for which the two spaces $(X, \mathcal{X})$ and $(Y, \mathcal{Y})$ happen to be the same.

We begin by proving three results, which generalize Theorems 8.1–8.3 respectively for this more abstract setting. All make use of the Monotone Class Lemma (Lemma 7.15).

THEOREM 8.4 Let $(X, \mathcal{X})$ and $(Y, \mathcal{Y})$ be measurable spaces; let P be a stochastic kernel on $\{X, \mathcal{Y}\}$; and let $F: X \times Y \to \overline{\mathbf{R}}_+$ be a nonnegative, $(\mathcal{X} \times \mathcal{Y})$-measurable function. Then the nonnegative function $TF: X \to \overline{\mathbf{R}}_+$ defined by

(2) $\displaystyle (TF)(x) = \int_Y F(x, y)P(x, dy), \quad \text{all } x \in X,$

is $\mathcal{X}$-measurable. That is, $T: M^+(X \times Y, \mathcal{X} \times \mathcal{Y}) \to M^+(X, \mathcal{X})$.

Proof. Choose $F \in M^+(X \times Y, \mathcal{X} \times \mathcal{Y})$. By Theorem 7.14 each x-section of F is a $\mathcal{Y}$-measurable function; hence the integral in (2) is well defined for each $x \in X$. Clearly TF is nonnegative. To show that TF is measurable, we will establish the result first for indicator functions of measurable rectangles; then for indicator functions of arbitrary measurable sets; then for measurable simple functions; and finally for arbitrary measurable functions.

First consider any indicator function for a measurable rectangle; that is, $F(x, y) = \chi_{A \times B}(x, y)$, where $A \in \mathcal{X}$ and $B \in \mathcal{Y}$. Then

$$(T\chi_{A \times B})(x) = \int_Y \chi_{A \times B}(x, y)P(x, dy)$$

$$= \int_Y \chi_A(x)\chi_B(y)P(x, dy)$$

$$= \chi_A(x)P(x, B), \quad \text{all } x \in X.$$

Thus $T\chi_{A \times B}$ is the product of $\mathcal{X}$-measurable functions and hence is $\mathcal{X}$-measurable. Clearly, the same argument applies if F is the indicator function for a finite union of disjoint measurable rectangles.

Let

$$\mathcal{E} = \{E \in \mathcal{X} \times \mathcal{Y}: T\chi_E \text{ is } \mathcal{X}\text{-measurable}\}.$$

As noted, $\mathcal{E}$ contains the algebra generated by the measurable rectangles. Next we will show that $\mathcal{E}$ is a monotone class; it will then follow from the Monotone Class Lemma that $\mathcal{E} = \mathcal{X} \times \mathcal{Y}$.

Let $\{E_n\}_{n=1}^{\infty}$ be an increasing sequence in $\mathcal{E}$, with $E = \cup_{n=1}^{\infty} E_n$. Then $\{\chi_{E_n}\}$ is an increasing sequence of nonnegative, measurable functions converging pointwise to χ_E. Hence by Theorem 7.4, χ_E is measurable, and by the Monotone Convergence Theorem,

$$(T\chi_E)(x) = \int_Y \chi_E(x, y)P(x, dy)$$

$$= \lim_{n \to \infty} \int_Y \chi_{E_n}(x, y)P(x, dy)$$

$$= \lim_{n \to \infty} (T\chi_{E_n})(x), \quad \text{all } x \in X.$$

Hence $T\chi_{E_n} \to T\chi_E$ pointwise. Since $\{T\chi_{E_n}\}$ is a sequence of measurable functions, it follows from Theorem 7.4 that $T\chi_E$ is measurable. Next, note that $E^c \in \mathcal{E}$ implies $E \in \mathcal{E}$. If $\{E_n\}$ is a decreasing sequence of sets, apply the argument above to the increasing sequence $\{E_n^c\}$, and use this fact. Hence $\mathscr{E}$ is a monotone class.

By the linearity of the integral, the result can be extended to all simple functions in $M^+(X \times Y, \mathscr{X} \times \mathscr{Y})$, and then by Theorem 7.5 and the Monotone Convergence Theorem to all functions in $M^+(X \times Y, \mathscr{X} \times \mathscr{Y})$. These arguments parallel exactly those used in the proof of Theorem 8.1, and we do not repeat them. ∎

COROLLARY *The operator T defined in (2) maps the space of bounded $(\mathscr{X} \times \mathscr{Y})$-measurable functions into the space of bounded $\mathscr{X}$-measurable functions; that is, $T: B(X \times Y, \mathscr{X} \times \mathscr{Y}) \to B(X, \mathscr{X})$.*

THEOREM 8.5 *Let $(W, \mathscr{W})$, $(X, \mathscr{X})$, and $(Y, \mathscr{Y})$ be measurable spaces; and let P_1 and P_2 be stochastic kernels on $\{W, \mathscr{X}\}$ and $\{X, \mathscr{Y}\}$ respectively. Then given any $w \in W$, there exists a unique probability measure $P_3(w, \cdot)$ on $(X \times Y, \mathscr{X} \times \mathscr{Y})$ such that*

$$(3) \qquad P_3(w, A \times B) = \int_A P_2(x, B) P_1(w, dx), \quad \text{all } A \in \mathscr{X}, B \in \mathscr{Y}.$$

Moreover, the function so defined has the property that $P_3(\cdot, C)$ is $\mathscr{W}$-measurable, for all $C \in \mathscr{X} \times \mathscr{Y}$. That is, P_3 is a stochastic kernel on $\{W, \mathscr{X} \times \mathscr{Y}\}$.

Proof. Fix $w \in W$; that (3) uniquely defines a probability measure on $\mathscr{X} \times \mathscr{Y}$ follows from Theorems 7.13 and 7.3.

To see that $P_3(\cdot, C)$ is $\mathscr{W}$-measurable, first let $C = A \times B$, with $A \in \mathscr{X}$ and $B \in \mathscr{Y}$. Then for $F(w, x) = \chi_A(x) P_2(x, B)$, it follows immediately from Theorem 8.4 that $P_3(\cdot, A \times B)$ is $\mathscr{W}$-measurable. Clearly, the argument also holds if C is the finite union of disjoint measurable rectangles. Let $\mathscr{E} = \{E \in \mathscr{X} \times \mathscr{Y}: P_3(\cdot, E) \text{ is } \mathscr{W}\text{-measurable}\}$. To complete the proof, it suffices to show that $\mathscr{E}$ is a monotone class; it will then follow from the Monotone Class Lemma that $\mathscr{E} = \mathscr{X} \times \mathscr{Y}$.

Let $\{E_n\}$ be an increasing sequence of sets in $\mathscr{E}$, with $E = \bigcup_{n=1}^{\infty} E_n$. Then $\{P_3(\cdot, E_n)\}$ is an increasing sequence of $\mathscr{W}$-measurable functions, converging pointwise to $P_3(\cdot, E)$. Hence $P_3(\cdot, E)$ is also $\mathscr{W}$-measurable. A similar argument holds if $\{E_n\}$ is a decreasing sequence. Hence $\mathscr{E}$ is a monotone class. ∎

When the hypotheses of Theorem 8.5 hold we say that P_3 is the *direct product* of P_1 and P_2, and we write $P_3 = P_1 \times P_2$.

THEOREM 8.6 *Let* $(W, \mathcal{W})$, $(X, \mathcal{X})$, *and* $(Y, \mathcal{Y})$ *be measurable spaces; let* P_1 *and* P_2 *be stochastic kernels on* $\{W, \mathcal{X}\}$ *and* $\{X, \mathcal{Y}\}$ *respectively; and let* $P_3 = P_1 \times P_2$ *be the stochastic kernel on* $\{W, \mathcal{X} \times \mathcal{Y}\}$ *defined by* (3). *Then for any function* $F \in M^+(X \times Y, \mathcal{X} \times \mathcal{Y})$,

(4) $$\int_{X \times Y} F(x, y) P_3(w, dx \times dy) = \int_X \left[\int_Y F(x, y) P_2(x, dy) \right] P_1(w, dx),$$

all $w \in W$.

Proof. We will prove the result by showing in turn that (4) holds for indicator functions of measurable rectangles, indicator functions of measurable sets, measurable simple functions, and measurable functions.

First, let $A \times B$ be any measurable rectangle in $\mathcal{X} \times \mathcal{Y}$, and let $F = \chi_{A \times B}$. Then as shown in the proof of Theorem 8.4,

$$\int_Y \chi_{A \times B}(x, y) P_2(x, dy) = \chi_A(x) P_2(x, B), \quad \text{all } x \in X.$$

Hence

$$\int_X \left[\int_Y \chi_{A \times B}(x, y) P_2(x, dy) \right] P_1(w, dx)$$

$$= \int_X \chi_A(x) P_2(x, B) P_1(w, dx)$$

$$= P_3(w, A \times B), \quad \text{all } w \in W.$$

Hence (4) holds if F is an indicator function of a measurable rectangle. Clearly the same argument holds if F is an indicator function for a finite union of disjoint measurable rectangles. Let

$$\mathscr{E} = \{E \in \mathcal{X} \times \mathcal{Y} : (4) \text{ holds for } F = \chi_E\}.$$

We have shown that $\mathscr{E}$ contains the algebra generated by the measurable rectangles. To complete the proof it suffices to show that $\mathscr{E}$ is a monotone class; it will then follow from the Monotone Class Lemma that $\mathscr{E} = \mathcal{X} \times \mathcal{Y}$.

Let $\{E_n\}_{n=1}^{\infty}$ be an increasing sequence in $\mathscr{E}$, with $E = \cup_{n=1}^{\infty} E_n$. Then $\{\chi_{E_n}\}$ is an increasing sequence of $(\mathcal{X} \times \mathcal{Y})$-measurable functions converging pointwise to χ_E; hence by Theorem 7.4, χ_E is also $(\mathcal{X} \times \mathcal{Y})$-measurable. Define the functions

$$g_n(x) = \int_Y \chi_{E_n}(x, y)P_2(x, dy), \quad n = 1, 2, \ldots, \text{ and}$$

$$g(x) = \int_Y \chi_E(x, y)P_2(x, dy).$$

By Theorem 8.4, all of these functions are $\mathcal{X}$-measurable; and by the Monotone Convergence Theorem, $g_n \to g$ pointwise. By hypothesis (4) holds for $F = \chi_{E_n}$, $n = 1, 2, \ldots$; that is,

$$\int_{X \times Y} \chi_{E_n}(x, y)P_3(w, dx \times dy) = \int_X \left[\int_Y \chi_{E_n}(x, y)P_2(x, dy) \right] P_1(w, dx),$$

all $w \in W$; $n = 1, 2, \ldots$.

Taking the limit as $n \to \infty$ and applying the Monotone Convergence Theorem to both sides, we find that

$$\int_{X \times Y} \chi_E(x, y)P_3(w, dx \times dy)$$

$$= \lim_{n \to \infty} \int_{X \times Y} \chi_{E_n}(x, y)P_3(w, dx \times dy)$$

$$= \lim_{n \to \infty} \int_X \left[\int_Y \chi_{E_n}(x, y)P_2(x, dy) \right] P_1(w, dx)$$

$$= \lim_{n \to \infty} \int_X g_n(x)P_1(w, dx)$$

$$= \int_X g(x)P_1(w, dx)$$

$$= \int_X \left[\int_Y \chi_{E_n}(x, y)P_2(x, dy) \right] P_1(w, dx), \quad \text{all } w \in W.$$

Hence (4) holds for χ_E, so $E \in \mathscr{E}$. If $\{E_n\}$ is a decreasing sequence in $\mathscr{E}$, apply the argument above to the increasing sequence $\{E_n^c\}$, and use the fact that $E^c \in \mathscr{E}$ implies $E \in \mathscr{E}$. Hence $\mathscr{E}$ is a monotone class; and by the

Monotone Class Lemma, (4) holds for all indicator functions of measurable sets.

The rest of the proof parallels exactly the proof of Theorem 8.3. The linearity of the integral is used to extend the result to all measurable simple functions. Then Theorem 7.5 and the Monotone Convergence Theorem are used to establish the result for all measurable functions. ∎

COROLLARY *Equation (4) holds for any function $F \in B(X \times Y, \mathcal{X} \times \mathcal{Y})$.*

Now recall that we want to establish that (1a) and (1b) hold if the function F is integrable. To do this we need the following result, which extends the conclusion in Theorem 8.6 to integrable functions.

THEOREM 8.7 *Let $(W, \mathcal{W})$, $(X, \mathcal{X})$, and $(Y, \mathcal{Y})$ be measurable spaces; let P_1 and P_2 be stochastic kernels on $\{W, \mathcal{X}\}$ and $\{X, \mathcal{Y}\}$ respectively; and let $P_3 = P_1 \times P_2$ be the stochastic kernel on $\{W, \mathcal{X} \times \mathcal{Y}\}$ defined by (3). If $F: X \times Y \to \overline{\mathbf{R}}$ is $P_3(\hat{w}, \cdot)$-integrable for some $\hat{w} \in W$, then (4) holds for $w = \hat{w}$.*

Proof. Fix $\hat{w} \in W$, and let $F: X \times Y \to \overline{\mathbf{R}}$ be $P_3(\hat{w}, \cdot)$-integrable. Then it follows by definition that F^+ and F^- are $P_3(\hat{w}, \cdot)$-integrable; that is, both have finite integrals. Hence by Theorem 8.6,

$$\int_X \left[\int_Y F^+(x, y)P_2(x, dy) \right] P_1(\hat{w}, dx)$$

$$= \int_{X \times Y} F^+(x, y)P_3(\hat{w}, dx \times dy) < \infty,$$

and similarly for F^-. Define the set K^+ by

$$K^+ = \{x \in X : \int_Y F^+(x, y)P_2(x, dy) = +\infty\},$$

and define K^- similarly. By Exercise 7.20c, $P_1(\hat{w}, K^+) = 0$ and $P_1(w, K^-) = 0$. Let $K = K^+ \cup K^-$. Then for $x \in X \backslash K$,

(5) $\qquad \int_Y F(x, y)P_2(x, dy) = \int_Y F^+(x, y)P_2(x, dy) - \int_Y F^-(x, y)P_2(x, dy)$

is finite-valued. Hence

$$\int_{X \times Y} F(x, y) P_3(\hat{w}, dx \times dy)$$

$$= \int_{X \times Y} F^+ P_3 - \int_{X \times Y} F^- P_3$$

$$= \int_X \left[\int_Y F^+ P_2 \right] P_1 - \int_X \left[\int_Y F^- P_2 \right] P_1$$

$$= \int_{X \setminus K} \left[\int_Y F^+ P_2 \right] P_1 - \int_{X \setminus K} \left[\int_Y F^- P_2 \right] P_1$$

$$= \int_{X \setminus K} \left[\int_Y F P_2 \right] P_1$$

$$= \int_X \left[\int_Y F(x, y) P_2(x, dy) \right] P_1(\hat{w}, dx),$$

where the first line uses the fact that F is $P_3(\hat{w}, \cdot)$-integrable; the second uses the fact that both F^+ and F^- are in $M^+(X \times Y, \mathcal{X} \times \mathcal{Y})$ and have finite integrals; the third uses Exercise 7.20b and the fact that $P_1(\hat{w}, K) = 0$; the fourth uses (5); and the last again uses Exercise 7.20b and the fact that $P_1(\hat{w}, K) = 0$. ∎

We are now ready to apply these results to the situation of interest. Let Q be a transition function on a measurable space $(Z, \mathcal{Z})$; let $z_0 \in Z$; and let $\{(Z^t, \mathcal{Z}^t, \mu^t(z_0, \cdot)\}$, $t = 1, 2, \ldots$, be the probability spaces defined in Section 8.2. The following result establishes a basic property of integrals with respect to the measures $\mu^t(z_0, \cdot)$.

THEOREM 8.8   *Let $(Z, \mathcal{Z})$, Q, $z_0 \in Z$, and $\{Z^t, \mathcal{Z}^t, \mu^t(z_0, \cdot)\}$ be as described, and fix $t \in \{2, 3, \ldots\}$. If the function $F: Z^t \to \overline{\mathbf{R}}$ is nonnegative and $\mathcal{Z}^t$-measurable or is $\mu^t(z_0, \cdot)$-integrable, then*

$$(6) \qquad \int_{Z^t} F(z^t) \mu^t(z_0, dz^t)$$

$$= \int_Z Q(z_0, dz_1) \int_Z Q(z_1, dz_2) \ldots \int_Z Q(z_{t-1}, dz_t) F(z_1 \ldots, z_t).$$

Proof. First notice that by repeated application of Theorems 7.14 and 8.4, the iterated integral on the right is well defined.

Let F be an indicator function of a measurable rectangle in $\mathfrak{X}^t$, that is, $F = \chi_{A_1 \times \ldots \times A_t}$. Then (6) follows immediately from the definition of $\mu^t(z_0, \cdot)$. It is also immediate that (6) holds if F is the indicator of a disjoint union of measurable rectangles. Let

$$\mathscr{E} = \{E \in \mathfrak{X}^t\colon (6) \text{ holds for } F = \chi_E\}.$$

Using an induction on the argument in the proof of Theorem 8.6 and then applying the Monotone Convergence Theorem, we find that $\mathscr{E}$ is a monotone class. Hence $\mathscr{E} = \mathfrak{X}^t$. The extension to all simple functions then follows from the linearity of the integral, and the extension to all measurable functions follows from Theorem 7.5 and the Monotone Convergence Theorem. The extension to all $\mu^t(z_0, \cdot)$-integrable functions can then be proved by using an induction on the argument in the proof of Theorem 8.7. ∎

The following exercise draws on this theorem to establish the properties that are of direct use later.

Exercise 8.8 a. Show that for $t = 1, 2, \ldots, \mu^t(\cdot, \cdot)$, is a stochastic kernel on $\{Z, \mathfrak{X}^t\}$.

b. Show that $Q \times \mu^{t-1} = \mu^t = \mu^{t-1} \times Q, t = 2, 3, \ldots$.

c. Show that for all $t \in \{2, 3, \ldots, \}$, all $z_0 \in Z$, and all $\mu^t(z_0, \cdot)$-integrable functions $F\colon Z^t \to \overline{\mathbf{R}}$, (1a) and (1b) hold.

The following exercise specializes Theorems 8.4–8.7 to the case where the shocks x and y are independent.

Exercise 8.9 Let $(X, \mathfrak{X}, \mu)$ and $(Y, \mathfrak{Y}, \nu)$ be probability spaces.

a. Show that there exists a unique probability measure λ on $(X \times Y, \mathfrak{X} \times \mathfrak{Y})$ such that $\lambda(A \times B) = \mu(A)\nu(B)$, all $A \in \mathfrak{X}, B \in \mathfrak{Y}$.

b. Show that for any nonnegative, $(\mathcal{X} \times \mathcal{Y})$-measurable function F (or any λ-integrable function F),

$$\int_{X \times Y} F(x, y)\lambda(dx \times dy) = \int_X \left[\int_Y F(x, y)\nu(dy) \right] \mu(dx).$$

$$= \int_Y \left[\int_X F(x, y)\mu(dx) \right] \nu(dy).$$

[The result in part (a) of this exercise is called the Product Measure Theorem. The result in part (b) for nonnegative functions is called Tonelli's Theorem, and the one for integrable functions is called Fubini's Theorem.]

8.4 Transitions Defined by Stochastic Difference Equations

In this section we look at two methods for defining a transition function for a stationary, first-order Markov process. We show that a first-order stochastic difference equation can be used to define a transition function and that a second- or higher-order Markov process can be written as a first-order process by suitably redefining the state space. The reader should note that similar arguments are used in Section 9.6 to show that for a stochastic dynamic program like the one described in the introduction, a transition function on the exogenous shocks and the optimal policy function together define a transition function on the state space of the system.

Let $\{w_t\}_{t=0}^{\infty}$, $w_t \in W$, be a sequence of independently and identically distributed random shocks; let $g: Z \times W \to Z$ be a given function; let z_0 be a given initial value; and let $\{z_t\}$ be defined by $z_{t+1} = g(z_t, w_t)$. The following theorem shows that the function g and the probability measure over the w_t's can be used to construct a transition function for the z_t's. As in the proof of Theorem 8.5, the third step in the proof draws upon the Monotone Class Lemma.

THEOREM 8.9 *Let $(W, \mathcal{W}, \mu)$ be a probability space, and let $(Z, \mathcal{Z})$ be a measurable space. Let $g: Z \times W \to Z$ be a measurable function, and define the correspondence $\Gamma: \mathcal{Z} \to Z \times W$ to be the inverse of g:*

$$\Gamma(A) = \{(z, w) \in Z \times W: g(z, w) \in A\}, \quad \text{all } A \in \mathcal{Z}.$$

Then $Q(z, A) = \mu([\Gamma(A)]_z)$ defines a transition function on $(Z, \mathcal{Z})$ (where for any set $C \in \mathcal{Z} \times \mathcal{W}$, C_z denotes the z-section of C).

Proof. First we must show that Q is well defined. To do this, it suffices to show that $[\Gamma(A)]_z \in \mathcal{W}$, all $z \in Z$, all $A \in \mathcal{Z}$. Since by hypothesis g is measurable, $\Gamma(A) \in \mathcal{Z} \times \mathcal{W}$, all $A \in \mathcal{Z}$. The desired result then follows from the fact, shown in Theorem 7.14, that any section of a measurable set is measurable.

Next we must show that for each $z \in Z$, $Q(z, \cdot)$ is a probability measure on $\mathcal{Z}$. Fix $z \in Z$. Clearly $Q(z, \emptyset) = \mu(\emptyset) = 0$, and $Q(z, Z) = \mu(W) = 1$. Also, for any disjoint sequence $\{A_i\}$ in $\mathcal{Z}$, the sets $C_i = \Gamma(A_i)$, $i = 1, 2, \ldots$, in $\mathcal{Z} \times \mathcal{W}$ are disjoint. Hence their z-sections are also disjoint, so

$$Q\left(z, \bigcup_{i=1}^{\infty} A_i\right) = \mu\left[\left(\bigcup_{i=1}^{\infty} C_i\right)_z\right] = \mu\left[\bigcup_{i=1}^{\infty} (C_i)_z\right]$$

$$= \sum_{i=1}^{\infty} \mu[(C_i)_z] = \sum_{i=1}^{\infty} Q(z, A_i).$$

Therefore $Q(z, \cdot)$ is countably additive.

Finally, we must show that for each $A \in \mathcal{Z}$, $Q(\cdot, A)$ is a $\mathcal{Z}$-measurable function. Since for each $A \in \mathcal{Z}$ the set $C = \Gamma(A)$ is in $\mathcal{Z} \times \mathcal{W}$, it suffices to show that the function $\mu(C_z)$, viewed as a function of z, is $\mathcal{Z}$-measurable for all $C \in \mathcal{Z} \times \mathcal{W}$. Let

$$\mathcal{E} = \{C \in \mathcal{Z} \times \mathcal{W} \colon \mu(C_z) \text{ is a measurable function of } z\}.$$

By the Monotone Class Lemma (Lemma 7.15), if suffices to show that $\mathcal{E}$ contains all finite unions of measurable rectangles and that $\mathcal{E}$ is a monotone class.

First, let $C = A \times B$. Then

$$\mu(C_z) = \begin{cases} \mu(B) & \text{if } z \in A \\ 0 & \text{if } z \notin A. \end{cases}$$

Since A is a measurable set, $\mu(C_z)$ is a measurable (simple) function of z. Hence each measurable rectangle is in $\mathcal{E}$.

Next we will show that if $E_1, \ldots, E_n$ are measurable rectangles, then $\cup_{i=1}^n E_i \in \mathscr{E}$. The proof is by induction. The claim holds for $n = 1$; suppose that it holds for $n - 1$. Then

$$\mu\left[\left(\bigcup_{i=1}^n E_i\right)_z\right] = \mu\left[\bigcup_{i=1}^n (E_i)_z\right]$$

$$= \mu\left[\bigcup_{i=1}^{n-1} (E_i)_z \cup (E_n)_z\right]$$

$$= \mu\left[\bigcup_{i=1}^{n-1} (E_i)_z\right] + \mu[(E_n)_z]$$

$$- \mu\left(\left[\bigcup_{i=1}^{n-1} (E_i)_z\right] \cap (E_n)_z\right)$$

$$= \mu\left[\left(\bigcup_{i=1}^{n-1} E_i\right)_z\right] + \mu[(E_n)_z]$$

$$- \mu\left[\left(\bigcup_{i=1}^{n-1} (E_i \cap E_n)\right)_z\right].$$

Since each argument of μ in the last line is in $\mathscr{E}$, each term in that line is a measurable function of z. Hence their sum is also a measurable function of z, so $\cup_{i=1}^n E_i$ is in $\mathscr{E}$.

Finally we will show that $\mathscr{E}$ is a monotone class. Let $E_1 \subseteq E_2 \subseteq \ldots$ be an increasing sequence of sets in $\mathscr{E}$, with $E = \cup_{i=1}^\infty E_i$. Note that this implies that the z-sections $(E_1)_z \subseteq (E_2)_z \subseteq \ldots$ form an increasing sequence in $\mathscr{W}$. Hence

$$(1) \qquad \mu(E_z) = \mu\left[\left(\bigcup_{i=1}^\infty E_i\right)_z\right] = \mu\left[\bigcup_{i=1}^\infty (E_i)_z\right] = \lim_{i \to \infty} \mu[(E_i)_z],$$

where the last equality uses Theorem 7.1. Since by hypothesis $\mu[(E_i)_z]$ is a measurable function of z, for each i, the last term on the right in (1) is the pointwise limit of a sequence of measurable functions. Hence by Theorem 7.4, it is itself a measurable function, and E is in $\mathscr{E}$. An analogous argument holds if $\{E_i\}$ is a nested decreasing sequence in $\mathcal{E}$. Hence $\mathcal{E}$ is a monotone class. ■

Exercise 8.10 Let (Z, ρ_z) and (W, ρ_w) be metric spaces, and let $\mathfrak{X}$ and $\mathcal{W}$ be the σ-algebras generated by the open sets. Show that if the function g in Theorem 8.9 is continuous, then Q has the Feller property. [*Hint.* Let $f \in C(Z)$. First show that

$$\int_Z f(z')Q(z, dz') = \int_W f[g(z, w)]\mu(dw);$$

and then use the Lebesgue Dominated Convergence Theorem to show that $z_n \to z$ implies that

$$\int_W f[g(z_n, w)]\mu(dw) \to \int_W f[g(z, w)]\mu(dw).]$$

The transition functions we have considered thus far have all been of the form $Q(a, A) = \Pr\{\tilde{z}_{t+1}(\omega) \in A \mid \tilde{z}_t(\omega) = a\}$. That is, we have allowed the probability measure for (the random outcome) $\tilde{z}_{t+1}(\omega)$ to depend on $\tilde{z}_t(\omega)$ but not on $\tilde{z}_{t-1}(\omega)$ or other lagged values. The following exercise shows that this limitation is not restrictive: any second- (or higher-) order Markov process—that is, one in which two (or more) lagged values affect the distribution of the current shock—can be viewed as a first-order process with an expanded state space.

Exercise 8.11 Let $(W, \mathcal{W})$ be a measurable space, and let $P: W \times W \times \mathcal{W} \to [0, 1]$ have the following properties:
   a. for each $(w, w') \in W \times W$, $P(w, w', \cdot): \mathcal{W} \to [0, 1]$ is a probability measure; and
   b. for each $A \in \mathcal{W}$, $P(\cdot, \cdot, A): W \times W \to [0, 1]$ is $(\mathcal{W} \times \mathcal{W})$-measurable.
Define the product space $(Z, \mathfrak{X}) = (W \times W, \mathcal{W} \times \mathcal{W})$. Show that

$$Q[(w, w'), A \times B] = \begin{cases} P(w, w', B) & \text{if } w' \in A \\ 0 & \text{if } w' \notin A; \end{cases}$$

all $w, w' \in W$; all $A, B \in \mathcal{W}$,

defines a transition function on $(Z, \mathfrak{X})$. [*Hint.* Use Theorem 7.13 and the Monotone Class Lemma.]

8.5 Bibliographic Notes

Doob (1953, chap. V) and Gihman and Skorohod (1974, chap. II, sects. 4 and 5) both contain excellent discussions of transition functions and Markov processes. A general proof that, given a transition function on a measurable space, there exists a corresponding stochastic process—the construction of $(Z^\infty, \mathfrak{L}^\infty, \mu^\infty(z_0, \cdot))$ in Section 8.2—is due to Ionescu-Tulcea. The proof may be found in Shiryayev (1984, Theorem 2, pp. 247–249), Neveu (1965, sect. V.1), or Gihman and Skorohod (1974, Theorem 3, pp. 81–82). Our discussion of stochastic kernels in Section 8.3 also draws heavily on the treatment in the lattermost. The proof of Theorem 8.9 follows the one in Futia (1982, Theorem 5.2), where a slightly more general version is given.

9   *Stochastic Dynamic Programming*

With the mathematical background in place, we are ready to study dynamic programming models that incorporate stochastic shocks. We study two specifications of the problem. The first of these parallels more closely the treatment of the deterministic model in Chapter 4, but the second is more general. The two approaches can be illustrated by two variations on the one-sector model of optimal growth.

Suppose that the one good, corn, can be consumed or used as seed. Output in any period depends on the quantity of seed planted and on the quantity of rainfall. Assume that the effect of rainfall is multiplicative. Rainfall is exogenously determined and stochastic, and may be serially correlated from year to year. The functional equation for optimal growth in this economy is

$$v(k, z) = \sup_{y \in [0, zf(k)]} \left\{ U[zf(k) - y] + \beta \int_Z v(y, z')Q(z, dz') \right\}.$$

In this equation the state variables are k, the quantity of seed corn planted in the spring, and z, the quantity of rainfall during the growing season. The only decision to be made is how much seed corn, y, to set aside for the following year. This decision is made in the fall, given $zf(k)$, the quantity of corn harvested. Since no further uncertainty intervenes between fall and spring, y is also the quantity planted in the spring.

Alternatively, consider an economy in which the quantity of rainfall does not fluctuate from year to year but in which there are mice in the storehouse where the seed corn is stored. The size of the mouse population is exogenously determined and stochastic, and may display serial correlation from year to year. Assume that the effect of mice is additive. With rainfall normalized to be unity, the functional equation for optimal growth in this economy is

$$v(k, z) = \sup_{y \in [0, f(k)]} \left\{ U[f(k) - y] + \beta \int_z v(y - z', z') Q(z, dz') \right\}.$$

As in the first model, the state variable k is the quantity of seed corn planted in the spring, and the only decision is how much seed corn, y, to set aside in the fall. In this case, however, the state variable next period depends on the random quantity z' consumed by the mice as well as on y. Since the value of z' is unknown when the storage decision is made, the decision-maker no longer has the power to choose a value for next period's state.

The important difference between these two problems is in the relative timing each period of the decision-making and the resolution of the uncertainty. In the first case the decision is made after the uncertainty is resolved, so we can view the decision-maker in each period as choosing directly the value of next period's state variable. In the second case the decision is made before the uncertainty is resolved, so we must view the decision-maker as choosing an action, and view the value of next period's state as a function of that action and of a random variable (and possibly of the current state).

The second structure is clearly more general: with an appropriate choice of an action space and a law of motion for the endogenous state variable, a model of the first type can always be viewed using the second structure. The reverse is not true. The first structure is a little simpler, however, and offers a more direct parallel to our formulation of the deterministic model in Chapter 4. Moreover, both the results and the lines of argument are very similar for the two structures. Our approach in this chapter is to study the first model in detail and then to indicate how the notation and arguments can be modified to fit the second.

The rest of this chapter is organized as follows. We begin in Section 9.1 by analyzing the relationship between problems stated in terms of sequences and the corresponding functional equations: the Principle of Optimality for stochastic dynamic programs. The results here are fairly general (in the sense that relatively few assumptions on the constraints and return function are required), although not as general as those for the deterministic model. The study of the functional equations, in Sections 9.2–9.4, then proceeds under substantially stronger assumptions. Bounded problems are treated in Section 9.2, and constant-returns-to-scale problems in Section 9.3. In Section 9.4 we provide a theorem for unbounded problems and show how it can be applied to linear-quadratic and logarithmic return functions. Stochastic Euler equations are discussed in Section 9.5. In Section 9.6 we show that the solution to a stochastic functional equation defines a transition function on the state space of the stochastic system; this motivates the study of convergence criteria for Markov processes in Chapters 11 and 12. Chapter 10 contains a variety of economic applications of the material in this chapter.

9.1 The Principle of Optimality

In this section we discuss the relationship between solutions to infinite-horizon programming problems that include stochastic shocks and solutions to the corresponding functional equations. The results connecting these two approaches are not quite as general as they are for deterministic problems, because measurability issues arise in the stochastic case that have no counterpart in deterministic settings.

Let $(X, \mathcal{X})$ and $(Z, \mathcal{Z})$ be measurable spaces, and let $(S, \mathcal{S}) = (X \times Z, \mathcal{X} \times \mathcal{Z})$ be the product space. The set X is the set of possible values for the endogenous state variable, Z is the set of possible values for the exogenous shock, and S is the set of possible states for the system. The evolution of the stochastic shocks is described by a stationary transition function Q on $(Z, \mathcal{Z})$.

We begin by considering decision problems in which in each period t, the decision-maker chooses the value for the endogenous state variable in the subsequent period. The constraints on this choice are described by a correspondence $\Gamma: X \times Z \to X$; that is, $\Gamma(x, z)$ is the set of feasible values for next period's endogenous state variable if the current state is (x, z). Let A be the graph of Γ:

$$A = \{(x, y, z) \in X \times X \times Z: y \in \Gamma(x, z)\}.$$

Let $F: A \to \mathbf{R}$ be the one-period return function; that is, $F(x, y, z)$ is the current-period return if the current state is (x, z) and $y \in \Gamma(x, z)$ is chosen as next period's endogenous state variable. Let $\beta \geq 0$ be the (constant) one-period discount factor. The givens for this problem are $(X, \mathcal{X})$, $(Z, \mathcal{Z})$, Q, Γ, F, and β.

Viewed in sequence form, the problem is as follows. In period 0, with the current state $s_0 = (x_0, z_0)$ known, the decision-maker chooses a value for x_1. In addition, he makes contingency plans for periods $t = 1, 2, \ldots$. He realizes that the decision to be carried out in period t can depend upon the information that will be available at that time. Thus, he chooses a sequence of functions, one for each period $t = 1, 2, \ldots$. The tth function in this sequence specifies a value for x_{t+1} as a function of the information that will be available in period t. For $t \geq 1$, this information is the sequence of shocks $(z_1, z_2, \ldots, z_t)$. He chooses this sequence of functions to maximize the expected discounted sum of returns, where the expectation is over realizations of the shocks. To spell this out precisely, we must decide what functions are available to the decision-maker and what probability measures are used to evaluate the returns they generate.

Define the product spaces $(Z^t, \mathscr{Z}^t)$, $t = 1, 2, \ldots$, and let $z^t = (z_1, \ldots, z_t) \in Z^t$ denote a partial history of shocks in periods 1 through t.

DEFINITION *A **plan** is a value $\pi_0 \in X$ and a sequence of measurable functions $\pi_t \colon Z^t \to X$, $t = 1, 2, \ldots$.*

The interpretation is that $\pi_t(z^t)$ is the value for x_{t+1} that will be chosen in period t if the partial history of shocks observed in periods 1 through t is z^t.

DEFINITION *A plan π is **feasible from** $s_0 \in S$ if*

(1a) $\pi_0 \in \Gamma(s_0)$,

(1b) $\pi_t(z^t) \in \Gamma[\pi_{t-1}(z^{t-1}), z_t]$,   all $z^t \in Z^t$, $t = 1, 2, \ldots$.

The constraints in (1a) and (1b) are the exact analogue of the feasibility constraints in the deterministic case, but the measurability requirements on the π_t's have no counterpart in the deterministic case. Let $\Pi(s_0)$ denote the set of plans that are feasible from s_0.

Our first question is, Under what conditions is $\Pi(s_0)$ nonempty, for all $s_0 \in S$? In the deterministic case, the set of feasible plans was nonempty if the correspondence Γ was nonempty. Here we must also ensure that the measurability requirements can be met. To do this we need the following assumption.

ASSUMPTION 9.1 Γ *is nonempty-valued and the graph of Γ is $(\mathscr{X} \times \mathscr{X} \times \mathscr{Z})$-measurable. In addition, Γ has a measurable selection; that is, there exists a measurable function $h: S \to X$ such that $h(s) \in \Gamma(s)$, all $s \in S$.*

Recall that for the case where X and Z are subsets of Euclidean spaces, Theorem 7.6 provides a sufficient condition for Γ to have a measurable selection. The following result follows immediately from this assumption.

LEMMA 9.1 *Let $(X, \mathscr{X})$, $(Z, \mathscr{Z})$, and Γ be given. Under Assumption 9.1, $\Pi(s_0)$ is nonempty for all $s_0 \in S$.*

Proof. Choose a measurable selection h from Γ. Fix $s_0 \in S$, and define π by

$$\pi_0 = h(s_0),$$

$$\pi_t(z^t) = h[\pi_{t-1}(z^{t-1}), z_t], \quad \text{all } z^t \in Z^t; \ t = 1, 2, \dots.$$

Clearly π satisfies (1a) and (1b) and π_0 is measurable. That each π_t, $t = 1$, $2, \dots$, is measurable then follows by induction from the fact that compositions of measurable functions are measurable (Exercise 7.31). Since $s_0 \in S$ was arbitrary, the desired result is established. ∎

A plan π constructed in this way by using the same measurable selection h from Γ in every period t is said to be *stationary* or *Markov*, since the action it prescribes for each period t depends only on the state $s_t = [\pi_{t-1}(z^{t-1}), z_t]$ in that period. Nonstationary plans can be constructed by using different measurable selections h_t in each period.

Next, consider how total, discounted, expected returns are calculated for a feasible plan. Given the transition function Q on $(Z, \mathscr{Z})$ and the initial state $(x_0, z_0) = s_0 \in S$, define the probability measures $\mu^t(z_0, \cdot): \mathscr{Z}^t \to [0, 1]$, $t = 1, 2, \dots$, as we did in Section 8.2. Recall that the domain of F is the set A, the graph of Γ. Let

$$\mathscr{A} = \{C \in \mathscr{X} \times \mathscr{X} \times \mathscr{Z}: C \subseteq A\}.$$

It is straightforward to show that under Assumption 9.1, $\mathscr{A}$ is a σ-algebra. Notice that if F is $\mathscr{A}$-measurable, then by Exercise 7.31, for any $s_0 \in S$ and any $\pi \in \Pi(s_0)$,

$$F[\pi_{t-1}(z^{t-1}), \pi_t(z^t), z_t] \text{ is } \mathscr{Z}^t\text{-measurable, for } t = 1, 2, \dots.$$

Hence for the stochastic case the following is the counterpart of Assumption 4.2.

ASSUMPTION 9.2 *$F: A \to \mathbf{R}$ is $\mathscr{A}$-measurable, and either (a) or (b) holds.*
a. $F \geq 0$ or $F \leq 0$.
b. For each $(x_0, z_0) = s_0 \in S$ and each plan $\pi \in \Pi(s_0)$,

$$F[\pi_{t-1}(z^{t-1}), \pi_t(z^t), z_t] \text{ is } \mu^t(z_0, \cdot)\text{-integrable, } t = 1, 2, \dots;$$

and the limit

$$F[x_0, \pi_0, z_0] + \lim_{n \to \infty} \sum_{t=1}^{n} \int_{Z^t} \beta^t F[\pi_{t-1}(z^{t-1}), \pi_t(z^t), z_t] \mu^t(z_0, dz^t)$$

exists (although it may be plus or minus infinity).

Notice that if (a) holds, then the limit in (b) is well defined.

Assumption 9.2 ensures that, for each $s_0 \in S$, we can define the functions $u_n(\cdot, s_0): \Pi(s_0) \to \mathbf{R}$, $n = 0, 1, \dots$, by

$$u_0(\pi, s_0) = F[x_0, \pi_0, z_0],$$

$$u_n(\pi, s_0) = F[x_0, \pi_0, z_0]$$

$$+ \sum_{t=1}^{n} \int_{Z^t} \beta^t F[\pi_{t-1}(z^{t-1}), \pi_t(z^t), z_t] \mu^t(z_0, dz^t).$$

Thus $u_n(\pi, s_0)$ is the sum of expected discounted returns in periods 0 through n from the plan π if the initial state is s_0. Assumption 9.2 also ensures that for each $s_0 \in S$ we can define $u(\cdot, s_0): \Pi(s_0) \to \overline{\mathbf{R}}$ to be the limit of this series as the horizon recedes:

$$u(\pi, s_0) = \lim_{n \to \infty} u_n(\pi, s_0).$$

Thus $u(\pi, s_0)$ is the (infinite) sum of expected discounted returns from the plan π if the initial state is s_0.

Under Assumptions 9.1 and 9.2, the function $u(\cdot, s)$ is well defined on the nonempty set $\Pi(s)$, for each $s \in S$. In this case we can define the supremum function $v^*: S \to \overline{\mathbf{R}}$ by

$$(2) \qquad v^*(s) = \sup_{\pi \in \Pi(s)} u(\pi, s).$$

That is, v^* is the unique function satisfying the following two conditions:

$$(3) \qquad v^*(s) \geq u(\pi, s), \quad \text{all } \pi \in \Pi(s);$$

$$(4) \qquad v^*(s) = \lim_{k \to \infty} u(\pi^k, s), \quad \text{for some sequence } \{\pi^k\}_{k=1}^\infty \text{ in } \Pi(s).$$

Now consider the functional equation corresponding to the sequence problem in (2):

$$(5) \qquad v(s) = v(x, z) = \sup_{y \in \Gamma(x,z)} \left[F(x, y, z) + \beta \int v(y, z')Q(z, dz') \right].$$

If there exists a function v satisfying (5), then we can also define the associated policy correspondence G by

$$(6) \qquad G(x, z) = \left\{ y \in \Gamma(x, z): v(x, z) = F(x, y, z) + \beta \int v(y, z')Q(z, dz') \right\}.$$

If G is nonempty and if there exists a measurable selection from G, then we say that π *is generated by G from s_0* if it is formed in the following way. Let $g_0, g_1, \ldots$ be a sequence of measurable selections from G, and define π by

$$\pi_0 = g_0(s_0);$$

$$\pi_t(z^t) = g_t[\pi_{t-1}(z^{t-1}), z_t], \quad \text{all } z^t \in Z^t, t = 1, 2, \ldots.$$

Since $g_t(s) \in G(s) \subseteq \Gamma(s)$, all $s \in S$, it is clear that π satisfies (1a) and (1b); and since each g_t is measurable, it is also clear that π is measurable (by the argument used in the proof of Lemma 9.1). Hence a plan π generated by G from s_0 is feasible from s_0.

Let Assumptions 9.1 and 9.2 hold, so that v^* is well defined, and consider the relationship between solutions to (2) and to (5) and (6). For the deterministic case we had two theorems connecting the supremum function v^* with solutions v to the functional equation, and two theorems connecting optimal plans (when they exist) with plans generated by the policy correspondence G (when that correspondence is nonempty). Theorem 4.2 showed that if the total discounted returns from any feasible plan are well defined, then the supremum function v^* satisfies the functional equation. Theorem 4.3 showed, conversely, that a solution v to the functional equation, if it satisfies a certain boundedness condition, is the supremum function. Theorems 4.4 and 4.5 showed that every optimal plan is generated by G and, conversely, that any plan generated by G and satisfying a boundedness condition is optimal.

For the stochastic case the results concerning the value function are somewhat weaker. First, there is no analogue to Theorem 4.2. Even under conditions ensuring that the supremum function v^* is well defined, that function may not be measurable. Hence the integral in the functional equation may not be well defined. Later in this section we will provide an example due to Blackwell that illustrates this fact. Similarly, because of measurability requirements it may be difficult to verify that (4) holds except by displaying a plan that attains the supremum. Thus the stochastic analogue to Theorem 4.3 requires that the policy correspondence G associated with the function v of interest be nonempty-valued and permit a measurable selection. Under these assumptions, a plan can be generated from G. The results in Theorems 4.4 and 4.5 do have close analogues in the stochastic case.

For the stochastic case, then, we have two main results. The first provides sufficient conditions for a solution v to the functional equation to be the supremum function, and for plans generated by the associated policy correspondence G to attain the supremum. It is the analogue of Theorems 4.3 and 4.5 for the deterministic model and uses a similar boundedness assumption.

THEOREM 9.2 Let $(X, \mathscr{X})$, $(Z, \mathscr{Z})$, Q, Γ, F, and β be given. Let Assumptions 9.1 and 9.2 hold, and let v^* be defined by (2). Let v be a measurable function satisfying the functional equation (5), and such that

(7) $$\lim_{t \to \infty} \int_{Z^t} \beta^t v[\pi_{t-1}(z^{t-1}), z_t] \mu^t(z_0, dz^t) = 0,$$

all $\pi \in \Pi(s_0)$, all $(x_0, z_0) = s_0 \in S$.

Let G be the correspondence defined by (6), and suppose that G is nonempty and permits a measurable selection. Then $v = v^*$, and any plan π^* generated by G attains the supremum in (2).

Proof. As noted above, under Assumptions 9.1 and 9.2, v^* is well defined. Suppose that $v: X \times Z \to \overline{\mathbf{R}}$ satisfies the stated hypotheses. To show that $v = v^*$, it suffices to show that v satisfies (3) and (4). Choose any $(x_0, z_0) = s_0 \in S$. Then for any $\pi \in \Pi(s_0)$,

$$v(s_0) = \sup_{y \in \Gamma(s_0)} \left[F(x_0, y, z_0) + \beta \int_Z v(y, z_1) Q(z_0, dz_1) \right]$$

$$\geq F(x_0, \pi_0, z_0) + \beta \int_Z v(\pi_0, z_1) Q(z_0, dz_1)$$

$$= u_0(\pi, s_0) + \beta \int_Z v(\pi_0, z_1) \mu^1(z_0, dz^1)$$

$$= u_0(\pi, s_0) + \beta \int_Z \left\{ \sup_{y \in \Gamma(\pi_0, z_1)} \left[F(\pi_0, y, z_1) \right. \right.$$

$$\left. \left. + \beta \int_Z v(y, z_2) Q(z_1, dz_2) \right] \right\} \mu^1(z_0, dz^1)$$

$$\geq u_0(\pi, s_0) + \beta \int_Z \left\{ F[\pi_0, \pi_1(z^1), z_1] \right.$$

$$\left. + \beta \int_Z v[\pi_1(z^1), z_2] Q(z_1, dz_2) \right\} \mu^1(z_0, dz^1)$$

$$= u_1(\pi, s_0) + \beta^2 \int_{Z^2} v[\pi_1(z^1), z_2] \mu^2(z_0, dz^2),$$

where the first and fourth lines each use the fact that v satisfies (5); the second and fifth each use the fact that π is feasible from s_0; the third uses the definitions of u_0 and μ^1; and the sixth uses the definition of u_1 and uses Exercise 8.8 to justify combining the two integrals into one operation. It then follows by induction that

$$v(s_0) \geq u_n(\pi, s_0) + \beta^{n+1} \int_{Z^{n+1}} v[\pi_n(z^n), z_{n+1}] \mu^{n+1}(z_0, dz^{n+1}),$$

$$n = 1, 2, 3, \ldots .$$

Taking the limit as $n \to \infty$ and using (7), we conclude that $v(s_0) \geq u(\pi, s_0)$. Since $\pi \in \Pi(s_0)$ was arbitrary, it follows that v satisfies (3).

To show that v also satisfies (4), let π^* be any plan generated by G from s_0; under the stated hypotheses for G there is at least one such plan. Then the argument above can be repeated with equality at every step. Hence (4) holds for the sequence $\pi^k = \pi^*$, $k = 1, 2, \ldots$.

Since $s_0 \in S$ was arbitrary, this establishes that $v = v^*$.   ∎

Our next main result, Theorem 9.4, is a partial converse to Theorem 9.2. It states that under somewhat stronger hypotheses a plan is optimal only if it is generated (a.e.) by G. But before proving this theorem we need one more definition and one preliminary result.

Given any $s_0 \in S$, $\pi \in \Pi(s_0)$, and $z_1 \in Z$, define the *continuation of π following z_1*, call it $C(\pi, z_1)$, as follows:

(8a) $C_0(\pi, z_1) = \pi_1(z_1)$,

(8b) $C_t(z_2^{t+1}; \pi, z_1) = \pi_{t+1}(z_1^{t+1})$,   all $z_2^{t+1} \in Z^t$, $t = 1, 2, \ldots$.

Thus, each function $C_t(\cdot; \pi, z_1) \colon Z^t \to X$, $t = 0, 1, 2, \ldots$, is simply the z_1-section of the function π_{t+1}. Hence by Theorem 7.14 these functions are measurable. Moreover, it is clear that they satisfy the feasibility constraints in (1a) and (1b). Hence for each $z_1 \in Z$, $C(\pi, z_1)$ is a feasible plan from (π_0, z_1).

Exercise 9.1   Show that if $\pi \in \Pi(s_0)$, then $u[C(\pi, z_1), (\pi_0, z_1)]$ is a measurable function of z_1. [*Hint.* Use Theorem 7.14 and Exercise 7.31.]

Our next result establishes that u, evaluated at a plan and its continuations, satisfies a recursive relation analogous to the one in the functional equation. The lemma requires the following strengthening of Assumption 9.2.

ASSUMPTION 9.3   *If F takes on both signs, there is a collection of nonnegative, measurable functions $L_t \colon S \to \mathbf{R}_+$, $t = 0, 1, \ldots$, such that for all $\pi \in \Pi(s_0)$ and all $s_0 \in S$*

$$|F(x_0, \pi_0, z_0)| \leq L_0(s_0);$$

$$|F[\pi_{t-1}(z^{t-1}), \pi_t(z^t), z_t]| \leq L_t(s_0),   \text{all } z^t \in Z^t, t = 1, 2, \ldots;$$

and

$$\sum_{t=0}^{\infty} \beta^t L_t(s_0) < \infty.$$

LEMMA 9.3 *Let* $(X, \mathscr{X})$, $(Z, \mathscr{Z})$, Q, Γ, F, *and* β *be given. Suppose that Assumptions 9.1–9.3 hold. Then for any* $(x_0, z_0) = s_0 \in S$ *and any* $\pi \in \Pi(s_0)$,

$$(9) \qquad u(\pi, s_0) = F(x_0, \pi_0, z_0) + \beta \int_Z u[C(\pi, z_1), (\pi_0, z_1)] Q(z_0, dz_1),$$

where for each $z_1 \in Z$, $C(\pi, z_1)$ *is the continuation of* π *following* z_1.

Proof. Let $(x_0, z_0) = s_0 \in S$ and $\pi \in \Pi(s_0)$ be given, and suppose that $F \geq 0$. Under Assumption 9.2, $u(\pi, s_0)$ is well defined, and

$$(10) \qquad u(\pi, s_0)$$

$$= F(x_0, \pi_0, z_0) + \lim_{n \to \infty} \sum_{t=1}^{n} \int_{Z^t} \beta^t F[\pi_{t-1}(z^{t-1}), \pi_t(z^t), z_t] \mu^t(z_0, dz^t).$$

For the second term on the right we have

$$\lim_{n \to \infty} \sum_{t=1}^{n} \int_{Z^t} \beta^t F[\pi_{t-1}(z^{t-1}), \pi_t(z^t), z_t] \mu^t(z_0, dz^t)$$

$$= \lim_{n \to \infty} \int_Z \left\{ \beta F[\pi_0, \pi_1(z_1), z_1] \right.$$

$$\left. + \sum_{t=2}^{n} \left[\int_{Z^{t-1}} \beta^t F[\pi_{t-1}(z^{t-1}), \pi_t(z^t), z_t] \mu^{t-1}(z_1, dz_2^t) \right] \right\} Q(z_0, dz_1)$$

$$= \int_Z \lim_{n \to \infty} \left\{ \beta F[\pi_0, \pi_1(z_1), z_1] \right.$$

$$\left. + \sum_{t=2}^{n} \left[\int_{Z^{t-1}} \beta^t F[\pi_{t-1}(z^{t-1}), \pi_t(z^t), z_t] \mu^{t-1}(z_1, dz_2^t) \right] \right\} Q(z_0, dz_1)$$

$$= \int_Z \beta \lim_{n \to \infty} \left\{ F[\pi_0, C_0(\pi, z_1), z_1] \right.$$

$$\left. + \int_{Z^1} \beta^t F[C_0(\pi, z_1), C_1(z_2; \pi, z_1), z_2] \mu^1(z_1, dz_2) \right.$$

$$+ \sum_{t=3}^{n} \left[\int_{Z^{t-1}} \beta^{t-1} F[C_{t-2}(z_2^{t-1}; \pi, z_1), C_{t-1}(z_2^t; \pi, z_1), z_t] \right.$$

$$\left. \times \mu^{t-1}(z_1, dz_2^t) \right] \bigg\} Q(z_0, dz_1)$$

$$= \beta \int_Z u[C(\pi, z_1), (\pi_0, z_1)] Q(z_0, dz_1),$$

where the first line uses Exercise 8.8 to justify breaking up the integral over Z^t into two parts, the second uses the Monotone Convergence Theorem (Theorem 7.8) to exchange the order of limit and integration (cf. Exercise 7.22), the third uses (8a) and (8b), and the last again uses the definition of u. Substituting into (10) then gives the desired result.

If $F \le 0$, the argument above can be applied to the function $-F$.

If F takes on both signs, then Assumption 9.3 holds. Define the sequence of functions $H_n: Z \to \mathbf{R}$ by

$$H_n(z_1) = \beta F[\pi_0, \pi_1(z_1), z_1]$$

$$+ \sum_{t=2}^{n} \left\{ \int_{Z^{t-1}} \beta^t F[\pi_{t-1}(z^{t-1}), \pi_t(z^t), z_t] \mu^{t-1}(z_1, dz_2^t) \right\},$$

$$n = 2, 3, \ldots .$$

Assumption 9.3 implies that there exists a constant $\bar{L} = \sum_{t=0}^{\infty} \beta^t L_t(s_0)$ with the property that $|H_n(z_1)| \le \bar{L}$, all $z_1 \in Z$, all n. Hence the argument above applies, with the Lebesgue Dominated Convergence Theorem (Theorem 7.10) justifying the change in the order of limit and integration. ■

The crucial steps in this proof are the use of Exercise 8.8 to break up the integration over Z^t into two steps, and the application of the Monotone Convergence Theorem or the Lebesgue Dominated Convergence Theorem to justify changing the order of limit and integration. Notice that it is the latter step that requires the assumption that either F takes on only one sign or else Assumption 9.3 holds. Clearly there are many variations on the latter assumption—variations involving more complicated bounds on F—that could also be used to justify this step.

With Lemma 9.3 in hand we are ready to prove the next main result of this section: if Lemma 9.3 applies, then any plan π^* that attains the supremum in (2) is generated (a.e.) by G.

THEOREM 9.4 *Let $(X, \mathcal{X})$, $(Z, \mathcal{Z})$, Q, Γ, F, and β be given. Let Assumptions 9.1–9.3 hold, and define v^* by (2). Assume that v^* is measurable and satisfies (5), and define the correspondence G by (6). Assume that G is nonempty and permits a measurable selection. Let $(x_0, z_0) = s_0 \in S$, and let $\pi^* \in \Pi(s_0)$ be a plan that attains the supremum in (2) for initial condition s_0. Then there exists a plan π^G generated by G from s_0 such that*

$$\pi_0^G = \pi_0^*, \quad \text{and}$$

$$\pi_t^G(z^t) = \pi_t^*(z^t), \quad \mu^t(z_0, \cdot)\text{-a.e.}, \quad t = 1, 2, \ldots.$$

Proof. Notice that under the stated hypotheses, Theorem 9.2 and Lemma 9.3 apply. Let π^* be a plan that attains the supremum in (2). Since G is defined by (6), it is sufficient to show that

(11a) $\quad v^*(s_0) = F(x_0, \pi_0^*, z_0) + \beta \int_Z v^*(\pi_0^*, z_1) Q(z_0, dz_1),$

(11b) $\quad v^*[\pi_{t-1}^*(z^{t-1}), z_t]$

$$= F[\pi_{t-1}^*(z^{t-1}), \pi_t^*(z^t), z_t] + \beta \int v^*[\pi_t^*(z^t), z_{t+1}] Q(z_t, dz_{t+1}),$$

$$\mu^t(z_0, \cdot)\text{-a.e.}, \quad t = 1, 2, \ldots.$$

Consider (11a). By hypothesis π^* satisfies

(12) $\quad v^*(s_0) = u(\pi^*, s_0) \geq u(\pi, s_0), \quad \text{all } \pi \in \Pi(s_0).$

Hence by Lemma 9.3 we can substitute from (9) to get

(13) $\quad F(x_0, \pi_0^*, z_0) + \beta \int u[C(\pi^*, z_1), (\pi_0^*, z_1)] Q(z_0, dz_1)$

$$\geq F(x_0, \pi_0, z_0) + \beta \int u[C(\pi, z_1), (\pi_0, z_1)] Q(z_0, dz_1),$$

$$\text{all } \pi \in \Pi(s_0).$$

In particular, (13) holds for any plan $\pi \in \Pi(s_0)$ with $\pi_0 = \pi_0^*$.

Choose a measurable selection g from G, and define the plan $\pi^g \in \Pi(s_0)$ as follows:

$$\pi_0^g = \pi_0^*, \quad \text{and}$$

$$\pi_t^g(z^t) = g[\pi_{t-1}^g(z^{t-1}), z_t], \quad \text{all } z^t \in Z^t, t = 1, 2, \ldots.$$

For each $z_1 \in Z$, the continuation $C(\pi^g, z_1)$ is a plan generated by G from (π_0^*, z_1). Hence by Theorem 9.2, $C(\pi^g, z_1)$ attains the supremum in (2) for $s = (\pi_0^*, z_1)$. That is,

$$(14) \qquad v^*(\pi_0^*, z_1) = u[C(\pi^g, z_1), (\pi_0^*, z_1)] \geq u[\pi, (\pi_0^*, z_1)],$$

$$\text{all } \pi \in \Pi(\pi_0^*, z_1), \text{ all } z_1 \in Z.$$

In particular, since $C(\pi^*, z_1) \in \Pi(\pi_0^*, z_1)$, all $z_1 \in Z$, (14) implies that

$$u[C(\pi^g, z_1), (\pi_0^*, z_1)] \geq u[C(\pi^*, z_1), (\pi_0^*, z_1)], \quad \text{all } z_1 \in Z;$$

and since $\pi^g \in \Pi(s_0)$ and $\pi_0^g = \pi_0^*$, (13) implies that

$$\int u[C(\pi^*, z_1), (\pi_0^*, z_1)]Q(z_0, dz_1)$$

$$\geq \int u[C(\pi^g, z_1), (\pi_0^*, z_1)]Q(z_0, dz_1).$$

By Exercise 7.24, these two inequalities together imply that

$$u[C(\pi^g, z_1), (\pi_0^*, z_1)] = u[C(\pi^*, z_1), (\pi_0^*, z_1)], \quad Q(z_0, \cdot)\text{-a.e.}$$

It then follows from (14) that

$$(15) \qquad v^*(\pi_0^*, z_1) = u[C(\pi^*, z_1), (\pi_0^*, z_1)], \quad Q(z_0, \cdot)\text{-a.e.}$$

Hence

$$v^*(s_0) = u(\pi^*, s_0)$$

$$= F(x_0, \pi_0^*, z_0) + \beta \int u[C(\pi^*, z_1), (\pi_0^*, z_1)]Q(z_0, dz_1)$$

$$= F(x_0, \pi_0^*, z_0) + \beta \int v^*(\pi_0^*, z_1)Q(z_0, dz_1),$$

where the second line uses Lemma 9.3, and the last uses (15) and Exercise 7.24. Hence (11a) holds, as was to be shown.

Use an analogous argument, with (15) in place of (12) as the starting point, to show that (11b) holds for $t = 1$, and continue by induction. ∎

The following exercise treats the case where F is bounded above or below, but not by zero, and Assumptions 9.2b and 9.3 fail. The exercise shows that if $\beta < 1$, then this case can be treated by an argument analogous to the one used if F takes on only one sign.

Exercise 9.2 Suppose that F is $\mathscr{A}$-measurable, F is uniformly bounded above or below (not necessarily by zero), and $\beta < 1$.

a. Show that $u(\cdot, s_0): \Pi(s_0) \to \overline{\mathbf{R}}$ is well defined. Show that if in addition Assumption 9.1 holds, then v^* is well defined.

b. Show that Theorem 9.2, Lemma 9.3, and Theorem 9.4 still hold.

These are the main results for the first formulation discussed in the introduction. Next we turn to a brief discussion of what can happen if the hypotheses of Theorem 9.2 fail. The main problem is that v^* may not be a measurable function, even if Γ and Q are well behaved and F is measurable. If this happens, the integral in the functional equation is not defined for $v = v^*$, so v^* does not satisfy the functional equation. To see that v^* may be nonmeasurable, consider the following example, taken from Blackwell (1965). Let $X = Z = [0, 1]$, with the Borel sets $\mathscr{X}$ and $\mathscr{Z}$, and let $\Gamma(s) = [0, 1]$, all $s \in S$. Thus Assumption 9.1 is satisfied. Let the transition function be

$$Q(z, C) = \begin{cases} 1 & \text{if } z \in C \\ 0 & \text{if } z \notin C, \end{cases} \quad \text{all } z \in Z, \text{ all } C \in \mathscr{Z}.$$

Hence the sequence of shocks $(z_0, z_1, \ldots)$ is a constant sequence with probability one. Let $E \subseteq X \times Z = [0, 1]^2$ be a Borel-measurable set with the following property: the projection of E onto Z, the set

$$\text{Proj}_z \, E = \{z \in Z: (y, z) \in E, \text{ for some } y \in X\},$$

is *not* Borel-measurable. (Unfortunately, sets E of this sort exist; see Behnke et al. 1974, pp. 465–474.) Define the return function F by

$$F(x, y, z) = \begin{cases} 1 & \text{if } (y, z) \in E \\ 0 & \text{if } (y, z) \notin E, \end{cases}$$

and let $0 < \beta < 1$; then clearly Assumption 9.2 holds. Moreover, for any initial state s_0, the optimum is attained by a feasible plan of the form

$$\pi_t(z^t) = \hat{y}, \quad \text{all } z^t \in Z^t, t = 1, 2, \ldots,$$

where $\hat{y}$ is chosen so that $(\hat{y}, z_0) \in E$, if any such $\hat{y}$ exists. That is, the optimum can always be attained by a policy that is constant over time. Since $\text{Proj}_z E$ is not a Borei set, however, the value function v^* is not measurable.

To see where the problem arises, define a *global plan* to be one that is defined for all initial states. That is, a global plan P is a sequence of measurable functions $P_t: S \times Z^t \to X, t = 0, 1, \ldots$. For any global plan P and any $s \in S$, let P^s denote the s-section of P; clearly any such section is a plan according to the original definition. Call a global plan *feasible* if for each $s \in S$, P^s is feasible from s. It is straightforward to show that, if P is a feasible global plan and if Assumption 9.2 holds, then $u(P^s, s)$ is a measurable function of s.

Now recall that if v^* is well defined it is the unique function satisfying (3) and (4). Suppose that this is the case, and for each $s \in S$, choose a sequence $\{\pi^{s,k}\}_{k=1}^{\infty}$ satisfying (4). These sequences can be used in the obvious way to define a sequence of functions $\{P^k\}_{k=1}^{\infty}$:

$$P_t^k(s, z^t) = \pi^{s,k}(z^t), \quad \text{all } s \in S; z^t \in Z^t; t = 0, 1, \ldots; k = 1, 2, \ldots.$$

Now the s-section of each function P^k is simply $\pi^{s,k}$ and hence is a feasible plan from $s \in S$. Hence we can define the functions $w^k: S \to \overline{\mathbf{R}}$ by

$$w^k(s) = u(P^{k,s}, s) = u(\pi^{s,k}, s), \quad \text{all } s \in S, k = 1, 2, \ldots.$$

Taking the limit as $k \to \infty$, we find that

$$\lim_{k \to \infty} w^k(s) = \lim_{k \to \infty} u(\pi^{s,k}, s), \quad \text{all } s \in S.$$

If each of the functions P^k is a global plan—that is, if it satisfies the measurability requirements—then each of the functions w^k is measurable. In this case the pointwise limit of these functions, v^*, is also measurable. However, the assumptions imposed thus far do not ensure that the P^k's satisfy the measurability requirements of a global plan.

In the remaining sections of this chapter, we will impose continuity restrictions on the return function F and on the correspondence Γ describing the feasibility constraints that are sufficient to ensure that v^* is continuous and that optimal policies exist. Before doing that, however, in the rest of this section we will discuss the relationship between solutions to sequence problems and to the corresponding functional equations for the second type of situation described in the introduction. The arguments are very similar to the ones above, and we will leave most of them as exercises.

Let $(X, \mathscr{X})$, $(Z, \mathscr{Z})$, $(S, \mathscr{S})$, Q, and β be as specified before. In addition, let $(Y, \mathscr{Y})$ be a measurable space. The set Y is the set of possible actions the decision-maker may take. In each period t, the decision-maker chooses an action from a specified subset of feasible alternatives in the set Y. The constraints on these choices are described by a correspondence $\Gamma: X \times Z \to Y$; that is, $\Gamma(x, z)$ is the set of feasible actions if the current state is (x, z). Define A to be the graph of Γ:

$$A = \{(x, y, z) \in X \times Y \times Z: y \in \Gamma(x, z)\}.$$

The one-period return function F is defined on this set, $F: A \to \mathbf{R}$; that is, $F(x, y, z)$ is the current-period return if the current state is (x, z) and the action $y \in \Gamma(x, z)$ is chosen.

We must also describe the evolution of the variable x. Let

$$D = \{(x, y) \in X \times Y: y \in \Gamma(x, z), \text{ for some } z \in Z\},$$

and let $\phi: D \times Z \to X$ be the law of motion for the state variable. That is, $x' = \phi(x, y, z')$ is the next period's value for the endogenous state variable, if x is the current value, the action y is taken, and z' is the value of next period's exogenous shock. Thus, the givens for this problem are $(X, \mathscr{X})$, $(Y, \mathscr{Y})$, $(Z, \mathscr{Z})$, Q, Γ, F, β, and ϕ.

Viewed in sequence form the problem is as follows. In period $t = 0$, with s_0 known, the decision-maker chooses an action y_0 and a sequence of functions describing actions to be taken in later periods. As before, the decision to be carried out in period t can depend upon the information available in that period, the partial history of shocks z^t.

DEFINITION *A **plan** is a sequence of functions* $\pi = \{\pi_t\}_{t=0}^{\infty}$, *where*

$\pi_t: Z^t \rightarrow Y$ is $\mathcal{Z}^t$-measurable, $t = 1, 2, \ldots$. A plan π is **feasible from** s_0 if in addition it satisfies

(1a') $\pi_0 \in \Gamma(s_0)$;

(1b') $\pi_t(z^t) \in \Gamma[x_t^\pi(z^t), z_t]$,   all $z^t \in Z^t, t = 1, 2, \ldots$.

where the functions $x_t^\pi: Z^t \rightarrow X, t = 1, 2, \ldots$, are defined recursively by

(16a) $x_1^\pi(z_1) = \phi(x_0, \pi_0, z_1)$,   all $z_1 \in Z$;

(16b) $x_t^\pi(z^t) = \phi[x_{t-1}^\pi(z^{t-1}), \pi_{t-1}(z^{t-1}), z_t]$,   all $z^t \in Z^t, t = 2, 3, \ldots$.

Thus, a plan consists of a sequence of functions describing the action y_t in each period t as a measurable function of the history of shocks z^t in periods 1 through t. A feasible plan is one that in addition satisfies the feasiblity constraints described by Γ, given the law of motion ϕ. For each $s_0 \in S$, let $\Pi(s_0)$ denote the set of all feasible plans from s_0; and for any plan $\pi \in \Pi(s_0)$, define $x^\pi = \{x_t^\pi\}_{t=1}^\infty$ as in (16).

Two conditions are needed to ensure that $\Pi(s)$ is nonempty. One is exactly analogous to the condition in Assumption 9.1; the other is a restriction on the law of motion ϕ.

ASSUMPTION 9.1' Γ *is nonempty-valued; the graph of* Γ *is* $(\mathcal{X} \times \mathcal{Y} \times \mathcal{Z})$-*measurable; and* Γ *has a measurable selection. That is, there exists a measurable function* $h: S \rightarrow Y$ *such that* $h(s) \in \Gamma(s)$, *all* $s \in S$. *In addition, the function* $\phi: D \times Z \rightarrow X$ *is measurable.*

Exercise 9.3 Show that under Assumption 9.1', $\Pi(s)$ is non-empty, all $s \in S$.

Next, consider how total discounted, expected returns are calculated for a feasible plan. Let the probability measures $\mu^t(z_0, \cdot)$ be as before, and let

$$\mathcal{A} = \{C \in \mathcal{X} \times \mathcal{Y} \times \mathcal{Z}: C \subseteq A\}.$$

The following is the counterpart of Assumption 9.2.

ASSUMPTION 9.2′ *F is 𝒜-measurable, and either (a) or (b) holds.*

  a. $F \geq 0$ or $F \leq 0$.

  b. *For each* $(x_0, z_0) = s_0 \in S$ *and each* $\pi \in \Pi(s_0)$,

$$F[x_t^\pi(z^t), \pi_t(z^t), z_t] \text{ is } \mu^t(z_0, \cdot)\text{-integrable}, \quad t = 1, 2, \ldots;$$

and the limit

$$F(x_0, \pi_0, z_0) + \lim_{n \to \infty} \sum_{t=1}^n \int_{Z^t} \beta^t F[x_t^\pi(z^t), \pi_t(z^t), z_t] \mu^t(z_0, dz^t)$$

exists (although it may be plus or minus infinity).

Note that, as before, if (a) holds the limit in (b) is well defined.

Under Assumption 9.2′, we can define the functions u_n and u as before:

$$u_0(\pi, s_0) = F(x_0, \pi_0, z_0);$$

$$u_n(\pi, s_0) = F(x_0, \pi_0, z_0) + \sum_{t=1}^n \int_{Z^t} \beta^t F[x_t^\pi(z^t), \pi_t(z^t), z_t] \mu^t(z_0, dz^t),$$

$$n = 1, 2, \ldots;$$

$$u(\pi, s_0) = \lim_{n \to \infty} u_n(\pi, s_0).$$

If Assumptions 9.1′ and 9.2′ both hold, then for each $s_0 \in S$, $u(\cdot, s_0)$ is well defined on the nonempty set $\Pi(s_0)$. In this case we can define the supremum function $v^*: S \to \overline{\mathbf{R}}$ by (2), so v^* is, as before, the unique function satisfying (3) and (4).

Now consider the corresponding functional equation and policy correspondence

(5′) $$v(s) = \sup_{y \in \Gamma(s)} \left\{ F(x, y, z) + \beta \int v[\phi(x, y, z'), z'] Q(z, dz') \right\},$$

(6′) $$G(s) = \left\{ y \in \Gamma(s): v(s) = F(x, y, z) + \beta \int v[\phi(x, y, z'), z'] Q(z, dz') \right\}.$$

If G is nonempty and if there exists at least one measurable selection from G, then we say that π *is generated by G from s_0* if it is formed in the following way. Let $g_0, g_1, \ldots$ be a sequence of measurable selections from G, and define π by

$$\pi_0 = g_0(x_0, z_0);$$

$$\pi_t(z^t) = g_t[x_t^\pi(z^t), z_t], \quad \text{all } z^t \in Z^t, t = 1, 2, \ldots .$$

It is clear that π satisfies (1a$'$) and (1b$'$), and since each g_t is measurable, clearly π is also measurable. Hence, any plan generated by G from s_0 is a feasible plan from s_0.

With this notation in place, we can establish the following result, the analogue of Theorem 9.2.

> **Exercise 9.4**   Let $(X, \mathcal{X})$, $(Y, \mathcal{Y})$, $(Z, \mathcal{Z})$, Q, Γ, F, β, and ϕ be given. Let Assumption 9.1$'$ and 9.2$'$ hold and let v^* be defined by (2). Let v be a (measurable) function satisfying (5$'$) and such that
>
> (7$'$) $\displaystyle \lim_{t \to \infty} \int_{Z^t} \beta^t v[x_t^\pi(z^t), z_t] \mu^t(z_0, dz^t) = 0,$
>
> all $\pi \in \Pi(x_0, z_0)$, all $(x_0, z_0) \in X \times Z$.
>
> Let G be the correspondence defined by (6$'$), and suppose that G is nonempty and permits at least one measurable selection. Show that $v = v^*$ and that any policy π^* generated by G attains the supremum in (2).

Given any feasible plan $\pi \in \Pi(s_0)$ and any fixed $z_1 \in Z$, define the *continuation of π following z_1*, call it $C(\pi, z_1)$, as we did before by (8). That is, $C(\pi, z_1)$ is the z_1-section of π. Clearly $C(\pi, z_1)$ is a feasible plan from $[\phi(x_0, \pi_0, z_1), z_1] \in S$. We then have the following analogue of Assumption 9.3.

ASSUMPTION 9.3$'$ *If F takes on both signs, there is a collection of nonnegative, measurable functions $L_t: S \to \mathbf{R}_+$, $t = 0, 1, \ldots$, such that for all $\pi \in \Pi(s_0)$*

and all $s_0 \in S$,

$$|F[x_0, \pi_0, z_0]| \le L_0(s_0);$$

$$|F[x_t^\pi(z^t), \pi_t(z^t), z_t]| \le L_t(s_0), \quad \text{all } z^t \in Z^t, t = 1, 2, \ldots;$$

and

$$\sum_{t=0}^{\infty} \beta^t L_t(s_0) < \infty.$$

Under this additional assumption we have the analogues of Theorems 9.3 and 9.4.

Exercise 9.5 Let $(X, \mathcal{X})$, $(Y, \mathcal{Y})$, $(Z, \mathcal{Z})$, Q, Γ, F, β, and ϕ be given, and suppose that Assumptions 9.1'–9.3' hold.
a. Show that

$$u(\pi, s_0) = F(x_0, \pi_0, z_0) + \beta \int_Z u[C(\pi, z_1), (x_1^\pi(z_1), z_1)]Q(z_0, dz_1),$$

all $(x_0, z_0) = s_0 \in S$, all $\pi \in \Pi(s_0)$.

b. Define v^* by (2), and assume that v^* is measurable and satisfies (5'). Define the correspondence G by (6'), and assume that G is non-empty and permits a measurable selection. Let $(x_0, z_0) = s_0 \in S$, and let $\pi^* \in \Pi(s_0)$ be a plan that attains the supremum in (2) for initial condition s_0. Show that there exists a plan π^G generated by G from s_0 such that

$$\pi_0^G = \pi_0^*, \quad \text{and}$$

$$\pi_t^G(z^t) = \pi_t^*(z^t), \quad \mu^t(z_0, \cdot)\text{-a.e.}, \quad t = 1, 2, \ldots.$$

9.2 Bounded Returns

In this section we study functional equations of the two forms discussed in the introduction to this chapter:

(1) $v(x, z) = \sup_{y \in \Gamma(x,z)} \left\{ F(x, y, z) + \beta \int_Z v(y, z')Q(z, dz') \right\},$ and

(2) $v(x, z) = \sup_{y \in \Gamma(x,z)} \left\{ F(x, y, z) + \beta \int_Z v[\phi(x, y, z'), z']Q(z, dz') \right\},$

under the assumption that the return function F is bounded and continuous, the discount factor β is strictly less than one, and the transition
function Q has the Feller property. Mathematically, the difference between the functional equation studied in Chapter 4 and (1) and (2) above
is the presence in the latter of the exogenous stochastic shocks z, z', and
the resulting integral with respect to $Q(z, \cdot)$. But it is shown below that,
under the same assumptions about X used in Chapter 4 and suitable
restrictions on the shocks, the required mathematical properties of the
function v are preserved under integration. Thus, the results for the
deterministic model carry over virtually without change. Our approach
in this section is first to study (1) and then to indicate how the arguments
can be modified to fit (2).

As in the last section, let $(X, \mathscr{X})$ and $(Z, \mathscr{Z})$ be measurable spaces of
possible values for the endogenous and exogenous state variables, re-
spectively; let $(S, \mathscr{S}) = (X \times Z, \mathscr{X} \times \mathscr{Z})$ be the product space; let Q be a
transition function on $(Z, \mathscr{Z})$; let $\Gamma: S \to X$ be a correspondence describing the feasibility constraints; let A be the graph of Γ; let $F: A \to \mathbf{R}$ be the
one-period return function; and let $\beta \geq 0$ be the discount factor. Thus,
the givens for the problem we will study are $(X, \mathscr{X}), (Z, \mathscr{Z}), Q, \Gamma, F,$ and β.
We will use A_z, A_{yz}, and so on to denote the sections of A.

Our first assumption, which restricts X, is precisely the one used
throughout Chapter 4. The second puts restrictions on Z and Q.

ASSUMPTION 9.4   *X is a convex Borel set in* $\mathbf{R}^l$, *with its Borel subsets* $\mathscr{X}$.

ASSUMPTION 9.5   *One of the following conditions holds:*
   a. Z is a countable set and $\mathscr{Z}$ *is the* σ-*algebra containing all subsets of Z; or*
   b. Z is a compact (Borel) set in $\mathbf{R}^k$, *with its Borel subsets* $\mathscr{Z}$, *and the transition*
      function Q on $(Z, \mathscr{Z})$ *has the Feller property.*

If $Z \subset \mathbf{R}^k$, we require that the Markov operator associated with Q map
the space of bounded continuous functions on Z into itself (cf. Section
8.1). If Z is a countable set, we use the discrete metric and all functions

on Z are continuous, so this requirement would be vacuous. Notice that a sequence $\{s_n = (x_n, z_n)\}$ in S converges to $s = (x, z) \in S$ if and only if $x_n \to x$ and $z_n \to z$. Therefore, if Z is a countable set, a function on S is continuous if and only if each z-section $f(\cdot, z): X \to \mathbf{R}$ is continuous. As before we take $C(S)$ to be the space of bounded continuous functions $f: S \to \mathbf{R}$ with the sup norm, $\|f\| = \sup_{s \in S} |f(s)|$. We stress, as we did in Chapter 4, that many of the results below apply much more broadly, and the arguments here can easily be adapted to other situations.

The following lemma shows that, under these two assumptions, integration preserves the required properties of the integrand in (1)—boundedness, continuity, monotonicity, and concavity. This lemma is the basis for showing that the arguments presented in Chapter 4 can be applied here as well.

LEMMA 9.5 *Let $(X, \mathcal{X})$, $(Z, \mathcal{Z})$, and Q satisfy Assumptions 9.4 and 9.5. If $f: X \times Z \to \mathbf{R}$ is bounded and continuous, then Mf defined by*

$$(Mf)(y, z) = \int f(y, z')Q(z, dz'), \quad \text{all } (y, z) \in X \times Z,$$

is also; that is, $M: C(S) \to C(S)$. If f is increasing (strictly increasing) in each of its first l arguments, then so is Mf; and if f is concave (strictly concave) jointly in its first l arguments, then so is Mf.

Proof. Suppose that f is bounded and continuous. Since for each $z \in Z$, $Q(z, \cdot)$ is a probability measure, it is clear that $\|Mf\| \le \|f\|$. Hence Mf is bounded. To see that Mf is continuous, choose a sequence $(y_n, z_n) \to (y, z)$. Then

$$|(Mf)(y, z) - (Mf)(y_n, z_n)|$$

$$\le |(Mf)(y, z) - (Mf)(y, z_n)| + |(Mf)(y, z_n) - (Mf)(y_n, z_n)|$$

(3) $$\le |(Mf)(y, z) - (Mf)(y, z_n)| + \int |f(y, z') - f(y_n, z')|Q(z_n, dz').$$

There are two possibilities, corresponding to the two possibilities for the space Z admitted by Assumption 9.5.

If Z is a countable set, then $z_n \to z$ implies that $z_n = z$ for all n sufficiently large. Hence as $n \to \infty$ the first term in (3) vanishes and $Q(z_n, \cdot) = Q(z, \cdot)$ is a fixed probability measure. Moreover, the functions $h_n(z') =$

$|f(y, z') - f(y_n, z')|$, $n = 1, 2, \ldots$, are all measurable; the sequence of functions $\{h_n\}$ converges pointwise to the zero function; and each term in the sequence is bounded above by the constant function $2\|f\|$. Hence by the Lebesgue Dominated Convergence Theorem (Theorem 7.10),

$$\lim_{n\to\infty} \int h_n(z')Q(z, dz') = \int \lim_{n\to\infty} h_n(z')Q(z, dz') = 0,$$

and the second term in (3) also vanishes.

Alternatively, suppose that Z is a compact set in $\mathbf{R}^k$. The fact that Q has the Feller property implies that the first term in (3) vanishes as $n \to \infty$. Moreover, since $y_n \to y$, it follows that there exists a compact set $D \subseteq X$ such that $y_n \in D$, all n, and $y \in D$. Since f is continuous, it is uniformly continuous on the compact set $D \times Z$. That is, for every $\varepsilon > 0$, there exists $N \geq 1$ such that

$$|f(y, z') - f(y_n, z')| < \varepsilon, \quad \text{all } n > N, \text{ all } z' \in Z.$$

Hence the second term in (3) vanishes as $n \to \infty$.

That weak monotonicity in y is preserved is obvious. To see that strict monotonicity is preserved, choose $y, \hat{y} \in X$ such that $y \leq \hat{y}$ and $y \neq \hat{y}$. Then $f(y, z') < f(\hat{y}, z')$, all $z' \in Z$. The desired conclusion then follows from Exercises 7.18 and 7.24.

To see that concavity is preserved, choose $y, \hat{y} \in X$, with $y \neq \hat{y}$, and for any $\theta \in (0, 1)$, let $y_\theta = \theta y + (1 - \theta)\hat{y}$. If f is concave in y, then

$$(Mf)(y_\theta, z) = \int f(y_\theta, z')Q(z, dz')$$

$$(4) \qquad\qquad \geq \int [\theta f(y, z') + (1 - \theta)f(\hat{y}, z')]Q(z, dz')$$

$$= \theta(Mf)(y, z) + (1 - \theta)(Mf)(\hat{y}, z),$$

$$\text{all } z \in Z, \text{ all } \theta \in (0, 1).$$

If f is strictly concave in y, then

$$f(y_\theta, z') > \theta f(y, z') + (1 - \theta)f(\hat{y}, z'), \quad \text{all } z' \in Z, \text{ all } \theta \in (0, 1),$$

and it follows from Exercises 7.18 and 7.24 that the inequality in (4) is also strict. ∎

In some situations the requirement that the set $Z \subset \mathbf{R}^k$ be compact is very unattractive. In fact, it can be dispensed with; but the proof of Lemma 9.5 becomes more complicated. We defer this proof until Section 12.6, when the required mathematical tools will have been developed.

With Lemma 9.5 in hand, it is straightforward to show that all of the results proved for deterministic dynamic programs have analogues when stochastic shocks are added. The next two assumptions are analogues to those used throughout Section 4.2.

ASSUMPTION 9.6 *The correspondence* $\Gamma: X \times Z \to X$ *is nonempty, compact-valued, and continuous.*

ASSUMPTION 9.7 *The function* $F: A \to \mathbf{R}$ *is bounded and continuous, and* $\beta \in (0, 1)$.

If Z is a countable set, we interpret Assumption 9.6 to mean that for each fixed $z \in Z$, the correspondence $\Gamma(\cdot, z): X \to X$ is nonempty, compact-valued, and continuous. Similarly, in this case Assumption 9.7 means that for each fixed $z \in Z$, the function $F(\cdot, \cdot, z): A_z \to \mathbf{R}$ (the z-section of F) is continuous.

The following exercise shows that under these assumptions, Theorems 9.2 and 9.4 hold.

Exercise 9.6 Show that under Assumptions 9.4–9.7, Assumptions 9.1–9.3 are satisfied. [*Hint.* Use the Measurable Selection Theorem (Theorem 7.6).]

Under these same assumptions, we have the following basic result.

THEOREM 9.6 *Let* $(X, \mathscr{X})$, $(Z, \mathscr{Z})$, Q, Γ, F, *and* β *satisfy Assumptions 9.4–9.7, and define the operator* T *on* $C(S)$ *by*

(5) $$(Tf)(x, z) = \sup_{y \in \Gamma(x,z)} \left\{ F(x, y, z) + \beta \int f(y, z') Q(z, dz') \right\}.$$

Then $T: C(S) \to C(S)$; T *has a unique fixed point* v *in* $C(S)$ *and for any* $v_0 \in C(S)$,

$$\|T^n v_0 - v\| \le \beta^n \|v_0 - v\|, \quad n = 1, 2, \ldots.$$

Moreover, the correspondence $G: S \to X$ *defined by*

(6) $$G(x, z) = \left\{ y \in \Gamma(x, z): v(x, z) = F(x, y, z) + \beta \int v(y, z')Q(z, dz') \right\},$$

is nonempty, compact-valued, and u.h.c.

Proof. Fix $f \in C(S)$. Then it follows from Lemma 9.5 that

$$(Mf)(y, z) = \int f(y, z')Q(z, dz')$$

is a bounded continuous function of (y, z). Moreover, since $Q(z, \cdot)$ is a probability measure, $M(f + c) = Mf + c$, for any constant function c. Hence the proof of Theorem 4.6 applies without change. ∎

To obtain sharper characterizations of the unique fixed point of T, more structure is needed. We examine in turn the consequences of monotonicity, concavity, and differentiability.

ASSUMPTION 9.8 *For each $(y, z) \in X \times Z$, $F(\cdot, y, z): A_{yz} \to \mathbf{R}$ is strictly increasing.*

ASSUMPTION 9.9 *For each $z \in Z$, $\Gamma(\cdot, z): X \to X$ is increasing in the sense that $x \le x'$ implies $\Gamma(x, z) \subseteq \Gamma(x', z)$.*

THEOREM 9.7 *Let $(X, \mathcal{X})$, $(Z, \mathcal{Z})$, Q, Γ, F, and β satisfy Assumptions 9.4– 9.9, and let v be the unique fixed point of the operator T in (5). Then for each $z \in Z$, $v(\cdot, z): X \to \mathbf{R}$ is strictly increasing.*

Proof. Let $C'(S) \subset C(S)$ be the set of bounded continuous functions f on S that are nondecreasing in their first l arguments, and let $C''(S) \subset C'(S)$ be the set of functions that are strictly increasing in those arguments. Since $C'(S)$ is a closed subspace of the complete metric space $C(S)$, by Corollary 1 to the Contraction Mapping Theorem (Theorem 3.2), it is sufficient to show that $T[C'(S)] \subseteq C''(S)$. Under Assumptions 9.8 and 9.9, Lemma 9.5 ensures that this is so. ∎

Next we consider concavity. Assumption 9.10 is a concavity restriction on F, and Assumption 9.11 is a convexity restriction on Γ.

ASSUMPTION **9.10** *For each $z \in Z$, $F(\cdot, \cdot, z): A_z \to \mathbf{R}$ satisfies*

$$F[\theta(x, y) + (1 - \theta)(x', y'), z] \geq \theta F(x, y, z) + (1 - \theta)F(x', y', z),$$

all $\theta \in (0, 1)$, and all $(x, y), (x', y') \in A_z$;

and the inequality is strict if $x \neq x'$.

ASSUMPTION **9.11** *For all $z \in Z$ and all $x, x' \in X$,*

$$y \in \Gamma(x, z) \quad \text{and} \quad y' \in \Gamma(x', z) \quad \text{implies}$$

$$\theta y + (1 - \theta)y' \in \Gamma[\theta x + (1 - \theta)x', z], \quad \text{all } \theta \in [0, 1].$$

Since the set X is convex, Assumption 9.11 is equivalent to assuming that for each $z \in Z$, the set A_z is convex. In particular, Assumption 9.11 implies that $\Gamma(s)$ is a convex set for each $s \in S$, and that there are no increasing returns.

THEOREM **9.8** *Let $(X, \mathscr{X})$, $(Z, \mathfrak{Z})$, Q, Γ, F, and β satisfy Assumptions 9.4–9.7 and 9.10–9.11; let v be the unique fixed point of the operator T in (5); and let G be the correspondence defined by (6). Then for each $z \in Z$, $v(\cdot, z): X \to \mathbf{R}$ is strictly concave and $G(\cdot, z): X \to X$ is a continuous (single-valued) function.*

Proof. Let $C'(S) \subset C(S)$ be the set of bounded continuous functions on S that are weakly concave jointly in their first l arguments, and let $C''(S) \subset C'(S)$ be the subset consisting of functions that are strictly concave jointly in those arguments. Since $C'(S)$ is a closed subspace of the complete metric space $C(S)$, by Corollary 1 to the Contraction Mapping Theorem (Theorem 3.2), it is sufficient to show that $T[C'(S)] \subseteq C''(S)$. Under Assumptions 9.10 and 9.11, Lemma 9.5 ensures that this is so. ∎

As it does in the deterministic case, concavity ensures that the sequence of approximate policy functions $\{g_n\}$ converges to the optimal policy function g.

THEOREM **9.9** *Let $(X, \mathscr{X})$, $(Z, \mathfrak{Z})$, Q, Γ, F, and β satisfy Assumptions 9.4–9.7 and 9.10–9.11; let $C'(S) \subset C(S)$ be the set of bounded continuous functions on S that are weakly concave jointly in their first l arguments; let $v \in C'(S)$ be the* *unique fixed point of the operator T in (5); and let g = G be the (single-valued) function defined by (6). Let $v_0 \in C'(S)$, and define $\{(v_n, g_n)\}$ by*

$$v_n = Tv_{n-1}, \quad \text{and}$$

$$g_n(x, z) = \underset{y \in \Gamma(x,z)}{\text{argmax}} \left\{ F(x, y, z) + \beta \int v_n(y, z')Q(z, dz') \right\},$$

$$n = 1, 2, \ldots.$$

Then $g_n \to g$ pointwise. If X and Z are both compact, then the convergence is uniform.

Proof. Let $C''(S) \subset C'(S)$ be as defined in the proof of Theorem 9.8; as shown there $T[C'(S)] \subseteq C''(S)$ and $v \in C''(S)$. Let $v_0 \in C'(S)$, and define the functions $\{f_n\}$ and f by

$$f_n(x, z, y) = F(x, y, z) + \beta \int v_n(y, z')Q(z, dz'), \quad n = 1, 2, \ldots,$$

and

$$f(x, z, y) = F(x, y, z) + \beta \int v(y, z')Q(z, dz').$$

Since $v_0 \in C'(S)$, each function v_n, $n = 1, 2, \ldots$, is in $C''(S)$, as is v. Hence for any $s \in S = X \times Z$, the functions $\{f_n(s, \cdot)\}$ and $f(s, \cdot)$ are all strictly concave in y. Therefore Theorem 3.8 applies. ∎

For concave problems with interior solutions, the differentiability of the value function can also be established.

ASSUMPTION 9.12   *For each fixed $z \in Z$, $F(\cdot, \cdot, z)$ is continuously differentiable in (x, y) on the interior of A_z.*

THEOREM 9.10   *Let $(X, \mathcal{X})$, $(Z, \mathcal{Z})$, Q, Γ, F, and β satisfy Assumptions 9.4–9.7 and 9.10–9.12; let $v \in C'(S)$ be the unique fixed point of the operator T in (5), and let $g = G$ be the function defined by (6). If $x_0 \in \text{int } X$ and $g(x_0, z_0) \in \text{int } \Gamma(x_0, z_0)$, then $v(\cdot, z_0)$ is continuously differentiable in x at x_0, with derivatives given by*

$$v_i(x_0, z_0) = F_i[x_0, g(x_0, z_0), z_0], \quad i = 1, \ldots, l.$$

Proof. Let $x_0 \in$ int X and $g(x_0, z_0) \in$ int $\Gamma(x_0, z_0)$. Then there is some open neighborhood D of x_0 such that $g(x_0, z_0) \in$ int $\Gamma(x, z_0)$, all $x \in D$. Hence we can define $W: D \to \mathbf{R}$ by

$$W(x) = F[x, g(x_0, z_0), z_0] + \beta \int v[g(x_0, z_0), z']Q(z_0, dz').$$

Clearly W is concave and continuously differentiable on D and

$$W(x) \leq v(x, z_0), \quad \text{all } x \in D,$$

with equality at x_0. Hence Theorem 4.10 applies, establishing the desired result. ∎

In some applications it is reasonable to expect that the value function is monotone in z as well as in x. Clearly this requires that Z be a set for which monotonicity is well defined; thus, if Z is a countable set, we will assume that $Z = \{1, 2, \ldots\}$. We will also need restrictions on F and Γ analogous to Assumptions 9.8 and 9.9, and an additional restriction on the transition function Q.

ASSUMPTION 9.13 *For each $(x, y) \in X \times X$, $F(x, y, \cdot): A_{xy} \to \mathbf{R}$ is strictly increasing.*

ASSUMPTION 9.14 *For each $x \in X$, $\Gamma(x, \cdot): Z \to X$ is increasing in the sense that $z \leq z'$ implies $\Gamma(x, z) \subseteq \Gamma(x, z')$.*

ASSUMPTION 9.15 *Q is monotone; that is, if $f: Z \to \mathbf{R}$ is nondecreasing, then the function $(Mf)(z) = \int f(z')Q(z, dz')$ is also nondecreasing.*

THEOREM 9.11 *Let $(X, \mathscr{X})$, $(Z, \mathscr{Z})$, Q, Γ, F, and β satisfy Assumptions 9.4–9.7 and 9.13–9.15; and let $v \in C(S)$ be the unique fixed point of the operator T in (5). Then for each $x \in X$, $v(x, \cdot): Z \to \mathbf{R}$ is strictly increasing.*

Proof. Let $C'(S) \subset C(S)$ be the set of bounded continuous functions on $X \times Z$ that are nondecreasing in z, and let $C''(S) \subset C'(S)$ be the subset consisting of functions that are strictly increasing in z. Since $C'(S)$ is a closed subspace of the complete metric space $C(S)$, by Corollary 1 to the Contraction Mapping Theorem, it is sufficient to show that $T[C'(S)] \subseteq C''(S)$.

Fix $x \in X$; suppose that $f(x, \cdot): Z \to \mathbf{R}$ is nondecreasing; and choose $z_1 < z_2$. Let $y_1 \in \Gamma(x, z_1)$ attain the maximum in (5) for $z = z_1$. Then

$$(Tf)(x, z_1) = F(x, y_1, z_1) + \beta \int f(y_1, z')Q(z_1, dz')$$

$$< F(x, y_1, z_2) + \beta \int f(y_1, z')Q(z_2, dz')$$

$$\leq \max_{y \in \Gamma(x, z_2)} \left[F(x, y, z_2) + \beta \int f(y, z')Q(z_2, dz') \right]$$

$$= (Tf)(x, z_2),$$

where the second line uses Assumptions 9.13 and 9.15 and the third uses Assumption 9.14. Hence $(Tf)(x, \cdot)$ is strictly increasing, as was to be shown. ∎

In the remainder of this section we show that the results above all have close parallels for the case where the functional equation has the form in (2). Let $(X, \mathscr{X})$, $(Z, \mathscr{Z})$, $(S, \mathscr{S})$, Q, and β be as specified above. In addition let $(Y, \mathscr{Y})$ be a measurable space of actions available to the decision-maker; let $\Gamma: X \times Z \to Y$ be a correspondence describing the feasibility constraints; let A be the graph of Γ; let $F: A \to \mathbf{R}$ be the one-period return function; let

$$D = \{(x, y) \in X \times Y: y \in \Gamma(x, z), \text{ for some } z \in Z\};$$

and let $\phi: D \times Z \to X$ be the law of motion for x.

To characterize solutions to the functional equation (2), we are interested in the operator T defined by

$$(7) \qquad (Tf)(x, z) = \sup_{y \in \Gamma(x, z)} \left[F(x, y, z) + \beta \int f[\phi(x, y, z'), z']Q(z, dz') \right].$$

Clearly we must retain Assumptions 9.4 and 9.5. We also need to restrict the set of feasible actions Y and to place a continuity assumption on the law of motion ϕ.

ASSUMPTION 9.16 *Y is a convex Borel set in $\mathbf{R}^m$, with its Borel subsets $\mathscr{Y}$.*

ASSUMPTION 9.17 $\phi\colon D \times Z \to X$ *is continuous.*

If Z is a countable set, then we interpret Assumption 9.17 to mean that for each $z \in Z$, the z-section of ϕ, the function $\phi(\cdot,\ \cdot,\ z)\colon D \to X$ is continuous. With these additional assumptions, we have the following parallel to Lemma 9.5.

LEMMA 9.5′ *Let $(X,\ \mathscr{X})$, $(Y,\ \mathscr{Y})$, $(Z,\ \mathscr{Z})$, Q, and ϕ satisfy Assumptions 9.4, 9.5, 9.16, and 9.17. Then for any continuous function $f\colon X \times Z \to \mathbf{R}$, the function $h\colon D \times Z \to \mathbf{R}$ defined by*

$$h(x,\ y,\ z) = \int f[\phi(x,\ y,\ z'),\ z']Q(z,\ dz')$$

is also continuous.

Proof. Let $u = (x,\ y)$ and define $\psi(u,\ z') = f[\phi(u,\ z'),\ z']$; since f and ϕ are continuous, so is ψ. It then follows from Lemma 9.5 that

$$h(u,\ z) = \int \psi(u,\ z')Q(z,\ dz')$$

is continuous. ∎

With this result in hand, it is straightforward to mimic the results in Exercise 9.6 and in Theorems 9.6–9.11; the required steps are presented in the following exercise. Note that the range of Γ is now Y, so A is now a subset of $X \times Y \times Z$. Rather than restate Assumptions 9.6–9.14, however, we merely note that the appropriate modifications must be made.

Exercise 9.7 a. Let $(X,\ \mathscr{X})$, $(Y,\ \mathscr{Y})$, $(Z,\ \mathscr{Z})$, Q, Γ, F, β, and ϕ satisfy Assumptions 9.4–9.7 and 9.16–9.17. Show that Assumptions 9.1′–9.3′ are satisfied.

b. Let the assumptions in part (a) hold, and let T be the operator defined in (7). Show that $T\colon C(S) \to C(S)$; that T has a unique fixed point $v \in C(S)$; and that for any $v_0 \in C(S)$,

$$\|T^n v_0 - v\| \leq \beta^n \|v_0 - v\|, \quad n = 1, 2, \ldots.$$

Also show that the correspondence $G: X \times Z \to Y$ defined by

$$G(x, z) = \left\{ y \in \Gamma(x, z): v(x, z) = F(x, y, z) \right.$$

$$\left. + \beta \int v[\phi(x, y, z'), z'] Q(z, dz') \right\},$$

is nonempty, compact-valued, and u.h.c.

c. Show that if, in addition, Assumptions 9.8 and 9.9 hold and ϕ is nondecreasing in each of its first l arguments, then v is strictly increasing in each of its first l arguments.

d. Suppose that, in addition to the assumptions in part (a), Assumptions 9.10 and 9.11 hold and that, for each $z' \in Z$, the function $\phi(\cdot, \cdot, z')$ is concave. Show that v is strictly concave jointly in its first l arguments and that G is a continuous (single-valued) function.

e. Show that under the assumptions in part (d) the sequence of policy functions $\{g_n\}$ defined as in Theorem 9.9 converges pointwise to the optimal policy function g; show that if $X \times Z$ is compact the convergence is uniform.

f. Let the assumptions in part (d) hold, let Assumption 9.12 hold, and assume that the law of motion $\phi(y, z')$ does not depend on x. Suppose that $(x_0, z_0) \in \text{int}(X \times Z)$ and $g(x_0, z_0) \in \text{int } \Gamma(x_0, z_0)$. Show that $v(\cdot, z_0)$ is differentiable in x at x_0 and that $v_i(x_0, z_0) = F_i[x_0, g(x_0, z_0), z_0]$, $i = 1, \ldots, l$.

g. Suppose that, in addition to the assumptions in part (a), Assumptions 9.13–9.15 hold. Show that $v(x, z)$ is strictly increasing in z.

9.3   Constant Returns to Scale

In Section 4.3 we noted that dynamic programs with constant returns to scale are often of economic interest but are, obviously, inconsistent with the assumption of bounded returns. We saw there, however, that for the deterministic model the arguments used in the bounded-returns case could be modified to fit the case of constant returns to scale. The same is true for the stochastic model, and the adaptation is completely analogous. We outline the argument in this section, leaving the main results as exercises.

As in the last section, we take as given $(X, \mathscr{X})$, $(Z, \mathscr{Z})$, Q, Γ, F, and β. We maintain Assumption 9.5 on the behavior of the shocks. To incorporate constant returns to scale, we replace Assumptions 9.4, 9.6, and 9.7 with the following. As before we take A to be the graph of Γ.

ASSUMPTION 9.18 $X \subset \mathbf{R}^l$ *is a convex cone, with its Borel subsets $\mathscr{X}$.*

ASSUMPTION 9.19 *The correspondence $\Gamma: X \times Z \to X$ is nonempty, compact-valued, and continuous; for any $(x, z) \in X \times Z$,*

$$y \in \Gamma(x, z) \text{ implies } \lambda y \in \Gamma(\lambda x, z), \quad \text{all } \lambda \geq 0;$$

and for some $\alpha \in (0, \beta^{-1})$,

$$\|y\|_l \leq \alpha \|x\|_l, \quad \text{all } y \in \Gamma(x, z), \text{ all } (x, z) \in X \times Z.$$

ASSUMPTION 9.20 *The function $F: A \to \mathbf{R}$ is continuous; for each $z \in Z$, the function $F(\cdot, \cdot, z): A_z \to \mathbf{R}$ is homogeneous of degree one; for some $0 < B < \infty$,*

$$|F(x, y, z)| \leq B(\|x\|_l + \|y\|_l), \quad \text{all } (x, y, z) \in A;$$

and the discount factor is $\beta \in (0, 1)$.

The next exercise shows that the Principle of Optimality holds under these assumptions.

Exercise 9.8 Show that under Assumptions 9.5 and 9.18–9.20, Assumptions 9.1–9.3 hold. [*Hint.* Show that

$$|F[\pi_{t-1}(z^{t-1}), \pi_t(z^t), z_t]| \leq \alpha^t B(1 + \alpha)\|x_0\|_l,$$

all $z^t \in Z^t$, $t = 1, 2, \ldots$, all $\pi \in \Pi(s_0)$, all $s_0 \in S$.]

The functional equation for this problem is

$$(1) \qquad v(x, z) = \sup_{y \in \Gamma(x,z)} \left[F(x, y, z) + \beta \int v(y, z') Q(z, dz') \right].$$

Paralleling the analysis in Section 4.3, we seek a solution to (1) in the space $H(S)$ of continuous functions $f: S = X \times Z \to \mathbf{R}$ that are homogeneous of degree one in x for each fixed z, and such that

(2) $\qquad \|f\| = \sup_{z \in Z} \sup_{\substack{x \in X \\ \|x\|_l \leq 1}} |f(x, z)| < \infty.$

Take $\|\cdot\|$ as the norm of this space. As shown in Exercise 4.7, $H(S)$ is a Banach space.

Assumption 9.5 requires that the Markov operator M associated with Q map the set $C(Z)$ of bounded continuous functions on Z into itself. For the case of bounded returns, we began in Lemma 9.5 by showing that if $(X, \mathcal{X})$, $(Z, \mathcal{Z})$, and Q satisfy Assumptions 9.4 and 9.5, then M also maps the space $C(S)$ of bounded continuous functions on $S = X \times Z$ into itself. For the case of constant returns to scale we need an analogous result. The argument is similar to the one used to prove Lemma 9.5. Note that for $C(Z)$ we use the sup norm, and for $H(S)$ we use the norm in (2).

Exercise 9.9   Let $(X, \mathcal{X})$, $(Z, \mathcal{Z})$, and Q satisfy Assumptions 9.18 and 9.5; let $S = X \times Z$; and let $H(S)$ be defined as above. Show that if $f \in H(S)$, then Mf defined by

$$(Mf)(y, z) = \int f(y, z')Q(z, dz')$$

is also in $H(S)$; that is, $M: H(S) \to H(S)$. Show that if f is quasi-concave (strictly quasi-concave) jointly in its first l arguments, then so is Mf.

With this result established, it is easy to show that the operator T associated with (1) takes $H(S)$ into itself. The next exercise is the analogue of Theorem 4.13.

Exercise 9.10   a. Let $(X, \mathcal{X})$, $(Z, \mathcal{Z})$, Q, Γ, F, and β satisfy Assumptions 9.5 and 9.18–9.20. Show that there is a unique function $v \in H(S)$ satisfying (1); that the associated policy correspondence $G: X \times Z \to X$ is nonempty, compact-valued and u.h.c.; and that for any $(x, z) \in X \times Z$,

$$y \in G(x, z) \text{ implies } \lambda y \in G(\lambda x, z), \quad \text{all } \lambda \geq 0.$$

b. Under what conditions is $v(\cdot, z): X \to \mathbf{R}$ strictly quasi-concave, for each $z \in Z$?

c. Verify that the monotonicity and differentiability arguments in Section 9.2 apply here as well.

9.4 Unbounded Returns

Since there was no very general theory for deterministic dynamic programs with unbounded return functions, none is to be expected if stochastic shocks are added. Yet as we noted in Section 4.4, both of our favorite parametric examples—linear-quadratic and logarithmic—involve returns that are unbounded. In this section, as in Section 4.4, we deal with this situation in an ad hoc fashion. Suppose that we have obtained a solution to the functional equation

$$(1) \qquad v(x, z) = \sup_{y \in \Gamma(x,z)} \left[F(x, y, z) + \beta \int v(y, z')Q(z, dz') \right],$$

and that the associated policy correspondence G is nonempty. We wish to know whether v is in fact the supremum function and whether plans generated by G are optimal.

Our treatment of this question in Section 4.4 (Theorem 4.14) rested on the fact that the supremum function satisfies the functional equation (Theorem 4.2). In the stochastic case, however, as we showed by example in Section 9.1, this need not be the case. Therefore we instead take an approach based on Theorem 9.2.

Let $\Pi(s)$, u, and v^* be as defined in Section 9.1. Under Assumptions 9.1 and 9.2, $\Pi(s)$ is nonempty and u and v^* are well defined. Recall that one of the hypotheses of Theorem 9.2 was that

$$(2) \qquad \lim_{t \to \infty} \beta^t \int_{Z^t} v[\pi_{t-1}(z^{t-1}), z_t]\mu^t(z_0, dz^t) = 0,$$

$$\text{all } \pi \in \Pi(s_0), \text{ all } (x_0, z_0) = s_0 \in S.$$

The difficulty with the unbounded case is that there may be some $s_0 \in S$ and $\pi \in \Pi(s_0)$ for which (2) does not hold. For each $s_0 \in S$, however, we can define $\hat{\Pi}(s_0)$ to be the subset of $\Pi(s_0)$ on which (2) does hold. Then define $\hat{v}: S \to \mathbf{R}$ by

$$\hat{v}(s) = \sup_{\pi \in \hat{\Pi}(s)} u(\pi, s).$$

Clearly $\hat{v} \leq v^*$. The following adaptation of Theorem 9.2 provides sufficient conditions for the two functions to be equal.

THEOREM 9.12   *Let $(X, \mathcal{X})$, $(Z, \mathcal{Z})$, Q, Γ, F, and β satisfy Assumptions 9.1
and 9.2. Let Π, u, and v^* be as defined in Section 9.1, and let $\hat{\Pi}$ and $\hat{v}$ be as
defined above. Suppose v is a measurable function satisfying (1), and that the
associated policy correspondence G is nonempty and permits a measurable selection. For each $s \in S$, let $\pi^*(\cdot; s)$ be a plan generated by G from s. Suppose in
addition that*

a. $\pi^*(\cdot; s) \in \hat{\Pi}(s)$, all $s \in S$; and
b. for any $s \in S$ and $\pi \in \Pi(s)$, there exists $\hat{\pi} \in \hat{\Pi}(s)$ such that $u(\hat{\pi}, s) \geq u(\pi, s)$.

Then

$$v^*(s) = \hat{v}(s) = v(s) = u[\pi^*(\cdot; s), s], \quad \text{all } s \in S.$$

Proof. Since (a) holds, it is a trivial adaptation of Theorem 9.2 to
show that

$$\hat{v}(s) = v(s) = u[\pi^*(\cdot; s), s], \quad \text{all } s \in S.$$

Clearly, $\hat{v}(s) \leq v^*(s)$, all $s \in S$. To establish the reverse inequality, suppose
that $\{\pi^k\}_{k=1}^{\infty}$ is a sequence in $\Pi(s)$ such that

$$\lim_{k \to \infty} u(\pi^k, s) = v^*(s).$$

Then by (b) there is a sequence $\{\hat{\pi}^k\}_{k=1}^{\infty}$ in $\hat{\Pi}(s)$ such that $u(\hat{\pi}^k, s) \geq
u(\pi^k, s)$, $k = 1, 2, \ldots$. Hence

$$\lim_{k \to \infty} u(\hat{\pi}^k, s) \geq v^*(s),$$

so $\hat{v} \geq v^*$. ∎

The practical usefulness of this result obviously depends on how easy
it is to verify conditions (a) and (b). In the stochastic unit elasticity and

linear-quadratic models we examine next, verifying these conditions is straightforward.

We consider first a stochastic growth model. Let $X = Z = \mathbf{R}_{++}$, with the Borel sets $\mathscr{X}$ and $\mathscr{Z}$. Let $\beta \in (0, 1)$, and let

$$\Gamma(x, z) = (0, zx^\alpha) \quad \text{and} \quad F(x, y, z) = \ln(zx^\alpha - y),$$

where $\alpha \in (0, 1)$. Let the exogenous shocks $\{z_t\}$ be independently and identically distributed, with $E[\ln(z)] = m$. This is the example considered in Exercise 2.6. To apply Theorem 9.12, we must verify that Assumptions 9.1 and 9.2 hold; find (v, G) and construct the plans $\pi^*(\cdot; s)$, all $s \in S$; and show that the hypotheses (a) and (b) hold.

Clearly Assumption 9.1 holds: $\Gamma(s) \neq \emptyset$ and there are lots of measurable selections (for example, all constant savings rate policies). To establish that Assumption 9.2 holds, note that for any $s_0 \in S$ and any $\pi \in \Pi(s_0)$,

$$(3) \qquad \ln[\pi_{t-1}(z^{t-1})] \leq \sum_{n=0}^{t-1} \alpha^{t-1-n} \ln(z_n) + \alpha^t \ln(x_0), \quad \text{and}$$

$$(4) \qquad F[\pi_{t-1}(z^{t-1}), \pi_t(z^t), z_t] \leq \alpha \ln[\pi_{t-1}(z^{t-1})] + \ln(z_t),$$

$$\text{all } z^t \in Z^t, t = 1, 2, \ldots.$$

Since $E[\ln(z)]$ is finite and $\alpha < 1$, the argument establishing that total returns are bounded above then parallels exactly the one used in Section 4.4, and we do not repeat it. Hence the limit in Assumption 9.2 exists (although it may be minus infinity).

We know from Exercise 2.6 that a solution v to (1) for this case is

$$(5) \qquad v(x, z) = A_0 + \frac{\alpha}{1 - \alpha\beta} \ln(x) + \frac{1}{1 - \alpha\beta} \ln(z),$$

and that the associated policy function is $g(x, z) = \alpha\beta zx^\alpha$. Hence, given any initial state $s_0 = (x_0, z_0)$, the plan $\pi^*(\cdot; s_0)$ generated by this policy can be calculated explicitly; in logs, it is

$$(6) \qquad \ln[\pi_{t-1}^*(z^{t-1}, s_0)] = \sum_{n=0}^{t-1} \alpha^{t-1-n}[\ln(\alpha\beta) + \ln(z_n)] + \alpha^t \ln(x_0).$$

It remains only to show that conditions (a) and (b) of Theorem 9.12 hold.

Exercise 9.11   Verify that the plans $\pi^*(\cdot; s_0)$, all $s_0 \in S$, defined in (6) satisfy condition (a) of Theorem 9.12. That is, show that (2) holds for each $\pi^*(\cdot; s_0)$, where v is given by (5).

To verify condition (b) we need to show that for any $s_0 \in S$, any plan in $\Pi(s_0)$ is weakly dominated by a plan in $\hat{\Pi}(s_0)$. We do this as follows: for each $s_0 \in S$, notice that $\pi^*(\cdot; s_0) \in \Pi(s_0)$ and that $u[\pi^*(\cdot; s_0), s_0]$ is finite. We will show that for any $\pi \in \Pi(s_0)$, either π is itself in $\hat{\Pi}(s_0)$, or else $u(\pi, s_0) = -\infty$ so π is dominated by $\pi^*(\cdot; s_0)$.

Let $s_0 \in S$ and $\pi \in \Pi(s_0)$ be arbitrary. By definition $\pi \in \hat{\Pi}(s_0)$ if and only if (2) holds. With v given by (5), condition (2) is

$$\lim_{t \to \infty} \beta^t \int_{Z^t} \left\{ A_0 + \frac{\alpha}{1 - \alpha\beta} \ln[\pi_{t-1}(z^{t-1})] \right.$$
$$\left. + \frac{1}{1 - \alpha\beta} \ln(z_t) \right\} \mu^t(z_0, dz^t) = 0.$$

It follows from the assumption on the z_t's that

$$\lim_{t \to \infty} \beta^t \int_{Z^t} \frac{1}{1 - \alpha\beta} \ln(z_t) \mu^t(z_0, dz^t) = \lim_{t \to \infty} \beta^t \frac{m}{1 - \alpha\beta} = 0.$$

Hence (2) holds if and only if

(7) $$\lim_{t \to \infty} \beta^t \int_{Z^t} \ln[\pi_{t-1}(z^{t-1})] \mu^t(z_0, dz^t) = 0.$$

That is, $\pi \in \hat{\Pi}(S_0)$ if and only if (7) holds. Now suppose that (7) fails. It follows from (4) that

$$u(\pi, s_0) \leq \sum_{t=0}^{\infty} \beta^t \int \left\{ \alpha\ln[\pi_{t-1}(z^{t-1})] + \ln(z_t) \right\} \mu^t(z_0, dz^t).$$

Since (7) fails, the series on the right diverges, but (3) implies that this series is bounded above. Hence the series must diverge to minus infinity: $u(\pi, s_0) = -\infty$; in this case π^* dominates π. Thus condition (b) is satisfied, and Theorem 9.12 implies that v given by (5) is the supremum function and that the plan given by (6) is optimal.

It is easy to apply Theorem 9.12 to this example because all of the plans in the set $\Pi(s)\backslash\hat{\Pi}(s)$ yield discounted returns of minus infinity. Hence it is easy to find plans in $\hat{\Pi}(s)$ that dominate them and thus to verify condition (b) of the theorem. The same feature carries over to many quadratic problems. We illustrate this using a modification of the quadratic example of Section 4.4.

Let $X = Z = \mathbf{R}$, with the Borel sets $\mathscr{X}$ and $\mathscr{Z}$. Let $\beta \in (0, 1)$; let $\Gamma(x, z) = \mathbf{R}$, all (x, z); and let $F: \mathbf{R}^3 \rightarrow \mathbf{R}$ be defined by

$$F(x, y, z) = zx - \frac{1}{2}bx^2 - \frac{1}{2}c(y - x)^2, \quad b, c > 0.$$

Let the transition function Q on $(Z, \mathscr{Z})$ be defined implicitly by the assumption that the shocks z_t follow the stochastic difference equation

$$z_{t+1} = \rho z_t + u_{t+1},$$

where $0 < \rho < 1$ and $\{u_t\}$ is a sequence of independent and identically distributed random variables with finite mean and variance. Let $\mu^t(z_0, \cdot)$ be the induced probability measures on Z^t, $t = 1, 2, \ldots$, as defined in Section 8.2.

Exercise 9.12 Show that under these assumptions, for any $z_0 \in \mathbf{R}$ there exist constants $A, B > 0$ such that

(8) $\quad \int |z_t| \, \mu^t(z_0, dz^t) < A \quad \text{and} \quad \int (z_t)^2 \mu^t(z_0, dz^t) < B, \quad \text{all } t.$

Following the interpretation used in Section 4.4, we can think of F as describing a firm's net revenue function. In this case, the marginal value product of capital, $z - bx$, is assumed to be subject to serially correlated stochastic shocks.

As in the previous example, to apply Theorem 9.12 we must verify that Assumptions 9.1 and 9.2 hold; find (v, G) and construct the plans $\pi^*(\cdot; s)$, all $s \in S$; and verify that hypotheses (a) and (b) of the theorem are satisfied.

Clearly Assumption 9.1 holds for this problem. To see that Assumption 9.2 holds, first note that (8) implies that the integrability requirements are satisfied for all t. Then note that for each $z \in \mathbf{R}$, $F(\cdot, \cdot, z)$ is bounded above by $z^2/2b$. Since $0 < \beta < 1$, it then follows that the required limit exists (although it may be minus infinity).

The following exercise characterizes v and G.

Exercise 9.13   a. Show that for Γ and F as specified, the functional equation (1) has a solution of the form

$$(9) \qquad v(x, z) = v_0 + v_1 z + v_2 x + v_3 zx - v_4 x^2,$$

where $v_4 > 0$. [There may be other functions satisfying (1) as well.]

b. Show that the associated policy correspondence is a single-valued function of the form

$$(10) \qquad g(x, z) = g_0 + g_1 x + g_2 z, \quad \text{where } 0 < g_1 < 1.$$

For any $s_0 \in S$, the plan $\pi^*(\cdot; s_0)$ can be constructed by simply solving the linear difference equation in (10).

Finally we must show that hypotheses (a) and (b) of Theorem 9.12 hold. To show that (a) holds we must show that for each $s_0 \in S$, the plan $\pi^*(\cdot; s_0)$ generated by g satisfies (2), where v is given by (9). That is, we must show that

$$(11) \qquad \lim_{t \to \infty} \beta^t \int_{Z^t} \{ v_0 + v_1 z_t + v_2 \pi^*_{t-1}(z^{t-1}; s_0) + v_3 z_t \pi^*_{t-1}(z^{t-1}; s_0)$$
$$- v_4 [\pi^*_{t-1}(z^{t-1}; s_0)]^2 \} \mu^t(z_0, dz^t) = 0, \quad \text{all } s_0 \in S.$$

Exercise 9.14   Show that (11) holds. [*Hint.* Use (8) and the fact that $0 < g_1 < 1$.]

To verify (b) we need to show that for any $s_0 \in S$, any plan $\pi \in \Pi(s_0)$ that does not satisfy (2) is dominated by one that does. Since (8) holds, evidently (2) holds for π if and only if

$$(12) \qquad \lim_{t \to \infty} \beta^t \int_{Z^t} \{ v_2 \pi_{t-1}(z^{t-1}) + v_3 z_t \pi_{t-1}(z^{t-1})$$
$$- v_4 [\pi_{t-1}(z^{t-1})]^2 \} \mu^t(z_0, dz^t) = 0.$$

To verify (b) we will show that if a plan $\pi \in \Pi(s_0)$ fails to satisfy (12), then it has total discounted returns equal to minus infinity.

For brevity let $E(\cdot)$ denote integration with respect to $\mu^t(z_0, \cdot)$ and suppress the argument of π_{t-1}. We first show that if $\pi \in \Pi(s_0)$ satisfies

(13) $\qquad \lim_{t \to \infty} \beta^t E\left[z_t \pi_{t-1} - \frac{b}{2}(\pi_{t-1})^2 \right] = 0,$

then

(14) $\qquad \lim_{t \to \infty} \beta^t E(z_t \pi_{t-1}) = 0 \quad \text{and} \quad \lim_{t \to \infty} \beta^t E(\pi_{t-1})^2 = 0.$

Suppose to the contrary that (13) holds and that $\beta^t E(\pi_{t-1})^2 \to m > 0$ along a subsequence. Then (13) would imply that along this same subsequence $\beta^t E(z_t \pi_{t-1}) \to bm/2$. Now for any constant $k > 0$,

$$0 \le E(k \beta^t \pi_{t-1} - z_t)^2$$

$$= k^2 \beta^{2t} E(\pi_{t-1})^2 - 2k\beta^t E(z_t \pi_{t-1}) + E(z_t^2), \quad t = 1, 2, \ldots .$$

The first term on the right converges to $k^2 \beta^t m$ along the subsequence under discussion. Since $0 < \beta < 1$, as $t \to \infty$ this term converges to zero along the subsequence. As shown in Exercise 9.12, the third is bounded by some constant $B > 0$, for all t. Finally, along the subsequence under discussion the second term converges to $-kbm < 0$, which can be made as large in absolute value as desired by choosing k large. This contradicts the fact that the sum of the three terms must be nonnegative. Hence (13) implies (14).

We can now use a similar argument to prove that (13) implies (12). For suppose that (13) holds; then using (14), we find that (12) can fail only if $\lim_{t \to \infty} \beta^t E_t(\pi_{t-1}) \ne 0$. But for any constant k,

$$0 \le E(k\beta^t \pi_{t-1} - 1)^2 = k^2 \beta^{2t} E(\pi_{t-1})^2 - 2k\beta^t E(\pi_{t-1}) + 1.$$

As before, the first term on the right converges to zero as $t \to \infty$, the third is a constant, and the second can be made negative and as large as desired in absolute value by suitable choice (positive or negative, as needed) of k, yielding a contradiction. Hence (13) implies (12).

To complete the argument, note that if $\pi \in \Pi(s_0)$ there are two possibilities. If (12) holds, then π is itself in $\hat{\Pi}(s_0)$. If (12) does not hold, then (13) does not hold, and it follows from the definition of F that

$$(15) \qquad \lim_{t \to \infty} \beta^t E[F(\pi_{t-1}, \pi_t, z_t)] \le \lim_{t \to \infty} \beta^t \left[E(z_t \pi_{t-1}) - \frac{b}{2} E(\pi_{t-1})^2 \right] \ne 0.$$

Let $\{t_j\}$ be the subsequence along which $\beta^t E[F(\pi_{t-1}, \pi_t, z_t)] \ge 0$. Recall that $F(\cdot, \cdot, z)$ is bounded above by $z^2/2b$ and that $E(z_t^2)$ is bounded above by a constant B. Hence $\beta^t E[F(\pi_{t-1}, \pi_t, z_t)] \to 0$ along this subsequence. Then (15) implies that among the remaining terms, which are all strictly negative, there is a subsequence that is bounded away from zero. That is, there exists $\varepsilon > 0$ and a subsequence $\{t_k\}_{k=1}^{\infty}$ such that $\beta^t E[F(\pi_{t-1}, \pi_t, z_t)] < -\varepsilon$ along this subsequence. Hence $u(\pi, s_0) = -\infty$, as was to be shown.

9.5 Stochastic Euler Equations

For stochastic optimization problems in sequence form, as described in Section 9.1, necessary conditions for an optimum can be derived using the same kind of reasoning we used in Section 4.5. It is customary to call these conditions *stochastic Euler equations* (even though they were unknown to Euler).

Let $(X, \mathcal{X})$, $(Z, \mathcal{Z})$, Q, Γ, F, and β satisfy Assumptions 9.1–9.3. Define the set of feasible plans $\Pi(s_0)$, all $(x_0, z_0) = s_0 \in S$ as in Section 9.1, and consider the problem

$$(1) \qquad \sup_{\pi \in \Pi(s_0)} \left\{ F(x_0, \pi_0, z_0) + \sum_{t=1}^{\infty} \beta^t \int_{Z^t} F[\pi_{t-1}(z^{t-1}), \pi_t(z^t), z_t] \mu^t(z_0, dz^t) \right\}.$$

Let $\pi = \{\pi_t\}$ be a feasible plan that attains the supremum in (1). Then necessary conditions for an optimum are that, for each $t \in \{0, 1, 2, \ldots\}$, there is a set $A^t \subseteq Z^t$ with $\mu^t(z_0, A^t) = 1$ such that

(2) $$\pi_t(z^t) = \underset{y}{\operatorname{argmax}} \left\{ F[\pi_{t-1}(z^{t-1}), y, z_t] \right.$$

$$\left. + \beta \int F[y, \pi_{t+1}(z^t, z_{t+1}), z_{t+1}] Q(z_t, dz_{t+1}) \right\}$$

s.t. $y \in \Gamma[\pi_{t-1}(z^{t-1}), z_t]$,   and

$$\pi_{t+1}(z^t, z_{t+1}) \in \Gamma(y, z_{t+1}), \quad \text{all } z_{t+1} \in Z; \text{ all } z^t \in A^t.$$

(The modified notation needed to cover the case $t = 0$ is obvious.) Suppose that F is concave and continuously differentiable. Choose $t \in \{0, 1, 2, \ldots\}$ and $z^t \in A^t$, and suppose that differentiating under the integral in (2) is legitimate. (This is true if F is integrable and each of the l partial derivatives F_x is absolutely integrable. See Lang 1983, p. 357, Lemma 2.2.) If for some $z^t \in A^t$,

$$\pi_t(z^t) \in \operatorname{int} \Gamma[\pi_{t-1}(z^{t-1}), z_t], \quad \text{and}$$

$$\pi_{t+1}(z^{t+1}) \in \operatorname{int} \Gamma[\pi_t(z^t), z_{t+1}], \quad \text{all } z_{t+1} \in Z,$$

then $\pi_t(z^t)$ must satisfy the first-order condition

(3) $$0 = F_y[\pi_{t-1}(z^{t-1}), \pi_t(z^t), z_t]$$

$$+ \beta \int F_x[\pi_t(z^t), \pi_{t+1}(z^{t+1}), z_{t+1}] Q(z_t, dz_{t+1}).$$

[Note that by following the procedure used in Section 4.5, the first-order conditions in (3) could also have been derived from the first-order and envelope conditions for the functional equation associated with (1).]

It is straightforward to develop a stochastic analogue to Theorem 4.15, showing that the Euler equations (3) together with an expected value version of the transversality condition are sufficient conditions for an optimal plan when the return is concave. Since we have already obtained an existence theory for these problems along other lines, we do not pursue this approach.

When the return function F is quadratic, stochastic Euler equations can be used to construct optimal plans. We sketch the basic ideas for the one-dimensional case, $X = \mathbf{R}$. Using F_{xx}, F_{xy}, and so on for the (constant) second derivatives of F, in the quadratic case (3) becomes

(4) $\qquad 0 = F_{xy}\pi_{t-1}(z^{t-1}) + F_{yy}\pi_t(z^t) + F_{yz}z_t$

$$+ \beta F_{xx}\pi_t(z^t) + \beta F_{xy} \int \pi_{t+1}(z^{t+1})Q(z_t, dz_{t+1})$$

$$+ \beta F_{xz} \int z_{t+1}Q(z_t, dz_{t+1}), \quad \mu^t(z_0, \cdot)\text{-a.e.}, \ t = 0, 1, \ldots .$$

For any $t \geq 0$, define the expectation operator E_t by

$$E_t(\pi_s | z^t) = \int_{Z^{s-t}} \pi_s(z^s)\mu^s(z_0^t, dz_{t+1} \times \ldots \times dz_s),$$

all $z^t \in Z^t$, all $s \geq t$.

Using the definition of μ^s then gives

$$E_t \left[\int \pi_{s+1}(z^{s+1})Q(z_s, dz_{s+1}) \big| z^t \right] = E_t(\pi_{s+1} | z^t).$$

Thus, for $t \geq 1$ and $s > t$, (4) implies

(5) $\qquad 0 = F_{xy}E_t(\pi_{s-1}|z^t) + F_{yy}E_t(\pi_s|z^t) + F_{yz}E_t(z_s|z^t)$

$$+ \beta F_{xx}E_t(\pi_s|z^t) + \beta F_{xy}E_t(\pi_{s+1}|z^t) + \beta F_{xz}E_t(z_{s+1}|z^t).$$

Equation (5) is a (deterministic) second-order linear difference equation with constant coefficients in the variables $\{E_t(\pi_s|z^t)\}_{s=t}^{\infty}$. The exogenous forcing variables $\{E_t(z_s|z^t)\}_{s=t+1}^{\infty}$ can be calculated using Q. One boundary condition is given by $E_t(\pi_t|z^t) = \pi_t$. A transversality condition provides a second. Thus (5) can be solved by standard linear methods to yield $\{E_t(\pi_s|z^t)\}$ for all $t \geq 1$ and $s \geq t$.

With the first term in this solution, $E_t(\pi_{t+1}|z^t)$, in place of the term $\int \pi_{t+1}(z^{t+1})Q(z_t, dz_{t+1})$, (4) becomes a first-order linear difference equation in the variables $\{\pi_t(z^t)\}$, in which the term $E_t(\pi_{t+1}|z^t)$, already solved for, plays the role of an exogenous forcing variable. Solving this equation then yields an explicit formula for the optimal plan.

Outside this linear context, however, stochastic Euler equations are not useful in the same way that deterministic Euler equations are. Recall that in Section 6.4 we used the linear approximation to a system of deterministic Euler equations, in the neighborhood of a steady state, to study the local stability of that steady state. Stochastic Euler equations cannot be used in the same way, since, as is shown in Chapters 11 and 12, the "steady state" of a stochastic system is a probability measure, not a point. Hence stochastic Euler equations cannot readily be used to establish stability properties in nonlinear models.

Aside from their possible use in constructing optimal plans, the Euler equations (3) have a great deal of empirical content. Equation (3) says that F_y evaluated at period t arguments plus the expected value of βF_x evaluated at period $t + 1$ arguments equals zero, where the expectation is conditioned on z^t, the information available in period t. Thus no other variables dated t or earlier should help to predict βF_x. This observation has led to a wide range of testing and estimation procedures based on (3).

9.6 Policy Functions and Transition Functions

In this section we prove two theorems that provide the motivation for our discussion in Chapters 11 and 12 of convergence results for Markov processes. Consider the functional equation

(1) $$v(x, z) = \sup_{y \in \Gamma(x,z)} \left[F(x, y, z) + \beta \int v(y, z')Q(z, dz') \right].$$

In Sections 9.2 and 9.3 we provided conditions under which an equation of this type has a unique solution v, and there is an associated (single-valued) policy function g describing the maximizing choice of y as a function of the state (x, z). Now suppose that the decision-maker follows the (unique) optimal policy function g. Then the behavior of the sequence $\{s_t\} = \{(x_t, z_t)\}$, from a given initial position $s_0 = (x_0, z_0)$, is described by the transition function Q and the function $g: X \times Z \to X$. What can be said about $\{s_t\}$?

In Theorem 9.13 we establish that if the function g is measurable, then $\{(x_t, z_t)\}$ is a Markov process, with a stationary transition function P on $(S, \mathscr{S})$ defined in terms of Q and g. In Theorem 9.14 we establish that if in addition Q has the Feller property and g is continuous, then P also has the Feller property. We then indicate how the results in Section 8.4 can be used to show that similar conclusions hold for the process $\{s_t\}$ defined by the transition function, policy function, and law of motion for the functional equation

$$(2) \qquad v(x, z) = \sup_{y \in \Gamma(x,z)} \left\{ F(x, y, z) + \beta \int v[\phi(x, y, z'), z'] Q(z, dz') \right\}.$$

Note that the proof of Theorem 9.13 is similar in overall structure to that of Theorem 8.5.

THEOREM 9.13   *Let $(X, \mathcal{X})$ and $(Z, \mathcal{Z})$ be measurable spaces; let $(S, \mathcal{S})$ be the product space; let Q be a transition function on $(Z, \mathcal{Z})$; and let $g: S \to X$ be a measurable function. Then*

$$(3) \qquad P[(x, z), A \times B] = \begin{cases} Q(z, B) & \text{if } g(x, z) \in A \\ 0 & \text{if } g(x, z) \notin A, \end{cases}$$

all $x \in X, z \in Z, A \in \mathcal{X}, B \in \mathcal{Z}$,

defines a transition function on $(S, \mathcal{S})$.

   Proof. Fix $(x, z) \in X \times Z$. It is clear that the function $P[(x, z), \cdot]$ defined in (3) on the measurable rectangles in $\mathcal{X} \times \mathcal{Z}$ satisfies the hypotheses of Theorem 7.13 and has $P[(x, z), X \times Z] = 1$. Hence by Theorems 7.13 and 7.3, $P[(x, z), \cdot]$ can be extended to a probability measure on all of $\mathcal{X} \times \mathcal{Z}$. To complete the proof we must show that for each $C \in \mathcal{S}$, the function $P(\cdot, C): S \to [0, 1]$ is measurable.
   Let $\mathcal{C} \subset \mathcal{S}$ be the algebra consisting of finite unions of measurable rectangles, and let $\mathcal{E} \subseteq \mathcal{S}$ be the family of sets C for which $P(\cdot, C)$ is a measurable function. By the Monotone Class Lemma (Lemma 7.15), it suffices to show that $\mathcal{E}$ contains $\mathcal{C}$ and that $\mathcal{E}$ is a monotone class.
   Fix $A \in \mathcal{X}$ and $B \in \mathcal{Z}$. Then we may rewrite (3) as

$$P[(x, z), A \times B] = Q(z, B)\chi_A[g(x, z)],$$

where χ_A is the indicator function for A. Since $Q(\cdot, B)$, $\chi_A(\cdot)$ and $g(\cdot)$ are all measurable functions, and since compositions and products of measurable functions are measurable, it follows that $P(\cdot, A \times B)$ is measurable. Hence $\mathcal{E}$ contains the measurable rectangles in $\mathcal{S}$. Since every set in $\mathcal{C}$ can be written as the finite union of disjoint measurable rectangles, it follows immediately that $\mathcal{C} \subseteq \mathcal{E}$.

To show that $\mathcal{E}$ is a monotone class, let $C_1 \subseteq C_2 \subseteq \ldots$ be an increasing sequence of sets in $\mathcal{E}$, with $C = \cup_{i=1}^{\infty} C_i$. Then for each $s \in S$, it follows from Theorem 7.1 that $P(s, C) = \lim_{n \to \infty} P(s, C_n)$. That is, $P(\cdot, C)$ is the pointwise limit of a sequence of measurable functions, and hence by Theorem 7.4 is measurable; therefore $C \in \mathcal{E}$. A similar argument applies if $\{C_i\}$ is a decreasing sequence. Therefore $\mathcal{E}$ is a monotone class. ∎

Recall that a transition function P on $(S, \mathcal{S})$ has the Feller property if the associated Markov operator M_P maps the space of bounded continuous functions on S into itself. The next theorem shows that if Q has the Feller property and if g is continuous, then P also has the Feller property. Its proof uses the following fact.

Exercise 9.15 Let $(X, \mathcal{X})$, $(Z, \mathcal{Z})$, $(S, \mathcal{S})$, Q, and g be as specified in Theorem 9.13, and let P be the transition function on $(S, \mathcal{S})$ defined by (3).

a. Show that if $f: S \to \mathbf{R}$ is a nonnegative, $\mathcal{S}$-measurable function, then

$$\int_{X \times Z} f(x', z') P[(x, z), dx' \times dz'] = \int_Z f[g(x, z), z'] Q(z, dz').$$

b. Show that this equality also holds if f is $P(s, \cdot)$-integrable.

THEOREM 9.14 Let $(X, \mathcal{X})$, $(Z, \mathcal{Z})$, and Q satisfy Assumptions 9.4 and 9.5; let $(S, \mathcal{S}) = (X \times Z, \mathcal{X} \times \mathcal{Z})$; and let $g: X \times Z \to X$ be continuous. Then the transition function P on $(S, \mathcal{S})$ defined by (3) has the Feller property.

Proof. Let M_Q and M_P be the Markov operators associated with Q and P, respectively; and let $f: S \to \mathbf{R}$ be any bounded continuous function. Then for any $(x, z) = s \in S$, it follows from Exercise 9.15 that

$$(M_P f)(s) = \int_S f(s') P(s, ds')$$

$$= \int_Z f[g(s), z'] Q(z, dz') = (M_Q f)[g(s), z].$$

The desired result then follows immediately from Lemma 9.5 and the fact that g is continuous. ∎

In some cases one might want to consider the sequence $\{x_t\}$ only. If $\{z_t\}$ is an i.i.d. sequence of shocks, then Theorem 8.9 establishes that the policy function g defines a transition function on $(X, \mathscr{X})$ and Exercise 8.10 establishes conditions under which that transition function has the Feller property. If the sequence $\{z_t\}$ is not i.i.d., then $\{x_t\}$ need not be a first-order Markov process. The following exercise illustrates this fact.

Exercise 9.16 Let $X = [0, 1]$; let $Z = \{0, 1\}$; let $Q(0, 0) = Q(1, 1) = .9$; let $Q(0, 1) = Q(1, 0) = .1$; and let $g(x, z) = \theta x + (1 - \theta)z$, where $\theta \in (0, 1)$. Let P be the transition function on $(X \times Z, \mathscr{X} \times \mathscr{Z})$ defined in Theorem 9.13. Show that for the random variables $\{(x_t, z_t)\}$ generated by P starting from some given initial point (x_0, z_0),

$$\Pr(x_{t+1} \in A \,|\, x_t, x_{t-1}) \text{ is } not \text{ equal to } \Pr(x_{t+1} \in A \,|\, x_t).$$

Finally, the following exercise deals with the case where the functional equation has the form in (2).

Exercise 9.17 Let $(X, \mathscr{X})$, $(Y, \mathscr{Y})$, and $(Z, \mathscr{Z})$ be measurable spaces; let Q be a transition function on $(Z, \mathscr{Z})$; and let $\phi: X \times Y \times Z \to X$ and $g: X \times Z \to Y$ be measurable functions. Define

$$H(x, z, A) = \{z' \in Z: \phi[x, g(x, z), z'] \in A\},$$

$$\text{all } x \in X, z \in Z, A \in \mathscr{X}.$$

a. Show that

$$P[(x, z), A \times B] = Q[z, B \cap H(x, z, A)],$$

$$\text{all } x \in X, z \in Z, A \in \mathscr{X}, B \in \mathscr{Z},$$

defines a transition function on $(S, \mathscr{S})$. [*Hint.* Recall the proof of Theorem 8.9.]

b. Show that if Assumptions 9.4, 9.5, 9.16, and 9.17 hold, and if g is continuous, then P has the Feller property.

9.7 Bibliographic Notes

Most of the references cited in Section 4.6 were also drawn upon in this chapter. In particular, Section 9.1 is based on Blackwell (1965). Bertsekas and Shreve (1978), Dynkin and Yushkevich (1979), and Gihman and Skorohod (1979) deal in detail with methods that apply when the hypotheses of Theorems 9.2 and 9.4 fail because of measurability problems.

On the differentiability of the value and policy functions, Blume, Easley, and O'Hara (1982) pursue a line that has no counterpart in deterministic models. Their idea is applicable to the second of the two formulations of stochastic dynamic programming introduced in Section 9.1. Assume that the exogenous shocks $\{z_t\}$ are i.i.d., with a distribution described by a continuous density q. Also assume that the shock z is an argument of the law of motion ϕ, but not of F or Γ. In this case the functional equation has the form

$$v(x) = \sup_{y \in \Gamma(x)} \left\{ F(x, y) + \beta \int v[\phi(x, y, z')]q(z')dz' \right\}.$$

Finally, assume that for each (x, y) the function $\phi(x, y, \cdot): Z \to X$ is one-to-one and continuously differentiable; let $h: X \times Y \times X \to Z$ denote the inverse. Under these conditions, we can use the change of variable $w = \phi(x, y, z')$ to rewrite the functional equation as

$$v(x) = \sup_{y \in \Gamma(x)} \left\{ F(x, y) + \beta \int v(w)q[h(x, y, w)]h_3(x, y, w)dw \right\},$$

where h_3 is the derivative of h with respect to its third argument. Notice that x appears on the right side of this equation only as an argument of the functions F, $q \cdot h$, and h_3, not of v. Hence if F, q, and ϕ are sufficiently smooth and if the maximum on the right is attained in the interior of $\Gamma(x)$, we can guarantee that the value and policy functions have derivatives of any order we like. The assumptions needed to carry this line to success are obviously more restrictive than those we have used in Section 9.2. But in applications where they hold, one has a great deal of information about the value function that is not available by any other means.

The use of the Euler equations to construct optimal plans in quadratic problems, discussed briefly in Section 9.5, is discussed more fully and is illustrated with examples in Sargent (1979). For the seminal use of direct empirical tests based on Euler equations, see Hall (1978).

10 Applications of Stochastic Dynamic Programming

In this chapter we illustrate how the methods developed in Chapter 9 can be used to study a variety of economic problems. Some are stochastic analogues to problems in Chapter 5, and it will sharpen your intuition to compare results. Others are problems with no, or with trivial, deterministic counterparts.

10.1 The One-Sector Model of Optimal Growth

A stochastic analogue to the optimal growth problem studied in Section 5.1 can be obtained by adding random shocks to the production function. For simplicity assume that these shocks enter multiplicatively. This specification leads to the problem

$$(1) \qquad \sup E \left\{ \sum_{t=0}^{\infty} \beta^t U[z_t f(x_t) - x_{t+1}] \right\}$$

$$\text{s.t.} \quad 0 \le x_{t+1} \le z_t f(x_t), \quad t = 0, 1, \ldots,$$

$$x_0 \ge 0 \quad \text{and} \quad z_0 \ge 0 \text{ given,}$$

where the expectation is over the sequence of shocks $\{z_t\}_{t=1}^{\infty}$. This problem is defined by the parameter β; the functions $U: \mathbf{R}_+ \to \mathbf{R}$ and $f: \mathbf{R}_+ \to \mathbf{R}$; and a specification for the sequence of shocks $\{z_t\}$. For the latter assume that

(Z1) $Z = [1, \bar{z}]$, where $1 < \bar{z} < +\infty$, with the Borel sets $\mathfrak{Z}$.
(Z2) $\{z_t\}$ is an i.i.d. sequence of shocks, each drawn according to the probability measure λ on $(Z, \mathfrak{Z})$.

288

We will also impose the restrictions on β, U, and f used in Section 5.1. To begin with, assume that (U1)–(U4) and (T1)–(T4) of that earlier problem hold. [Notice that, as in the deterministic problem, the monotonicity restrictions on U and f justify solving out for consumption in (1).]

Exercise 10.1 a. Replace $E(\cdot)$ in (1) with a precisely specified sum of integrals. Describe precisely the set of feasible plans for (1).

The functional equation corresponding to (1) is

$$(2) \qquad v(x, z) = \max_{0 \le y \le zf(x)} \left\{ U[zf(x) - y] + \beta \int v(y, z')\lambda(dz') \right\}.$$

Under Assumptions (T1)–(T4), we can define $\bar{x}$ as the unique positive value satisfying $\bar{x} = \bar{z}f(\bar{x})$. It is obviously convenient to restrict the capital stock to lie in the interval $X = [0, \bar{x}]$ and to take v as defined on $S = X \times Z$.

Exercise 10.1 b. Show that there exists a unique bounded continuous function v satisfying (2) and that the associated optimal policy correspondence G is nonempty, compact-valued, and u.h.c. What can be said about the relationship between the pair (v, G) and the solution to the sequence problem in part (a)?

c. Show that v is strictly increasing and strictly concave in its first argument and that G is a continuous single-valued function; call this function g.

d. Show that g has the form $g(x, z) = h[zf(x)]$, where h is continuous and strictly increasing. Notice that this implies that g is strictly increasing in both of its arguments. Show that the optimal consumption policy $c(x, z) = zf(x) - g(x, z)$ is also strictly increasing in both of its arguments.

e. Assume in addition that (U5) and (T5) hold. Show that if $g(x, z) \in (0, zf(x))$, then v is continuously differentiable at (x, z), with derivatives

$$v_x(x, z) = U'[zf(x) - g(x, z)]zf'(x) \quad \text{and}$$

$$v_z(x, z) = U'[zf(x) - g(x, z)]f(x).$$

Next, suppose that instead of (Z2) we have

(Z3) *Q is a transition function on $(Z, \mathfrak{Z})$, and Q has the Feller property. The sequence of random shocks $\{z_t\}$ is a Markov process generated by Q.*

Exercise 10.1   f. Show that if (Z2) is replaced by (Z3), the conclusions in (a)–(c) are unchanged. Does the policy function g take the form in part (d) in this case? Is g necessarily increasing in z? Show that if Q is monotone, then v and g are both increasing in z. Which parts of (e) still hold?

10.2   Optimal Growth with Two Capital Goods

Consider the following modification of the model above. Let (U1)–(U5) and (Z1)–(Z2) hold, but suppose that there are two types of capital, x_1 and x_2. Assume that there is a single output and that the production function $f: \mathbf{R}_+^2 \to \mathbf{R}$ satisfies (T1) and (T3)–(T5). Assume that capital depreciates completely within each period and that output can be consumed or used as either type of capital. The technology constraints are then

$$0 \le y_1, y_2 \quad \text{and} \quad y_1 + y_2 \le zf(x_1, x_2).$$

Exercise 10.2   a. What additional restriction on f ensures that the set of sustainable capital stocks is compact?

b. State the optimal growth problem for this economy in sequence form; state the corresponding functional equation. Show that there exists a unique bounded continuous function v satisfying the functional equation and that v is strictly increasing, strictly concave, and once differentiable in its first two arguments. Show that the associated policy correspondence is a continuous, single-valued function, g.

c. Show that if $\partial f/\partial x_1$ is increasing in x_2 and $\partial f/\partial x_2$ is increasing in x_1, then $g(s) = [g_1(s), g_2(s)]$ is strictly increasing in all its arguments.

d. Show that this model can be reformulated in terms of only one endogenous state variable and that the analysis in Section 10.1 applies to the reformulated model.

10.3   Optimal Growth with Many Goods

In this problem we show that the methods in Chapter 9 can be used to analyze the standard many-sector optimal growth model under uncertainty. This model is the obvious generalization of the two above to include an arbitrary number of consumption and capital goods.

Let $(Z, \mathscr{Z})$ and Q be a measurable space and transition function that satisfy Assumption 9.5; let $(Z^t, \mathscr{Z}^t)$ and $\mu^t(z_0, \cdot)$, $z_0 \in Z$, $t = 1, 2, \ldots$, be as defined in Section 8.2.

Consider an economy in which in every period and every state of the world there are l capital goods and M consumption goods. A consumption allocation for the representative consumer in this economy is a sequence $c = \{c_t\}_{t=0}^{\infty}$, where $c_t: Z^t \rightarrow \mathbf{R}_+^M$ is a $\mathscr{Z}^t$-measurable function, all t. The preferences of the representative consumer are given by

(1) $$u(c) = \sum_{t=0}^{\infty} \beta^t \int_{Z^t} U[c_t(z^t)] \mu^t(z_0, dz^t),$$

where $U: \mathbf{R}_+^M \rightarrow \mathbf{R}$ is bounded, continuous, strictly increasing, and strictly concave, and where $\beta \in (0, 1)$.

Let $(X, \mathscr{X})$, with $X \subset \mathbf{R}_+^l$ satisfy Assumption 9.4. The technology is described by a correspondence $\Phi: X \times Z \rightarrow \mathbf{R}_+^M \times X$, where $(c, y) \in \Phi(x, z)$ means that the pair (c, y) of consumption goods and end-of-period capital goods is jointly producible given the pair (x, z) of beginning-of-period capital goods and current technology shock. Assume that

   a. Φ is nonempty, compact-valued, convex-valued, and continuous;

   b. if $x, x' \in X$, $z \in Z$, $x \leq x'$, and $(c, y) \in \Phi(x, z)$, then $(c, y) \in \Phi(x', z)$;

   c. if $x, x' \in X$, $z \in Z$, $\theta \in [0, 1]$, $(c, y) \in \Phi(x, z)$, and $(c', y') \in \Phi(x', z)$, then $[\theta c + (1 - \theta)c', \theta y + (1 - \theta)y'] \in \Phi[\theta x + (1 - \theta)x', z]$.

To apply the analysis of Section 9.2, define the correspondence Γ: $X \times Z \rightarrow X$, the set $A \subset X \times X \times Z$, and the return function $F: A \rightarrow \mathbf{R}$ by

$$\Gamma(x, z) = \{y \in X: (c, y) \in \Phi(x, y) \text{ for some } c \in \mathbf{R}_+^M\};$$

$$A = \{(x, y, z) \in X \times X \times Z: y \in \Gamma(x, z)\};$$

$$F(x, y, z) = \max_{c \in \mathbf{R}_+^M} U(c) \quad \text{s.t.} \quad (c, y) \in \Phi(x, z).$$

Exercise 10.3 a. Show that Γ, A, and F are well defined and satisfy Assumptions 9.6–9.11.

It then follows immediately from Theorems 9.6–9.8 that there exists a unique solution to the functional equation

$$v(x, z) = \max_{y \in \Gamma(x,z)} \left[F(x, y, z) + \beta \int v(y, z')Q(z, dz') \right];$$

that for each fixed $z \in Z$, $v(\cdot, z)$ is strictly increasing in each of its first l arguments and strictly concave jointly in its first l arguments; and that the optimal policy function g is continuous and single-valued.

Given $(x_0, z_0) \in X \times Z$, define π^* to be the plan generated by g from (x_0, z_0):

$$\pi_0^* = g(x_0, z_0),$$

$$\pi_t^*(z^t) = g[\pi_{t-1}^*(z^{t-1}), z_t], \quad \text{all } z^t \in Z^t, \text{ all } t;$$

and γ^* to be the consumption plan corresponding to π^*:

$$\gamma_t^*(z^t) = \underset{c \in \mathbf{R}_+^M}{\operatorname{argmax}} \ U(c)$$

s.t. $[c, \pi_t^*(z^t)] \in \Phi[\pi_{t-1}^*(z^{t-1}), z_t], \quad \text{all } z^t \in Z^t, \text{ all } t.$

Exercise 10.3 b. Show that (γ^*, π^*) is a solution to the problem: maximize (1), given (x_0, z_0), and subject to the feasibility constraint $(c_t, x_{t+1}) \in \Phi(x_t, z_t)$, all z^t, all t.

10.4 Industry Investment under Uncertainty

Consider an industry in which costs of production and of investment are known with certainty and are constant over time, but in which exogenous shocks to demand follow a stationary, first-order Markov process. In addition, the technologies for both production and investment display constant returns to scale. Here we begin studying the problem of total (consumers' plus producers') surplus maximization for this industry; we complete the analysis in Section 13.4, where the issue of convergence to a stationary distribution is addressed. Then in Section 16.4 we show that the results of the surplus-maximization model can be interpreted as the competitive equilibrium of an industry with many small producers, each with the same (constant-returns-to-scale) technology.

Let $Z = [\underline{z}, \bar{z}]$ be an interval in $\mathbf{R}_+$, with its Borel subsets $\mathcal{Z}$. The exogenous state variable $z \in Z$ is an index of the strength of demand. Specifically, demand is described by the inverse demand curve $D: \mathbf{R}_+ \times Z \to \mathbf{R}_+$. That is, $p = D(q, z)$ is the market-clearing price when q is the aggregate quantity supplied and z is the state of demand. Assume that D is continuous, strictly decreasing in q, and strictly increasing in z, with

$$D(0, z) > 0 \quad \text{and} \quad \lim_{q \to \infty} D(q, z) = 0, \quad \text{all } z \in Z.$$

Define $U: \mathbf{R}_+ \times Z \to \mathbf{R}_+$ as the integral

$$U(q, z) = \int_0^q D(v, z)dv, \quad \text{all } q \in \mathbf{R}_+, z \in Z.$$

$U(q, z)$ is total consumers' surplus (the area under the demand curve) when q is the quantity consumed and z is the state of demand. Assume that U is uniformly bounded; that is, for some $A < \infty$,

$$\lim_{q \to \infty} U(q, z) \le A, \quad \text{all } z \in Z.$$

The endogenous state variable for the system is x, the total industry capital stock. Output is produced using capital as the only input, so that there are no direct costs of production. Without loss of generality we can choose units so that aggregate industry output is equal to the aggregate industry capital stock, $q = x$.

Investment costs are the only costs, and the unit cost of investment is assumed to depend on the (percentage) rate of increase in the capital stock. Specifically, if the current capital stock is $x > 0$ and next period's stock is $y > 0$, then the cost of investment is $xc(y/x)$. Assume that $c: \mathbf{R}_+ \to \mathbf{R}_+$ is continuously differentiable and that for some $\delta \in (0, 1)$, $c(a) = 0$ on $[0, 1 - \delta]$ and c is strictly increasing and strictly convex on $(1 - \delta, +\infty)$. (See Figure 10.1.) The parameter δ is interpreted as the rate of depreciation of capital. Note that since δ is strictly less than one, for $x > 0$ the strictly positive capital stock $y = (1 - \delta)x$ can be carried over at no cost. Since costs of investment are not defined for $x = 0$, we will exclude that point from the state space and let $X = \mathbf{R}_{++}$.

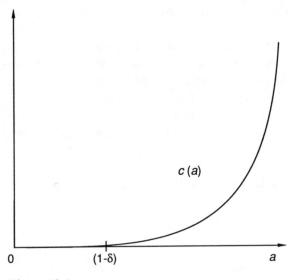

Figure 10.1

Also note that since there are constant returns to scale in both production and investment, the distribution of the capital stock over firms does not matter. For our purposes here, it may be easier to think of this problem as one involving just one firm. We return to this issue in Section 16.4, where we show that the solution developed here can be interpreted as a competitive equilibrium outcome.

Let Q be a transition function on $(Z, \mathfrak{Z})$; assume that Q is monotone and has the Feller property. Given an initial value $z_0 \in Z$, the evolution of demand conditions over time is described by the transition function Q. Assume that the interest rate $r > 0$ is constant over time. Consider the problem of maximizing total expected discounted consumers' plus producers' surplus, given the initial state (x_0, z_0):

(1) $$\sup E \left\{ \sum_{t=0}^{\infty} (1 + r)^{-t} [U(x_t, z_t) - x_t c(x_{t+1}/x_t)] \right\}.$$

Exercise 10.4   a. Give a precise statement of the problem in (1) in sequence form, and show that the supremum function for that problem is well defined. What can be said about the relationship between the supremum function and solutions to the functional equation

(2) $$v(x, z) = \sup_{y \in X} \left[U(x, z) - xc(y/x) + (1 + r)^{-1} \int v(y, z')Q(z, dz') \right]?$$

What can be said about the relationship between optimal plans for the sequence problem and the policy correspondence for (2)?

Our next task is to establish the existence and uniqueness of a function $v: X \times Z \to \mathbf{R}$ satisfying (2) and to characterize that function as precisely as possible. Note that since $X = \mathbf{R}_{++}$, the maximization in (2) is over a set that is neither closed nor bounded. To sidestep this problem, it is useful to define $\Gamma: \mathbf{R}_{++} \to \mathbf{R}_{++}$ by

$$\Gamma(x) = [(1 - \delta')x, M], \quad x \in (0, M],$$

$$\Gamma(x) = [(1 - \delta')x, x], \quad x \in (M, +\infty).$$

where $\delta < \delta' < 1$, and M is a suitably chosen (very large) number.

Exercise 10.4 b. Show that there exists a unique bounded continuous function $v: X \times Z \to \mathbf{R}_+$ satisfying

(2') $$v(x, z) = \max_{y \in \Gamma(x)} \left[U(x, z) - xc(y/x) + (1 + r)^{-1} \int v(y, z')Q(z, dz') \right].$$

Show that the function v satisfying (2') also satisfies (2).
 c. Show that v is strictly increasing in both arguments and strictly concave in its first argument. Show that the optimal policy correspondence associated with v is a (single-valued) continuous function; call this function g. Show that for each $(x, z) \in X \times Z$, $g(x, z)$ lies in the interior of the set $\Gamma(x)$. Show that for each $z \in Z$, $v(\cdot, z)$ is continuously differentiable on X.
 d. Show that for each $z \in Z$, $g(x, z)$ is strictly increasing in x, but with a slope strictly less than one. (Refer to Figure 10.2.) Notice that these facts imply that the growth rate in aggregate capacity, $g(x, z)/x$, is strictly decreasing in current capacity x.
 e. Show that for each $x \in X$, $g(x, z)$ is nondecreasing in z, and is strictly increasing at points where gross investment is strictly positive: where

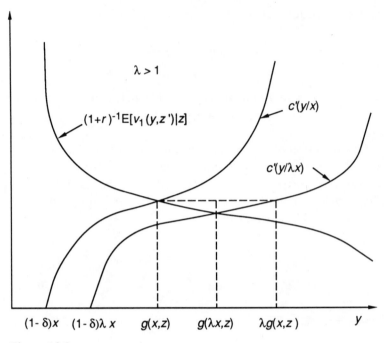

Figure 10.2

$g(x, z) > (1 - \delta)x$. (Refer to Figure 10.3.) Notice that these facts imply that the growth rate in aggregate capacity, $g(x, z)/x$, is strictly increasing in the state of current demand, z.

Next, consider the long-run behavior of the aggregate capital stock under the assumption that the demand shocks are i.i.d. That is, suppose that there is a probability measure μ on $(Z, \mathscr{Z})$ such that $Q(z, \cdot) = \mu(\cdot)$, all $z \in Z$.

Exercise 10.4   f.   Which, if any, of the conclusions in parts (a)–(e) are changed under the assumption of i.i.d. shocks to demand? Show that under this assumption, the optimal policy function does not depend on z; that is, it can be written as simply $g(x)$. Hence for any $x_0 > 0$ the unique optimal plan is given by the deterministic difference equation $x_{t+1} = g(x_t)$, $t = 0, 1, \ldots$. Show that for any $x_0 > 0$ the optimal sequence $\{x_t\}$ converges to a stationary point $\hat{x}$ that is independent of x_0. Under what assumptions on demand and costs is $\hat{x}$ strictly positive?

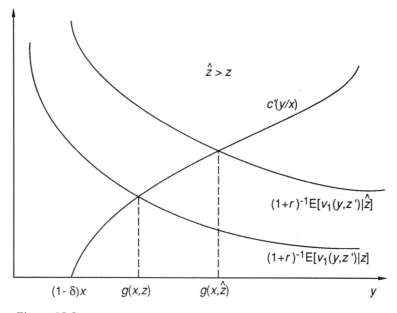

Figure 10.3

10.5 Production and Inventory Accumulation

In markets for many agricultural commodities, inventories play an important role in smoothing the stochastic shocks to supply that result from fluctuations in the weather. In this section we study the determination of consumption, production, and inventories in such a setting. Here, as in Section 10.4, we study the problem of maximizing total (consumers' plus producers') surplus. As noted there, the arguments to be discussed in Chapter 15 can be used to show that the solution to this problem can be interpreted as a competitive equilibrium allocation.

Assume that demand is constant over time and is described by the inverse demand curve $D: \mathbf{R}_+ \to \mathbf{R}_+$. That is, $D(q)$ is the market-clearing price when $q > 0$ is the quantity supplied. Assume that D is continuous and strictly decreasing, with $0 < D(0) < \infty$, and $\lim_{q \to \infty} D(q) = 0$. Define the integral $U: \mathbf{R}_+ \to \mathbf{R}_+$ by

$$U(q) = \int_0^q D(v)dv, \quad \text{all } q \in \mathbf{R}_+,$$

so that U describes total consumers' surplus (the area under the demand curve). Assume that $\lim_{q\to\infty} U(q) < \infty$.

The technology is as follows. In each period t, the planner must decide how to allocate the beginning-of-period stock of goods x_t (stocks carried over from last period plus the current harvest) between final consumption c_t and end-of-period stocks y_t to be carried over to the next period. He must also decide how much input n_t (labor and so on) to devote to production.

Let $\phi(y)$ denote the cost of holding (end-of-period) inventories of $y \geq 0$ units; assume that $\phi: \mathbf{R}_+ \to \mathbf{R}_+$ is strictly increasing, strictly convex, and continuously differentiable, with $\phi(0) = 0$ and $\phi'(0) = 0$. Let $c(n)$ denote the cost of devoting inputs of $n \geq 0$ to production; assume that $c: \mathbf{R}_+ \to \mathbf{R}_+$ is strictly increasing, strictly convex, and continuously differentiable, with $c(0) = 0$ and $c'(0) = 0$.

The uncertainty in this model concerns the size of the harvest. Let $\Omega = [\underline{\omega}, \bar{\omega}]$ be an interval in $\mathbf{R}_+$, let $\mathscr{F}$ be the Borel sets of Ω, and let μ be a probability measure on $(\Omega, \mathscr{F})$. Assume that $n_{t-1}\omega_t$ is the size of the harvest if n_{t-1} is the input in period $t-1$ and ω_t is the realization of the random shock in period t. The shocks are i.i.d. over time, with probabilities given by μ.

Exercise 10.5 a. Cost and output have been specified as strictly convex and linear functions respectively of the quantity of input n. Show, by redefining "units of input" (in a nonlinear fashion), that this is equivalent to specifying cost and output as linear and strictly concave respectively in the "quantity of input."

Let x_t, y_t, n_t, and ω_t be as described above. Then the surplus-maximization problem is

(1) $$\sup_{\{y_t, n_t\}} E\left\{\sum_{t=0}^{\infty} \beta^t[U(x_t - y_t) - \phi(y_t) - c(n_t)]\right\}$$

s.t. $x_{t+1} = y_t + n_t\omega_{t+1}$,   all t,

$y_t, n_t \geq 0$,   all t,

given x_0.

Exercise 10.5 b. Give a precise statement of the problem in (1) in sequence form, and show that the supremum function for that problem is well defined. What can be said about the relationship between the supremum function and solutions to the functional equation

$$(2) \qquad v(x) = \sup_{y,n \geq 0} \left[U(x - y) - \phi(y) - c(n) + \beta \int v(y + n\omega)\mu(d\omega) \right]?$$

What can be said about the relationship between optimal plans for the sequence problem and the policy correspondence for (2)? Explain briefly why the current value of the exogenous shock does not appear as a state variable in (2).

c. Show that there exists a unique bounded continuous function $v: \mathbf{R}_+ \to \mathbf{R}_+$ satisfying (2). What argument is needed to take care of the fact that the maximization is over an unbounded set? Show that v is strictly increasing and strictly concave. Let $Y(x)$ and $N(x)$ denote the maximizing values of y and n, respectively, as functions of x. Show that Y and N are single-valued and continuous. Show that v is differentiable and that $v'(x) = U'[x - Y(x)]$.

To characterize the behavior of consumption, labor input, and inventories more sharply, it is useful to look at the first-order conditions

$$(3) \qquad U'[x - Y(x)] + \phi'[Y(x)] \geq \beta \int v'[Y(x) + N(x)\omega] \, d\mu,$$
$$\text{with equality if } Y(x) > 0;$$

$$(4) \qquad c'[N(x)] \geq \beta \int \omega v'[Y(x) + N(x)\omega] \, d\mu,$$
$$\text{with equality if } N(x) > 0.$$

Exercise 10.5 d. Show that consumption, $c(x) = x - Y(x)$, is strictly increasing in the beginning-of-period stock, x.

Storage and production are both ways of increasing the total supply of goods next period. Next we will show that a higher beginning-of-period stock x leads to more storage and less production.

Exercise 10.5 e. Let $x_2 > x_1$. Suppose that $Y(x_2) \leq Y(x_1)$ and $Y(x_1) > 0$. Use (3) to show that this implies that

$$(5) \qquad \int v'[Y(x_1) + N(x_1)\omega] \, d\mu > \int v'[Y(x_2) + N(x_2)\omega] \, d\mu,$$

and hence that $N(x_2) > N(x_1)$. Use (4) to show that this, in turn, implies that

(6) $$\int \omega v'[Y(x_1) + N(x_1)\omega]\, d\mu < \int \omega v'[Y(x_2) + N(x_2)\omega]\, d\mu.$$

Next we will use (5) and (6) to obtain a contradiction to the hypothesis that $Y(x_2) \leq Y(x_1)$ and $Y(x_1) > 0$. Define

$$\gamma(\omega) = v'[Y(x_2) + N(x_2)\omega] - v'[Y(x_1) + N(x_1)\omega].$$

Since $Y(x_2) \leq Y(x_1)$ and $N(x_2) > N(x_1)$, it follows immediately that

$$\gamma(\omega) \gtreqless 0 \text{ as } \omega \lesseqgtr A, \quad \text{where } A = [Y(x_1) - Y(x_2)]/[N(x_2) - N(x_1)] > 0.$$

Then (5) and (6) respectively state that $E[\gamma(\omega)] < 0$ and $E[\gamma(\omega)\omega] > 0$.

Exercise 10.5 f. Show that this is a contradiction.

Hence if $x_2 > x_1$, then either $Y(x_2) > Y(x_1)$ or $Y(x_2) = Y(x_1) = 0$.

Exercise 10.5 g. Show that $N(x) > 0$, all x, so that (4) always holds with equality. Use this fact and the result established in part (e) to show that $x_2 > x_1$ implies that $N(x_2) < N(x_1)$. How would this result be changed if $c'(0) > 0$?

10.6 Asset Prices in an Exchange Economy

In this problem we study the determination of equilibrium asset prices in a pure exchange economy. There are a finite number of productive assets, each in fixed supply, that produce random quantities of the single consumption good each period; we call these dividends. Thus, an asset is a claim to a stochastic dividend stream. We normalize units of assets so that there is one unit of each asset per consumer. There are a large number of consumers, all with identical tastes and with equal endowments of all the assets. The consumption good is not storable.

In each period there are spot markets for the single consumption good and for shares in the assets. Since all agents are identical, the competitive equilibrium quantities are trivial: in each period each consumer holds one unit of each asset and consumes all of the dividends (consumption goods) produced by those assets. That is, although competitive markets open each period, no consumer actually chooses a non-zero trade. Our goal is to characterize the prices that support this allocation as a competitive equilibrium.

The preferences of the representative consumer over random consumption sequences are

(1) $$E\left[\sum_{t=0}^{\infty} \beta^t U(c_t)\right],$$

where $U: \mathbf{R}_+ \to \mathbf{R}$ is bounded, continuously differentiable, strictly increasing, and strictly concave, with $U(0) = 0$, and where $\beta \in (0, 1)$.

There are $i = 1, \ldots, k$ productive assets. Let Z be a compact subset of $\mathbf{R}_+^k$, with its Borel subsets $\mathscr{Z}$. Dividends in any period are described by a vector $z = (z_1, \ldots, z_k) \in Z$, where z_i denotes the dividend (the quantity of current consumption good) paid by one unit of asset i. The dividends follow a Markov process, with stationary transition function Q on $(Z, \mathscr{Z})$, and Q has the Feller property.

Ownership of assets is determined by trading on a competitive stock market, where in each period the current consumption good and shares in all of the assets are traded. Prices in each period are normalized so that the price of the current consumption good is unity. Our goal is to characterize asset prices in a stationary competitive equilibrium. In any such equilibrium, asset prices in each period are described by a (stationary) function $p: Z \to \mathbf{R}_+^k$, where $p(z) = [p_1(z), \ldots, p_k(z)]$ is the vector of asset prices that prevail if the current state of the economy is $z \in Z$. Each consumer takes the function p as given. (Note that we are making use of the fact that in equilibrium the distribution of wealth across consumers does not change. If consumers were heterogeneous in either preferences or endowments of assets or both, then in general the distribution of wealth would change over time, and the joint distribution of tastes and wealth would be another state variable.)

The consumer's asset holdings in any period are described by a vector $x = (x_1, \ldots, x_k) \in \mathbf{R}_+^k$. His problem, viewed in period 0, is as follows. Given the price function p, the initial state of the economy z_0, and his initial asset holdings x_0, he wants to choose a sequence of plans for consumption and end-of-period asset holdings that maximizes his present discounted expected utility (1) subject to the constraints

$$c_t + p(z_t) \cdot x_{t+1} \leq [z_t + p(z_t)] \cdot x_t, \quad \text{all } z^t, \text{ all } t,$$

$$c_t, x_{t+1} \geq 0, \quad \text{all } z^t, \text{ all } t.$$

Exercise 10.6 a. Formulate the consumer's problem in sequence form. Show that given any continuous price function p, the supremum function v^{p*} for the consumer's problem is well defined.

In order to study the functional equation corresponding to the problem in (a), it is convenient to impose an upper bound on the consumer's holdings of any asset. Since we know that in equilibrium the consumer chooses to hold exactly one unit of each asset, any bound $\bar{x} > 1$ is nonbinding in equilibrium. Then let $X = [0, \bar{x}]^k$ with its Borel subsets $\mathscr{X}$, and define the correspondence $\Gamma: X \times Z \to X$ by

$$\Gamma(x, z) = \{y \in X: p(z) \cdot y \leq [z + p(z)] \cdot x\}.$$

Thus $\Gamma(x, z)$ is the set of feasible end-of-period portfolios if the consumer's beginning-of-period portfolio is x and the current state is z. For simplicity, we consider the case where all assets have strictly positive dividends in all states, $Z \subset \mathbf{R}^k_{++}$, and hence the price function is strictly positive in all states.

Exercise 10.6 b. Show that for any continuous, strictly positive function $p: Z \to \mathbf{R}_{++}$, there exists a unique bounded continuous function $v^p: X \times Z \to \mathbf{R}_+$ such that

$$v^p(x, z) = \max_{y \in \Gamma(x,y)} \left\{ U[z \cdot x + p(z) \cdot (x - y)] + \beta \int v^p(y, z')Q(z, dz') \right\}.$$

Show that for each $z \in Z$, v^p is strictly increasing and weakly concave in x. Show that the associated policy correspondence G^p is nonempty, compact-valued, convex-valued, and u.h.c. Explain briefly why v^p is only weakly concave in x, and why there may be multiple optimal portfolios. Show that for any $(x, z) \in X \times Z$,

$$p(z) \cdot y = p(z) \cdot y', \quad \text{all } y, y' \in G^p(x, z).$$

c. Let p be any continuous, strictly positive price function, and let (v^p, G^p) be as defined in part (b). Fix $(x, z) \in X \times Z$. Show that if $x \in \text{int } X$ and if $G^p(x, z) \cap \text{int } \Gamma(x, z)$ is nonempty, then $v^p(\cdot, z)$ is differentiable with respect to x at (x, z), with derivatives given by

(1) $v_i^p(x, z) = \partial v^p(x, z)/\partial x_i = U'[z \cdot x + p(z) \cdot (x - y)][z_i + p_i(z)],$

        $i = 1, \ldots, k$, all $y \in G^p(x, z)$.

Show that if $G^p(x, z) \cap \text{int } \Gamma(x, z)$, is nonempty, then

(2) $U'[z \cdot x + p(z) \cdot (x - y)]p_i(z) = \beta \int v_i^p(y, z')Q(z, dz'),$

        $i = 1, \ldots, k$, all $y \in G^p(x, z)$.

  To compute the equilibrium prices for this economy, we will use the fact that (1) and (2) hold at equilibrium and that we know the equilibrium quantities in advance. Specifically, we know that if each consumer begins with one unit of each asset, then in equilibrium he must choose to hold that same portfolio in every successive period, under any realization for the endowment shocks, and hence consume the dividends from that portfolio. Note that since $Z \subset \mathbf{R}_{++}^k$ it follows that $z \cdot 1 > 0$, all $z \in Z$, so $1 \in \text{int } \Gamma(1, z)$, all $z \in Z$.
  Suppose that p^* is an equilibrium price function and that p^* is continuous. Let v^* be the value function described in (b), and let $v_i^*, i = 1, \ldots, k$, denote the partial derivatives of v^*.

  Exercise 10.6   d. Show that

(3) $v_i^*(1, z) = U'(z \cdot 1)[z_i + p_i^*(z)], \quad i = 1, \ldots, k; \quad \text{and}$

(4) $U'(z \cdot 1)p_i^*(z) = \beta \int v_i^*(1, z')Q(z, dz'), \quad i = 1, \ldots, k.$

Substituting from (3) into (4) to eliminate the v_i^*'s, we find that

(5) $U'(z \cdot 1)p_i^*(z) = \beta \int U'(z' \cdot 1)[z_i' + p_i^*(z')]Q(z, dz'), \quad i = 1, \ldots, k.$

Any continuous function p^* satisfying (5) is an equilibrium price function. Our final task is to show that there exists exactly one such function.

To this end, define the functions

$$h_i(z) = \beta \int U'(z' \cdot \underline{1}) z_i' Q(z, dz'), \quad i = 1, \ldots, k.$$

Then finding an equilibrium price function $p^*(z) = [p_1^*(z), \ldots, p_k^*(z)]$ is equivalent to finding functions $\phi_1(z), \ldots, \phi_k(z)$ satisfying the k (independent) functional equations

$$(6) \qquad \phi_i(z) = h_i(z) + \beta \int \phi_i(z') Q(z, dz'), \quad i = 1, \ldots, k.$$

If a solution to (6) can be found, then $p_i^*(z) = \phi_i(z)/U'(z \cdot \underline{1}), i = 1, \ldots, k,$ is a solution to (5).

Exercise 10.6   e. Show that for each $i = 1, \ldots, k$, there exists a unique bounded continuous function ϕ_i satisfying (6). Show that each ϕ_i is strictly positive. Express the solution $\phi_i(z)$ in terms of the function h_i and the iterates Q^n of the transition function.

f. What is the interpretation of (5)? What can be said about asset prices in the case where utility is linear, $U(c) = c$? What can be said in the case where there are a very large number of assets, with i.i.d. returns?

g. How can dividends and asset prices of zero be incorporated?

10.7   A Model of Search Unemployment

Consider a worker who begins each period with a current wage offer and has two alternative actions. He can work at that wage or he can search for a new wage offer. If he chooses to search, he earns nothing during the current period, and his new wage is drawn according to some fixed probability measure. He cannot divide his time within a period between searching and working. Moreover, if a worker chooses to work during the current period, then with probability $1 - \theta$ the same wage is available to him next period. But with probability θ he will lose his job at the beginning of next period and begin next period with a "wage" of zero.

The worker does not value leisure, and his preferences over random consumption sequences $\{c_t\}$ are given by

$$E\left[\sum_{t=0}^{\infty} \beta^t U(c_t)\right].$$

The worker cannot borrow or lend, so his consumption is equal to his earnings during each period.

The decision problem for this worker is defined by β, U, θ, and the probability distribution over new wage offers. Assume that $0 < \beta < 1$, and let $U: \mathbf{R}_+ \to \mathbf{R}_+$ be continuously differentiable, strictly increasing, and strictly concave, with $U(0) = 0$ and $U'(0) < \infty$. Assume that all wage offers lie in the interval $W = [0, \bar{w}]$, and let f be a density on that interval.

It is possible, but awkward, to set up this problem in sequence form. To do so we need two exogenous state variables. The first is $d \in D = \{0, 1\}$, where $d = 0$ or 1 is interpreted respectively as meaning that the worker does or does not lose his job at the beginning of the current period, given that he chose to work last period. The second is $z \in Z = [0, \bar{w}]$, where z is interpreted as the worker's current wage offer, given that he chose to search last period. In addition there is one endogenous state variable, the current wage $w \in W$. In each period, given his current wage offer w, the worker chooses an action $y \in Y = \{0, 1\}$, where $y = 0$ or 1 is interpreted respectively as meaning that the worker chooses to search or to work at his current job.

Exercise 10.7   a. What is the law of motion $\phi: W \times Y \times D \times Z \to W$ for this model? That is, describe w_{t+1} in terms of $(w_t, y_t, d_{t+1}, z_{t+1})$.

b. Formulate the worker's decision problem as a choice of functions mapping partial histories $(d^t, z^t) = [(d_1, z_1), \ldots, (d_t, z_t)]$ of exogenous shocks into actions and current wage offers that satisfy the law of motion above, given the initial state (w_0, d_0, z_0). Show that the supremum function v^* for this problem is well defined and depends only on w_0 (not on d_0 or z_0).

The recursive formulation of this problem is much simpler and more natural. For notational convenience, drop the asterisk and let v be the supremum function for the problem in (b). Suppose that a worker's current wage offer is w, that he chooses to work at this wage for one period, and that he will follow an optimal policy (if one exists) forever after. Then his expected present discounted value of utility is

$$U(w) + \beta[(1 - \theta)v(w) + \theta v(0)].$$

If he chooses to search instead, his expected utility is

$$0 + \beta \int_0^{\bar{w}} v(w')f(w')dw'.$$

Combining these possibilities, we find that v must satisfy

$$(1) \quad v(w) = \max \left\{ U(w) + \beta[(1 - \theta)v(w) + \theta v(0)], \beta \int_0^{\bar{w}} v(w')f(w')dw' \right\}.$$

Exercise 10.7   c. Show that there exists a unique bounded continuous function v satisfying (1) and that v is the supremum function for the problem in part (b). Show that v is weakly increasing.

The value function v can be characterized more sharply by exploiting special features of (1). First, define

$$(2) \qquad A = \beta \int_0^{\bar{w}} v(w')f(w')dw',$$

and note that $v(0) = A$.

Exercise 10.7   d. Show that there is a unique $w^* \in W$ such that

$$v(w^*) = U(w^*) + \beta[(1 - \theta)v(w^*) + \theta A] = A.$$

It follows from part (d) that w^* is the unique value satisfying

$$(3) \qquad U(w^*) = (1 - \beta)A.$$

Exercise 10.7   e. Show that v has the form

$$(4) \qquad v(w) = \begin{cases} A & \text{if } w < w^* \\ \dfrac{U(w) + \beta\theta A}{1 - \beta(1 - \theta)} & \text{if } w \geq w^*, \end{cases}$$

as shown in Figure 10.4.

Equation (4) gives the solution v to (1) in terms of A and w^*. The value of A is in turn given in terms of v by (2), and the value of w^* by (3).

Exercise 10.7   f. Use (2) and (4) to show that

$$(5) \qquad (1 - \beta)A = \frac{\beta}{1 + \beta\theta - \beta F(w^*)} \int_{w^*}^{\bar{w}} U(w)f(w)dw;$$

where $F(w) = \int_0^w f(w')dw'$ is the cumulative distribution function corresponding to f.

Equations (3) and (5) are now two equations in the unknown parameters w^* and A. Combining them to eliminate A gives

(6) $$[1 + \beta\theta - \beta F(w^*)]U(w^*) = \beta \int_{w^*}^{\bar{w}} U(w)f(w)\,dw.$$

Exercise 10.7 g. Show that there is a unique value w^* satisfying (6).

Parts (d)–(g) completely characterize the value function v: it is given by (4) with w^* as determined in part (g) and A then given by (3) or (5). From (1) we see that the optimal decision rule for the worker is simply: if the current wage is at least w^*, work; if not, search. Call w^* the *reservation wage*.

Exercise 10.7 h. How does the reservation wage depend on the parameters β and θ?
   i. What can be said about the effect of changes in the variance of the wage distribution on the expected utility of the worker?

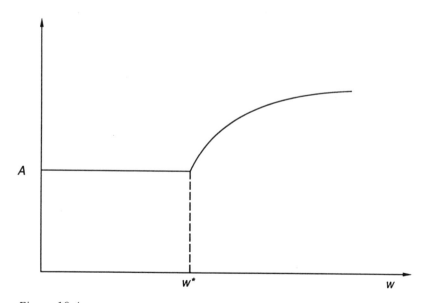

Figure 10.4

10.8   The Dynamics of the Search Model

Let $W = [0, \overline{w}]$ with its Borel subsets $\mathcal{W}$, and let μ be a probability measure on $(W, \mathcal{W})$. Let $w^* \in (0, \overline{w}]$, and let $A = [w^*, \overline{w}]$. In the search model of the last problem, we showed that if a worker follows an optimal strategy, then his wage offers $\{w_t\}$ are a Markov process on $(W, \mathcal{W})$ with transition function

(1a) $P(w, B) = \mu(B)$,   all $B \in \mathcal{W}$, if $w \in A^c$;

(1b) $P(w, B) = \begin{cases} 0 & \text{if } 0 \notin B \text{ and } w \notin B \\ \theta & \text{if } 0 \in B \text{ and } w \notin B \\ 1 - \theta & \text{if } 0 \notin B \text{ and } w \in B \\ 1 & \text{if } 0 \in B \text{ and } w \in B, \end{cases}$ if $w \in A$.

Here $W = [0, \overline{w}]$ is the set of possible wage offers; μ is the probability measure over wage offers if the worker is searching; $A = [w^*, \overline{w}]$ is the set of acceptable wage offers; and $A^c = [0, w^*)$ is the set of unacceptable offers. (We adopt the convention that the worker accepts the wage w^*.) Here we study the long-run behavior of this Markov process. That is, we ask: Given an initial probability measure λ_0 on $(W, \mathcal{W})$, what can we say about the sequence of probability measures $\lambda_n = T^{*n}\lambda_0$, $n = 1, 2, \ldots$, where T^* is the adjoint operator associated with P (cf. Section 8.1)? Because the transition function P is so simple, it is possible to answer this question very explicitly using ad hoc arguments.

Let λ_0 be an initial probability measure on $(W, \mathcal{W})$, and define the sequence $\{\lambda_t\}$ as above. Then the probability that the worker is unemployed (searching) in any period t is $\lambda_t(A^c)$. We begin by determining the sequence $\{\lambda_t(A^c)\}_{t=0}^{\infty}$ of unemployment probabilities. To do this, we note that the probability that the worker is unemployed in period $t + 1$ is equal to the probability that he is unemployed in period t and draws an unacceptable wage, plus the probability that he is employed in period t and loses his job. Hence, as (1a) and (1b) imply,

$$\lambda_{t+1}(A^c) = \int P(w, A^c)\lambda_t(dw)$$

$$= \lambda_t(A^c)\mu(A^c) + \lambda_t(A)\theta$$

$$= \lambda_t(A^c)\mu(A^c) + [1 - \lambda_t(A^c)]\theta$$

(2) $$= \theta + \lambda_t(A^c)[\mu(A^c) - \theta], \quad t = 0, 1, \ldots.$$

That is, the sequence $\{\lambda_t(A^c)\}$ is described by the first-order difference equation (2).

Exercise 10.8   a. Show that the difference equation (2) is stable and that

(3) $$\lim_{t \to \infty} \lambda_t(A^c) = \frac{\theta}{\theta + \mu(A)}.$$

b. Let $C \subseteq A^c$ be any measurable set of unacceptable wage offers. Use the same reasoning as above to show that if $0 \in C$, then

$$\lambda_{t+1}(C) = \theta + \lambda_t(A^c)[\mu(C) - \theta], \quad t = 0, 1, \ldots, \quad \text{and}$$

(4) $$\lim_{t \to \infty} \lambda_t(C) = \frac{\theta}{\theta + \mu(A)}\mu(C) + \frac{\mu(A)}{\theta + \mu(A)}\theta.$$

Show that if $0 \notin C$, then

$$\lambda_{t+1}(C) = \lambda_t(A^c)\mu(C), \quad t = 0, 1, \ldots, \quad \text{and}$$

(5) $$\lim_{t \to \infty} \lambda_t(C) = \frac{\theta}{\theta + \mu(A)}\mu(C).$$

For any measurable set $C \subseteq A$, the probabilities are also easily determined. The probability that in period $t + 1$ the worker has a wage in the set $C \subseteq A$ is simply the probability that he is searching in period t and draws a wage in the set C, plus the probability that he had a wage in the set C last period and retained his job. Thus, as (1a) and (1b) imply,

$$\lambda_{t+1}(C) = \int P(w, C)\lambda_t(dw)$$

$$= \lambda_t(A^c)\mu(C) + \lambda_t(C)[1 - \theta], \quad t = 0, 1, \ldots.$$

Exercise 10.8   c. Show that for any measurable set $C \subseteq A$ of acceptable wage offers,

(6) $$\lim_{t \to \infty} \lambda_t(C) = \frac{\theta}{\theta + \mu(A)}\frac{\mu(C)}{\theta}.$$

d. Interpret the results in (3)–(6). What is the average wage for employed workers in this economy? What is the distribution of the length of unemployment spells?

10.9   Variations on the Search Model

Once the basic structure of the search model in Sections 10.7 and 10.8 is understood, it is easy to think of variations that capture realistic features that are abstracted from in the original version. It would be tedious to work through all such variations in detail, but it is instructive to think some of them through at least to the point of formulating the appropriate analogue to the functional equation.

Exercise 10.9   a. Suppose wage offers follow a Markov process with transition function Q on $(W, \mathcal{W})$. Assume that Q is monotone and has the Feller property. How does this change the functional equation [Equation (1) in Section 10.7] and Figure 10.4?

b. Suppose the worker is endowed with one unit of time each period, which he divides between l_t units of leisure and $1 - l_t$ units of work or search. His utility function is $U(c_t, l_t)$. He can choose his hours, if he works at all. Thus, if his current wage is w_t and he chooses to work $1 - l_t$ units of time, his current consumption (equal to his current earnings) is $c_t = (1 - l_t)w_t$. If he searches, the probability of obtaining *any* offer is $1 - l_t$, so with probability l_t he draws a wage offer of zero. Reformulate the functional equation for this case.

c. Suppose that the job-loss probability θ is zero, but that each worker spends exactly $T + 1$ periods in the work force. Specifically, a worker enters the labor force at age $t = 0$ with no job (an initial wage offer of zero) and hence will spend at least one period searching. The objective function for a worker just entering the labor force is thus $E[\sum_{t=1}^{T} \beta^t U(c_t)]$. What is the functional equation for the value $v_t(w)$ for a worker of age t who begins with a wage offer w? What can be said about the sequence $w_1^*, \ldots, w_T^*$ of age-specific reservation wages?

d. Retain the assumptions of part (c), and assume the following demographics. In each period, all age $T + 1$ workers retire, and an equal number of age zero workers enter. Thus, in each period there are an equal number of workers at each of the ages $t = 0, 1, \ldots, T$. What do the age-specific unemployment rates look like for such an economy? What is the shape of the age-earnings profile, the sequence of age-specific average wages? What shapes of age-specific unemployment rate functions could one obtain by combining this model with the original model of Section 10.7?

e. Suppose that $x \in X = [0, 1]$ is an index of labor market conditions and that $f(\cdot, x)$, $x \in X$, is a family of density functions on the interval $W = [0, \bar{w}]$. Thus $f(\cdot, x)$ describes the distribution of offers the worker faces if market conditions are x. Assume that this family of density functions has the monotone likelihood ratio property. That is, for any $x' > x$, the ratio $f(w, x')/f(w, x)$ is increasing in w. Let $g: X \to \mathbf{R}_+$ also be a density function.

Modify the search model in Section 10.7 as follows. Assume that whenever a worker becomes unemployed, there is a random draw of x from the distribution given by g. The value of x is fixed as long as the worker continues searching, but the worker does not observe x directly. (He does know that it is a random draw from the distribution g.) However, the worker can make inferences about x based on the wage offers he observes. Thus the worker can use Bayes's rule to update his beliefs about x while he is searching.

How must the functional equation (1) in Section 10.7 be modified to incorporate x? How does the reservation wage of a worker who has been searching for n periods depend on the offers he has received?

10.10 A Model of Job Matching

Rather than thinking of a job as being characterized by its wage rate, one may think of it as being described by a productivity variable that is specific to a particular worker-task "match." Here is a simple, discrete version of this idea.

A worker must choose among a continuum of possible tasks. At any given task, in any period he produces a return of 1 with probability θ or 0 with probability $1 - \theta$. Returns on a given task are serially independent. There is no way to tell one's proficiency θ at a particular task short of trying it out, but one's θ on any task is drawn from a known distribution with the density function μ on [0, 1]. Once a worker chooses a task, he can keep it as long as he wants or he can leave it and draw a new task from μ.

Suppose a worker has engaged in a specific task for n periods and has achieved $k \in \{0, 1, \ldots, n\}$ successes. His probability of a success at this task in any future period, conditional on k successes in n trials to date, is then given by the density $f(\theta, n, k)$. For any (θ, n, k), an application of Bayes's rules gives

$$f(\theta, n, k) = \frac{\binom{n}{k} \theta^k (1 - \theta)^{n-k} \mu(\theta)}{\int_0^1 \binom{n}{k} u^k (1 - u)^{n-k} \mu(u) \, du},$$

since given θ, the probability of k successes in n independent trials is given by the binomial formula. Then the expected return $\pi(n, k)$ on the next trial, if he remains on this task, is

$$\pi(n, k) = \int_0^1 \theta f(\theta, n, k) \, d\theta = \frac{\int_0^1 \theta^{k+1} (1 - \theta)^{n-k} \mu(\theta) \, d\theta}{\int_0^1 \theta^k (1 - \theta)^{n-k} \mu(\theta) \, d\theta}.$$

Exercise 10.10   a. Suppose μ is the uniform density on $[0, 1]$; that is, $\mu(\theta) = 1$, all $\theta \in [0, 1]$. Show that $f(\theta, n, k)$ is the beta density with parameters $(k + 1, n + 1 - k)$:

$$f(\theta, n, k) = \frac{\Gamma(n + 2)}{\Gamma(k + 1)\Gamma(n + 1 - k)} \theta^k (1 - \theta)^{n-k},$$

where $\Gamma(x) = \int_0^\infty t^{x-1} e^{-t} dt$.

b. Suppose μ is the beta density with parameters (α, β); that is,

$$\mu(\theta) = \frac{\Gamma(\alpha + \beta)}{\Gamma(\alpha)\,\Gamma(\beta)} \theta^{\alpha-1} (1 - \theta)^{\beta-1}, \quad \theta \in (0, 1),$$

[so part (a) is the special case $\alpha = \beta = 1$]. Show that

$$f(\theta, n, k) = \frac{\Gamma(\alpha + \beta + n)}{\Gamma(\alpha + k)\Gamma(\beta + n - k)} \theta^{\alpha+k-1} (1 - \theta)^{\beta+n-k-1}.$$

c. Show that if μ is as specified in (b), then

$$\pi(n, k) = \frac{\alpha + k}{\alpha + \beta + n}.$$

d. Show that $\pi(n, k)$ as given in (c) satisfies

$$0 < \pi(n, k) < 1, \quad \pi(n, k + 1) > \pi(n, k),$$

$$\pi(n + 1, k) < \pi(n, k), \quad \pi(n + 1, k + 1) > \pi(n, k),$$

$$k = 0, 1, \ldots, n; \, n = 1, 2, \ldots.$$

e. Show that if $\{k_n\}$ is a sequence of positive integers with $k_n \leq n$ and $\lim_{n \to \infty} k/n = p$, then $\lim_{n \to \infty} \pi(n, k_n) = p$. Do these properties hold for an arbitrary density μ with $\mu(\theta) > 0$ on $(0, 1)$?

Now consider the decision problem of a worker who has been engaged on a given task for n periods and has produced $k \leq n$ successes. Let $v(n, k)$ denote the expected present value, with the discount factor β, of his earnings under optimal behavior. If he remains at his present task, he has an expected current return of $\pi(n, k)$ (his success probability), a probability of $\pi(n, k)$ of moving to state $(n + 1, k + 1)$, and a probability of $1 - \pi(n, k)$ of moving to $(n + 1, k)$. If he chooses a new task, his expected current return is $\pi(0, 0) = \int_0^1 \theta \mu(\theta) d\theta$, and he moves to the state $(1, 1)$ with probability $\pi(0, 0)$ or to $(1, 0)$ with probability $1 - \pi(0, 0)$. Hence $v(n, k)$ must satisfy

$$(1) \qquad v(n, k) = \max \{\pi(n, k) + \beta[\pi(n, k)v(n + 1, k + 1)$$

$$+ [1 - \pi(n, k)]v(n + 1, k)],$$

$$\pi(0, 0) + \beta[\pi(0, 0)v(1, 1) + [1 - \pi(0, 0)]v(1, 0)]\}.$$

The domain of v is thus the triangular array D of integers $n = 0, 1, \ldots,$ $k = 0, 1, \ldots, n$, and the range of v is the interval $[0, 1/(1 - \beta)]$. Let S be the space of functions $f: D \to [0, 1/(1 - \beta)]$, with the norm

$$\|f\| = \sup_{(n,k) \in D} |f(n, k)|.$$

Exercise 10.10 f. Prove that there is a unique $v \in S$ satisfying (1).

g. Prove that if $\pi(n, k)$ has the properties in part (d), then $v(n, k)$ is nonincreasing in n for each fixed k, nondecreasing in k for each fixed n; and if $\{k_n\}$ is a sequence of positive integers with $k_n \le n$ and $\lim_{n \to \infty} k_n/n = p$, then

$$\lim_{n \to \infty} v(n, k_n) = \max\left\{\frac{p}{1 - \beta}, v(0, 0)\right\}.$$

The policy correspondence, which takes states (n, k) into choices 1 (stay on the job) and 0 (leave), is multivalued for some states (n, k). (Which ones?) Let us select a policy function by assuming that the worker stays on the job if he is indifferent.

Exercise 10.10   h. Prove that there exists a sequence $\{j_n\}_{n=1}^\infty$ of integers such that the optimal policy is given by

$$g(n, k) = \begin{cases} 1 \text{ if } k \ge j_n \\ 0 \text{ if } k < j_n. \end{cases}$$

Show that this sequence satisfies

$$j_1 = 1 \quad \text{and} \quad j_{n+1} \ge j_n, \quad n = 1, 2, \ldots.$$

i. What is the average wage in this economy for workers with job seniority n, for $n \in \{0, 1, 2, \ldots\}$?

10.11   Job Matching and Unemployment

If we interpret the wage rate in the search model of Section 10.7 as a worker's expected return on a specific task, that model and the job-matching model of Section 10.10 are obviously complementary. Suppose, for example, that workers in Section 10.7 do not immediately draw a new task the period after they leave one but instead must spend one period unemployed.

Exercise 10.11   a. Modify the functional equation of Section 10.7 to suit this new situation. How are the answers to parts (f), (g), and (h) of Exercise 10.7 affected?

b. What does this model imply about unemployment rates as a function of age?

Suppose, to elaborate further, we interpret job search as an activity designed to obtain advance information on the random variable θ characterizing a worker's proficiency on a particular task. How might one formulate such a testing activity? Under what conditions might workers utilize such a testing technology (as opposed to hands-on experience, as assumed in Section 10.7) if it were available?

10.12 Bibliographic Notes

The one-sector growth model with independent shocks of Section 10.1 was first studied by Brock and Mirman (1972). Further developments are reported in Mirman and Zilcha (1975), which contains a proof of the differentiability of the value function, and in Danthine and Donaldson (1981). Brock and Mirman (1973) consider the undiscounted case, analogous to Ramsey's original (1928) deterministic analysis. Donaldson and Mehra (1983) study the case of serially correlated production shocks.

The model of industry investment under uncertainty in Section 10.4 is taken from Lucas and Prescott (1971). The inventory model of Section 10.5 is closely related to Danthine (1977) and Scheinkman and Schechtman (1983).

The model of asset pricing in Section 10.6 is based on Lucas (1978). See also Breeden (1979), Cox, Ingersoll, and Ross (1985), and LeRoy (1973). For an excellent example of empirical implementation of asset-pricing models of this type, see Hansen and Singleton (1983).

The model of search unemployment in Sections 10.7–10.9 is from McCall (1970), which in turn draws on Stigler (1961). A useful survey of more recent developments on this topic is Lippman and McCall (1976a,b). See also Mortensen's (1970) seminal paper. Albrecht and Axell (1984) contains an interesting application of this theory.

The job-matching model of Sections 10.10–10.11 is a discrete-time version of the one introduced in Jovanovic (1979).

11 Strong Convergence of Markov Processes

In Chapter 9 we studied dynamic programming problems that incorporated exogenous stochastic shocks and related them to problems posed in terms of sequences. In this chapter and the three that follow, we take up the question of characterizing the long-run behavior of the state variables for such models and of comparing their predictions with observed time series.

Recall that in problems of the type studied in Chapter 9, the endogenous state variables $\{x_t\}$, the decision variables $\{y_t\}$, and the exogenous shocks $\{z_t\}$ take values in measurable spaces $(X, \mathscr{X})$, $(Y, \mathscr{Y})$, and $(Z, \mathscr{Z})$ respectively. The dynamics of the system are then determined as follows. The exogenous shocks $\{z_t\}$ follow a Markov process defined by an exogenously given transition function Q on $(Z, \mathscr{Z})$; the actions $\{y_t\}$ are described by an endogenously determined optimal policy function $g: X \times Z \to Y$, so $y_t = g(x_t, z_t)$; and the state variables $\{x_t\}$ are described by the exogenously given law of motion $\phi: X \times Y \times Z \to X$ (a measurable function), so

$$(1) \qquad x_{t+1} = \phi[x_t, g(x_t, z_t), z_{t+1}].$$

If $(Y, \mathscr{Y}) = (X, \mathscr{X})$ and $\phi(x, y, z) = y$, then (1) is just $x_{t+1} = g(x_t, z_t)$. In Sections 9.2–9.4 we established that various sets of conditions are sufficient to ensure that the policy function g is measurable. Then in Section 9.6 we showed that if g is measurable, the pair of variables $\{s_t = (x_t, z_t)\}$ jointly follows a Markov process on the product space $(S, \mathscr{S}) = (X \times Z, \mathscr{X} \times \mathscr{Z})$, with a transition function P that is determined by Q, g, and ϕ.

The behavior through time of the state variable $\{s_t\}$ is then simply determined by P, and the study of such a system is not in any way simplified by the fact that one set of state variables, x_t, is endogenous and another, z_t, exogenous. In this chapter and the next, then, we examine the general mathematical issues involved in deducing facts about the long-run behavior of a Markov process $\{s_t\}$ from properties of its transition function P. In Chapter 13, which is concerned with economic applications of this theory, we consider various ways of establishing properties of P from properties of Q, g, and ϕ. Finally, in Chapter 14 we study the long-run behavior of the time series generated by such a system, a law of large numbers.

What questions about the process $\{s_t\}$ are we interested in? In the study of deterministic systems in Chapter 6, we were concerned with the behavior of a sequence $\{x_t\}$ governed by a deterministic difference equation, $x_{t+1} = g(x_t)$. We were interested in finding conditions under which the system had a unique stationary point and converged to that point from any initial value. The idea, of course, was that under those conditions, the stationary point was the model's prediction about the long-run behavior of the system, regardless of the initial conditions.

In this chapter we develop analogous conditions for a stochastic process $\{s_t\}$ governed by a transition function P. It is clear, however, that the notion of a stationary point will have to be replaced with something more complicated, since Markov processes do not, in general, converge to a constant value. Clearly, too, a different notion of convergence will be needed.

Recall from Section 8.1 that for any transition function P on a measurable space $(S, \mathcal{S})$, there is an associated operator T^* that maps the set of probability measures on $(S, \mathcal{S})$, call it $\Lambda(S, \mathcal{S})$, into itself. This operator is defined so that if $\lambda_0 \in \Lambda(S, \mathcal{S})$ is the probability measure over the state in period 0, then the probability measures over the states in all subsequent periods are given recursively by $\lambda_t = T^*\lambda_{t-1}$, $t = 1, 2, \ldots$. (If the system starts out at a point s, then λ_0 is simply a unit mass at s.) Thus convergence of the stochastic process $\{s_t\}$ means convergence, in some sense, of the sequence of probability measures $\{\lambda_t\}$, given λ_0, and the analogue of a stationary state is a limiting probability measure.

The issues involved in defining convergence for a sequence of probability measures are subtle, and we put off discussion of them until later. But the notion of stationarity we will use is easy to define. We call a probability measure λ^* an *invariant probability measure* if it has the following property: if λ^* is the probability measure over the state s_t in period t, then it is also the probability measure over the state s_{t+1} in period $t + 1$. That is, a probability measure λ^* is invariant if and only if it is a fixed point of the operator T^*, $\lambda^* = T^*\lambda^*$.

In this chapter and the next, we develop various sets of conditions on P sufficient to ensure that one or more of the following hold: that at least one invariant probability measure exists, and at most a finite number; that from any initial λ_0, the sequence of long-run average probabilities $\{(1/T)\Sigma_{t=0}^{T-1}\lambda_t\}$ converges to one of these invariant measures; that the invariant measure is unique; and that from any initial probability measure λ_0, the sequence $\{\lambda_t\}$, and not just the sequence of long-run averages, converges to the unique invariant measure.

In the next section we address these questions for the case of finite Markov chains, Markov processes on a state space S with a finite number of elements. All of the basic types of behavior possible for more general Markov processes can be illustrated with Markov chains, and this is done in a series of examples. Then a series of general results for chains is established in a very simple, self-contained way.

When we turn to extensions of this theory to more general state spaces, we face a decision as to what we want the term "convergence" to mean for a sequence $\{\lambda_t\}$ of probability measures. This issue is introduced in Section 11.2, where two notions of convergence, called *strong* and *weak,* are defined. The theory of strong convergence of Markov processes is developed in close analogy to the theory of Markov chains, so we turn to it first. In Section 11.3 we discuss alternative ways of characterizing strong convergence; then in Section 11.4 we establish several results about the strong convergence of Markov processes on arbitrary measurable spaces. These results, Theorems 11.9, 11.10, and 11.12, are the main results of this chapter. They establish, under successively stronger assumptions about the transition function P, results on the existence or uniqueness or both of an invariant measure and strong convergence of the sequence $\{(1/T)\Sigma_{t=0}^{T-1}\lambda_t\}$ or the sequence $\{\lambda_t\}$ or both.

The restrictions on the transition function P needed to establish strong convergence of a Markov process on an arbitrary state space, although easy to state, can be difficult to verify in economic applications. Moreover, as is shown by example in Section 11.2, strong convergence is in some cases more than one might reasonably ask for. For both reasons, there is a need for convergence results that, if weaker, are also more easily applied. In Chapter 12 we study the weak convergence of Markov processes, arriving at a convergence result, Theorem 12.14, that is based on conditions quite different from those used in this chapter.

We are also interested in knowing how values of various parameters affect the behavior of the system. Specifically, we want to look at the following comparative statics question. Suppose that the function g in (1) depends on a vector of parameters θ, so $y_t = g(x_t, z_t; \theta)$, where $\theta \in \Theta \subseteq \mathbf{R}^n$. Suppose, too, that for every $\theta \in \Theta$, there exists a unique invariant measure $\lambda^*(\cdot; \theta)$. We want to find conditions under which the expected value of a function under the invariant measure, $\int f(s)\lambda^*(ds; \theta)$, is continuous in θ, for every function f in a suitable class. This topic is addressed in Section 12.5.

In Chapter 13 we look at economic applications of the results developed in Chapters 11 and 12. Analyzing these models involves developing arguments that establish the desired properties of the transition function P from properties of the functions Q, g, and ϕ.

Finally, in Chapter 14 we look at the long-run properties of the time series generated by systems governed by Markov processes. Suppose that it can be established that for the system of interest, the sequence of long-run average probabilities $\{(1/T)\Sigma_{t=0}^{T-1}\lambda_t\}$ converges, in some sense, to an invariant measure λ^*. Then it seems reasonable to expect that for any real-valued function f in some suitable class, the sample average of the sequence of real numbers $\{f(s_t)\}$ converges, in the ordinary sense, to the expected value of f with respect to this invariant measure. That is, we expect that

$$\lim_{T \to \infty} \frac{1}{T} \sum_{t=0}^{T-1} f(s_t) = \int f(s)\lambda^*(ds),$$

holds for most of the sample paths—that is, for most of the sequences of realizations $\{s_t\}$—that one might obtain. Convergence statements of this type are called laws of large numbers. In Chapter 14 we develop such a law for Markov processes.

11.1 Markov Chains

In this section we discuss convergence for the case where the state space S consists of a finite number of elements, $S = \{s_1, \ldots, s_l\}$, and $\mathcal{S}$ consists of all subsets of S. A Markov process on a finite state space is called a **Markov chain**. Although the models discussed in Chapter 9 do not have finite state spaces, beginning with this case is useful, since many of the types of behavior possible for general Markov processes can be illustrated with a finite state space. Hence Markov chains are useful for illustrating various kinds of "bad" behavior and for examining the assumptions needed to rule them out. Moreover, many of the arguments used to establish existence, uniqueness, and convergence results for finite chains have close parallels in the general case. Since finite Markov chains are easy to analyze in a self-contained way, this is how we begin. Section 11.4 then parallels this one very closely, establishing analogous results for general state spaces.

The rest of this section is organized as follows. First, the notation is set and several terms are defined. Then we present five examples that illustrate various types of behavior. The analysis then proceeds to a more general level, and three results are established. Theorem 11.1 proves the existence of at least one invariant distribution and convergence of the sequence of long-run average probabilities, from any initial state, to one of these; Theorem 11.2 provides a necessary and sufficient condition for the uniqueness of the invariant distribution; and Theorem 11.4 provides a necessary and sufficient condition for the convergence of the sequence of probabilities, not just the averages, to this unique limit. Theorem 11.4 is, for our purposes, the most important of these results, and the reader may wish to skip to it immediately after studying the examples.

When S is the finite set $\{s_1, \ldots, s_l\}$, a probability measure on $(S, \mathcal{S})$ is represented by a vector p in the l-dimensional unit simplex: $\Delta^l = \{p \in \mathbf{R}^l : p \geq 0 \text{ and } \Sigma_{i=1}^l p_i = 1\}$. (All vectors here are row vectors.) Similarly, a transition function P is represented by an $l \times l$ matrix $\Pi = [\pi_{ij}]$, where $\pi_{ij} = P(s_i, \{s_j\})$. Note that the elements of Π are nonnegative and that each row sum is unity. Any such matrix is called a **Markov matrix** or a **stochastic matrix**. For $i = 1, \ldots, l$, let $e_i \in \Delta^l$ denote the vector with a one in the ith position and zeros elsewhere.

First consider one-step transitions. If the current state is s_i, the probability distribution over next period's state is given by the ith row of Π, $\pi_{i\cdot} = (\pi_{i1}, \ldots, \pi_{il})$. That is, if the probability distribution over the current state is e_i, then the distribution over next period's state is $e_i\Pi = \pi_{i\cdot}$. More generally, if $p \in \Delta^l$ is the probability distribution over the state in period t, then the distribution over the state in period $t + 1$ is given by $\hat{p} = (\hat{p}_1, \ldots, \hat{p}_l)$, where

$$\hat{p}_j = \sum_{i=1}^l p_i \pi_{ij}, \quad j = 1, \ldots, l.$$

Since $\Sigma_j \hat{p}_j = \Sigma_i p_i \Sigma_j \pi_{ij} = 1$, it follows that $\hat{p} \in \Delta^l$. In matrix notation then, $\hat{p} = p\Pi$, and we have shown that if Π is an $l \times l$ Markov matrix and $p \in \Delta^l$, then $p\Pi \in \Delta^l$.

Applying the same argument again, we find that if the probability distribution over the state in period t is $p \in \Delta^l$, then the probability distribution over the state two periods ahead is $(p\Pi)\Pi = p(\Pi \cdot \Pi) = p\Pi^2$. Continuing by induction, we find that the n-step transition probabilities are given by the matrix Π^n, for $n = 0, 1, 2, \ldots$, where we take Π^0 to be the identity matrix. It is straightforward to verify that if Π is a Markov matrix, then so is Π^n, for $n = 2, 3, \ldots$. Thus, if the initial state is s_i, then the probability distribution over states n periods ahead is given by $e_i\Pi^n$, the ith row of Π^n. To understand the long-run behavior of the system, then, we must study the behavior of the sequence $\{\Pi^n\}_{n=0}^{\infty}$. Before beginning the formal analysis, it is useful to look at examples that illustrate various possibilities.

Example 1 Let $l = 2$, and suppose that

$$\Pi = \begin{bmatrix} 3/4 & 1/4 \\ 1/4 & 3/4 \end{bmatrix}.$$

A set $E \subseteq S$ is called an **ergodic set** if $p(s_i, E) = 1$, for $s_i \in E$, and if no proper subset of E has this property. In this example, the only ergodic set is S itself. Moreover, it is easy to verify by direct calculation that

$$\Pi^2 = \begin{bmatrix} 5/8 & 3/8 \\ 3/8 & 5/8 \end{bmatrix},$$

$$\Pi^3 = \begin{bmatrix} 9/16 & 7/16 \\ 7/16 & 9/16 \end{bmatrix},$$

$$\Pi^4 = \begin{bmatrix} 17/32 & 15/32 \\ 15/32 & 17/32 \end{bmatrix}.$$

Clearly the sequence $\{\Pi^n\}$ is converging, and pretty rapidly, and

$$\lim_{n \to \infty} \Pi^n = \begin{bmatrix} 1/2 & 1/2 \\ 1/2 & 1/2 \end{bmatrix}.$$

Notice how we use the word *converge* here: we say that the sequence of $l \times l$ matrices $\{\Pi^n\}$ converges to Q if each of the l^2 sequences of elements converges. In this example the probability distribution over the state converges to $p^* = (1/2, 1/2)$ for all initial probability distributions p_0. Note, too, that if the probability distribution over the initial state is p^*, then it is also p^* in every successive period. A vector with this property is called an **invariant distribution.** Note that each row of the limit matrix in this example is the invariant distribution, p^*.

Example 2   Let $l = 3$, and suppose that Π has the form

$$\Pi = \begin{bmatrix} 1 - \gamma & \gamma/2 & \gamma/2 \\ 0 & 1/2 & 1/2 \\ 0 & 1/2 & 1/2 \end{bmatrix},$$

where $\gamma \in (0, 1)$. If the system starts out in state s_1, then in the next period with probability $(1 - \gamma)$ it stays in that state, and with probability γ it leaves. Given that it leaves, it is equally likely to go to state s_2 or s_3. Note that if it leaves the state s_1, it cannot return. A state is called **transient** if there is a positive probability of leaving and never returning. If the initial state is s_2 or s_3, the situation is similar to that in Example 1; here $E = \{s_2, s_3\}$ is the only ergodic set.

By direct calculation we find that in this example

$$\Pi^n = \begin{bmatrix} (1 - \gamma)^n & \delta_n/2 & \delta_n/2 \\ 0 & 1/2 & 1/2 \\ 0 & 1/2 & 1/2 \end{bmatrix},$$

where $\delta_n = 1 - (1 - \gamma)^n$. Since $\gamma \in (0, 1)$, it follows that

$$\lim_{n \to \infty} \Pi^n = \begin{bmatrix} 0 & 1/2 & 1/2 \\ 0 & 1/2 & 1/2 \\ 0 & 1/2 & 1/2 \end{bmatrix}.$$

Thus, with probability one the system eventually leaves the state s_1 and enters the ergodic set. Note that in this case, as in Example 1, $\{\Pi^n\}$ converges, and each row of the limit matrix is an invariant distribution.

Example 3 Next suppose that Π has the form

$$\Pi = \begin{bmatrix} 0 & \Pi_1 \\ \Pi_2 & 0 \end{bmatrix},$$

where Π_1 and Π_2 are $k \times (l - k)$ and $(l - k) \times k$ Markov matrices respectively, each with strictly positive elements. Then

$$\Pi^{2n} = \begin{bmatrix} (\Pi_1\Pi_2)^n & 0 \\ 0 & (\Pi_2\Pi_1)^n \end{bmatrix} \quad \text{and}$$

$$\Pi^{2n+1} = \begin{bmatrix} 0 & (\Pi_1\Pi_2)^n\Pi_1 \\ (\Pi_2\Pi_1)^n\Pi_2 & 0 \end{bmatrix}$$

for even- and odd-numbered transitions respectively. If the system begins in a state in the set $C_1 = \{s_1, \ldots, s_k\}$, then after any even number of steps it is back in the set C_1, and after any odd number of steps it is in the set $C_2 = \{s_{k+1}, \ldots, s_l\}$. If the system starts out in C_2, the reverse is true. In this example, as in the first, there is only one ergodic set, all of S, but that ergodic set has **cyclically moving subsets**. Obviously $\{\Pi^n\}$ does not converge in this case, but the two subsequences for odd and even steps do.

For example, suppose that $k = l - k = 2$ and that Π_1 and Π_2 are both equal to Π of Example 1. Then as n increases,

$$\Pi^{2n} \rightarrow \begin{bmatrix} 1/2 & 1/2 & 0 & 0 \\ 1/2 & 1/2 & 0 & 0 \\ 0 & 0 & 1/2 & 1/2 \\ 0 & 0 & 1/2 & 1/2 \end{bmatrix} \quad \text{and}$$

$$\Pi^{2n+1} \rightarrow \begin{bmatrix} 0 & 0 & 1/2 & 1/2 \\ 0 & 0 & 1/2 & 1/2 \\ 1/2 & 1/2 & 0 & 0 \\ 1/2 & 1/2 & 0 & 0 \end{bmatrix}$$

for even- and odd-numbered transitions. Thus $\{\Pi^n\}$ does not converge.

On the other hand, the following average does:

$$\lim_{N \to \infty} \frac{1}{N} \sum_{n=0}^{N-1} \Pi^n = \begin{bmatrix} 1/4 & 1/4 & 1/4 & 1/4 \\ 1/4 & 1/4 & 1/4 & 1/4 \\ 1/4 & 1/4 & 1/4 & 1/4 \\ 1/4 & 1/4 & 1/4 & 1/4 \end{bmatrix}.$$

Note, too, that each row of this limit matrix, $p^* = (1/4, 1/4, 1/4, 1/4)$, is an invariant distribution.

Example 4   Next suppose that Π has the form

$$\Pi = \begin{bmatrix} \Pi_1 & 0 \\ 0 & \Pi_2 \end{bmatrix},$$

where Π_1 and Π_2 are Markov matrices of dimension $k \times k$ and $(l - k) \times (l - k)$ respectively, each with strictly positive elements. The n-step transitions are then given by

$$\Pi^n = \begin{bmatrix} \Pi_1^n & 0 \\ 0 & \Pi_2^n \end{bmatrix}.$$

Thus, if the system starts out in the set $E_1 = \{s_1, \ldots, s_k\}$, then it stays in that set forever. The same is true if the system starts out in the set $E_2 = \{s_{k+1}, \ldots, s_l\}$. In this case, then, there are two ergodic sets. Clearly the sequence $\{\Pi^n\}$ converges if and only if $\{\Pi_1^n\}$ and $\{\Pi_2^n\}$ both converge. Suppose that Π_1 and Π_2 are both as specified in Example 1. Then

$$\lim_{n \to \infty} \Pi^n = \begin{bmatrix} 1/2 & 1/2 & 0 & 0 \\ 1/2 & 1/2 & 0 & 0 \\ 0 & 0 & 1/2 & 1/2 \\ 0 & 0 & 1/2 & 1/2 \end{bmatrix}.$$

Thus there are two invariant distributions, $p_1^* = (1/2, 1/2, 0, 0)$ and $p_2^* = (0, 0, 1/2, 1/2)$, and the system converges to one or the other, depending on the initial state. Note, too, that all convex combinations of p_1^* and p_2^* are invariant distributions as well.

Example 5 Finally, consider a case where there are three states, and

$$
\Pi = \begin{bmatrix} 1 - \gamma & \alpha\gamma & \beta\gamma \\ 0 & 1 & 0 \\ 0 & 0 & 1 \end{bmatrix},
$$

where $\alpha, \beta, \gamma \in (0, 1)$ and $\alpha + \beta = 1$. Here, as in Example 2, s_1 is a transient state; however, there are two ergodic sets: $E_1 = \{s_2\}$ and $E_2 = \{s_3\}$. If the system starts out in state s_1 and leaves, the conditional probability of going to E_1 is α and to E_2 is β. If the state is s_2 or s_3, it remains constant forever after.

The n-step transition matrix in this case is

$$
\Pi^n = \begin{bmatrix} (1 - \gamma)^n & \alpha\delta_n & \beta\delta_n \\ 0 & 1 & 0 \\ 0 & 0 & 1 \end{bmatrix},
$$

where $\delta_n = 1 - (1 - \gamma)^n$. Since $\gamma \in (0, 1)$, it then follows that

$$
\lim_{n \to \infty} \Pi^n = \begin{bmatrix} 0 & \alpha & \beta \\ 0 & 1 & 0 \\ 0 & 0 & 1 \end{bmatrix}.
$$

In this case $\{\Pi^n\}$ converges; each row of the limit matrix is an invariant distribution; and the row corresponding to the transient state is a convex combination of the rows corresponding to the ergodic sets.

These five examples illustrate all possible types of limiting behavior for finite Markov chains. We will establish this fact in the remainder of the section, studying the existence and uniqueness of an ergodic set, the existence and uniqueness of an invariant distribution, and the convergence of the sequences $\{(1/n)\sum_{k=0}^{n-1}\Pi^k\}_{n=1}^{\infty}$ or $\{\Pi^k\}_{k=0}^{\infty}$ or both. Theorems 11.1, 11.2, and 11.4 deal with these questions under successively stronger assumptions about Π.

Let $S = \{s_1, \ldots, s_l\}$, let the stochastic matrix $\Pi = [\pi_{ij}]$ define the transition probabilities, and let $\Pi^n = [\pi_{ij}^{(n)}]$ denote the powers of Π. [Note that $\pi_{ij}^{(n)}$ is *not* in general equal to $(\pi_{ij})^n$.] Our first result requires no further restrictions on Π.

THEOREM 11.1 Let $S = \{s_1, \ldots, s_l\}$ be a finite set, and let the stochastic matrix Π define transition probabilities on S. Then

    a. S can be partitioned into $M \geq 1$ ergodic sets and a transient set.

    b. The sequence $\{(1/n)\Sigma_{k=0}^{n-1}\Pi^k\}_{n=1}^{\infty}$ converges to a stochastic matrix Q. That is, $\lim_{n\to\infty}(1/n)\Sigma_{k=0}^{n-1}p_k = p_0Q$, for any sequence $\{p_k\} = \{p_0\Pi^k\}$ where $p_0 \in \Delta^l$.

    c. Each row of Q is an invariant distribution, so p_0Q is an invariant distribution for each $p_0 \in \Delta^l$; and every invariant distribution for Π is a convex combination of the rows of Q.

Proof of (a). Call j a *consequent* of i if $\pi_{ij}^{(n)} > 0$ for some $n \geq 1$. Call s_i a *transient* state if it has at least one consequent j for which $\pi_{ji}^{(n)} = 0$, all $n \geq 1$. Thus, a state is transient if and only if there is a positive probability of not returning to it. Call a state i *recurrent* if for every j that is a consequent of i, i is also a consequent of j.

To show that S can be partitioned as claimed, we will begin by showing that S has at least one recurrent state. Suppose the contrary. Then $\pi_{ii}^{(n)} \neq 1$, $i = 1, \ldots, l$ (otherwise s_i would be recurrent). Since s_1 is transient, there exists a state—call it s_2—and $N \geq 1$ such that $\pi_{12}^{(N)} > 0$ and $\pi_{21}^{(n)} = 0$, $n = 1, 2, \ldots$. Then since $\pi_{22}^{(n)} \neq 1$, $\pi_{21}^{(n)} = 0$, $n = 1, 2, \ldots$, and s_2 is transient, there exists a state—call it s_3—and $N' \geq 1$ such that $\pi_{23}^{(N')} > 0$ and $\pi_{32}^{(n)} = 0$, $n = 1, 2, \ldots$. Moreover, since $0 = \pi_{32}^{(n+N)} \geq \pi_{31}^{(n)}\pi_{12}^{(N)}$, $n = 1, 2, \ldots$, it follows that $\pi_{31}^{(n)} = 0$, $n = 1, 2, \ldots$. Continuing by induction, we conclude that $\pi_{ll} \neq 1$ and $\pi_{lj} = 0$, $j = 1, \ldots, l-1$, which contradicts the fact that Π is a stochastic matrix.

Next we will show that if the state s_i is recurrent and j is a consequent of i, then i is a consequent of j and s_j is also recurrent. Suppose that s_i is recurrent and that j is a consequent of i. Since s_i is recurrent, not transient, it follows that $\pi_{ji}^{(N)} > 0$ for some $N \geq 1$, so i is a consequent of j. Next, suppose that k is a consequent of j. Then $\pi_{jk}^{(L)} > 0$, for some $L \geq 1$. But this implies that $\pi_{ik}^{(N+L)} \geq \pi_{ij}^{(N)}\pi_{jk}^{(L)} > 0$, so k is a consequent of i. Since s_i is recurrent, it then follows that $\pi_{ki}^{(K)} > 0$, for some $K \geq 0$. Hence $\pi_{kj}^{(K+N)} \geq \pi_{ki}^{(K)}\pi_{ij}^{(N)} > 0$, so j is a consequent of k. Since k was an arbitrary consequent of j, it follows that j is recurrent.

Hence the set S can be partitioned as follows. First, let F be the set of all transient states. Then partition the recurrent states into disjoint sets $E_1, E_2, \ldots, E_M$, by assigning two states to the same set if and only if they are consequents of each other. Since there is at least one recurrent state, there is at least one such set. Moreover, by construction, $s_i \in E_m$ implies that $\Sigma_{j \in E_m}\pi_{ij} = 1$ and that no subset of E_m has this property. Hence each set E_m is ergodic. Note that once the state enters one of the ergodic sets, it remains in that set forever.

Proof of (b). Next consider the average probabilities over n-step horizons. Let $p_0 = (p_{01}, \ldots, p_{0l})$ be a probability distribution over states in period 0. Then $p_k = p_0\Pi^k$ is the probability distribution over states in period k, for $k = 1, 2, \ldots$; and the average over these distributions for the first n periods is given by

$$\frac{1}{n}\sum_{k=0}^{n-1} p_k = \frac{1}{n}\sum_{k=0}^{n-1} p_0\Pi^k = p_0\left[\frac{1}{n}\sum_{k=0}^{n-1}\Pi^k\right].$$

Define $A^{(n)} = (1/n)\sum_{k=0}^{n-1}\Pi^k$, and note that since it is an average of stochastic matrices, each $A^{(n)}$ is itself a stochastic matrix. We will first characterize the behavior of the long-run average probabilities by examining the behavior of $A^{(n)}$ as $n \to \infty$ and then will show that if S is a finite set, the sequence $\{A^{(n)}\}$ converges.

First we will show that there exists a subsequence—call it n_k—such that $\{A^{(n_k)}\}$ converges. To see this, note that each of the sequences $\{a_{ij}^{(n)}\}_{n=1}^{\infty}$, $i, j = 1, \ldots, l$, lies on the compact interval $[0, 1]$. Hence there exists a subsequence of the n's—call it n'—for which $\{a_{11}^{(n')}\}$ converges. Then, by the same reasoning, there exists a subsequence of the n's, call it n'', for which $\{a_{12}^{(n'')}\}$ also converges, etc. Since there are only a finite number of elements to consider, continuing by induction establishes the desired conclusion. Note, too, that this argument establishes that every subsequence of $\{A^{(n)}\}$ contains a convergent subsequence.

Let Q be the limit of some convergent subsequence $\{A^{(n_k)}\}$:

$$\lim_{k \to \infty} \frac{1}{n_k}\sum_{m=0}^{n_k-1}\Pi^m = Q.$$

Then pre- and postmultiplying by Π, we find that

$$\lim_{k \to \infty} \frac{1}{n_k}\sum_{m=1}^{n_k}\Pi^m = Q\Pi = \Pi Q.$$

Since the two averages in these equations differ only by the terms Π^0/n_k and Π^{n_k}/n_k, both of which go to zero as $k \to \infty$, the two limits are equal. Hence $Q = Q\Pi = \Pi Q$. This fact in turn implies that $Q = Q\Pi^n = \Pi^n Q$, all n.

We have defined Q to be the limit of the subsequence $\{A^{(n_k)}\}$. From the remaining terms in $\{A^{(n)}\}$ we can extract another convergent subsequence; call its limit A. Then since $Q = Q\Pi^n = \Pi^n Q$, $n = 1, 2, \ldots$, it follows that $Q = QA = AQ$, and, with the roles of Q and A reversed, that $A = AQ = QA$. Hence $A = Q$. Since the choice of subsequences converging to A and Q was arbitrary, it follows that

$$Q = \lim_{n\to\infty} \frac{1}{n} \sum_{k=0}^{n-1} \Pi^k,$$

and hence that

$$p_0 Q = \lim_{n\to\infty} \frac{1}{n} \sum_{k=0}^{n-1} p_0 \Pi^k, \quad \text{all } p_0 \in \Delta^l.$$

Proof of (c). Finally we will show that each of the rows of Q is an invariant distribution and that every invariant distribution is a convex combination of these rows.

As shown above $Q\Pi = Q$; that is $\Sigma_{k=1}^l q_{ik}\pi_{kj} = q_{ij}$, $i, j = 1, \ldots, l$. Hence each row of Q is an invariant distribution. Conversely, suppose that $r = (r_1, \ldots, r_l)$ is an invariant distribution. Then

$$\sum_{i=1}^l r_i \pi_{ij}^{(n)} = r_j, \quad j = 1, \ldots, l; n = 1, 2, \ldots;$$

so

$$\frac{1}{N} \sum_{n=0}^{N-1} \left[\sum_{i=1}^l r_i \pi_{ij}^{(n)} \right] = \sum_{i=1}^l r_i \left[\frac{1}{N} \sum_{n=0}^{N-1} \pi_{ij}^{(n)} \right] = r_j,$$

$$j = 1, \ldots, l; N = 1, 2, \ldots.$$

Taking the limit as $N \to \infty$, we obtain $\Sigma_{i=1}^l r_i q_{ij} = r_j, j = 1, \ldots, l$, so r is a convex combination of the rows of Q. ∎

This theorem applies to all of the five examples above, and they illustrate the variety of behavior that is consistent with its conclusions. There may be one ergodic set or more than one, and in addition there may be a transient set; the sequence $\{\Pi^k\}$ may or may not converge, but the sequence of averages $\{A^{(n)}\} = \{(1/n)\Sigma_{k=0}^{n-1} \Pi^k\}$ necessarily converges; and the rows of the limiting matrix Q are invariant distributions. For the case of finite chains, then, given any initial probability distribution, the long-run average probabilities over states converge. In particular, if the initial state is s_i, then the long-run average probabilities are given by the ith row of the matrix Q. If p_0 is an initial probability distribution over states, then the long-run average probabilities are given by $p_0 Q$. Note that we have not ruled out the possibility of multiple ergodic sets or cyclically moving subsets within any ergodic set.

There is a close connection between the M ergodic sets and the M invariant distributions described in Theorem 11.1. To see it note that we can, without loss of generality, order the states so that all of the transient states come first, and the states in each ergodic class appear in a block. With this ordering of the states, the transition matrix Π takes the (almost block diagonal) form

	F	E_1	E_2	$\ldots$	E_M
F	R_{00}	R_{01}	R_{02}	$\ldots$	R_{0M}
E_1	0	R_{11}	0	$\ldots$	0
E_2	0	0	R_{22}	$\ldots$	0
$\vdots$	$\vdots$	$\vdots$	$\vdots$	$\ddots$	$\vdots$
E_M	0	0	0	$\ldots$	R_{MM}

Note that each matrix $R_{11}, \ldots, R_{MM}$ is a stochastic matrix; hence Theorem 11.1 applies to each one, and we can define

$$Q_j = \lim_{N\to\infty} \frac{1}{N} \sum_{n=0}^{N-1} R_{jj}^n, \quad j = 1, \ldots, M.$$

On the other hand, R_{00} is not a stochastic matrix; otherwise F would be an ergodic set. That is, R_{00} has at least one row sum that is strictly less than one.

Exercise 11.1 Show that when Π has the form above, Q has the form

	F	E_1	E_2	$\cdots$	E_M
F	0	$w_1 Q_1$	$w_2 Q_2$	$\cdots$	$w_M Q_M$
E_1	0	Q_1	0	$\cdots$	0
E_2	0	0	Q_2	$\cdots$	0
$\vdots$	$\vdots$	$\vdots$	$\vdots$	$\ddots$	$\vdots$
E_M	0	0	0	$\cdots$	Q_M

,

where the rows within each matrix Q_j are all identical and where the column vectors w_j sum to the unit vector. Show that the ith element in w_j is the probability of a transition, eventually, from the ith transient state to the set E_j.

Since all the rows within each matrix Q_i are identical, it follows that if the system begins in any state in the ergodic class E_i, the long-run average probabilities are the same. The same is true if the initial position is described by any probability distribution that assigns zero probability to all states outside of E_i. The M distinct rows of the matrices $Q_1, \ldots, Q_M$ correspond to the M ergodic classes. The first block of rows, those corresponding to initial states in F, are convex combinations of the others. If the system begins in a transient state, then the long-run average probabilities are determined by the probability of eventually getting into each of the various ergodic classes. Thus in the case of a finite state space we can, for an arbitrary transition matrix Π, establish the existence of at least one ergodic class and, accordingly, one invariant distribution.

To obtain sharper results, we must impose additional structure on the transition matrix Π. The next theorem provides a necessary and sufficient condition to ensure that there is a unique ergodic class. That is, it rules out cases like Examples 4 and 5.

THEOREM 11.2 *Let $S = \{s_1, \ldots, s_l\}$ be a finite set, and let the stochastic matrix Π define transition probabilities on S. Then Π has a unique ergodic set if and only if there exists a state s_j such that the following holds: for every*

$i \in \{1, \ldots, l\}$, *there exists $n \geq 1$ such that $\pi_{ij}^{(n)} > 0$. In this case Π has a unique invariant distribution, call it p^*; each row of Q is equal to p^*; and for any $p_0 \in \Delta^l$, $p_0 Q = p^*$.*

Proof. Suppose that the stated condition holds for some state s_j. Then s_j cannot be transient and is a consequent of every state s_i, $i = 1, \ldots, l$. Hence there is at most one ergodic set. The other claims then follow immediately from Theorem 11.1.

Conversely, suppose that there is only one ergodic class, E, and choose $s_j \in E$. Since every element of E is a consequent of j, it follows that the stated condition holds for every $s_i \in E$. Consider next any $s_i \in F$. For some $s_k \in E$ and $n \geq 1$, $\pi_{ik}^{(n)} > 0$; otherwise s_i is not transient. Since j is a consequent of k, $\pi_{kj}^{(m)} > 0$ for some $m \geq 1$. Hence $\pi_{ij}^{(n+m)} \geq \pi_{ik}^{(n)} \pi_{kj}^{(m)} > 0$. ∎

Our final result provides a condition that, in addition to ensuring the uniqueness of the ergodic set, rules out cyclically moving subsets within the ergodic set. That is, it rules out cases like Example 3. Under this condition the sequence $\{\Pi^k\}$, not just the sequence of long-run averages, converges to Q. Since by Theorem 11.2 each row of Q is equal to the unique invariant distribution p^*, it then follows that the sequence of distributions $\{p_0 \Pi^k\}$ converges to p^* for all $p_0 \in \Delta^l$. Moreover the convergence is at a geometric rate that is uniform in p_0.

There are many ways to establish this result; the proof we will present is based on the Contraction Mapping Theorem. The idea is to show that if for some $N \geq 1$, Π^N defines a contraction mapping on Δ^l, then the unique fixed point of this mapping is the vector p^* and the convergence of $\{p_0 \Pi^k\}$ is as claimed. We will also show that the converse is true: if $\{p_0 \Pi^k\} \to p^*$, all $p_0 \in \Delta^l$, then for some $N \geq 1$, Π^N defines a contraction mapping on Δ^l. Lemma 11.3 provides a sufficient condition for Π to define a contraction mapping on Δ^l; Theorem 11.4 uses this condition to obtain the conclusions described above.

To apply the Contraction Mapping Theorem we must show that Δ^l is a complete metric space, for an appropriately chosen metric, and that the transition matrix Π defines an operator taking Δ^l into itself. For the rest of this section let $\|\cdot\|_\Delta$ denote the norm on $\mathbf{R}^l$ defined by

$$\|x\|_\Delta = \sum_{j=1}^{l} |x_j|.$$

Recall from Exercises 3.4c and 3.6a that with this metric $(\mathbf{R}^l, \|\cdot\|_\Delta)$ is a complete metric space and Δ^l is a closed subset. Hence $(\Delta^l, \|\cdot\|_\Delta)$ is also a complete metric space. Then as was shown above, for any $l \times l$ Markov matrix Π, the operator T^* defined by $T^*p = p\Pi$ takes Δ^l into itself.

LEMMA 11.3   *Let Π be an $l \times l$ Markov matrix, and for $j = 1, \ldots, l$, let $\varepsilon_j = \min_i \pi_{ij}$. If $\Sigma_{j=1}^l \varepsilon_j = \varepsilon > 0$, then the mapping $T^*: \Delta^l \to \Delta^l$ defined by $T^*p = p\Pi$ is a contraction of modulus $1 - \varepsilon$.*

Proof. Let $p, q \in \Delta^l$. Then

$$\|T^*p - T^*q\|_\Delta = \|p\Pi - q\Pi\|_\Delta$$

$$= \sum_{j=1}^l \left| \sum_{i=1}^l (p_i - q_i)\pi_{ij} \right|$$

$$= \sum_{j=1}^l \left| \sum_{i=1}^l (p_i - q_i)(\pi_{ij} - \varepsilon_j) + \sum_{i=1}^l (p_i - q_i)\varepsilon_j \right|$$

$$\leq \sum_{j=1}^l \sum_{i=1}^l |p_i - q_i|(\pi_{ij} - \varepsilon_j) + \sum_{j=1}^l \varepsilon_j \left| \sum_{i=1}^l (p_i - q_i) \right|$$

$$= \sum_{i=1}^l |p_i - q_i| \sum_{j=1}^l (\pi_{ij} - \varepsilon_j) + 0$$

$$= (1 - \varepsilon)\|p - q\|_\Delta. \quad \blacksquare$$

THEOREM 11.4   *Let $S = \{s_1, \ldots, s_l\}$ be a finite set, and let the stochastic matrix Π define transition probabilities on S. For $n = 1, 2, \ldots$, let $\varepsilon_j^{(n)} = \min_i \pi_{ij}^{(n)}$, $j = 1, \ldots, l$, and let $\varepsilon^{(n)} = \Sigma_{j=1}^l \varepsilon_j^{(n)}$. Then S has a unique ergodic set with no cyclically moving subsets if and only if for some $N \geq 1$, $\varepsilon^{(N)} > 0$. In this case $\{p_0\Pi^k\}$ converges to a unique limit $p^* \in \Delta^l$, for all $p_0 \in \Delta^l$, and convergence is at a geometric rate that is independent of p_0.*

Proof. If $\varepsilon^{(N)} > 0$ then by Lemma 11.3, $T^{*N}: \Delta^l \to \Delta^l$ defined by $T^*p = p\Pi^N$ is a contraction of modulus $1 - \varepsilon^{(N)}$. Since Δ^l is a closed subset of a complete metric space, it follows from the Contraction Mapping Theorem (Theorem 3.2) that T^{*N} has a unique fixed point—call it p^*—and that

$$\|p_0\Pi^{kN} - p^*\|_\Delta \leq (1 - \varepsilon^{(N)})^k \|p_0 - p^*\|_\Delta, \quad k = 1, 2, \ldots, \text{ all } p_0 \in \Delta^l.$$

Conversely, suppose that $\{p_0\Pi^n\} \to p^*$, all $p_0 \in \Delta^l$. Then $\{\Pi^n\} \to (p^*, \ldots, p^*)'$, so for some $N \geq 1$ sufficiently large there is at least one column j for which $\pi_{ij}^{(N)} > 0$, all i. Then $\varepsilon^{(N)} \geq \varepsilon_j^{(N)} > 0$. ∎

Hence for the case where the state space S is finite, we have a very simple condition that is both necessary and sufficient for convergence to a unique stationary distribution. Moreover, in this case convergence is at a geometric rate that is uniform in the initial distribution.

It is worthwhile to summarize briefly the steps in the analysis above. First we defined Δ^l, the set of all probability distributions on S, and showed that a transition matrix Π defines a mapping T^* of Δ^l into itself. Specifically, we saw that if $p_0 \in \Delta^l$ is the distribution over the initial state, then $p_n = p_0\Pi^n$ is the distribution over the state n periods later, and $(1/n)\Sigma_{k=0}^{n-1} p_k = p_0A^{(n)}$ is the average of the distributions over the first n periods. The main results were

1. S can always be partitioned into $M \geq 1$ ergodic sets and a transient set, and the sequence $\{A^{(n)}\}$ always converges to a stochastic matrix Q. Moreover, the rows of Q are invariant distributions; hence for any $p_0 \in \Delta^l$, the sequence $\{(1/n)\Sigma_{k=0}^{n-1}p_0\Pi^k\} = \{(1/n)\Sigma_{k=0}^{n-1}p_k\}$ converges to p_0Q, an invariant distribution. Finally, all invariant distributions can be formed as convex combinations of the rows of Q.

2. If the additional hypothesis of Theorem 11.2 holds, then there is a unique ergodic set. In this case all of the rows of Q are identical, and the vector p^* in each row is the unique invariant distribution.

3. If the additional hypothesis of Theorem 11.4 holds, then the unique ergodic class has no cyclically moving subsets, and the sequence $\{\Pi^n\}$ converges to Q. Hence for any $p_0 \in \Delta^l$, the sequence $\{p_n\} = \{p_0\Pi^n\}$ converges to p^*. Moreover, the rate of convergence is geometric and is uniform in p_0.

In Section 11.4 we show that all of these results have analogues in general state spaces. However, there are possibilities that arise in infinite state spaces that do not have counterparts in the finite-state Markov chains we have treated so far. We conclude this section with two examples of infinite-state Markov processes that illustrate these possibilities.

Example 6 Let $S = \{s_1, s_2, \ldots\}$, and suppose that the transition matrix Π is the infinite-dimensional identity matrix. Then there are an infinite number of ergodic sets, each of the sets $E_i = \{s_i\}$, $i = 1, 2, \ldots$; and corresponding to each is an invariant distribution, the probability vectors e_i, $i = 1, 2, \ldots$. Clearly this possibility arises whenever the state space is infinite.

Example 7   Let $S = \{s_1, s_2, \ldots\}$, and let

$$
\Pi = \begin{bmatrix} 0 & 1 & 0 & 0 & \cdots \\ 0 & 0 & 1 & 0 & \cdots \\ 0 & 0 & 0 & 1 & \cdots \\ \vdots & \vdots & \vdots & \vdots & \ddots \end{bmatrix}.
$$

In this case all of the states are transient. There is no ergodic set and hence no invariant distribution. Note that in this case the sequence $\{\Pi^k\}$ converges to the zero matrix: all of the probability "wanders off to infinity."

To extend the results in the theorems above to more general state spaces, then, we must find assumptions that rule out cases like these. Before turning to these issues, however, we need to discuss the notion of convergence for measures in those spaces.

11.2   Convergence Concepts for Measures

In the last section we examined conditions under which a sequence of probability distributions $\{p_n\}$ on a finite space, generated from an initial distribution p_0 by the recursive formula $p_{n+1} = p_n\Pi$, would converge to a limiting distribution p^* as $n \to \infty$. In that discussion $\{p_n\}$ and p^* were elements of $\mathbf{R}^l$, so the term "convergence" could be made precise using any of the many equivalent norms for $\mathbf{R}^l$. Our use of the particular norm $\|p\| = \Sigma_i|p_i|$ was important for establishing facts about the *rate* of convergence in Lemma 11.3 and Theorem 11.4, but not for the other results. In the rest of this chapter and the next, our concern is with sequences $\{\lambda_n\}$ of probability measures on a fixed measurable space $(S, \mathscr{S})$, and with questions about the convergence of such a sequence to a limiting measure λ. When $(S, \mathscr{S})$ is an arbitrary measurable space, there is considerable latitude in defining convergence of a sequence of probability measures. Therefore, it is useful to begin by reviewing some of the issues involved in defining convergence for measures.

Let $(S, \mathscr{S})$ be a measurable space; let $\Lambda(S, \mathscr{S})$ be the set of probability measures on $(S, \mathscr{S})$; and let $\{\lambda_n\}_{n=1}^{\infty}$ and λ be measures in $\Lambda(S, \mathscr{S})$. Two basic approaches can be used in defining convergence concepts for sequences of probability measures. The first is based on measures of sets, the second on the expected values of functions. As we show below, however, all of the standard notions of convergence can be characterized using either approach.

First consider the possibilities for defining convergence in terms of measures of sets. One criterion is simply

(1) $\lim\limits_{n\to\infty} \lambda_n(A) = \lambda(A)$,   all $A \in \mathcal{S}$.

If (1) holds, we say that λ_n *converges setwise* to λ. This criterion can be weakened by choosing a family of sets $\mathcal{A} \subset \mathcal{S}$ and requiring only that (1) hold for sets in $\mathcal{A}$. An appropriate choice of $\mathcal{A}$ leads to a different, strictly weaker, notion of convergence. Alternatively we can strengthen the definition in (1) by requiring, in addition, some sort of uniformity in the rate of convergence.

A second way to think about convergence of measures is in terms of the behavior of the expected values of functions. Let $(S, \mathcal{S})$ and $\Lambda(S, \mathcal{S})$ be as specified above, and let $B(S, \mathcal{S})$ be the set of bounded measurable functions $f: S \to \mathbf{R}$. Then given $\{\lambda_n\}$ and λ in $\Lambda(S, \mathcal{S})$, we might want to use as a criterion the requirement that

(2) $\lim\limits_{n\to\infty} \int f\, d\lambda_n = \int f\, d\lambda$,   all $f \in B(S, \mathcal{S})$.

Obviously (2) implies (1), since the indicator function of each set in $\mathcal{S}$ is in $B(S, \mathcal{S})$. The converse is also true.

Exercise 11.2   Show that (1) implies (2).

Thus (2) is an alternative and completely equivalent way to characterize setwise convergence.

The criterion (2) can be weakened by choosing a smaller family of functions and requiring only that (2) hold for functions in this smaller family. As before, if the smaller family is appropriately chosen, a different, strictly weaker, definition of convergence is obtained. Alternatively, (2) can be strengthened by requiring some sort of uniformity in the rate of convergence.

As the discussion thus far should suggest, whether convergence of probability measures is defined in terms of measures of sets or in terms of expected values of functions is purely a matter of convenience. As we saw above for setwise convergence, and will see later for other convergence concepts, the definitions of interest can be expressed either way.

We still have not resolved the question of choosing a convergence concept. Is setwise convergence the "right" concept? Or should we use something stronger? Or something weaker? This question does not have a single answer, but it is important to understand clearly what the various concepts do and do not entail. A particularly useful example in this regard is the following deterministic system.

Let $S = [0, 1]$, and consider the deterministic process governed by the difference equation $s_{t+1} = s_t/2$. This system is globally asymptotically stable, converging to the stationary point $s^* = 0$ from any initial point $s_0 \in S$. Now let $\mathcal{S}$ be the Borel sets of S, and let P be the transition function on $(S, \mathcal{S})$ defined by $P(s, \{s/2\}) = 1$, so that P corresponds precisely to the deterministic process. Let λ_n be the probability measure that is a unit mass at the point $1/2^n$, for $n = 0, 1, 2, \ldots$. Then starting the system at the point $s_0 = 1$ is exactly the same as taking λ_0 to be the probability measure over the state in period $t = 0$, and $\{\lambda_n\}_{n=1}^{\infty}$ is the sequence of probability measures over the state in subsequent periods. What can we say about the sequence $\{\lambda_n\}$? Clearly the only candidate for a limiting measure is a unit mass at zero; call this measure λ. However, if we take the measurable function

$$f(s) = \begin{cases} 1 & \text{if } s = 0 \\ 0 & \text{if } s \neq 0, \end{cases}$$

then $\int f \, d\lambda_n = 0$, $n = 0, 1, 2, \ldots$, but $\int f \, d\lambda = 1$. Thus, (2) fails: the sequence $\{\lambda_n\}$ does not converge setwise to λ or to anything else.

It seems perverse to define convergence for stochastic systems in a way that excludes our notion of convergence for deterministic systems. We can see what the problem is by recalling the definition of convergence for deterministic systems. A sequence $\{s_n\}$ in a space S converges to s if the distance between s_n and s goes to zero as n gets large. Our ordinary definition of convergence thus requires a metric on the space S, and we count on the metric to capture our idea of what it means for two points to be "close." Stated somewhat differently, we choose our metric so that if s_n is close to s, then functions of the state—at least, the ones we care about—take on similar values whether the state is s_n or s. That is, we choose the metric on S so that functions of interest are continuous in the chosen metric. Then the fact that $\{s_n\}$ converges to s implies that $\{f(s_n)\}$ converges to $f(s)$, for all functions f of interest. Notice that in the example above, for any continuous function f,

$$\lim_{n\to\infty} \int f \, d\lambda_n = \lim_{n\to\infty} f(1/2^n) = f(0) = \int f \, d\lambda.$$

This example and others like it motivate the following concept of convergence.

DEFINITION *Let (S, ρ) be a metric space; let $\mathcal{S}$ be the Borel sets of S; let $\{\lambda_n\}$ and λ be measures in $\Lambda(S, \mathcal{S})$; and let $C(S)$ be the space of bounded, continuous, real-valued functions on S. Then $\{\lambda_n\}$ **converges weakly** to λ if*

$$(3) \qquad \lim_{n\to\infty} \int f \, d\lambda_n = \int f \, d\lambda, \quad \text{all } f \in C(S).$$

Thus, in the deterministic example above, the sequence $\{\lambda_n\}$ does converge weakly to λ.

Clearly (2) implies (3), but in general (3) does not imply (2). That is, setwise convergence implies weak convergence, but in general the reverse is not true. (The exception occurs when ρ is the discrete metric, so $\mathcal{S}$ is the family of all subsets of S. In this case every function is both measurable and continuous, $B(S, \mathcal{S}) = C(S)$, and setwise convergence and weak convergence are equivalent. This is why the issue of choosing a convergence concept did not arise in our treatment in Section 11.1 of systems with a finite state space.)

Weak convergence is very often all that we really care about in the context of describing the dynamics of an economic system. Accordingly, we make a detailed study of it in Chapter 12. In the remainder of this chapter, however, we look briefly at a stronger concept than setwise convergence. This concept is easily stated in terms of a strengthening of (2).

DEFINITION *Let $(S, \mathcal{S})$ be a measurable space and let $\{\lambda_n\}$ and λ be measures in $\Lambda(S, \mathcal{S})$. Then $\{\lambda_n\}$ **converges strongly** to λ if (2) is satisfied, and if in addition the rate of convergence is uniform for all $f \in B(S, \mathcal{S})$ such that $\|f\| = \sup_{s\in S}|f(s)| \leq 1$.*

The uniformity condition in this definition may look odd. It looks less so when restated as a strengthening of (1), as will be done later.

There are two reasons for beginning with a study of strong convergence. First, since strong convergence implies weak convergence, establishing the former is one way of establishing the latter. Second, the results established in Section 11.1 for finite state spaces have very close parallels in terms of strong convergence results for arbitrary state spaces, and it is instructive to see what conditions are needed in the more general case.

In Section 11.3 we characterize strong convergence in terms of measures of sets. Then in Section 11.4 we study the issue of strong convergence for Markov processes with an arbitrary state space. We show there that all of the results obtained in Section 11.1 for finite Markov chains have quite close parallels. In particular, we provide a fairly simple condition that is both necessary and sufficient for the strong convergence of a Markov process to a unique limiting measure, independent of the initial measure. In Chapter 12 we take up the study of weak convergence, again beginning with a study of alternative characterizations and proceeding to the study of Markov processes. We will not make further use of the concept of setwise convergence.

11.3   Characterizations of Strong Convergence

In this section and the next, let $(S, \mathcal{S})$ be an arbitrary measurable space, let $\Lambda(S, \mathcal{S})$ be the set of probability measures on $(S, \mathcal{S})$, and let $B(S, \mathcal{S})$ be the space of bounded, measurable functions $f: S \to \mathbf{R}$ with the sup norm, $\|f\| = \sup_{s \in S} |f(s)|$. The main results in this section are as follows. We first define a norm, the total variation norm, on the set $\Lambda(S, \mathcal{S})$ and show (Theorem 11.6) that convergence in this norm is equivalent to the uniform convergence of measures of all sets in $\mathcal{S}$. We then show (Theorem 11.7) that convergence in the total variation norm is also equivalent to strong convergence as defined in the last section. Taken together then, these two theorems show that, as for setwise convergence, strong convergence has equivalent characterizations in terms of measures of sets or in terms of integrals of functions. Finally, we show (Theorem 11.8) that endowed with the total variation norm, the set $\Lambda(S, \mathcal{S})$ is a complete metric space. This last result is drawn upon in our study of strong convergence of Markov processes in Section 11.4, where we apply the Contraction Mapping Theorem.

In order to define the norm of interest, we must introduce the appropriate vector space. To do this, we need the following definition.

DEFINITION *For any two finite measures* λ_1, λ_2 *on a measurable space* $(S, \mathcal{S})$, *the set function* $\nu: \mathcal{S} \to \mathbf{R}$ *defined by* $\nu(C) = \lambda_1(C) - \lambda_2(C)$, *all* $C \in \mathcal{S}$, *is called a* **signed measure** *on* $\mathcal{S}$.

We will use $\Phi(S, \mathcal{S})$ to denote the space of signed measures on $(S, \mathcal{S})$. It is straightforward to show that $\Phi(S, \mathcal{S})$ is a vector space. We define the **total variation norm** on this space by

$$(1) \qquad \|\lambda\| = \sup \sum_{i=1}^{k} |\lambda(A_i)|,$$

where the supremum is over all finite partitions of S into disjoint measurable subsets.

> **Exercise 11.3** Show that $\Phi(S, \mathcal{S})$ is a vector space, and that (1) defines a norm on $\Phi(S, \mathcal{S})$.

The set $\Lambda(S, \mathcal{S})$ is a subset of the vector space $\Phi(S, \mathcal{S})$; and for any measures λ_1, λ_2 in $\Lambda(S, \mathcal{S})$, the signed measure $\lambda_1 - \lambda_2$ is in $\Phi(S, \mathcal{S})$. Hence (1) defines a metric on the space $\Lambda(S, \mathcal{S})$. We then have the following definition.

DEFINITION *The sequence of probability measures* $\{\lambda_n\}$ **converges in the total variation norm** *to the probability measure* λ *if* $\lim_{n \to \infty} \|\lambda_n - \lambda\| = 0$.

In the next lemma we use the decomposition described in Lemma 7.12 to characterize the value of $\|\lambda_1 - \lambda_2\|$ for any probability measures $\lambda_1, \lambda_2 \in \Lambda(S, \mathcal{S})$. Recall that Lemma 7.12 shows how, given measures λ_1 and λ_2 in $\Lambda(S, \mathcal{S})$, to construct a partition of S into two measurable sets, B and B^c, such that λ_1 exceeds λ_2 on B and λ_2 exceeds λ_1 on B^c. The proof of Lemma 11.5 uses the fact that we can evaluate $\|\lambda_1 - \lambda_2\|$ in terms of the measures of the sets B and B^c. Theorem 11.6 then draws on this result to show that convergence in the total variation norm is equivalent to the uniform convergence of the measures of all sets in $\mathcal{S}$.

LEMMA 11.5 *For any two probability measures* $\lambda_1, \lambda_2 \in \Lambda(S, \mathcal{S})$,

$$\|\lambda_1 - \lambda_2\| = 2 \sup_{A \in \mathcal{S}} |\lambda_1(A) - \lambda_2(A)|.$$

Proof. Let $\lambda_1, \lambda_2 \in \Lambda(S, \mathscr{S})$ be given. By Lemma 7.12, we can write λ_1, λ_2 as $\lambda_i = \lambda + \alpha_i$, $i = 1, 2$, where λ, α_1, and α_2 are nonnegative measures, and where α_1 and α_2 are mutually singular, $\alpha_1 \perp \alpha_2$. By construction,

$$|\lambda_1(A) - \lambda_2(A)| = |\alpha_1(A) - \alpha_2(A)|, \quad \text{all } A \in \mathscr{S},$$

so

$$\|\lambda_1 - \lambda_2\| = \|\alpha_1 - \alpha_2\|.$$

Moreover, since $\alpha_1 \perp \alpha_2$, there are measurable sets B, B^c such that α_1 is concentrated on B and α_2 on B^c. Also, since $\lambda_1(S) = \lambda_2(S) = 1$, it follows that $\alpha_1(S) = \alpha_2(S) = 1 - \lambda(S)$. Hence $\alpha_1(B) = \alpha_1(S) = \alpha_2(S) = \alpha_2(B^c)$ and $\alpha_1(B^c) = \alpha_2(B) = 0$. It then follows that

$$\|\lambda_1 - \lambda_2\| = \|\alpha_1 - \alpha_2\| = |\alpha_1(B)| + |\alpha_2(B^c)| = 2|\alpha_1(B)|$$

$$= 2 \sup_{A \in \mathscr{S}} |\alpha_1(A) - \alpha_2(A)| = 2 \sup_{A \in \mathscr{S}} |\lambda_1(A) - \lambda_2(A)|. \quad \blacksquare$$

THEOREM 11.6   *Let $\{\lambda_n\}$ and λ be measures in $\Lambda(S, \mathscr{S})$. Then*

$$(2) \qquad \lim_{n \to \infty} \|\lambda_n - \lambda\| = 0,$$

if and only if

$$(3) \qquad \lim_{n \to \infty} |\lambda_n(A) - \lambda(A)| = 0, \quad \text{all } A \in \mathscr{S},$$

and the latter convergence is uniform in A.

Proof. Let $\{\lambda_n\}$ and λ be given, and suppose that (2) holds. Then for every $\varepsilon > 0$, there exists $N_\varepsilon > 0$ such that

$$\|\lambda_n - \lambda\| < \varepsilon, \quad \text{all } n > N_\varepsilon.$$

It then follows immediately from Lemma 11.5 that for every $\varepsilon > 0$,

$$(4) \qquad |\lambda_n(A) - \lambda(A)| < \varepsilon/2, \quad \text{all } A \in \mathscr{S}, \text{ all } n > N_\varepsilon.$$

That is, (3) holds and the rate of convergence is uniform in A.

Conversely, suppose that the latter holds. That is, for every $\varepsilon > 0$, there exists $N_\varepsilon > 0$ such that (4) holds. Then for every $\varepsilon > 0$,

$$\|\lambda_n - \lambda\| = 2 \sup_{A \in \mathscr{S}} |\lambda_n(A) - \lambda(A)| < \varepsilon, \quad \text{all } n > N_\varepsilon,$$

so (2) holds. ∎

Theorem 11.6 characterizes convergence in the total variation norm in terms of the uniform convergence of the measures of all sets in $\mathscr{S}$. The next theorem shows that convergence in the total variation norm is also equivalent to strong convergence as defined in Section 11.2. The proof of this theorem illustrates very clearly the close relationship between measures of sets and integrals of functions: statements about measures of sets translate directly into statements about integrals of characteristic functions, and vice versa. The rest is then simply a matter of showing that the statements of interest that hold for characteristic functions also hold for all simple functions and for all bounded measurable functions.

THEOREM 11.7 *Let $\{\lambda_n\}$ and λ be measures in $\Lambda(S, \mathscr{S})$. Then*

$$\lim_{n \to \infty} \|\lambda_n - \lambda\| = 0$$

if and only if

(5) $$\lim_{n \to \infty} \left| \int f \, d\lambda_n - \int f \, d\lambda \right| = 0, \quad \text{all } f \in B(S, \mathscr{S}),$$

and the convergence is uniform for all functions with $\|f\| \le 1$.

Proof. Suppose that $\lim_{n \to \infty} \|\lambda_n - \lambda\| = 0$. Then for any $\varepsilon > 0$, there exists $N_\varepsilon \ge 1$ such that $n > N_\varepsilon$ implies

$$\sup \sum_{i=1}^{k} |\lambda_n(A_i) - \lambda(A_i)| < \varepsilon,$$

where the supremum is over all finite measurable partitions of S.

Consider any measurable simple function ϕ. Then ϕ can be written as $\phi(s) = \sum_{i=1}^{k} c_i \chi_{A_i}(s)$, all $s \in S$, where $A_1, \ldots, A_k$ is a measurable partition of S. Hence

$$\left| \int \phi \, d\lambda_n - \int \phi \, d\lambda \right| \le \sum_{i=1}^{k} |c_i| \, |\lambda_n(A_i) - \lambda(A_i)|$$

$$\le \|\phi\| \, \varepsilon, \quad \text{all } n > N_\varepsilon.$$

Hence (5) holds for all simple functions; and since N_ε does not depend on ϕ, the convergence is uniform for all simple functions with $\|\phi\| \le 1$.

Next consider any bounded measurable function f. By Theorem 7.5, the positive and negative parts of f—call them f^+ and f^-—can each be written as the limit of an increasing sequence of nonnegative, measurable, simple functions. Let $\{\phi_k^+\}$ and $\{\phi_k^-\}$ be such sequences, and let $\phi_k = \phi_k^+ - \phi_k^-$, all k. Note that $\|\phi_k\| \le \|f\|$, all k. Then it follows from the argument above that for any $\varepsilon > 0$, there exists $N_\varepsilon \ge 1$ such that

$$(6) \qquad \left| \int \phi_k \, d\lambda_n - \int \phi_k \, d\lambda \right| \le \|\phi_k\| \varepsilon \le \|f\| \varepsilon, \quad \text{all } n > N_\varepsilon, \text{ all } k.$$

Hence

$$\left| \int f \, d\lambda_n - \int f \, d\lambda \right| = \left| \lim_{k \to \infty} \int \phi_k \, d\lambda_n - \lim_{k \to \infty} \int \phi_k \, d\lambda \right|$$

$$= \lim_{k \to \infty} \left| \int \phi_k \, d\lambda_n - \int \phi_k \, d\lambda \right|$$

$$\le \|f\| \varepsilon, \quad \text{all } n > N_\varepsilon,$$

where the first line follows from the Lebesgue Dominated Convergence Theorem (Theorem 7.10), the second from the fact that for each fixed $n > N_\varepsilon$, $\{\int \phi_k \, d\lambda_n\}_{k=1}^{\infty}$ and $\{\int \phi_k \, d\lambda\}_{k=1}^{\infty}$ are convergent sequences of real numbers, and the last from (6). Hence $\lim_{n \to \infty} \|\lambda_n - \lambda\| = 0$ implies that (5) holds. If $\|f\| \le 1$, then all the simple functions in the approximating sequences have $\|\phi_k\| \le 1$. Hence the rate of convergence is uniform for all measurable functions with $\|f\| \le 1$.

Conversely, suppose that (5) holds and that the rate of convergence is uniform for $\|f\| \le 1$. Then for every $\varepsilon > 0$, there exists $N_\varepsilon > 0$ such that for simple functions ϕ with $\|\phi\| \le 1$,

$$\left| \int \phi \, d\lambda_n - \int \phi \, d\lambda \right| < \varepsilon, \quad \text{all } n > N_\varepsilon.$$

Let $A_1, \ldots, A_k$ be any finite measurable partition of S, and consider the family (with 2^k members) of simple functions of the form $\phi(s) = \Sigma_{i=1}^k c_i \chi_{A_i}(s)$, where $c_i = +1$ or -1 for each i. Then for any $n > N_\varepsilon$, there exists a function ϕ in this family for which

$$\sum_{i=1}^k |\lambda_n(A_i) - \lambda(A_i)| = \sum_{i=1}^k c_i[\lambda_n(A_i) - \lambda(A_i)]$$

$$= \left| \int \phi \, d\lambda_n - \int \phi \, d\lambda \right| < \varepsilon.$$

Since this is true for any partition $A_1, \ldots, A_k$, it follows that

$$\|\lambda_n - \lambda\| = \sup \sum_{i=1}^k |\lambda_n(A_i) - \lambda(A_i)| \leq \varepsilon, \quad \text{all } n > N_\varepsilon. \quad \blacksquare$$

Taken together, Theorems 11.6 and 11.7 show that there are three equivalent ways of characterizing strong convergence of a sequence of measures $\{\lambda_n\}$ in $\Lambda(S, \mathcal{S})$: as convergence in the total variation norm, as uniform convergence of the measures of all sets in $\mathcal{S}$, and as convergence of the integrals of all bounded measurable functions, where the convergence is uniform for functions with $\|f\| \leq 1$. Thus the terms *norm convergence* and *convergence in the total variation norm* are used interchangeably with *strong convergence*.

To establish a necessary and sufficient condition for convergence in the total variation norm, we use—as we did in Theorem 11.4—an argument based on the Contraction Mapping Theorem. Hence we need the following result.

LEMMA 11.8 *The space of probability measures $\Lambda(S, \mathcal{S})$ with the total variation norm is a complete metric space.*

Proof. Let $\{\lambda_n\}$ be a Cauchy sequence in Λ. Then for every $\varepsilon > 0$, there exists $N_\varepsilon \geq 1$ such that $\|\lambda_n - \lambda_m\| < \varepsilon$, all $n, m > N_\varepsilon$. By Lemma 11.5, this fact implies that

(7) $\qquad |\lambda_n(A) - \lambda_m(A)| < \varepsilon/2, \quad \text{all } n, m > N_\varepsilon, \text{ all } A \in \mathcal{S}.$

Hence for each $A \in \mathcal{S}$, $\{\lambda_n(A)\}$ is a Cauchy sequence in $\mathbf{R}_+$ and thus converges. Let $\lambda(A) = \lim_{n \to \infty} \lambda_n(A)$, all $A \in \mathcal{S}$.

Next we will show that λ is a probability measure. Clearly $\lambda(\emptyset) = 0$, $\lambda(S) = 1$, and $\lambda(A) \geq 0$, all $A \in \mathcal{S}$. To see that λ is countably additive, let $\{A_i\}$ be any disjoint sequence in $\mathcal{S}$, with $A = \cup_{i=1}^{\infty} A_i$. Since each λ_n is countably additive, $\lambda_n(A) = \sum_{i=1}^{\infty} \lambda_n(A_i)$, all n. Taking the limit as $n \to \infty$, we have

$$\lambda(A) = \lim_{n \to \infty} \lambda_n(A) = \lim_{n \to \infty} \sum_{i=1}^{\infty} \lambda_n(A_i)$$

$$= \sum_{i=1}^{\infty} \lim_{n \to \infty} \lambda_n(A_i) = \sum_{i=1}^{\infty} \lambda(A_i).$$

Hence λ is countably additive.

Finally, we must show that $\lim_{n \to \infty} \|\lambda_n - \lambda\| = 0$. Fix $\varepsilon > 0$. Then it follows from (7) that

$$|\lambda_n(A) - \lambda(A)| = \lim_{m \to \infty} |\lambda_n(A) - \lambda_m(A)|$$

$$\leq \varepsilon/2, \quad \text{all } n > N_\varepsilon, \text{ all } A \in \mathcal{S}.$$

Hence by Lemma 11.5, $\|\lambda_n - \lambda\| \leq \varepsilon$, all $n > N_\varepsilon$. ∎

11.4 Sufficient Conditions

In this section we apply the results of Section 11.3 to show that, under appropriate restrictions, the results obtained for Markov chains in Section 11.1 go through virtually unchanged for general state spaces. Throughout this section: $(S, \mathcal{S})$ is a measurable space; P is a transition function on $(S, \mathcal{S})$; T is the Markov operator associated with P; T^* is the adjoint of T; $\Lambda(S, \mathcal{S})$ is the space of probability measures on $(S, \mathcal{S})$; and $\|\cdot\|$ denotes the total variation norm on $\Lambda(S, \mathcal{S})$. In this section convergence of a sequence of probability measures will always mean convergence in the total variation norm.

We concluded Section 11.1 with two examples of badly behaved infinite-state Markov processes. In Example 6 there were an infinite number of ergodic sets and invariant distributions, and in Example 7 there were none. Theorem 11.1 showed that if the state space S is a finite set, these two types of behavior are ruled out; but it is clear that if S is an arbitrary set, they are possible. We begin the present section with an additional condition, due to Doeblin, that rules out these, and other, "bad" examples.

Theorem 11.9 shows that Doeblin's condition is sufficient to establish the existence of a finite number $M \geq 1$ of ergodic sets and the convergence for each $\lambda_0 \in \Lambda(S, \mathcal{Y})$ of the sequence of averages $\{(1/N) \sum_{n=0}^{N-1} (T^{*n})\lambda_0\}$ to an invariant measure $\lambda^* \in \Lambda(S, \mathcal{Y})$, where λ^* may depend on λ_0. As in the case of Markov chains, there are $M \geq 1$ invariant probability measures, corresponding to the M ergodic sets; and all invariant probability measures of T^* are convex combinations of these. Thus, Theorem 11.9 provides an analogue for arbitrary state spaces to the result proved in Theorem 11.1 for Markov chains.

Theorems 11.10 and 11.12 then provide analogues to Theorems 11.2 and 11.4. Theorem 11.10 shows that, as in the case of Markov chains, one additional assumption is sufficient to rule out multiple ergodic sets. Theorem 11.12 uses the Contraction Mapping Theorem to show that a strengthening of Doeblin's condition, called Condition M, is necessary and sufficient to establish that the sequence $\{T^{*n}\lambda_0\}$ converges at a geometric rate to a unique limit λ^* for all $\lambda_0 \in \Lambda(S, \mathcal{Y})$. Clearly this rules out both multiple ergodic sets and cyclically moving subsets.

In many applications of interest to us, the most useful methods for establishing Doeblin's condition are also sufficient to establish Condition M. Thus Theorem 11.12 is, for our purposes, the most useful result in this section. The other results are presented primarily for completeness.

We begin with a statement of Doeblin's condition.

CONDITION D   *There is a finite measure ϕ on $(S, \mathcal{Y})$, an integer $N \geq 1$, and a number $\varepsilon > 0$, such that if $\phi(A) \leq \varepsilon$, then $P^N(s, A) \leq 1 - \varepsilon$, all $s \in S$.*

The condition says that for some finite measure ϕ and some integer N, the following is true: for sets A of small ϕ-measure, the probability of a transition to A in N steps, $P^N(s, A)$, is bounded away from one uniformly in s and A. It is crucial that ϕ be a finite measure. Note, too, that if Condition D holds for (ϕ, ε, N), then it also holds for (ϕ, ε, N'), for all $N' \geq N$. (Why?) The following exercise illustrates ways to verify that Doeblin's condition holds and provides examples of cases where it is violated.

Exercise 11.4   Let $(S, \mathscr{S})$ be a measurable space, and let P be a transition function. Show that in each of the following cases, P satisfies Condition D.

a. $S = \{s_1, \ldots, s_l\}$ is a finite set, and $\mathscr{S}$ consists of all subsets of S.

b. $S = \{s_1, s_2, \ldots\}$ is a countable set, $P = [p_{ij}]$ is a stochastic matrix, and $\sum_j p_{ij}$ converges uniformly in i.

c. There is a point $s_0 \in S$, an integer $N \geq 1$, and a number $\varepsilon > 0$, such that $P^N(s, \{s_0\}) > \varepsilon$, all $s \in S$.

d. There exists a finite measure ϕ on $(S, \mathscr{S})$ and an integer $N \geq 1$, such that $P^N(s, A) \leq \phi(A)$, all $s \in S$, $A \in \mathscr{S}$.

e. There is a finite measure μ on $(S, \mathscr{S})$, and a measurable function $p\colon S \times S \to \mathbf{R}_+$, where p is uniformly bounded away from zero, such that

$$P(s, A) = \int_A p(s, s')\mu(ds'), \quad \text{all } s \in S, A \in \mathscr{S}.$$

f. P is as specified in part (e), except that p is measurable and bounded above.

g. $P(s, A) = \alpha P_1(s, A) + (1 - \alpha)P_2(s, A)$, where P_1 and P_2 are transition functions on $(S, \mathscr{S})$, $\alpha \in (0, 1)$, and P_1 satisfies Condition D.

Show that in each of the following cases P does *not* satisfy Condition D.

h. $S = \{s_1, s_2, \ldots\}$ is countably infinite, $\mathscr{S}$ consists of all subsets of S, and $P(s_i, \{s_i\}) = 1$, $i = 1, 2, \ldots$.

i. $(S, \mathscr{S})$ is as specified in part (h), and $P(s_i, \{s_{i+1}\}) = 1$, $i = 1, 2, \ldots$.

j. $S = [0, 1]$, with the Borel sets $\mathscr{S}$, and

$$P(s, A) = \begin{cases} 1 & \text{if } s/2 \in A \\ 0 & \text{otherwise.} \end{cases}$$

Suppose the transition function P satisfies Condition D for some triple (ϕ, N, ε). We will define an ergodic set for such a P and show, as we did in Theorem 11.1 for finite chains, that S can be partitioned into a finite number $M \geq 1$ of ergodic sets and a transient set. Call E a *consequent set of* s if $P^n(s, E) = 1$, $n = 1, 2, \ldots$. Note that $\phi(E) \geq \varepsilon$ for every set E that is a consequent set of any s. (Why?) Call a set E *invariant* if E is a consequent set of every $s \in E$. Call an invariant set *ergodic* if it contains no other invariant subset of smaller ϕ-measure.

We show first that every consequent set contains an ergodic set.

Let $s_0 \in S$, let E be a consequent set of s_0, and define $F_n = \{s \in E: P^n(s, E) < 1\}$. Then for each n, $E - F_n$ is also a consequent set of s_0. Hence $E' = \bigcap_{n=1}^{\infty} (E - F_n)$ is a consequent set of s_0 and is also an invariant set.

If E' is an ergodic set, we are finished. If not, then there exists a point $s_1 \in E'$ and a set $E_1 \subset E'$ such that E_1 is a consequent set of s_1, and $\phi(E_1) < \phi(E')$. Repeating the argument gives a nested decreasing sequence of sets $E' \supset E_1 \supset E_2 \supset \ldots$, with $\phi(E') > \phi(E_1) > \phi(E_2) > \ldots \geq \varepsilon$. If the sequence is finite, then the last element is an ergodic set. If the sequence is infinite, then $\bigcap_{n=1}^{\infty} E_n$ is an ergodic set. This establishes the existence of at least one ergodic set.

Next, note that if E_i and E_j are invariant sets, then $E_i \cap E_j$ is also an invariant set, or else empty. Thus, if E_i and E_j are ergodic sets, it must be that either $\phi(E_i \cap E_j) = \phi(E_i) = \phi(E_j)$, or else $E_i \cap E_j = \emptyset$. That is, any two ergodic sets either differ by a set of ϕ-measure zero or are disjoint. Hence S can be partitioned as claimed.

Finally, since each ergodic set has ϕ-measure of at least $\varepsilon > 0$, it follows that there are at most $\phi(S)/\varepsilon$ such sets. Hence Doeblin's condition implies that there exists at least one ergodic set and, since ϕ is a finite measure, at most a finite number. Doeblin's condition is thus sufficient to rule out cases, like Examples 6 and 7 of Section 11.1, with an infinite number of ergodic sets or with none at all. The following theorem shows that if P satisfies Doeblin's condition, then the other results established in Theorem 11.1 for Markov chains also hold.

THEOREM 11.9 *Let $(S, \mathcal{S})$ be a measurable space, let P be a transition function on $(S, \mathcal{S})$, and suppose that P satisfies Doeblin's condition for (ϕ, N, ε). Then*

a. *S can be partitioned into a transient set and M ergodic sets, where $1 \leq M \leq \phi(S)/\varepsilon$;*

b. *$\lim_{N \to \infty} (1/N) \sum_{n=1}^{N} T^{*n} \lambda_0$ exists for each $\lambda_0 \in \Lambda$, and for each λ_0 the limit is an invariant measure of T^*; and*

c. *there are M invariant measures corresponding to the M ergodic sets, and every invariant measure of T^* can be written as a convex combination of these.*

Part (a) of this theorem has been proved in the preceding discussion. There are two ways (at least) to prove parts (b) and (c). The first method uses arguments analogous to those in the proof of Theorem 11.1. These arguments draw on fairly sophisticated ideas of abstract operator theory, and pursuing this idea would take us far afield. (See Neveu 1965, sect. V.3, for a proof along these lines.) The other method of proof relies on constructing explicit bounds on the probabilities involved. No single step in this proof is very difficult, but the entire proof is quite long. (See Doob 1953, sect. V.5, for a proof along these lines.) We do not present either proof here.

Our next theorem provides sufficient conditions for the ergodic set to be unique.

THEOREM 11.10 *Let $(S, \mathscr{S})$ be a measurable space, let P be a transition function on $(S, \mathscr{S})$, and assume that P satisfies Condition D for (ϕ, ε, N). Suppose in addition that if A is any set of positive ϕ-measure, then for each $s \in S$ there exists $n \geq 1$ such that $P^n(s, A) > 0$. Then*

a. *S has only one ergodic set;*

b. *T^* has only one invariant measure, call it λ^*; and*

c. *$\lim_{N \to \infty} (1/N) \sum_{n=1}^{N} T^{*n}\lambda_0 = \lambda^*$, for all $\lambda_0 \in \Lambda(S, \mathscr{S})$.*

Proof. If the stated condition holds, then clearly there is only one ergodic set. Parts (b) and (c) then follow immediately from Theorem 11.9. ∎

Next we look at a condition that is necessary and sufficient to establish the strong convergence of the sequence of probability measures $\{T^{*N}\lambda_0\}$, and not just the sequence of averages, to a unique limit λ^*, independent of λ_0, and at a uniform rate. Like the proof of Theorem 11.4 for Markov chains, the following proof is based on the Contraction Mapping Theorem.

It was shown in Exercise 8.4 that for any $N \geq 1$, the operator T^{*N} maps the set of probability measures $\Lambda(S, \mathscr{S})$ into itself; and it was shown in Lemma 11.8 that the space $\Lambda(S, \mathscr{S})$, with the total variation norm, is a complete metric space. As will be shown in Lemma 11.11, the following strengthening of Condition D is sufficient for the operator T^{*N} associated with P to be a contraction, for some $N \geq 1$.

CONDITION M *There exists $\varepsilon > 0$ and an integer $N \geq 1$ such that for any $A \in \mathscr{S}$, either $P^N(s, A) \geq \varepsilon$, all $s \in S$, or $P^N(s, A^c) \geq \varepsilon$, all $s \in S$.*

Exercise 11.5 Let $(S, \mathscr{S})$ be a measurable space, and let P be a transition function.

a. Show that the examples in parts (c) and (e) of Exercise 11.4 satisfy Condition M.

b. Show that if P satisfies Condition M, then it satisfies Condition D.

c. Let $S = \{s_1, s_2\}$, and let

$$P(s_i, A) = \begin{cases} 1 & \text{if } s_i \in A \\ 0 & \text{otherwise,} \quad i = 1, 2. \end{cases}$$

Show that P satisfies Condition D but does *not* satisfy Condition M.

LEMMA 11.11 *Let $(S, \mathscr{S})$ be a measurable space; let $\Lambda(S, \mathscr{S})$ be the space of probability measures on $(S, \mathscr{S})$; let P be a transition function on $(S, \mathscr{S})$; and let T^* be the adjoint operator associated with P. If P satisfies Condition M for $N \geq 1$ and $\varepsilon > 0$, then T^{*N} is a contraction of modulus $(1 - \varepsilon)$ on the space $\Lambda(S, \mathscr{S})$ with the total variation norm.*

Proof. Suppose P satisfies Condition M for $N \geq 1$ and $\varepsilon > 0$. Choose any $\lambda_1, \lambda_2 \in \Lambda(S, \mathscr{S})$. By Lemma 7.12, we can choose finite positive measures λ, α_1, and α_2 such that $\lambda_i = \lambda + \alpha_i, i = 1, 2$, and $\alpha_1 \perp \alpha_2$. Then using Lemma 11.5, we have

$$\|T^{*N}\lambda_1 - T^{*N}\lambda_2\| = \|T^{*N}\alpha_1 - T^{*N}\alpha_2\|$$

$$= 2 \sup_{A \in \mathscr{S}} \left| \int P^N(s, A)\alpha_1(ds) - \int P^N(s, A)\alpha_2(ds) \right|.$$

Fix any $A, A^c \in \mathscr{S}$, and without loss of generality suppose that $P^N(s, A) \geq \varepsilon$, all $s \in S$. Then

$$2 \left| \int P^N(s, A)\alpha_1(ds) - \int P^N(s, A)\alpha_2(ds) \right| \leq 2(1 - \varepsilon)\alpha_1(S)$$

$$= (1 - \varepsilon) \|\alpha_1 - \alpha_2\|$$

$$= (1 - \varepsilon) \|\lambda_1 - \lambda_2\|,$$

where the first line uses the fact that $\alpha_1(S) = 1 - \lambda(S) = \alpha_2(S)$, and the second uses the fact that $\alpha_1 \perp \alpha_2$. Since $A \in \mathcal{S}$ was arbitrary it follows that

$$\|T^{*N}\lambda_1 - T^{*N}\lambda_2\| \le (1 - \varepsilon)\|\lambda_1 - \lambda_2\|. \qquad \blacksquare$$

Using this lemma, it is straightforward to show that Condition M is necessary and sufficient for the strong convergence of a Markov process to a unique invariant measure, independent of the initial measure λ_0, at a geometric rate that is uniform in λ_0. For any $s \in S$, let δ_s denote the probability measure that is a unit mass at the point s.

THEOREM 11.12 *Let $(S, \mathcal{S})$ be a measurable space; let $\Lambda(S, \mathcal{S})$ be the space of probability measures on $(S, \mathcal{S})$, with the total variation norm; let P be a transition function on $(S, \mathcal{S})$; and let T^* be the adjoint operator associated with P. If P satisfies Condition M for $N \ge 1$ and $\varepsilon > 0$, then there exists a unique probability measure $\lambda^* \in \Lambda(S, \mathcal{S})$ such that*

(1) $$\|T^{*Nk}\lambda_0 - \lambda^*\| \le (1 - \varepsilon)^k \|\lambda_0 - \lambda^*\|,$$

all $\lambda_0 \in \Lambda(S, \mathcal{S})$, $k = 1, 2, \ldots$.

Conversely, if (1) holds, then Condition M is satisfied for some $N \ge 1$ and $\varepsilon > 0$.

Proof. Suppose that Condition M holds for $N \ge 1$ and $\varepsilon > 0$. Then by Lemma 11.11, $T^{*N}: \Lambda(S, \mathcal{S}) \to \Lambda(S, \mathcal{S})$ is a contraction of modulus $1 - \varepsilon$. Since $\Lambda(S, \mathcal{S})$ is complete (Lemma 11.8), the conclusions then follow from the Contraction Mapping Theorem (Theorem 3.2).

Conversely, suppose that (1) holds. Choose $s \in S$. Using Lemma 11.5, we have for all $A \in \mathcal{S}$,

$$2\,|P^{Nk}(s, A) - \lambda^*(A)| \le \|P^{Nk}(s, \cdot) - \lambda^*\|$$

$$= \|T^{*Nk}\delta_s - \lambda^*\|$$

$$\le (1 - \varepsilon)^k \|\delta_s - \lambda^*\|$$

$$\le 2(1 - \varepsilon)^k.$$

Choose K sufficiently large that $(1 - \varepsilon)^K \le 1/4$. Let A, $A^c \in \mathcal{S}$ be given, and without loss of generality suppose that $\lambda^*(A) \geq 1/2$. Then $|P^{NK}(s, A) - \lambda^*(A)| \leq 1/4$, so $P^{NK}(s, A) \geq 1/4$. Since $s \in S$ was arbitrary, Condition M holds for $\hat{N} = NK$ and $\hat{\varepsilon} = 1/4$. ∎

The main attraction of this convergence result is that Condition M is easy to verify in some applications. This fact is illustrated in Sections 13.1, 13.2, and 13.5.

11.5 Bibliographic Notes

Many excellent treatments of Markov chains are available. The material in Section 11.1 is based on Doob (1953, sect. V.2). Kemeny and Snell (1960), Chung (1967), and Kemeny, Snell, and Knapp (1976) are also excellent sources. Green (1976) contains a result related to Theorem 11.4. Some writers use the term *Markov chain* to refer to any Markov process with a discrete *time* parameter, regardless of the nature of the state space. What we call a Markov chain is then referred to as a *finite state Markov chain*.

Condition D is due to Doeblin; it is discussed in detail in Doob (1953, sect. V.5), where a proof of Theorem 11.9 can also be found. An alternative line of proof uses the fact that Doeblin's condition holds if and only if the operator associated with the transition function is quasi-compact. A proof of this fact is available in Futia (1982, Theorem 4.9). Neveu (1965, sect. V.3) contains a proof of Theorem 11.9 based on this fact. Both lines of proof also establish that convergence is at a uniform geometric rate. Tweedie (1975) provides an alternative—and quite different—set of sufficient conditions for convergence, conditions that may hold when the rate of convergence is not uniform.

We are grateful to C. Ionescu Tulcea for bringing to our attention Condition M. It is discussed in Onicescu (1969), where Theorem 11.12 also appears. The proof offered here, based on the Contraction Mapping Theorem, is new.

See Dynkin (1965), Rosenblatt (1971), and Gihman and Skorohod (1974) for more extensive treatments of general Markov processes.

12   Weak Convergence of
Markov Processes

In this chapter we continue our study of the convergence of Markov processes. As in Chapter 11, we will be concerned with sequences $\{\lambda_n\}_{n=0}^\infty$ of probability measures defined by $\lambda_{n+1} = T^*\lambda_n$, where λ_0 is a fixed initial probability measure and T^* is the operator associated with a fixed transition function P. Recall that a probability measure λ^* is said to be *invariant* under T^* if it is a fixed point of T^*, that is, if $\lambda^* = T^*\lambda^*$. In Theorem 11.12 we provided a necessary and sufficient condition on P for convergence in the total variation norm of the sequence $\{\lambda_n\}$ to a unique invariant measure λ^*, for all initial probability measures λ_0. For the reasons discussed in Section 11.2, however, strong convergence is in many situations more than we expect or care about. Thus, in the present chapter we develop conditions that are sufficient to establish the weak convergence of the sequence $\{\lambda_n\}$ to a unique invariant measure. These conditions are considerably different from those required for strong convergence, and, as some of the applications in Chapter 13 illustrate, they are often extremely easy to verify.

Since weak convergence is defined in terms of continuous functions, we must impose much more structure on the state space $(S, \mathcal{S})$ here than we did in Chapter 11, where it was any measurable space. In Section 12.1, which contains general results on the characterization of weak convergence, we assume that (S, ρ) is a metric space and $\mathcal{S}$ is the σ-algebra generated by the open sets of S. In the sections that follow we further restrict the analysis and assume that S is a Borel subset of a finite-dimensional Euclidean space.

We begin in Section 12.1 by characterizing weak convergence in terms of the convergence of measures of certain families of sets. The goal here is to find one or more families of sets $\mathcal{A} \subset \mathcal{S}$ such that convergence of the measures of sets in $\mathcal{A}$ implies weak convergence. We also establish that the limiting measure λ of any weakly convergent sequence $\{\lambda_n\}$ is unique. Then in Section 12.2 we establish the one-to-one relationship between probability measures on $(\mathbf{R}^l, \mathscr{B}^l)$ and distribution functions on $\mathbf{R}^l$. The results of both sections are then drawn on in Section 12.3, where we characterize weak convergence in terms of distribution functions. This characterization is in turn used to prove Helly's Theorem, a very general result establishing the existence of weakly convergent subsequences. In Section 12.4 we draw on Helly's Theorem to prove two convergence results for a particular class of Markov processes, those that are monotone.

We then address the following question: If the transition function P depends on a vector of parameters θ, what can be said about the dependence of the invariant measure on that parameter vector? In Section 12.5 we establish sufficient conditions for the invariant measure to depend continuously on θ. Finally, we tie up the loose end that was left hanging in Chapter 9. Section 12.6 shows that we can drop the assumption, used in Lemma 9.5, that the exogenous shocks lie in a compact set.

12.1 Characterizations of Weak Convergence

In this section we will be concerned with characterizing weak convergence of probability measures in terms of the convergence of the measures of certain families of sets. Throughout the section we assume that (S, ρ) is a metric space with its Borel sets $\mathscr{S}$. That is, given (S, ρ), $\mathscr{S}$ is defined as follows. Let $b(x, \varepsilon)$ denote the open ball in S of radius ε about x: that is, $b(x, \varepsilon) = \{s \in S : \rho(s, x) < \varepsilon\}$. A set $A \subseteq S$ is open if for every $x \in A$ there exists $\varepsilon > 0$ such that $b(x, \varepsilon) \subseteq A$. The family of Borel sets $\mathscr{S}$ is the σ-algebra generated by the open sets. The interior of a set $A \subseteq S$ is the set

$$\mathring{A} = \{x \in A : b(x, \varepsilon) \subseteq A, \text{ for some } \varepsilon > 0\},$$

and the closure of A is the set

$$\overline{A} = \{x \in S : x_n \to x, \text{ for some sequence } \{x_n\} \text{ in } A\}.$$

A set A is closed if $\overline{A} = A$.

Note that if S is a Borel set of $\mathbf{R}^l$, then a set A may be open when viewed as a subset of S, but not when viewed as a subset of $\mathbf{R}^l$. When we want to stress the distinction, we say that A is *open relative to S*, or *relatively open*. Similarly, we will refer to the *interior of A relative to S* and the *closure of A relative to S*, when we wish to stress the fact that these sets are defined using S.

Exercise 12.1   Let S be a Borel set in $\mathbf{R}^l$.
a. Show that $\mathscr{S} = \{A \subseteq S : A \in \mathscr{B}^l\}$.
b. Show that A is open relative to S if $A = A' \cap S$ for some open set $A' \in \mathscr{B}^l$.
c. Show that the interior of A relative to S is open relative to S.
d. Show that if A is open relative to S, then $\mathring{A} = A$.

Let $C(S)$ be the set of bounded continuous functions on S; and let $\Lambda(S, \mathscr{S})$ be the set of probability measures on $(S, \mathscr{S})$. Recall that a sequence $\{\lambda_n\}$ of probability measures is said to *converge weakly* to a probability measure λ, written $\lambda_n \Rightarrow \lambda$, if

$$\lim_{n \to \infty} \int f \, d\lambda_n = \int f \, d\lambda, \quad \text{all } f \in C(S).$$

We will develop methods for verifying weak convergence by showing that

$$\lim_{n \to \infty} \lambda_n(A) = \lambda(A), \quad \text{all } A \in \mathscr{A},$$

where $\mathscr{A}$ is a suitable subclass of the sets in $\mathscr{S}$.

We begin by proving two preliminary lemmas. Lemma 12.1 shows that the measure of any closed set can be approximated by the integrals of continuous functions, and Lemma 12.2 shows that the integral of any continuous function can be approximated by the sums of measures of closed sets. These two lemmas are then used to establish our first main result, Theorem 12.3, which provides four equivalent ways of characterizing weak convergence. Theorems 12.4 and 12.5 then draw on this result to characterize smaller families of sets $\mathscr{A}$ that are sufficient to imply weak convergence. Finally, Theorem 12.6 and its corollaries show that two measures are equal if they assign the same value to every closed set or if they assign the same expected value to every continuous function. This result implies immediately that if $\{\lambda_n\}$ is a weakly convergent sequence of measures, then the limit λ is unique.

Our first two lemmas show the intimate connection between measures of closed sets and integrals of continuous functions. The first draws on the following exercise.

Exercise 12.2 Let (S, ρ) be a metric space. For $A \subset S$, $A \neq \emptyset$, and $s \in S$, define $\rho(s, A) = \inf_{x \in A} \rho(s, x)$.

a. Show that $|\rho(x, A) - \rho(y, A)| \leq \rho(x, y)$, all $x, y \in S$, $A \subset S$.

b. Show that for any $A \subset S$, the function $\rho(\cdot, A): S \to \mathbf{R}_+$ is uniformly continuous.

c. Show that $\overline{A} = \{s \in S: \rho(s, A) = 0\}$.

LEMMA 12.1 *Given any closed set $F \in \mathscr{S}$, there exists a decreasing sequence of continuous functions $\{f_n\}$ such that $f_n(s) = 1$, all $s \in F$, all n, and*

$$\lim_{n \to \infty} \int f_n \, d\lambda = \lambda(F), \quad \text{all } \lambda \in \Lambda(S, \mathscr{S}).$$

Proof. The proof is by construction. Let F be given, and define the sets

$$F_n = \{s \in S: \rho(s, F) \leq 1/n\}, \quad n = 1, 2, \dots.$$

Then define the sequence of functions $\{f_n\}$ by

$$f_n(s) = \begin{cases} 1 - n\rho(s, F) & \text{if } \rho(s, F) \leq 1/n \\ 0 & \text{if } \rho(s, F) > 1/n, \quad \text{all } s \in S, n = 1, 2, \dots. \end{cases}$$

It follows from part (b) of Exercise 12.2 that each function f_n is continuous. Moreover, for each n,

$$f_n(s) = 1, s \in F; \quad f_n(s) = 0, s \in F_n^c; \quad 0 \leq f_n(s) \leq 1, s \in S;$$

so

(1) $$\lambda(F) = \int_F f_n \, d\lambda \leq \int_S f_n \, d\lambda \leq \lambda(F_n), \quad \text{all } \lambda \in \Lambda(S, \mathscr{S}), \text{ all } n.$$

Also, it follows from part (c) of Exercise 12.2 and the fact that F is closed, that $\cap_{n=1}^{\infty} F_n = \overline{F} = F$. Since $\{F_n\}$ is a decreasing sequence of sets, it then follows from Theorem 7.1 that $\lim_{n\to\infty}\lambda(F_n) = \lambda(F)$. Taking the limit in (1) as $n \to \infty$ then establishes the result. ∎

Figure 12.1 shows one of the functions f_n for the case where $S = \mathbf{R}$ and $F = [a, b]$.

The next lemma shows that the integral of any bounded measurable function can be approximated by the sums of measures of appropriate sets. If the function is continuous, the approximation can be done with closed sets.

LEMMA 12.2 *Let f be any bounded measurable function; let a, b be such that $a \le f(s) < b$, all $s \in S$; and let $c = b - a$. Then for every $\varepsilon > 0$, there exists an integer $k \ge 1$ and a family of sets $\{F_i\}_{i=1}^{k}$ in $\mathscr{S}$ such that*

(2)
$$a + \frac{c}{k}\sum_{i=1}^{k}\mu(F_i) \le \int f\,d\mu \le a + \frac{c}{k}\sum_{i=1}^{k}\mu(F_i) + \varepsilon,$$

all $\mu \in \Lambda(S, \mathscr{S})$.

If f is continuous, the sets $\{F_i\}$ can be chosen to be closed.

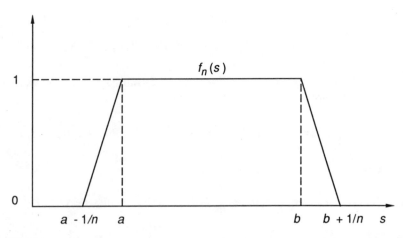

Figure 12.1

Proof. First we will show that the claim holds if $0 \leq f(s) < 1$, all $s \in S$. In this case we may take $a = 0$, $b = 1$, and $c = 1$. For each integer $k \geq 1$, define the sets

(3) $F_{ki} = \{s \in S: i/k \leq f(s)\}, \quad i = 0, 1, \ldots, k.$

Then to establish the desired result, it suffices to show that

(4) $$\frac{1}{k} \sum_{i=1}^{k} \mu(F_{ki}) \leq \int f \, d\mu \leq \frac{1}{k} + \frac{1}{k} \sum_{i=1}^{k} \mu(F_{ki}),$$

all $\mu \in \Lambda(S, \mathcal{S})$, $k = 1, 2, \ldots$.

Fix k, and—dropping the first subscript—consider the sets F_i, $i = 0, 1, \ldots, k$. Note that they are nested and decreasing, with $F_0 = S$ and $F_k = \emptyset$. Also note that if f is continuous, then each set F_i is closed. The sets $(F_{i-1} \backslash F_i)$, $i = 1, \ldots, k$, form a partition of S, and

$$\frac{i-1}{k} \leq f(s) < \frac{i}{k}, \quad \text{all } s \in (F_{i-1} \backslash F_i), i = 1, \ldots, k.$$

Hence for any $\mu \in \Lambda(S, \mathcal{S})$, we have

$$\sum_{i=1}^{k} \frac{i-1}{k} \mu(F_{i-1} \backslash F_i) \leq \int f \, d\mu \leq \sum_{i=1}^{k} \frac{i}{k} \mu(F_{i-1} \backslash F_i), \quad \text{or}$$

$$\sum_{i=1}^{k} \left(\frac{i-1}{k}\right) [\mu(F_{i-1}) - \mu(F_i)]$$

$$\leq \int f \, d\mu \leq \sum_{i=1}^{k} \frac{i}{k} [\mu(F_{i-1}) - \mu(F_i)], \quad \text{or}$$

$$\frac{1}{k} \sum_{i=1}^{k} \mu(F_i) \leq \int f \, d\mu \leq \frac{1}{k} + \frac{1}{k} \sum_{i=1}^{k} \mu(F_i),$$

as was to be shown.

Next let f be any bounded, measurable function, with $a \leq f(s) < b$, all $s \in S$; let $c = b - a$; and fix $\varepsilon > 0$. Define the function $\hat{f}(s) = [f(s) - a]/c$; and let $\hat{\varepsilon} = \varepsilon/c$. A family of sets $\{F_i\}_{i=1}^k$ for which (2) holds can be found by applying the argument above to $(\hat{f}, \hat{\varepsilon})$. ∎

With these two lemmas in hand, we are ready to prove our first main result, which provides several characterizations of weak convergence. We use the notation ∂A to denote the **boundary** of a set A, the set of points that are limits of both sequences in A and sequences in A^c.

THEOREM 12.3 *Let $\{\lambda_n\}$ and λ be probability measures on $(S, \mathcal{S})$. Then the following four conditions are equivalent:*

a. $\lim_{n \to \infty} \int f \, d\lambda_n = \int f \, d\lambda$, all $f \in C(S)$;

b. for every closed set F, $\lim \sup_{n \to \infty} \lambda_n(F) \leq \lambda(F)$;

c. for every open set G, $\lim \inf_{n \to \infty} \lambda_n(G) \geq \lambda(G)$;

d. $\lim_{n \to \infty} \lambda_n(A) = \lambda(A)$, for every set $A \in \mathcal{S}$ with $\lambda(\partial A) = 0$.

Proof. (a) $\Rightarrow$ (b). Suppose that (a) holds, and let F be a closed set. Then by Lemma 12.1, given any $\varepsilon > 0$ there exists a continuous function f such that

$$\lambda_n(F) \leq \int f \, d\lambda_n, \text{ all } n, \text{ and } \int f \, d\lambda \leq \lambda(F) + \varepsilon.$$

Taking the limit as $n \to \infty$ and using (a), we find that

$$\lim \sup_{n \to \infty} \lambda_n(F) \leq \lim_{n \to \infty} \int f \, d\lambda_n = \int f \, d\lambda \leq \lambda(F) + \varepsilon.$$

Since $\varepsilon > 0$ was arbitrary, (b) follows.

(b) $\Rightarrow$ (a). Suppose that (b) holds, and let f be a continuous function with $0 \leq f(s) < 1$, all $s \in S$. For each integer $k \geq 1$, define the sets $\{F_{ki}\}_{i=0}^k$ as in (3). Then as shown in the proof of Lemma 12.2, (4) holds. Hence

$$\int f \, d\lambda_n \leq \frac{1}{k} + \frac{1}{k} \sum_{i=1}^{k} \lambda_n(F_{ki}), \text{ all } n, k.$$

Since f is continuous, the sets F_{ki} are all closed. Therefore, fixing k, taking the limit as $n \to \infty$, and using (b), we obtain

$$\limsup_{n \to \infty} \int f \, d\lambda_n \leq \frac{1}{k} + \limsup_{n \to \infty} \frac{1}{k} \sum_{i=1}^{k} \lambda_n(F_{ki})$$

$$\leq \frac{1}{k} + \frac{1}{k} \sum_{i=1}^{k} \limsup_{n \to \infty} \lambda_n(F_{ki})$$

$$\leq \frac{1}{k} + \frac{1}{k} \sum_{i=1}^{k} \lambda(F_{ki}).$$

Using (4) again, we find that

$$\frac{1}{k} \sum_{i=1}^{k} \lambda(F_{ki}) \leq \int f \, d\lambda.$$

Using these two inequalities and letting $k \to \infty$, we conclude that

$$\limsup_{n \to \infty} \int f \, d\lambda_n \leq \int f \, d\lambda.$$

Similarly, for the continuous function $g = 1 - f$, we have

$$1 - \liminf_{n \to \infty} \int f \, d\lambda_n = \limsup_{n \to \infty} \int g \, d\lambda_n \leq \int g \, d\lambda = 1 - \int f \, d\lambda.$$

Combining these two results gives

$$\limsup_{n \to \infty} \int f \, d\lambda_n \leq \int f \, d\lambda \leq \liminf_{n \to \infty} \int f \, d\lambda_n,$$

so (a) holds.

If $a \leq f < b$, apply the argument above to the function $\hat{f} = (f - a)/(b - a)$. The linearity of the integral then implies that the conclusion also holds for f.

(b) $\Leftrightarrow$ (c). This follows immediately from complementation.

(b) $\Rightarrow$ (d). Suppose that (b) holds, and let $A \in \mathcal{S}$ be any set with $\lambda(\partial A) = 0$. Since $\lambda(\partial A) = 0$, it follows that $\lambda(\mathring{A}) = \lambda(A) = \lambda(\overline{A})$. Then since $\mathring{A}$ is open and $\overline{A}$ is closed and since (c) holds if (b) does, it follows that

$$\lambda(A) = \lambda(\mathring{A}) \le \liminf_{n \to \infty} \lambda_n(\mathring{A}) \le \liminf_{n \to \infty} \lambda_n(A)$$

$$\le \limsup_{n \to \infty} \lambda_n(A) \le \limsup_{n \to \infty} \lambda_n(\overline{A}) \le \lambda(\overline{A}) = \lambda(A).$$

(d) $\Rightarrow$ (b). Suppose (d) holds, and let F be any closed set. For distinct δ's, the boundaries of the closed sets $\{s \in S : \rho(s, F) \le \delta\}$ are disjoint. Hence only a countable number of them can have positive measure under λ, and—avoiding these—we can choose a decreasing sequence $\{\delta_k\}$ converging to zero such that

$$\lambda(\partial F_k) = 0 \text{ for } F_k = \{s \in S : \rho(s, F) \le \delta_k\}, \quad k = 1, 2, \ldots .$$

Since $F \subset F_k$, for each k, it follows that $\lambda_n(F) \le \lambda_n(F_k)$, all n, k. Then holding k fixed, taking the limit as $n \to \infty$, and using (d), we have

(5) $$\limsup_{n \to \infty} \lambda_n(F) \le \lim_{n \to \infty} \lambda_n(F_k) = \lambda(F_k), \quad \text{all } k.$$

Since $\{F_k\}$ is a nested, decreasing sequence, with $F = \cap_{k=1}^{\infty} F_k$, it follows from Theorem 7.1 that $\lambda(F) = \lim_{k \to \infty} \lambda(F_k)$. Hence, taking the limit in (5) as $k \to \infty$ we find that (b) holds. ∎

The next result uses criterion (c) of Theorem 12.3 to establish an alternative sufficient condition for weak convergence in terms of the measures of certain families of sets.

THEOREM 12.4 *Let $\{\lambda_n\}$ and λ be probability measures on $(S, \mathscr{S})$, and let $\mathscr{A} \subseteq \mathscr{S}$ be a family of sets such that*
   a. *$\mathscr{A}$ is closed under finite intersection; and*
   b. *each open set in $\mathscr{S}$ is a countable union of sets in $\mathscr{A}$.*
Then $\lambda_n(A) \to \lambda(A)$, all $A \in \mathscr{A}$ implies $\lambda_n \Rightarrow \lambda$.

Proof. Let $\mathscr{A}$ satisfy (a) and (b), and let $\{\lambda_n\}$ and λ be probability measures, with $\lim_{n \to \infty} \lambda_n(A) = \lambda(A)$, all $A \in \mathscr{A}$. If $A_1, \ldots, A_m$ lie in $\mathscr{A}$, then by (a) so do their intersections, and hence by the inclusion-exclusion formula, for each $n = 1, 2, \ldots,$

$$\lambda_n \left(\bigcup_{i=1}^m A_i \right) = \sum_i \lambda_n(A_i) - \sum_i \sum_j \lambda_n(A_i \cap A_j)$$

$$+ \sum_i \sum_j \sum_k \lambda_n(A_i \cap A_j \cap A_k) - \ldots.$$

Taking the limit as $n \to \infty$, we obtain

$$(6) \qquad \lim_{n \to \infty} \lambda_n \left(\bigcup_{i=1}^m A_i \right) = \sum_i \lambda(A_i) - \sum_i \sum_j \lambda(A_i \cap A_j) + \ldots$$

$$= \lambda \left(\bigcup_{i=1}^m A_i \right).$$

Let G be any open set, and choose $\{A_i\}_{i=1}^\infty$ in $\mathcal{A}$ such that $\cup_{i=1}^\infty A_i = G$; by hypothesis (b), this can be done. Then given any $\varepsilon > 0$, there exists $m \geq 1$ such that $\lambda(G) - \varepsilon < \lambda(\cup_{i=1}^m A_i)$. It then follows from (6) that

$$\lambda(G) - \varepsilon < \lambda \left(\bigcup_{i=1}^m A_i \right) = \lim_{n \to \infty} \lambda_n \left(\bigcup_{i=1}^m A_i \right) \leq \liminf_{n \to \infty} \lambda_n(G).$$

Since the open set G and $\varepsilon > 0$ were arbitrary, condition (c) of Theorem 12.3 follows. ∎

Theorem 12.5 and its corollary apply this result to obtain a useful criterion for weak convergence in a finite-dimensional Euclidean space or subset thereof. The proof draws on the following fact. Let S be a Borel set in $\mathbf{R}^l$. If $\{A_\eta\}_{\eta \in H}$ is a family of relatively open sets in S, then there exists a countable subfamily, call it $\{A_i\}_{i=1}^\infty$ such that $\cup_{i=1}^\infty A_i = \cup_{\eta \in H} A_\eta$. (See Royden 1968, Proposition 9, p. 40.) We stress again that $\mathring{A}$ denotes the interior of A relative to S, and $b(x, \varepsilon)$ denotes a ball that is open relative to S.

THEOREM 12.5 *Let $S \subseteq \mathbf{R}^l$ be a Borel set, with its Borel subsets $\mathcal{S}$. Let $\{\lambda_n\}$ and λ be probability measures on $(S, \mathcal{S})$, and let $\mathcal{A} \subset \mathcal{S}$ be a family of sets such that*

　　a. $\mathcal{A}$ is closed under finite intersection; and

b. for every $x \in S$ and $\varepsilon > 0$, there exists $A \in \mathcal{A}$ such that $x \in \mathring{A} \subseteq A \subseteq b(x, \varepsilon)$.

Then $\lambda_n(A) \to \lambda(A)$, all $A \in \mathcal{A}$ implies that $\lambda_n \Rightarrow \lambda$.

Proof. Let $\mathcal{A}$ satisfy the stated hypotheses. In view of (a), it is sufficient to show that $\mathcal{A}$ satisfies condition (b) of Theorem 12.4.

Let $G \in \mathcal{G}$ be any open set. For each $x \in G$, there exists $\varepsilon_x > 0$ such that $b(x, \varepsilon_x) \subseteq G$. It then follows from (b) that there exists $A_x \in \mathcal{A}$ such that $x \in \mathring{A}_x \subseteq A_x \subseteq b(x, \varepsilon_x) \subseteq G$. Since this is true for each $x \in G$, it follows that

$$G = \bigcup_{x \in G} x \subseteq \bigcup_{x \in G} \mathring{A}_x \subseteq \bigcup_{x \in G} A_x \subseteq \bigcup_{x \in G} b(x, \varepsilon_x) \subseteq G,$$

so that $\bigcup_{x \in G} \mathring{A}_x = G$. Hence there exists a countable selection of the sets $\mathring{A}_x$—call it $\{\mathring{A}_i\}_{i=1}^{\infty}$—such that $G = \bigcup_{i=1}^{\infty} \mathring{A}_i$. Therefore $G = \bigcup_{i=1}^{\infty} A_i$; and since G was an arbitrary open set, $\mathcal{A}$ satisfies (b) of Theorem 12.4. ∎

The following corollary shows that for $S \subset \mathbf{R}^l$, the finite intersections of open balls, excluding those with boundaries of positive λ-measure, can serve as the class $\mathcal{A}$ in Theorem 12.5.

COROLLARY *Let $S \subseteq \mathbf{R}^l$ be a Borel set, with its Borel subsets $\mathcal{G}$, and let $\{\lambda_n\}$ and λ be probability measures on $(S, \mathcal{G})$. If $\lim_{n \to \infty} \lambda_n(A) = \lambda(A)$ for each set A that is a finite intersection of open balls with $\lambda(\partial A) = 0$, then $\lambda_n \Rightarrow \lambda$.*

Proof. Since for fixed x, the boundaries of the open balls $b(x, \varepsilon)$ are disjoint for distinct ε's, at most countably many of them have positive λ-measure. Hence the hypotheses of Theorem 12.5 are satisfied by the family $\mathcal{A}$ consisting of finite intersection of open balls with boundaries of λ-measure zero. ∎

A class of sets $\mathcal{A}$ with the property that

$$\lambda_n(A) \to \lambda(A) \text{ for all } A \in \mathcal{A} \text{ with } \lambda(\partial A) = 0 \text{ implies } \lambda_n \Rightarrow \lambda,$$

is called a ***convergence-determining class***. Thus the corollary states that the finite intersections of open balls are a convergence-determining class for $S \subset \mathbf{R}^l$. Note that if $\mathcal{A} \subset \mathcal{G}$ is a convergence-determining class and

$\lambda(A) = \mu(A)$ for all $A \in \mathscr{A}$, then $\lambda = \mu$ on $\mathscr{S}$. (Why?) Later, when we discuss distribution functions on $\mathbf{R}^l$, we draw on Theorem 12.5 again to show that the family of half-open rectangles of the form $(a, b]$ are a convergence-determining class.

Our final result establishes a very important property of probability measures on an arbitrary metric space (S, ρ). Its usefulness is illustrated in the two corollaries that follow, which show that any probability measure on such a space is completely determined by its values on closed sets, or by the expected value it assigns to continuous functions.

THEOREM 12.6 *Let λ be a probability measure on a metric space (S, ρ), with the Borel sets $\mathscr{S}$. Then for any set $B \in \mathscr{S}$ and any $\varepsilon > 0$, there exists a closed set A and an open set C such that $A \subseteq B \subseteq C$, and $\lambda(C) - \lambda(A) < \varepsilon$.*

Proof. Let $(S, \mathscr{S})$ be given. First, consider the case where B is closed. Let $A = B$, and define the sequence $\{C_k\}$ of open sets by $C_k = \{s: \rho(s, B) < 1/2^k\}$. Then $\{C_k\}$ is a nested, decreasing sequence of sets, with $B = \cap_{k=1}^{\infty} C_k$. Hence it follows from Theorem 7.1 that $\lambda(B) = \lim_{k \to \infty} \lambda(C_k)$. Hence for any $\varepsilon > 0$, there exists k sufficiently large such that $C = C_k$ has the required properties.

Let $\mathscr{G}$ be the family of sets B for which an appropriate A and C can be chosen. We have shown that $\mathscr{G}$ contains all the closed sets. Hence it is sufficient to show that $\mathscr{G}$ is a σ-algebra: that it is closed under complementation and countable union.

Let $B \in \mathscr{G}$, and fix $\varepsilon > 0$. Then there is a closed set A and an open set B such that $A \subseteq B \subseteq C$ and $\lambda(C) - \lambda(A) < \varepsilon$. Hence C^c is closed and A^c is open, with $C^c \subseteq B^c \subseteq A^c$ and

$$\lambda(A^c) - \lambda(C^c) = [1 - \lambda(A)] - [1 - \lambda(C)] = \lambda(C) - \lambda(A) < \varepsilon.$$

Hence $\mathscr{G}$ is closed under complementation.

Finally, choose a sequence $\{B_n\}_{n=1}^{\infty}$ in $\mathscr{G}$, let $B = \cup_{n=1}^{\infty} B_n$, and fix $\varepsilon > 0$. Then for each set B_n, we can choose a closed set A_n and an open set C_n such that $A_n \subseteq B_n \subseteq C_n$ and $\lambda(C_n) - \lambda(A_n) \leq \varepsilon/2^{n+1}$. Let $C = \cup_{n=1}^{\infty} C_n$, and let $A = \cup_{n=1}^{N} A_n$, where N is chosen sufficiently large that $\lambda(\cup_{n=1}^{\infty} A_n \backslash A) = \lambda(\cup_{N+1}^{\infty} A_n \cap A^c) < \varepsilon/2$. Then A is closed and C is open, with $A \subseteq B \subseteq C$, and

$$\lambda(C) - \lambda(A) = \lambda(C \backslash A) = \lambda \left(\bigcup_{n=1}^{\infty} C_n \backslash \bigcup_{n=1}^{N} A_n \right)$$

$$\leq \lambda \left[\bigcup_{n=1}^{\infty} (C_n \backslash A_n) \cup \left(\bigcup_{N+1}^{\infty} A_n \cap A^c \right) \right]$$

$$\leq \sum_{n=1}^{\infty} \lambda(C_n \backslash A_n) + \lambda \left(\bigcup_{N+1}^{\infty} A_n \cap A^c \right)$$

$$= \sum_{n=1}^{\infty} [\lambda(C_n) - \lambda(A_n)] + \lambda \left(\bigcup_{N+1}^{\infty} A_n \cap A^c \right) < \varepsilon.$$

Hence $\mathscr{G}$ is closed under countable union. ∎

This theorem shows that any probability measure on a metric space is completely determined by the values it assigns to closed sets. Given the measure of each closed set, the measure of each open set C is determined by $\lambda(C) = 1 - \lambda(C^c)$. Then, since every set B can be "squeezed" between a closed set A and an open set C, with $\lambda(C) - \lambda(A)$ arbitrarily small, the measure assigned to every set is determined.

COROLLARY 1   *Let λ and μ be probability measures. If $\lambda(A) = \mu(A)$, for every closed set A, then $\lambda = \mu$.*

Theorem 12.6 also implies that a probability measure is completely determined by the values it assigns to integrals of continuous functions. To see this, note that Lemma 12.1 implies that if λ and μ assign the same values to integrals of all continuous functions, then they also assign the same values to the measures of all closed sets. Hence Corollary 1 applies and $\lambda = \mu$.

COROLLARY 2   *Let λ and μ be probability measures. If $\int f \, d\lambda = \int f \, d\mu$, all $f \in C(S)$, then $\lambda = \mu$.*

An immediate consequence of either of these corollaries is that if a sequence of probability measures $\{\lambda_n\}$ converges weakly, then the limiting measure is unique.

12.2   Distribution Functions

Given any probability measure λ on $(\mathbf{R}^l, \mathscr{B}^l)$, the function F defined by

(1) $F(x) = \lambda((-\infty, x]),$ all $x \in \mathbf{R}^l,$

is called the corresponding **distribution function**. [By $x < y$, we will mean that $x_i < y_i$, $i = 1, \ldots, l$; and by $x \leq y$, that $x_i \leq y_i$, $i = 1, \ldots, l$. By $(a, b]$, we will mean $\{x \in \mathbf{R}^l: a < x \leq b\}$.] When the state space is $\mathbf{R}^l$, it is often convenient to deal with distribution functions rather than probability measures.

In this section we show that for any probability measure λ on $(\mathbf{R}^l, \mathcal{B}^l)$ there is a unique corresponding distribution function F, and that F has certain properties. Conversely, for any function F on $\mathbf{R}^l$ with these properties, there is a unique corresponding probability measure λ on $(\mathbf{R}^l, \mathcal{B}^l)$. Finally, the theorem shows that F is continuous from above at a point x if and only if the boundary of the set $(-\infty, x]$ has λ-measure zero. These results (Theorem 12.7) are drawn on in the next section, where we characterize weak convergence of a sequence of probability measures in terms of the corresponding sequence of distribution functions.

We write $\varepsilon \downarrow 0$ if $\varepsilon > 0$ and $\varepsilon \to 0$, and write $\varepsilon \uparrow 0$ if $\varepsilon < 0$ and $\varepsilon \to 0$. A function $F: \mathbf{R}^l \to \mathbf{R}$ is *continuous from above at x* if $F(x) = \lim_{\varepsilon \downarrow 0} F(x + \varepsilon \underline{1})$, where $\underline{1} = (1, 1, \ldots, 1)$ and is *continuous from below at x* if $F(x) = \lim_{\varepsilon \uparrow 0} F(x + \varepsilon \underline{1})$. Recall that F is *continuous at x* if for every $\varepsilon > 0$ there exists $\delta > 0$ such that $\|x - y\| < \delta$ implies $|F(x) - F(y)| < \varepsilon$. If F is continuous at x, then clearly it is continuous from above and from below at x. The following exercise provides a converse that applies to distribution functions.

Exercise 12.3   Let $F: \mathbf{R}^l \to \mathbf{R}$ be nondecreasing. Show that if F is continuous from above and from below at x, then F is continuous at x.

The following theorem establishes the properties of distribution functions and the one-to-one relationship between probability measures and distribution functions.

THEOREM 12.7   *a. For any probability measure λ on $(\mathbf{R}^l, \mathcal{B}^l)$ the distribution function $F: \mathbf{R}^l \to [0, 1]$ given by (1) has the following properties:*
(D1) F is weakly increasing, $F(x) \to 0$ as any coordinate $x_i \to -\infty$, and $F(x) \to 1$ as all coordinates $x_i \to +\infty$;
(D2) F is everywhere continuous from above;
(D3) for each l-dimensional rectangle $(a, b]$,

$$\sum_{j=1}^{2^l} \pm F(a + \theta_j d) = \sum_{j=1}^{2^l} \pm F(a_1 + \theta_{j1}d_1, \ldots, a_l + \theta_{jl}d_l) \geq 0,$$

where $d = b - a$, where the sum is over the 2^l vectors θ_j composed of zeros and ones, and the sign is plus if the number of zeros is even, minus if it is odd.

  b. For any function $F: \mathbf{R}^l \to [0, 1]$ satisfying (D1)–(D3), there exists a unique probability measure λ on $(\mathbf{R}^l, \mathcal{B}^l)$ satisfying (1).

  c. For any pair F, λ satisfying (1), F is continuous from below at x if and only if the boundary of the set $(-\infty, x]$ has λ-measure zero.

Proof of (a). Let λ be given, and define F by (1). It is immediate from (1) that (D1) holds. To see that (D2) holds, fix $x \in \mathbf{R}^l$, and let $\{\varepsilon_k\}$ be a positive sequence converging to zero. Define the sets A_k by $A_k = (-\infty, x + \varepsilon_k \underline{1}]$, $k = 1, 2, \ldots$. Since $\{A_k\}$ is a nested, decreasing family, with $(-\infty, x] = \cap_{k=1}^\infty A_k$, Theorem 7.1 implies that

$$F(x) = \lambda((-\infty, x]) = \lambda\left(\bigcap_{k=1}^\infty A_k\right) = \lim_{k\to\infty} \lambda(A_k) = \lim_{k\to\infty} F(x + \varepsilon_k \underline{1}),$$

so that F is continuous from above at x. Finally, to see that (D3) holds, note for any rectangle $(a, b]$,

$$\sum_{j=1}^{2^l} \pm F(a + \theta_j d) = \sum_{j=1}^{2^l} \pm \lambda(-\infty, a + \theta_j d] = \lambda((a, b]).$$

Figure 12.2 illustrates the case where $l = 2$.

  Proof of (b). Suppose that $F: \mathbf{R}^l \to [0, 1]$ satisfies (D1)–(D3). The Borel sets in $\mathbf{R}^l$ are generated by the algebra $\mathcal{A}$ consisting of finite unions of half-open rectangles: sets of the form $(a, b]$, $(-\infty, b]$, $(a, +\infty)$, $(-\infty, +\infty)$. (Cf. Exercise 7.6.) Hence it follows from the Caratheodory Extension Theorem (Theorem 7.2) that to construct a probability measure λ on $(\mathbf{R}^l, \mathcal{B}^l)$, it suffices to define λ on $\mathcal{A}$ and show that λ is countably additive on $\mathcal{A}$.

  For the half-open rectangles, define λ by

(2) $\lambda((-\infty, b]) = F(b)$, $\lambda((a, b]) = \Sigma \pm F(a + \theta_j d)$,

   $\lambda((-\infty, +\infty)) = 1$, $\lambda((a, +\infty)) = \Sigma \pm F(a + \theta_j d)$.

Clearly λ satisfies (1). The intersection of two rectangles is itself a rectan-

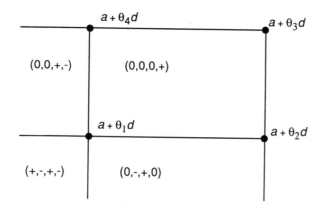

$$\theta_1 = (0,0), \quad \theta_2 = (1,0), \quad \theta_3 = (1,1), \quad \theta_4 = (0,1)$$

Figure 12.2

gle, so the measure of any such set is given by one of the formulas above. Finally, any set in $\mathscr{A}$ that is the finite union of rectangles can be written as the finite union of disjoint rectangles. Suppose that A is such a set, and $\cup_{i=1}^{I} A_i = A = \cup_{j=1}^{J} B_j$ are two ways of expressing it. The argument establishing that these two sums are equal is exactly like that used in the proof of Theorem 7.13, and we define $\lambda(A)$ to be their common value.

To see that λ is countably additive on $\mathscr{A}$, let $A = \cup_{n=1}^{\infty} A_n$, where A and $\{A_n\}$ are in $\mathscr{A}$, and the A_n's are disjoint. We must show that $\lambda(A) = \sum_{n=1}^{\infty} \lambda(A_n)$. We do this in detail for the case $l = 1$ and indicate briefly how the argument can be extended. Since any set $A \in \mathscr{A}$ is the finite union of disjoint intervals, it suffices to consider the case where A is an interval. Let $A = (a, b]$, and consider any sequence of disjoint intervals $(a_n, b_n]$ with $\cup_{n=1}^{\infty} (a_n, b_n] = (a, b]$. Without loss of generality, we may order the intervals so that $b = b_1 \geq a_1 = b_2 \geq \ldots = a$. Then we have

$$\sum_{n=1}^{\infty} \lambda((a_n, b_n]) = \sum_{n=1}^{\infty} [F(b_n) - F(a_n)] = \sum_{n=1}^{\infty} [F(b_n) - F(b_{n+1})]$$

$$= \lim_{N \to \infty} \sum_{n=1}^{N} [F(b_n) - F(b_{n+1})] = F(b_1) - \lim_{N \to \infty} F(b_{N+1})$$

$$= F(b) - F(a) = \lambda(a, b],$$

where the next-to-last step uses the facts that $\{b_n\}$ is a decreasing sequence converging to a and that F is continuous from above.

The key step in this argument is the cancellation of terms, and this cancellation also holds in higher dimensions. Let $(a, b]$ be a rectangle in $\mathbf{R}^l$, and let $\{(a_n, b_n]\}$ be a disjoint sequence of rectangles whose union is $(a, b]$. Then

$$\sum_{n=1}^{\infty} \lambda((a_n, b_n]) = \sum_{n=1}^{\infty} \left[\sum_{j=1}^{2^l} \pm F(a_n + \theta_j d_n) \right],$$

and all of the terms on the right cancel except those corresponding to the 2^l vertices of the rectangle $(a, b]$. [For $l = 2$, this corresponds, as shown in Figure 12.3 to the fact that every vertex in the interior of $(a, b]$ is counted either two or four times, with plus and minus signs canceling; every vertex along an edge of $(a, b]$ is counted exactly twice, again with signs canceling; and each of the four vertices of $(a, b]$ is counted exactly once.]

Finally, note that since (1) implies (2), λ is uniquely defined on $\mathcal{A}$;

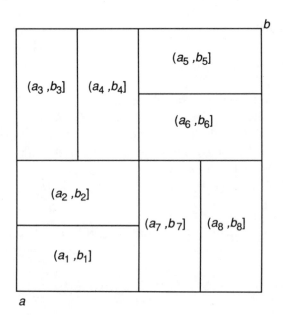

Figure 12.3

hence the Hahn Extension Theorem (Theorem 7.3) implies that the extension of λ to all of $\mathcal{B}^l$ is unique.

Proof of (c). Fix x; let $\{\varepsilon_k\}$ be a decreasing sequence converging to zero; and let $B_k = (-\infty, x - \varepsilon_k \underline{1}], k = 1, 2, \ldots$. Then B_k is a nested increasing family, with $\cup_{k=1}^{\infty} B_k = (-\infty, x)$. Hence by Theorem 7.1,

$$\lambda((-\infty, x)) = \lambda\left(\bigcup_{k=1}^{\infty} B_k\right) = \lim_{k \to \infty} \lambda(B_k) = \lim_{k \to \infty} F(x - \varepsilon_k \underline{1}).$$

Since $F(x) = \lambda((-\infty, x])$, it follows immediately that F is continuous from below at x if and only if $\lambda((-\infty, x]) = \lambda((-\infty, x))$. ∎

12.3 Weak Convergence of Distribution Functions

In the last section we showed that if the state space is a finite-dimensional Euclidean space, then there is a one-to-one correspondence between distribution functions and probability measures. Hence arguments can be made in terms of either, as convenience dictates. This fact motivates the two results we prove below. The first, Theorem 12.8, characterizes weak convergence in terms of distribution functions. Theorem 12.9, Helly's Theorem, then draws on this result to establish a very general result for the existence of weakly convergent subsequences, given any sequence $\{F_n\}$ of distribution functions. A corollary to this theorem provides a simple sufficient condition for the convergence of the sequence $\{F_n\}$ itself, rather than a subsequence.

The next theorem draws on Theorems 12.3 and 12.7 to establish the connection between weak convergence of a sequence of measures and convergence of the corresponding sequence of distribution functions. The basic idea is that the rectangles of the form $(a, b]$ are a convergence-determining class.

THEOREM 12.8 *Let $\{\lambda_n\}$ and λ be probability measures on $(\mathbf{R}^l, \mathcal{B}^l)$, and let $\{F_n\}$ and F be the corresponding distribution functions. Then $\lambda_n \Rightarrow \lambda$ if and only if*

(1) $\lim_{n \to \infty} F_n(x) = F(x)$ *at all continuity points of F.*

Proof. Suppose that $\lambda_n \Rightarrow \lambda$. Let $\{F_n\}$ and F be the corresponding distribution functions, and choose any point x at which F is continuous. It then follows from Theorem 12.7 that the boundary of the set $(-\infty, x]$ has λ-measure zero. Hence

$$\lim_{n\to\infty} F_n(x) = \lim_{n\to\infty} \lambda_n((-\infty, x]) = \lambda((-\infty, x]) = F(x),$$

where the second equality follows from part (d) of Theorem 12.3. Hence (1) holds.

Conversely, suppose that (1) holds. Recall that a *hyperplane* in $\mathbf{R}^l$ is a set of the form $\mathbf{R}^{i-1} \times a_i \times \mathbf{R}^{l-i}$, $i \in \{1, \ldots, l\}$, $a_i \in \mathbf{R}$. For each fixed i, at most a countable number of these can have positive measure under λ. That is, for each $i = 1, \ldots, l$, the set

$$Z_i = \{a_i \in \mathbf{R}: \lambda(\mathbf{R}^{i-1} \times a_i \times \mathbf{R}^{l-i}) = 0\},$$

differs from $\mathbf{R}$ by at most a countable set.

An interval of the form $(a, b]$ in $\mathbf{R}^l$ is determined by the $2l$ hyperplanes containing its faces. Let $\mathscr{A}$ be the class of intervals for which all these hyperplanes have λ-measure zero. That is,

$$\mathscr{A} = \{(a, b] \subset \mathbf{R}^l: a_i, b_i \in Z_i, i = 1, \ldots, l\}.$$

Clearly $\mathscr{A}$ satisfies the hypotheses of Theorem 12.5.

To complete the proof, it suffices to show that $\lambda(A) = \lim_{n\to\infty} \lambda_n(A)$, all $A \in \mathscr{A}$. To see this, note that each interval $(a, b] \in \mathscr{A}$ has the property that each vertex of $(a, b]$ is an element of $Z_1 \times Z_2 \times \ldots \times Z_l$ and is therefore a continuity point of F. Hence

$$\lambda((a, b]) = \sum_{j=1}^{2^l} \pm F(a + \theta_j d) = \sum_{j=1}^{2^l} \pm \lim_{n\to\infty} F_n(a + \theta_j d)$$

$$= \lim_{n\to\infty} \sum_{j=1}^{2^l} \pm F_n(a + \theta_j d) = \lim_{n\to\infty} \lambda_n((a, b]),$$

where $d = b - a$ and the θ_j's are as specified before. ∎

Theorem 12.8 is an extremely useful result, since it is often easier to work with distribution functions rather than with probability measures.

If the state space is a subset of $\mathbf{R}^l$, the corresponding distribution function is defined as follows. First note that if S is a Borel subset of $\mathbf{R}^l$, then for any probability measure $\lambda \in \Lambda(S, \mathcal{S})$,

(2) $\qquad \hat{\lambda}(A) = \lambda(A \cap S), \quad$ all $A \in \mathcal{B}^l$,

defines a natural extension of λ to a measure $\hat{\lambda} \in \Lambda(\mathbf{R}^l, \mathcal{B}^l)$. It is easy to show that the weak convergence of a sequence of probability measures defined on $(S, \mathcal{S})$ is equivalent to the weak convergence of the corresponding sequence defined on $(\mathbf{R}^l, \mathcal{B}^l)$.

Exercise 12.4 Let $S \subset \mathbf{R}^l$ be a Borel set; let $\{\lambda_n\}$, λ be probability measures on $(S, \mathcal{S})$; and let $\{\hat{\lambda}_n\}$, $\hat{\lambda}$ be the corresponding probability measures on $(\mathbf{R}^l, \mathcal{B}^l)$. Show that $\lambda_n \Rightarrow \lambda$ if and only if $\hat{\lambda}_n \Rightarrow \hat{\lambda}$. [*Hint.* Use Exercise 12.1b and part (b) of Theorem 12.3.]

Thus, Theorem 12.8 and Exercise 12.4, taken together, imply that the weak convergence of a sequence of probability measures on any Borel subset $(S, \mathcal{S})$ of $\mathbf{R}^l$ is equivalent to the weak convergence of the corresponding sequence of distribution functions. The following exercise establishes a consequence of this fact that we use later.

Exercise 12.5 Let $S = [a, b] \subset \mathbf{R}^l$, and let $\mathcal{A} = \{A = [a, x]: x \in S\}$.
a. Let $\{\lambda_n\}$ and λ be measures in $\Lambda(S, \mathcal{S})$, and suppose that

$$\lim_{n \to \infty} \lambda_n(A) = \lambda(A), \quad \text{all } A \in \mathcal{A}.$$

Show that $\lambda_n \Rightarrow \lambda$. [*Hint.* Use Exercise 12.4 and Theorem 12.8.]
b. Let $\lambda, \mu \in \Lambda(S, \mathcal{S})$. Show that if $\int f \, d\lambda = \int f \, d\mu$, for all continuous, monotone functions f, then $\lambda = \mu$. [*Hint.* For each $A \in \mathcal{A}$, look at the sequence of continuous functions constructed as they were in the proof of Theorem 12.1. Then apply the result established in part (a).]

Our next result, Helly's Theorem, provides another illustration of the advantage of working with distribution functions. Before stating it, however, we need the following definition. Let (S, ρ) be a metric space, with its Borel sets $\mathcal{S}$, and let $\lambda \in \Lambda(S, \mathcal{S})$ be a probability measure on $(S, \mathcal{S})$.

The **support** of Λ is the smallest set A that is closed (relative to S) and such that $\lambda(A) = 1$. To see that the support is well defined, note that S itself is closed and $\lambda(S) = 1$. Moreover, if A and B are closed sets with $\lambda(A) = \lambda(B) = 1$, then $A \cap B$ is also closed and $\lambda(A \cap B) = 1$. (Why?) Finally, note that the latter argument can be extended to any family of closed sets, each of λ-measure unity.

Helly's Theorem establishes that for any sequence $\{F_n\}$ of distribution functions on $(\mathbf{R}^l, \mathscr{B}^l)$, all having support contained in the same compact set, there exists a subsequence that converges weakly to a distribution function F. The main idea of the proof is as follows. Let Z be the set of points in $\mathbf{R}^l$ with rational coordinates. First construct a subsequence of $\{F_n\}$ that converges pointwise on the set Z, and use the pointwise limit of this subsequence to define a function G on Z. Then extend this function to all of $\mathbf{R}^l$, and, finally, alter it to make it continuous from above. The resulting function is the desired distribution function F, and the subsequence of $\{F_n\}$ used in its construction converges weakly to it.

THEOREM 12.9 (*Helly's Theorem*)   *Let $\{F_n\}$ be a sequence of distribution functions on $(\mathbf{R}^l, \mathscr{B}^l)$, with the following property:*

(3)   *for some $\underline{a}, \bar{b} \in \mathbf{R}^l$, $F_n(\underline{a}) = 0$ and $F_n(\bar{b}) = 1, n = 1, 2, \ldots$*

Then there exists a distribution function F with $F(\underline{a}) = 0$ and $F(\bar{b}) = 1$, and a subsequence of $\{F_n\}$ that converges weakly to F.

Proof. Let $Z = \{z_i\}_{i=1}^{\infty}$ be an enumeration of the points in $\mathbf{R}^l$ with rational coordinates. Consider the sequence of real numbers $\{F_n(z_1)\}$. Since this sequence is contained in the closed interval $[0, 1]$, it contains a convergent subsequence. That is, there exists a subsequence $\{F_n^{(1)}\}$ of $\{F_n\}$ such that $\{F_n^{(1)}(z_1)\}$ converges. Next consider the sequence of real numbers $\{F_n^{(1)}(z_2)\}$. Since this sequence is also contained in the closed interval $[0, 1]$, it also contains a convergent subsequence. That is, there exists a subsequence $\{F_n^{(2)}\}$ of $\{F_n^{(1)}\}$ such that $\{F_n^{(2)}(z_i)\}$ converges, $i = 1, 2$. Continuing by induction, we can for each $N = 1, 2, \ldots$ find a subsequence $\{F_n^{(N)}\}$ of $\{F_n\}$ that converges on the points $z_1, \ldots, z_N$. Hence the sequence $\{F_N^{(N)}\}_{N=1}^{\infty}$ converges at all the points of $\mathbf{R}^l$ with rational coordinates.

Let $G(z_i) = \lim_{N \to \infty} F_N^{(N)}(z_i)$, $i = 1, 2, \ldots$. On the rest of $\mathbf{R}^l$, let $G(x) = \inf_{z_i > x} G(z_i)$. Clearly G satisfies property (D1) of Theorem 12.7. To see that it satisfies (D3), first note that since each function $F_N^{(N)}$ is a distribution function, (D3) holds for $F_N^{(N)}$. Hence for a and b with rational coordinates,

$$\sum_{j=1}^{2^l} \pm G(a + \theta_j d) = \lim_{N \to \infty} \sum_{j=1}^{2^l} \pm F_N^{(N)}(a + \theta_j d) \geq 0,$$

where $d = b - a$, and the θ_j's are as specified before. If a or b or both have some irrational coordinates, choose sequences $\varepsilon_i \downarrow 0$ and $\hat{\varepsilon}_i \downarrow 0$ in $\mathbf{R}^l$ such that $a + \varepsilon_i$ and $(b - a) + \hat{\varepsilon}_i$ have rational coordinates for each i, and

$$G(a + \theta_j d) = \lim_{i \to \infty} G(a + \varepsilon_i + \theta_j d + \theta_j \hat{\varepsilon}_i), \quad j = 1, \ldots, 2^l.$$

Then

$$\sum_{j=1}^{2^l} \pm G(a + \theta_j d) = \lim_{i \to \infty} \sum_{j=1}^{2^l} \pm G(a + \varepsilon_i + \theta_j d + \theta_j \hat{\varepsilon}_i) \geq 0.$$

Hence G also satisfies (D3) of Theorem 12.7. However, G need not be continuous from above.

To make it so, define the function F by

$$F(x) = \lim_{\varepsilon \downarrow 0} G(x + \varepsilon \underline{1}), \quad x \in \mathbf{R}^l,$$

where $\underline{1} = (1, 1, \ldots, 1)$. If G is continuous at x, then $F(x) = G(x)$; otherwise, $F(x)$ is the right-hand limit of G at x. Clearly F satisfies (D1) and (D2) of Theorem 12.7. To see that it also satisfies (D3), note that since G satisfies (D3),

$$\sum_{j=1}^{2^l} \pm F(a + \theta_j d) = \lim_{\varepsilon \downarrow 0} \sum_{j=1}^{2^l} \pm G(a + \varepsilon \underline{1} + \theta_j d) \geq 0.$$

Finally, note that if F is continuous at x, then so is G, so $F(x) = G(x) = \lim_{N \to \infty} F_N^{(N)}(x)$. Hence by Theorem 12.8, $\{F_N^{(N)}\}$ converges weakly to F. ∎

The following corollary simply restates Helly's Theorem in terms of probability measures.

COROLLARY 1 *Let $\{\lambda_n\}$ be a sequence of probability measures on $(\mathbf{R}^l, \mathcal{B}^l)$, with the following property:*

for some $\underline{a}, \bar{b} \in \mathbf{R}^l$, $\lambda_n((-\infty, \underline{a}]) = 0$ and

$$\lambda_n((-\infty, \bar{b}]) = 1, n = 1, 2, \ldots .$$

Then there exists a probability measure λ with $\lambda((-\infty, \underline{a}]) = 0$ and $\lambda((-\infty, \bar{b}]) = 1$, and a subsequence of $\{\lambda_n\}$ that converges weakly to λ.

To see that the assumption of support in a common compact set cannot be dropped altogether, consider the following sequence of distributions on the real line:

$$F_n(x) = \begin{cases} 0 & \text{if } x < n \\ 1 & \text{if } x \geq n. \end{cases}$$

The sequence $\{F_n\}$ converges pointwise to the zero function, which is not a distribution function. The assumption can be relaxed, however, as shown in the next exercise. The exercise also shows how the result can be extended to the case where S is a closed subset of $\mathbf{R}^l$.

Exercise 12.6 a. Show that the conclusion of Theorem 12.9 holds under the following weaker condition: for every $\varepsilon > 0$, there exists $\underline{a}(\varepsilon)$ and $\bar{b}(\varepsilon)$ such that $F_n[\bar{b}(\varepsilon)] - F_n[\underline{a}(\varepsilon)] > 1 - \varepsilon$, all n.
  b. Let $\{\lambda_n\}$ be a sequence of probability measures on $(\mathbf{R}^l, \mathcal{B}^l)$, and suppose that for every $\varepsilon > 0$ there exists a compact set K such that $\lambda_n(K) > 1 - \varepsilon$, all n. Show that $\{\lambda_n\}$ has a weakly convergent subsequence.
  c. Show that the result in part (b) holds if the state space is $(S, \mathcal{S})$, where S is a closed subset of $\mathbf{R}^l$.

Given any sequence of distribution functions $\{F_n\}$, all with support in the compact set $[\underline{a}, \bar{b}]$, Helly's Theorem ensures the existence of a weakly convergent subsequence. With one additional assumption on the sequence $\{F_n\}$, this conclusion can be strengthened. Call a sequence of distribution functions $\{F_n\}$ *monotone* if $F_{n+1} \leq F_n$, all n, or $F_{n+1} \geq F_n$, all n. The following corollary shows that if the sequence $\{F_n\}$ is monotone, then it converges weakly to a limiting distribution function F.

COROLLARY 2 *Let $\{F_n\}$ be a monotone sequence of distribution functions on $\mathbf{R}^l$, satisfying (3). Then $\{F_n\}$ converges weakly to a distribution function F.*

Proof. Since (3) holds, $\{F_n\}$ converges pointwise to a function G satisfying properties (D1) and (D3) of Theorem 12.7. Construct F from G as in the last step of the proof above; the arguments there show that F satisfies (D1)–(D3) and that $\{F_n\}$ converges weakly to F. ∎

12.4 Monotone Markov Processes

In this section we draw on the ideas developed above to establish sufficient conditions for the weak convergence of a Markov process. Except where explicitly stated, throughout this section we take the state space to be a Borel set of a Euclidean space, $S \subseteq \mathbf{R}^l$, with its Borel subsets $\mathcal{S}$. We take P to be a transition function on $(S, \mathcal{S})$, $T: B(S, \mathcal{S}) \to B(S, \mathcal{S})$ to be the associated operator on bounded measurable functions, and $T^*: \Lambda(S, \mathcal{S}) \to \Lambda(S, \mathcal{S})$ to be the associated operator on probability measures. We phrase arguments in terms of P, T, T^*, or their iterates as convenience dictates; all of these were defined in Section 8.1. We also make use of the notation $\langle f, \lambda \rangle = \int f \, d\lambda$ introduced there.

We prove two main results. These make use of two assumptions on P—the Feller property and monotonicity—that were introduced in Section 8.1 and are discussed in more detail below. Theorem 12.10 establishes that if the state space S is compact and P has the Feller property, then there exists an invariant measure. The proof of this result draws on Helly's Theorem. Then in Theorem 12.12, we establish that if, in addition, P is monotone and satisfies a mixing condition, then the invariant measure is unique and the sequence $\{T^{*n}\lambda_0\}$ converges weakly to it for any initial probability measure λ_0. Although the latter set of assumptions may at first glance seem rather restrictive, they are satisfied in a wide variety of economic contexts, as the examples in Chapter 13 show.

Recall from Section 8.1 that a transition function P has the *Feller property* if for any bounded continuous function f, the function Tf defined by

$$(Tf)(s) = \int f(s')P(s, ds'), \quad \text{all } s,$$

is also continuous. That is, P has the Feller property if the operator T

satisfies $T[C(S)] \subseteq C(S)$. The following exercise provides alternative characterizations of the Feller property in terms of P and T^*. Note that both of the latter involve the notion of weak convergence.

Exercise 12.7 Show that the following statements are equivalent:
a. $f \in C(S)$ implies $Tf \in C(S)$ (the Feller property);
b. $s_n \to s$ implies $P(s_n, \cdot) \Rightarrow P(s, \cdot)$; and
c. $\lambda_n \Rightarrow \lambda$ implies $T^*\lambda_n \Rightarrow T^*\lambda$.
[*Hint.* Use Theorem 8.3. Note that the results in this exercise hold for any metric space.]

To establish the existence of an invariant measure when $S \subset \mathbf{R}^l$, we might choose an arbitrary initial probability measure λ_0 and look at the sequence $\{T^{*n}\lambda_0\}$. Corollary 1 to Helly's Theorem ensures that if S is a compact set, then this sequence has a weakly convergent subsequence. Although the limiting measure λ of this subsequence might seem to be a candidate for an invariant measure, in the presence of cyclically moving subsets it will not be. The following example illustrates the problem. Recall that for any $s \in S$, δ_s denotes the probability measure that is a unit mass at the point s.

Exercise 12.8 Let $S = [0, 1]$, and consider the difference equation $s_{t+1} = 1 - s_t$.
a. What is the transition function P corresponding to this difference equation? Show that P has the Feller property.
b. Show that for any initial probability measure $\lambda_0 = \delta_s$, where $s \neq 1/2$, the sequence $\{T^{*n}\lambda_0\}$ has two subsequences converging to two distinct limits. Show that neither of these limits is an invariant measure.
c. What are the invariant measures for this system?

This exercise suggests that, as in Theorems 11.1 and 11.9, an invariant measure might be obtained by looking at the sequence $\{(1/N)\sum_{n=0}^{N-1} T^{*n}\lambda_0\}_{N=1}^{\infty}$ of N-period averages, since averaging eliminates cycles. The following theorem shows that this is indeed the case.

THEOREM 12.10 *If $S \subset \mathbf{R}^l$ is compact and P has the Feller property, then there exists a probability measure that is invariant under P.*

Proof. Choose any $\lambda_0 \in \Lambda(S, \mathcal{S})$, and consider the sequence $\{\mu_N\}$ in $\Lambda(S, \mathcal{S})$ defined by

$$\mu_N = \frac{1}{N} \sum_{n=0}^{N-1} T^{*n} \lambda_0.$$

By Corollary 1 to Helly's Theorem (Theorem 12.9), there exists a probability measure μ and a subsequence $\{\mu_{N_k}\}$ of $\{\mu_N\}$ such that $\{\mu_{N_k}\}$ converges weakly to μ.

Let f be a continuous function on S. Note that since P has the Feller property, Tf is also continuous; and since S is compact, f is bounded. Fix $\varepsilon > 0$. Since $\mu_{N_k} \Rightarrow \mu$ and since f and Tf are both continuous, it follows that for some $K_1 \geq 1$ sufficiently large,

$$|\langle f, \mu_{N_k}\rangle - \langle f, \mu\rangle| < \varepsilon/3 \quad \text{and}$$

$$|\langle Tf, \mu_{N_k}\rangle - \langle Tf, \mu\rangle| < \varepsilon/3, \quad \text{all } k \geq K_1.$$

Moreover, for any $N \geq 1$,

$$|\langle f, \mu_N\rangle - \langle Tf, \mu_N\rangle| = \left|\left\langle f, \frac{1}{N}\sum_{n=0}^{N-1} T^{*n}\lambda_0\right\rangle - \left\langle Tf, \frac{1}{N}\sum_{n=0}^{N-1} T^{*n}\lambda_0\right\rangle\right|$$

$$= \left|\frac{1}{N}\sum_{n=0}^{N-1}\langle f, T^{*n}\lambda_0\rangle - \frac{1}{N}\sum_{n=0}^{N-1}\langle Tf, T^{*n}\lambda_0\rangle\right|$$

$$= \left|\frac{1}{N}\sum_{n=0}^{N-1}\left(\langle f, T^{*n}\lambda_0\rangle - \langle f, T^{*(n+1)}\lambda_0\rangle\right)\right|$$

$$= \left|\frac{1}{N}\left(\langle f, \lambda_0\rangle - \langle f, T^{*N}\lambda_0\rangle\right)\right|$$

$$\leq 2\|f\|/N,$$

where the third line uses Theorem 8.3. Hence for some K_2 sufficiently large,

$$|\langle f, \mu_{N_k}\rangle - \langle Tf, \mu_{N_k}\rangle| < \varepsilon/3, \quad \text{all } k \geq K_2.$$

Using the triangle inequality and the three bounds above, we conclude that for any $\varepsilon > 0$ there exists $K \geq 1$ such that

$$|\langle f, \mu \rangle - \langle Tf, \mu \rangle|$$

$$\leq |\langle f, \mu \rangle - \langle f, \mu_{N_k} \rangle| + |\langle f, \mu_{N_k} \rangle - \langle Tf, \mu_{N_k} \rangle|$$

$$+ |\langle Tf, \mu_{N_k} \rangle - \langle Tf, \mu \rangle|$$

$$< \varepsilon, \quad \text{all } k \geq K.$$

Since $\varepsilon > 0$ was arbitrary, it follows that

$$(1) \qquad \langle f, \mu \rangle = \langle Tf, \mu \rangle = \langle f, T^*\mu \rangle,$$

where the second equality again uses Theorem 8.3. Since f is an arbitrary continuous function, (1) holds for all $f \in C(S)$. Hence by Corollary 2 to Theorem 12.6, $\mu = T^*\mu$. ∎

Notice that the example in Exercise 12.8 satisfies the hypotheses of this theorem. That is, Theorem 12.10 does not rule out the existence of multiple invariant measures or cycles. To rule out these possibilities and guarantee convergence of the sequence $\{T^{*n}\lambda_0\}$ to a unique invariant measure requires stronger assumptions.

Recall from Section 8.1 that for $S \subseteq \mathbf{R}^l$, a transition function P on $(S, \mathcal{S})$ is **monotone** if for any bounded, increasing function f, the function Tf is also increasing. (Here we use *increasing* in the weak sense.) Thus we defined monotonicity of a Markov process in terms of the way the operator T acts on increasing functions. The assumption that P is monotone is used in establishing the stronger convergence result in Theorem 12.12 below. As with the Feller property, however, monotonicity has equivalent characterizations in terms of P or T^*, and it is useful to look at them. In particular, for our purposes it is useful to characterize monotone processes in terms of T^*.

To do this, we first need to define the following partial ordering on the set $\Lambda(S, \mathcal{S})$ of probability measures.

DEFINITION   Let $\lambda, \mu \in \Lambda(S, \mathcal{S})$. Then μ **dominates** λ if $\langle f, \mu \rangle \geq \langle f, \lambda \rangle$ for any increasing function $f \in B(S, \mathcal{S})$.

That is, μ dominates λ if any bounded increasing function f, when integrated against μ, gives a value that is at least as high as the one obtained when it is integrated against λ. If μ dominates λ, we will write $\mu \geq \lambda$. The following exercise shows that in $\mathbf{R}^1$ monotonicity of the distribution functions and dominance of probability measures are equivalent, but that in higher dimensions, the latter is stronger.

Exercise 12.9 a. Let $S \subseteq \mathbf{R}^l$, and let $\lambda, \mu \in \Lambda(S, \mathcal{S})$. Show that if $\mu \geq \lambda$, then the corresponding distribution functions satisfy $F_\mu(s) \leq F_\lambda(s)$, all $s \in S$.

b. Show that for $\mathbf{R}^1$ the converse is also true.

c. Give an example in $\mathbf{R}^2$ where the converse does *not* hold.

The next result, which we use later, draws on this exercise. It shows that if a sequence of probability measures is "squeezed" between two other sequences, both converging weakly to the same limit, then it also converges weakly to that limit.

Exercise 12.10 Let $S = [a, b] \subset \mathbf{R}^l$; and let $\{\mu_{1n}\}$, $\{\mu_{2n}\}$, and $\{\lambda_n\}$ be sequences in $\Lambda(S, \mathcal{S})$, with $\mu_{1n} \leq \lambda_n \leq \mu_{2n}$, all n. Show that if $\mu_{in} \Rightarrow \mu$, $i = 1, 2$, then $\lambda_n \Rightarrow \mu$. [*Hint.* Let $\{F_{1n}\}, \{F_{2n}\}, F$, and $\{G_n\}$ be the distribution functions corresponding to $\{\mu_{1n}\}, \{\mu_{2n}\}, \mu$, and $\{\lambda_n\}$ respectively, and let $X \subseteq [a, b]$ be the set of points at which F is continuous. Use part (a) of Exercise 12.9 and Theorem 12.8.]

Using the notion of dominance for probability measures, we have the following alternative characterizations of monotonicity for a Markov process in terms of T^* and P.

Exercise 12.11 Show that the following statements are equivalent:

a. $f \in B(S, \mathcal{S})$ and f increasing implies Tf increasing (monotonicity);

b. $\lambda, \mu \in \Lambda(S, \mathcal{S})$ and $\mu \geq \lambda$ implies $T^*\mu \geq T^*\lambda$; and

c. $s, s' \in S$ and $s \geq s'$ implies $P(s, \cdot) \geq P(s', \cdot)$.

[*Hint.* Use Theorem 8.3.]

This exercise shows that a Markov process is monotone if and only if T^* preserves dominance relationships between probability measures.

We call a sequence $\{\lambda_n\}$ of probability measures **monotone** if they are ordered by dominance, that is, if $\lambda_{n+1} \geq \lambda_n$, all n, or $\lambda_{n+1} \leq \lambda_n$, all n. The next exercise shows that if S is a closed, bounded rectangle $[a, b] \subset \mathbf{R}^l$ and if P is monotone and has the Feller property, then the sequences $\{T^{*n}\delta_a\}$ and $\{T^{*n}\delta_b\}$ converge weakly to invariant measures.

Exercise 12.12   Let $S = [a, b] \subset \mathbf{R}^l$. Show that if P is monotone and has the Feller property, then the sequences $\{T^{*n}\delta_a\}$ and $\{T^{*n}\delta_b\}$ are monotone increasing and decreasing sequences respectively, and they converge weakly to (possibly different) invariant measures. [*Hint.* Use monotonicity to show that each sequence converges weakly. Then use the Feller property to show that each limit is an invariant measure.]

Are the hypotheses of Exercise 12.12—compactness, monotonicity, and the Feller property—enough to ensure weak convergence to a unique invariant measure? The following example shows that they are not: there still may be multiple ergodic sets.

Exercise 12.13   Let $S = [a, b] \subset \mathbf{R}$, and let $h: S \to S$ and $H: S \to S$ be the two functions shown in Figure 12.4. Consider the following transition function:

$$P(s, A) = \frac{\mu(A \cap [h(s), H(s)])}{\mu([h(s), H(s)])},$$

where μ denotes Lebesgue measure on $\mathbf{R}$. That is, for each $s \in S$, $P(s, \cdot)$ is the measure corresponding to a uniform density on the interval $[h(s), H(s)]$.

a. Show that P is monotone and has the Feller property.

b. Show that the indicated sets E_1 and E_2 are distinct ergodic sets, and that the set F is a transient set.

c. Show that the sequences $\{T^{*n}\delta_a\}$ and $\{T^{*n}\delta_b\}$ do not have the same limit.

Exercise 12.13 shows that to ensure uniqueness of the invariant measure, we must impose enough "mixing" on the transition function to rule the kind of behavior shown in Figure 12.4. This is done in Assumption

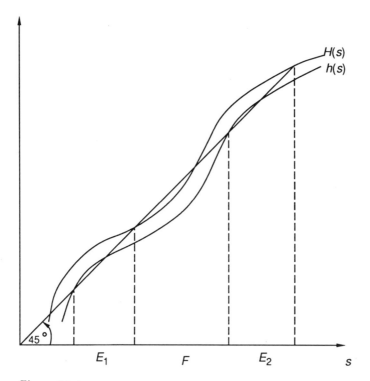

Figure 12.4

12.1 below. Lemma 12.11 then shows that if this condition holds, the expected value of any bounded, measurable, nondecreasing function is bounded above and below in a particular way. Theorem 12.12 then draws on this result to establish sufficient conditions for uniqueness of the invariant measure λ^*, and weak convergence of the sequence $\{T^{*n}\lambda_0\}$ to λ^* for any initial probability measure λ_0.

ASSUMPTION 12.1 *There exists $c \in S$, $\varepsilon > 0$, and $N \geq 1$ such that $P^N(a, [c, b]) \geq \varepsilon$ and $P^N(b, [a, c]) \geq \varepsilon$.*

Exercise 12.14 Show that if P is monotone and satisfies Assumption 12.1 for (c, ε, N), then

$$P^N(s, [a, c]) \geq \varepsilon \quad \text{and} \quad P^N(s, [c, b]) \geq \varepsilon, \quad \text{all } s \in S.$$

LEMMA 12.11   *Let $S = [a, b] \subset \mathbf{R}^l$. Assume that P is monotone and satisfies Assumption 12.1 for (c, ε, N). Then for any bounded, measurable, nondecreasing function f,*

(2) $\varepsilon f(c) + (1 - \varepsilon)f(a) \leq (T^N f)(s) \leq \varepsilon f(c) + (1 - \varepsilon)f(b), \quad$ *all $s \in S$.*

Proof. Let $A = [a, c]$; then by Assumption 12.1 and Exercise 12.14, $P^N(s, A) \geq \varepsilon$, all $s \in S$. Hence

$$(T^N f)(s) = \int_A f(s')P^N(s, ds') + \int_{A^c} f(s')P^N(s, ds')$$

$$\leq f(c)P^N(s, A) + f(b)P^N(s, A^c)$$

$$\leq \varepsilon f(c) + (1 - \varepsilon)f(b),$$

where the last line uses the fact that $f(c) \leq f(b)$ and $P^N(s, A) \geq \varepsilon$. This establishes the second inequality in (2); a similar argument establishes the first. ∎

We are now ready to prove our final result.

THEOREM 12.12   *Let $S = [a, b] \subset \mathbf{R}^l$. If P is monotone, has the Feller property, and satisfies Assumption 12.1, then P has a unique invariant probability measure λ^*, and $T^{*n}\lambda_0 \Rightarrow \lambda^*$, all $\lambda_0 \in \Lambda(S, \mathscr{S})$.*

Proof. By Exercise 12.12, the sequences $\{T^{*n}\delta_a\}$ and $\{T^{*n}\delta_b\}$ both converge weakly, and their limits λ_a^* and λ_b^* are invariant measures. Since $\delta_a \leq \lambda_0 \leq \delta_b$, all $\lambda_0 \in \Lambda(S, \mathscr{S})$, and T^* is monotone, it follows that

$$T^{*n}\delta_a \leq T^{*n}\lambda_0 \leq T^{*n}\delta_b, \quad n = 1, 2, \ldots, \text{ all } \lambda_0 \in \Lambda(S, \mathscr{S}).$$

If $\lambda_a^* = \lambda_b^*$, then it follows immediately from Exercise 12.10 that the sequence $\{T^{*n}\lambda_0\}$ also converges weakly to this common limiting measure. Hence it suffices to show that $\lambda_a^* = \lambda_b^*$.

Suppose that P satisfies the stated hypotheses, and let (c, ε, N) be values for which Assumption 12.1 holds. Since the sequence $\{T^{*n}\delta_a\}$

converges weakly to λ_a^*, it follows that for any continuous function f,

$$\langle f, \lambda_a^* \rangle = \lim_{n \to \infty} \langle f, T^{*n}\delta_a \rangle = \lim_{n \to \infty} \langle T^n f, \delta_a \rangle$$

$$= \lim_{n \to \infty} (T^n f)(a) = \lim_{n \to \infty} (T^{Nn} f)(a).$$

Similarly,

$$\langle f, \lambda_b^* \rangle = \lim_{n \to \infty} (T^{Nn} f)(b).$$

Next we will show that if f is nondecreasing, these two limits are equal. Specifically, we will show by induction that

(3) $\qquad (T^{Nn} f)(b) - (T^{Nn} f)(a) \le (1 - \varepsilon)^n [f(b) - f(a)], \quad n = 0, 1, 2, \ldots .$

Clearly (3) holds for $n = 0$. Suppose that it holds for $n \ge 0$. Then

$$[T^{N(n+1)} f](b) - [T^{N(n+1)} f](a)$$

$$= [T^N (T^{Nn} f)](b) - [T^N (T^{Nn} f)](a)$$

$$\le \varepsilon(T^{Nn} f)(c) + (1 - \varepsilon)(T^{Nn} f)(b) - \varepsilon(T^{Nn} f)(c) - (1 - \varepsilon)(T^{Nn} f)(a)$$

$$= (1 - \varepsilon)[(T^{Nn} f)(b) - (T^{Nn} f)(a)]$$

$$\le (1 - \varepsilon)^{n+1} [f(b) - f(a)],$$

where the third line uses Lemma 12.11. Hence $\langle f, \lambda_a^* \rangle = \langle f, \lambda_b^* \rangle$ for any continuous, nondecreasing function f. It then follows from part (b) of Exercise 12.5 that $\lambda_a^* = \lambda_b^*$. ∎

12.5 Dependence of the Invariant Measure on a Parameter

We have thus far taken the transition function P on $(S, \mathcal{S})$ to be fixed. In applications, however, we are often interested in how the behavior of the system depends on various parameters. For transition functions that arise as the solutions to stochastic dynamic programs, these might be parameters affecting the exogenous shocks or the preferences or technology of the decision-maker. In this section we study the way parameters that alter the transition function P affect the long-run behavior of the system.

Let the state space be $S \subseteq \mathbf{R}^l$, with its Borel sets $\mathcal{S}$, and assume that the parameters of interest can be described by a vector θ taking values in a set $\Theta \subseteq \mathbf{R}^m$. For each $\theta \in \Theta$, let P_θ be a transition function on $(S, \mathcal{S})$, and let T_θ and T_θ^* be the operators associated with P_θ. Let $C(S)$ be the space of bounded continuous function on S, and let $\Lambda(S, \mathcal{S})$ be the space of probability measures on $(S, \mathcal{S})$. We then have the following result.

THEOREM 12.13 *Assume that*

   a. S is compact;

   b. if $\{(s_n, \theta_n)\}$ is a sequence in $S \times \Theta$ converging to (s_0, θ_0), then the sequence $\{P_{\theta_n}(s_n, \cdot)\}$ in $\Lambda(S, \mathcal{S})$ converges weakly to $P_{\theta_0}(s_0, \cdot)$; and

   c. for each $\theta \in \Theta$, T_θ^* has a unique fixed point $\mu_\theta \in \Lambda(S, \mathcal{S})$.

If $\{\theta_n\}$ is a sequence in Θ converging to θ_0, then the sequence $\{\mu_{\theta_n}\}$ converges weakly to μ_{θ_0}.

Proof. Let $\{\theta_n\}$ be a sequence in Θ converging to θ_0; and let $\{(P_n, T_n, T_n^*, \mu_n)\}$ and (P_0, T_0, T_0^*, μ_0) be the corresponding transition functions, operators, and invariant probability measures. Let (a)–(c) hold, and let $\hat{\Theta} \subseteq \Theta$ be a compact set containing $\{\theta_n\}$ and θ_0.

For any continuous function f, (b) implies that

$$(T_\theta f)(s) = \int f(s') P_\theta(s, s')$$

is continuous in (s, θ), and (a) implies that it is uniformly continuous on the compact set $S \times \hat{\Theta}$.

Fix $f \in C(S)$. Since $\{\theta_n\}$ and θ_0 lie in $\hat{\Theta}$, and $\theta_n \to \theta_0$, it follows from the uniform continuity of $(T_\theta f)(s)$ on $S \times \hat{\Theta}$ that for every $\varepsilon > 0$ there exists $N \geq 1$ such that

$$|(T_n f)(s) - (T_0 f)(s)| < \varepsilon, \quad \text{all } s \in S, \text{ all } n \geq N.$$

That is,

$$\|T_n f - T_0 f\| < \varepsilon, \quad \text{all } n \geq N,$$

so $T_n f$ converges to $T_0 f$ in the sup norm.

Next, since S is compact, it follows from Helly's Theorem (Theorem 12.9) that $\{\mu_n\}$ has a weakly convergent subsequence. Let $\{\mu_{n_k}\}$ be such a subsequence, and let $\hat{\mu}$ be its limit. Then for any function $f \in C(S)$,

(1) $|\langle f, \hat{\mu} \rangle - \langle T_0 f, \hat{\mu} \rangle|$

$$\leq |\langle f, \hat{\mu} \rangle - \langle f, \mu_{n_k} \rangle| + |\langle f, \mu_{n_k} \rangle - \langle T_0 f, \mu_{n_k} \rangle|$$

$$+ |\langle T_0 f, \mu_{n_k} \rangle - \langle T_0 f, \hat{\mu} \rangle|.$$

Since f and $T_0 f$ are continuous and since $\{\mu_{n_k}\}$ converges weakly to $\hat{\mu}$, the first and third terms on the right in (1) approach zero as $k \to \infty$. For the second term, we have

$$|\langle f, \mu_{n_k} \rangle - \langle T_0 f, \mu_{n_k} \rangle| = |\langle f, T_{n_k}^* \mu_{n_k} \rangle - \langle T_0 f, \mu_{n_k} \rangle|$$

$$= |\langle T_{n_k} f, \mu_{n_k} \rangle - \langle T_0 f, \mu_{n_k} \rangle|$$

$$\leq \|T_{n_k} f - T_0 f\|,$$

where the first line uses the fact that μ_{n_k} is a fixed point of $T_{n_k}^*$, and the second uses Theorem 8.3. Since $\{T_{n_k} f\}$ converges to $T_0 f$ in the sup norm, this establishes that the second term in (1) also approaches zero as $k \to \infty$. Since $f \in C(S)$ was arbitrary, it then follows that

$$\langle f, \hat{\mu} \rangle = \langle T_0 f, \hat{\mu} \rangle = \langle f, T_0^* \hat{\mu} \rangle, \quad \text{all } f \in C(S),$$

where the second equality uses Theorem 8.3. Hence by Corollary 2 to Theorem 12.6, $\hat{\mu} = T_0^* \hat{\mu}$. Since μ is the unique fixed point of T_0^* in $\Lambda(S, \mathscr{S})$, it follows that $\hat{\mu} = \mu$. That is, $\{\mu_{n_k}\}$ converges weakly to μ_0.

By the same argument, every subsequence of $\{\mu_n\}$ has a further subsequence converging weakly to μ_0. Hence $\{\mu_n\}$ converges weakly to μ_0. ∎

12.6 A Loose End

In Section 9.2 we analyzed stochastic dynamic programs under two alternative assumptions about the form of the state space $(Z, \mathfrak{Z})$ for the exogenous shocks. We assumed either that Z was a countable set or that Z was a compact, convex subset of a finite-dimensional Euclidean space $\mathbf{R}^k$. As we noted there, it is often convenient to take Z to be all of $\mathbf{R}^k$ or $\mathbf{R}^k_+$. Since neither of these sets is compact, however, the argument given in the proof of Lemma 9.5 does not then hold.

In this section we provide an alternative proof of Lemma 9.5 that allows us to drop the assumption that Z is compact. The proof of this lemma uses the fact that if a transition function Q on $(\mathbf{R}^k, \mathscr{B}^k)$ has the Feller property, then for any sequence $\{z_n\}$ converging to z, the sequence of probability measures $\{Q(z_n, \cdot)\}$ converges weakly to $Q(z, \cdot)$.

LEMMA 12.14 *Let X and Z be convex subsets of $\mathbf{R}^l$ and $\mathbf{R}^k$, respectively, with their Borel subsets $\mathscr{X}$ and $\mathfrak{Z}$; let Q be a transition function on $(Z, \mathfrak{Z})$; and assume that Q has the Feller property. Then for any bounded continuous function $f: X \times Z \to \mathbf{R}$, the function Tf defined by*

$$(Tf)(y, z) = \int f(y, z')Q(z, dz'), \quad \text{all } (y, z) \in X \times Z,$$

is also bounded and continuous. If f is increasing (strictly increasing) in its first l arguments, then so is Tf; if f is concave (strictly concave) in its first l arguments, then so is Tf.

Proof. It is sufficient to show that for any bounded continuous function f, if $(y_n, z_n) \to (y, z)$, then

(1) $$\lim_{n\to\infty} \int |f(y, z') - f(y_n, z')|Q(z_n, dz') = 0;$$

the rest of the proof is exactly as presented in Lemma 9.5.

Let f be a bounded continuous function on $X \times Z$, and let $(y_n, z_n) \to (y, z)$. For each $\varepsilon > 0$, define

$$A_n(\varepsilon) = \{z' \in Z: |f(y, z') - f(y_n, z')| > \varepsilon\}, \quad n = 1, 2, \ldots,$$

and

$$E_k(\varepsilon) = \bigcup_{n=k}^{\infty} A_n(\varepsilon), \quad k = 1, 2, \ldots.$$

Notice that for each $\varepsilon > 0$, $\{E_k(\varepsilon)\}_{k=1}^{\infty}$ is a nested, decreasing sequence of sets. Moreover, since f is continuous and $y_n \to y$, for each fixed $z' \in Z$, the sequence (of real numbers) $\{f(y_n, z')\}$ converges to $f(y, z')$. Hence, for each $\varepsilon > 0$ and $z' \in Z$, $z' \notin A_n(\varepsilon)$, all n sufficiently large. Therefore, $\cap_{k=1}^{\infty} E_k(\varepsilon) = \emptyset$, all $\varepsilon > 0$.

Now fix k and consider the sets $E_k(\varepsilon)$, $\varepsilon > 0$. The boundaries of these sets are given by

$$\partial[E_k(\varepsilon)] = \{z' \in Z: |f(y, z') - f(y_n, z')| \leq \varepsilon,$$

all $n \geq k$, with equality for some $n\}$.

Hence for fixed k, the boundaries are distinct for different ε's; therefore at most a countable number of them have positive measure under $Q(z, \cdot)$. For each $k \geq 1$, let Δ_k be this countable set:

$$\Delta_k = \{\varepsilon > 0: Q(z, \partial[E_k(\varepsilon)]) > 0\}, \quad k = 1, 2, \ldots.$$

Since each set Δ_k is countable, so is their union $\Delta = \cup_{k=1}^{\infty} \Delta_k$.

Since $z_n \to z$ and Q has the Feller property, it follows that the sequence of probability measures $\{Q(z_n, \cdot)\}$ converges weakly to $Q(z, \cdot)$. It then follows from part (d) of Theorem 12.3 that for any $\varepsilon > 0$ that is *not* in Δ,

$$\lim_{n \to \infty} Q[z_n, E_k(\varepsilon)] = Q[z, E_k(\varepsilon)], \quad \text{all } k \geq 1.$$

We can now evaluate (1) as follows. For any $n \geq 1$ and $\varepsilon > 0$,

$$\int_Z |f(y, z') - f(y_n, z')| Q(z_n, dz')$$

$$= \int_{A_n(\varepsilon)} |f(y, z') - f(y_n, z')| Q(z_n, dz')$$

$$+ \int_{A_n^c(\varepsilon)} |f(y, z') - f(y_n, z')| Q(z_n, dz')$$

$$\leq 2\|f\| Q[z_n, A_n(\varepsilon)] + \varepsilon$$

$$\leq 2\|f\| Q[z_n, E_k(\varepsilon)] + \varepsilon, \quad \text{all } k \leq n.$$

Now choose any $\varepsilon > 0$ not in Δ, and any $k \geq 1$. Taking the limit as $n \to \infty$, we find that

$$\limsup_{n \to \infty} \int_Z |f(y, z') - f(y_n, z')| Q(z_n, dz')$$

$$\leq \lim_{n \to \infty} 2\|f\| \, Q[z_n, E_k(\varepsilon)] + \varepsilon$$

$$= 2\|f\| \, Q[z, E_k(\varepsilon)] + \varepsilon, \quad \text{all } k \geq 1, \text{ all } \varepsilon \notin \Delta.$$

Taking the limit on the right as $k \to \infty$ then gives

$$\limsup_{n \to \infty} \int_Z |f(y, z') - f(y_n, z')| Q(z_n, dz')$$

$$\leq 2\|f\| \lim_{k \to \infty} Q[z, E_k(\varepsilon)] + \varepsilon$$

$$= 0 + \varepsilon,$$

where the last line uses Theorem 7.1 and the fact that $\{E_k(\varepsilon)\}$ is a decreasing sequence with $\cap_{k=1}^{\infty} E_k(\varepsilon) = \emptyset$. Since this holds for every $\varepsilon > 0$ not in the countable set Δ, it follows that (1) holds. ∎

12.7   Bibliographic Notes

Our discussion of weak convergence in Section 12.1–12.3 is based on Billingsley (1968, chap. 1 and app. II), which is an excellent source for results on weak convergence in a variety of spaces. Billingsley (1979, chap. 5) contains much complementary material, including a good discussion of Helly's Theorem. Feller (1971, chap. VIII) contains a good discussion of convergence of distribution functions.

A one-dimensional version of Theorem 12.12, the monotonicity result in Section 12.4, is proved in Theorem 1 of Razin and Yahav (1979). Hopenhayn and Prescott (1987) strengthen this result by dropping the assumption that the transition function has the Feller property. See Torres (1988) for an excellent discussion of monotonicity in its various forms.

The analysis in Section 12.5 follows closely that in Manuelli (1985).

13   Applications of Convergence Results
       for Markov Processes

This chapter consists of applications of the convergence results for Markov processes reviewed in Chapters 11 and 12. Some of the economic models discussed here were introduced in Chapter 10, and we draw on results established there; others are new.

13.1   A Discrete-Space (s, S) Inventory Problem

The linear inventory problem discussed in Section 5.14 can also be formulated with stochastic demand. Let the manager begin the period with a stock x. He must immediately decide whether to place an order or not. If he does order, he can bring his stock up to any level y at a cost of $c_0 + c_1(y - x)$. After this decision is made, total demand for the product, call it z, is drawn from a known distribution. The manager then earns revenues of pz if his inventory exceeds z, and p times his inventory otherwise. It is a natural conjecture, on the basis of the analysis in Section 5.14, that the solution to this problem takes the form of an (s, S) policy, where s is the stock level below which it is optimal to place an order and S is the optimal size of total inventories after an order is placed. But this conjecture is false unless more structure is placed on the distribution of demand.

In this section we add such structure. We study an integer version of the problem that is similar to the one studied in Section 5.15 and examine the dynamics of the finite-state Markov chain that optimally managed inventories follow. In Section 13.2 we consider a situation in which demand has a continuous distribution. There we simply assume that an (s, S) policy is followed—ignoring the question of whether it is optimal—and study the resulting Markov process.

Let product demand z take on the value 1 with probability θ, or 0 with probability $1 - \theta$. We consider integer-valued stocks only: $x = 0, 1, 2, \ldots$. Then clearly an optimal policy has $s = 0$: there is no reason for the manager to place an order before he has stocked out, since one unit meets the maximum possible demand. Let $v(x)$ be the expected, present discounted value of profits if the current stock is x and an optimal ordering policy is followed. Then v must satisfy the functional equation

(1) $$v(x) = \theta[p + \beta v(x - 1)] + (1 - \theta)\beta v(x), \quad x = 1, 2, \ldots,$$

and the value $v(0)$ must satisfy

(2) $$v(0) = \max_{y \in \{1,2,\ldots\}} [-c_0 - c_1 y + v(y)].$$

Exercise 13.1   a. Show that under suitable restrictions on the parameters of the problem there is a function v satisfying (1) and (2), and a finite optimal order size S that solves (2). Characterize S in terms of $c_0, c_1, \beta, p,$ and θ.

Given S, optimally managed inventories are a Markov process with the state space $\{0, 1, 2, \ldots\}$.

Exercise 13.1   b. What is the transition matrix for this process? What are the ergodic and transient sets? Are there any cyclically moving subsets?
    c. Prove that this process has a unique invariant distribution and that the system converges to it from any initial distribution. Characterize this invariant distribution in terms of S.

13.2   A Continuous-State (s, S) Process

In this section we retain the other features of the model above but assume that demand takes values in the interval $Z = [0, \bar{z}]$. It is easy enough to write out the functional equation for this problem (try it), but, as one might guess from Section 5.14, the analysis is hard going. Here we simply assume that an (s, S) policy is followed and focus on characterizing the dynamics of inventories given this assumption.

Let $\mathfrak{Z}$ denote the Borel sets of Z, and let μ be a probability measure on $(Z, \mathfrak{Z})$. Assume that the sequence of demands $\{z_t\}$ is i.i.d., with common distribution μ each period. It is natural to assume that $s < \bar{z}$ (why?), and we will do so. Under these assumptions, inventories $\{x_t\}$ are a Markov process with state space $X = [0, \infty)$. In particular,

$$(1) \qquad x_{t+1} = \begin{cases} \max\{x_t - z_t, 0\} & \text{if } x_t > s \\ \max\{S - z_t, 0\} & \text{if } x_t \le s. \end{cases}$$

Exercise 13.2 a. Write the transition probability $P(x, A)$ corresponding to (1) for the case when A is an interval. Show that this is sufficient to define a transition function on $(X, \mathfrak{X})$. Does P have the Feller property?

As in the last section, the ergodic set for this problem is $[0, S]$ and the transient set is (S, ∞). Since any invariant measure for the process is concentrated on $[0, S]$, it is convenient to begin by studying the process on the smaller state space consisting of $[0, S]$ and its Borel subsets. After studying the convergence of the process on this state space, we can treat behavior on (S, ∞) by side arguments. This simplifying device is a standard.

For this process, we can apply Theorem 11.12 to prove that there exists a unique invariant measure λ^*, and that for any initial measure λ on $[0, S]$, the sequence $\{T^{*n}\lambda\}$ converges strongly to λ^*. We do this by verifying the hypotheses of Condition M via the sufficient condition given in Exercise 11.5a.

Exercise 13.2 b. Show that there is an integer $N \ge 1$ and an $\varepsilon > 0$ such that

$$P^N(x, \{0\}) \ge \varepsilon, \quad \text{all } x \in [0, S].$$

13.3 The One-Sector Model of Optimal Growth

Consider again the stochastic growth model with independent shocks studied in Section 10.1. For present purposes it is convenient to take output rather than the capital stock as the state variable and to use the second of the two formulations of a stochastic dynamic programming problem introduced in Section 9.1. The functional equation for the optimal growth problem is then

$$(1) \qquad v(x) = \max_{0 \leq y \leq x} \left[U(x - y) + \beta \int v[f(y)z] \, \mu(dz) \right].$$

Thus x is the quantity of output available (after production has taken place) in the current period, y is the quantity carried over as capital to be used in production next period, and $x - y$ is the quantity consumed. Next period, a shock z to the technology is drawn from the distribution μ. Then $f(y)z$ units of output are available next period, the new state.

We maintain Assumptions (U1)–(U5) from Section 5.1 on preferences and Assumptions (Z1)–(Z2) from Section 10.1 on the shocks. We add the following assumption, which ensures that μ assigns positive probability to all nondegenerate subintervals of $Z = [1, \bar{z}]$:

(Z3) for some $\alpha > 0$, $\mu((a, b]) \geq \alpha(b - a)$,   all $(a,b] \subset Z$.

We also maintain Assumptions (T1)–(T5) from Section 5.1 on the production function f, with the following important exception. We modify (T2) so that positive output is producible even with no capital: $f(0) > 0$. We also assume that $\beta f'(0) > 1$. The reason for these two assumptions will soon be clear.

As we did in Section 10.1, let $\bar{x} > 0$ be the unique value satisfying $\bar{x} = \bar{z} f(\bar{x})$; and let $X = [0, \bar{x}]$, with its Borel subsets $\mathcal{X}$.

Exercise 13.3   a. Show that there is a unique bounded continuous function $v \colon X \to \mathbf{R}$ satisfying (1) and that v is strictly increasing and strictly concave.

b. Show that the associated policy function $g \colon X \to X$ is single-valued, continuous, and strictly increasing, with $g(0) = 0$ and $0 < g(x) < x$, all $0 < x \leq \bar{x}$. Show that the consumption function $c \colon X \to X$ defined by $c(x) = x - g(x)$ is also strictly increasing.

c. Show that v is continuously differentiable, with $v'(x) = U'[x - g(x)]$.

Using the definition of the consumption function in part (b) and the result in part (c), we can combine the first-order and envelope conditions for (1) to get

(2) $U'[c(x)] = \beta \int U'(c[f(g(x))z])f'[g(x)]z\mu(dz).$

The policy function g defines a Markov process on X, corresponding to the stochastic difference equation

$$x_{t+1} = f[g(x_t)]z_{t+1}.$$

By Theorem 8.9, the functions f and g and the probability measure μ together define a transition function—call it P—on $(X, \mathscr{X})$; in addition, since f and g are continuous, it follows from Exercise 8.10 that P has the Feller property. Finally, since X is compact, it follows from Theorem 12.10 that P has at least one invariant measure.

The rest of this section consists of applying Theorem 12.12 to establish that this invariant measure—call it λ^*—is unique and that the system converges weakly to it from any initial condition: $T^{*n}\lambda_0 \Rightarrow \lambda^*$, all $\lambda_0 \in \Lambda(X, \mathscr{X})$. We begin with the following result.

Exercise 13.3   d. Show that P is monotone.

In view of (d), it remains only to verify that Assumption 12.1 holds. Let z^* be the mean of μ: $z^* = \int z\,\mu(dz)$, and define $x^* \in X$ as the unique value satisfying $\beta f'[g(x^*)]z^* = 1$. We will show that Assumption 12.1 holds for the interval $X = [0, \bar{x}]$ and the point x^*.

For any $x \in X$ and $z \in Z$, define the sequence $\{\phi_n(x, z)\}$ by

$$\phi_0(x, z) = x,$$

$$\phi_{n+1}(x, z) = f[g(\phi_n(x, z))]z, \quad n = 0, 1, 2, \ldots.$$

That is, $\phi_n(x, z)$ is the quantity of goods available at the beginning of period n if x is the quantity at the beginning of period 0, the stochastic shock takes the constant value $z_t = z$ every period, and the investment policy g is followed every period. Notice that since f and g are continuous and strictly increasing, the functions $\phi_n: X \times Z \to X$, $n = 1, 2, \ldots$, are also continuous and strictly increasing.

From (Z3) and from the fact that each function $\phi_n(x, \cdot)$ is strictly increasing in z, we conclude that

(3a) $P^n\big(x, (\phi_n(x, \bar{z} - \delta), \phi_n(x, \bar{z})]\big) \geq \alpha^n \delta^n$,

(3b) $P^n\big(x, (\phi_n(x, 1), \phi_n(x, 1 + \delta)]\big) \geq \alpha^n \delta^n$,

all $0 < \delta < \bar{z} - 1$, $n = 1, 2, \ldots$, all $x \in X$.

The rest of the proof consists of verifying Assumption 12.1 by considering (3a) for the case $x = 0$ and (3b) for the case $x = \bar{x}$.

Consider the sequence $\{\phi_n(0, \bar{z})\}_{n=0}^\infty$. Since

(4) $\phi_0(0, \bar{z}) = 0 < f(0)\bar{z} = f[g(0)]\bar{z} = \phi_1(0, \bar{z})$,

it follows by induction from the monotonicity of f and g that this sequence is nondecreasing. Since it is bounded above by $\bar{x}$, it converges to a value $\xi \in X$. By the continuity of f and g, $\xi = f[g(\xi)]\bar{z}$. Hence

$$U'[c(\xi)] = \beta \int U'[c(f[g(\xi)]z)]f'[g(\xi)]z\mu(dz)$$

$$= \beta f'[g(\xi)] \int U'[c(\xi z/\bar{z})]z\mu(dz)$$

$$> \beta f'[g(\xi)]U'[c(\xi)] \int z\mu(dz)$$

$$= \beta f'[g(\xi)]U'[c(\xi)]z^*,$$

where the first line follows from the first-order condition (2), the second from the fact above about ξ, the third from the concavity of U and the fact that $z/\bar{z} < 1$, and the last from the definition of z^*. Hence $1 > \beta f'[g(\xi)]z^*$, which in turn implies that $\xi > x^*$.

Next choose $N \geq 1$ such that $\phi_N(0, \bar{z}) > x^*$, and $\delta > 0$ such that $\phi_N(0, \bar{z} - \delta) > x^*$. Then $x^* < \phi_N(0, \bar{z} - \delta) < \phi_N(0, \bar{z}) \leq \bar{x}$. Hence

$$P^N\big(0, (x^*, \bar{x}]\big) \geq P^N\big(0, (\phi_N(0, \bar{z} - \delta), \phi_N(0, \bar{z})]\big) \geq \alpha^N \delta^N,$$

as was to be shown.

Exercise 13.3   e. Show that for some $N \geq 1$ and $\delta > 0$,

$$P^N\big(\bar{x}, (0, x^*]\big) \geq P^N\big(\bar{x}, (\phi_N(\bar{x}, 1), \phi_N(\bar{x}, 1 + \delta)]\big) \geq \alpha^N \delta^N.$$

The restriction $f(0) > 0$ is clearly necessary for this result, since otherwise the inequality in (4) does not hold. If $f(0) = 0$, then the singleton $\{0\}$

is an ergodic set for P. Thus even if it can be established—by an argument like the one above—that there is another ergodic set in X, the invariant measure is not unique. One way to deal with this situation [if one insists on assuming that $f(0) = 0$] is to find conditions under which it can be shown that $f[g(\varepsilon)] \geq \varepsilon$, for some $\varepsilon > 0$. Then one can take the state space to be $X = [\varepsilon, \bar{x}]$ and apply exactly the argument used above. We leave this as an exercise, but the reader is warned that it is by no means routine.

13.4 Industry Investment under Uncertainty

Recall the model of a surplus-maximizing industry subject to stochastic demand shocks considered in Section 10.4. The long-run average behavior of investment in such an industry can be studied using methods similar to those applied in the last section. The functional equation for the industry problem was

$$(1) \qquad v(x, z) = \max_{y \in X} \left[F(x, z) - xc(y/x) + (1 + r)^{-1} \int v(y, z')Q(z, dz') \right],$$

where $X = \mathbf{R}_{++}$ and where $Z = [\underline{z}, \bar{z}]$ is a compact interval in $\mathbf{R}_{++}$. We continue to assume that the functions F, c, and Q satisfy the restrictions stated in Section 10.4.

In Section 10.4 we assumed that Q was monotone and had the Feller property. Here we assume, in addition, that Q has the following property:

$(2) \qquad$ for some $N \geq 1$ and $\alpha > 0$,

$$Q^N(z, (a, b]) \geq \alpha(b - a), \quad \text{all } z \in Z, \text{ all } \underline{z} \leq a \leq b \leq \bar{z}.$$

Clearly (2) implies that Assumption 12.1 (in Section 12.4) is satisfied, where z^* can be any point in the interior of the interval Z. Then by Theorems 12.10 and 12.12, Q has an invariant measure μ^*, say, and if T^* is the Markov operator associated with Q, then $T^{*n}\mu \Rightarrow \mu^*$ for all $\mu \in \Lambda(Z, \mathcal{Z})$.

In parts (d) and (e) of Exercise 10.4 we showed that the policy function $g(x, z)$ for the dynamic program (1) is continuous and has two properties: for each $z \in Z$, $g(\cdot, z)$ is strictly increasing in x with a slope less than one; and for each fixed $x \in X$, $g(x, \cdot)$ is nondecreasing in z. Under these conditions, there exist unique values $0 < \underline{x}$ and $0 < \bar{x}$ satisfying

$$\underline{x} = g(\underline{x}, \underline{z}) \quad \text{and} \quad \bar{x} = g(\bar{x}, \bar{z}),$$

respectively. Clearly these values also satisfy $\underline{x} \leq \bar{x}$; let $\hat{X} = [\underline{x}, \bar{x}]$.

In part (f) of Exercise 10.4 we found that if $Q(z, \cdot)$ does not depend on z (that is, if the shocks are i.i.d.), then the optimal time path for industry capital is deterministic. In that case, $\underline{x} = \bar{x}$ and $\hat{X}$ consists of a single point: the stationary point of this deterministic difference equation. Here we consider the case where Q is any monotone transition function.

Let $\underline{s} = (\underline{x}, \underline{z})$ and $\bar{s} = (\bar{x}, \bar{z})$. We will first study the Markov process defined by Q and g on the state space $[\underline{s}, \bar{s}] = \hat{S} = \hat{X} \times Z$. Let $\hat{\mathcal{S}}$ be the Borel sets of $\hat{S}$. By Theorem 9.13, the function g and the transition function Q together define a transition function $\hat{P}$ on $(\hat{S}, \hat{\mathcal{S}})$.

Exercise 13.4   a. Show that $\hat{P}$ is monotone and has the Feller property.

By Theorem 12.10, it follows immediately from this exercise that $\hat{P}$ has an invariant measure. To establish uniqueness, we need to verify that Assumption 12.1 holds on the set $\hat{S}$.

Exercise 13.4   b. Prove that there exists a point $s^* \in \hat{S}$, an integer $N \geq 1$, and a number $\varepsilon > 0$ such that

$$\hat{P}^N(\underline{s}, [s^*, \bar{s}]) > \varepsilon \quad \text{and} \quad \hat{P}^N(\bar{s}, [\underline{s}, s^*]) > \varepsilon.$$

By Theorem 12.12, this establishes the uniqueness of an invariant measure λ^* on $(\hat{S}, \hat{\mathcal{S}})$ and the weak convergence of $T^{*n}\lambda$ to λ^* for all $\lambda \in \Lambda(\hat{S}, \hat{\mathcal{S}})$.

Now we return to the original state space $S = X \times Z$, where $X = \mathbf{R}_{++}$. The policy function g and the transition function Q define a transition function—call it P—on this larger space with its Borel sets $\mathcal{S}$. Let T^* be the associated Markov operator.

Exercise 13.4   c. Show that $T^{*n}\lambda \Rightarrow \lambda^*$ for all $\lambda \in \Lambda(S, \mathcal{S})$.

13.5 Equilibrium in a Pure Currency Economy

In many applications of economic interest, the object under study is the frequency distribution of a characteristic in the population. In the stationary state for such a model, the frequency distribution is invariant over time, so there is no uncertainty at the aggregate level. Prices and aggregate per capita variables are thus constant over time. If there are stochastic shocks at the individual level, however, so each individual faces a stochastic optimization problem, individual positions within the population change from period to period. In such a case the invariant measure for the Markov process of interest describes the population every period as well as the experience of each individual averaged over time. In this section we study an economy of this type in which currency is the only security held.

Consider an economy with a large number of households, each composed of one worker and one shopper. In each period each worker produces y units of consumption goods. However, a household cannot consume what it produces itself; rather, it must sell what it produces to other households and purchase what it consumes from other households. Trading takes place as follows. Each worker-shopper pair begins the period with some initial holdings of fiat money. The shopper goes out and uses all or part of this money to buy goods from other households. The worker stays at home and produces y units of output, which he or she sells to other households in exchange for fiat money. Consumption occurs at the end of the period when the shopper returns. Unspent currency plus receipts from the sale of goods determine the pair's initial cash balances at the beginning of the next day. There is no technology for enforcing credit contracts; hence no household is willing to extend credit.

All households have identical preferences ex ante, but each period each pair experiences a stochastic shock to its preferences. These shocks take values in a closed interval on the real line and will be denoted by $z \in Z = [\underline{z}, \bar{z}]$. The shocks are independent over time and across households. Let $\mathfrak{Z}$ be the Borel sets of Z, and let μ, a probability measure on $(Z, \mathfrak{Z})$, describe the distribution of the shocks. A pair's preferences are given by

$$E\left[\sum_{t=0}^{\infty} \beta^t U(c_t, z_t)\right],$$

where $0 < \beta < 1$ and where $U: \mathbf{R}_+ \times Z \to \mathbf{R}$ is bounded and continuously differentiable. Assume, in addition, that for each fixed $z \in Z$, $U(\cdot, z)$ is strictly increasing and strictly concave and that for each fixed $c \in \mathbf{R}_+$, $U_1(c, \cdot)$ is strictly increasing in z. That is, larger values of z are associated with higher marginal utilities at every level of consumption. We require μ to satisfy the same assumption we used in Section 13.3:

$$\text{for some } \alpha > 0, \quad \mu((a, b]) \geq \alpha(b - a), \quad \text{all } (a, b] \subset Z.$$

Assume that the price level p is constant over time, and consider the decision problem facing a typical household. Let M denote their beginning-of-period nominal money balances, and let $m = M/p$ denote their real balances. Then their decision problem can be written as

(1) $$v(m, z) = \max_{c, m' \geq 0} \left[U(c, z) + \beta \int v(m', z') \, \mu(dz') \right]$$

s.t. $m' + c - m - y \leq 0,$

$c - m \leq 0.$

The first constraint is that real balances at the beginning of next period plus current consumption cannot exceed current real balances plus real income from the sale of goods. (Note that both purchases and sales of goods have a real price of unity.) The second constraint is that the shopper's expenditures on the consumption good cannot exceed the pair's beginning-of-period cash balances. This constraint reflects the fact that, under the given description of trading, it is impossible for the pair to use currency obtained from the sale of current-period goods for the purchase of current-period goods. Current-period receipts can be used only for the purchase of goods in future periods.

The dynamic programming problem in (1) can be studied using the techniques developed in Chapter 9. The next exercises establish the main facts about (1).

Exercise 13.5   a. Show that there is a unique bounded continuous function v satisfying (1).

b. Show that for each $z \in Z$, $v(\cdot, z)$ is strictly increasing, strictly concave, and continuously differentiable in m. [*Hint.* To establish differentiability at the point where the cash-in-advance constraint just binds, show that the left and right derivatives are equal.]

c. Show that there is a continuous function $g(m, z)$ describing end-of-period real balances.

In order to study the evolution of a pair's real balances over time, we must characterize the policy function g more sharply. Since $c(m, z) = m + y - g(m, z)$, this argument will also characterize the optimal consumption policy.

Exercise 13.5 d. Show that for each fixed $z \in Z$, there exists some $\phi(z) > 0$ such that $g(\cdot, z) = y$ on $[0, \phi(z)]$, and $g(\cdot, z)$ is strictly increasing on $[\phi(z), \infty)$.

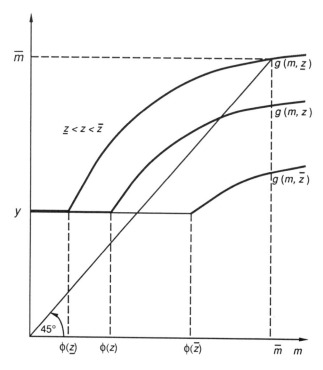

Figure 13.1

e. Show that for each fixed $z \in Z$, $c(\cdot, z)$ is strictly increasing on $[0, \infty)$ and hence that

$$m_1 < m_2 \text{ implies } 0 \le g(m_2, z) - g(m_1, z) < m_2 - m_1.$$

f. Show that there exists $\overline{m} > 0$ such that $g(\overline{m}, \underline{z}) = \overline{m}$.
g. Show that $\phi(\overline{z}) \ge y$. That is, $g(\cdot, \overline{z}) = y$ on $[0, y]$.
h. Show that for each $m \ge 0$, $g(m, \cdot)$ is weakly decreasing in z.

These exercises establish that the policy function g has the qualitative features displayed in Figure 13.1: the functions $g(\cdot, z)$ are ordered, as shown; each is constant on an interval $[0, \phi(z)]$ and strictly increasing with a slope less than unity on $[\phi(z), \infty)$; and each cuts the 45° line.

By Theorem 8.9, the function g and the measure μ together define a transition function P on $(\mathbf{R}_+, \mathcal{B}_+)$. Evidently the ergodic sets of this process are contained in the set $X = [y, \overline{m}]$, so it is convenient to treat X with its Borel subsets $\mathcal{X}$ as the state space of the process.

Exercise 13.5 i. Show that the Markov process on $(X, \mathcal{X})$ defined by P—that is, by g and μ—satisfies the hypotheses of Theorem 12.12.

Let λ^* denote the unique stationary probability measure on $(X, \mathcal{X})$.

The analysis thus far has dealt with consumption and real balances for a single household, with the price level p exogenously fixed and constant over time. Next we will show how the equilibrium price level p is determined for a long-run stationary equilibrium. Let M be the (exogenously given) per capita supply of nominal money balances. In market equilibrium in this economy the per capita demand for real cash balances, averaged over households, must equal per capita balances supplied M/p. But in the long run the average per capita demand over households is given by the stationary probability measure λ^*. Hence p must satisfy

$$(2) \qquad \int m \, \lambda^*(dm) = M/p.$$

Exercise 13.5 j. Show that (2) holds if and only if p satisfies

$$\int \int g(m, z)\mu(dz)\lambda^*(dm) = M/p,$$

where g is the pair's optimal policy function.

Note that if the initial distribution of money balances across households is different from λ^*, then the price level will not be constant over time. To study the evolution of the price level in this case, one would need to go back and re-solve the household's problem for situations where the price level is changing over time. This would not be an easy exercise.

13.6 A Pure Currency Economy with Linear Utility

The model of the last section has an intriguing structure when utility is linear, and in this case both the value function and the invariant measure can be calculated explicitly. Let $Z = [0, 1]$, and let $U(c, z) = zc$. Note that because U is unbounded, this model is not quite a special case of the last one. Hence we must analyze it from scratch.

The household's functional equation is now

(1) $$v(m, z) = \max_{m'} \left[(m + y - m')z + \beta \int v(m', z') \, \mu(dz') \right]$$

s.t. $y \le m' \le m + y$.

Exercise 13.6   a. Prove that for some $\zeta \in (0, 1)$ and $A > 0$,

$$v(m, z) = \begin{cases} \zeta m + A & \text{if } z < \zeta \\ zm + A & \text{if } z \ge \zeta, \end{cases}$$

satisfies (1), and

$$g(m, z) = \begin{cases} m + y & \text{if } z < \zeta \\ y & \text{if } z \ge \zeta, \end{cases}$$

is the associated policy function. Characterize ζ and A in terms of μ and β.

Let $X = [y, +\infty)$, with its Borel subsets $\mathcal{X}$. The policy function g and the measure μ define a transition function on $(X, \mathcal{X})$.

Exercise 13.6   b. Prove that the ergodic set for this process consists of y and its integer multiples.

In view of (b), the invariant distribution is a discrete probability distribution $\{\pi_i\}_{i=1}^{\infty}$, where $\pi_i = \Pr\{m = yi\}$.

      Exercise 13.6   c. Calculate π_i, $i = 1, 2, \ldots$.

An interesting variation on this model, or on the last one, is obtained by assuming that instead of holding the nominal money supply M constant, the monetary authority increases or decreases the money supply at a constant percentage rate via lump sum transfers. Try it. What can be said about the efficiency of equilibria in these models? How would their structure be altered if these monetary transfers were uniform across agents at a point in time but were stochastically chosen over time?

13.7   A Pure Credit Economy with Linear Utility

The households in the economies of Sections 13.5 and 13.6 can enjoy quite different consumption streams if we let them engage in securities trading. Recall that each household receives an endowment of y each period. Define one unit of the asset to be a claim to this endowment stream. Then a household's beginning-of-period state is defined by its current preference shock z and its asset holdings w. Of course, asset holdings must be nonnegative. Let Ψ_t, a probability measure on $\mathbf{R}_+$, denote the distribution of households by asset holdings at the beginning of period t. Then average holdings must satisfy

$$(1) \qquad \int w \, \Psi_t(dw) = 1, \quad t = 0, 1, 2, \ldots.$$

This general problem can be studied under the assumptions on preferences of Section 13.5 or of Section 13.6; we will look only at the latter case. In this case, household (w, z) wishes to maximize $E[\sum_{t=0}^{\infty} \beta^t z_t c_t]$, where the expectation is taken with respect to the i.i.d. shocks z_t, and where the probability measure μ for the shocks satisfies the assumptions that it did in the last two problems.

Suppose that the price of the asset, in terms of the consumption good, is constant over time, and let q denote this price. Then the functional equation for this problem is

(2) $v(w, z) = \max_{w'} \left\{ [(y + q)w - qw']z + \beta \int v(w', z')\, \mu(dz') \right\}$

s.t. $0 \le w' \le (1 + yq^{-1})w$.

Exercise 13.7   a. Solve (2) explicitly. Show that the optimal policy function has the form

(3) $w' = g(w, z) = \begin{cases} 0 & \text{if } z \ge \zeta \\ (1 + yq^{-1})w & \text{if } z < \zeta. \end{cases}$

Characterize the value ζ in terms of μ, β, and q.

Look at the behavior implied by (3)! Each period, a fraction $\mu([\zeta, 1])$ of the households sell their entire future income streams and consume the proceeds immediately. In doing this, they in effect leave the system forever. The policy function g given by (3), together with μ, define a Markov transition function and an associated operator T^*, just as they do in earlier problems in this chapter. Yet in this case we have the following result.

Exercise 13.7   b. Let Ψ_0 be a probability measure over wealth satisfying (1). Show that the sequence $\{T^{*n}\Psi_0\}$ does not converge weakly to an invariant measure.

Nevertheless, we can establish the following result. Note that in an equilibrium for this economy, (1) must hold.

Exercise 13.7   c. Show that for any initial probability measure Ψ_0 that satisfies (1), there is an equilibrium with a constant asset price q. In this equilibrium, the policy (3) with fixed cutoff ζ is optimal for households at each date, and (1) is satisfied for $\Psi_t = T^{*t}\Psi_0$, $t = 1, 2, \ldots$. Characterize the equilibrium price q in terms of β and μ. Show that it is independent of Ψ_0.

13.8   An Equilibrium Search Economy

In this problem we examine another economy in which individuals—in this case individual markets rather than individual agents—are subject to idiosyncratic shocks but in which the system has no aggregate uncertainty. It offers a model of search unemployment that is quite different from the one studied in Section 10.8.

We determine the general equilibrium in an economy consisting of a continuum of spatially separated markets, or "islands." Each island is subject to serially correlated productivity shocks that are independent across islands; there is no aggregate uncertainty. At the beginning of a period, a fixed population of infinitely lived workers is distributed in some way across the islands. Shocks are realized on each island, with each island's shock being common knowledge to workers on every island. Each worker then decides whether to stay where he is, earning a competitively determined local wage (in the form of a single consumption good that must be consumed on the spot), or to migrate to another island of his own choosing. If he chooses to migrate, his earnings (consumption) for the current period are zero, but he begins the following period on the new island. We interpret the fraction of workers in transit as the unemployment rate for the economy. Our objective is to determine the stationary equilibrium unemployment rate, the distribution of workers over islands, and the distribution of wages.

For most of our analysis we focus attention on a single island, taking the opportunities in the outside world as parametrically given. For this analysis it is convenient to think of an economy composed of one small island and two large "continents," one rich and one poor. The wage rate on each continent is constant over time, and the two rates differ by an amount that leaves workers on the poor continent just indifferent between staying where they are and forgoing consumption for one period to migrate to the rich continent. Think of the rich continent as the place to which workers on the island migrate if the local productivity shock is low enough and the poor continent as the place from which new workers arrive if local productivity is high enough. When we have completed the analysis of the economy composed of one island and two continents, we will return to the problem of determining the equilibrium in an economy composed of many islands.

The exogenous factors in the economy with one island and two continents are the stochastic process describing productivity shocks on the island, the technology for producing consumption goods on the island, workers' preferences, and the (constant) wage rates on the two continents. Given these, a stationary competitive equilibrium consists of a description of the decision rule workers use to decide when to relocate, the size of the labor force employed and the wage paid on the island as a function of its current state, and the equilibrium joint distribution of productivity shocks and labor force size on the island.

Exogenous Shocks In each period the island receives a productivity shock $z \in Z = [\underline{z}, \bar{z}]$. The sequence of shocks form a Markov process with transition function $Q: Z \times \mathcal{Z} \to [0, 1]$, where Q is monotone, has the Feller property, and satisfies the mixing assumption (2) that we used in Section 13.4. Let $\mu: \mathcal{Z} \to [0, 1]$ be the unique stationary probability measure for Q.

Technology The technology on the island is described by a function $f: \mathbf{R}_+ \times Z \to \mathbf{R}_+$, where $f(x, z)$ is the marginal product of labor when x is the size of the work force employed and z is the island's current productivity shock. The function f is continuous, and there exists some $\bar{x} > 0$ such that f has the following properties:

(F1) For each $z \in Z, f(\cdot, z): [0, \bar{x}] \to \mathbf{R}_+$ is strictly decreasing, with $f(0, z)$ finite and $f(\bar{x}, z) = 0$.

(F2) For each $x \in [0, \bar{x}], f(x, \cdot): Z \to \mathbf{R}_+$ is strictly increasing.

Define $X = [0, \bar{x}]$.

Preferences Workers do not value leisure, and their utility is linear in consumption:

$$(1) \qquad u(c) = \mathrm{E}\left[\sum_{t=0}^{\infty} \beta^t c_t\right],$$

where $0 < \beta < 1$.

At the beginning of each period, the state of the island is completely described by $(x, z) \in X \times Z$, where x is the size of its beginning-of-period work force and z is the value of its current-period technology shock.

Competitive Equilibrium A stationary competitive equilibrium consists of

(E1) a function $v: X \times Z \to \mathbf{R}_+$ describing the expected discounted wage stream of a worker currently residing on the island, as a function of the current state;

(E2) a function $g: X \times Z \to X$ describing the size of the end-of-period work force on the island, as a function of the current state;

(E3) an invariant measure $\lambda: \mathscr{X} \times \mathscr{X} \to [0, 1]$ describing the distribution of the state over time.

Note that v, g, and λ will all depend on the wage rates on the two continents.

In each period each worker either can work in his current place of residence or can experience a period of unemployment while moving. To study this choice, let $v: X \times Z \to \mathbf{R}_+$ be the function describing the expected present value of the wage stream for a worker currently residing on the island, as a function of the state of the island. If the worker chooses to remain on the island, $v(x, z)$ equals the current wage plus the expected value of the wage stream from next period on, discounted to the present. If the worker chooses to move, $v(x, z)$ equals the present discounted value of the wage stream from next period on. Note that with preferences given by (1), the discount factor is β.

We assume throughout that a worker on the island is paid his marginal product, and that a worker on either continent earns a constant wage. Let w be the wage rate on the rich continent and βw the wage on the poor one. This specification ensures that there is no incentive for direct migration from the poor continent to the rich one: the one period of lost earnings exactly offsets the higher wage paid on the rich continent. Let $\theta = w\beta/(1 - \beta)$, so that θ is the present value of the wage stream either of a worker currently on the poor continent or of a potential immigrant to the rich continent. (The distribution of profits does not affect workers' incentives and therefore will not be specified. It does, of course, affect the distribution of income and consumption.)

To develop the functional equation for v, for fixed $\theta \geq 0$, note that there are three qualitative situations for the island: it might be that some or all current workers leave, or that all current workers stay but no new workers arrive, or that all current workers stay and, in addition, new workers arrive. The island will never have workers leaving and arriving in the same period. It is convenient to consider the three cases separately.

Case A   Some or all current workers leave; no workers arrive. Suppose that for some (x, z),

$$(2a) \qquad f(x, z) + \beta \int v(x, z')Q(z, dz') < \theta.$$

This inequality says that if all workers were to stay on the island in state (x, z), each would have an expected wage stream strictly less than the present value of moving to the rich continent. Hence at least some workers choose to depart. The departing workers earn the expected return from search, θ. Remaining workers earn no less, since they have the option to leave, and no more, since departing workers have the option to remain. Hence

(3a) $\qquad v(x, z) = \theta$ if (2a) holds.

Clearly no worker on the poor continent has an incentive to move to the island when it is in this state.

    Case B   All current workers remain; no additional workers arrive. Suppose that

(2b) $\qquad \beta \int v(x, z')Q\,(z, dz') \le \theta \le f(x, z) + \beta \int v(x, z')Q(z, dz').$

Condition (2b) says that, if all current workers stay and no additional workers arrive, then the expected value of each current worker exceeds the value of moving to the rich continent; hence none chooses to depart. Condition (2b) also says that the expected value of a worker arriving from the poor continent is less than what he would earn by remaining on the poor continent; hence none chooses to arrive. Therefore, when (2b) holds, the entire current work force chooses to stay, but no new workers choose to arrive. Hence employment in the current period is x and the initial size of the work force in the next period is also x. Thus

(3b) $\qquad v(x, z) = f(x, z) + \beta \int v(x, z')Q(z, dz')$ if (2b) holds.

    Case C   All current workers remain; some additional workers arrive. Suppose that

(2c) $\qquad \theta < \beta \int v(x, z')Q(z, dz').$

Condition (2c) says that if no new workers were to arrive, the discounted wage stream from next period on of workers on the island would be greater than θ. Hence workers on the poor continent move to the island when it is in this state. The number of new workers arriving on the island is just enough to drive the expected present value (discounted to the present) of wages from tomorrow on down to θ. Thus for arriving workers and for the workers currently on the island, the expected present value of the wage stream from next period on is θ. Clearly no worker leaves the island when it is in this state, so the entire current work force is employed this period. Hence for any worker currently on the island,

(3c) $v(x, z) = f(x, z) + \theta$ if (2c) holds.

Combining (3b) and (3c), we find that

$$v(x, z) = f(x, z) + \min\left\{\theta, \beta \int v(x, z')Q(z, dz')\right\},$$

if (2b) or (2c) holds. Combining this equation with (3a) then yields

(4) $v(x, z) = \max\left\{\theta, \left[f(x, z) + \min\left\{\theta, \beta \int v(x, z')Q(z, dz')\right\}\right]\right\}.$

Exercise 13.8   a. Show that for any $\theta > 0$ there exists a unique bounded continuous function $v: X \times Z \to \mathbf{R}_+$ satisfying (4) and that v is bounded above by $\max\{\theta, f(0, \bar{z})/(1 - \beta)\}$. Show that $v(x, z)$ is nonincreasing in x and nondecreasing in z.

Next consider what the work force will be on the island next period, as a function of the island's current state. Given the function v satisfying (4), the inequalities in (2a)–(2c) partition the state space $X \times Z$ into three regions. Define $g: X \times Z \to X$ as follows:

(5a) $f[g(x, z), z] + \beta \int v[g(x, z), z']Q(z, dz') \le 0,$

            with equality if $g(x, z) > 0$,   if (2a) holds;

(5b) $g(x, z) = x,$ if (2b) holds;

(5c) $\beta \int v[g(x, z), z']Q(z, dz') = 0,$ if (2c) holds.

Exercise 13.8 b. Show that g is nondecreasing in x and z. Show that for any $z \in Z$,

$$|g(x, z) - g(x', z)| \le |x - x'|, \quad \text{all } x, x' \in X.$$

c. Show that g is continuous on $X \times Z$.

For fixed $z \in Z$, $g(\cdot, z)$ is as shown in Figure 13.2.

By Theorem 9.13, the function g defined by (5a)–(5c), together with the transition function Q, define a transition function P on $(X \times Z, \mathcal{X} \times \mathcal{Z})$ that describes the law of motion for the state. By part (c) of Exercise 13.8 and Theorem 9.14, P has the Feller property. If the island is currently in state (x, z), then next period it will have a population of size $x' = g(x, z)$ and a randomly drawn productivity shock z' with distribution given by $Q(z, \cdot)$.

The set $S = X \times Z$ is compact and P has the Feller property, so by Theorem 12.10, P has an invariant measure. But our assumptions to this point leave open the possibility that, as z fluctuates, earning prospects on

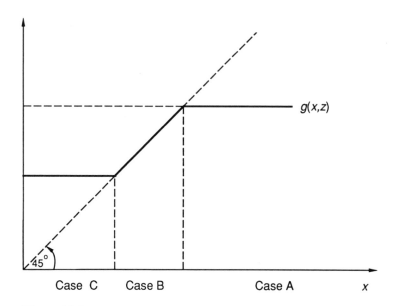

Figure 13.2

the island never become attractive enough to induce immigration or discouraging enough to induce emigration. If there is an interval of initial x values for which this is true, there is a corresponding multiplicity of invariant measures for (x, z). To prove that there exists a unique invariant measure, then, we must ensure that for θ values in a relevant range there is always some incentive for migration.

Define $w: X \times Z \to \mathbf{R}_+$ by

$$w(x, z) = f(x, z) + \beta \int w(x, z')Q(z, dz').$$

Thus, $w(x, z)$ is the expected discounted wage stream of a worker on the island if the population is constant at x (no migration) and the current productivity shock is z. Note that

$$w(\bar{x}, z) = 0, \quad \text{all } z \in Z.$$

In addition, we assume that

(6) $w(x, \underline{z}) < \beta \int w(x, z')Q(\bar{z}, dz'), \quad \text{all } x \in [0, \bar{x}).$

This inequality says that, given any fixed population size $x \in [0, \bar{x})$, with no possibility for migration, it is always better to start work tomorrow on an island that has current shock $\bar{z}$ than to start work today on an island that has current shock $\underline{z}$. Note that (6) is a joint restriction on f, Q, and β. It is violated if f depends too little on its second argument, if Q displays too little serial correlation, or if β is too close to zero.

> **Exercise 13.8**   d. Show that if (6) holds, then for any $\theta > 0$, P has a unique invariant measure λ on $\mathcal{X} \times \mathcal{Z}$. [*Hint*. Show that if (6) holds, then for all θ sufficiently large,
>
> (7) $v(x, z; \theta) = \theta \quad \text{and} \quad g(x, z, \theta) = 0, \quad \text{all } (x, z) \in X \times Z.$
>
> Let $\bar{\theta}$ be the smallest θ such that (7) holds. Let $\Theta = (0, \bar{\theta})$. Show that for all $\theta \in \Theta$, $v(\cdot, \cdot; \theta)$ is such that (2a) and (2c) hold over some regions of the state space.]

There are other conditions that might be employed in order to ensure uniqueness. For example, there may be a few workers that enter or leave the work force for reasons other than current market conditions.

Exercise 13.8 e. Modify the model so that each period a fraction γ of the workers currently on the island leave for idiosyncratic reasons such as health. Establish that the invariant measure is unique in the model so modified.

In Exercise 13.8d we have obtained a complete characterization of the stationary equilibrium in the economy composed of one island and two continents, taking as given the value of the parameter θ. We now return to the economy consisting of a continuum of islands, all with the same structure as the island just studied, with productivity shocks that are independent across islands. To determine the equilibrium in this system, we reinterpret the parameter θ as the present value of earnings for a worker who migrates to the best available alternative island. As in the analysis just completed, individual workers treat θ as given to them; for each worker, it plays the role of a competitive market price. Thus, the analysis of the functional equation (4) and of the Markov process it gives rise to continue to apply, both conditional on θ. But now we wish to determine θ endogenously, as the value that equates the average work force on an island to the exogenously given average population per island, N.

Let λ_θ denote the invariant measure found in Exercise 13.8d, where the notation emphasizes its dependence on θ. We seek a value for θ such that

$$D(\theta) = \int x\, \lambda_\theta(dx \times dz) = N.$$

To establish the existence of a value θ satisfying this equation, we first establish the following facts.

Exercise 13.8 f. Show that $D(0) = \bar{x}$ and that for some $\bar{\theta}$ sufficiently large, $\theta \geq \bar{\theta}$ implies $D(\theta) = 0$.

g. Show that D is continuous by verifying the hypotheses of Theorem 12.13.

We can establish that there is at most one positive equilibrium value for θ by showing that $D(\theta)$ is strictly decreasing for $\theta > 0$. Let T_θ be the Markov operator associated with P_θ, and let T_θ^* be its adjoint. We have shown, in Exercise 13.8c, that

$$D(\theta) = \int x \, \lambda_\theta(dx \times dz) = \lim_{n \to \infty} \int x \, (T_\theta^{*n}\lambda_0)(dx \times dz),$$

for any initial measure λ_0 on $\mathscr{X} \times \mathscr{Z}$. (Why?) Then it follows from Theorem 8.3 that

$$D(\theta) = \lim_{n \to \infty} \int (T_\theta^n x)\lambda_0(dx \times dz).$$

Exercise 13.8 h. Use the definition of T_θ in terms of the policy function $g_\theta(x, z)$ to show that $D(\theta)$ is nonincreasing. How can this argument be strengthened to show that $D(\theta)$ is strictly decreasing when $\theta > 0$?

13.9 Bibliographic Notes

Scarf (1959) contains counterexamples to the conjecture that the stochastic linear inventory problem always has a solution of the (s, S) form. That paper also provides conditions on the probability measure μ for the shocks that are sufficient to ensure that an (s, S) policy is optimal. Iglehart (1963) also provides sufficient conditions for the optimality of (s, S) policies. Caplin (1985) analyzes a Markov chain arising from (s, S) policies in a formulation that is more general than the one in Section 13.1.

Section 13.2 is in the spirit of chapter 14 of Arrow, Karlin, and Scarf (1958), where characteristics of the stochastic processes for inventories are derived taking the parameters s and S as given. Examples of explicit solutions for the invariant distributions of such processes are also provided.

The stochastic growth model in Section 13.3 is taken from Brock and Mirman (1972). See also the other references in Section 10.13. The proof of convergence used here, based on monotonicity, is from Razin and Yahav (1979). Brock and Mirman provide an argument that also applies when $f(0) = 0$. Majumdar and Radner (1983) study the existence of stationary equilibria in a much more general setting.

The model of industry investment under uncertainty in Section 13.4 is from Lucas and Prescott (1971). The convergence argument here, based on monotonicity, is new. Sargent (1980) studies a general equilibrium investment problem in which the nonnegativity constraint on gross investment is crucial.

The model of a pure currency economy in Section 13.5 is taken from Lucas (1980). See also the earlier, similar model of Foley and Hellwig (1975). Again, the convergence proof here is new. The linear utility version in Section 13.6 is from Taub (1988a). Taub (1988b) studies a credit economy similar to the one studied in Section 13.7.

The model of the search economy in Section 13.8 is based on Lucas and Prescott (1974), but the analysis here is quite different.

14   Laws of Large Numbers

In Chapters 11 and 12 we developed methods for characterizing the long-run behavior of a recursive system in terms of the sequence of probability measures on the state space in successive periods implied by the model. As the applications in Chapter 13 showed, this type of analysis gives a good deal of insight into the outcomes such models generate. By itself, however, it does not form a basis for systematic empirical work. In this chapter we carry the analysis a little further and show how recursive models can be used as the bases for empirical studies.

Suppose that we are interested in whether a certain model is consistent with a set of data, where the data are simply time series for some observable function(s) of the state. That is, the data are sequences of the form $\{f(s_n)\}$, where s_n is the state in period n, and where $f: S \rightarrow \mathbf{R}$ is a fixed, real-valued function. Then we must decide what properties for such sequences are implied by the theoretical model. To study this issue, we adopt the same framework we used in Chapters 11 and 12.

Let $(S, \mathcal{S})$ be a measurable space; let $\Lambda(S, \mathcal{S})$ be the space of probability measures on $(S, \mathcal{S})$; let P be a transition function on $(S, \mathcal{S})$; and let T^* be the operator on probability measures associated with P (cf. Section 8.1). Given an arbitrary initial probability measure λ_0, define the sequence $\{\lambda_n\}$ recursively by $\lambda_{n+1} = T^*\lambda_n$, $n = 0, 1, \ldots$. In Chapters 11 and 12 we developed conditions on $(S, \mathcal{S})$ and P sufficient to ensure the strong and weak convergence of the sequence of averages $\{(1/N) \sum_{n=1}^{N} \lambda_n\}$ or the sequence $\{\lambda_n\}$ itself to an invariant probability measure—a fixed point of T^*. Thus, Chapters 11 and 12 dealt with the convergence of sequences of probability measures, objects that are not directly observable.

Suppose that the sequence $\{(1/N) \sum_{n=1}^{N} \lambda_n\}$ converges weakly to a unique invariant probability measure λ^*, for all λ_0. Then for any continuous function f and any initial state s_0, it is natural to take the expected value $\int f \, d\lambda^*$ as a prediction about the long-run average behavior of the observed values of f, that is, as a prediction about $(1/N) \sum_{n=1}^{N} f(s_n)$ as $N \to \infty$. In this chapter we develop the language needed to make this statement more precise and provide conditions under which the desired conclusion holds.

To begin, we need several definitions. Let $(\Omega, \mathcal{F}, \mu)$ be a probability space, and let $\{f_n\}_{n=1}^{\infty}$ and f be random variables (measurable, real-valued functions) on $(\Omega, \mathcal{F})$. Recall that we say that $\{f_n\}$ converges to f *almost everywhere* (*a.e.* or *μ-a.e.*) if there is a set $A \in \mathcal{F}$ with $\mu(A) = 0$ such that

$$\lim_{n \to \infty} f_n(\omega) = f(\omega), \quad \text{all } \omega \in A^c.$$

In probabilistic settings this is also referred to as convergence *almost surely* (*a.s.*). In this chapter we will also make use of a weaker notion of convergence for such a sequence. We say that $\{f_n\}$ converges to f *in probability* (*in pr.*) if

$$\lim_{n \to \infty} \mu(\{\omega \in \Omega : |f_n(\omega) - f(\omega)| > \varepsilon\}) = 0, \quad \text{all } \varepsilon > 0.$$

This limiting property is also called convergence *in measure*. Notice that both definitions require that we specify in advance a fixed probability measure μ on $(\Omega, \mathcal{F})$; let $E(\cdot)$ denote integration with respect to this fixed measure. If the sequence of random variables $\{f_n\}$ is such that

(1) $$\frac{1}{N} \sum_{n=1}^{N} [f_n - E(f_n)] \to 0$$

in pr., we say that $\{f_n\}$ satisfies a *weak law of large numbers*. If the convergence in (1) is a.e., we say that $\{f_n\}$ satisfies a *strong law of large numbers*.

Our objective in this chapter is to establish a strong law for Markov processes. To do this, we must first decide how such a law is to be stated. Let $(S, \mathcal{S})$, P, and s_0 be given; let $[S^{\infty}, \mathcal{S}^{\infty}, \mu^{\infty}(s_0, \cdot)] = (\Omega, \mathcal{F}, \mu)$ be the probability space of infinite sequences defined in Section 8.2; and for each $(s_1, s_2, \ldots) = \omega \in \Omega$, let $\sigma_n(\omega) = s_n$ denote the nth component of ω. Then for any function $f : S \to \mathbf{R}$, define the sequence of functions $\hat{f}_n : \Omega \to \mathbf{R}$ by $\hat{f}_n(\omega) = f[\sigma_n(\omega)] = f(s_n)$, $n = 1, 2, \ldots$. Now suppose that $(S, \mathcal{S})$ and P are such that $\{(1/N) \sum_{n=1}^{N} \lambda_n\}$ converges weakly to a unique invariant probability measure λ^*, for all λ_0. Then in particular, that sequence converges if λ_0 puts probability one on the point s_0. Hence

$$\lim_{N \to \infty} \frac{1}{N} \sum_{n=1}^{N} E[\hat{f}_n(\omega)] = \lim_{N \to \infty} \frac{1}{N} \sum_{n=1}^{N} E\{f[\sigma_n(\omega)]\}$$

$$= \lim_{N \to \infty} \frac{1}{N} \sum_{n=1}^{N} \int f(s_n) \, d\lambda_n$$

$$(2) \qquad\qquad\qquad = \int f(s) \, d\lambda^*,$$

where $E(\cdot)$ denotes integration with respect to $\mu^{\infty}(s_0, \cdot)$. Since s_0 and f were arbitrary, (2) holds for all $s_0 \in S$ and $f \in C(S)$. Hence we say that a Markov process satisfies a strong law of large numbers if it has the weak convergence property described above and if

$$(3) \qquad \lim_{N \to \infty} \frac{1}{N} \sum_{n=1}^{N} f(s_n) - \int f \, d\lambda^* = 0 \quad \text{a.e.,} \quad \text{all } f \in C(S), \text{ all } s_0 \in S.$$

In this chapter we show that (3) holds if S is a compact set in a finite-dimensional Euclidean space and the transition function P has the Feller property.

In Section 14.1 we develop a series of laws of large numbers, dealing first with uncorrelated random variables and then with variables that display a certain type of correlation. Then in Section 14.2 we apply the latter result to Markov processes. Some of the arguments developed in this chapter are rather long and difficult, and none of them will be used elsewhere in the book. Thus, skipping this chapter on first reading causes no loss in continuity.

14.1   Definitions and Preliminaries

In this section we prove several laws of large numbers, culminating in a strong law of large numbers for a class of correlated random variables. We begin with a series of preliminary results, Lemmas 14.1–14.3, that provide alternative sufficient conditions for convergence a.e. Then in Theorem 14.4 we use Chebyshev's inequality to prove a weak law of large numbers for uncorrelated random variables, and in Theorem 14.5 we strengthen this result to obtain a strong law. Finally, in Theorem 14.6 we provide a strong law for a class of correlated random variables, a result we draw on in the next section to prove a strong law for Markov processes.

Throughout this section, we take $(\Omega, \mathscr{F}, \mu)$ to be a fixed probability space and let $E(\cdot)$ denote integration over Ω with respect to the measure μ. That is, for any random variable f on $(\Omega, \mathscr{F})$, $E(f) = \int f \, d\mu$. We also adopt a shorthand notation, standard in probability theory, and use $\mu(f$ has property $X)$ to denote $\mu(\{\omega \in \Omega : f(\omega)$ has property $X\})$.

Our first result is an alternative characterization of convergence a.e.

LEMMA 14.1 $f_n \to f$ *a.e. if and only if*

(1) $\lim\limits_{m \to \infty} \mu(|f_n - f| \le \varepsilon, \text{ all } n \ge m) = 1, \quad \text{all } \varepsilon > 0.$

Proof. Define the sets

$$A = \{f_n(\omega) \to f(\omega)\}; \quad \text{and}$$

$$A_m(\varepsilon) = \{|f_n - f| \le \varepsilon, \text{ all } n \ge m\}, \quad \text{all } \varepsilon > 0, m = 1, 2, \ldots.$$

Then to prove the lemma, it suffices to show that

$$\mu(A) = 1 \text{ if and only if } \lim\limits_{m \to \infty} \mu[A_m(\varepsilon)] = 1, \quad \text{all } \varepsilon > 0.$$

First note that for any fixed $\varepsilon > 0$, $\{A_m(\varepsilon)\}$ is a nested increasing sequence of sets. Note, too, that if $\omega \in A$, then $\omega \in A_m(\varepsilon)$ for all m sufficiently large. Hence $A \subseteq \cup_{m=1}^{\infty} A_m(\varepsilon)$. Suppose that $\mu(A) = 1$. Then using Theorem 7.1, we find that

$$1 \ge \lim\limits_{m \to \infty} \mu[A_m(\varepsilon)] = \mu\left[\bigcup_{m=1}^{\infty} A_m(\varepsilon)\right] \ge \mu(A) = 1, \quad \text{all } \varepsilon > 0.$$

Conversely, suppose that $\lim_{m \to \infty} \mu[A_m(\varepsilon)] = 1$, all $\varepsilon > 0$. Let $A(\varepsilon) = \cup_{m=1}^{\infty} A_m(\varepsilon)$. Then Theorem 7.1 implies that

$$\mu[A(\varepsilon)] = \mu \left[\bigcup_{m=1}^{\infty} A_m(\varepsilon) \right] = \lim_{m \to \infty} \mu[A_m(\varepsilon)] = 1, \quad \text{all } \varepsilon > 0.$$

Let $\{\varepsilon_k\}$ be a decreasing sequence converging to zero. Then $\{A(\varepsilon_k)\}$ is a nested decreasing sequence of sets, and $A = \cap_{k=1}^{\infty} A(\varepsilon_k)$. Hence, applying Theorem 7.1 again, we obtain

$$\mu(A) = \mu \left[\bigcap_{k=1}^{\infty} A(\varepsilon_k) \right] = \lim_{k \to \infty} \mu[A(\varepsilon_k)] = 1. \quad \blacksquare$$

Let $\{A_n\}$ be any sequence of sets in $\mathcal{F}$. Then we define the measurable set $\limsup A_n$ by

$$\limsup A_n = \bigcap_{m=1}^{\infty} \bigcup_{n=m}^{\infty} A_n.$$

Thus ω is an element of $\limsup A_n$ if and only if it is contained in an infinite number of the sets A_n. Stated a little differently, the event $\limsup A_n$ occurs if and only if infinitely many of the events in the sequence $\{A_n\}$ occur. In this case we say that the events A_n occur *infinitely often (i.o.)*. Note that $\{\cup_{n=m}^{\infty} A_n\}$ is a nested, decreasing sequence of sets. Hence

$$(2) \qquad \mu(A_n \text{ i.o.}) = \mu(\limsup A_n) = \mu \left(\bigcap_{m=1}^{\infty} \bigcup_{n=m}^{\infty} A_n \right) = \lim_{m \to \infty} \mu \left(\bigcup_{n=m}^{\infty} A_n \right),$$

where the last step uses Theorem 7.1.

The next lemma, a fairly immediate consequence of (2) and Lemma 14.1, provides a slightly different characterization of convergence a.e.

LEMMA 14.2 $f_n \to f$ *a.e. if and only if*

$$\mu(|f_n - f| > \varepsilon \text{ i.o.}) = 0, \quad \text{all } \varepsilon > 0.$$

Proof. Let $A_n(\varepsilon) = \{|f_n - f| > \varepsilon\}$, $n = 1, 2, \ldots$, all $\varepsilon > 0$. Then (2) implies that

$$\mu(|f_n - f| > \varepsilon \text{ i.o.}) = \mu[A_n(\varepsilon) \text{ i.o.}]$$

$$= \lim_{m \to \infty} \mu\left[\bigcup_{n=m}^{\infty} A_n(\varepsilon)\right], \quad \text{all } \varepsilon > 0.$$

Hence by Lemma 14.1, it suffices to show that (1) holds if and only if $\lim_{m \to \infty} \mu[\bigcup_{n=m}^{\infty} A_n(\varepsilon)] = 0$, all $\varepsilon > 0$. This conclusion follows directly from the fact that

$$\{|f_n - f| \le \varepsilon, \text{ all } n \ge m\} = \bigcap_{n=m}^{\infty} A_n^c(\varepsilon) = \left[\bigcup_{n=m}^{\infty} A_n(\varepsilon)\right]^c,$$

$$m = 1, 2, \ldots, \text{ all } \varepsilon > 0. \quad \blacksquare$$

The next result draws on this lemma to provide a sufficient condition for convergence a.e.

LEMMA **14.3** *If*

$$\sum_{n=1}^{\infty} \mu(|f_n - f| > \varepsilon) < \infty, \text{ all } \varepsilon > 0,$$

then $f_n \to f$ *a.e.*

Proof. By Lemma 14.2, it suffices to show that for any sequence of sets $\{A_n\}$ in $\mathcal{F}$,

$$\sum_{n=1}^{\infty} \mu(A_n) < \infty \text{ implies } \mu(A_n \text{ i.o.}) = 0.$$

To establish the latter, note that for any sequence of sets $\{A_n\}$ in $\mathcal{F}$,

$$\mu\left(\bigcup_{n=m}^{\infty} A_n\right) \le \sum_{n=m}^{\infty} \mu(A_n), \quad m = 1, 2, \ldots.$$

Moreover,

$$\sum_{n=1}^{\infty} \mu(A_n) < \infty \text{ implies } \lim_{m \to \infty} \sum_{n=m}^{\infty} \mu(A_n) = 0.$$

Hence using (2), we have

$$\mu(A_n \text{ i.o.}) = \lim_{m \to \infty} \mu \left(\bigcup_{n=m}^{\infty} A_n \right) \leq \lim_{m \to \infty} \sum_{n=m}^{\infty} \mu(A_n) = 0. \quad \blacksquare$$

It follows directly from Lemma 14.1 that convergence almost every-where implies convergence in probability; so a "strong law" is indeed stronger than a "weak law." The converse, however, is not true.

Exercise 14.1 Let $(\Omega, \mathcal{F}, \mu)$ be the unit interval $[0, 1)$, with the Borel subsets and Borel measure. For each $n \geq 1$ and $1 \leq i \leq n$, define

$$f_{ni}(\omega) = \begin{cases} 1 & \text{if } \omega \in [(i-1)/n, i/n) \\ 0 & \text{otherwise.} \end{cases}$$

Consider the sequence of random variables $(f_{11}, f_{21}, f_{22}, f_{31}, f_{32}, f_{33}, \ldots)$.
  a. Show that this sequence does not converge at any point of Ω and, hence, does not converge a.e.
  b. Show that this sequence converges in pr. to the random variable that is identically zero.
  c. Identify a subsequence that converges a.e.

Exercise 14.2 Let $(\Omega, \mathcal{F}, \mu)$ be a probability space and let $\{f_n\}$ and f be random variables.
  a. Let $\{\varepsilon_n\}$ be a sequence of positive numbers converging to zero. Show that if $\sum_{n=1}^{\infty} \mu(|f_n - f| > \varepsilon_n) < +\infty$, then $f_n \to f$ a.e. [*Hint.* Adapt the proof of Lemma 14.3.]
  b. Show that if $f_n \to f$ in pr., then there exists a subsequence $\{f_{n_k}\}$ converging to f a.e. [*Hint.* Let $n_1 > 1$ satisfy $\mu(|f_{n_1} - f| > 1) \leq 1/2$. Then define the sequence $\{n_k\}$ inductively by $n_k > n_{k-1}$ and $\mu(|f_{n_k} - f| > 1/k) \leq 1/2^k$, and apply the result in part (a).]

We turn next to three laws of large numbers. Theorems 14.4 and 14.5 are weak and strong laws respectively for uncorrelated random variables. These are presented to make clear the ideas behind the proof of Theorem 14.6, a strong law for a class of correlated random variables, which is the result we draw on in the next section.

The proof of Theorem 14.4 uses the fact that for any random variable h with $E(h^2) < \infty$:

$$E(h^2) = \int_\Omega h^2 \, d\mu \geq \int_{|h| \geq \varepsilon} h^2 \, d\mu \geq \varepsilon^2 \mu(|h| \geq \varepsilon), \quad \text{all } \varepsilon > 0,$$

from which it follows that

(3) $\qquad \mu(|h| \geq \varepsilon) \leq E(h^2)/\varepsilon^2, \quad \text{all } \varepsilon > 0.$

This fact is called **Chebyshev's inequality**.

We also need to recall the definition of uncorrelated random variables.

DEFINITION *A sequence of random variables $\{f_k\}$ is **uncorrelated** if*

$$E(f_k^2) < \infty, k = 1, 2, \ldots, \quad \text{and} \quad E(f_j f_k) = E(f_j)E(f_k), \quad \text{all } j \neq k.$$

For any sequence of uncorrelated random variables, it follows immediately that

(4) $\qquad E\{[f_j - E(f_j)][f_k - E(f_k)]\} = 0, \quad \text{all } j \neq k.$

Using (3) and (4), we can establish the following weak law of large numbers for uncorrelated random variables.

THEOREM 14.4 *Let $\{f_k\}$ be a sequence of uncorrelated random variables with $E\{[f_k - E(f_k)]^2\} < M$, all k, for some $M < \infty$. Then*

(5) $\qquad \dfrac{1}{n} \displaystyle\sum_{k=1}^{n} [f_k - E(f_k)] \to 0 \quad \text{in pr.}$

Proof. Let $h_k = [f_k - E(f_k)]$, $k = 1, 2, \ldots$. Then (4) implies that $E(h_j h_k) = 0$, all $j \neq k$, so the partial sums satisfy

(6) $$E\left[\left(\sum_{k=1}^{n} h_k\right)^2\right] = \sum_{k=1}^{n} E(h_k^2) + \sum_{\substack{j,k=1 \\ j \neq k}}^{n} E(h_j h_k)$$

$$\leq nM + 0.$$

It then follows from Chebyshev's inequality that

(7) $$\mu\left(\left|\sum_{k=1}^{n} h_k\right| \geq n\varepsilon\right) \leq nM/n^2\varepsilon^2 = M/n\varepsilon^2, \quad \text{all } \varepsilon > 0.$$

Hence

$$\lim_{n \to \infty} \mu\left(\left|\frac{1}{n}\sum_{k=1}^{n} h_k\right| \geq \varepsilon\right) \leq \lim_{n \to \infty} M/n\varepsilon^2 = 0, \quad \text{all } \varepsilon > 0,$$

so that (5) holds. ∎

Our next result shows that under the same hypotheses, (5) holds a.e.

THEOREM 14.5 *Let $\{f_k\}$ be a sequence of uncorrelated random variables, with $E\{[f_k - E(f_k)]^2\} < M$, all k, for some $M < \infty$. Then (5) holds a.e.*

Proof. Let $h_k = [f_k - E(f_k)]$, $k = 1, 2, \ldots$, and define the partial sums $g_n = \sum_{k=1}^{n} h_k$, $n = 1, 2, \ldots$. We wish to show that $g_n/n \to 0$ a.e. As shown in (7),

(8) $$\mu(|g_n| \geq n\varepsilon) \leq M/n\varepsilon^2, \quad \text{all } \varepsilon > 0.$$

We would like to apply Lemma 14.3, but summing (8) over n gives

$$\sum_{n=1}^{\infty} \mu(|g_n| \geq n\varepsilon) \leq \frac{M}{\varepsilon^2} \sum_{n=1}^{\infty} \frac{1}{n},$$

and the series on the right does not converge. Instead, we apply a device called the *method of subsequences*.

Consider the subsequence $n_k = k^2$, $k = 1, 2, \ldots$. Summing (8) along this subsequence, we find that

$$\sum_{k=1}^{\infty} \mu(|g_{k^2}| > k^2 \varepsilon) \leq \frac{M}{\varepsilon^2} \sum_{k=1}^{\infty} \frac{1}{k^2} < \infty, \quad \text{all } \varepsilon > 0.$$

Hence it follows from Lemma 14.3 that the subsequence $\{g_{k^2}/k^2\}$ converges to zero a.e.

The rest of the proof consists of showing that each term in the sequence $\{g_n/n\}$ is close to a neighboring term in the sequence $\{g_{k^2}/k^2\}$. Define

$$D_{k,n} = |g_n - g_{k^2}|, \quad \text{all } k \geq 1, n = k^2 + 1, \ldots, (k+1)^2 - 1.$$

Then for each (k, n),

$$E(D_{k,n}^2) = E(|g_n - g_{k^2}|^2) = E\left(\left|\sum_{i=k^2+1}^{n} h_i\right|^2\right)$$

$$\leq E\left(\sum_{i=k^2+1}^{(k+1)^2-1} h_i^2\right) + 0 \leq 2kM,$$

where we have again used the fact that the h_i's are uncorrelated. Hence by Chebyshev's inequality,

(9) $\quad \mu(D_{k,n} \geq k^2 \varepsilon) \leq 2kM/k^4 \varepsilon^2 = 2M/k^3 \varepsilon^2, \quad \text{all } \varepsilon > 0, \text{ all } k, n.$

For each $k \geq 1$, let $Z_k = \max_n D_{k,n}$, where the maximization is over $n \in \{k^2 + 1, \ldots, (k+1)^2 - 1\}$. Then (9) implies that

$$\mu(Z_k \geq k^2 \varepsilon) \leq 2M/k^3 \varepsilon^2, \quad \text{all } \varepsilon > 0, \text{ all } k.$$

Hence, using the same argument as above, we find that

$$\sum_{k=1}^{\infty} \mu\left(\frac{1}{k^2} Z_k \geq \varepsilon\right) \leq \frac{2M}{\varepsilon^2} \sum_{k=1}^{\infty} \frac{1}{k^3} < \infty,$$

so that $Z_k/k^2 \to 0$ a.e. ∎

Next we show that a variation on Theorem 14.5 holds for a certain class of correlated random variables. Note that a key step in the proofs of Theorems 14.4 and 14.5 involved using (4) to establish that the cross terms in (6) are all zero. For the correlated random variables of interest here, we simply replace the unconditional mean $E(f_k)$ in (4) with an appropriately chosen conditional mean.

THEOREM 14.6 Let $(\Omega, \mathcal{F}, \mu)$ be a probability space; let $\{f_k, \mathcal{A}_k\}$ be a sequence of random variables and σ-algebras such that for $k = 0, 1, \ldots$,

  a. $\mathcal{A}_k \subset \mathcal{A}_{k+1} \subset \mathcal{F}$;
  b. f_k is $\mathcal{A}_k$-measurable;
  c. $E\{[f_k - E(f_k|\mathcal{A}_{k-1})]^2\} < M$, all k, for some $M < \infty$.
Then

$$\lim_{n \to \infty} \frac{1}{n} \sum_{k=1}^{n} [f_k - E(f_k|\mathcal{A}_{k-1})] = 0 \quad \text{a.e.}$$

Proof. Define the random variables

$$\phi_k = E(f_k|\mathcal{A}_{k-1}), \quad k = 1, 2, \ldots.$$

By Theorem 14.5, it suffices to show that $\{f_k - \phi_k\}$ is a sequence of uncorrelated random variables. To see this, first note that

$$E(\phi_k|\mathcal{A}_{k-1}) = \phi_k = E(f_k|\mathcal{A}_{k-1}) \quad \text{a.e.,} \quad \text{all } k.$$

Hence for $j < k$,

$$E[(f_j - \phi_j)(f_k - \phi_k)|\mathcal{A}_{k-1}] = (f_j - \phi_j)E[(f_k - \phi_k)|\mathcal{A}_{k-1}]$$

$$= 0 \quad \text{a.e.}$$

Therefore

$$E[(f_j - \phi_j)(f_k - \phi_k)] = 0, \quad \text{all } j \neq k. \quad \blacksquare$$

14.2 A Strong Law for Markov Processes

In this section, we establish a strong law of large numbers for a fairly wide class of Markov processes. This result, Theorem 14.7, is easy to state and interpret, but the proof is rather involved. Therefore, to make the structure of the argument as clear as possible we proceed as follows. First we state Theorem 14.7 and present the basic steps in the proof. At this point we draw on two main lemmas. We then prove the two lemmas. The first, Lemma 14.8, is an application of Theorem 14.6. The second, Lemma 14.9, uses some facts about function spaces and rests, in turn, on several supporting arguments.

Let (S, ρ) be a metric space, with its Borel sets $\mathscr{S}$; let $C(S)$ be the space of bounded continuous functions on S; and let $\Lambda(S, \mathscr{S})$ be the space of probability measures on $(S, \mathscr{S})$. Let P be a transition function on $(S, \mathscr{S})$; and let T, T^* be the associated Markov operator and adjoint. Throughout this section, we maintain the following assumptions.

ASSUMPTION 14.1 *S is a compact subset of a finite-dimensional Euclidean space $\mathbf{R}^l$.*

ASSUMPTION 14.2 *T has the Feller property. That is, $T: C(S) \to C(S)$.*

ASSUMPTION 14.3 *There exists a unique probability measure λ^* such that $\{(1/N) \Sigma_{n=1}^{N} T^{*n}\lambda_0\}$ converges weakly to λ^*, for all $\lambda_0 \in \Lambda(S, \mathscr{S})$.*

Let $\Omega = S^\infty = S \times S \times \ldots$ be the infinite product of the state space, and let $\mathscr{F} = \mathscr{S}^\infty = \mathscr{S} \times \mathscr{S} \times \ldots$ be the σ-algebra defined in Section 8.2. As shown there, for any fixed $s_0 \in S$, the transition function P induces a probability measure—call it $\mu(s_0, \cdot)$—on $(\Omega, \mathscr{F})$. Finally, for any $(s_1, s_2, \ldots) = \omega \in \Omega$, let $\sigma_n(\omega) = s_n$ denote the nth component of ω. The rest of this section is devoted to a proof of the following strong law of large numbers for Markov processes.

THEOREM 14.7 *Let $(S, \mathscr{S})$, P, T, and T^* satisfy Assumptions 14.1–14.3. Then for any $s_0 \in S$ and any continuous function $f: S \to \mathbf{R}$,*

$$\lim_{N \to \infty} \frac{1}{N} \sum_{n=1}^{N} f[\sigma_n(\omega)] = \int f \, d\lambda^*, \quad \mu(s_0, \cdot)\text{-a.e.}$$

Proof. Fix $s_0 \in S$ and $f \in C(S)$. For any integers N, M,

$$\left| \frac{1}{N} \sum_{n=1}^{N} f[\sigma_n(\omega)] - \int f \, d\lambda^* \right|$$

$$\leq \left| \frac{1}{N} \sum_{n=1}^{N} f[\sigma_n(\omega)] - \frac{1}{N} \sum_{n=1}^{N} \left[\frac{1}{M} \sum_{m=1}^{M} (T^m f)[\sigma_n(\omega)] \right] \right|$$

$$+ \left| \frac{1}{N} \sum_{n=1}^{N} \left[\frac{1}{M} \sum_{m=1}^{M} (T^m f)[\sigma_n(\omega)] \right] - \int f \, d\lambda^* \right|$$

(1) $$\leq \frac{1}{M} \sum_{m=1}^{M} \left| \frac{1}{N} \sum_{n=1}^{N} f[\sigma_n(\omega)] - \frac{1}{N} \sum_{n=1}^{N} (T^m f)[\sigma_n(\omega)] \right|$$

$$+ \left| \frac{1}{N} \sum_{n=1}^{N} \left[\frac{1}{M} \sum_{m=1}^{M} (T^m f)[\sigma_n(\omega)] \right] - \int f \, d\lambda^* \right|, \quad \text{all } \omega \in \Omega.$$

To prove the theorem, it suffices to establish that each of the two terms in (1) converges to zero $\mu(s_0, \cdot)$-a.e. as $N \to \infty$. Two entirely separate arguments are needed.

For the first term in (1), observe that for any $1 \leq m < N$,

$$\left| \frac{1}{N} \sum_{n=1}^{N} f[\sigma_n(\omega)] - \frac{1}{N} \sum_{n=1}^{N} (T^m f)[\sigma_n(\omega)] \right|$$

$$= \frac{1}{N} \left| \sum_{n=1}^{N} f[\sigma_n(\omega)] - \sum_{n=m+1}^{m+N} (T^m f)[\sigma_{n-m}(\omega)] \right|$$

(2) $$\leq \frac{1}{N} \left| \sum_{n=1}^{m} f[\sigma_n(\omega)] \right| + \frac{1}{N} \left| \sum_{n=N+1}^{N+m} (T^m f)[\sigma_{n-m}(\omega)] \right|$$

$$+ \frac{1}{N} \left| \sum_{n=m+1}^{N} \{ f[\sigma_n(\omega)] - (T^m f)[\sigma_{n-m}(\omega)] \} \right|, \quad \text{all } \omega \in \Omega.$$

The first two terms in (2) are easily handled. Since T is a Markov operator and $f \in C(S)$, $\|T^m f\| \leq \|f\| < \infty$, all $m \geq 1$. Hence for any fixed $m \geq 1$, each of those terms is bounded above by $m\|f\|/N$.

The argument for the third term draws on the following lemma, which is proved later.

LEMMA 14.8 *Let μ be a probability measure on $(\Omega, \mathcal{F}) = (S^\infty, \mathcal{S}^\infty)$; let $\sigma_n(\omega) = s_n$, all n, all $\omega \in \Omega$; and let f be a bounded measurable function on S. Then for any $m \geq 1$,*

$$(3) \qquad \lim_{N \to \infty} \frac{1}{N} \left| \sum_{n=m+1}^{N} [f(\sigma_n) - (T^m f)(\sigma_{n-m})] \right| = 0, \quad \mu\text{-a.e.}$$

Lemma 14.8 implies that for any fixed $s_0 \in S$ and $f \in C(S)$ and for any $m \geq 1$, there exists a set $A_m \in \mathcal{F}$, with $\mu(s_0, A_m) = 0$, with the following property: for every $\varepsilon > 0$, there exists $N_m(\varepsilon) > m$ such that

$$(4) \qquad \frac{1}{N} \left| \sum_{n=m+1}^{N} [f(\sigma_n) - (T^m f)(\sigma_{n-m})] \right| \leq \varepsilon/4,$$

$$\text{all } N \geq N_m(\varepsilon), \text{ all } \omega \in A_m^c.$$

Next, consider the second term in (1). To handle this term, we use the following lemma, which is also proved later.

LEMMA 14.9 *Let Assumptions 14.1–14.3 hold, and let $f \in C(S)$. Then for any $\varepsilon > 0$, there exists $M(\varepsilon) \geq 1$ such that*

$$\left| \frac{1}{M} \sum_{m=1}^{M} (T^m f)(s) - \int f \, d\lambda^* \right| \leq \varepsilon/4, \quad \text{all } M \geq M(\varepsilon), \text{ all } s \in S.$$

Lemma 14.9 says that the sequence of functions $\{(1/M)\Sigma_{m=1}^{M}(T^m f)\}$ converges, in the sup norm, to the constant function with value $\int f \, d\lambda^*$. It follows immediately from this lemma that

(5) $$\left| \frac{1}{M} \sum_{m=1}^{M} (T^m f)[\sigma_n(\omega)] - \int f \, d\lambda^* \right| \leq \varepsilon/4,$$

all $M \geq M(\varepsilon)$, all $\omega \in \Omega$, all $n \geq 1$.

Given Lemmas 14.8 and 14.9, the proof of Theorem 14.7 proceeds as follows. Recall that $s_0 \in S$ and $f \in C(S)$ are fixed. For $m = 1, 2, \ldots$, choose a set $A_m \in \mathcal{F}$, with $\mu(s_0, A_m) = 0$, such that (4) holds; by Lemma 14.8, this is possible. Let $A = \cup_{m=1}^{\infty} A_m$, and note that $\mu(s_0, A) = 0$. Then fix $\varepsilon > 0$, and choose $M(\varepsilon)$ such that (5) holds; by Lemma 14.9, this is possible. Then for each $m = 1, \ldots, M(\varepsilon)$, choose $N_m(\varepsilon)$ such that (4) holds, where the A_m's are the ones already selected; by Lemma 14.8, this is possible, and $N_m(\varepsilon) > m$, all m. Finally, choose

$$N^*(\varepsilon) \geq \max \{N_1(\varepsilon), \ldots, N_{M(\varepsilon)}, 4M(\varepsilon)\|f\|/\varepsilon\},$$

and note that $N^*(\varepsilon) > M(\varepsilon)$.

Next, substitute from (2) into (1), and set $M = M(\varepsilon)$ to find that

$$\left| \frac{1}{N} \sum_{n=1}^{N} f[\sigma_n(\omega)] - \int f(s) \, d\lambda^* \right|$$

$$\leq \frac{1}{M(\varepsilon)} \sum_{m=1}^{M(\varepsilon)} \left\{ \frac{2m\|f\|}{N} \right.$$

$$+ \frac{1}{N} \left| \sum_{n=m+1}^{N} \{f[\sigma_n(\omega)] - (T^m f)[\sigma_{n-m}(\omega)]\} \right| \right\}$$

$$+ \left| \frac{1}{N} \sum_{n=1}^{N} \left[\frac{1}{M(\varepsilon)} \sum_{m=1}^{M(\varepsilon)} (T^m f)[\sigma_n(\omega)] \right] - \int f \, d\lambda^* \right|,$$

all $\omega \in \Omega$, all $N > M(\varepsilon)$.

It follows from (4) and (5) that the right side of this equation is less than ε, for all $\omega \in A^c$ and all $N \geq N^*(\varepsilon)$. Since $\varepsilon > 0$ was arbitrary, this completes the proof. ∎

It remains to prove Lemmas 14.8 and 14.9. The proof of the former is an application of Theorem 14.6, the strong law of large numbers for correlated random variables that we established in the last section.

Proof of Lemma 14.8. Let μ be a probability measure on $(\Omega, \mathcal{F})$, and let f be a bounded measurable function on S. Then for any $n \geq m + 1$,

$$f(\sigma_n) - (T^m f)(\sigma_{n-m}) = \sum_{j=0}^{m-1} [(T^j f)(\sigma_{n-j}) - (T^{j+1} f)(\sigma_{n-j-1})],$$

all $\omega \in \Omega$.

Hence for any $N \geq m + 1$,

$$\frac{1}{N} \left| \sum_{n=m+1}^{N} [f(\sigma_n) - (T^m f)(\sigma_{n-m})] \right|$$

$$= \frac{1}{N} \left| \sum_{n=m+1}^{N} \sum_{j=0}^{m-1} [(T^j f)(\sigma_{n-j}) - (T^{j+1} f)(\sigma_{n-j-1})] \right|$$

$$\leq \sum_{j=0}^{m-1} \left| \frac{1}{N} \sum_{n=m+1}^{N} [(T^j f)(\sigma_{n-j}) - (T^{j+1} f)(\sigma_{n-j-1})] \right|, \quad \text{all } \omega \in \Omega.$$

We will show that each of the m terms on the right side converges to zero μ-a.e. as $N \to \infty$.

Fix $0 \leq j \leq m - 1$, and define the functions g_n^j, $n = 0, 1, \ldots$, by

$$g_n^j = \begin{cases} 0 & n = 0, 1, \ldots, m, \\ (T^j f)(\sigma_{n-j}) & n = m + 1, m + 2, \ldots. \end{cases}$$

Let $\hat{\mathcal{G}}^k$, $k = 0, 1, \ldots$ be the σ-algebras of Ω defined in Section 8.2, and let

$$\mathcal{A}_n^j = \begin{cases} \hat{\mathcal{G}}^0 & n = 0, 1, \ldots, m - 1, \\ \hat{\mathcal{G}}^{n-j} & n = m, m + 1, \ldots. \end{cases}$$

Then $\mathscr{A}_n^j \subseteq \mathscr{A}_{n+1}^j \subseteq \mathscr{F}$, $n = 0, 1, \ldots$, and each function g_n^j is $\mathscr{A}_n^j =$ measurable. Moreover,

$$(T^j f)(\sigma_{n-j}) - (T^{j+1} f)(\sigma_{n-j-1}) = g_n^j - E(g_n^j | \mathscr{A}_{n-1}^j),$$

$$n = m + 1, m + 2, \ldots.$$

Hence

$$\frac{1}{N} \left| \sum_{n=m+1}^{N} [(T^j f)(\sigma_{n-j}) - (T^{j+1} f)(\sigma_{n-j-1})] \right|$$

$$= \frac{1}{N} \left| \sum_{n=1}^{N} [g_n^j - E(g_n^j | \mathscr{A}_{n-1}^j)] \right|, \quad \text{all } \omega \in \Omega.$$

Hence to establish that (3) holds, it suffices to show that

(6) $$\lim_{N \to \infty} \frac{1}{N} \left| \sum_{n=1}^{N} [g_n^j - E(g_n^j | \mathscr{A}_{n-1}^j)] \right| = 0, \quad \mu\text{-a.e.}$$

Since f is bounded,

$$E\{[g_n^j - E(g_n^j | \mathscr{A}_{n-1}^j)]^2\} \le 4\|f\|^2, \quad n = 1, 2, \ldots.$$

Thus, the sequence $\{g_n^j, \mathscr{A}_n^j\}_{n=1}^{\infty}$ satisfies the hypotheses of Theorem 14.6. Hence (6) holds. ∎

The proof of Lemma 14.9, to which we turn next, involves no probability theory. Rather, it rests on a number of results about linear operators on normed linear spaces and about the duals of normed linear spaces. (The reader who is unfamiliar with the concept of a dual of a normed linear space is invited to skip ahead at this point and read the material about dual spaces in Section 15.1.) The proof of Lemma 14.10 is developed as follows.

First we state, without proof, a standard minimum norm duality result; this is Theorem 14.10. We then draw on this theorem to establish Lemma 14.11. This lemma and another, Lemma 14.12, are used in the proof of Lemma 14.13, which is a specialization of a result known as the

Norms Ergodic Lemma. Then in Theorem 14.14 we state, without proof, a version of the Riesz Representation Theorem. Finally, we draw on the latter two results to prove Lemma 14.9.

Let X be a normed linear space with norm $\|\cdot\|_X$. The space of all continuous linear functionals $\mu: X \to \mathbf{R}$ is called the **dual space** of X and is denoted by X^*. (See Exercise 15.2 for examples of the duals of some normed linear spaces.) We use the notation $\langle x, \mu \rangle$ to denote the value of the functional μ at the point $x \in X$. Define the norm $\|\cdot\|_{X^*}$ on X^* by

$$\|\mu\|_{X^*} = \sup_{\substack{x \in X \\ \|x\|_X \leq 1}} \langle x, \mu \rangle.$$

The assumption that μ is continuous implies that $\|\mu\|_{X^*}$ is finite (Theorem 15.1).

Next, we must define linear operators on X and develop some of their properties.

DEFINITION   *A mapping T of a normed linear space X into itself is called a* **linear operator** *on X if $T(\alpha x + \beta y) = \alpha Tx + \beta Ty$, all $x, y \in X$, all $\alpha, \beta \in \mathbf{R}$.*

Let L be the space of linear operators $T: X \to X$, and define the norm $\|\cdot\|_L$ on L by

$$\|T\|_L = \sup_{\substack{x \in X \\ \|x\|_X \leq 1}} \|Tx\|_X.$$

It is clear from the definition of $\|\cdot\|_L$ that for any linear operator T,

$$\|Tx\|_X \leq \|T\|_L \cdot \|x\|_X, \quad \text{all } x \in X.$$

When there is no possibility for confusion, we will drop the subscripts on the various norms.

For any $T \in L$, define the subset TX of X by

$$TX = \{y \in X: y = Tx \text{ for some } x \in X\}.$$

Thus TX is the image set under T of the whole space X. It is clear that TX is a subspace of X; that is, TX is a linear space contained in X. Let $\overline{TX}$ denote the closure of this set under the norm $\|\cdot\|_X$.

The proof of our first preliminary result draws on the following duality theorem.

THEOREM 14.10 *(Minimum Norm Duality)* *Let X be a normed linear space; let $x \in X$; and let M be any subspace of X. Then*

$$\inf_{y \in M} \|x - y\| = \max_{\substack{\mu \in X^* \\ \|\mu\| \leq 1}} \langle x, \mu \rangle \quad \text{s.t.} \quad \langle y, \mu \rangle = 0, \quad \text{all } y \in M,$$

and the maximum is attained for some $\mu^* \in X^*$.

See Luenberger (1969, pp. 136–137) for a proof.

LEMMA 14.11 *Let X be a normed linear space; let $T: X \rightarrow X$ be a linear operator; let $\{x_n\}$ be a sequence in TX; and suppose that for some $x \in X$,*

$$(7) \qquad \lim_{n \to \infty} \langle x_n, \mu \rangle = \langle x, \mu \rangle, \quad \text{all } \mu \in X^*.$$

Then $x \in \overline{TX}$.

Proof. Let X, T, $\{x_n\}$, and x satisfy the stated hypotheses. Since T is linear, TX is a subspace of X. Hence Theorem 14.10 implies that there exists $\mu^* \in X^*$ such that

$$d = \inf_{y \in TX} \|x - y\| = \langle x, \mu^* \rangle \quad \text{and} \quad \langle y, \mu^* \rangle = 0, \quad \text{all } y \in TX.$$

Therefore, since $\{x_n\}$ lies in TX, $\langle x_n, \mu^* \rangle = 0$, all n. It then follows from (7) that $d = \langle x, \mu^* \rangle = 0$, and hence that $x \in \overline{TX}$. ∎

Our next result makes use of the following exercise.

Exercise 14.3 Let X be a normed linear space, and let $T: X \rightarrow X$ be a linear operator.
   a. Define the operators $T^k: X \rightarrow X$ by $T^0 x = x$, and $T^k x = T(T^{k-1}x)$, $k = 1, 2, \ldots$. Show that each operator T^k is linear and that if $\|T\| \leq 1$, then $\|T^k\| \leq 1$, $k = 2, 3, \ldots$.
   b. Define the operators $H_n: X \rightarrow X$ by

$$(8) \qquad H_n x = \frac{1}{n} \sum_{k=1}^{n} T^{k-1}x, \quad n = 1, 2, \ldots.$$

Show that each operator H_n is linear and that, if $\|T\| \le 1$, then $\|H_n\| \le 1$, $n = 1, 2, \ldots$.

LEMMA 14.12 *Let X be a normed linear space; let $T: X \to X$ be a linear operator with $\|T\| = 1$; and let (8) define the linear operators $H_n: X \to X$, $n = 1, 2, \ldots$. Let $I: X \to X$ be the identity map. Then*

$$\lim_{n \to \infty} \|H_n x\| = 0, \quad \text{all } x \in \overline{(T - I)X}.$$

Proof. We first establish the result for $x \in (T - I)X$. If $x \in (T - I)X$, then $x = (T - I)y$ for some $y \in X$. Hence

$$H_n x = H_n(T - I)y$$

$$= \frac{1}{n} \sum_{k=1}^{n} T^{k-1}(T - I)y$$

$$= \frac{1}{n} \left(\sum_{k=1}^{n} T^k y - \sum_{k=1}^{n} T^{k-1}y \right)$$

$$= \frac{1}{n}(T^n y - y).$$

Hence

$$\lim_{n \to \infty} \|H_n x\|_X = \lim_{n \to \infty} \frac{1}{n} \|T^n y - y\|_X$$

$$\le \lim_{n \to \infty} \frac{1}{n} (\|T^n y\|_X + \|y\|_X)$$

$$\le \lim_{n \to \infty} \frac{1}{n} (\|T^n\|_L \cdot \|y\|_X + \|y\|_X)$$

$$\le \lim_{n \to \infty} \frac{2}{n} \|y\|_X$$

$$= 0,$$

where the fourth line uses Exercise 14.3a.

Now suppose that $x \in \overline{(T - I)X}$. Then for any $\varepsilon > 0$, there exists $x' \in (T - I)X$ with $\|x - x'\| < \varepsilon$, and $y' \in X$ with $x' = (T - I)y'$. Then

$$\|H_n x\|_X \leq \|H_n x'\|_X + \|H_n(x - x')\|_X$$

$$\leq \|H_n x'\|_X + \|H_n\|_L \cdot \|x - x'\|_X$$

$$\leq \|H_n x'\|_X + \varepsilon,$$

where the last line uses Exercise 14.3b. Since $\varepsilon > 0$ was arbitrary and $\|H_n x'\|_X \to 0$, this completes the proof. ∎

Our next result draws upon Lemmas 14.11 and 14.12.

LEMMA 14.13 (*Norms Ergodic Lemma*)   *Let X be a normed linear space; let $T: X \to X$ be a linear operator with $\|T\| = 1$; and let the operators H_n be defined by (8). Suppose that $\bar{x} \in X$ is a fixed point of T and that $x \in X$ satisfies*

(9) $$\lim_{n \to \infty} \langle H_n x, \mu \rangle = \langle \bar{x}, \mu \rangle, \quad \text{all } \mu \in X^*.$$

Then

$$\lim_{n \to \infty} \|H_n x - \bar{x}\| = 0.$$

Proof. Let X, T, and $\{H_n\}$ be as specified, and let $I: X \to X$ be the identity map. Note that

$$(H_n - I) = (T - I)\left(\frac{n - 1}{n} I + \frac{n - 2}{n} T + \cdots + \frac{1}{n} T^{n-2}\right), \quad \text{all } n.$$

(Just carry out the multiplication on the right.) That is,

$$(H_n - I)x \in (T - I)X, \quad \text{all } x \in X, \text{ all } n.$$

Let $\bar{x}$ be a fixed point of T, let $x \in X$ satisfy (9), and let $y_n = (H_n - I)x$, $n = 1, 2, \ldots$. Then

$$\langle y_n, \mu \rangle = \langle (H_n - I)x, \mu \rangle = \langle H_n x, \mu \rangle - \langle x, \mu \rangle, \quad \text{all } n, \text{ all } \mu \in X^*.$$

Taking the limit and using (9), we find that

$$\lim_{n \to \infty} \langle y_n, \mu \rangle = \langle \bar{x}, \mu \rangle - \langle x, \mu \rangle = \langle \bar{x} - x, \mu \rangle, \quad \text{all } \mu \in X^*.$$

Since $y_n \in (T - I)X$, all n, it follows from Lemma 14.11 that $(x - \bar{x}) \in \overline{(T - I)X}$. And since $\|T\| = 1$, it follows that

$$0 = \lim_{n \to \infty} \|H_n(x - \bar{x})\| = \lim_{n \to \infty} \|H_n x - H_n \bar{x}\| = \lim_{n \to \infty} \|H_n x - \bar{x}\|,$$

where the first equality uses Lemma 14.12 and the last uses the fact that, since $\bar{x}$ is a fixed point of T, it is also a fixed point of H_n, for all n. ∎

Let $S \subset \mathbf{R}^l$ be a subset of a finite-dimensional Euclidean space, with its Borel subsets $\mathscr{S}$, and let $C(S)$ be the space of bounded continuous functions $f : S \to \mathbf{R}$. Recall (see Exercise 3.4e) that $C(S)$, with the sup norm, is a normed linear space. In our application of Theorem 14.13, $C(S)$ is the space of interest. Let P be a transition function on $(S, \mathscr{S})$, and let T be the Markov operator associated with P. Assume that T has the Feller property (Assumption 14.2).

Exercise 14.4   Show that under Assumption 14.2, $T: C(S) \to C(S)$ is a linear operator; that $\|T\|_L = 1$; and that every constant function is a fixed point of T.

To apply Theorem 14.13, we must also identify the dual space of $C(S)$. The next result states that $\Phi(S, \mathscr{S})$, the space of signed measures on $(S, \mathscr{S})$ introduced in Section 11.3, is the dual space of $C(S)$. Recall that signed measures must be finite.

THEOREM 14.14 (*Riesz Representation Theorem*)   *Let $S \subset \mathbf{R}^l$ be a compact set, with its Borel subsets $\mathscr{S}$; let $C(S)$ be the space of bounded continuous functions $f : S \to \mathbf{R}$; and let $\Phi(S, \mathscr{S})$ be the space of signed measures on $(S, \mathscr{S})$. If $T: C(S) \to \mathbf{R}$ is a continuous linear functional on $C(S)$, there exists a unique signed measure $\nu \in \Phi(S, \mathscr{S})$ such that $Tf = \int f \, d\nu$, all $f \in C(S)$.*

For a proof of this theorem, see Royden (1968, Theorem 8, pp. 310–311).

We are now ready to establish our final result.

Proof of Lemma 14.9. Let $(S, \mathscr{S})$, T, and T^* satisfy Assumptions 14.1–14.3, and let $C(S)$ be the space of bounded continuous functions on S. Under Assumption 14.1, $C(S)$ is a normed linear space and, by Theorem 14.14, its dual is the space $\Phi(S, \mathscr{S})$ of signed measures on $(S, \mathscr{S})$. Under Assumptions 14.1 and 14.2, it follows from Exercise 14.4 that $T: C(S) \to C(S)$ is a linear operator, with $\|T\| = 1$. Define the linear operators $H_n: C(S)$, $n = 1, 2, \ldots$, by (8). By Assumption 14.3, there is a unique probability measure $\lambda^* \in \Lambda(S, \mathscr{S})$ such that

$$(10) \qquad \lim_{n \to \infty} \int (H_n f)(s) \, d\lambda = \int f \, d\lambda^*, \quad \text{all } f \in C(S), \text{ all } \lambda \in \Lambda(S, \mathscr{S}).$$

Let $\nu \in \Phi(S, \mathscr{S})$ be a signed measure on $(S, \mathscr{S})$. Then there exist probability measures $\lambda_1, \lambda_2 \in \Lambda(S, \mathscr{S})$ and constants $\alpha_1, \alpha_2 \in \mathbf{R}_+$ such that $\nu(A) = \alpha_1 \lambda_1(A) - \alpha_2 \lambda_2(A)$, all $A \in \mathscr{S}$. Hence

$$\int H_n f \, d\nu = \alpha_1 \int H_n f \, d\lambda_1 - \alpha_2 \int H_n f \, d\lambda_2, \quad \text{all } n, \text{ all } f \in C(S).$$

It then follows from (10) that

$$\lim_{n \to \infty} \int H_n f \, d\nu = \alpha_1 \lim_{n \to \infty} \int H_n f \, d\lambda_1 - \alpha_2 \lim_{n \to \infty} \int H_n f \, d\lambda_2$$

$$= (\alpha_1 - \alpha_2) \int f \, d\lambda^*, \quad \text{all } f \in C(S).$$

Now fix $f \in C(S)$, and let $\bar{f}$ denote the constant function with value $\int f \, d\lambda^*$. Then

$$\lim_{n \to \infty} \langle H_n f, \nu \rangle = (\alpha_1 - \alpha_2) \langle f, \lambda^* \rangle$$

$$= (\alpha_1 - \alpha_2) \langle \bar{f}, \lambda^* \rangle$$

$$= \langle \bar{f}, \nu \rangle, \quad \text{all } \nu \in \Phi(S, \mathscr{S}).$$

By Exercise 14.4, any constant function $\bar{f}$ is a fixed point of T. Hence Lemma 14.13 implies that

$$\lim_{n \to \infty} \|H_n f - \bar{f}\| = 0.$$

This fact completes the proof of Lemma 14.9, and—in case the reader has lost sight of the point of all this—of Theorem 14.7. ∎

14.3 Bibliographic Notes

The strong law of large numbers proved in this chapter is due to Breiman (1960). Our proof follows exactly that given in his paper. We have drawn on Chung (1974, chaps. 4 and 5) in Section 14.1. Our treatment of the Norms Ergodic Lemma in Section 14.2 is taken from Loève (1977, sect. 35).

PART IV

Competitive Equilibrium

15   Pareto Optima and
         Competitive Equilibria

Thus far we have been concerned with methods for studying a variety of dynamic optimization problems, both deterministic and stochastic. In these problems a single decision-maker (a consumer, firm, or social planner) maximizes an objective function (utility, profits, or social welfare) subject to a set of constraints (technological or market opportunities or both). If the decision-maker is a consumer or a firm, the solution to this optimization problem is sometimes the object of direct interest. In other cases our ultimate interest is in the behavior of an economic system composed of two or more such agents trading on a specified set of markets. In this chapter and the three that follow, we examine methods for analyzing the competitive equilibria of such systems. Two approaches are developed.

The first draws upon the two fundamental theorems of welfare economics. As we suggested in Chapter 2 and will show more formally below, there is a wide class of situations in which the "invisible hand" ensures that the sets of Pareto-optimal allocations and competitive equilibrium allocations coincide exactly. In these situations we can interpret certain normative models of optimal decision-making (from the point of view of a hypothetical "benevolent social planner") as positive models of equilibrium outcomes. This approach is developed in the present chapter and the one that follows.

In situations where competitive equilibria are not Pareto-optimal, an entirely different approach is needed. This second approach, which is based upon a direct analysis of the first-order conditions from individual agents' optimization problems, is developed in Chapters 17 and 18.

In the rest of this chapter we study in more detail the device of exploiting the connection between competitive equilibria and Pareto optima. To do this we develop the connections somewhat differently from the way we did Chapter 2, where we simply checked that some first-order conditions matched. That approach can, under suitable convexity assumptions, be made rigorous. But we do not pursue it, because there are many situations in which Pareto-optimal and competitive equilibrium allocations coincide but in which this fact is difficult or impossible to verify by a comparison of first-order conditions. Fortunately, much more powerful methods are available. Our task in this chapter is to describe these methods and to see how they apply to the dynamic problems we are interested in.

The general plan can be illustrated diagrammatically. Figure 15.1 displays indifference curves for a consumer whose utility $U(l, c)$ depends on his leisure l and his goods consumption c. He is endowed with one unit of leisure and has access to the production technology $c = f(1 - l)$, so Y is the set of feasible (l, c) pairs. It is clear that the point (l^0, c^0) maximizes U over Y and hence is a Pareto-optimal allocation. It is also a competitive equilibrium at the relative prices given by the slope of the straight line passing through (l^0, c^0). One way to see this is to observe that an indifference curve is tangent to the production possibility frontier at this point, so the first-order condition for an optimum is satisfied. Then note that the straight line to which these curves are mutually tangent is an equilibrium price, so (l^0, c^0) satisfies the first-order condi-

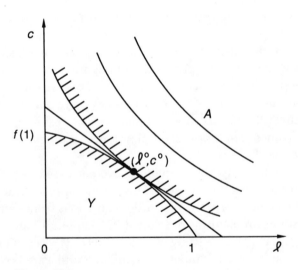

Figure 15.1

tions for an equilibrium, too. If the functions U and f are concave and differentiable, this approach is perfectly respectable.

A somewhat different way of establishing the same thing is as follows. To see that (l^0, c^0) is Pareto optimal, simply note that the set of allocations preferred to (l^0, c^0) consists of the interior of the set A. Since none of these points is feasible—since Y and the interior of A do not intersect—(l^0, c^0) is a Pareto optimum. To see that this allocation is also a competitive equilibrium, at the relative price p, refer to Figure 15.2.

We need to check two conditions. The first is whether the allocation (l^0, c^0) is utility maximizing for the consumer over his budget set B. The

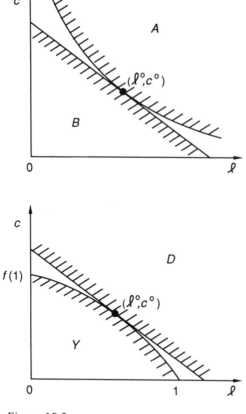

Figure 15.2

argument that this is so is the same as the one above: B and the interior of A do not intersect. The second is whether (l^0, c^0) is profit maximizing for the firm at the given prices and with the given technology. The allocations that yield higher profit are simply those in the interior of the set D. Since Y and the interior of D do not intersect, none of these is feasible.

Note that the latter approach uses the fact that the sets A and Y are convex, with a shared point (l^0, c^0) and a line separating the two sets. Since the convexity of A and Y is equivalent to the concavity of U and f— the assumptions used in the first approach—for this one-person, two-good economy there is little at stake in the choice between the two points of view (aside from the fact that the latter does not require differentiability). The approach based on convex sets and separating lines (or planes, or hyperplanes) is much more powerful, however; and we need to exploit this extra power because the models discussed in Chapters 4 and 9 all involve infinite-dimensional commodity spaces.

There is no single idealization of a competitive economy that encompasses all the particular models one might ever run across, but the welfare theorems discussed in this chapter apply to such a wide range of models that it is useful to have as abstract a statement as possible. Arrow (1951) provided the first modern treatment of this topic, idealizing the commodity allocations chosen by consumers and firms as points in a finite-dimensional Euclidean space. Debreu (1954) extended this analysis to commodity spaces that are required only to be normed vector spaces. It is clear from even the simple examples in Chapter 2 that to study models with an infinite time horizon or with random shocks that take on infinitely many values, we need this broader idea of a commodity space.

To discuss the competitive equilibria of economies in which the commodity space is an arbitrary normed vector space, we must first decide what is to be meant by a price system in such an economy. For reasons that will become clear below, the most useful approach is to take price systems to be continuous linear functionals on the commodity space. For a given commodity space, the set of possible price systems is then the dual space, the space of all continuous linear functionals. Thus, we begin in Section 15.1 by discussing some of the main facts about the relationship between various normed vector spaces and their duals. We also provide a statement of the Hahn-Banach Theorem, the infinite-dimensional version of the separation theorem for convex sets illustrated in Figure 15.1.

In Section 15.2 we draw on these results to review Debreu's (1954) treatment of the relationship between Pareto optima and competitive equilibria, the two fundamental theorems of welfare economics, in a context where the commodity space is taken to be an arbitrary normed vector space. Then in Section 15.3 we discuss the issues involved in deciding which particular normed vector spaces are suited for applications involving time and uncertainty. Finally, in Section 15.4 we discuss conditions under which equilibrium price systems for such economies can be represented as inner products and hence be given a natural economic interpretation.

15.1 Dual Spaces

To discuss competitive equilibrium, we need to decide what we mean by a price system. If the commodity space is a finite-dimensional Euclidean space $\mathbf{R}^K$, the obvious way to do this is simply to take the price of each commodity, $k = 1, \ldots, K$, to be a number $p_k \in \mathbf{R}$. A price system is then a vector $p = (p_1, \ldots, p_K) \in \mathbf{R}^K$, and the value of any commodity point x is the inner product $p \cdot x = \Sigma_k p_k x_k$. Hence a price system in this case is a mapping from the commodity space $\mathbf{R}^K$ into $\mathbf{R}$; and since $p \cdot (\alpha x + \beta y) = \alpha(p \cdot x) + \beta(p \cdot y)$, for any $\alpha, \beta \in \mathbf{R}$ and any $x, y \in \mathbf{R}^K$, the mapping is linear.

The generalization of this idea to a commodity space that is an arbitrary normed vector space is given in the following definition.

DEFINITION *A **linear functional** on a normed vector space $(S, \|\cdot\|_s)$ is a function $\phi: S \to \mathbf{R}$ satisfying*

$$\phi(\alpha x + \beta y) = \alpha\phi(x) + \beta\phi(y), \quad \text{all } x, y \in S, \text{ all } \alpha, \beta \in \mathbf{R}.$$

*The linear functional ϕ is **continuous** if $\|x_n - x\|_s \to 0$ implies $|\phi(x_n) - \phi(x)| \to 0$. It is **bounded** if there exists a constant M such that $|\phi(x)| \leq M\|x\|_s$, for all $x \in S$. The **norm** of a bounded linear functional ϕ is then defined to be*

$$(1) \qquad \|\phi\|_d = \inf\{M \in \mathbf{R}_+: |\phi(x)| \leq M\|x\|_s, \text{ all } x \in S\}$$

$$= \sup_{\|x\|_s \leq 1} |\phi(x)|.$$

When there is no possibility for confusion, we drop the subscripts on the norms and refer to S, rather than $(S, \|\cdot\|_s)$, as a normed vector space.

The following theorem offers two useful ways of identifying continuous linear functionals.

THEOREM 15.1 *Let S be a normed vector space, and let ϕ be a linear functional on S. Then*

    a. if ϕ is continuous at any point in S, it is continuous on all of S; and

    b. ϕ is continuous if and only if it is bounded.

Proof. (a) Suppose that ϕ is continuous at $s \in S$, and let $\{x_n\}$ be a sequence in S converging to $x \in S$. Define the sequence $\{s_n\}$ by $s_n = s + x_n - x$, $n = 1, 2, \ldots$. By the linearity of ϕ,

$$\phi(x_n) = \phi(x) + \phi(s_n) - \phi(s), \quad n = 1, 2, \ldots .$$

Therefore, taking the limit and using the continuity of ϕ at s, we obtain

$$\lim_{n \to \infty} \phi(x_n) = \phi(x) + \lim_{n \to \infty} \phi(s_n) - \phi(s)$$

$$= \phi(x).$$

(b) Suppose that ϕ is bounded, with $\|\phi\| = M$. Then for any sequence $\{x_n\}$ converging to θ, we have

$$\lim_{n \to \infty} |\phi(x_n)| \leq \lim_{n \to \infty} M\|x_n\| = 0,$$

so ϕ is continuous at θ. Hence by part (a) it is continuous on all of S.

Conversely, suppose that ϕ is continuous. Then there exists some $0 < M < \infty$ such that $\|x\| \leq 1/M$ implies $\phi(x) \leq 1$. Then for any $x \neq \theta$,

$$|\phi(x)| = |\phi(x/M\|x\|)|M\|x\| \leq M\|x\|.$$

Hence $\|\phi\| \leq M$. ∎

For any normed vector space S, the space S^* of all continuous linear functionals on S is called the **dual** of S. Addition and scalar multiplication on S^* are defined in the obvious way, and since

$$a\phi + b\psi \in S^*, \quad \text{for all } \phi, \psi \in S^*, \text{ and all } a, b \in \mathbf{R},$$

S^* is a vector space. With the norm defined in (1), $(S^*, \|\cdot\|_d)$ is a normed vector space. It is not too difficult to show that $(S^*, \|\cdot\|_d)$ is also complete, even if S is not. That is, every dual space is a Banach space.

Exercise 15.1 Let S be a normed vector space. Show that the dual space S^* is complete.

We turn next to some standard examples of normed vector spaces and their duals.

Example 1 Let S be the finite-dimensional Euclidean space $\mathbf{R}^n$, with the norm $\|x\| = (\Sigma_{i=1}^n |x_i|^2)^{1/2}$. Clearly any $y \in \mathbf{R}^n$ defines a continuous linear functional on S through the inner product

$$\phi(x) = y \cdot x = \sum_{i=1}^n y_i x_i.$$

The converse is true as well. To see this, let ϕ be any continuous linear functional. For $i = 1, \ldots, n$, let $e_i = (0, \ldots, 0, 1, 0, \ldots, 0)$ be the vector with a one as the ith component and zeros elsewhere. Define $y \in \mathbf{R}^n$ by

$$y_i = \phi(e_i), \quad i = 1, \ldots, n.$$

Then the linearity of ϕ implies that $\phi(x) = \Sigma_{i=1}^n y_i x_i = y \cdot x$, all $x \in \mathbf{R}^n$, and we say that the inner product $y \cdot x$ *represents* ϕ. In this example there is a one-to-one correspondence between S^* and $\mathbf{R}^n$, and we refer to either as the dual space.

Example 2 For $1 \le p < \infty$, the space l_p consists of all sequences $x = (x_1, x_2, \ldots)$, $x_n \in \mathbf{R}$, that are bounded in the norm

(2) $\qquad \|x\|_p = \left(\sum_{i=1}^\infty |x_i|^p \right)^{1/p}.$

When $p = \infty$, (2) is interpreted as

$$\|x\|_\infty = \sup_i |x_i|,$$

and the corresponding space is called l_∞. For any $1 < p < \infty$, define the conjugate index $q = p/(p - 1)$, so that $1/p + 1/q = 1$; for $p = 1$, take $q = \infty$. Then using arguments similar to those above, we can show that, for

$1 \le p < \infty$, the dual of l_p is l_q. That is, any $y = (y_1, y_2, \ldots) \in l_q$ defines a continuous linear functional on l_p by the inner product

$$\phi(x) = y \cdot x = \sum_{i=1}^{\infty} y_i x_i;$$

and, conversely, any continuous linear functional on l_p has such a representation.

Exercise 15.2   a. Show that the dual of l_2 is l_2.
b. Show that the dual of l_1 is l_∞.

The space that is of the most interest to us is l_∞. Its dual contains l_1, as the next exercise shows.

Exercise 15.3   Show that every $y \in l_1$ defines a continuous linear functional on l_∞ through the inner product $\phi(x) = y \cdot x = \sum_{i=1}^{\infty} y_i x_i$.

But the dual of l_∞ also contains elements that are not in l_1. In Section 15.3 we provide an example of such a functional.

Example 3   Let c_0 be the subspace of l_∞ consisting of all sequences converging to zero: $c_0 = \{(x_1, x_2, \ldots) \in l_\infty : x_n \to 0\}$.

Exercise 15.4   Verify that c_0 is a normed vector space, and show that l_1 is the dual of c_0.

Example 4   Let $(Z, \mathfrak{L}, \mu)$ be a measure space; and, for $1 \le p < \infty$, consider the space of all real-valued, measurable functions that are bounded in the norm

(3) $$\|x\|_p = \left[\int |x(z)|^p \, d\mu(z) \right]^{1/p}.$$

The pair $[(Z, \mathfrak{L}, \mu), \|\cdot\|_p]$ does not quite work as a normed vector space, since it is possible that $\|x\|_p = 0$ and $x \neq \theta$. We can avoid this difficulty as follows.

Consider the set of measurable functions on $(Z, \mathfrak{L}, \mu)$ that are bounded in the norm in (3); call this set B_p. For any $x, x' \in B_p$, we say that the function x is **equivalent** to the function x' if $x(z) = x'(z)$, μ-a.e. Similarly, for any $x \in B_p$, we define the **equivalence class** containing x to be the subset of B_p consisting of all functions x' such that $x = x'$ μ-a.e. Clearly the equivalence relation is transitive: if $x, x', x'' \in B_p$, with $x = x'$, μ-a.e. and $x' = x''$, μ-a.e., then $x = x''$, μ-a.e. This transitivity ensures that each function in B_p belongs to exactly one equivalence class. That is, the equivalence relation defines a partition on B_p. Moreover, for the norm defined in (3), $\|x - x'\| = 0$ if and only if x and x' are in the same equivalence class.

Therefore we define $L_p(Z, \mathfrak{L}, \mu)$, for $1 \leq p < \infty$, to be the space of equivalence classes of measurable functions, with the norm in (3). (It is standard to write simply L_p if the underlying space is $\mathbf{R}^1$ with the Lebesgue sets and Lebesgue measure.) The space $L_\infty(Z, \mathfrak{L}, \mu)$ is defined analogously to l_∞. It is the space of all equivalence classes of measurable, real-valued functions that are bounded in the **essential supremum norm** (ess sup norm). This norm is defined by

$$\|x\|_\infty = \text{ess sup } |x(z)|$$

$$= \inf_{y = x \; \mu\text{-a.e.}} \sup_z |y(z)|.$$

Equivalently,

$$\|x\|_\infty = \inf_{A \subset Z, \; \mu(A) = 0} \sup_{z \in Z \backslash A} |x(z)|.$$

$$= \inf\{M : \mu\{z : |x(z)| > M\} = 0\}.$$

[Although all of the $L_p(Z, \mathfrak{L}, \mu)$ spaces have equivalence classes of functions as elements, we will follow standard usage and speak interchangeably of x and the equivalence class containing x.]

By arguments analogous to those for the l_p spaces, it can be shown that for $1 \leq p < \infty$, the dual of $L_p(Z, \mathfrak{L}, \mu)$ is $L_q(Z, \mathfrak{L}, \mu)$, where $1/p + 1/q = 1$. That is, each $y \in L_q(Z, \mathfrak{L}, \mu)$ defines a continuous linear functional on $L_p(Z, \mathfrak{L}, \mu)$ through the inner product

$$\phi(x) = \int y(z)x(z) \, d\mu(z);$$

and conversely, any continuous linear functional on $L_p(Z, \mathfrak{L}, \mu)$ has such a representation.

The space that is of interest to us later is $L_\infty(Z, \mathfrak{L}, \mu)$, and its dual, like that of l_∞, is more complicated. Every element of $L_1(Z, \mathfrak{L}, \mu)$ defines a continuous linear functional on $L_\infty(Z, \mathfrak{L}, \mu)$, but the converse is not true.

Exercise 15.5 a. Show that any function $f \in L_1(Z, \mathfrak{L}, \mu)$ defines a continuous linear functional on $L_\infty(Z, \mathfrak{L}, \mu)$ through the inner product

$$\phi(x) = \int f(z)x(z) \, d\mu(z).$$

b. Show that each such functional can also be represented by a signed measure ν on $(Z, \mathfrak{L})$ that is absolutely continuous with respect to μ. [*Hint.* Use Exercise 7.21.]

The dual of $L_\infty(Z, \mathfrak{L}, \mu)$ is larger than $L_1(Z, \mathfrak{L}, \mu)$, as the example of Section 15.3 will show. To see this, let $Z = \{1, 2, \ldots\}$; let $\mathfrak{L}$ be the σ-algebra consisting of all subsets of Z; and let μ be any probability measure with $\mu(A) > 0$, all $A \in \mathfrak{L}$. Then $L_\infty(Z, \mathfrak{L}, \mu)$ consists of all bounded functions $f: Z \to \mathbf{R}$, and hence is equivalent to l_∞. In Section 15.3 we discuss the l_p and $L_p(Z, \mathfrak{L}, \mu)$ spaces in more detail and show why l_∞ and $L_\infty(Z, \mathfrak{L}, \mu)$ are particularly useful for establishing certain facts about the models discussed in Chapters 4 and 9, respectively.

Our interest in linear functionals stems from our interest in making precise the connections between Pareto-optimal allocations and competitive equilibria. In particular, we want to be able to state conditions under which any Pareto-optimal allocation can, for a suitable choice of prices, be supported as a competitive equilibrium. In the example displayed in Figure 15.1, proving this claim amounted to finding a price line tangent to the sets A and Y at the point (l^0, c^0). The basic mathematical idea illustrated there is the Hahn-Banach Theorem, a "separation theorem" for convex sets. This theorem comes in many different forms; the one we will use is as follows.

THEOREM 15.2 (*Geometric form of the Hahn-Banach Theorem*)   *Let S be a normed vector space, and let A, B $\subset$ S be convex sets. Assume that*

> *either   B has an interior point*
>
> *or   S is finite dimensional,*

and that A does not contain any interior points of B. Then there exists a continuous linear functional ϕ, not identically zero on S, and a constant c such that

$$\phi(y) \leq c \leq \phi(x), \quad \text{all } x \in A, \text{ all } y \in B.$$

The proof is rather long and we omit it. (Luenberger 1969 contains a good discussion of the Hahn-Banach Theorem in its various forms.)

The restriction that, if S is infinite-dimensional, then B must have an interior point merits some discussion. Since it is not needed in finite-dimensional spaces, we cannot "see" why it is needed geometrically. The following example illustrates that the restriction is needed in infinite-dimensional spaces.

Let S be the space of infinite sequences $\{x_t\}$, with

$$\|x\| = \sum_{t=0}^{\infty} \beta^t |x_t| < \infty,$$

where $\beta \in (0, 1)$. Let B be the convex set

$$B = \{x \in S: |x_t| \leq 1, t = 0, 1, 2, \ldots\}.$$

There is an obvious sense in which the point $\theta = (0, 0, \ldots)$ is in the middle of the set B. However, as the next exercise shows, it is not in the interior of B.

Exercise 15.6 Show that θ is not in the interior of B.

Hence $A = \{\theta\}$ is a convex set that does not contain any interior points of B. But it is clear that the only continuous linear functional ϕ on S such that $\phi(x) \leq 0$, for all $x \in B$, is the zero functional.

15.2 The First and Second Welfare Theorems

In this section we first define Pareto optima and competitive equilibria for economies where the commodity space is an arbitrary normed vector space. We then state and prove the two fundamental theorems of welfare economics establishing the connections between the two. Theorem 15.3 is the First Welfare Theorem, the famous "invisible hand" result showing that competitive equilibria are Pareto optimal. Theorem 15.4, the Second Welfare Theorem, then draws on the Hahn-Banach Theorem to establish that any Pareto optimum can, for suitably chosen prices, be supported as a competitive equilibrium.

Let S be a vector space, with norm $\|\cdot\|$. There are I consumers, indexed $i = 1, \ldots, I$. Consumer i chooses among commodity points in a set $X_i \subseteq S$, evaluating them according to a utility function $u_i: X_i \to \mathbf{R}$. There are J firms, indexed $j = 1, \ldots, J$. Firm j chooses among points in a set $Y_j \subseteq S$ describing its technological possibilities, evaluating them according to total profits. Note that the set

$$Y = \Sigma_j Y_j = \{\bar{y} \in S : \bar{y} = \Sigma_j y_j \text{ with } y_j \in Y_j, \text{ all } j\},$$

describes the technological possibilities for the economy as a whole.

The interaction between firms and consumers in this economy involves consumers supplying factors of production and consuming final goods (negative and positive components respectively of the x_i's), and firms demanding factors of production and supplying final goods (negative and positive components, respectively, of the y_j's). The totals are constrained by $\Sigma_i x_i - \Sigma_j y_j = 0$. (The alternative assumption that $\Sigma_i x_i - \Sigma_j y_j \leq 0$ assumes free disposal. We prefer to build this assumption, when it is wanted, into our description of the technology.) An $(I + J)$-tuple $[(x_i), (y_j)]$ describing the consumption x_i of each consumer and the production y_j of each firm is an ***allocation*** for this economy. An allocation is called ***feasible*** if $x_i \in X_i$, all i; $y_j = Y_j$, all j; and $\Sigma_i x_i - \Sigma_j y_j = 0$.

The idea of Pareto optimality needs no modification in moving from a Euclidean commodity space to this more abstract setting.

DEFINITION   *An allocation $[(x_i), (y_j)]$ is **Pareto optimal** if it is feasible and if there is no other feasible allocation $[(x_i'), (y_j')]$ such that $u_i(x_i') \geq u_i(x_i)$, all i; and $u_i(x_i') > u_i(x_i)$, some i.*

In this section we follow Debreu (1954) and *define* a price system to be a continuous linear functional $\phi: S \to \mathbf{R}$, since this definition allows us to apply the Hahn-Banach Theorem. The difficulties of economic interpretation this definition gives rise to are treated in Sections 15.3 and 15.4.

DEFINITION   *An allocation $[(x_i^0), (y_j^0)]$ together with a continuous linear functional $\phi: S \to \mathbf{R}$ is a **competitive equilibrium** if*

(E1) $[(x_i^0), (y_j^0)]$ is feasible;
(E2) for each i, $x \in X_i$ and $\phi(x) \leq \phi(x_i^0)$ implies $u_i(x) \leq u_i(x_i^0)$; and
(E3) for each j, $y \in Y_j$ implies $\phi(y) \leq \phi(y_j^0)$.

Condition (E2) states that for each consumer i, given the price system ϕ, the allocation x_i^0 is utility maximizing. Condition (E3) states that at these same prices, for each firm j, the allocation y_j^0 is profit maximizing.

Notice that this definition of a competitive equilibrium makes no reference to the endowments of individual agents [except obliquely through the requirement that $\phi(x) \leq \phi(x_i^0)$] and gives no description of how the profits, if any, earned by firms are distributed among consumers. This omission may seem odd, but for our immediate purposes it makes no difference. In Theorem 15.3 we begin with a competitive equilibrium; so we know the value $\phi(x_i^0)$ of consumer i's consumption. Knowing the value of his consumption is equivalent to knowing the value of his income, and the sources of this income are immaterial. In Theorem 15.4 we start with a Pareto-optimal allocation and find a system of supporting prices. These prices assign a value to each agent's consumption or production; and with the allocation so valued it is clear that many different endowment and ownership arrangements are consistent with the same equilibrium. Of course, if one were concerned with establishing the existence of an equilibrium with given endowments, the above definition would not be useful.

The First Welfare Theorem requires no additional assumptions on the technology and only a nonsatiation condition for consumers.

THEOREM 15.3 (*First Welfare Theorem*)   *Suppose that for each i and each $x \in X_i$, there exists a sequence $\{x_n\}$ in X_i converging to x, such that $u_i(x_n) > u_i(x)$, $n = 1, 2, \ldots$. If $[(x_i^0), (y_j^0), \phi]$ is a competitive equilibrium, then the allocation $[(x_i^0), (y_j^0)]$ is Pareto optimal.*

Proof. Let $[(x_i^0), (y_j^0), \phi]$ be a competitive equilibrium. First we will show that under the stated condition,

(1)   for each i, $u_i(x) = u_i(x_i^0)$ implies $\phi(x) \geq \phi(x_i^0)$.

Suppose to the contrary that

$$u_i(x) = u_i(x_i^0) \text{ and } \phi(x) < \phi(x_i^0).$$

Let $\{x_n\}$ be a sequence in X_i converging to x, such that

$$u_i(x_n) > u_i(x) = u_i(x_i^0), \quad i = 1, 2, \ldots .$$

The continuity of ϕ implies that for all n sufficiently large, $\phi(x_n) < \phi(x_i^0)$, contradicting condition (E2) in the definition of a competitive equilibrium. Hence (1) holds.

Next, suppose that there exists a feasible allocation $[(x_i'), (y_j')]$ such that $u_i(x_i') \geq u_i(x_i^0)$, all i, with strict inequality for some i. Since $[(x_i'), (y_j')]$ is feasible, $x_i' \in X_i$, all i. Hence by condition (E2),

(2)   for each i, $u_i(x_i') > u_i(x_i^0)$ implies $\phi(x_i') > \phi(x_i^0)$.

Since either (1) or (2) holds for each i and since (2) holds for some i, if we sum and use the fact that ϕ is linear, we find that

$$\phi\left(\sum_i x_i'\right) = \sum_i \phi(x_i') > \sum_i \phi(x_i^0) = \phi\left(\sum_i x_i^0\right).$$

Both allocations are feasible, so it follows that

$$\sum_j \phi(y_j') = \phi\left(\sum_j y_j'\right) = \phi\left(\sum_i x_i'\right) > \phi\left(\sum_i x_i^0\right)$$

$$= \phi\left(\sum_j y_j^0\right) = \sum_j \phi(y_j^0),$$

contradicting condition (E3). ∎

The Second Welfare Theorem is a converse to the first. As we will see below, it requires several additional assumptions, because a competitive equilibrium is a more complicated object than a Pareto optimum. It is an allocation together with a price system, so the Second Welfare Theorem takes the form: "Given a Pareto-optimal allocation, there exists a price system such that. . ." It is establishing the existence of a suitable price system that has no counterpart in the First Welfare Theorem. This part of the argument draws on the Hahn-Banach Theorem (Theorem 15.2). To apply this result to the economic problem at hand, we need to ensure the convexity of the relevant sets (A and Y in Figure 15.1) and, for infinite-dimensional commodity spaces, the existence of an interior point. The following assumptions are sufficient for these purposes.

ASSUMPTION 15.1 *For each i, X_i is convex.*

ASSUMPTION 15.2 *For each i, if $x, x' \in X_i$, $u_i(x) > u_i(x')$, and $\theta \in (0, 1)$, then $u_i[\theta x + (1 - \theta)x'] > u_i(x')$.*

ASSUMPTION 15.3 *For each i, $u_i: X_i \to \mathbf{R}$ is continuous.*

ASSUMPTION 15.4 *The set $Y = \Sigma_j Y_j$ is convex.*

ASSUMPTION 15.5 *Either the set $Y = \Sigma_j Y_j$ has an interior point, or S is finite dimensional.*

THEOREM 15.4 (*Second Welfare Theorem*) *Let Assumptions 15.1–15.5 be satisfied, let $[(x_i^0), (y_j^0)]$ be a Pareto-optimal allocation, and assume that for some $h \in \{1, \dots, I\}$ there is $\hat{x}_h \in X_h$ with $u_h(\hat{x}_h) > u_h(x_h^0)$. Then there exists a continuous linear functional $\phi: S \to \mathbf{R}$, not identically zero on S, such that*

(3)   *for each i, $x \in X_i$ and $u_i(x) \geq u_i(x_i^0)$ implies $\phi(x) \geq \phi(x_i^0)$;*

(4)   *for each j, $y \in Y_j$ implies $\phi(y) \leq \phi(y_j^0)$.*

Proof. Let $[(x_i^0), (y_j^0)]$ be a Pareto-optimal allocation. Define the sets

$$A_i = \{x \in X_i: u_i(x) \geq u_i(x_i^0)\}, \quad i = 1, \dots, I.$$

Let $A = \Sigma_i A_i$ and $Y = \Sigma_j Y_j$; we will show that the sets A and Y satisfy the hypotheses of the Hahn-Banach Theorem (Theorem 15.2). Under Assumptions 15.1–15.3, each set A_i is convex, and hence their sum A is also convex. Under Assumptions 15.4 and 15.5, Y is convex and has an interior point if S is infinite dimensional. Finally, we must show that no interior point of Y lies in A.

Suppose to the contrary that $y \in \text{int } Y$ and $y \in A$. Then for some $(x_1, \dots, x_I)$, with $x_i \in A_i$, all i, we have $y = \Sigma_i x_i$. Note that

$$u_i(x_i) \geq u_i(x_i^0), \quad \text{all } i.$$

By hypothesis, there exists $h \in (1, \ldots, I)$, and $\hat{x}_h \in X_h$ such that

$$u_h(\hat{x}_h) > u_h(x_h^0).$$

Let $x_h^\theta = \theta \hat{x}_h + (1 - \theta)x_h, \theta \in (0, 1)$. By Assumptions 15.1 and 15.2,

$$x_h^\theta \in X_h \text{ and } u_h(x_h^\theta) > u_h(x_h^0), \quad \text{all } \theta \in (0, 1).$$

Let $y^\theta = \Sigma_{i \neq h} x_i + x_h^\theta$. Since $y \in \text{int } Y$, it follows that, for $\varepsilon > 0$ sufficiently small, $y^\varepsilon \in Y$. In this case the allocation $[(x_1, \ldots, x_{h-1}, x_h^\varepsilon, x_{h+1}, \ldots, x_I), y^\varepsilon]$ is feasible and satisfies

$$x_i \in X_i, \text{ all } i, \quad u_i(x_i) \geq u_i(x_i^0), \text{ all } i \neq h, \quad \text{and } u_h(x_h^\varepsilon) > u_h(x_h^0),$$

contradicting the Pareto optimality of $[(x_i^0), (y_j^0)]$. Hence no interior point of Y lies in A.

Thus, Theorem 15.2 applies to A and Y, and there exists a continuous linear functional ϕ, not identically zero, and a constant c such that $\phi(y) \leq c \leq \phi(x)$, all $y \in Y$, $x \in A$. Clearly this linear functional satisfies (3) and (4). ∎

Although (4) is precisely the profit-maximization condition (E3) in the definition of a competitive equilibrium, (3) says only that at the prices ϕ, x_i^0 is a *cost-minimizing* choice for consumers over the set A_i of allocations weakly preferred to x_i^0. This is weaker than condition (E2), which requires that x_i^0 be *utility maximizing* over the budget set $\{x_i \in X_i: \phi(x_i) \leq \phi(x_i^0)\}$. The following supplementary result provides the missing link.

REMARK *Let the hypotheses of Theorem 15.4 hold; let $\phi: S \rightarrow \mathbf{R}$ be a continuous linear functional satisfying (3) and (4); and suppose in addition that*

for each i, there exists $x_i' \in X_i$ such that $\phi(x_i') < \phi(x_i^0)$.

Then $[(x_i^0), (y_j^0), \phi]$ is a competitive equilibrium.

Proof. It suffices to show that (E2) holds. By hypothesis, for each i there exists $x_i' \in X_i$ such that $\phi(x_i') < \phi(x_i^0)$. Now suppose that

$$x_i \in X_i \text{ and } \phi(x_i) \leq \phi(x_i^0).$$

Let

$$x_i^\theta = \theta x_i' + (1 - \theta)x_i, \quad \text{all } \theta \in (0, 1).$$

By Assumption 15.1, $x_i^\theta \in X_i$, all $\theta \in (0, 1)$; and by the linearity of ϕ,

$$\phi(x_i^\theta) = \theta\phi(x_i') + (1 - \theta)\phi(x_i) < \phi(x_i^0), \quad \text{all } \theta \in (0, 1).$$

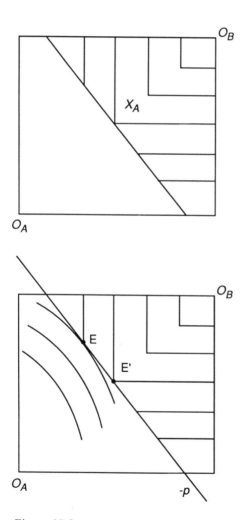

Figure 15.3

Hence it follows by contraposition from (3) that $u_i(x_i^\theta) < u_i(x_i^0)$, all $\theta \in (0, 1)$. Hence by Assumption 15.3, $u_i(x_i) = \lim_{\theta \to 0} u_i(x_i^\theta) \leq u_i(x_i^0)$. ∎

Figure 15.3 illustrates a case where Theorem 15.4 holds but the Remark fails. Consumer A's consumption set is the closed, convex set X_A, and B's is the entire positive orthant. Consumer A's indifference curves form right angles, and B's are smooth and strictly convex, both as shown. The allocation at E is clearly Pareto optimal but cannot be supported as a competitive equilibrium: the only price ratio at which E is utility maximizing for consumer B is the indicated ratio p; but at that price ratio, consumer A prefers the allocation E'.

15.3   Issues in the Choice of a Commodity Space

The two welfare theorems of the last section establish that if Assumptions 15.1–15.5 are satisfied, then the set of competitive equilibrium allocations and the set of Pareto-optimal allocations coincide exactly. Since the latter are simply solutions to the appropriate constrained optimization problems, with weighted sums of consumers' utilities as the objective, these optimization problems provide a very convenient way to study competitive equilibria. In this section we look at particular issues that arise when optimization problems of the type studied in Chapters 4 and 9 are viewed in this way.

Specifically we look at the issues involved in ensuring that Assumptions 15.1–15.5 hold and that the continuous linear functional provided by Theorem 15.4 can be interpreted as a set of prices in the usual sense of the word. In some cases this interpretation requires care in choosing the commodity space $(S, \|\cdot\|)$. The economic model itself generally determines the set S, but the choice of an appropriate norm can be more difficult.

Two considerations play a role in the decision. The first is that the norm chosen determines whether any given function u_i is continuous and whether any given set Y has an interior point. The norm on S must be chosen so that Assumptions 15.3 and 15.5 hold for the preferences and technologies of interest. The second issue is that the choice of the norm determines the class of continuous linear functionals on S. It is convenient if the norm can be chosen so that every continuous linear functional has an inner product representation, since Theorem 15.4

then guarantees the existence of a set of prices in the usual sense. As we will see below, however, these two desiderata sometimes conflict.

In the rest of this section we look at three specific classes of models: a deterministic, one-period model; a deterministic, infinite-horizon model; and a stochastic, one-period model. The first of these provides an example where both criteria are satisfied by any of a wide variety of norms. The last two show how the two criteria can come into conflict. In Section 15.4 we pursue the consequences of dropping the second. There we look at situations where Theorem 15.4 applies but the continuous linear functional it provides may not have an inner product representation. We show how, in these cases, additional assumptions on the preferences and technology can be imposed to guarantee the existence of a price system with an inner product representation.

In static models with no uncertainty, we generally take $S = \mathbf{R}^K$, and $x = (x_1, \ldots, x_K) \in S$ is interpreted as a list of quantities of K different goods. Since this space is finite dimensional, we do not have to worry about the existence of an interior point for Y. Moreover, all the norms on this space that one might reasonably think of—for example, $(\Sigma_k |x_k|^p)^{1/p}$, $p \geq 1$; $\Sigma_k \alpha_k |x_k|$, $\alpha_k > 0$, all k; $\max_k |x_k|$; and so forth—have the feature that a sequence $\{x_n\}$ in $\mathbf{R}^K$ converges to x if and only if $\{x_{nk}\}$ converges to x_k, for $k = 1, \ldots, K$. Hence any function u_i that is continuous in one of these norms is continuous in all of them. Finally, as was shown in Section 15.1, every linear functional on a finite-dimensional Euclidean space has an inner product representation, $\phi(x) = p \cdot x$, and conversely.

Dynamic models with a finite number of periods and stochastic models with a finite number of states-of-the-world have exactly the same mathematical properties, since the commodity space is still a finite-dimensional Euclidean space. However, infinite-horizon dynamic models and stochastic models with an infinite number of states raise a new set of mathematical issues. We turn to these now.

In the one-sector model of optimal growth, an allocation is an infinite sequence $x = (x_0, x_1, \ldots)$. As we saw in Section 15.1, all of the l_p spaces consist of such elements, so this family seems to offer many possibilities for commodity spaces. However, working with any of the l_p spaces other than l_∞ causes serious difficulties. In the first place, if $1 \leq p < \infty$, then $x \in l_p$ only if the series $\Sigma_{t=0}^\infty |x_t|^p$ converges, which requires $\lim_{t \to \infty} x_t = 0$. Although one has some flexibility in interpreting the zero point, this condition is obviously a severe restriction on the kind of dynamics that can be considered. The next exercise illustrates a second difficulty: none of the l_p spaces with p finite can have a production set in the positive orthant with an interior point. Among the l_p spaces, only l_∞ has a positive orthant with interior points.

Exercise 15.7   a. Show that for $1 \le p < \infty$, the positive orthant of l_p has no interior points.
   b. Show that the positive orthant of l_∞ has a nonempty interior.

Within the l_p family, Theorem 15.4 can be applied only if l_∞ is chosen as the commodity space. The following example shows that functionals on l_∞ that are not in l_1 can arise in models satisfying Assumptions 15.1–15.5.

   Consider an infinite-horizon economy with one consumption good. The commodity space S is l_∞, and x_t is interpreted as units of the single good available in period t. The production set is

$$Y = \{y \in S: 0 \le y_t \le 1 + 1/t, \text{ all } t\};$$

the consumption set is

$$X = \{x \in S: x_t \ge 0, \text{ all } t\};$$

and preferences $u: S \to \mathbf{R}$ are defined by

(1) $u(x) = \inf_t x_t.$

Exercise 15.8   Show that this economy satisfies Assumptions 15.1–15.5.

One Pareto-optimal allocation in this economy is $x_t^0 = y_t^0 = 1 + 1/t, t = 1, 2, \ldots$. By Theorem 15.4, then, there is a continuous linear functional $\phi: S \to \mathbf{R}$, not identically zero on S, such that x^0, y^0, and ϕ together satisfy

(2) $x \in X$ and $u(x) \ge u(x^0)$ implies $\phi(x) \ge \phi(x^0)$;

(3) $y \in Y$ implies $\phi(y) \le \phi(y^0)$.

Suppose it were the case that this functional could be written

(4) $$\phi(x) = \sum_{t=1}^{\infty} p_t x_t,$$

for some sequence $\{p_t\}$. If $p_t < 0$ for any t, then (3) would be violated, since replacing y_t^0 with 0 would yield a higher-profit element of Y. Since not all of the p_t's can be zero, $p_t > 0$ for some t. Now consider the sequence $\underline{1} = (1, 1, 1, \ldots)$. Clearly $\underline{1} \in X$; and for the preferences in (1), $u(\underline{1}) = u(x^0)$. But if $p_t > 0$ for any t, then

$$\phi(\underline{1}) = \sum_{t=1}^{\infty} p_t < \sum_{t=1}^{\infty} p_t\left(1 + \frac{1}{t}\right) = \phi(x^0),$$

so (2) is violated. Thus $\phi(x)$ cannot take the form given in (4); rather, the equilibrium valuation must "put all of its weight at infinity."

As economists, we do not want to talk about "prices at infinity," so this case poses a problem. The solution must involve ruling out preferences, like those in (1), that put extreme emphasis on outcomes—in this case, consumption arbitrarily far in the future—that our economic instincts tell us actual consumers do not put much weight on. But we want to do this in a way that does not compromise the wide applicability of the theory.

As Exercise 15.8 shows, continuity in the sup norm does not rule out the preferences in (1). The l_p spaces with $1 \leq p < \infty$ are not useful alternatives for this problem, since none of them contains Y as a subset. What about the space of sequences $\{x_t\}$ with

(5) $$\|x\| = \sum_{t=1}^{\infty} \beta^t |x_t| < \infty,$$

where $\beta \in (0, 1)$? Continuity in this norm rules out the preferences in (1); here the norm of the space itself expresses the idea that consumption in the distant future ought not to matter very much.

Exercise 15.9   Show that the preferences in (1) are not continuous if the norm in (5) is used.

But this line also fails: as shown in Exercise 15.6, the positive orthant
then has no interior point, so Assumption 15.5 is violated.

These examples illustrate something of a theoretical bind. We want to
choose a commodity space for infinite-horizon problems to which we can
apply Theorem 15.4. To do this we require that the production set Y
have an interior, which dictates the use of l_∞. But a linear functional on l_∞
need not have an inner product representation: it need not lie in l_1. In
other words, it may not have an economic interpretation as a price
system. The approach we use in the next section is to use l_∞ as the
commodity space but to impose stronger assumptions on the preferences and technology. Under these stronger assumptions, we are able to
construct from the functional ϕ of Theorem 15.4 a related, but possibly
different, functional that *is* in l_1 and also serves as an equilibrium price
system.

Exactly the same issues arise in stochastic models. Let $(Z, \mathfrak{X}, \mu)$ be a
probability space, where $z \in Z$ describes the state-of-the-world. If there
are K commodities in each state, then an allocation is a $\mathfrak{X}$-measurable
function $x: Z \to \mathbf{R}^K$, where $x(z)$ is a K-vector of contingent claims to goods
to be delivered if the state $z \in Z$ occurs. Hence we want the set S to be the
set of all such functions. We then must choose a suitable norm for S and
use elements of the dual space as price systems.

For exactly the reasons already discussed, we want to take the com-
modity space to be the space $L_\infty(Z, \mathfrak{X}, \mu)$ of essentially bounded equivalence classes of functions, with the ess sup norm defined in Section 15.1.
The difficulty then is that not every continuous linear functional on
$L_\infty(Z, \mathfrak{X}, \mu)$ can be represented as an inner product of the form

$$\phi(x) = \int p(z)x(z) \, d\mu(z),$$

where $p \in L_1(Z, \mathfrak{X}, \mu)$. To see this, note that the example above can be
interpreted as a one-period model of uncertainty, where $t \in \{0, 1, \ldots\}$
indicates the state-of-the-world, and $\beta^t/(1 - \beta)$ is the probability that the
tth state occurs. Using $L_\infty(Z, \mathfrak{X}, \mu)$ as the commodity space raises exactly
the same set of difficulties as does using l_∞. In the next section we show
one way these difficulties can be dealt with.

15.4 Inner Product Representations of Prices

We have seen that if the commodity space is l_∞ or $L_\infty(Z, \mathfrak{X}, \mu)$, the linear functional ϕ the existence of which is asserted in Theorem 15.4 need not have an inner product representation. In this section we show that in these and similar cases we can, by imposing additional requirements on the preferences and technology, strengthen Theorem 15.4 to ensure the existence of prices, that is, of a linear functional that can be represented as an inner product. We deal first with time and then with uncertainty, and then comment briefly on combining both.

Consider an infinite-horizon economy. Let the normed vector space $(X, \|\cdot\|_x)$ be the one-period commodity space, which we take to be the same for each period. Let $S = X \times X \times \ldots$ be the space of sequences $x = (x_0, x_1, \ldots)$, $x_t \in X$, with the norm

$$\|x\|_s = \sup_t \|x_t\|_x < \infty.$$

For any $x = (x_0, x_1, \ldots) \in S$, let $x^T \in S$ denote the truncated sequence $x^T = (x_0, \ldots, x_T, \theta, \theta, \ldots)$. In Lemma 15.5 these truncations are used to show that every continuous linear functional ϕ on S can be decomposed into a "well-behaved" part, ψ, and a part that puts "weight at infinity," the rest. The lemma shows how to construct ψ given ϕ. Then in Theorem 15.6 it is shown that with the preferences and technology suitably restricted, the functional ψ is also an equilibrium price system.

L E M M A 15.5 *Let ϕ be a continuous linear functional on the normed vector space $(S, \|\cdot\|_s)$ defined above. Then*

(1) $\qquad \psi(x) = \lim_{T \to \infty} \phi(x^T), \quad \text{all } x \in S,$

defines a continuous linear functional on S, and ψ can be written as

(2) $\qquad \psi(x) = \sum_{t=0}^{\infty} \psi_t(x_t), \quad \text{all } x \in S,$

where each ψ_t is a continuous linear functional on X.

Proof. We must show that the limit in (1) exists for all $x \in S$ and that ψ so defined is a continuous linear functional. First note that since ϕ is continuous, it follows from Theorem 15.1 that $\|\phi\| < \infty$.

If $x = \theta$, then clearly $\psi(\theta) = 0$. Suppose $x \neq \theta$. For each $t = 0, 1, \ldots$, let $\underline{x}_t = (\theta, \ldots, \theta, x_t, \theta, \ldots)$; let

$$y_t = \begin{cases} x_t & \text{if } \phi(\underline{x}_t) \geq 0 \\ -x_t & \text{if } \phi(\underline{x}_t) < 0; \end{cases}$$

and let $\underline{y}_t = (\theta, \ldots, \theta, y_t, \theta, \ldots)$. Then for all T,

$$\phi(x^T) = \sum_{t=0}^{T} \phi(\underline{x}_t) \leq \sum_{t=0}^{T} |\phi(\underline{x}_t)| = \sum_{t=0}^{T} \phi(\underline{y}_t) = \phi(y^T)$$

$$\leq \|\phi\| \|y^T\|_s = \|\phi\| \|x^T\|_s \leq \|\phi\| \|x\|_s.$$

That is, the series $\sum_{t=0}^{T} |\phi(\underline{x}_t)|$ is bounded above by $\|\phi\| \|x\|_s$ and hence converges. It follows that the series $\sum_{t=0}^{T} \phi(\underline{x}_t)$ also converges, so $\psi(x)$ is well defined.

Clearly ψ is linear, and $\psi(x) \leq \|\phi\| \|x\|_s$, all $x \in S$; hence $\|\psi\| \leq \|\phi\| < \infty$, so ψ is bounded. It then follows from Theorem 15.1 that ψ is continuous.

Finally, let X^* be the dual of X, and define the continuous linear functionals $\psi_t \in X^*$, $t = 0, 1, \ldots$, by

$$\psi_t(x_t) = \phi(\underline{x}_t).$$

Then (2) follows immediately from (1). ∎

If X is the finite-dimensional Euclidean space $\mathbf{R}^K$, then, as shown in Section 15.1, each linear functional ψ_t has an inner product representation: $\psi_t(x_t) = p_t \cdot x_t$ for some $p_t = (p_{t1}, \ldots, p_{tK}) \in \mathbf{R}^K$. Hence, for this case, the linear functional ψ can be written as an inner product

$$(3) \qquad \psi(x) = \sum_{t=0}^{\infty} \psi_t(x_t) = \sum_{t=0}^{\infty} p_t \cdot x_t = \sum_{t=0}^{\infty} \sum_{k=1}^{K} p_{tk} x_{tk}.$$

Next we show that under somewhat stronger assumptions on the preferences and technology, the linear functional ϕ given in Theorem 15.4

defines—by means of (1)—a functional ψ that is a competitive equilibrium price system and does not put any "weight at infinity." We need two
additional assumptions. The commodity space S and the definitions of
truncated sequences are as above. Note that the X_i's and Y_j's are subsets
of S, not of X.

ASSUMPTION 15.6 *For each i, $x \in X_i$ implies $x^T \in X_i$, for all T sufficiently
large; and for each j, $y \in Y_j$ implies $y^T \in Y_j$, for all T sufficiently large.*

ASSUMPTION 15.7 *For each i, if x, $x' \in X_i$ and $u_i(x) > u_i(x')$, then
$u_i(x^T) > u_i(x')$, for all T sufficiently large.*

Assumption 15.6 says that truncated feasible sequences are feasible for
consumers and producers, if the truncation is sufficiently far in the
future. Assumption 15.7 is a continuity requirement on preferences to
the effect that sufficiently distant consumption is "discounted" in a very
weak sense.

> **Exercise 15.10** Let $C \subseteq X$ be a convex set with $\theta \in C$, and let $X_i =$
> $C \times C \times \ldots .$
>   a. Show that X_i satisfies Assumptions 15.1 and 15.6.
>   b. Let $U_i: C \to \mathbf{R}$ be a bounded function satisfying Assumptions 15.2
> and 15.3, and let $\beta \in (0, 1)$. Show that $u_i: X_i \to \mathbf{R}$ defined by $u_i(x) =$
> $\Sigma_{t=0}^{\infty} \beta^t U_i(x_t)$ satisfies Assumptions 15.2, 15.3, and 15.7.
>   c. Let $C = \mathbf{R}_+^n$, and let $W: C \times \mathbf{R}_+ \to \mathbf{R}_+$ be an aggregator function, as
> defined in Section 5.11. Show that the fixed point u_W of the operator T_W
> defined there satisfies Assumptions 15.2, 15.3, and 15.7.

> **Exercise 15.11** Let $S = l_\infty$.
>   a. Show that the preferences $u(x) = \inf_t x_t$ do not satisfy Assumption
> 15.7.
>   b. Let $c_0 \subset l_\infty$ be the subspace consisting of all sequences converging to
> zero. Then Assumption 15.6 requires that for each i, $x \in X_i$ implies that
> the tail of the sequence $\{x^T\}$ lies in $X_i \cap c_0$. Show that Assumption 15.7
> then holds if and only if $u_i(x) = \lim_{T \to \infty} u_i(x^T)$.

Our next theorem shows that under these two additional assumptions,
if $[(x_i^0), (y_j^0), \phi]$ is a competitive equilibrium, then so is $[(x_i^0), (y_j^0), \psi]$,
where ψ is defined by (1).

THEOREM 15.6   *Let S be the normed vector space defined above; let Assumptions 15.1–15.7 hold; let* $[(x_i^0), (y_j^0), \phi]$ *be a feasible allocation and continuous linear functional such that*

(4)   for each i, $x \in X_i$ and $u_i(x) \geq u_i(x_i^0)$ implies $\phi(x) \geq \phi(x_i^0)$;

(5)   for each j, $y \in Y_j$ implies $\phi(y) \leq \phi(y_j^0)$;

and suppose that for each i there exists $\hat{x}_i \in X_i$ *such that* $u_i(\hat{x}_i) > u_i(x_i^0)$. *Let ψ be the continuous linear functional defined by (1). Then (4) and (5) also hold with ψ in place of ϕ.*

Proof. We first verify that

(6)   for each i, $x \in X_i$ and $u_i(x) \geq u_i(x_i^0)$ implies $\psi(x) \geq \phi(x_i^0)$; and

(7)   for each j, $y \in Y_j$ implies $\psi(y) \leq \phi(y_j^0)$.

Fix i, and suppose that $x \in X_i$ with $u_i(x) \geq u_i(x_i^0)$. By hypothesis, there exists $\hat{x}_i \in X_i$ such that $u_i(\hat{x}_i) > u_i(x_i^0)$. Define

$$x^\theta = \theta\hat{x}_i + (1 - \theta)x, \quad \text{all } \theta \in (0, 1).$$

By Assumptions 15.1 and 15.2,

$$x^\theta \in X_i \quad \text{and} \quad u_i(x^\theta) > u_i(x_i^0), \quad \text{all } \theta \in (0, 1).$$

Fix $\theta \in (0, 1)$; by Assumptions 15.6 and 15.7,

$$x^{\theta T} \in X_i \quad \text{and} \quad u_i(x^{\theta T}) > u_i(x_i^0), \quad \text{all } T \text{ sufficiently large.}$$

Then it follows from (4) that for all T sufficiently large,

$$\phi(x_i^0) \leq \phi(x^{\theta T}) = \theta\phi(\hat{x}_i^T) + (1 - \theta)\phi(x^T).$$

As shown in Lemma 15.5, the limit on the right side is well defined as $T \to \infty$; hence, taking the limit and using the definition of ψ, we find that

$$\phi(x_i^0) \leq \theta\psi(\hat{x}_i) + (1 - \theta)\psi(x).$$

Since this holds for each $\theta \in (0, 1)$, taking the limit as $\theta \to 0$ we find that $\phi(x_i^0) \leq \psi(x)$, establishing (6).

Let $y \in Y_j$. Then for all T sufficiently large, it follows from Assumption 15.6 and (5) that $y^T \in Y_j$ and $\psi(y^T) = \phi(y^T) \leq \phi(y_j^0)$. Letting $T \to \infty$ establishes (7).

Now, from (6) and (7), it follows that

$$\psi(x_i^0) \geq \phi(x_i^0), \quad \text{all } i, \quad \text{and}$$

$$\psi(y_j^0) \leq \phi(y_j^0), \quad \text{all } j.$$

Summing over i and j and recalling that $x^0 = \Sigma_i x_i^0 = \Sigma_j y_j^0 = y^0$, we obtain

$$\psi(x^0) \geq \phi(x^0) = \phi(y^0) \geq \psi(y^0) = \psi(x^0),$$

so $\psi(x^0) = \phi(x^0) = \phi(y^0) = \psi(y^0)$. It then follows from the inequalities above that

$$\psi(x_i^0) = \phi(x_i^0), \quad \text{all } i, \quad \text{and}$$

$$\psi(y_j^0) = \phi(y_j^0), \quad \text{all } j.$$

Then (6) and (7) respectively imply that ϕ can be replaced with ψ in (4) and (5). ∎

Under Assumptions 15.1–15.7, Theorems 15.4 and 15.6 together imply that for any Pareto-optimal allocation $[(x_i^0), (y_j^0)]$, there exists a continuous linear functional ψ such that (4) and (5) hold (with ψ in place of ϕ) and such that ψ does not put any "weight at infinity." That is, $\psi(x) = \lim_{T \to \infty} \psi(x^T)$, all $x \in S$. If, in addition, ψ satisfies the hypotheses of the Remark following Theorem 15.4, then $[(x_j), (y_j), \psi]$ is a competitive equilibrium. If the one-period commodity space X is simply $\mathbf{R}^K$, then Theorems 15.4 and 15.6 give conditions under which Pareto-optimal allocations can be supported as competitive equilibria by price systems of the form given in (3).

Similar arguments can be used in models involving uncertainty. We consider first a one-period model. Let $(Z, \mathcal{Z}, \mu)$ be a probability space. For ease of exposition, we consider a one-good economy and take the commodity space to be $L_\infty(Z, \mathcal{Z}, \mu)$. As above, we proceed in two steps. First we show that given any continuous linear functional ϕ on $L_\infty(Z, \mathfrak{L}, \mu)$, we can construct a continuous linear functional ψ that is the "well-behaved" part of ϕ. We then impose additional assumptions on the preferences and technology that ensure that ψ also satisfies the conclusions of Theorem 15.4.

As above, we work with truncated allocations, in this case truncating over events. Given $x \in L_\infty(Z, \mathfrak{L}, \mu)$ and $A \in \mathfrak{L}$, define $x^A \in L_\infty(Z, \mathfrak{L}, \mu)$ by

$$x^A(z) = \begin{cases} 0 & \text{if } z \in A, \\ x(z) & \text{otherwise.} \end{cases}$$

Thus, x^A simply truncates the function (allocation) x to zero over the set A. The analogue of Lemma 15.5 is the following result.

LEMMA 15.7　*For any continuous linear functional ϕ on $L_\infty(Z, \mathfrak{L}, \mu)$, there is a nested, decreasing sequence of sets $A_1 \supset A_2 \supset \ldots$ in $\mathfrak{L}$, with $\lim_{n\to\infty} \mu(A_n) = 0$, and a continuous linear functional ψ such that*

$$\psi(x) = \lim_{n\to\infty} \phi(x^{A_n}), \quad \text{all } x \in L_\infty(Z, \mathfrak{L}, \mu).$$

Moreover, there exists a function $p \in L_1(Z, \mathfrak{L}, \mu)$ such that

$$\psi(x) = \int p(z)x(z)d\mu, \quad \text{all } x \in L_\infty(Z, \mathfrak{L}, \mu).$$

We omit the proof, which follows directly from Theorems 1.22 and 1.24 in Yosida and Hewitt (1952).

To apply this result we need to add two assumptions, the analogues of Assumptions 15.6 and 15.7. We use the shorthand notation $A_n \downarrow 0$ to indicate that $\{A_n\}$ is a nested, decreasing sequence of sets in $\mathfrak{L}$, with $\lim_{n\to\infty} \mu(A_n) = 0$.

ASSUMPTION 15.8　*For each i, if $x \in X_i$ and $A_n \downarrow 0$, then $x^{A_n} \in X_i$, for all n sufficiently large; and for each j, if $y \in Y_j$ and $A_n \downarrow 0$, then $y^{A_n} \in Y_j$, for all n sufficiently large.*

ASSUMPTION 15.9　*For each i, if $x, x' \in X_i$, $u_i(x) > u_i(x')$, and $A_n \downarrow 0$, then for all n sufficiently large, $u_i(x^{A_n}) > u_i(x')$.*

Assumption 15.8 requires that *conditionally* truncated feasible allocations be feasible, provided the truncation probability is sufficiently small. Assumption 15.9 requires that consumers value truncated consumption sequences almost as highly as the corresponding untruncated sequences, provided the truncation probability is sufficiently small.

Exercise 15.12 Let $X_i \subset L_\infty(Z, \mathfrak{X}, \mu)$ satisfy Assumptions 15.1 and 15.8. Let μ_i be any probability measure on $(Z, \mathfrak{X})$ that is absolutely continuous with respect to μ; and let $U_i: \mathbf{R} \to \mathbf{R}$ satisfy Assumptions 15.2 and 15.3. Show that if $u_i: X_i \to \mathbf{R}$ has the form $u_i(x) = \int U_i[x(z)]\, d\mu_i(z)$, then u_i satisfies Assumptions 15.2, 15.3, and 15.9.

Using Lemma 15.7 and these two additional assumptions, we then have the following result.

THEOREM 15.8 *Let $(Z, \mathfrak{X}, \mu)$ be a probability space; let S be the normed vector space $L_\infty(Z, \mathfrak{X}, \mu)$; let Assumptions 15.1–15.5 and 15.8–15.9 hold; let $[(x_i^0), (y_j^0), \phi]$ be a feasible allocation and a continuous linear functional such that (4) and (5) hold; and suppose that for each i there exists $\hat{x}_i \in X_i$ such that $u_i(\hat{x}_i) > u_i(x_i^0)$. Let ψ be the continuous linear functional given by Lemma 15.7. Then (4) and (5) hold with ψ in place of ϕ.*

The proof parallels exactly that of Theorem 15.6, and we do not repeat it. Note, too, that this argument holds for any finite number of goods.

For models like the ones in Chapter 9 that combine an infinite time horizon and uncertainty, the arguments above must be combined. First, note that it is straightforward to modify Lemma 15.5, Assumptions 15.6 and 15.7, and Theorem 15.6 to allow for commodity spaces that are different in each period. Let $(X_t, \|\cdot\|_t)$, $t = 0, 1, \dots$, be a sequence of normed vector spaces; and define the normed vector space $(S, \|\cdot\|_s)$ by $S = X_0 \times X_1 \times \dots$ and

(8) $$\|x\|_s = \sup_t \|x_t\|_t.$$

Define truncated sequences as before. Then Lemma 15.5 goes through with only notational modifications: for any continuous linear functional ϕ on S, (1) defines a continuous linear functional ψ on S, and ψ can be written as in (2), where for each t, ψ_t is a continuous linear functional on

$(X_t, \|\cdot\|_t)$. Theorem 15.6 also goes through as before: under the same hypotheses, if $[(x_i^0), (y_j^0), \phi]$ satisfy (4) and (5), then $[(x_i^0), (y_j^0), \psi]$ also satisfy (4) and (5), where ψ is defined by (1).

The rest of the argument consists of applying Lemma 15.7 and Theorem 15.8. We illustrate this application with the one-good, stochastic optimal growth model. Let $(Z^t, \mathfrak{X}^t, \mu^t)$, $t = 0, 1, \ldots$, be a sequence of probability spaces; for each t, let $X_t = L_\infty(Z^t, \mathfrak{X}^t, \mu^t)$; and let $S = X_0 \times X_1 \times \ldots$ with the norm in (8). Then for each fixed t, Lemma 15.7 applies. To apply Theorem 15.8, we must assume that the analogues of Assumptions 15.8 and 15.9 hold for each t. For any $x = (x_0, x_1, \ldots) \in S$, let $x^{A_{tn}} = (x_0, \ldots, x_{t-1}, x_t^{A_{tn}}, x_{t+1}, \ldots) \in S$. Use $A_{tn} \downarrow 0$ to indicate that $\{A_{tn}\}_{n=1}^\infty$ is a nested, decreasing sequence of sets in $\mathfrak{X}^t$, with $\lim_{n\to\infty} \mu^t(A_{tn}) = 0$.

ASSUMPTION 15.8' *For each i, t, if $x \in X_i$ and $A_{tn} \downarrow 0$, then $x^{A_{tn}} \in X_i$, for all n sufficiently large; and for each j, t, if $y \in Y_j$ and $A_{tn} \downarrow 0$, then $y^{A_{tn}} \in Y_j$, for all n sufficiently large.*

ASSUMPTION 15.9' *For each i, t, if $x, x' \in X_i$, $u_i(x) > u_i(x')$, and $A_{tn} \downarrow 0$, then for all n sufficiently large, $u_i(x^{A_{tn}}) > u_i(x')$.*

We then have the following result.

THEOREM 15.9 *Let S be the normed vector space defined above; let Assumptions 15.1–15.7 and 15.8'–15.9' hold; let $[(x_i^0), (y_j^0), \phi]$ be a feasible allocation and a continuous linear functional such that (4) and (5) hold; and suppose that for each i, there exists $\hat{x}_i \in X_i$ such that $u_i(\hat{x}_i) > u_i(x_i^0)$. Then there exists a continuous linear functional ν on S such that (4) and (5) hold with ν in place of ϕ and such that ν can be written as*

$$(9) \qquad \nu(x) = \sum_{t=0}^\infty \int_{Z^t} p_t(z^t) x_t(z^t) \, d\mu^t(z^t), \quad \text{all } x \in S,$$

where $p_t \in L_1(Z^t, \mathfrak{X}^t, \mu^t)$, all t.

Proof. Let ψ be the continuous linear functional on S defined by (1), and let $\{\psi_t\}$ be the continuous linear functionals on the spaces $\{X_t\}$ such that (2) holds. As noted above, minor modifications of Lemma 15.5 and Theorem 15.6 ensure that these are well defined and that (4) and (5) hold with ψ in place of ϕ. That is,

(10)　　　for each i, $x \in X_i$ and $u_i(x) \geq u_i(x_i^0)$ implies

$$\psi(x) = \sum_{t=0}^{\infty} \psi_t(x_t) \geq \sum_{t=0}^{\infty} \psi_t(x_{it}^0) = \psi(x_i^0);$$

(11)　　　for each j, $y \in Y_j$ implies

$$\psi(y) = \sum_{t=0}^{\infty} \psi_t(y_t) \leq \sum_{t=0}^{\infty} \psi_t(y_{jt}^0) = \psi(y_j^0).$$

For each ψ_t, it follows from Lemma 15.7 that there exists $A_{tn} \downarrow 0$ and a continuous linear functional ν_t such that

(12)　　　$\nu_t(x_t) = \lim_{n \to \infty} \psi_t(x_t^{A_{tn}})$,　all $x_t \in X_t$.

Define the continuous linear functional ν on S by

$$\nu(x) = \sum_{t=0}^{\infty} \nu_t(x_t), \quad \text{all } x \in S.$$

Next we will verify that

(13)　　　for each i, $x \in X_i$ and $u_i(x) \geq u_i(x_i^0)$ implies

$$\nu(x) = \sum_{t=0}^{\infty} \nu_t(x_t) \geq \sum_{t=0}^{\infty} \psi_t(x_{it}^0) = \psi(x_i^0);$$

(14)　　　for each j, $y \in Y_j$ implies

$$\nu(y) = \sum_{t=0}^{\infty} \nu_t(y_t) \leq \sum_{t=0}^{\infty} \psi_t(y_{jt}^0) = \psi(y_j^0).$$

Fix i, and suppose that $x \in X_i$ with $u_i(x) \geq u_i(x_i^0)$. By hypothesis, there exists $\hat{x}_i \in X_i$ such that $u_i(\hat{x}_i) > u_i(x_i^0)$. Define

$$x_\theta = \theta\hat{x}_i + (1 - \theta)x, \quad \text{all } \theta \in (0, 1).$$

By Assumptions 15.1 and 15.2,

$$x^\theta \in X_i \text{ and } u_i(x^\theta) > u_i(x_i^0), \quad \text{all } \theta \in (0, 1).$$

Fix $\theta \in (0, 1)$; then by Assumptions 15.6 and 15.7, for some $\hat{T}(\theta)$ sufficiently large,

$$x^{\theta T} \in X_i \text{ and } u_i(x^{\theta T}) > u_i(x_i^0), \quad \text{all } T \geq \hat{T}(\theta).$$

For each ψ_t, let $A_{tn} \downarrow 0$ be the sequence used in defining ν_t in (12). For any function $x \in S$, let $x^{Tn} \in S$ denote the function that is truncated to zero in all components past the Tth, and on the sets A_{tn}, for $t = 0, 1, \ldots, T$. That is,

$$x^{Tn} = (x_0^{A_{0n}}, x_1^{A_{1n}}, \ldots, x_T^{A_{Tn}}, 0, 0, \ldots).$$

Fix $T \geq \hat{T}(\theta)$; then it follows from repeated application of Assumptions 15.8′ and 15.9′ that for some $N(T)$ sufficiently large,

$$x^{\theta Tn} \in X_i \text{ and } u_i(x^{\theta Tn}) > u_i(x_i^0), \quad \text{all } n \geq N(T).$$

Hence it follows from (10) and the definition of the ν_t's that

$$\sum_{t=0}^\infty \psi_t(x_{it}^0) \leq \sum_{t=0}^T \psi_t(x_t^{\theta A_{tn}}) = \sum_{t=0}^T \nu_t(x_t^{\theta A_{tn}}), \quad \text{all } n \geq N(T).$$

Since the right side converges as $n \to \infty$, it follows that

$$\sum_{t=0}^\infty \psi_t(x_{it}^0) \leq \sum_{t=0}^T \nu_t(x_t^\theta), \quad \text{all } T \geq \hat{T}(\theta).$$

Then since the right side converges as $T \to \infty$, it follows that

$$\sum_{t=0}^\infty \psi_t(x_{it}^0) \leq \sum_{t=0}^\infty \nu_t(x_t^\theta), \quad \text{all } \theta \in (0, 1).$$

Then from the linearity of the ν_t's, it follows that

$$\sum_{t=0}^\infty \psi_t(x_{it}^0) \leq \theta \sum_{t=0}^\infty \nu_t(\hat{x}_t) + (1 - \theta) \sum_{t=0}^\infty \nu_t(x_t), \quad \text{all } \theta \in (0, 1).$$

Taking the limit as $\theta \to 0$, we then find that

$$\psi(x_i^0) = \sum_{t=0}^{\infty} \psi_t(x_{it}^0) \le \sum_{t=0}^{\infty} \nu_t(x_t) = \nu(x),$$

which establishes (13).

Next let $y \in Y_j$. Then by Assumption 15.6, there exists some $\hat{T}$ such that $y^T \in Y_j$, for all $T \ge \hat{T}$. Fix $T \ge \hat{T}$; then by Assumption 15.8', there exists some $N(T)$ such that $y^{Tn} \in Y_j$, for all $n \ge N(T)$. It then follows from (11) and the definition of the ν_t's that

$$\sum_{t=0}^{\infty} \psi_t(y_{jt}^0) \ge \sum_{t=0}^{T} \psi_t(y_t^{A_m}) = \sum_{t=0}^{T} \nu_t(y_t^{A_m}), \quad \text{all } n \ge N(T).$$

Taking the limit as $n \to \infty$ and then as $T \to \infty$ establishes (14).

From (13) and (14), it can be established that

$$\psi(x_i^0) = \nu(x_i^0), \quad \text{all } i, \quad \text{and}$$

$$\psi(y_j^0) = \nu(y_j^0), \quad \text{all } j;$$

the argument parallels exactly the one in the proof of Theorem 15.6. It then follows from these equalities together with (13) and (14) that (4) and (5) hold with ν in place of ϕ.

Finally, by Lemma 15.7, each ν_t can be represented by a function $p_t \in L_1(Z^t, \mathscr{L}^t, \mu^t)$; hence ν can be written as shown in (9). ∎

15.5 Bibliographic Notes

Luenberger (1969, chap. 5) contains an excellent discussion of dual spaces, including many of the most common examples, and of the Hahn-Banach Theorem.

The two fundamental welfare theorems reviewed in Section 15.2 date from Arrow (1951), where a set-theoretic formulation of both theorems was given for the first time and where the separation theorem for convex sets was first used to prove the second theorem. Theorems 15.3 and 15.4 and the Remark all appear in that paper, essentially as here except for the restriction to $\mathbf{R}^n$. The extension of these results to commodity spaces that are arbitrary normed vector spaces was first made in Debreu (1954), and our treatment follows his very closely. The main difference is that we assume a continuous utility function rather than a preference ordering for each consumer.

Jones (1986) contains a set of examples illuminating the problems that can arise in infinite-dimensional commodity spaces. These examples illustrate very nicely where certain norms (or more generally, certain topologies) cause difficulties. As the examples in Section 15.3 show, many potentially interesting commodity spaces lack interior points. Some recent work has been devoted to developing new arguments—arguments that do not involve the Hahn-Banach Theorem—for establishing the existence of supporting prices: see Mas-Colell (1986a,b) and Back (1988).

For the commodity space l_∞, Bewley (1972) first studied the existence of competitive equilibria supported by prices in l_1. In his treatment the role of Assumptions 15.6 and 15.7 is played by the assumption that preferences are continuous in the Mackey topology. The appendix of that paper contains a proof that expected utility has this continuity property. The treatment in Section 15.4 follows closely the one in Prescott and Lucas (1972). Brown and Lewis (1981) showed that Mackey-continuity of preferences is equivalent to Assumptions 15.6 and 15.7, as well as to similar assumptions that treat the "tails" in different ways.

16 Applications of Equilibrium Theory

An immediate consequence of the theory reviewed in Chapter 15 is that the solutions to certain planning problems can be interpreted as competitive equilibria of economies with a large number of consumers who have identical preferences and identical endowments, and a large number of firms that have identical constant-returns-to-scale technologies. The variables in such an economy are thought of as per capita magnitudes. Since the consumers have identical preferences, solving the social planner's problem is equivalent to finding the symmetric Pareto-optimal allocations. The First Welfare Theorem then ensures that all symmetric competitive equilibria are symmetric Pareto optima and hence are solutions to the planning problem. The Second Welfare Theorem ensures that all symmetric Pareto optima, and hence all solutions to the planning problem, are, for suitable prices, supportable as competitive equilibria. The models in Sections 16.1–16.4 illustrate various ways in which this type of argument can be applied.

In Sections 16.5 and 16.6 we look at the issue of representing competitive equilibrium prices as inner products. In Section 16.5 we consider a more general form of truncation than the one in Assumptions 15.6 and 15.7. This generalization permits a strengthening of Theorem 15.6 that is useful in some applications. In Section 16.6 we give a cautionary example that highlights a limitation on the applicability of Theorem 15.6.

In Section 16.7 we show that the Pareto-optimal allocations for a growth model with many heterogeneous consumers can be obtained by the methods of dynamic programming. We also show that the theory of Chapter 15 can be applied to characterize equilibrium prices in this case, just as it can in economies with identical consumers.

16.1   A One-Sector Model of Growth under Certainty

Consider the deterministic one-sector growth model that we studied in Sections 5.1 and 6.1. There is one produced good, which can be consumed or used as capital, and one nonproduced good, which is in fixed supply each period and is used as a factor of production. Here we interpret the latter resource as land. In each period the representative household consumes goods, and the representative firm uses land and capital to produce goods. Hence an allocation for this economy consists of

   a. a consumption sequence $x = \{x_t\}_{t=0}^{\infty}$ for the representative consumer, where $x_t \in \mathbf{R}_+$ is consumption of goods in period t; and
   b. a production sequence $y = \{y_t\}_{t=0}^{\infty}$ for the representative firm, where $y_t \in \mathbf{R}_+$ is the supply of consumption goods in period t.

If the firm's technology is bounded, it is appropriate to limit attention to bounded sequences; that is the case we consider here. We can then take the commodity space to be l_{∞}.

The consumption set for the representative consumer is the positive orthant of l_{∞}, $X = l_{\infty}^+$. His preferences over this set are given by

$$u(x) = \sum_{t=0}^{\infty} \beta^t U(x_t),$$

where $U: \mathbf{R}_+ \to \mathbf{R}$. Assume that U is bounded, continuous, strictly increasing, and strictly concave, and that $\beta \in (0, 1)$.

Each firm has an initial endowment of one unit of land and $\hat{k} > 0$ units of capital, both interpreted as the economy-wide stocks per capita. Each firm also has access to the same constant-returns-to-scale production function $F: \mathbf{R}_+^2 \to \mathbf{R}_+$. Since the supply of land is one unit per capita, it is convenient to define $f: \mathbf{R}_+ \to \mathbf{R}_+$ by $f(k) = F(k, 1) + (1 - \delta)k$, where $\delta \in (0, 1]$ is the depreciation rate. As noted above, we assume that f is bounded. Then the production set Y is given by

$$Y = \{y \in l_{\infty}^+: \text{there exists } k \in l_{\infty}^+ \text{ such that } k_0 = \hat{k}, \text{ and}$$

$$k_{t+1} + y_t \leq f(k_t), \text{ all } t\}.$$

Assume that f is continuous, strictly increasing, and strictly concave, with $f(0) = 0$; note that since f is bounded, $f(\bar{k}) = \bar{k}$ for some $\bar{k} > 0$.

The maximization problem studied in Section 5.1 is, in this notation: choose $x \in X \cap Y$ to maximize $u(x)$. Clearly the solution is a symmetric Pareto-optimal allocation; we wish to show that it is also supportable as a competitive equilibrium.

Exercise 16.1 a. Show that under the restrictions on β, U, and f stated above, this economy has exactly one symmetric Pareto-optimal allocation. [*Hint.* Use the result of Exercise 5.1.] What does the First Welfare Theorem (Theorem 15.3) then imply about the number of symmetric competitive equilibrium allocations?

b. Show that under the restrictions on β, U, and f stated above, u, X, and Y satisfy Assumptions 15.1–15.5. Make clear exactly how each of the restrictions is used. What does the Second Welfare Theorem (Theorem 15.4) then imply about the existence of a symmetric competitive equilibrium?

c. Show that under the stated restrictions Assumptions 15.6 and 15.7 are also satisfied. What does Theorem 15.6 then imply about the existence of equilibrium prices that are representable by $p \in l_1$?

Let (x^0, y^0) be the unique symmetric Pareto-optimal allocation for this economy, and let $p \in l_1$ represent a continuous linear functional supporting it as a competitive equilibrium. Then the consumer's budget constraint can be written as $p \cdot x \le p \cdot x^0$. (Note that since $p \cdot x^0 = p \cdot y^0$ is the value of the firm's revenue stream, the right side of the budget constraint can be interpreted as the value of the consumer's share holdings in the profits of the representative firm.) Alternatively, the sequence $r = \{r_t\}_{t=0}^{\infty}$ of one-period real interest rates can be defined by

$$1/(1 + r_t) = p_{t+1}/p_t, \quad t = 0, 1, \ldots;$$

and the budget constraint can be written as

$$x_0 + \sum_{t=1}^{\infty} \left(\prod_{s=0}^{t-1} \frac{1}{1 + r_s} \right) x_t \le x_0^0 + \sum_{t=1}^{\infty} \left(\prod_{s=0}^{t-1} \frac{1}{1 + r_s} \right) x_t^0.$$

With a little more structure on preferences, we can use these interest rates to calculate equilibrium prices explicitly.

Exercise 16.1   d. Assume that U and f are continuously differentiable, and let (x^0, y^0, p) and r be as specified above. Express the sequence of equilibrium real interest rates $\{r_t\}$ in terms of marginal rates of substitution and transformation. Show that the sequence r is uniquely determined and hence that relative prices in equilibrium are uniquely determined.

The allocation and prices (x^0, y^0, p) can be interpreted as the competitive equilibrium of a market held in period 0, in which claims to infinite sequences of dated goods are exchanged. Alternatively, suppose that agents trade in a sequence of spot markets and that each agent has rational expectations (perfect foresight) about future spot prices. We show next that the allocation (x^0, y^0) is also a competitive equilibrium under the latter market structure. The analysis here is carried out for a particularly simple structure of spot markets; many others are possible.

Recall that in period 0 each firm is endowed with one unit of land and $\hat{k}$ units of capital and each household owns one firm. If (x^0, y^0) is to be the equilibrium allocation under sequential trading on spot markets, then it must be the case that all firms have equal capital : land ratios and that each household owns one firm in every subsequent period as well. In this case the state of the system in any period t is fully described by the economy-wide capital : land ratio, k_t, and all spot prices are functions of this state variable.

Suppose that in each period there are spot markets for claims to next period's consumption good and for shares in firms, all priced in units of the current consumption good. A competitive equilibrium then consists of functions describing prices for claims to future consumption and for shares in firms, the investment by each firm, and the consumption and savings of each household, all as functions of the current state of the economy. Formally, an equilibrium consists of functions $(g, q, \psi, h, \Omega, \omega)$, where

$g(k)$	is the economy-wide law of motion for the state variable;
$q(k)$	is the price, when the state is k, of a claim to one unit of next period's consumption good;
$\psi(k, z)$	is the market value before the current dividend has been paid, in terms of the current consumption good, when the state is k, of a firm that owns one unit of land and z units of capital;

$h(k, z)$ is the investment undertaken, when the state is k, by a firm
that owns one unit of land and z units of capital;

$\Omega(k, a)$ is the value, when the state is k, of the maximized objective
function for a household whose initial assets are a;

$\omega(k, a)$ is the savings undertaken, when the state is k, by a household whose initial assets are a.

In equilibrium the representative household has assets $a = \psi(k, k)$ and
the representative firm has $z = k$ units of capital; but to determine
equilibrium prices, it is essential to be able to evaluate the consequences
of individual deviations from equilibrium behavior.

In each period, firms sell consumption goods to households at a price
of unity, pay the receipts from those sales to shareholders as dividends,
and retain all unsold output as capital. The firm takes the price functions
q and ψ as given, as well as the economy-wide law of motion g and the
current value k of the economy-wide capital stock. Its own current capital stock z is also given. Hence the decision problem facing the firm is as
follows: given k and z, choose the quantity of capital to accumulate (and
hence the quantity of consumption goods to sell) to maximize the return
to current shareholders. Formally, its problem is described by the functional equation

(1) $\psi(k, z) = \max_{0 \le z' \le f(z)} \{f(z) - z' + q(k)\psi[g(k), z']\}.$

The representative household owns assets and in each period makes a
consumption-savings decision. (Since there is no uncertainty, all assets
must pay the same one-period rate of return.) Households, like firms,
take the functions g, q, and ψ as given. A household thus faces the
decision problem: given the current state k and its own asset holdings a
(measured in units of the current consumption good), choose a level for
current consumption and the quantity of assets to hold for next period.
Formally, its problem is described by the functional equation

(2) $\Omega(k, a) = \max_{0 \le a' \le a/q(k)} \{U[a - q(k)a'] + \beta\Omega[g(k), a']\}.$

These considerations motivate the following definition of a *recursive
competitive equilibrium* as a set of functions $(g, q, \psi, h, \Omega, \omega)$ such that

(R1) ψ satisfies the functional equation (1), and h is the associated optimal policy function;

(R2) Ω satisfies the functional equation (2), and ω is the associated optimal policy function;

(R3) $h(k, k) = g(k)$, all $k > 0$;

(R4) $\omega[k, \psi(k, k)] = \psi[g(k), g(k)]$, all $k > 0$.

Conditions (R1) and (R2) express maximizing behavior by firms and households. Condition (R3) says that the function h leads to investment decisions by firms that are compatible with the law of motion g. Condition (R4) is a little more complicated. It says that if the current state of the economy is k, a household whose beginning-of-period assets consist of ownership of one representative firm, valued at $\psi(k, k)$ in terms of current goods, chooses end-of-period assets equal to $\psi[g(k), g(k)]$, the end-of-period value of one firm. Thus, condition (R4) says that the savings function ω of households is such that the market for shares in firms and hence, by Walras's law, the market for current consumption both clear.

To show that the allocation (x^0, y^0) is an equilibrium for the sequential trading structure, we proceed as follows. Let g be the policy function for the dynamic programming problem

(3) $v(k) = \max_{0 \le k' \le f(k)} \{U[f(k) - k'] + \beta v(k')\},$

and define $c(k) = f(k) - g(k)$, all $k > 0$. In view of the two welfare theorems and the nature of this economy, it is a natural conjecture that the optimal policy function g for this planning problem is also the economy-wide law of motion for capital in a recursive competitive equilibrium. We pursue this idea in the rest of this section.

The first-order and envelope conditions for (2) suggest that the equilibrium price of a claim to consumption goods one period hence must be

(4) $q(k) = \beta f'(k)U'(c[g(k)])/U'[c(k)].$

Exercise 16.1   e. Show that, given the functions g and q defined by (3) and (4), there is a unique bounded continuous function ψ satisfying (1) and that the associated optimal policy function h is a single-valued continuous function. Show that there is a unique bounded continuous function Ω satisfying (2) and that the associated optimal policy function ω is a single-valued continuous function.

f. Show that if all firms use the decision rule h and all households use the decision rule ω, then conditions (R3) and (R4) in the definition of a recursive competitive equilibrium hold.

g. Explain why parts (e) and (f) of this exercise establish that (x^0, y^0) is the equilibrium allocation in the economy with sequential trading.

The equilibrium for the recursive economy with a series of spot markets is thus the same as the equilibrium for the corresponding economy in which infinite sequences are traded in one grand market meeting in period 0. The recursive formulation suggests a very different market interpretation, however, one that seems much closer to ordinary experience.

16.2   A Many-Sector Model of Stochastic Growth

The solutions to the models of optimal growth under uncertainty studied in Sections 10.1–10.3 and again in Section 13.1 can also be given a market interpretation. Here we use the more general setup of Section 10.3, specializing it when useful.

Recall that there are l capital goods and M consumption goods each period. Let the measurable space $(Z, \mathfrak{Z})$, the transition function Q, the initial state $\hat{z} \in Z$, the product spaces $(Z^t, \mathfrak{Z}^t)$, the probability measures μ^t, the set $X \subseteq \mathbf{R}_+^l$, the correspondence $\Phi: X \times Z \rightarrow \mathbf{R}_+^M \times X$, and the function u be as described in Section 10.3, and let them satisfy the assumptions stated there. Let

$$S^M = \{c = \{c_t\}_{t=0}^{\infty}: \text{for each } t, \ c_t: Z^t \rightarrow \mathbf{R}^M \text{ is a } \mathfrak{Z}^t\text{-measurable,}$$

essentially bounded function, with

$$\|c\| = \sup_t \{\text{ess sup } \|c_t\|\} < \infty\}.$$

The normed vector space S^M is the commodity space. The consumption set C for the representative consumer in this economy is the positive orthant of S^M, and $u: C \rightarrow \mathbf{R}$ as described in Section 10.3 represents the consumer's preferences. Define S^l analogously to S^M. Given the initial capital stock $\hat{x} \in \mathbf{R}^l_+$, the production set $Y \subset S^M$ for this economy is defined by

$$Y = \{c \in S^M : \text{there exists a sequence } x = \{x_t\}_{t=0}^\infty \in S^l_+ \text{ such that}$$

$$x_0 = \hat{x}, \text{ and } (c_t, x_{t+1}) \in \Phi(x_t, z_t), \text{ all } t, \text{ all } z^t\}.$$

Exercise 16.2   a. Show that (C, u, Y) satisfy Assumptions 15.1–15.7 and 15.8′–15.9′.

b. Let $\gamma^* \in C$ be as defined in Section 10.3. Show that there exists a continuous linear functional ν such that $(\gamma^*, \gamma^*, \nu)$ is a competitive equilibrium and that ν can be represented as

$$\nu(c) = \sum_{t=0}^\infty \left\{ \int_{Z^t} \left[\sum_{m=1}^M p_{tm}(z^t) c_{tm}(z^t) \right] d\mu^t(z^t) \right\}, \quad \text{all } c \in S^M.$$

With these facts established, it is not difficult to develop prices for arbitrary securities. We use the recursive formulation of equilibrium introduced in Section 16.1, letting the representative consumer trade away from the equilibrium allocation by buying or selling the security whose price we wish to calculate. Since the consumer is already in a complete market equilibrium, he never chooses to exercise this option. This fact allows us to calculate the formula for the price of the security.

We consider one-period securities first. For simplicity, we restrict attention to a single consumption good, $M = 1$. Both the price and the returns from the security will be expressed in terms of this good. (Alternatively, we could pick one of M consumer goods as the good being claimed, as in ordinary commodities futures markets.) Let $f : Z \to \mathbf{R}_+$ be a bounded measurable function. Any such function defines a one-period security, where $f(z')$ is interpreted as the return per unit of the security if next period's state is z'. Let $q(x, z)$ be the price of one unit of this security if it is purchased in state (x, z).

Let g be the policy function for the optimal growth model of Section 10.3, and let c be the associated consumption function:

$$c(x, z) = \underset{c \in \mathbf{R}_+}{\text{argmax }} U(c) \quad \text{s.t. } [c, g(x, z)] \in \Phi(x, z).$$

Let $w(A, x, z)$ be the maximized present discounted utility, if the current state is (x, z), of a consumer who has a claim in perpetuity to $c(x, z)$ units of consumption whenever state (x, z) occurs, and in addition a claim to A units of the current consumption good. He can divide this claim between an increment δ (possibly negative) to his current consumption and a purchase at the price $q(x, z)$ of b units of the security. To ensure that maximization is over a compact set, we give the consumer a credit limit of $-\infty < B < 0$. This constraint does not bind in equilibrium. Then w must satisfy

(1) $$w(A, x, z) = \max_{\delta, b} \left\{ U[c(x, z) + \delta] \right.$$

$$\left. + \beta \int w[bf(z'), g(x, z), z']Q(z, dz') \right\}$$

s.t. $\delta + q(x, z)b = A$,

$c(x, z) + \delta \geq 0$,

$b \geq B$.

Exercise 16.2 c. Show that there exists a unique bounded continuous function w satisfying (1).

d. Assume that U is differentiable. Show that if $c(\hat{x}, \hat{z}) > 0$ for some fixed $(\hat{x}, \hat{z}) \in X \times Z$, then $w(\cdot, \hat{x}, \hat{z})$ is differentiable in its first argument and $w_1(0, \hat{x}, \hat{z}) = U'[c(\hat{x}, \hat{z})]$.

We maintain the assumption that U is differentiable in the rest of the problem.

The first-order condition for (1) is

$$U'[c(x, z) + A - q(x, z)b]q(x, z)$$

$$= \beta \int w_1[bf(z'), g(x, z), z']f(z')Q(z, dz'),$$

and in equilibrium it must be the case that $A = b = 0$. Using this fact and combining the first-order and envelope conditions, we obtain

(2) $$U'[c(x, z)]q(x, z) = \beta \int U'(c[g(x, z), z'])f(z')Q(z, dz').$$

Since the functions c and g have been solved for already, (2) character-izes the function $q(x, z)$ that expresses the price, as a function of the current state, of the security with returns $f(\cdot)$. This formula can easily be specialized to particular cases.

Exercise 16.2   e. What is the price of a claim to one unit of con-sumption one period hence with certainty? What is the price of a bond that pays one unit if the event $E \in \mathcal{X}$ occurs and zero otherwise?

f. Lottery tickets (pure gambles) can also be priced with (2). Suppose that z consists of two components, $z = (z_1, z_2) \in Z_1 \times Z_2 = Z$, that are independent Markov processes. That is, there exist transition functions $Q_i: Z_i \times \mathcal{X}_i \to [0, 1]$, $i = 1, 2$, such that

$$Q[(z_1, z_2), A_1 \times A_2] = Q_1(z_1, A_1)Q_2(z_2, A_2).$$

Suppose that f depends only on z_1 and that the technology depends only on z_2 [so that $c(x, z)$ and $g(x, z)$ do not vary with z_1]. What is the price of the security f?

Securities that yield a finite or infinite sequence of returns over time can also be priced in this way. For example, consider an asset whose dividend payment $f(x, z)$ in each period is a function of the state. Then its price after payment of the dividend, $q(x, z)$, is also a function of the current state.

Exercise 16.2   g. Show, by reasoning analogous to that above, that

(3) $U'[c(x, z)]q(x, z)$

$$= \beta \int U'(c[g(x, z), z'])\{f[g(x, z), z'] + q[g(x, z), z']\}Q(z, dz').$$

h. If $f_1, \ldots, f_n$ are securities with prices $q_1, \ldots, q_n$, what is the price of the security $f = \Sigma_i f_i$?

Part (h) of Exercise 16.2 is one version of the celebrated Modigliani-Miller Theorem. To see this, simply interpret $f_1, \ldots, f_n$ as the returns to the various holders of the firm's liabilities: f_1 as returns to bond holders, f_2 as returns to trade creditors, f_3 as returns to preferred shareholders, f_4

as returns to owners of common stock, and so on. Then f is the entire earnings stream of the firm, and the theorem says that the value of the enterprise does not depend on its capital structure, that is, on the way its earnings are divided among various kinds of claimants.

If we let $c_t = c(x_t, z_t)$, $q_t = q(x_t, z_t)$, and so on, we can write (3) simply as

$$(3') \qquad U'(c_t)q_t = \beta E_t[U'(c_{t+1})(f_{t+1} + q_{t+1})],$$

where $E_t(\cdot)$ denotes an expectation conditioned on (x_t, z_t). If $U'(c_t) = U'(c_{t+1})$, $\beta = 1$, and $f_{t+1} = 0$, then this formula reduces to

$$q_t = E_t(q_{t+1}).$$

A stochastic process $\{q_t\}$ that has this property is called a *martingale*, and this condition is often referred to as the martingale property of stock prices. When are the three conditions used to derive this property likely to hold? For actively traded securities like common stocks, prices vary a lot from day to day, whereas consumption by typical households is relatively smooth. That is, c_t is approximately constant, so $U'(c_t)$ is also approximately constant. If time is measured in days or weeks, then $\beta \approx 1$ is not a bad approximation. Finally, dividend payments are announced publicly in advance, so days when $f_{t+1} \neq 0$ can be identified and excluded from the data. It is exactly applications of this character in which the martingale property has received its strongest empirical confirmation.

Even if $\{q_t\}$ is not itself a martingale, (3') always implies the martingale property for *some* time series. Specifically, define

$$w_{t+1} = \beta U'(c_{t+1})(f_{t+1} + q_{t+1}) - U'(c_t)q_t, \quad t = 0, 1, \ldots;$$

and let $W_t = \Sigma_{s=1}^t w_s$. Then $\{W_t\}_{t=1}^\infty$ is a martingale.

16.3 An Economy with Sustained Growth

The commodity spaces used in Sections 16.1 and 16.2 contain only bounded paths for capital and consumption goods. Hence these models cannot be used, as they stand, to study economies where consumption per person is growing without bound. In this problem we study a modeling device that accommodates unbounded growth.

Consider the deterministic economy of Section 16.1, with a Cobb-Douglas technology and exogenous technological change:

(1) $k_{t+1} + y_t \leq \gamma^t k_t^\alpha,$

where $\gamma > 1$ and $0 < \alpha < 1$. Given $k_0 > 0$, one feasible path is

$$k_{t+1} = y_t = \frac{1}{2} \gamma^t k_t^\alpha, \quad t = 0, 1, 2, \ldots.$$

For this path, neither $y = \{y_t\}_{t=0}^\infty$ nor $k = \{k_t\}_{t=0}^\infty$ lies in l_∞.

A useful commodity space in this situation is a space of sequences with growth rates that are uniformly bounded. For any $\theta \geq 1$, define the normed linear space

$$S_\theta = \{x = \{x_t\}_{t=0}^\infty \colon \|x\|_\theta = \sup_t |\theta^{-t} x_t| < \infty\}.$$

Also define $Y = \{y = \{y_t\} \colon (1) \text{ holds for some } \{k_t\} = k \geq 0\}$.

Exercise 16.3   a. For what values of θ is Y a subset of S_θ?

b. For which of these values of θ does the set Y have an interior point when viewed as a subset of S_θ?

In what follows we let θ denote the unique value such that $Y \subset S_\theta$ and Y has a nonempty interior under the norm $\|\cdot\|_\theta$.

With the new norm $\|\cdot\|_\theta$, we need to reexamine the continuity of the function $u(x) = \sum_{t=0}^\infty \beta^t U(x_t)$ defined on a suitable subset X of S_θ.

Exercise 16.3   c. Show that if $X = S_\theta^+$ and $U \colon \mathbf{R}_+ \to \mathbf{R}$ is continuous and bounded, then u is continuous in the norm $\|\cdot\|_\theta$.

Frequently, the current-period utility functions that are most convenient to work with when consumption is growing without bound are unbounded on $\mathbf{R}_+$. For example, the constant relative risk aversion (CRRA) functions, $U(x) = (x^{1-\sigma} - 1)/(1 - \sigma)$ are unbounded above on $\mathbf{R}_{++}$ if $\sigma \leq 1$ and unbounded below if $\sigma \geq 1$.

Exercise 16.3 d. Let the consumption set X be defined, for some $a > 0$, by

$$X = \{x \in S_\theta : \inf_t |\theta^{-t} x_t| \geq a\}.$$

Show that if U is CRRA with $\beta \theta^{1-\sigma} < 1$, then u is bounded and continuous on X.

This choice of X is unnatural in the way it is designed to exclude the origin. But with luck, the lower bound on consumption is not binding.

The specifications of the space S_θ and its subsets X and Y for this growth problem are obviously very specific to the functional forms chosen for technology and preferences. Now we are in a position to apply Theorems 15.3 and 15.4, but with all this specificity, we no longer need them!

Exercise 16.3 e. For the version of the one-sector growth model specified in this problem, show directly that (i) if (x, y, p) is a competitive equilibrium, then $x = y$ and (x, y) is a Pareto-optimal allocation, and (ii) if x is a Pareto-optimal allocation, then there exists p such that (x, x, p) is a competitive equilibrium.

16.4 Industry Investment under Uncertainty

In this problem we consider again the industry investment model described in Section 10.4. There we established the existence of a unique solution to the problem of maximizing the expected discounted value of total industry (consumers' plus producers') surplus, developed some qualitative features of the surplus-maximizing allocation, and suggested that this allocation could serve as a model of a rational expectations equilibrium for the industry. In this problem, we develop the connection between surplus-maximizing allocations and industry equilibrium allocations more formally.

To do this, we first define a suitable commodity space and describe the production sets for firms in the industry. Then we define surplus-maximizing allocations and industry equilibria. We then use a direct argument to show that an industry equilibrium allocation is surplus maximizing and that any surplus-maximizing allocation can be supported as an industry equilibrium. Finally, we sketch an alternative approach in which a synthetic consumer is constructed so that this partial equilibrium problem can be viewed as a general equilibrium model and Theorems 15.3 and 15.4 can be applied.

Let the set Z, the transition function Q, and the functions D, U, and c be as defined in Section 10.4. Since the technology displays constant returns to scale, there is no further loss in generality in assuming that there is a single representative firm in the industry. Let the firm's initial capital stock k_0 and the initial demand shock z_0 both be given.

Let $(Z^t, \mathcal{Z}^t, \mu^t)$, $t = 1, 2, \ldots$, be as defined in Section 8.2, given the initial state z_0, and for each t let $L_\infty(Z^t, \mathcal{Z}^t, \mu^t)$ denote the space of equivalence classes of measurable functions that are bounded in the ess sup norm. We take as the commodity space L for this problem the space of sequences $(q, I) = \{(q_t, I_t)\}_{t=0}^\infty$, where $q_t, I_t \in L_\infty(Z^t, \mathcal{Z}^t, \mu^t)$, all t, that are bounded in the norm

$$\|(q, I)\| = \sup_t \{\text{ess} \sup_{z^t} |q_t(z^t)| + \text{ess} \sup_{z^t} |I_t(z^t)|\}.$$

The interpretation of a point (q, I) in the commodity space is that q_t and I_t denote the levels of production and investment respectively in period t, both expressed as functions of the history z^t of shocks.

The production set Y for the single firm in the industry lies in L_+, the nonnegative orthant of L. Three additional requirements define Y: the beginning-of-period capital stock in each period t is at least as great as the depreciated stock carried over from the previous period (so gross investment is nonnegative); production in each period t is no greater than the firm's beginning-of-period capital stock; and gross investment in each period is sufficient to cover net additions to the capital stock. The beginning-of-period capital stock in period 0, $k_0 \geq 0$, is given. For $t = 0, 1, \ldots$, we use $k_{t+1} \in L_\infty(Z^t, \mathcal{Z}^t, \mu^t)$ to denote its beginning-of-period capital stock in period $t + 1$, as a function of the history of shocks through period t. With this notation, the production set Y can be defined as follows:

(1) $Y = \{(q, I) \in L_+ : \text{there exists } k = \{k_{t+1}\}_{t=0}^\infty \text{ such that:}$

$$k_{t+1} \in L_\infty(Z^t, \mathcal{Z}^t, \mu^t), \ t = 0, 1, \ldots;$$

$$k_1 \geq (1 - \delta)k_0; \quad q_0 \leq k_0; \quad I_0 = k_0 c(k_1/k_0);$$

$$k_{t+1}(z^t) \geq (1 - \delta)k_t(z^{t-1}), \quad t = 1, 2, \ldots, \text{ all } z^t;$$

$$q_t(z^t) \leq k_t(z^{t-1}), \quad t = 1, 2, \ldots, \text{ all } z^t;$$

$$I_t(z^t) = k_t(z^{t-1})c[k_{t+1}(z^t)/k_t(z^{t-1})], \quad t = 1, 2, \ldots, \text{ all } z^t\}.$$

We define an *industry equilibrium* as an allocation (q, I) together with a sequence of prices $p = \{p_t\}_{t=0}^{\infty}$, with $p_t \in L_1^+(Z^t, \mathscr{Z}^t, \mu^t)$, all t, such that

(I1) $(q, I) \in Y$;
(I2) $p_t = D(q_t, z_t)$, all t, all z^t;

(I3) $\mathrm{E}\left\{\sum_{t=0}^{\infty}(1 + r)^{-t}[p_t q_t - I_t]\right\} \geq \mathrm{E}\left\{\sum_{t=0}^{\infty}(1 + r)^{-t}[p_t q_t' - I_t']\right\}$,

   all $(q', I') \in Y$.

That is, an equilibrium allocation must be feasible, it must be market clearing at equilibrium prices [remember that $D(q, z) = U_1(q, z) = \partial U(q, z)/\partial q$ is the market inverse demand function], and it must maximize the expected discounted value of profits at equilibrium prices.

As we did in Section 10.4, we define a *surplus-maximizing allocation* as an allocation (q, I) such that condition (I1) holds and

(I4) $\mathrm{E}\left\{\sum_{t=0}^{\infty}(1 + r)^{-t}[U(q_t, z_t) - I_t]\right\} \geq \mathrm{E}\left\{\sum_{t=0}^{\infty}(1 + r)^{-t}[U(q_t', z_t) - I_t']\right\}$,

   all $(q', I') \in Y$.

That is, a surplus-maximizing allocation must be feasible and must maximize total (consumers' plus producers') surplus over all feasible allocations.

Exercise 16.4   a. Reformulate the definitions of a surplus-maximizing allocation and of an industry equilibrium for the case when there are J identical firms in the industry.

In Section 10.4 we showed that there is a unique surplus-maximizing allocation. Here we want to establish that, at the prices given by condition (I2), this allocation is also the unique industry equilibrium. One way to do this is to establish analogues to Theorems 15.3 and 15.4 by methods specific to this particular problem. To this end we first establish the following result.

Exercise 16.4   b. Show that if (q, I, p) is an industry equilibrium, then (q, I) is a surplus-maximizing allocation. [*Hint*. Use the fact that the concavity of U implies

$$U(q'_t, z_t) \le U(q_t, z_t) + U_1(q_t, z_t)(q'_t - q_t), \quad \text{all } (q_t, q'_t, z_t),$$

to show that conditions (I2) and (I3) imply condition (I4).]

Together with the results of Section 10.4, Exercise 16.4b implies that there is at most one industry equilibrium. To show that there is exactly one industry equilibrium, we use this fact together with the next result.

Exercise 16.4   c. Show that if (q, I) is a surplus-maximizing allocation and p is defined by condition (I2), then (q, I, p) is an industry equilibrium. [*Hint*. Let (q, I) be a surplus-maximizing allocation, and for any $(q', I') \in Y$ define $f: [0, 1] \to \mathbf{R}$ by

$$f(\theta) = \mathrm{E}\left\{\sum_{t=0}^{\infty} (1 + r)^{-t}\{U[(1 - \theta)q_t + \theta q'_t, z_t]\right.$$

$$\left. - [(1 - \theta)I_t + \theta I'_t]\}\right\}.$$

Since Y is convex, f is well defined; and since (q, I) is optimal, $\theta = 0$ maximizes f over the interval $[0, 1]$. Use the first-order condition for a maximum to complete the argument.]

The result in Exercise 16.4c is the analogue, for this problem, to Theorem 15.4. It is much easier to establish, however: since condition (I2) provides a candidate for the supporting prices, the Hahn-Banach Theorem is not needed. Note that with differentiable, strictly concave preferences, we could have taken this same approach in Sections 16.1–16.3. Alternatively, as we next show, we can apply Theorems 15.3 and 15.4 to the present problem.

The idea is to invent a synthetic consumer, whose marginal conditions are equivalent to condition (I2). Let $X = L_+$ be the consumption set for this consumer. Define his preferences on X by

$$u(q, I) = E\left\{\sum_{t=0}^{\infty} (1 + r)^{-t}\{U[q_t(z^t), z_t] - I_t(z^t)\}\right\},$$

where the expectation is over the z_t's given z_0.

Exercise 16.4 d. Show that the pair (X, u) satisfies Assumptions 15.1–15.3. Show that Y as defined in (1) satisfies Assumptions 15.4 and 15.5.

For the economy defined by (X, u, Y), surplus-maximizing allocations as defined above are clearly Pareto optimal.

Exercise 16.4 e. Apply Theorems 15.3–15.6 to prove the results in parts (b) and (c) of this exercise.

16.5 Truncation: A Generalization

In this problem we prove a generalization of Theorem 15.6 that is useful when the zero element θ is not an element of the consumption set of some or all consumers. Recall that the main idea of Theorem 15.6 was that under Assumptions 15.6 and 15.7, if x is in X_i, then for all T sufficiently large the truncated allocation $x^T = (x_1, x_2, \ldots, x_T, 0, 0, \ldots)$ is also in X_i and yields almost as much utility. For one-period utility functions that are not well defined at zero, this approach fails. But an analogous result can be obtained by truncating to a point other than zero.

For simplicity take l_∞ to be the commodity space. Let ϕ be a continuous linear functional on l_∞, and let $\psi: l_\infty \to \mathbf{R}$ be defined by

(1) $\psi(x) = \lim_{T \to \infty} \phi(x^T)$.

As shown in the first part of Lemma 15.5, this limit exists. The following result plays the role of the second part of that lemma.

Exercise 16.5   a. Show that for any $x, a \in l_\infty$,

$$(2) \qquad \lim_{T \to \infty} \phi(x_1, \ldots, x_T, a_{T+1}, a_{T+2}, \ldots) - \psi(x) = \phi(a) - \psi(a).$$

The idea behind this result is that each side of (2) expresses the "weight at infinity" that the linear functional ϕ assigns to the point $a \in l_\infty$.

In place of Assumptions 15.6 and 15.7, we need the following.

ASSUMPTION 16.1   *There exists an allocation $[(a_i), (b_j)]$ such that*
  a. *for each i, if $x_i \in X_i$, then for all T sufficiently large, $x_i^T = (x_{i1}, \ldots, x_{iT},$
     $a_{i,T+1}, a_{i,T+2}, \ldots) \in X_i$;*
  b. *for each j, if $y_j \in Y_j$, then for all T sufficiently large, $y_j^T = (y_{j1}, \ldots, y_{jT},$
     $b_{j,T+1}, b_{j,T+2}, \ldots) \in Y_j$;*
  c. *$\Sigma_i a_i = \Sigma_j b_j$;*
  d. *for each i, if $x_i, \hat{x}_i \in X_i$ and $u(x_i) > u(\hat{x}_i)$, then for all T sufficiently large,*
     $u(x_{i1}, \ldots, x_{iT}, a_{i,T+1}, a_{i,T+2}, \ldots) > u(\hat{x}_i)$.

Note that the allocation $[(a_i), (b_j)]$ need not be feasible. However, it is useful to think of a_i as a subsistence allocation for agent i.

Let Assumptions 15.1–15.5 and 16.1 hold; let $[(x_i^0), (y_j^0), \phi]$ be a feasible allocation and a continuous linear functional such that

$$(3) \qquad \text{for each } i, x \in X_i \text{ and } u_i(x) \geq u_i(x_i^0) \text{ implies } \phi(x) \geq \phi(x_i^0);$$

$$(4) \qquad \text{for each } j, y \in Y_j \text{ implies } \phi(y) \leq \phi(y_j^0);$$

and suppose that for each i there exists $\hat{x}_i \in X_i$ such that $u_i(\hat{x}_i) > u(x_i^0)$. Let ψ be the continuous linear functional defined by (1).

Exercise 16.5   b. Show that for each i, $x \in X_i$ and $u(x) \geq u(x_i^0)$ implies

$$\psi(x) + [\phi(a_i) - \psi(a_i)] \geq \phi(x_i^0);$$

and for each j, $y \in Y_j$ implies

$$\psi(y) + [\phi(b_j) - \psi(b_j)] \le \phi(y_j^0).$$

c. Show that

$$\phi(\Sigma_i x_i^0) - \psi(\Sigma_i x_i^0) = \phi(\Sigma_i a_i) - \psi(\Sigma_i a_i); \quad \text{and}$$

$$\phi(\Sigma_j y_j^0) - \psi(\Sigma_j y_j^0) = \phi(\Sigma_j b_j) - \psi(\Sigma_j b_j).$$

d. Show that

$$\phi(x_i^0) = \psi(x_i^0) + [\phi(a_i) - \psi(a_i)], \text{ all } i; \quad \text{and}$$

$$\phi(y_j^0) = \psi(y_j^0) + [\phi(b_j) - \psi(b_j)], \text{ all } j.$$

e. Show that (3) and (4) hold with ψ in place of ϕ.

16.6 A Peculiar Example

The following example illustrates what Theorem 15.4, the Remark following that theorem, and Theorem 15.6 do *not* say about supporting prices. The example consists of a pure exchange economy with one household, so the unique Pareto-optimal allocation is for the household to consume the entire endowment. Thus, the only interesting questions involve the existence and qualitative properties of prices supporting this allocation as a competitive equilibrium.

The commodity space is l_∞, and the household's consumption set is $X = l_\infty^+$, the positive orthant of l_∞. The household's preferences are represented by the utility function $u: X \to \mathbf{R}$ defined by

$$u(x) = \sum_{t=1}^{\infty} \frac{1}{2^t} [1 - \exp(-x_t 2^t)].$$

Note that u is bounded, continuous, strictly increasing, and strictly concave, with

$$\frac{\partial u(x)}{\partial x_t} = \exp(-x_t 2^t) > 0, \quad \frac{\partial^2 u(x)}{\partial x_t^2} = -2^t \exp(-x_t 2^t) < 0, \quad \text{all } t.$$

The aggregate production possibility set is

$$Y = \{y \in l_\infty : y_t \le 2^{-t}, \text{ all } t\}.$$

Note that the production set includes the entire negative orthant. Clearly, the unique Pareto-optimal allocation for this economy is given by $x^* = y^* = (\frac{1}{2}, \frac{1}{4}, \frac{1}{8}, \ldots)$. The question, then, is whether this allocation can be supported as a competitive equilibrium, and if so, what the supporting prices look like.

The following result is easy to establish.

Exercise 16.6   a. Show that Assumptions 15.1–15.7 are satisfied.

It follows immediately that Theorems 15.4 and 15.6 hold. Thus by Theorem 15.4 there exists a continuous linear function on l_∞, not identically zero, such that

(1) $x \in X$ and $u(x) \ge u(x^*)$ implies $\phi(x) \ge \phi(x^*)$;

(2) $y \in Y$ implies $\phi(y) \le \phi(y^*)$.

For any $x \in l_\infty$, let x^T denote the truncated sequence $x^T = (x_1, \ldots, x_T, 0, 0, \ldots)$. Lemma 15.5 implies that $\psi: l_\infty \to \mathbf{R}$ defined by

(3) $\psi(x) = \lim_{T \to \infty} \phi(x^T), \quad \text{all } x \in l_\infty,$

is also a continuous linear functional, and Theorem 15.6 implies that (1) and (2) hold with ψ in place of ϕ. Finally, since X is the entire positive orthant of l_∞, the Remark following Theorem 15.4 implies that if $\phi(x^*) \ne 0$, then (x^*, y^*, ϕ) is a competitive equilibrium. In the rest of this section we characterize in more detail the continuous linear functionals ϕ and ψ satisfying (1) and (2), and determine whether any of them constitute competitive equilibrium prices.

An obvious candidate for a competitive equilibrium is to take ϕ to be the continuous linear functional corresponding to the price vector $p = (p_0, p_1, p_2, \ldots)$, where each price p_t is proportional to the marginal utility of consumption in period t. Since

$$\left. \frac{\partial u(x)}{\partial x_t} \right|_{x=x^*} = \exp(-x_t^* 2^t) = \exp(-1), \quad \text{all } t,$$

any price vector of the form $p = (c, c, c, \ldots)$, for some $c > 0$, would seem to be a natural candidate to support x^* as a competitive equilibrium.

Exercise 16.6 b. Show that a price vector p of this form does *not* define a continuous linear functional on l_∞. [*Hint.* Use Theorem 15.1.]

c. Let ϕ be any continuous linear functional satisfying (1) and (2), and let ψ be the continuous linear functional defined by (3). Show that $\psi(x) = 0$, all $x \in l_\infty$.

d. Suppose that for this example we take the commodity space to be l_1. Show that in this case the production set Y has an empty interior. Show that (x^*, y^*, p) is a competitive equilibrium, where $p \in l_\infty$ is any price vector of the form $p = (c, c, \ldots)$, $c > 0$.

16.7 An Economy with Many Consumers

Although most of the dynamic applications of the theory of Chapter 15—including all of the applications so far in this chapter—deal with one-consumer economies, the theory can deal with any finite number of agents, with preferences differing among them. In this section we treat a fairly general deterministic, recursive system with many agents, a generalization of the two-consumer exchange economy studied in Section 5.13.

The commodity space is S^l, the set of sequences $c = \{c_t\}_{t=0}^{\infty}$ such that

$$\|c\| = \sup_t \|c_t\|_E < \infty,$$

where $c_t \in \mathbf{R}^l$, all t, and $\|\cdot\|_E$ is the Euclidean norm on $\mathbf{R}^l$.

There are $i = 1, \ldots, I$ consumers, each with the consumption set $C = S_+^l$. Consumer i has preferences induced by an aggregator function W_i: $\mathbf{R}_+^l \times \mathbf{R}_+ \to \mathbf{R}_+$ that is assumed to satisfy conditions (W1)–(W5) of

Section 5.11. In Exercise 5.11d we showed that any such aggregator function defines a utility function $u_i: C \to \mathbf{R}_+$, the unique fixed point of the operator T_{W_i} defined there. We also showed that u_i is bounded and continuous in the sup norm, is increasing and concave, and satisfies

$$|u_i(c) - u_i(c^n)| \leq \beta^n \|u_i\|, \quad \text{all } c \in C,$$

where $c^n = (c_0, c_1, \ldots, c_n, 0, 0, \ldots)$ and where $\|u_i\| = \sup_{c \in C} |u_i(c)|$. Thus C and u_i satisfy Assumptions 15.1–15.3 and 15.6–15.7.

Next we construct the production set $Y \subset S^l_+$; the method of construction ensures that the resulting technology is recursive. Assume that the state of the system in any period is characterized by a vector $\kappa \in \mathbf{R}^p_+$ of capital goods. Production during the period yields a vector $\gamma \in \mathbf{R}^l$ of current consumption goods and a vector $y \in \mathbf{R}^p$ of beginning-of-period capital stocks for the following period. Feasible production within any period is thus characterized by a correspondence $\Phi: \mathbf{R}^p \to \mathbf{R}^l \times \mathbf{R}^p$. This correspondence is restricted as follows.

(T1) Φ *is continuous;*
(T2) *for each* κ, $\Phi(\kappa)$ *is compact and convex;*
(T3) $(\gamma, y) \in \Phi(\kappa)$ *and* $0 \leq (\gamma', y') \leq (\gamma, y)$ *implies* $(\gamma', y') \in \Phi(\kappa)$;
(T4) $\kappa' \leq \kappa$ *implies* $\Phi(\kappa') \subseteq \Phi(\kappa)$;
(T5) $(\gamma, y) \in \Phi(\kappa)$, $(\gamma', y') \in \Phi(\kappa')$, *and* $\theta \in [0, 1]$ *implies*

$$[\theta\gamma + (1 - \theta)\gamma', \theta y + (1 - \theta)y'] \in \Phi[\theta\kappa + (1 - \theta)\kappa'];$$

(T6) *the set* $M = \{\kappa \in \mathbf{R}^p: (0, \kappa) \in \Phi(\kappa)\}$ *has a nonempty interior;*
(T7) *if* κ *is an interior point of* M, *then* $(\gamma, \kappa) \in \Phi(\kappa)$ *for some* $\gamma \gg 0$.

Assumptions (T1)–(T3) restrict current-period production possibilities, given κ, and (T4) and (T5) restrict the way Φ varies with κ. As we will see shortly, Assumptions (T6) and (T7) ensure that the production set in the sense of Chapter 15 has a nonempty interior.

We use the production correspondence Φ to define the production set Y for a given initial capital vector $\hat{k}$ exactly as we did in Sections 16.1 and 16.2:

$$Y(\hat{k}) = \{c \in S^l_+: \text{there exists } k \in S^p_+ \text{ with } k_0 = \hat{k}, \text{ and}$$

$$\text{such that } (c_t, k_{t+1}) \in \Phi(k_t), t = 0, 1, 2, \ldots\}.$$

Thus $Y(\hat{k})$ is the set of consumption sequences that are feasible given the initial capital stock $\hat{k}$.

Exercise 16.7 a. Show that for any $\hat{k} \in \mathbf{R}^\ell_+$, $Y(\hat{k})$ is closed and convex and satisfies Assumption 15.6. Show that if $\hat{k}$ is an interior point of the set M defined in Assumption (T6), then $Y(\hat{k})$ has an interior point.

If preferences satisfy assumptions (W1)–(W5), if the technology satisfies assumptions (T1)–(T7), and if $\hat{k}$ is an interior point of M, then the economy defined by $C, u_1, \ldots, u_I$, and $Y(\hat{k})$ satisfies Assumptions 15.1–15.7. Hence in this case the First and Second Welfare Theorems (Theorems 15.3 and 15.4) apply, as does Theorem 15.6. The rest of this problem is concerned with the construction of this economy's Pareto-optimal allocations, which thus coincide with its competitive equilibrium allocations.

As we did in Chapter 15, we will use the notation $[(c_i), y]$ to denote an allocation. We call an allocation *feasible from* $\hat{k}$ if $c_i \in C$, all i, $y \in Y(\hat{k})$, and $\Sigma_i c_i = y$. We begin by defining this economy's *utility possibility set*:

(1) $U(\hat{k}) = \{z \in \mathbf{R}^I_+ : z_i = u_i(c_i),$ all i, for some allocation

          $[(c_i), y]$ that is feasible from $\hat{k}\}$.

Next, let Δ^I denote the unit simplex in $\mathbf{R}^I$, and define the *support function* $v: \mathbf{R}^p \times \Delta^I \to \mathbf{R}_+$ of U by

$$v(\kappa, \theta) = \sup_{z \in U(\kappa)} \sum_{i=1}^I \theta_i z_i.$$

From the definition of U, it follows that we can also write

(2) $v(\kappa, \theta) = \sup_{c_1, \ldots, c_I} \sum_{i=1}^I \theta_i u_i(c_i)$

     s.t. $c_i \geq 0,$ all $i,$

     $\Sigma_i c_i \in Y(\kappa).$

Exercise 16.7 b. Prove that an allocation is Pareto optimal if and only if it attains the supremum in (2).

We next formulate a functional equation for the support function v and analyze it using the methods of Chapter 4. The utility that consumer i receives from the allocation c_i is the utility he gets from the first term in the sequence, c_{i0}, and from the remaining terms $(c_{i1}, c_{i2}, \ldots)$. Evaluated in terms of the aggregator function W_i, his utility from c_i is

$$u_i(c_i) = W_i[c_{i0}, u_i(c_{i1}, c_{i2}, \ldots)].$$

The feasible I-vectors of utilities from next period on, $u_i(c_{i1}, c_{i2}, \ldots)$, $i = 1, 2, \ldots, I$, are the points z' in the set $U(k_1)$, where k_1 is next period's vector of capital stocks. Hence (2) may be rewritten as

(3) $\qquad v(\kappa, \theta) = \sup_{\gamma, z', \kappa'} \sum_{i=1}^{I} \theta_i W_i(\gamma_i, z_i')$

$\qquad$ s.t. $z' \in U(\kappa')$,

$\qquad (\Sigma_i \gamma_i, \kappa') \in \Phi(\kappa)$.

Since U is defined by (1), (3) is a functional equation in the unknown function v. But the constraint that z' must lie in $U(\kappa')$ is equivalent to a statement about z' and the support function $v(\kappa', \cdot)$.

Exercise 16.7 c. Prove that for any $\kappa \in \mathbf{R}_+^\ell$, $z \in U(\kappa)$ if and only if $v(\kappa, \theta) \geq \theta \cdot z$, for all $\theta \in \Delta^I$.

In view of this exercise, (3) may be rewritten as

(4) $\qquad v(\kappa, \theta) = \sup_{\gamma, z', \kappa'} \sum_{i=1}^{I} \theta_i W_i(\gamma_i, z_i')$

$\qquad$ s.t. $v(\kappa', \theta') \geq \theta' \cdot z'$, all $\theta' \in \Delta^I$,

$\qquad (\Sigma_i \gamma_i, \kappa') \in \Phi(\kappa)$.

Let F be the space of bounded continuous functions $f : \mathbf{R}_+^\ell \times \Delta^I \to \mathbf{R}_+$. Let T be the operator on F defined by the constrained optimization problem in (4). That is, (4) says that $v = Tv$.

Exercise 16.7   d. Show that applying T to any $f \in F$ involves, for each $(\kappa, \theta) \in \mathbf{R}^{\varrho}_+ \times \Delta^I$, maximizing a continuous function over a compact, convex set.

    e. Show that $T: F \rightarrow F$.

    f. Show that T is a contraction with modulus $\beta = \max_i \beta_i$, where β_i is the bound on the slope of W_i postulated in condition (W3) of Section 5.11.

The proof of part (f) is an application of Blackwell's sufficient conditions (Theorem 3.3). To show that T is monotone is trivial; to show that it has the discounting property $T(f + a) \leq Tf + \beta a$ is not, so we provide an extended hint. Let $f \in F$ and $(\kappa, \theta) \in \mathbf{R}^{\varrho}_+ \times \Delta^I$ be given. Choose $a > 0$. Let $(\gamma^a, z^a, \kappa^a)$ attain $T(f + a)$ at (κ, θ). Define the sets U, U^a, and B as follows.

$$U = \{z' \in \mathbf{R}^I_+ : f(\kappa^a, \theta') \geq \theta' \cdot z', \quad \text{all } \theta' \in \Delta^I\},$$

$$U^a = \{z' \in \mathbf{R}^I_+ : f(\kappa^a, \theta') + a \geq \theta' \cdot z', \quad \text{all } \theta' \in \Delta^I\},$$

$$B = \{z' \in \mathbf{R}^I_+ : z' \leq z'' + a\underline{1}, \quad \text{some } z'' \in U\},$$

where $\underline{1}$ is the I-vector $(1, 1, \ldots, 1)$. Draw the sets U and U^a for the case $I = 2$. Then prove that $U^a = B$.

    With the result in part (f) established, the existence of a unique solution $v \in F$ to (4) is immediate.

Exercise 16.7   g. Prove that the policy correspondence for (4) is u.h.c. and convex valued.

    How do we know that resource allocations generated by the optimal policy correspondence solve the originally stated maximum problem in (2)? This is a Principle of Optimality issue. This problem is not a special case of that treated in Section 4.1, but it can be addressed by the same methods. Try it!

16.8   Bibliographic Notes

The growth models in Sections 16.1 and 16.2 were introduced in Chapters 5 and 10; see the references cited there. Prescott and Mehra (1980) treat equilibrium in the stochastic model from a recursive point of view.

The equilibrium interpretation of the stochastic growth model forms the basis for a burgeoning recent literature on real business cycle theory. See the original papers of Kydland and Prescott (1982) and Long and Plosser (1983). McCallum (1989) contains a helpful survey of this literature.

The results on asset pricing in Section 16.2 are samplings from a vast literature. The general framework used here is from Lucas (1978) and Brock (1982). The Modigliani-Miller Theorem was first advanced by those authors in their 1958 paper. Hirshleifer (1966) provided the first proof using the contingent-claim framework used here. Samuelson (1965) contains the first theoretical derivation of the martingale property for an equilibrium price series. See Fama (1965) for a pioneering and highly successful empirical application.

Section 16.3 is based on Mehra and Prescott (1985). See Jones and Manuelli (1987) and Rebelo (1987) for further results on sustained growth.

Section 16.4 is based on Lucas and Prescott (1971).

The argument in Section 16.5 was developed in Prescott and Rios-Rull (1988), where it is applied to a model of search.

The example in Section 16.6 is from Gilles, Marshall, and Sonstelie (1987). Similar examples can be found in Mas-Colell (1975) and in Jones (1984).

The economy with many consumers studied in Section 16.7 is adapted from Lucas and Stokey (1984). See Dana and Le Van (1988) for more recent developments along this line. The idea of recursively constructing utility possibility sets is also useful in noncooperative games; see Abreu, Pearce, and Stacchetti (1986).

17   Fixed-Point Arguments

In earlier chapters we used recursive methods to study economic models
of three types. First, we analyzed decision problems faced by a single
agent: decisions about consumption and savings, about job search, about
portfolio choice, and so on. In these cases we used the techniques developed in Chapters 4 and 9 to study properties of the agent's maximal
expected utility and of his associated optimal decision rule. We also
studied systems composed of many agents in which the system taken as a
whole implicitly solves an optimization problem. Examples in this category include the models of growth, industry investment, and inventory
accumulation. In these cases we used the techniques developed in Chapters 4 and 9 to characterize Pareto-optimal allocations, and then we drew
on the two welfare theorems of Chapter 15 to establish that those were
exactly the competitive equilibrium allocations as well. Finally, we looked
at models composed of many agents in which individual agents maximize, but the system as a whole does not. The models of a pure currency
economy and of a search economy presented in Chapter 13 fall into this
category. In these cases we used the techniques developed in Chapters 4
and 9 to study the behavior of individual agents, but we established the
existence of a competitive equilibrium and characterized its properties
by looking directly at the equilibrium conditions.

In this chapter we continue our study of models of the last type,
systems where individual agents maximize but the system as a whole—
because of some distortion, externality, or absence of markets—does
not. Although this category includes a wide range of interesting models,
they are models not amenable to analysis by any single approach. In
cases where the two fundamental welfare theorems do not apply, and
competitive equilibria cannot be characterized by studying a "social planner's problem," no widely applicable approach to the study of equilibria

is available. Instead, particular models must be studied one at a time, exploiting their special structure as ingenuity—in formulation as well as in analysis—permits.

There are, however, some basic mathematical results, fixed-point theorems, that are useful in many different contexts. One of these, the Contraction Mapping Theorem, has been used repeatedly in earlier chapters. Another, the Brouwer Fixed-Point Theorem, is useful in finite-dimensional applications. A third, the Schauder Fixed-Point Theorem, is an infinite-dimensional version of Brouwer's Theorem. Finally, the existence of one or more fixed points can sometimes be established by showing that the operator of interest is monotone.

In this chapter we present these fixed-point results and show by example how they can be used to establish the existence of equilibria in recursive models. To this end, we begin in Section 17.1 by introducing a simple overlapping-generations model. In Sections 17.2–17.5 we discuss in turn the four fixed-point results and apply each of them to this model. In Section 17.6 we look at a variation on the overlapping-generations model that has a different information structure, and apply each of our fixed-point results to it.

An important feature of the model studied in this chapter is that its only state variable is exogenous. Models with endogenous state variables, such as physical capital, raise a different set of technical problems and are discussed in Chapter 18.

17.1 An Overlapping-Generations Model

Consider an infinitely lived economy with a constant population. Each individual lives for two periods, working when he is young and consuming when he is old. His von Neumann-Morgenstern utility function is $U(l, c) = -H(l) + V(c)$, where l is his supply of labor when young and c is his consumption when old. There is a single, nonstorable consumption good, which is produced using labor as the only input. An exogenous random variable x, which follows a first-order Markov process, affects the technology. Specifically, if l units of labor are used, output y is given by $y = xl$, so the technology shows constant returns to scale each period. Finally, fiat money, of which there is a fixed supply M, is the only store of value. In each period, the young agents produce goods and sell them to the old in exchange for fiat money; this market is perfectly competitive.

This economy is competitive, but it does not satisfy the conditions of Chapter 15 under which competitive equilibrium allocations and Pareto-optimal allocations coincide. (Why not?) Nevertheless, we can define a stationary competitive equilibrium for this economy and then study the existence, uniqueness, and properties of such equilibria by direct methods.

In this economy the technology shock x is the only state variable. Let x be an element of a closed, bounded interval $[a, b] = X \subset \mathbf{R}_{++}$; let $\mathscr{X}$ be the Borel subsets of X; and let $\pi: X \times \mathscr{X} \to [0, 1]$ be a transition function. Define a stationary competitive equilibrium in which money is valued to be a price function $p: X \to \mathbf{R}_+$ and a labor supply function $n: X \to \mathbf{R}_+$ such that

$$(1) \qquad n(x) \in \underset{l}{\operatorname{argmax}} \left\{ -H(l) + \int V\left[\frac{xlp(x)}{p(x')}\right] \pi(x, dx') \right\}, \quad \text{all } x \in X;$$

$$(2) \qquad xn(x) = M/p(x), \quad \text{all } x \in X.$$

The first condition is that given the price function p and the current state x, a young individual's optimal labor supply is $n(x)$. The labor he supplies produces $xn(x)$ units of output, which he sells for $xn(x)p(x)$ units of money. In his old age he uses all his money balances to buy goods, but since the price of goods next period is random, so is his consumption $xn(x)p(x)/p(x')$. The second condition is that the supply and demand for goods, and hence, by Walras's Law, for money are equal in every state.

In order to analyze this system, we need to place restrictions on the functions H and V. The following assumption, although stronger than necessary, is very convenient.

ASSUMPTION 17.1 *H: $[0, L) \to \mathbf{R}_+$ is twice continuously differentiable, strictly increasing, and strictly convex, with*

$$H'(0) = 0 \quad \text{and} \quad \lim_{l \to L} H'(l) = +\infty.$$

V: $\mathbf{R}_+ \to \mathbf{R}_+$ is twice continuously differentiable, strictly increasing, and strictly concave.

(Note that labor supply is assumed to be bounded below by zero and above by $L < +\infty$.)

Exercise 17.1   Show that under Assumption 17.1, given any measurable price function $p: X \to \mathbf{R}_+$ that is uniformly bounded away from zero, and any $x \in X$, the unique solution $n(x)$ to the consumer's problem (1) satisfies the first-order condition

$$H'[n(x)] = \int \frac{xp(x)}{p(x')} V' \left[\frac{xn(x)p(x)}{p(x')} \right] \pi(x, dx').$$

Show that the solution is always strictly positive: $n(x) > 0$, all x.

Multiplying this first-order condition by $n(x)$ and substituting from (2) to eliminate $p(x)$ and $p(x')$, we obtain

(3) $n(x)H'[n(x)] = \int x'n(x')V'[x'n(x')] \pi(x, dx'),$ all $x \in X.$

Given any strictly positive, measurable function n satisfying (3), for the price function $p(x) = M/xn(x)$ the pair (n, p) is a stationary competitive equilibrium. Hence questions about the existence and uniqueness of a stationary equilibrium are essentially questions about the existence and uniqueness of a strictly positive function n satisfying (3).

Define $\zeta: [0, L) \to \mathbf{R}_+$ by $\zeta(l) = lH'(l)$ and $\phi: \mathbf{R}_+ \to \mathbf{R}_+$ by $\phi(y) = yV'(y)$, so that (3) can be written as

(4) $\zeta[n(x)] = \int \phi[x'n(x')] \pi(x, dx').$

Equation (4) is a single equation in the unknown function $n(x)$. In some respects it appears simpler than the functional equations we studied in Chapters 4 and 9, since it does not involve a maximization operator. It is not a special case of the equations we have examined earlier, however, so our concern in this chapter is with methods suitable for analyzing it and other equations of the same general type.

It is instructive to begin the analysis of (4) by considering first the special case of serially independent shocks. In this case the right side of (4) does not depend on x, so a solution is simply a number $n > 0$ satisfying

(5) $\zeta(n) = \int \phi(x'n) \pi(dx').$

We then have the following result. (To distinguish the highly specific results we use as illustrations, we call them propositions.)

PROPOSITION 1 *Let $X = [a, b] \subset \mathbf{R}_{++}$, with its Borel subsets $\mathcal{X}$, and let π be a probability measure on $(X, \mathcal{X})$. Let H and V satisfy Assumption 17.1, and define ζ and ϕ we did as above. Then (5) has a unique solution $n > 0$.*

Proof. Under Assumption 17.1, the function ζ is once continuously differentiable, with $\zeta'(l) = H'(l) + lH''(l)$. Hence ζ is strictly increasing, with

$$\zeta(0) = 0; \quad \zeta'(0) = 0; \quad \zeta'(l) > 0, \text{ all } l \in (0, L); \quad \text{and}$$

$$\lim_{l \to L} \zeta(l) = +\infty.$$

Moreover, the elasticity of ζ is greater than one,

(6) $$\frac{l\zeta'(l)}{\zeta(l)} = \frac{H'(l) + lH''(l)}{H'(l)} \geq 1, \quad \text{all } l \in [0, L),$$

with equality only at $l = 0$.

The function ϕ is once continuously differentiable, with $\phi'(y) = V'(y) + yV''(y)$. Hence ϕ may be either increasing or decreasing but is strictly increasing at zero, $\phi'(0) = V'(0) > 0$. Moreover, its elasticity is less than one,

(7) $$\frac{y\phi'(y)}{\phi(y)} = \frac{V'(y) + yV''(y)}{V'(y)} \leq 1, \quad \text{all } y \geq 0,$$

with equality only at $y = 0$.

There are two cases to consider, shown in Figure 17.1, where $\zeta(l)$ and $E[\phi(x'l)] = \int \phi(x'l) \pi(dx')$ are graphed as functions of l. Note that their derivatives are $\zeta'(l)$ and $E[x'\phi'(x'l)]$ respectively. If $\phi(0) > 0$, then at $l = 0$ we have $\zeta(0) = 0 < E[\phi(0)] = \phi(0)$, as shown in the top panel of Figure 17.1. If $\phi(0) = 0$, then at $l = 0$ we have $\zeta(0) = 0 = E[\phi(0)] = \phi(0)$. Since $0 < \phi'(0)$, however, it follows that $\zeta'(0) = 0 < E[x'\phi'(0)]$, so that $\zeta(l) < E[\phi(x'l)]$ in the neighborhood of $l = 0$, as shown in the bottom panel of Figure 17.1. Since both functions are continuous, and since $\lim_{l \to L} \zeta(l) = +\infty$ and $E[\phi(x'L)] < +\infty$, the existence of a solution $n > 0$ follows immediately in either case.

To establish uniqueness, first note that for any $l > 0$,

$$\phi(xl) > 0, \quad \text{all } x \in X, \quad \text{and} \quad \int \frac{\phi(x'l)}{E[\phi(xl)]} \pi(dx') = 1.$$

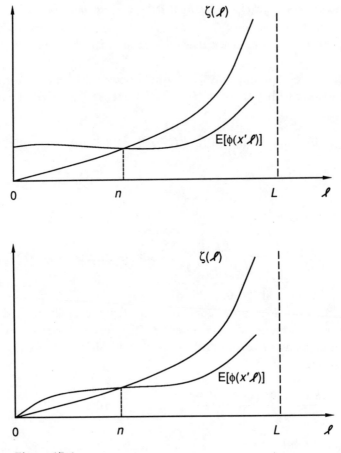

Figure 17.1

Hence it follows from (6) and (7) that

$$\frac{l\zeta'(l)}{\zeta(l)} > 1 > \int \frac{x'l\phi'(x'l)}{\phi(x'l)} \frac{\phi(x'l)}{E[\phi(xl)]} \pi(dx'), \quad \text{all } l > 0,$$

where the second inequality uses the fact that the integral on the right is a convex combination of terms that are less than one. Suppose $n > 0$ satisfies (5). Then $\zeta(n) = E[\phi(xn)]$, and if we use this fact to cancel terms in the inequality above we find that

$$\zeta'(n) > E[x'\phi'(x'n)].$$

Therefore, at any intersection the $\zeta(l)$ curve crosses the $E[\phi(xl)]$ curve from below. Hence the two curves cross only once, as shown in the figures, and there is only one strictly positive solution. ∎

For the case of independent shocks, then, the existence and uniqueness of the solution to (4) follows in a straightforward way from fairly standard assumptions on preferences. To study the case when shocks are serially correlated, it is convenient to put (4) into a slightly different form.

Under Assumption 17.1, the function ζ is continuous, strictly increasing, and onto. Hence the inverse function ζ^{-1}: $\mathbf{R}_+ \to [0, L)$ is well defined, continuous, strictly increasing, and onto. Therefore a bounded, continuous, strictly positive function n^*: $X \to [0, L)$ satisfies (4) if and only if the bounded, continuous, strictly positive function f^*: $X \to \mathbf{R}_{++}$ defined by $f^*(x) = \zeta[n^*(x)]$ satisfies

(8) $$f^*(x) = \int \phi[x'\zeta^{-1}(f^*(x'))] \, \pi(x, dx'), \quad \text{all } x \in X.$$

To study the existence of solutions to (8), we define the operator T on functions f: $X \to \mathbf{R}_{++}$ by

(9) $$(Tf)(x) = \int \phi[x'\zeta^{-1}(f(x'))] \, \pi(x, dx').$$

A function f^* satisfies (8) if and only if it is a fixed point of T. Hence the problem of finding equilibria of the overlapping-generations model has been converted into one of finding strictly positive functions f^* that are fixed points of the operator T defined in (9). In the next sections we pursue four different, mutually complementary strategies.

The first strategy, followed in Section 17.2, is to seek conditions sufficient to ensure that the operator T is a contraction mapping. The required conditions are restrictions on preferences stronger than those stated in Assumption 17.1.

The second approach is to make the state space finite. That is, let the state space be $X = \{x_1, \dots, x_m\}$, with transitions described by $\pi_{ij} = \Pr\{x_j | x_i\}$, and let n_j denote labor supply in state x_j. Then the operator defined in (9) takes vectors $f = (f_1, \ldots, f_m)$ into vectors $Tf = (T_1 f, \ldots, T_m f)$. In this case (9) takes the form

$$(10) \qquad T_i f = \sum_{j=1}^{m} \phi[x_j \zeta^{-1}(f_j)] \pi_{ij}, \quad i = 1, \ldots, m,$$

and the equation $f = Tf$ is simply a system of m equations in m unknowns. That is, the operator T maps a subset of $\mathbf{R}^m$ into itself. The basic existence theorem for fixed points of such operators is Brouwer's Theorem. We review this result and apply it to (10) in Section 17.3.

In systems where the state variables are all exogenous, as they are in this example, this strategy is attractive. Little is lost by the restriction to a finite state space, since any bounded space can be approximated as closely as one wishes. In systems with endogenous state variables, however, the restriction to a finite state space is very awkward. As a preliminary step to studying such systems, we would like to have sufficient conditions for the existence of a fixed point of the operator T defined in (9) when X is a bounded interval.

When X is a bounded interval, the operator T maps the space $C(X)$ of bounded continuous functions into itself. The basic existence result for fixed points of operators of this sort is Schauder's Theorem. We review this result and apply it to our model in Section 17.4.

In Section 17.5 we present a fixed-point theorem that applies when the operator T in (9) is monotone. We also show that monotonicity leads to a constructive method for locating fixed points and a computationally useful method for establishing uniqueness.

In Section 17.6, we treat an overlapping-generations model similar to the one introduced above, except that the economy is subject to monetary as well as real disturbances, and agents have only partial information on contemporaneous realizations of these shocks. We show that the methods of the earlier sections are readily adapted to situations of this type.

17.2   An Application of the Contraction Mapping Theorem

In this section we show how the Contraction Mapping Theorem can be used to establish the existence and uniqueness of an equilibrium in the overlapping-generations model described above. We begin by proving two preliminary lemmas. The first gives sufficient conditions for an operator like that defined in (9) of the last section to be a contraction. The second gives sufficient conditions for a closely related operator involving logarithms to be a contraction. We conclude by applying the latter to our overlapping-generations model.

Let (X, ρ) be a metric space with its Borel sets $\mathscr{X}$, and let π be a transition function on $(X, \mathscr{X})$. Let $D \subset \mathbf{R}$; let $F \subset C(X)$ be the space of bounded continuous functions $f: X \to D$, with the sup norm; and let $G: X \times X \times D \to D$ be a (single-valued) function. We will show how the Contraction Mapping Theorem can be applied to locate the fixed points of the operator T on F defined by

(1) $(Tf)(x) = \displaystyle\int G[x, x', f(x')]\, \pi(x, dx'), \quad$ all $x \in X$.

Clearly, (9) of the previous section is a special case of (1), with $G(x, x', y) = \phi[x'\zeta^{-1}(y)]$.

The following exercise establishes conditions under which $T: F \to F$ and F is a complete metric space.

> **Exercise 17.2**   Let $(X, \mathscr{X}), \rho, \pi, D, F$, and G be as specified above.
>
> a. Assume that D is convex, that G is continuous, and that π has the Feller property. Show that the operator T defined in (1) maps F into itself.
>
> b. Assume that D is closed. Show that F with the sup norm is a complete metric space.

Using this result we can prove the following lemma.

LEMMA 17.1   *Let the hypotheses of Exercise 17.2a,b hold. In addition, assume that for each $(x, x') \in X \times X$, G is continuously differentiable on D, and assume that there exists $0 \le \beta < 1$ such that*

(2) $|G_3(x, x', y)| \le \beta, \quad$ all $(x, x', y) \in X \times X \times D.$

Let T be the operator on F defined by (1). Then T has a unique fixed point $f^* \in F$, and

$$\|T^n f_0 - f^*\| \le \beta^n \|f_0 - f^*\|, \quad \text{all } f_0 \in F.$$

Proof. As shown in Exercise 17.2, $T: F \to F$ and F is a complete metric space. Hence it is sufficient to show that T is a contraction of modulus β.

Fix $f, g \in F$. Then for any $(x, x') \in X \times X$, the Mean Value Theorem applied to G implies that for some $\theta \in [0, 1]$,

$$G[x, x', f(x')] - G[x, x', g(x')]$$

$$= G_3[x, x', \theta f(x') + (1 - \theta)g(x')][f(x') - g(x')].$$

It follows from this fact and (2) that

$$|(Tf)(x) - (Tg)(x)| \leq \int |G[x, x', f(x')] - G[x, x', g(x')]| \, \pi(x, dx')$$

$$\leq \beta \int |f(x') - g(x')| \, \pi(x, dx')$$

$$\leq \beta \|f - g\|, \quad \text{all } x \in X.$$

Hence

$$\|Tf - Tg\| \leq \beta \|f - g\|.$$

Since f and g were arbitrary elements of F, it follows that T is a contraction of modulus β. ∎

Lemma 17.1 applies only if the derivative of G with respect to its third argument is uniformly less than one in absolute value. Unfortunately, it is easy to verify that under Assumption 17.1, the overlapping-generations model in the last section need not satisfy (2).

Exercise 17.3 Let $X = [a, b] \subset \mathbf{R}_{++}$, let $D = \mathbf{R}_+$, and let H and V satisfy Assumption 17.1. Define ζ and ϕ as we did before, and let $G(x, x', y) = \phi[x'\zeta^{-1}(y)]$. Show that (2) does not hold.

But recall that Assumption 17.1 does imply that the elasticity of ϕ is less than one and that of ζ greater than one. This fact suggests using logarithms as an alternative line of attack.

Taking logs of both sides of (1), we find that f^* is a fixed point of T if and only if

$$\ln[f^*(x)] = \ln \left\{ \int G[x, x', f^*(x')] \, \pi(x, dx') \right\}, \quad \text{all } x \in X.$$

Obviously, to do this we must require that f^* and G take only strictly positive values; that is, we must require that $D \subset \mathbf{R}_{++}$. In this case we can define

$$\hat{D} = \ln(D) = \{\hat{d} \in \mathbf{R} : \hat{d} = \ln(d), \text{ some } d \in D\}.$$

Let $\hat{F} \subset C(X)$ be the set of continuous functions $f \colon X \to \hat{D}$, with the sup norm. Then letting $g(x) = \ln[f(x)]$, we are led to consider the operator $\hat{T}$ on $\hat{F}$ defined by

$$(3) \qquad (\hat{T}g)(x) = \ln \left\{ \int G[x, x', e^{g(x')}] \, \pi(x, dx') \right\}, \quad \text{all } x \in X.$$

Clearly, f^* is a fixed point of the operator T defined in (1) if and only if $g^* = \ln(f^*)$ is a fixed point of $\hat{T}$. Note that if D is closed and convex, then so is $\hat{D}$. The following exercise is the analogue of Exercise 17.2.

Exercise 17.4 Let the hypotheses of Exercise 17.2a,b hold. Assume in addition that $D \subset \mathbf{R}_{++}$, and let $\hat{D}$ and $\hat{F}$ be as defined above.
a. Show that the operator $\hat{T}$ defined in (3) maps $\hat{F}$ into itself.
b. Show that $\hat{F}$ is a complete metric space.

We then have the following analogue of Lemma 17.1.

LEMMA 17.2 *Let the hypotheses of Exercise 17.2a,b hold, with $D \subset \mathbf{R}_{++}$. In addition, assume that for each $(x, x') \in X \times X$, G is continuously differentiable on D, and assume that there exists some $0 \le \beta < 1$ such that*

$$(4) \qquad \left| \frac{yG_3(x, x', y)}{G(x, x', y)} \right| \le \beta, \quad \text{all } (x, x', y) \in X \times X \times D.$$

Define $\hat{D}$ and $\hat{F}$ as we did above, and let $\hat{T}$ be the operator on $\hat{F}$ defined by (3). Then $\hat{T}$ has a unique fixed point $g^* \in \hat{F}$, and

$$\|\hat{T}^n g_0 - g^*\| \le \beta^n \|g_0 - g^*\|, \quad \text{all } g_0 \in \hat{F}.$$

Proof. As shown in Exercise 17.4, $\hat{T} \colon \hat{F} \to \hat{F}$ and $\hat{F}$ is a complete metric space. Hence it is sufficient to show that $\hat{T}$ is a contraction of modulus β.
Fix $g, h \in \hat{F}$, and define $w \colon X \times X \to R$ by

$$w(x, x') = \frac{G[x, x', e^{h(x')}]}{\int G[x, u, e^{h(u)}] \, \pi(x, du)}.$$

Clearly $w(x, x') > 0$ and $\int w(x, x') \, \pi(x, dx') = 1$, all $x, x' \in X$. Therefore,

$$(\hat{T}g)(x) - (\hat{T}h)(x)$$

$$= \ln \left\{ \int G[x, x', e^{g(x')}] \, \pi(x, dx') \right\} - \ln \left\{ \int G[x, x', e^{h(x')}] \, \pi(x, dx') \right\}$$

$$= \ln \left\{ \frac{\int G[x, x', e^{g(x')}] \, \pi(x, dx')}{\int G[x, u, e^{h(u)}] \, \pi(x, du)} \right\}$$

$$= \ln \left\{ \int w(x, x') \frac{G[x, x', e^{g(x')}]}{G[x, x', e^{h(x')}]} \, \pi(x, dx') \right\}$$

$$\leq \sup_{x,x'} \left\{ \ln \left\{ \frac{G[x, x', e^{g(x')}]}{G[x, x', e^{h(x')}]} \right\} \right\}$$

$$= \sup_{x,x'} \left\{ \ln \{ G[x, x', e^{g(x')}] \} - \ln \{ G[x, x', e^{h(x')}] \} \right\}$$

$$\leq \beta \sup_{x'} [g(x') - h(x')]$$

$$\leq \beta \| g - h \|, \quad \text{all } x \in X,$$

where the next-to-last line involves applying the Mean Value Theorem to the function $\gamma(x, x', y) = \ln[G(x, x', e^y)]$ and using the hypothesis (4). Repeating the analysis with the roles of g and h reversed establishes that

$$\| \hat{T}g - \hat{T}h \| \leq \beta \| g - h \|.$$

Since g and h were arbitrary elements of $\hat{F}$, it follows that $\hat{T}$ is a contraction of modulus β. ∎

Note that the operators in (1) and (3) are related by

$$\hat{T}[\ln(f)](x) = \ln(Tf)(x), \quad \text{all } x \in X, \text{ all } f \in F.$$

Fix $f_0 \in F$, and define the sequence $\{f_n\}$ by $f_n = Tf_{n-1}$, $n = 1, 2, \ldots$. Lemma 17.1 provides a sufficient condition for the existence of a value $0 \leq \beta < 1$ such that

$$\| f_{n+1} - f_n \| = \| Tf_n - Tf_{n-1} \| \leq \beta \| f_n - f_{n-1} \|, \quad \text{all } n,$$

where β can be chosen independently of f_0. Alternatively, Lemma 17.2 provides a sufficient condition for the existence of a value $0 \le \beta < 1$ such that

$$\|\ln(f_{n+1}) - \ln(f_n)\| \le \beta\|\ln(f_n) - \ln(f_{n-1})\|, \quad \text{all } n,$$

where β can be chosen independently of f_0. The two lemmas look at the same sequence. The difference between them is simply that they use different metrics.

Lemma 17.2 can be used to establish the existence and uniqueness of an equilibrium with strictly positive labor supply for our overlapping-generations model. A key step in the proof involves the construction of a closed, convex set D that is bounded away from the origin. The proof also requires an additional restriction on preferences.

ASSUMPTION 17.2 *For some* $0 \le \beta < 1$,

(5) $$1 - \beta \le -yV''(y)/V'(y) \le 1 + \beta, \quad \text{all } y \in \mathbf{R}_+.$$

PROPOSITION 2 *Let* $X = [a, b] \subset \mathbf{R}_{++}$, *with its Borel subsets* $\mathscr{X}$; *let* π *be a transition function on* $(X, \mathscr{X})$; *and assume that* π *has the Feller property. Let* H *and* V *satisfy Assumptions 17.1 and 17.2, and define* ζ *and* ϕ *as we did in Section 17.1. Then there is a unique bounded, continuous, strictly positive function* $f^*: X \to \mathbf{R}_{++}$ *satisfying*

(6) $$f^*(x) = \int \phi[x'\zeta^{-1}(f^*(x'))] \, \pi(x, dx'), \quad \text{all } x \in X.$$

Proof. The proof will be an application of Lemma 17.2. First we must construct a suitable set D. Since $\zeta'(0) = 0$ and $\zeta'(l) > 0$ if $l > 0$, it follows that ζ^{-1} is continuously differentiable on $\mathbf{R}_{++}$, with $\lim_{y\to 0}\zeta^{-1\prime}(y) = +\infty$, as shown in Figure 17.2. For $k = 1, 2, \ldots$, define the sequence $\{\varepsilon_k\}$ by

$$\varepsilon_k = \min\{\varepsilon > 0: \zeta^{-1}(\varepsilon) = k\varepsilon\}.$$

Since ζ^{-1} is continuous, strictly increasing, and bounded above by L, this sequence is well defined and strictly decreasing, as shown in Figure 17.2. Moreover, the sequence $\{k\varepsilon_k\}$ is also decreasing.

Recall that $X = [a, b]$, where $a > 0$. Define $C = aV'(bL)$, and note that $C > 0$. Choose any $K > 1/C$. Since ζ^{-1} is increasing and V' is decreasing,

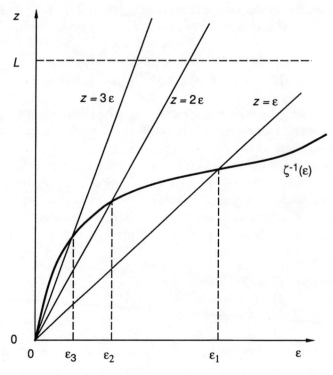

Figure 17.2

it follows that

(7) $\phi[x'\zeta^{-1}(y)] = x'\zeta^{-1}(y)V'[x'\zeta^{-1}(y)]$

$\geq a\zeta^{-1}(\varepsilon_K)V'(bL)$

$= K\varepsilon_K C$

$> \varepsilon_K, \quad \text{all } x' \in X, \text{all } y \geq \varepsilon_K.$

Define the closed, convex set $D = [\varepsilon_K, +\infty) \subset \mathbf{R}_{++}$, and define $\hat{D}$ and $\hat{F}$ as we did above.

Define the function $G(x, x', y) = \phi[x'\zeta^{-1}(y)]$; then f^* satisfies (6) if and only if $\ln(f^*)$ is a fixed point of the operator $\hat{T}$ defined in (3). We will use

Lemma 17.2 to establish the existence and uniqueness of a fixed point of the latter.

It follows immediately from (7) that $G: X \times X \times D \to D$; clearly the hypotheses of Exercise 17.4 hold; and it follows immediately from Assumption 17.1 that $G(x, x', \cdot)$ is continuously differentiable in y. It only remains to be shown that G satisfies (4).

Recall from the proof of Proposition 1 that $l\zeta'(l)/\zeta(l) \geq 1$, all $l \in [0, L)$. From this fact it follows immediately that $y\zeta^{-1\prime}(y)/\zeta^{-1}(y) \leq 1$, all $y \in D$. In addition, Assumption 17.2 implies that $|y\phi'(y)/\phi(y)| \leq \beta$, all $y \in \mathbf{R}_+$. Hence it follows from the definition of G that for any $x, x' \in X$,

$$\left| \frac{yG_3(x, x', y)}{G(x, x', y)} \right| = \left| \frac{x'\zeta^{-1}(y)\phi'[x'\zeta^{-1}(y)]}{\phi[x'\zeta^{-1}(y)]} \right| \left| \frac{y\zeta^{-1\prime}(y)}{\zeta^{-1}(y)} \right|$$

$$\leq \beta, \quad \text{all } y \in D.$$

That is, G satisfies (4).

Hence Lemma 17.2 applies, and the operator $\hat{T}$ defined in (3) has a unique fixed point $g^* \in \hat{F}$. Moreover, since any $K > 1/C$ could have been used to define the set D, the solution is unique. Hence $f^* = e^{g^*}$ is the only bounded, continuous, strictly positive solution to (6). ∎

Notice that Assumption 17.2 is equivalent to requiring that for some $\varepsilon > 0$, the index of relative risk aversion $-yV''/V'$ be bounded below by ε and above by $2 - \varepsilon$, for all $y \in \mathbf{R}_+$. Since the strict monotonicity and strict concavity of V imply that $0 < -yV''(y)/V'(y)$, Assumption 17.1 ensures that the index of relative risk aversion is strictly positive. This restriction was needed to establish the existence and uniqueness of a solution in the case of serially independent shocks. The first inequality in (5) is a slight strengthening of this restriction, since it requires that the bound away from zero be uniform. The second inequality in (5), which places an upper bound on the curvature of V, is entirely new; nothing like it was required in the case of serially independent shocks. The stronger restrictions in Assumption 17.2 are needed to prove Proposition 2 because the Contraction Mapping Theorem implies not only the existence and uniqueness of the fixed point f^*, but also the convergence of the sequence $\hat{T}^n[\ln(f_0)]$ to $\ln(f^*)$ at a uniform geometric rate, for any f_0. This convergence requires not only that the two curves in Figure 17.1

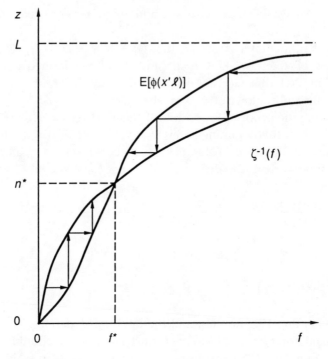

Figure 17.3

cross exactly once but also that their intersection be stable under the adjustment process indicated by the arrows in Figure 17.3, and, in addition, that the rate of convergence, in terms of the logarithms, be uniform. In the next two sections we will see that these stronger restrictions on the degree of relative risk aversion can be dispensed with if we take a different mathematical approach to the problem of existence.

17.3   The Brouwer Fixed-Point Theorem

It is quite easy to convince oneself by diagram (see Figure 17.4) that any continuous function mapping the unit interval into itself must cross the 45° line at least once; that is, that any such function has at least one fixed point. The Brouwer Fixed-Point Theorem extends this conclusion to arbitrary closed, bounded, convex subsets of a finite-dimensional space.

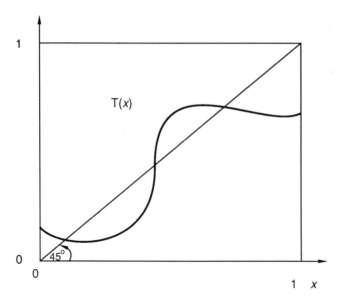

Figure 17.4

THEOREM 17.3 (*Brouwer Fixed-Point Theorem*) *Let F be a nonempty, closed, bounded, convex subset of a finite-dimensional, normed vector space. If T is a continuous mapping of F into itself, then T has a fixed point in F.*

We omit the proof, and instead turn directly to the application of this result to functional equations of the type discussed in the previous section.

Let $X = \{x_1, \ldots, x_m\}$ be a finite set, and let $\Pi = [\pi_{ij}]$ be an $m \times m$ stochastic matrix. Let $D \subset \mathbf{R}$ be a nonempty, closed, bounded, convex set; and let $F = D \times \ldots \times D = D^m$. Let $G: X \times X \times D \to D$, and assume that G is continuous in its third argument. Define the operator T on F by

$$(T_i f)(x) = \sum_{j=1}^{m} G(x_i, x_j, f_j)\pi_{ij}, \quad i = 1, \ldots, m,$$

where $f = (f_1, \ldots, f_m) \in F$. To apply Brouwer's Theorem, simply note that $F \subset \mathbf{R}^m$ is nonempty, closed, bounded, and convex; that $T: F \to F$; and that T is a continuous mapping.

In the last section we saw that using a logarithmic transformation was sometimes useful in applying the Contraction Mapping Theorem. It is easy to show that such a transformation is *not* useful if Brouwer's Theorem is to be applied. To see this, assume that $D \subset \mathbf{R}_{++}$, let $\hat{D} = \ln(D)$, and define $\hat{F} = \hat{D}^m$. Let $g(x) = \ln[f(x)]$, and consider the operator $\hat{T}$ on $\hat{F}$ defined by

$$(\hat{T}_i g)(x) = \ln \left[\sum_{j=1}^{m} G(x_i, x_j, e^{g_j}) \pi_{ij} \right], \quad i = 1, \ldots, m.$$

Note that $\hat{F}$ and $\hat{T}$ satisfy the hypotheses of Brouwer's Theorem if and only if F and T do.

We can apply Brouwer's Theorem to our overlapping-generations model if we assume that the number of states is finite. A key step in the proof is the construction of a suitable set F. We know from direct analysis that there may exist an equilibrium in which labor supply is identically zero. Since our goal is to establish the existence of an equilibrium in which labor supply is strictly positive, we draw upon the argument used in the proof of Proposition 2 to bound labor supply away from zero. Notice that to apply Brouwer's Theorem we also need to bound F above.

PROPOSITION 3 *Let $X = \{x_1, \ldots, x_m\}$ be a finite set in $\mathbf{R}_{++}$, and let $\Pi = [\pi_{ij}]$ be an $m \times m$ stochastic matrix. Let H and V satisfy Assumption 17.1, and define ζ and ϕ as we did in Section 17.1. Then there exists a strictly positive vector $f^* = (f_1^*, \ldots, f_m^*) \in \mathbf{R}_{++}^m$ satisfying*

(1) $f_i^* = \sum_{j=1}^{m} \phi[x_j \zeta^{-1}(f_j^*)] \pi_{ij}, \quad i = 1, \ldots, m.$

Proof. Define the operator T on $\mathbf{R}_+^m$ by

(2) $T_i f = \sum_{j=1}^{m} \phi[x_j \zeta^{-1}(f_j)] \pi_{ij}, \quad i = 1, \ldots, m.$

We will establish the claim by applying Brouwer's Theorem to T.

To do this, we first must choose a suitable set $F \subset \mathbf{R}_+^m$. Without loss of generality, assume that $x_1 < x_2 < \ldots < x_m$. Define $C = x_1 V'(x_m L)$, define the sequence $\{\varepsilon_k\}$ as we did in the proof of Proposition 2, and choose any $K > 1/C$. Then as shown in the proof of Proposition 2,

$$\phi[x_j\zeta^{-1}(y)] > \varepsilon_K, \quad \text{all } x_j, \text{ all } y \geq \varepsilon_K.$$

Next, let $z = x_1\zeta^{-1}(\varepsilon_K)$ and $Z = x_m L$, and define $B = \max_{y \in [z,Z]} \phi(y)$. Since ζ^{-1} is monotone, it follows that

$$\phi[x_j\zeta^{-1}(y)] \leq B, \quad \text{all } x_j, \text{ all } y \geq \varepsilon_K.$$

Define $F = [\varepsilon_K, B]^m$. Clearly F is nonempty, closed, bounded, and convex, and the operator T defined in (2) maps the set F into itself.

Finally, under Assumption 17.1 the functions ϕ and ζ^{-1} are both continuous. Hence T is continuous, and the desired result follows from Brouwer's Theorem. ∎

For problems like this one, with no endogenous state variables, restricting the state space to be finite is not unreasonable. In models with endogenous state variables, however, such a restriction is much less tenable and often introduces more complications than it eliminates. In these situations an infinite-dimensional analogue to Brouwer's Theorem is needed. It is provided in the Schauder Fixed-Point Theorem.

17.4   The Schauder Fixed-Point Theorem

We are often interested in finding fixed points of an operator T mapping a space $C(X)$ of bounded continuous functions into itself. If the set X is a finite set, then the space $C(X)$ is finite dimensional, and as shown in the preceding section, Brouwer's Theorem provides one way of establishing the existence of at least one fixed point of T. But if X is not a finite set, Brouwer's Theorem cannot be used. In this section we discuss the Schauder Fixed-Point Theorem, an extension of Brouwer's Theorem to infinite-dimensional spaces. For simplicity, we simply state a version of Schauder's Theorem that applies to spaces of bounded continuous functions.

Let X be a bounded subset of $\mathbf{R}^l$, and let $C(X)$ be the space of bounded continuous (real-valued) functions on X, with the sup norm.

DEFINITION *A subset F of C(X) is **equicontinuous** if for every ε > 0 there exists δ > 0 such that*

$$|x - y| < \delta \text{ implies } |f(x) - f(y)| < \varepsilon, \quad \text{all } f \in F.$$

That is, the family F is equicontinuous if each function in F is uniformly continuous and if the continuity is uniform for all functions in F. We then have the following result, which we state without proof.

THEOREM 17.4 (*Schauder Fixed-Point Theorem*) *Let X be a bounded subset of $\mathbf{R}^l$, and let C(X) be the space of bounded continuous functions on X, with the sup norm. Let $F \subset C(X)$ be nonempty, closed, bounded and convex. If the mapping $T: F \to F$ is continuous and the family $T(F)$ is equicontinuous, then T has a fixed point in F.*

The following exercise illustrates how Schauder's Theorem can be used.

Exercise 17.5 a. Consider the differential equation and boundary condition

$$\frac{dx(t)}{dt} = f[x(t)], \quad t \in [0, 1]; \quad x(0) = c.$$

Show that if f is continuous, this equation has a solution on $[0, 1]$.
    b. Find two solutions on $[0, 1]$ to the equation

$$\frac{dx(t)}{dt} = [x(t)]^{1/2}, \quad t \in [0, 1]; \quad x(0) = 0.$$

c. Which condition(s) of Exercise 3.8 does this equation violate?

Before applying Schauder's Theorem to our overlapping-generations model, we need to prove one more preliminary result. Lemma 17.5 gives a sufficient condition for the equicontinuity of a family of functions defined as conditional expectations by using a transition function. This lemma requires the following continuity assumption on the transition function.

ASSUMPTION 17.3 *Let X be a bounded Borel set of $\mathbf{R}^l$, with its Borel subsets $\mathcal{X}$; and let π be a transition function on $(X, \mathcal{X})$. For every ε > 0 there exists δ > 0* *such that*

$$|x - \hat{x}| < \delta \text{ implies } \|\pi(x, \cdot) - \pi(\hat{x}, \cdot)\|_{\text{TV}} < \varepsilon, \text{ all } x, \hat{x} \in X;$$

where $\|\cdot\|_{\text{TV}}$ denotes the total variation norm.

Assumption 17.3 can be viewed as a twofold strengthening of the Feller property. Recall that π has the Feller property if for any sequence $\{x_n\}$ converging to a point x_0, the sequence of probability measures $\{\pi(x_n, \cdot)\}$ converges weakly to the probability measure $\pi(x_0, \cdot)$. Assumption 17.3 strengthens this condition by requiring that the sequence $\{\pi(x_n, \cdot)\}$ converge to $\pi(x_0, \cdot)$ in norm (that is, strongly) rather than weakly, and that the rate of convergence be uniform.

Under Assumption 17.3 we have the following result.

LEMMA 17.5 *Let $(X, \mathcal{X})$ and π satisfy Assumption 17.3. Let $D \subset \mathbf{R}$ be nonempty, closed, bounded, and convex; and let $F \subset C(X)$ be the set of bounded continuous functions $f: X \to D$. Let $G: X \times X \times D \to D$ be a continuous function, and assume that G is uniformly continuous in its first argument. Define the operator T on F by*

(1) $$(Tf)(x) = \int G[x, x', f(x')]\pi(x, dx'), \quad \text{all } x \in X, f \in F.$$

Then the family of continuous functions $T(F)$ is bounded and equicontinuous.

Proof. Let $B > 0$ be a bound on the interval D. Then clearly it is also a bound on the functions in F and in $T(F)$. To see that the family $T(F)$ is equicontinuous, note that for any $f \in F$ and any $x, \hat{x} \in X$,

$$|(Tf)(x) - (Tf)(\hat{x})|$$

$$\leq \left| \int \{G[x, x', f(x')] - G[\hat{x}, x', f(x')]\} \, \pi(x, dx') \right|$$

$$+ \left| \int G[\hat{x}, x', f(x')]\pi(x, dx') - \int G[\hat{x}, x', f(x')]\pi(\hat{x}, dx') \right|$$

(2) $$\leq \int |G[x, x', f(x')] - G[\hat{x}, x', f(x')]| \, \pi(x, dx')$$

$$+ B\|\pi(x, \cdot) - \pi(\hat{x}, \cdot)\|_{\text{TV}}.$$

Choose any $\varepsilon > 0$. Since G is uniformly continuous in its first argument, there exists $\delta_1 > 0$ such that

$$\|x - \hat{x}\| < \delta_1 \text{ implies } |G(x, x', y) - G(\hat{x}, x', y)| < \varepsilon/2,$$

all $x' \in X$, all $y \in D$.

And since π satisfies Assumption 17.3, there exists $\delta_2 > 0$ such that

$$\|x - \hat{x}\| < \delta_2 \text{ implies } \|\pi(x, \cdot) - \pi(\hat{x}, \cdot)\|_{\text{TV}} < \varepsilon/2B.$$

Hence it follows from (2) that

$$\|x - \hat{x}\| < \min\{\delta_1, \delta_2\} \text{ implies}$$

$$|(Tf)(x) - (Tf)(\hat{x})| < \varepsilon, \quad \text{all } f \in F.$$

Therefore the family $T(F)$ is equicontinuous. ∎

With Lemma 17.5 established, to apply Schauder's Theorem to (1) it suffices to show that T is continuous as an operator. In general, establishing this may require an additional restriction on G.

Exercise 17.6   Let $(X, \mathcal{X})$, π, D, F, and G satisfy the hypotheses of Lemma 17.5, and in addition assume that G is uniformly continuous in its third argument. Show that T as defined in (1) is a continuous operator.

To conclude this section, we apply Schauder's Theorem to our over-lapping-generations model. Note that the proof is very similar to the one based on Brouwer's Theorem.

PROPOSITION 4 *Let $(X, \mathcal{X})$ and π satisfy Assumption 17.3, with $X = [a, b] \subset \mathbf{R}_{++}$. Let H and V satisfy Assumption 17.1, and define ζ and ϕ as we did in Section 17.1. Then there exists a continuous, strictly positive function $f^*: X \to \mathbf{R}_{++}$ satisfying*

$$f^*(x) = \int \phi[x'\zeta^{-1}(f^*(x'))]\pi(x, dx'), \quad \text{all } x \in X.$$

Proof. Define the operator T by

(3) $\qquad (Tf)(x) = \int \phi[x'\zeta^{-1}(f(x'))]\pi(x, dx'), \quad$ all $x \in X$.

We will establish the claim by applying Schauder's Theorem to T.

To do this we first must choose a suitable set $F \subset C(X)$. As we did in the proof of Proposition 2, define the sequence $\{\varepsilon_k\}$, define $C = aV'(bL)$, and choose any $K > 1/C$. Then as shown there,

(4) $\qquad \phi[x'\zeta^{-1}(y)] > \varepsilon_K, \quad$ all $x' \in X$, all $y \geq \varepsilon_K$.

Let $z = a\zeta^{-1}(\varepsilon_K)$ and $Z = bL$, and define $B = \max_{y \in [z, Z]} \phi(y)$. Since ζ^{-1} is monotone, it follows that

(5) $\qquad \phi[x'\zeta^{-1}(y)] \leq B, \quad$ all $x' \in X$, all $y \geq \varepsilon_K$.

Let $F \subset C(X)$ be the space of continuous functions $f: X \rightarrow [\varepsilon_K, B]$. Clearly F is nonempty, closed, bounded, and convex.

Next we must show that T maps F into itself. Since for each $x \in X$, $\pi(x, \cdot)$ is a probability measure, it follows immediately from (4) and (5) that Tf takes values in $[\varepsilon_K, B]$. Moreover, since π has the Feller property and ϕ, ζ^{-1}, and f are continuous, it follows that Tf is continuous. Hence $T: F \rightarrow F$.

Next we must show that $T(F)$ is an equicontinuous family. By Lemma 17.5, this conclusion follows from the fact that the family F is bounded, the integrand in (3) does not depend on x, and π satisfies Assumption 17.3.

Finally, we must show that T is continuous as an operator. Consider a sequence $\{f_i\}$ in F converging (in the sup norm) to f. For every $\gamma > 0$ there exists $N(\gamma) \geq 1$ such that

$$|f_i(x') - f(x')| < \gamma, \quad \text{all } x' \in X, \text{ all } i \geq N(\gamma).$$

Also, since ζ^{-1} is continuous, it is uniformly continuous on the compact set $[\varepsilon_K, B]$. Hence for every $\delta > 0$ there exists $\gamma(\delta) > 0$ such that

$$|y_i - y| < \gamma(\delta) \text{ implies } |\zeta^{-1}(y_i) - \zeta^{-1}(y)| < \delta.$$

Moreover, since ϕ is continuous, it is uniformly continuous on the compact set $[z, Z]$. Hence for every $\nu > 0$, there exists $\delta(\nu) > 0$ such that

$$|\xi_i - \xi| < \delta(\nu) \text{ implies } |x'\xi_i - x'\xi| < b\delta(\nu) \quad \text{and}$$

$$|\phi(x'\xi_i) - \phi(x'\xi)| < \nu, \quad \text{all } x' \in X.$$

Using these three conditions together, we find that for every $\nu > 0$ there exists $M(\nu) = N[\gamma(\delta(\nu))]$ such that

$$|\phi[x'\zeta^{-1}(f_i(x'))] - \phi[x'\zeta^{-1}(f(x'))]| < \nu, \quad \text{all } x' \in X, \text{all } i \geq M(\nu).$$

Hence

$$|(Tf_i)(x) - (Tf)(x)|$$

$$\leq \int |\phi[x'\zeta^{-1}(f_i(x'))] - \phi[x'\zeta^{-1}(f(x'))]| \, \pi(x, dx')$$

$$< \nu, \quad \text{all } x \in X, \text{all } i \geq M(\nu).$$

That is, $\{Tf_i\}$ converges to Tf in the sup norm. Hence T is continuous as an operator, and it follows from Schauder's Theorem that T has a fixed point in F. ∎

The key steps in applying Schauder's Theorem to operators of the form in (1) are choosing a nonempty, closed, bounded, convex set $F \subset C(X)$ such that T maps F into itself; ensuring that $T(F)$ is equicontinuous; and ensuring that T is continuous as an operator. Notice that the first and last of these steps have exact analogues in applications of Brouwer's Theorem, since the continuity of T as an operator plays the same role as the continuity of T required in Brouwer's Theorem. The second step—establishing that $T(F)$ is an equicontinuous family—had no counterpart in the finite case, because, if X is a finite set, this assumption is trivially satisfied. This specialization of Schauder's Theorem is exactly Brouwer's Theorem.

It is instructive to compare the assumptions and conclusions of Proposition 2, where the Contraction Mapping Theorem was applied, with those of Proposition 4. The former required much stronger assumptions on preferences but, in return, established uniqueness as well as existence. It is interesting that Proposition 2 did not require any restrictions on the transition function π, because the Contraction Mapping Theorem does not involve equicontinuity. In contrast, Assumption 17.3 or something similar would generally seem to be required in applications of Schauder's Theorem.

For the same reasons as discussed above in the context of Brouwer's Theorem, logarithmic transformations are not useful if Schauder's Theorem is to be applied. As the following exercise shows, however, in any given context there may be more than one way to apply Schauder's Theorem.

Exercise 17.7 An equilibrium of our overlapping-generations model can also be characterized as a function $n^*: X \to [0, L)$ satisfying

$$n^*(x) = \zeta^{-1} \left[\int \phi(x'n^*(x')) \, \pi(x, dx') \right], \quad \text{all } x \in X.$$

(Why?) Show that the operator defined by the right side of this equation has a fixed point.

17.5 Fixed Points of Monotone Operators

If an operator $T: F \to F$ is a contraction mapping, then for any initial point $f_0 \in F$ the limit of the sequence $\{T^n f_0\}_{n=1}^{\infty}$ is the unique fixed point of T. Proofs based on the Contraction Mapping Theorem establish uniqueness as well as existence and are constructive in the sense that they provide an algorithm for locating the fixed point computationally. Moreover, the algorithm converges at a geometric rate. If an operator T satisfies the hypotheses of Brouwer's or Schauder's Theorem but is not a contraction, then only existence is established: there may be several fixed points of T; and for an arbitrary point $f_0 \in F$, the sequence $\{T^n f_0\}$ need not converge.

In this section we look at operators that satisfy hypotheses similar to those of Brouwer's or Schauder's Theorem and in addition have a certain monotonicity property. We show that existence and uniqueness results and a computational algorithm are all available for such operators. We then apply this result to the overlapping-generations model discussed in earlier sections.

We begin with the following preliminary lemma, which shows that if for some $f_0 \in F$ the sequence $\{T^n f_0\}$ converges pointwise, then the limiting function is a fixed point of T. The hypotheses required for this result are weaker than those required for Schauder's Theorem—F need not be bounded or convex—because the lemma applies only *if* there is a sequence $\{T^n f_0\}$ that is pointwise convergent.

LEMMA 17.6 *Let $X \subset \mathbf{R}^l$ be a bounded set; let $C(X)$ be the space of bounded continuous functions on X, with the sup norm; and let $F \subset C(X)$ be closed. Assume that the operator $T: F \to F$ is continuous and that $T(F)$ is an equicontinuous family. Suppose in addition that for some $f_0 \in F$, the sequence of functions $\{T^n f_0\}$ converges pointwise. Then the limiting function $f = \lim_{n \to \infty} T^n f_0$ is in F and is a fixed point of T.*

Proof. Let $f_0 \in F$, and suppose that $T^n f_0 \to f$ pointwise. We will show that $T^n f_0 \to f$ uniformly (in the sup norm); the desired results will then follow from the facts that F is closed and T is a continuous operator.

First note that $f_n \in T(F) \subseteq F$, $n = 1, 2, \ldots$, and that

(1) $|f(x') - f(x)| \le |f(x') - f_n(x')| + |f_n(x') - f_n(x)| + |f_n(x) - f(x)|,$

all $x, x' \in X$, $n = 1, 2, \ldots$.

Fix $\varepsilon > 0$, and choose $\delta > 0$ such that

(2) $\|x' - x\| < \delta$ implies $|f_n(x') - f_n(x)| < \varepsilon,$ $n = 1, 2, \ldots$;

since $\{f_n\} \subset T(F)$ and $T(F)$ is an equicontinuous family, this is possible. Now fix $x, x' \in X$. Since $f_n \to f$ pointwise, for any $\Delta > 0$ there exists $N \ge 1$, which may depend on x and x', such that

(3a) $|f(x') - f_n(x')| < \Delta/2,$ and

(3b) $|f_n(x) - f(x)| < \Delta/2,$ all $n \ge N.$

Then substituting from (2) and (3) into (1), we find that

$$\|x' - x\| < \delta \text{ implies } |f(x') - f(x)| < \varepsilon + \Delta.$$

Since $\Delta > 0$ was arbitrary, it follows that

(4) $\qquad \|x' - x\| < \delta$ implies $|f(x') - f(x)| < \varepsilon.$

And since δ was chosen independently of x and x', (4) holds for all $x, x' \in X$. Hence f is uniformly continuous.

To see that $f_n \to f$ uniformly, choose any $\varepsilon > 0$. Then choose $\delta > 0$ such that (2) holds and select a finite set $A = \{x_1, x_2, \ldots, x_l\} \subset X$ such that

(5) $\qquad \min_{x_i \in A} \|x - x_i\| < \delta, \quad$ all $x \in X;$

since X is bounded, this is possible. Then choose $M \geq 1$, which may depend on the choice of A, such that

(6) $\qquad |f(x_i) - f_n(x_i)| < \varepsilon, \quad$ all $x_i \in A$, all $n \geq M;$

since A is a finite set and $f_n \to f$ pointwise, this is possible. Next, note that

(7) $\qquad |f(x) - f_n(x)| \leq |f(x) - f(x_i)| + |f(x_i) - f_n(x_i)| + |f_n(x_i) - f_n(x)|,$

$\qquad$ all $x \in X$, all $x_i \in A$, $n = 1, 2, \ldots.$

Fix $x \in X$ and let $x_{i*} \in A$ be an element that attains the minimum in (5). Then it follows from (2) and (4) that

(8a) $\qquad |f_n(x) - f_n(x_{i*})| < \varepsilon, \quad n = 1, 2, \ldots, \quad$ and

(8b) $\qquad |f(x_{i*}) - f(x)| < \varepsilon.$

Therefore, setting $i = i*$ in (7) and substituting from (6) and (8), we find that

(9) $\qquad |f(x) - f_n(x)| < 3\varepsilon, \quad$ all $n \geq M.$

Since A and M were chosen independently of x, (9) holds for all $x \in X$. That is, $\|f - f_n\| < 3\varepsilon$, all $n \geq M$. Since $\varepsilon > 0$ was arbitrary, it follows that $f_n \to f$ uniformly; then since F is closed, it follows that $f \in F$.

Finally, to see that f is a fixed point of T, note that

$$f = \lim_{n \to \infty} T^{n+1} f_0 = \lim_{n \to \infty} Tf_n = T(\lim_{n \to \infty} f_n) = Tf,$$

where the third equality uses the fact that T is a continuous operator. ∎

Lemma 17.6 shows that *if* the sequence of functions $\{T^n f_0\}$ converges pointwise, then the limiting function f is a fixed point of T. Thus the lemma is useful only if we can identify conditions under which the sequence $\{T^n f_0\}$ converges. In the rest of this section we show that monotonicity of the operator T is useful in this respect.

Let $X \subset \mathbf{R}^l$ be a bounded set, let F be a set of real-valued functions on X, and let T be an operator taking F into itself. We call T *monotone* if

$$f, g \in F \text{ and } f \geq g \text{ implies } Tf \geq Tg,$$

where $f \geq g$ means that $f(x) \geq g(x)$, all $x \in X$. In the next theorem this property is used in conjunction with the hypotheses of Lemma 17.6 to verify that certain operators have fixed points.

THEOREM 17.7 *Let $X \subset \mathbf{R}^l$ be a bounded set; let $C(X)$ be the space of bounded continuous functions on X, with the sup norm; and let $F \subset C(X)$ be closed and bounded. Assume that the operator $T: F \to F$ is continuous and monotone and that $T(F)$ is an equicontinuous family. Suppose there exists $f_0 \in F$ such that either $f_0 \leq Tf_0$ or $f_0 \geq Tf_0$. Then the limit $f = \lim T^n f_0$ exists, f is in F, and f is a fixed point of T.*

Proof. By Lemma 17.6, it suffices to show that the sequence of functions $\{T^n f_0\}$ converges pointwise. Suppose that $f_0 \leq Tf_0$; then it follows by induction that the sequence $\{T^n f_0\}$ is weakly increasing. Since the set F is closed and bounded, it also follows that the limiting function $f = \lim T^n f_0$ exists. A similar argument applies if $f_0 \geq Tf_0$. ∎

The following corollary illustrates how Theorem 17.7 can be used. It shows that if T is monotone and if f_0 and g_0 are minimal and maximal elements of F, then every fixed point h of T satisfies

$$\lim T^n f_0 = f \leq h \leq g = \lim T^n g_0.$$

COROLLARY   *Let X, F, and T satisfy the hypotheses of Theorem 17.7. If $f_0 \leq h_0$ for all $h_0 \in F$, then $\lim T^n f_0 = f \leq h$ for all fixed points h of T in F. A similar conclusion holds with the inequalities reversed.*

Proof. Suppose that $f_0 \leq h_0$, all $h_0 \in F$. Then $f_0 \leq Tf_0$, and Theorem 17.7 implies that $f = \lim T^n f_0 \in F$ exists and is a fixed point of T. Suppose that h is a fixed point of T. Since $f_0 \leq h$ and T is monotone, it follows that $Tf_0 \leq Th = h$. Hence by induction, $T^n f_0 \leq h$, $n = 1, 2, \ldots$, and taking the limit we find that $f \leq h$. A similar argument holds with the inequalities reversed.   ∎

This corollary provides a useful computational check on the multiplicity of fixed points. If f and g are the fixed points obtained by applying T to minimal and maximal elements of F respectively, and if it should turn out that $f = g$, then this function is the unique fixed point of T.

Now consider the assumptions that are needed to apply Theorem 17.7 and its corollary to functional equations of the type discussed in the earlier sections. As before let $X \subset \mathbf{R}^l$ be a bounded set, let π be a transition function on $(X, \mathscr{X})$, and let π satisfy Assumption 17.3. Let $D = [a, b] \subset \mathbf{R}$ be a nonempty, closed, bounded interval; and let $F \subset C(X)$ be the family of functions $f: X \to D$. Let $G: X \times X \times D \to D$ be a continuous function, and assume that G is uniformly continuous in its first and last arguments. Consider the operator T on F defined by

$$(Tf)(x) = \int G[x, x', f(x')] \pi(x, dx'), \quad \text{all } x \in X.$$

Under the stated conditions, F is closed and bounded, T maps F into itself, $T(F)$ is equicontinuous (by Lemma 17.5), and T is a continuous operator (by Exercise 17.6). Moreover, the functions $f_0(x) = a$ and $g_0(x) = b$, all $x \in X$, satisfy $f_0 \leq h_0 \leq g_0$, all $h_0 \in F$. Hence, to apply Theorem 17.7 it suffices to show that T is monotone. Clearly this is so if G is weakly increasing in its third argument.

We conclude this section by applying Theorem 17.7 and its corollary to the overlapping-generations model discussed earlier. The following additional assumption on preferences is required.

ASSUMPTION 17.4 $-yV''(y)/V'(y) \leq 1$, all $y \in \mathbf{R}_+$.

It is instructive to compare Assumptions 17.2 and 17.4. Note that the monotonicity and concavity of V (Assumption 17.1) imply that

$$0 < -yV''(y)/V'(y), \quad \text{all } y \in \mathbf{R}_+,$$

and that Assumption 17.2 can be restated as a requirement that, for some $\varepsilon > 0$,

$$\varepsilon < -yV''(y)/V'(y) \leq 2 - \varepsilon, \quad \text{all } y \in \mathbf{R}_+.$$

Hence Assumption 17.4 involves dropping the uniformity requirement on the lower bound but strengthening the upper bound substantially. In this particular example, the additional assumption on preferences needed to ensure monotonicity is stronger, almost, than the one needed to apply the Contraction Mapping Theorem.

PROPOSITION 5 *Let $(X, \mathcal{X})$ and π satisfy Assumption 17.3, with $X = [a, b]$ $\subset \mathbf{R}_{++}$. Let H and V satisfy Assumptions 17.1 and 17.4, and define ζ and ϕ as we did in Section 17.1. Then the operator T on $C(X)$ defined by*

$$(Tf)(x) = \int \phi[x'\zeta^{-1}(f(x'))]\pi(x, dx')$$

has at least one fixed point.

Also, define $\{\varepsilon_k\}$, K, and B as we did in the proof of Proposition 4; and define the constant functions $f_0(x) = \varepsilon_K$ and $g_0(x) = B$, all $x \in X$. Then the sequences $\{T^n f_0\}$ and $\{T^n g_0\}$ converge to fixed points of T; and if

$$\lim T^n f_0 = f = g = \lim T^n g_0,$$

then this function is the unique fixed point of T.

Proof. Let $F \subset C(X)$ be as specified in the proof of Proposition 4. Clearly, F is closed and bounded, $T: F \to F$ is continuous, and $T(F)$ is equicontinuous. Recall that ζ^{-1} is strictly increasing, and note that Assumption 17.4 implies that ϕ is nondecreasing. Hence the operator T is monotone, and the desired conclusions follow immediately from Theorem 17.7 and its corollary. ∎

Other (more interesting) applications of monotonicity are discussed in Chapter 18.

17.6 Partially Observed Shocks

To close this chapter, we show how the methods developed in the previous sections can be applied to a model in which the contemporaneous shock is only partially observed. The example we consider is the "islands" model studied in Lucas (1972), which incorporates both real and monetary shocks. First we show that the competitive equilibria of this system correspond to the fixed points of a certain operator on a space of bounded continuous functions. We then show how the four fixed-point theorems described in the earlier sections—the Contraction Mapping Theorem, Brouwer's Theorem, Schauder's Theorem, and the monotonicity theorem—can be applied to this operator.

We begin with a description of the economy, which is a modification of the overlapping-generations example used in the earlier sections of the chapter. As before, each individual lives for two periods. When young, he works and sells the output he produces in exchange for money balances, which he carries over to the following period. When old, he uses all of his money balances to buy goods, which he consumes. As before, preferences over labor-consumption pairs have the form $U(l, c) = -H(l) + V(c)$.

In contrast to the earlier example, there are no stochastic shocks to the production technology. In each period labor can be used to produce output on a one-for-one basis: $y = l$. However, there are two sources of uncertainty in this economy that had no counterparts in the earlier model.

The first source of uncertainty is real and arises from the fact that the economy consists of two distinct "islands," with no trade possible between them. In each period the members of the young generation are assigned randomly to one of the two islands, with the proportion $\theta/2$ going to one and $1 - \theta/2$ to the other. Members of the old generation are reassigned randomly to the two islands, with half going to each, in a way that equates the aggregate quantity of money in the two markets.

The second source of uncertainty is nominal and arises from the fact that in each period the government injects (or withdraws) money from the system by paying interest on (or taxing) money holdings of the old.

In particular, xm are the posttransfer money balances of an old individual who has accumulated balances m when young.

Thus, the nominal and real shocks to the system in any period are fully described by the exogenously determined pair (x, θ). Let $X \times \Theta$ denote the state space. We assume that the pair (x_t, θ_t) is independently and identically distributed over time and that within each period the nominal and real components of the shock are independently drawn from distribution functions Ψ and G on X and Θ, respectively. We use the following assumption on the shocks.

ASSUMPTION 17.5 $x \in X = [\underline{x}, \bar{x}]$, where $0 < \underline{x} < \bar{x} < \infty$; and $\theta \in \Theta = [\underline{\theta}, \bar{\theta}]$, where $0 < \underline{\theta} < \bar{\theta} < 2$. The distribution functions Ψ and G have continuous densities, ψ and g, respectively.

Assume that the contemporaneous shocks (x, θ) are not directly observed by any member of the young generation but are observed with a one-period lag. Then the pretransfer money supply in period t—call it $M_t = M_0 \prod_{s=1}^{t-1} x_s$—is known to all. The money price of goods in period t will depend on the current state (x_t, θ_t) but will also depend—in a neutral way—on the pretransfer, perfectly observed money stock M_t. Thus, in any stationary equilibrium for this economy, the price level in any period t will be given by $P_t = M_t p(x_t, \theta_t)$, where $p(x, \theta)$ is a (real, not nominal) price function.

As in the model analyzed earlier, we define a stationary equilibrium for this economy as a price function $p: X \times \Theta \to \mathbf{R}_+$ and a labor supply function $n: X \times \Theta \to [0, L]$. For this economy, the equilibrium conditions are

(1) $n(x, \theta) \in \underset{l \in [0,L]}{\mathrm{argmax}}$

$$\left\{ -H(l) + \underset{\tilde{x}, \tilde{\theta}}{\mathrm{E}} \left\{ \underset{x', \theta'}{\mathrm{E}} \left\{ V\left[\frac{x' l p(\tilde{x}, \tilde{\theta})}{\tilde{x} p(x', \theta')} \right] \middle| p(\tilde{x}, \tilde{\theta}) = p(x, \theta) \right\} \right\} \right\},$$

(2) $n(x, \theta) p(x, \theta) = x/\theta$,   all $(x, \theta) \in X \times \Theta$.

Condition (1) says that $n(x, \theta)$ is the optimal labor supply for a young individual in state (x, θ), given the information available to him. What information is this? The agent cannot observe the current state (x, θ). But he does observe the value of the price function p evaluated at the current state, and therefore he knows that the current state is in the subset of $X \times \Theta$ where price is equal to $p(x, \theta)$. Thus from his point of view the current state is a random variable, $(\tilde{x}, \tilde{\theta})$, for which he knows the distribution but not the current realization. Since the state is independently and identically distributed, next period's state (x', θ') is also a random variable with a known distribution. His optimal labor supply $n(x, \theta)$ maximizes his conditional expected lifetime utility, given this information.

His choice entails producing $n(x, \theta)$ units of output, which he sells at the known price $p(\tilde{x}, \tilde{\theta})M_t$, acquiring total revenues of $n(x, \theta)p(\tilde{x}, \tilde{\theta})M_t$. Hence in the following period he has random posttransfer money balances of $x'n(x, \theta)p(\tilde{x}, \tilde{\theta})M_t$, which he uses to buy goods at the random price $p(x', \theta')M_{t+1} = p(x', \theta')M_t\tilde{x}$. His random consumption of goods when old is thus $x'n(x, \theta)p(\tilde{x}, \tilde{\theta})/\tilde{x}p(x', \theta')$.

Condition (2) is a market-clearing condition. For the market with the fraction θ of the young, it equates the real balances acquired by each young agent in payment for the labor he supplies to the average balances per young agent held by the old.

Notice that any two states (x, θ) and $(\hat{x}, \hat{\theta})$ that lead to the same price level are indistinguishable to the young agent. Hence the set of utility-maximizing values for labor supply in (1) is the same in both states. Suppose that H and V satisfy Assumption 17.1, so that (1) is strictly concave in l and the maximizing value is unique. Then

$$p(x, \theta) = p(\hat{x}, \hat{\theta}) \text{ implies } n(x, \theta) = n(\hat{x}, \hat{\theta}),$$

and the market-clearing condition (2) then implies that $x/\theta = \hat{x}/\hat{\theta}$ for any such pair of states. This equality implies that any equilibrium must be of the form $p(x, \theta) = \rho(x/\theta)$ and $n(x, \theta) = \eta(x/\theta)$. If there is a solution of this form for which ρ is monotone, then the price reveals the ratio x/θ. Thus, our strategy for establishing the existence of an equilibrium is as follows. We will look for functions (ρ, η) of the form above that satisfy (1) and (2) when the conditioning information in (1) is taken to be the ratio x/θ. If such a pair can be found, and if ρ is monotone, then (ρ, η) describes an equilibrium.

Define $z = x/\theta$; under Assumption 17.5, $z \in Z = [\underline{z}, \bar{z}] = [\underline{x}/\bar{\theta}, \bar{x}/\underline{\theta}]$, where $0 < \underline{z} < \bar{z} < \infty$. The distribution function for z—call it Π—is then given by

$$\Pi(z) = \Pr\{x/\theta \le z\} = \int_{\underline{\theta}}^{\bar{\theta}} \int_{\underline{x}}^{z\theta} g(\theta)\psi(x)\,dx\,d\theta = \int_{\underline{\theta}}^{\bar{\theta}} g(\theta)\Psi(z\theta)\,d\theta,$$

and Π has a continuous density:

$$\pi(z) = \Pi'(z) = \int_{\underline{\theta}}^{\bar{\theta}} g(\theta)\theta\psi(z\theta)\,d\theta.$$

The following exercise shows that we can also derive the conditional distribution function $G(\cdot|z)$ for θ given z, for any $z \in Z$.

Exercise 17.8   a. Derive the conditional distribution function $G(\cdot|z)$: $\Theta \to [0, 1]$, $z \in Z$. Show that for each $z \in \text{int } Z$, $G(\cdot|z)$ has a continuous density $g(\cdot|z)$.
   b. Show that if $z_n \to z$, then $G(\cdot|z_n)$ converges weakly to $G(\cdot|z)$.

We can use the distribution functions Π and $G(\cdot|z)$ to rewrite (1). Substituting η for n, ρ for p, and z for x/θ, we can write (1) as

$$\eta(z) = \underset{l \in [0,L)}{\text{argmax}} \left\{ -H(l) + \int_{\Theta} \int_{Z} \int_{\Theta} V \left[\frac{\theta' z' l \rho(z)}{\bar{\theta} z \rho(z')} \right] \right.$$

$$\left. \times G(d\theta'|z')\,\pi(dz')\,G(d\bar{\theta}|z) \right\}.$$

Under Assumption 17.1, the solution to this maximization problem is interior and hence must satisfy the first-order condition

(3) $\eta(z)H'[\eta(z)]$

$$= \int_{\Theta} \int_{Z} \int_{\Theta} \frac{\theta'}{\bar{\theta}} \eta(z')V' \left[\frac{\theta'}{\bar{\theta}} \eta(z') \right] G(d\theta'|z')\,\pi(dz')\,G(d\bar{\theta}|z),$$

where (2) has been used to eliminate ρ.

As we did in the earlier sections, define $\zeta(l) = lH'(l)$ and $\phi(y) = yV'(y)$, and recall that under Assumption 17.1 ζ is invertible. Then use (3) to define an operator T on $C(Z)$ by

(4) $$(Tf)(z) = \int_\Theta \int_Z \int_\Theta \phi \left[\frac{\theta'}{\bar{\theta}} \zeta^{-1}(f(z')) \right] G(d\theta'|z') \, \pi(dz') \, G(d\tilde{\theta}|z).$$

Clearly η satisfies (3) if and only if $f(z) = \zeta[\eta(z)]$ is a fixed point of T. A fixed point f corresponds to an equilibrium if the price function ρ associated with $\eta = \zeta^{-1}[f]$ is monotone. Thus the problem of locating equilibria has been reduced to one of locating the fixed points of T in (4) and then verifying that the corresponding price function is invertible.

One approach to finding fixed points of T is to apply the Contraction Mapping Theorem as was done in Proposition 2. Note that the restrictions on preferences needed here are exactly the ones used there.

PROPOSITION 6 *Let H and V satisfy Assumptions 17.1 and 17.2; let X, Θ, Ψ, and G satisfy Assumption 17.5; let $Z = [\underline{x}/\bar{\theta}, \bar{x}/\underline{\theta}]$; and define Π and G $(\cdot|z)$ as we did in Exercise 17.8. Then the operator T defined in (4) has a unique fixed point in $C(Z)$.*

The proof of this result parallels the proof of Proposition 2, but it is not quite an application of Lemma 17.2 because the information structure of this economy is more complicated. The main steps are
1. Find a closed, convex set $D \subset \mathbf{R}_{++}$ such that the operator T defined in (4) maps the space F of bounded continuous functions $f: Z \to D$ into itself. Define $\hat{D}$, $\hat{F}$, and $\hat{T}$ as we did in the proof of Proposition 2.
2. Apply the Mean Value Theorem as we did in the proof of Lemma 17.2, to show that $\hat{T}$ is a contraction with modulus β.

We leave the details as an exercise.

Exercise 17.9 Complete the proof of Proposition 6.

An alternative to the approach taken in Proposition 6 is to apply Brouwer's or Schauder's Theorem. This alternative approach allows us to dispense with Assumption 17.2, but it also means that we obtain no information about the uniqueness of an equilibrium of the desired form. The application of Schauder's Theorem is more difficult here than it was in Section 17.5, however, because—as the following exercise shows—

Assumption 17.5 does not imply that the analogue to Assumption 17.3 holds.

Exercise 17.10   Let X, Θ, Ψ, and G satisfy Assumption 17.5; and let Z, Π, and $G(\cdot|z)$ be as specified in Exercise 17.8. Show by example that if $z_n \to z$, $\{G(\cdot|z_n)\}$ may not converge to $G(\cdot|z)$ in the total variation norm.

But Assumption 17.3 was simply a means to an end. For the problem at hand, another line of argument is available for establishing equicontinuity. To illustrate it, we consider the special case where x and θ both have uniform distributions.

ASSUMPTION 17.6   *G and Ψ are uniform distributions.*

PROPOSITION 7   *Let H and V satisfy Assumption 17.1; and let X, Θ, Ψ, and G satisfy Assumptions 17.5 and 17.6. Then T has a fixed point in $C(Z)$.*

The proof of this result uses Schauder's Theorem, so the steps in the argument parallel those in the proof of Proposition 4:
1. Choose a nonempty, closed, bounded, convex set $D \subset \mathbf{R}_{++}$, and let $F \subset C(Z)$ be the space of continuous functions $f: Z \to D$.
2. Show that $T: F \to F$.
3. Show that T is a continuous operator.
4. Show that the family $T(F)$ is equicontinuous.

Exercise 17.11   Carry out Steps 1–3.

Note that Assumption 17.6 does not simplify any of these three steps: they can as easily be carried out under Assumption 17.5 alone. The proof that $T(F)$ is equicontinuous (Step 4) is more difficult, and we write it out in some detail.

First we need to establish the following preliminary result.

Exercise 17.12   Let X, Θ, Ψ, and G satisfy Assumptions 17.5 and 17.6. Show that $G(\cdot|z)$ is the uniform distribution on $[a(z), b(z)]$ where

(5) $a(z) = \max\{\underline{x}/z, \underline{\theta}\}$ and $b(z) = \min\{\bar{x}/z, \bar{\theta}\}$.

Next, note that for any $f \in F$, we can define the function $\phi_f\colon \Theta \to D$ by

$$\phi_f(\tilde{\theta}) = \int_Z \int_\Theta \phi\left(\frac{\theta'}{\tilde{\theta}}\, \zeta^{-1}[f(z')]\right) G(d\theta'|z')\,\pi(dz').$$

Then it follows immediately from (4) and Exercise 17.12 that

(6a) $(Tf)(z) = \dfrac{1}{b(z) - a(z)} \displaystyle\int_{a(z)}^{b(z)} \phi_f(\tilde{\theta})\, d\tilde{\theta}, \quad \text{if } z \in (\underline{z}, \bar{z});$

(6b) $(Tf)(\underline{z}) = \phi_f(\bar{\theta}); \quad \text{and} \quad (Tf)(\bar{z}) = \phi_f(\underline{\theta}).$

To show that $T(F)$ is an equicontinuous family, we will show that for each $f \in F$, Tf is piecewise continuously differentiable and that there is a bound—uniform over functions in $T(F)$—on these derivatives. Thus each function Tf is Lipschitz, and there is a Lipschitz constant that holds uniformly for all functions in $T(F)$. The following exercise, which establishes a uniform bound on the derivative of ϕ_f, for all $f \in F$, will be useful in this regard.

Exercise 17.13   Show that there exists $0 < B < \infty$ such that

$$|\phi_f'(\theta)| < B, \quad \text{all } \theta \in \Theta, \text{ all } f \in F.$$

Next define the set $\hat{Z} = Z - \{\underline{x}/\bar{\theta}, \bar{x}/\underline{\theta}, \underline{x}/\underline{\theta}, \bar{x}/\bar{\theta}\}$. It follows from (6a) that for any $f \in F$, Tf is differentiable on $\hat{Z}$, with

(7) $(Tf)'(z) = \dfrac{\{\phi_f[b(z)] - (Tf)(z)\}b'(z) - \{\phi_f[a(z)] - (Tf)(z)\}a'(z)}{b(z) - a(z)},$

all $z \in Z$.

The rest of the proof consists of showing that this derivative satisfies a Lipschitz condition on each of three subintervals of Z. If $\underline{x}/\underline{\theta} < \bar{x}/\bar{\theta}$, as shown in Figure 17.5, these three intervals are

$$I_1 = (\underline{x}/\bar{\theta}, \underline{x}/\underline{\theta}), \quad I_2 = (\underline{x}/\underline{\theta}, \bar{x}/\bar{\theta}), \quad I_3 = (\bar{x}/\bar{\theta}, \bar{x}/\underline{\theta}).$$

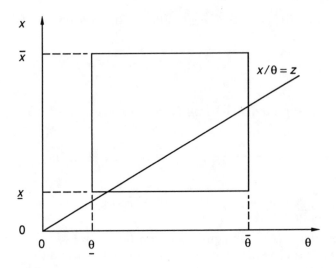

Figure 17.5

If $\underline{x}/\underline{\theta} > \bar{x}/\bar{\theta}$, the roles of $\underline{x}/\underline{\theta}$ and $\bar{x}/\bar{\theta}$ are reversed, and if $\underline{x}/\underline{\theta} = \bar{x}/\bar{\theta}$, there are only two intervals.

First, consider the limiting value of the derivative as z approaches the end-point value $\underline{z} = \underline{x}/\bar{\theta}$. Note that $b(z) = \bar{\theta}$ in this neighborhood and that $a(z) \rightarrow \bar{\theta}$ as $z \rightarrow \underline{x}/\bar{\theta}$. Hence the denominator in (7) approaches zero as $z \rightarrow \underline{x}/\bar{\theta}$. In addition, $\phi_f[a(z)] \rightarrow \phi_f(\bar{\theta})$ and $(Tf)(z) \rightarrow \phi_f(\bar{\theta})$ as $z \rightarrow \underline{x}/\bar{z}$. Hence the numerator in (8) also approaches zero. Thus, applying L'Hôspital's rule, we find that

$$\lim_{z \rightarrow \underline{x}/\bar{\theta}} (Tf)'(z) = \lim_{z \rightarrow \underline{x}/\bar{\theta}} \{\phi_f'[a(z)]a'(z) - (Tf)'(z)\},$$

so

$$|(Tf)'(\underline{x}/\bar{\theta})| = |\phi_f'[a(\underline{x}/\bar{\theta})]a'(\underline{x}/\bar{\theta})|/2 \leq B\bar{\theta}^2/2\underline{x},$$

where B is the bound established in Exercise 17.13. Hence $(Tf)'(z)$ is bounded as $z \rightarrow \underline{x}/\bar{\theta}$. A completely analogous argument holds as $z \rightarrow \bar{x}/\underline{\theta}$.

Next, consider the case as z approaches $\underline{x}/\underline{\theta}$ from below, $z \uparrow \underline{x}/\underline{z}$. Then the left derivative of (Tf) at $z = \underline{x}/\underline{\theta}$ is given by (6a), when we use the left derivatives of $a(z)$ and $b(z)$. These are

$$\lim_{z \uparrow \underline{x}/\underline{\theta}} a'(z) = \lim_{z \uparrow \underline{x}/\underline{\theta}} (-\underline{x}/z^2) = -\underline{\theta}^2/\underline{x}, \quad \text{and}$$

$$\lim_{z \uparrow \underline{x}/\underline{\theta}} b'(z) = 0.$$

Hence the left derivative of (Tf) at $z = \underline{x}/\underline{\theta}$ is

$$(Tf)'(z) = \frac{\{\phi_f[a(z)] - (Tf)(z)\}a'(z)}{b(z) - a(z)},$$

which is bounded.

Similar arguments hold as z approaches $\underline{x}/\underline{\theta}$ from above and as it approaches $\bar{x}/\bar{\theta}$ from above and below. Hence Tf satisfies a Lipschitz condition, with a uniform Lipschitz constant for all $f \in F$. It follows that $T(F)$ is equicontinuous, completing the proof of Proposition 7.

If Z is a finite set, an analogue to Proposition 7 using Brouwer's Theorem can be formulated. The proof involves Steps 1–3 only and is otherwise the same as the proof of Proposition 7.

Finally, consider the issue of monotonicity. As seen in the earlier model, T is monotone if Assumption 17.4 also holds; the proof is similar to the proof of Proposition 5, and we do not repeat it. As noted before, however, the assumptions needed to establish that T is monotone are almost as strong—and in some respects stronger—than those needed to ensure that $\hat{T}$ is a contraction.

Thus far we have considered lines of argument establishing the existence of a solution η to the functional equation (3). Establishing the existence of a competitive equilibrium requires one more step, however.

As noted earlier in this section, a function η satisfying (3) corresponds to an equilibrium for the economic model only if the associated price function $\rho(z) = z/\eta(z)$ is strictly increasing. None of our existence arguments guarantees that this is so. Our final result shows that if, in addition to the hypotheses of Proposition 6 or 7, preferences satisfy Assumption 17.4, then the price function ρ associated with any solution η of (3) is monotone. Although it is disappointing to find that Assumption 17.4 is needed after all, the study of monotonicity for this particular model provides a good illustration of the way an equation like (3) can be used to characterize solutions after existence has already been established.

PROPOSITION 8   *Let H and V satisfy Assumptions 17.1 and 17.4; and let
X, Θ, Ψ, and G satisfy Assumptions 17.5. Let η be a solution to (3), and let
$\rho(z) = z/\eta(z)$. Then ρ is strictly increasing.*

To establish this result, it is useful to define the functions $\xi: \Theta \to D$ and
$J: (\underline{z}, \bar{z}) \to D$ by

$$\xi(\theta) = \int_Z \int_\Theta \phi \left[\frac{\theta'}{\theta} \eta(z') \right] G(d\theta'|z') \, \pi(dz'),$$

$$J(z) = \frac{1}{b(z) - a(z)} \int_{a(z)}^{b(z)} \xi(\theta) \, d\theta,$$

where $a(z)$ and $b(z)$ are as defined in (5). In terms of the function J, (3)
can be restated as

$$\eta(z)H'[\eta(z)] = J(z), \quad \text{all } z \in Z.$$

We leave the remainder of the proof as an exercise.

Exercise 17.14   a. Show that ρ is strictly increasing if and only if
$z\eta'(z)/\eta(z) < 1$.
  b. Show that $z\eta'(z)/\eta(z) < 1$ if $zJ'(z)/J(z) < 1$.
  c. Show that Assumptions 17.1 and 17.4 together imply that

$$0 \le \frac{y\phi'(y)}{\phi(y)} \le 1,$$

and hence that

$$-1 \le \frac{\theta\xi'(\theta)}{\xi(\theta)} \le 0.$$

[*Hint.* Recall the function w used in the proof of Lemma 17.2.]
  d. Show that

$$-1 \le \frac{\theta\xi'(\theta)}{\xi(\theta)} \le 0 \text{ implies } \frac{zJ'(z)}{J(z)} \le 1.$$

[*Hint.* Use the fact that part (c) implies $\theta\xi(\theta)$ is increasing in θ.]

Thus, to prove that a solution to (3) is an equilibrium, we need to impose Assumption 17.4 after all. Since Assumption 17.2, the restriction needed to apply the Contraction Mapping Theorem, is a very mild strengthening of that hypothesis, Proposition 7 is, in the end, of little substantive interest. Note that we arrive at this conclusion because we have assumed that agents' only source of information about the ratio x/θ is their observation of the price $\rho(x/\theta)$. If, instead, we imagine that each agent is simply given accurate information about the value x/θ, then any solution to (3) can be interpreted as an equilibrium.

17.7 Bibliographic Notes

See Labadie (1984) for an application of Brouwer's Theorem, very similar to the one in Section 17.3, to a nonmonetary overlapping-generations model. The model in Section 17.6 is adapted from Lucas (1972).

There are several entirely different ways to prove Brouwer's Theorem. A proof based on simplices can be found in Burger (1963, Appendix) or in Border (1985, chap. 6). A very intuitive proof, but one that uses some topology, is given in Milnor (1965, pp. 13–15). A discussion and proof of Schauder's Theorem and a nice treatment of monotone operators are provided in Hutson and Pym (1980). Istratescu (1981, chap. 5) also contains a proof of Schauder's Theorem and some generalizations. Zeidler (1986) contains a detailed treatment of fixed-point theorems (vol. 1) and of monotone operators (vol. 2).

Throughout this chapter we have confined our attention to recursive competitive equilibria. If we had been dealing with economies where the two welfare theorems held, this restriction would have been innocuous. The set of competitive equilibrium allocations for such systems is exactly the set of solutions to the social planner's problem, so the results in Sections 4.1 and 9.1 establishing the equivalence between recursive and sequence formulations of single-agent decision problems apply. For systems where the welfare theorems fail, however, this equivalence need not hold. The monetary economies we studied in this chapter and the taxed economies we study in the next all fall into this category. For economies like these, defining competitive equilibrium in terms of sequences—or even defining it recursively with larger state space—can lead to a larger set of equilibria. For examples of some of the kinds of equilibrium behavior that are possible under broader definitions, see Cass and Shell (1983), Kehoe and Levine (1985), and Muller and Woodford (1988).

18   Equilibria in Systems
with Distortions

In Chapter 17 we introduced several fixed-point arguments and showed how they could be used to establish the existence of equilibria in situations where the economy as a whole did not solve an optimization problem. As noted there, these arguments are needed in situations where competitive equilibrium allocations are not Pareto optimal and hence cannot be studied by analyzing an associated Pareto problem.

In this chapter we do not introduce any new fixed-point theorems; instead, we further illustrate how the theorems of Chapter 17 can be applied. Recall that in the two specific economies studied in Chapter 17 the only state variables were exogenous shocks. In the current chapter we show how similar arguments can be used in models with endogenous state variables. In particular, we look at a growth model in which distorting taxes break the connection between Pareto-optimal and competitive equilibrium allocations. (The economies considered in Chapter 17 were overlapping-generations models, and the ones to be considered below have identical, infinitely lived agents, but for our purposes this is not the critical distinction. It is the presence of endogenous state variables that complicates the arguments in the present section.)

Recall (cf. Sections 5.1 and 16.1) that for the optimal growth model without taxes, dynamic programming techniques can be used to characterize competitive equilibria directly. Since the competitive equilibrium allocation is Pareto optimal, the economy implicitly solves the problem of maximizing the representative consumer's utility. Thus, an easy method for characterizing competitive equilibria in these situations is to solve this optimization problem explicitly.

In the presence of taxes, externalities, or other distortions, this type of attack fails. Moreover, there is no single method of analysis that succeeds for all distorted economies. Rather, there is an array of approaches, any one of which may or may not be useful in any specific application. In the next three sections, we illustrate three alternative lines of argument that can be useful and discuss the strengths and weaknesses of each.

In Section 18.1 we describe in detail the growth model with distorting taxes that is used throughout the chapter, and we show that for certain kinds of taxes the competitive equilibrium of the distorted (taxed) economy solves the planning problem for a wholly fictional "pseudo-economy." In this case the methods of Chapter 4 can be used even though a tax wedge leads to a deviation between Pareto-optimal and competitive equilibrium allocations.

Unfortunately, the indirect pseudo-economy device of Section 18.1 has very limited applicability. In Sections 18.2 and 18.3 we explore two other approaches for establishing the existence of a competitive equilibrium for a taxed economy, approaches that are useful when the pseudo-economy method is not applicable. Both of these approaches are based on a direct analysis of the first-order conditions for the representative consumer's dynamic optimization problem. The first is a local analysis that makes use of the Contraction Mapping Theorem; the second is a global analysis that makes use of the Schauder Fixed-Point Theorem and the monotonicity result of Theorem 17.7.

18.1 An Indirect Approach

Assume that there are many consumers, all with identical preferences described by the current-period utility function U and the discount factor β. Let f denote the production function (gross of depreciated capital). Then the functional equation for the optimally planned economy is

(1) $v(k) = \max_{y} \{U[f(k) - y] + \beta v(y)\}.$

Let g be the optimal policy function corresponding to (1). Then the total discounted utility of the representative consumer is maximized if all consumers adopt a policy of saving $g(k)$ and consuming $f(k) - g(k)$ per capita, whenever the capital stock per capita is equal to k. That is, g describes a Pareto-optimal allocation in which all of the consumers are given equal weight.

As shown in Section 16.1, this allocation also describes the competitive equilibrium of an economy in which all consumers have equal initial holdings of capital. That is, if all consumers have equal endowments of capital, then in the unique competitive equilibrium each saves $g(k)$ and consumes $f(k) - g(k)$ whenever the capital stock per capita is k.

To see this connection directly, note that each individual agent in this economy can be viewed as solving a dynamic programming problem. Specifically, consider the problem faced by one agent, who anticipates that all other agents in the economy will use the savings rule described by the function g. Suppose, too, that this particular agent begins with initial capital holdings of x, whereas all other agents in the economy begin with initial capital holdings of k. This one agent must choose his current consumption c and end-of-period assets y such that their sum is less than the sum of his wage income, $f(k) - kf'(k)$, and his earnings on capital, $xf'(k)$. Hence the maximum present discounted value of his utility is described by the value function $V(x, k; g)$ satisfying the functional equation

$$(2) \qquad V(x, k; g) = \max_{y} \{U[f(k) + (x - k)f'(k) - y] + \beta V[y, g(k); g]\}.$$

Call the policy function for this problem $G(x, k; g)$, where the notation emphasizes that the individual's value and action depend both on the state (x, k) and on the way he expects others to behave, g.

As noted above, for this economy Pareto-optimal and competitive equilibrium allocations coincide. Moreover, if all agents receive equal weight in the social welfare function or, in the competitive economy, if all begin with equal endowments of capital, then all agents have equal consumption and equal capital holdings in every subsequent period as well. Therefore, given the unique value function v satisfying (1) and the associated policy function g, the unique value function $V(\cdot, \cdot; g)$ satisfying (2) and the associated policy function $G(\cdot, \cdot; g)$ satisfy $V(k, k; g) = v(k)$ and $G(k, k; g) = g(k)$, identically in k.

Exercise 18.1 Show that

$$V(k, k; g) = v(k) \text{ and } G(k, k; g) = g(k), \quad \text{all } k.$$

In the rest of this section and in those that follow, we consider modifications to this model obtained by introducing flat-rate taxes and associated government spending programs. To begin, consider the case where there is a flat-rate tax of $\theta \in (0, 1)$ on income from capital, the proceeds of which are returned to consumers in the form of a lump-sum subsidy. [The word *income* is being used here in a rather misleading way. Since $f(k)$ includes undepreciated capital, the tax is on both the one-period rental returns on capital and the undepreciated capital remaining at the end of the period. Realistically, the latter is much larger, so it is probably more accurate to think of the tax we use here as a wealth tax.] Then the consumer's after-tax income, including his lump-sum subsidy, is $f(k) + (1 - \theta)(x - k)f'(k)$, and his functional equation is

(3) $W(x, k; g)$

$$= \max_y \{U[f(k) + (1 - \theta)(x - k)f'(k) - y] + \beta W[y, g(k); g]\}.$$

It is clear that the function $V(\cdot, \cdot; g)$ does not satisfy (3) and hence that the consumer's policy function for the latter is not $G(\cdot, \cdot; g)$, even if we restrict attention to the locus where $x = k$. That is, the savings function g from the optimal growth model does not describe competitive equilibrium savings in the taxed economy.

Instead, an equilibrium for the taxed economy is an aggregate savings function h for the economy as a whole and an optimal policy function $H(\cdot, \cdot; h)$ for the individual such that $H(k, k; h) = h(k)$, identically in k. That is, in equilibrium it must be optimal for the representative agent to behave the way everyone else does. To construct an equilibrium, we conjecture that the savings function of the representative consumer is a continuous function—call it h. The optimization problem facing the typical agent in this economy is then given by (3), but with h in place of g. The first-order and envelope conditions for this problem are then

(4) $U'[f(k) + (1 - \theta)(x - k)f'(k) - H(x, k; h)]$

$$= \beta W_1[H(x, k; h), h(k); h],$$

(5) $W_1(x, k; h)$

$$= (1 - \theta)f'(k)U'[f(k) + (1 - \theta)(x - k)f'(k) - H(x, k; h)].$$

Define $\phi(k) = W_1(k, k; h)$. In equilibrium, $x = k$ and $H(k, k; h) = h(k)$, so (4) and (5) imply

(6) $U'[f(k) - h(k)] = \beta\phi[h(k)]$,

(7) $\phi(k) = (1 - \theta)f'(k)U'[f(k) - h(k)]$.

These two equations constitute a pair of functional equations in the unknown functions h and ϕ. If a solution can be found, the functions $W(\cdot, \cdot; h)$ and $H(\cdot, \cdot; h)$ can then be obtained by using (3).

In Sections 18.2 and 18.3, we consider two different methods for obtaining solutions (h, ϕ) directly from (6) and (7). We call such approaches *direct methods*. For the particular fiscal policy under study here, however, it turns out that (6) and (7) can be interpreted as the first-order and envelope conditions for a fictional planning problem. In this case, simply exploiting this observation leads to an easy *indirect method* for characterizing the equilibrium.

Consider an economy that has the same preferences and technology as outlined above, but with no taxes, and in which the discount rate is $\hat{\beta} = (1 - \theta)\beta$. For this economy, the competitive equilibrium solves the dynamic programming problem

(8) $w(k) = \max_{y} \{U[f(k) - y] + \hat{\beta}w(y)\}$.

Under standard assumptions, there exists a unique function w satisfying (8), and both w and the associated optimal policy function $\hat{h}$ are completely characterized by the first-order and envelope conditions

(9) $U'[f(k) - \hat{h}(k)] = \hat{\beta}w'[\hat{h}(k)]$,

(10) $w'(k) = f'(k)U'[f(k) - \hat{h}(k)]$.

Now compare (6) and (7) with (9) and (10). Clearly the pair of functions $\phi(k) = (1 - \theta)w'(k)$ and $h(k) = \hat{h}(k)$ satisfies (6) and (7). Since the functions w and $\hat{h}$ are readily obtained by the methods of Chapter 4, this indirect method is an easy way of obtaining solutions to (6) and (7).

It is also clear from the analysis above that this method does not work unless the proceeds of the tax are returned to consumers. If they are not rebated, there is no alternative to a straightforward attack on the first-order conditions. Such methods are the subject of the next two sections.

Exercise 18.2 Consider a growth model with a tax rate of θ on capital income, the proceeds of which are returned to consumers as a lump-sum subsidy, and a tax rate of α on all income, the proceeds of which are thrown away. Show that the tax-distorted economy behaves like an undistorted economy with the production function $F(k) = (1 - \alpha)f(k)$ and the discount factor $\hat{\beta} = \beta(1 - \theta - \alpha)/(1 - \alpha)$.

18.2 A Local Approach Based on First-Order Conditions

In cases where the indirect approach described in the previous section fails, a direct attack on the first-order conditions is required. In this section, we pursue one such approach, one closely related to the local analysis of the Euler equations presented in Section 6.4. In Section 18.3, we take a different line, one that involves a global analysis. We consider the tax problem for the deterministic one-sector model studied in Section 18.1, except that in this section and the next we assume that the tax proceeds are not returned to consumers.

Suppose the proceeds of the tax on capital are thrown away. Then it is convenient to define the after-tax income function $\psi(k) = f(k) - \theta k f'(k)$. The analogues to the equilibrium conditions (6) and (7) in the last section are then

(1) $U'[\psi(k) - g(k)] = \beta\phi[g(k)]$,

(2) $\phi(k) = (1 - \theta)f'(k)U'[\psi(k) - g(k)]$.

These equations differ from the earlier pair only in that private-sector disposable income is $\psi(k)$ rather than $f(k)$. A competitive equilibrium for this economy is characterized by a savings function g and a marginal value of capital function ϕ satisfying (1) and (2). We proceed under the following restrictions on tastes, technology, and taxes.

ASSUMPTION **18.1**
   a. $\beta \in (0, 1)$;
   b. $U: \mathbf{R}_+ \to \mathbf{R}$ *is twice continuously differentiable, strictly increasing, and strictly concave;*

   c. $\theta \in (0, 1)$;
   d. $f: \mathbf{R}_+ \to \mathbf{R}_+$ is twice continuously differentiable, strictly increasing, and
      strictly concave, with $f(0) > 0$ and $\lim_{k \to 0} f'(k) > 1/\beta(1 - \theta)$;
   e. for some $\bar{k} > 0$, $\psi(k) - k = f(k) - \theta k f'(k) - k$ is strictly positive on $(0, \bar{k})$
      and strictly negative on $(\bar{k}, \infty)$.

Part (d) of this assumption is needed to ensure that the capital stock does not converge to zero in the long run, and part (e) is needed to ensure that it remains bounded in the long run. The value $\bar{k}$ is the maximum capital stock maintainable out of after-tax income, and (e) ensures that it is possible to maintain any smaller, positive capital stock and simultaneously to have positive consumption. We seek solutions g and ϕ on the interval $K = [0, \bar{k}]$.

For $x \in K$, $y \in [0, \psi(x)]$, and $z \in [0, \psi(y)]$, define the function

$$(3) \qquad F(x, y, z) = U'[\psi(x) - y] - \beta(1 - \theta) f'(y) U'[\psi(y) - z],$$

where the right side is obtained from (1) and (2) by putting y in place of $g(x)$ and z in place of $g^2(x) = g[g(x)]$ and by eliminating ϕ between equations. In terms of F, a competitive equilibrium is a function g satisfying

$$(4) \qquad F[k, g(k), g^2(k)] = 0, \quad \text{all } k \in K,$$

with ϕ then defined by (1) or (2). Equation (4) is thus a single functional equation in the unknown function g. [Note that F could also be viewed as defining a second-order difference equation, $F(k_t, k_{t+1}, k_{t+2}) = 0$, that could be studied by the methods of Chapter 6.]

Our first result describes the stationary points of the unknown function g.

PROPOSITION 1 *If g is a continuous function satisfying (4), then g has exactly one stationary point, the value k^* defined by*

$$(5) \qquad 1 = \beta(1 - \theta) f'(k^*).$$

Proof. Let $g: K \to K$ be a continuous function satisfying (4); then Brouwer's Fixed-Point Theorem (Theorem 17.3) implies that g has at least one stationary point. To see that the stationary point is unique, suppose that g has a stationary point at k^*. Then

$$0 = F[k^*, g(k^*), g^2(k^*)]$$

$$= F(k^*, k^*, k^*)$$

$$= U'[\psi(k^*) - k^*] - \beta(1 - \theta)f'(k^*)U'[\psi(k^*) - k^*],$$

so that k^* must satisfy (5). Part (d) of Assumption 18.1 implies that there exists a unique value k^* with this property. ∎

Since we are confining our search for solutions to (4) to continuous functions, we can—without further loss of generality—confine our attention to functions that have a stationary point at k^*.

With k^* defined by (5), define the polynomial function

$$P(\lambda) = F_1^* + F_2^*\lambda + F_3^*\lambda^2,$$

where $F_i^* = F_i(k^*, k^*, k^*)$, $i = 1, 2, 3$. In terms of U and f, these derivatives are

(6a) $\qquad F_1^* = U''(c^*)[\beta^{-1} - \theta k^*f''(k^*)],$

(6b) $\qquad F_2^* = -U''(c^*)[1 + \beta^{-1} - \theta k^*f''(k^*)] - \beta(1 - \theta)f''(k^*)U'(c^*),$

(6c) $\qquad F_3^* = U''(c^*),$

where $c^* = \psi(k^*) - k^*$ is stationary consumption. From (6), it is readily verified that $P(0) < 0$, $P(1) > 0$, and $\lim_{\lambda \to \infty} P(\lambda) < 0$. Hence P has two real roots, one between zero and one and the other exceeding one. Call the smaller root λ^*. It is easily verified that $P(F_1^*/F_3^*) > 0$, so $\lambda^* < F_1^*/F_3^*$.

Next note that since $F_2^* > 0$, it follows from the Implicit Function Theorem that there is an open rectangle $I \times I$ containing (k^*, k^*) and a continuously differentiable function $H: I \times I \to \mathbf{R}_+$ such that

(7) $\qquad F[x, H(x, z), z] = 0, \quad$ all $(x, z) \in I \times I.$

Let $C(I)$ be the space of bounded continuous functions $h: I \to \mathbf{R}$, with the sup norm. Define the operator T on $C(I)$ by

(8) $(Th)(k) = H[k, h^2(k)], \quad$ all $k \in I$.

Clearly fixed points of T are solutions to (4) on I.

The rest of this section is organized as follows. First we prove that for some set $I' \subseteq I$ and for some set $D \subseteq C(I')$, the operator T maps D into itself; this is Proposition 2. Then in Proposition 3 we establish that T is a contraction mapping on D and hence has a unique fixed point. In Proposition 4 we provide a sharper characterization of this fixed point.

For any $\varepsilon > 0$, define the interval $I_\varepsilon = [k^* - \varepsilon, k^* + \varepsilon]$. Then for any $\lambda \in (0, 1)$, define $D_\lambda(I_\varepsilon)$ to be the set of continuous functions on I_ε that have a stationary point at k^* and that satisfy a Lipschitz condition with constant λ:

$$D_\lambda(I_\varepsilon) = \{h \in C(I_\varepsilon): h(k^*) = k^*, \text{ and}$$

$$|h(k) - h(k')| \le \lambda |k - k'|, \text{ all } k, k' \in I_\varepsilon\}.$$

Note that since $h(k^*) = k^*$ and $0 < \lambda < 1$, it follows that $h: I_\varepsilon \to I_\varepsilon$, all $h \in D_\lambda(I_\varepsilon)$. We then have the following result.

PROPOSITION 2   *Let β, U, θ, and f satisfy Assumption 18.1; and let F, k^*, λ^*, I, and H be defined as above. For any $\lambda \in (\lambda^*, 1)$, there exists some $\varepsilon > 0$ such that $I_\varepsilon \subset I$ and $T: D_\lambda(I_\varepsilon) \to D_\lambda(I_\varepsilon)$, where T is the operator defined in (8).*

Proof. Choose $\lambda \in (\lambda^*, 1)$. First note that for any choice of $\varepsilon > 0$, the continuity of H implies immediately that Th is continuous, for all $h \in D_\lambda(I_\varepsilon)$. Moreover, since $F(k^*, k^*, k^*) = 0$, it is also immediate that $(Th)(k^*) = k^*$, all $h \in D_\lambda(I_\varepsilon)$. Therefore it suffices to show that for an appropriate choice of ε the required Lipschitz condition holds.

Since $\lambda \in (\lambda^*, 1)$, it follows that

$$P(\lambda) = F_1^* + F_2^* \lambda + F_3^* \lambda^2 > 0.$$

Then since the derivatives of H, evaluated at (k^*, k^*), are $H_1^* = -F_1^*/F_2^* > 0$ and $H_2^* = -F_3^*/F_2^* > 0$, it also follows that

$$H_1^* + H_2^* \lambda^2 = -\frac{1}{F_2^*}(F_1^* + F_3^* \lambda^2) < \lambda.$$

Hence there exist some $m_1 > H_1^*$ and $m_2 > H_2^*$ such that $m_1 + m_2\lambda^2 < \lambda$. Then since H_1 and H_2 are continuous on I, there exists some $\varepsilon > 0$ such that $I_\varepsilon \subset I$, and

$$0 < H_1(x, z) \leq m_1 \text{ and } 0 < H_2(x, z) \leq m_2, \quad \text{all } (x, z) \in I_\varepsilon \times I_\varepsilon.$$

Choose any $h \in D_\lambda(I_\varepsilon)$. Then for any $k, k' \in I_\varepsilon$,

$$|(Th)(k) - (Th)(k')| = |H[k, h^2(k)] - H[k', h^2(k')]|$$

$$\leq m_1|k - k'| + m_2|h^2(k) - h^2(k')|$$

$$\leq m_1|k - k'| + m_2\lambda|h(k) - h(k')|$$

$$\leq (m_1 + m_2\lambda^2)|k - k'|$$

$$\leq \lambda|k - k'|,$$

where the third line uses the fact that $h \in D_\lambda(I_\varepsilon)$. Hence Th satisfies the required Lipschitz condition, as was to be shown. ∎

Proposition 2 shows that for any $\lambda \in (\lambda^*, 1)$, there exists an interval I_ε containing k^* such that $T: D_\lambda(I_\varepsilon) \to D_\lambda(I_\varepsilon)$. Our next task is to show that for some such pair (λ, I_ε), T has a fixed point in $D_\lambda(I_\varepsilon)$. In Chapter 17 we suggested that there are (at least) three potential arguments for accomplishing this: Schauder's Fixed-Point Theorem (Theorem 17.4), the monotonicity result (Theorem 17.7), and the Contraction Mapping Theorem (Theorem 3.2).

First consider the application of Schauder's Theorem. Note that I_ε is a bounded set and that $D_\lambda(I_\varepsilon) \subset C(I_\varepsilon)$ is nonempty, closed, bounded, and convex. Moreover, $D_\lambda(I_\varepsilon)$ is itself an equicontinuous family. In light of Proposition 2, it only remains to be shown that T is continuous as an operator. This proof is not difficult, and we leave it as an exercise.

Exercise 18.3 Let Assumption 18.1 hold, and let $\lambda \in (\lambda^*, 1)$. Define $I_\varepsilon > 0$ as we did in the proof of Proposition 2, so that $T: D_\lambda(I_\varepsilon) \to D_\lambda(I_\varepsilon)$. Show that the operator T is continuous.

Next consider the application of Theorem 17.7. Since T is continuous, it suffices to show that T is monotone and that there exists some

$h_0 \in D_\lambda(I_\varepsilon)$ such that either $h_0 \leq Th_0$ or $h_0 \geq Th_0$. This, too, is straight-forward, and we leave it as an exercise.

Exercise 18.4   a. Let Assumption 18.1 hold, and let $\lambda \in (\lambda^*, 1)$. Define $I_\varepsilon > 0$ as we did in the proof of Proposition 2, so that $T: D_\lambda(I_\varepsilon) \to D_\lambda(I_\varepsilon)$. Show that the operator T is monotone.
   b. Show that the functions $\lim T^n \underline{h}$ and $\lim T^n \overline{h}$ are fixed points of T, where $\underline{h}(k) = k^* - \varepsilon$ and $\overline{h}(k) = k^* + \varepsilon$, all $k \in I_\varepsilon$.

Finally we have the following result, which shows that for an appropriate choice of λ and I_ε, T is a contraction mapping on $D_\lambda(I_\varepsilon)$.

PROPOSITION 3   *Let β, U, θ, and f satisfy Assumption 18.1, and let F, k^*, λ^*, I, and H be defined as before. For any $\lambda \in (\lambda^*, 1)$, there exists $\varepsilon > 0$ such that T is a contraction on $D_\lambda(I_\varepsilon)$.*

Proof. Fix $\lambda \in (\lambda^*, 1)$, and define m_1 and m_2 as we did in the proof of Proposition 2. Then note that since $\lambda^* < F_1^*/F_3^*$ and $H_2^* = -F_3^*/F_2^*$, it follows that

$$H_2^*(1 + \lambda^*) < -(F_1^* + F_3^*)/F_2^* < 1,$$

where the second inequality uses the expressions in (6). Hence we can choose $\delta < 1$ and $\hat{m}_2 > H_2^*$ such that $\hat{m}_2(1 + \lambda^*) < \delta$. Let $M_2 = \min \{m_2, \hat{m}_2\}$, and choose $\varepsilon > 0$ such that $I_\varepsilon \subseteq I$ and such that

$$H_1(x, z) < m_1 \text{ and } H_2(x, z) < M_2, \text{ all } (x, z) \in I_\varepsilon \times I_\varepsilon.$$

Since H_2 is continuous, this choice is possible. We will show that T is a contraction of modulus δ on $D_\lambda(I_\varepsilon)$.
   As shown in the proof of Proposition 2, $T: D_\lambda(I_\varepsilon) \to D_\lambda(I_\varepsilon)$. To prove that T is a contraction with modulus δ, choose any h, $\hat{h} \in D_\lambda(I_\varepsilon)$. Then

$$|(Th)(k) - (T\hat{h})(k)|$$

$$= |H[k, h^2(k)] - H[k, \hat{h}^2(k)]|$$

$$\leq M_2|h^2(k) - \hat{h}^2(k)|$$

$$\le M_2\{|h[h(k)] - \hat{h}[h(k)]| + |\hat{h}[h(k)] - \hat{h}[\hat{h}(k)]|\}$$

$$\le M_2\{\|h - \hat{h}\| + \lambda|h(k) - \hat{h}(k)|\}$$

$$\le M_2(1 + \lambda)\|h - \hat{h}\|$$

$$\le \delta\|h - \hat{h}\|, \quad \text{all } k \in I_\varepsilon.$$

Since h and $\hat{h}$ were arbitrary, the desired result follows. ∎

Since $D_\lambda(I_\varepsilon)$ with the sup norm is a complete metric space, Proposition 3 together with the Contraction Mapping Theorem implies the existence of a unique fixed point of T in $D_\lambda(I_\varepsilon)$. This function—call it g—is a solution to the functional equation (4) on the interval I_ε. It is the unique solution within the class of functions that have k^* as a stationary point and satisfy a Lipschitz condition with constant $\lambda \in (\lambda^*, 1)$.

Notice that in addition to proving the existence of an equilibrium savings function g, Propositions 2 and 3 also imply the local stability of k^*. Since the fixed point g of T satisfies $g(k^*) = k^*$ and $|g(k) - g(k')| \le \lambda|k - k'|$, all $k, k' \in I_\varepsilon$, it follows that $\lim_{t\to\infty} k_t = k^*$ for all solutions to $k_{t+1} = g(k_t)$ with $k_0 \in I_\varepsilon$.

The next result provides a sharper characterization of the equilibrium savings and consumption functions. The proof rests on Corollary 1 to the Contraction Mapping Theorem.

PROPOSITION 4 *Let Assumption 18.1 hold, let (λ, I_ε) be any pair such that T is a contraction on $D_\lambda(I_\varepsilon)$, and let g be the unique fixed point of T in $D_\lambda(I_\varepsilon)$. Then g is strictly increasing on I_ε.*

Proof. Suppose that T is a contraction on $D_\lambda(I_\varepsilon)$. Let $D'_\lambda(I_\varepsilon)$ be the subset of $D_\lambda(I_\varepsilon)$ containing functions h that are nondecreasing; clearly $D'_\lambda(I_\varepsilon)$ is closed. Let $D''_\lambda(I_\varepsilon)$ be the subset of $D'_\lambda(I_\varepsilon)$ containing functions h that are strictly increasing. By Corollary 1 to the Contraction Mapping Theorem (Theorem 3.2), it suffices to show that $T[D'_\lambda(I_\varepsilon)] \subseteq D''_\lambda(I_\varepsilon)$. That is, it suffices to show that if h is nondecreasing, then Th is strictly increasing.

To see this, note that it follows from (7) and (8) that Th satisfies

$$F[k, (Th)(k), h^2(k)] = 0, \quad \text{all } k \in I_\varepsilon.$$

Moreover, it follows from (3) that F is strictly decreasing in its first and third arguments and strictly increasing in its second. Now suppose that h is nondecreasing, and choose k, $k' \in I_\varepsilon$, with $k' > k$. Then it follows immediately that $(Th)(k') > (Th)(k)$. ∎

In the next section we pursue an alternative line of attack on (4) that uses an operator defined in a slightly different way.

18.3   A Global Approach Based on First-Order Conditions

The approach taken in the last section involved a local argument to establish the existence of an equilibrium savings function g in a neighborhood of the stationary point k^*. In this section we show that under slightly stronger assumptions, the existence of an equilibrium can be established by applying Schauder's Theorem to a different operator. We also show that the new operator is monotone, so a simple computational algorithm for locating fixed points is available. We first conduct the analysis in the deterministic context used in the last section and then briefly discuss the extension to stochastic models.

Recall that the equilibrium condition for the one-sector growth model with a flat-tax of θ on capital is

$$(1) \qquad U'[\psi(k) - g(k)] = \beta(1 - \theta)f'[g(k)]U'\{\psi[g(k)] - g[g(k)]\},$$

where, as before, we define the after-tax income function $\psi = f - \theta k f'$. We assume throughout this section that the preferences, technology, and tax rate θ satisfy Assumption 18.1 and, in addition, have the following property.

ASSUMPTION 18.2 $f'(0) = A < \infty$ and $\lim_{c \to 0} U'(c) = \infty$.

As before we take $K = [0, \bar{k}]$, where $\bar{k}$ is the maximum sustainable capital stock defined in part (e) of Assumption 18.1. Note that Proposition 1 still applies, since the equilibrium condition (1) has not changed. Define k^* as we did in Proposition 1. As before, we restrict our attention to equilibria characterized by continuous functions, and hence we can—without further loss of generality—limit attention to functions that have a stationary point at k^*. In fact, we will confine attention to an even smaller set of functions. Since Schauder's Theorem says nothing about uniqueness, there is no particular virtue in working with a large space. On the contrary, using a smaller space sharpens the characterization of the equilibrium.

Let $C(K)$ be the set of continuous functions $h: K \to \mathbf{R}$. Then define the following subset of $C(K)$:

$$F = \{h \in C(K): h \text{ satisfies } (2)-(6)\},$$

where

(2) $0 \le h(k) \le \psi(k)$, all $k \in K$;

(3) h and $\psi - h$ are nondecreasing;

(4) $h(k) \ge k$, all $k < k^*$;

(5) $h(k^*) = k^*$;

(6) $h(k) \le k$, all $k > k^*$.

The restrictions on h implied by (2)–(6) are depicted in Figure 18.1. Since $\psi(k) = f(k) - \theta k f'(k)$, it follows that

$$\psi'(k) = (1 - \theta)f'(k) - \theta k f''(k)$$

$$> (1 - \theta)f'(k), \quad \text{all } k \in K;$$

so ψ is strictly increasing. Moreover, since $\beta(1 - \theta)f'(k^*) = 1$ and f is strictly concave, it follows that $\psi'(k) > 1/\beta > 1$, for $k \le k^*$. Finally, since $\psi(0) = f(0) > 0$ and since the derivative of ψ exceeds unity on $[0, k^*]$, it follows that $\psi(k^*) > k^*$. Hence the functions $\psi(k)$ and $\psi(k) - [\psi(k^*) - k^*]$ are as shown in Figure 18.1. The bounds in (2) and (4)–(6) imply that any function $h \in F$ must lie in areas A and B–C. In addition, since $\psi - h$ must be nondecreasing, the slope of h is bounded above by the slope of ψ. This fact in turn implies that h cannot lie in region C. Thus functions in F must lie in regions A and B, with slopes bounded below by zero and above by the slope of ψ.

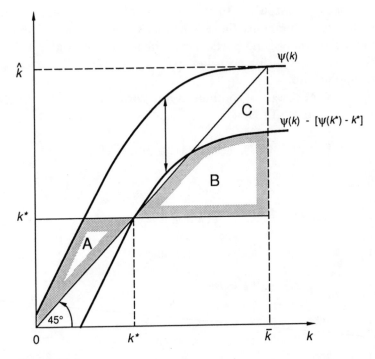

Figure 18.1

Our first objective is to use Schauder's Theorem to show that there is a function g in F satisfying (1). Note that the set K is bounded and that the family of functions F is nonempty, closed, bounded, and convex. We can use the equilibrium condition (1) to define the following operator T on F:

(7) $U'[\psi(k) - (Th)(k)]$

    $= \beta(1 - \theta)f'[(Th)(k)]U'\{\psi[(Th)(k)] - h[(Th)(k)]\}.$

Exercise 18.5 Prove that T is well defined and that $T: F \to F$. [*Hint*. Use Figure 18.2.]

To apply Schauder's Theorem, we only need to verify that T is continuous and that $T(F)$ is an equicontinuous family. To do this, we first prove that F is itself an equicontinuous family. This result implies that

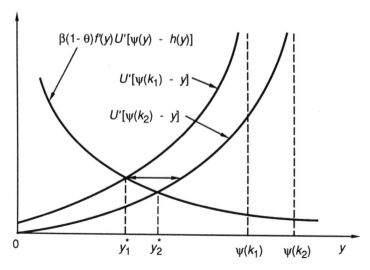

Figure 18.2

$T(F)$ is equicontinuous and is also useful in showing that T is a continuous operator.

PROPOSITION 5 *F is an equicontinuous family.*

Proof. For all $h \in F$ and all k, $k' \in K$ with $k' > k$, (3) implies that

$$0 \le h(k') - h(k) \le \psi(k') - \psi(k).$$

The function ψ is continuously differentiable on the compact interval K; so by the Mean Value Theorem,

$$|\psi(k') - \psi(k)| \le A|k' - k|,$$

where $A < \infty$ is as specified in Assumption 18.2. Combining these two facts gives the desired result. ∎

With Proposition 5 established, the continuity of the operator T is also straightforward.

Exercise 18.6   Prove that T is continuous. [*Hint.* First prove that if $\{g_n\}$ and g are in F and $g_n \to g$ in the sup norm, then $Tg_n \to Tg$ pointwise. Then use the fact that K is compact and F is equicontinuous to establish the desired result.]

Proposition 5 and Exercise 18.6 complete the verification of the hypotheses of Schauder's Theorem. We have thus established that T has a fixed point in F.

In fact, much more can be said about the operator T.

Exercise 18.7   Prove that T is monotone; that is, if $h, \hat{h} \in F$ and $\hat{h} \geq h$, then $T\hat{h} \geq Th$. [*Hint.* Modify Figure 18.2.]

The monotonicity of T is especially useful in this context, because F has both a smallest and a largest element. Specifically, Figure 18.1 shows that the functions

$$\underline{h}(k) = \begin{cases} k, & \text{if } k \leq k^*, \\ k^*, & \text{if } k > k^*, \end{cases}$$

and

$$\bar{h}(k) = \begin{cases} \min\{\psi(k), k^*\}, & \text{if } k \leq k^*, \\ \min\{k, \psi(k) - [\psi(k^*) - k^*]\}, & \text{if } k > k^*, \end{cases}$$

are minimal and maximal elements, respectively, of F. Thus, Exercise 18.7 and Theorem 17.7 together imply that $\lim T^n\underline{h}$ and $\lim T^n\bar{h}$ are both fixed points of T. Moreover, the corollary to Theorem 17.7 implies that if the two limits coincide, then that common limit g is the unique fixed point of T.

Finally, we discuss briefly how the analysis above can be modified to include exogenous shocks. Specifically, assume that exogenous shocks affect the production technology. Let $\Xi = \{\xi_1, \ldots, \xi_J\}$ be a finite set, and let $\Pi = [\pi_{ij}]$ be a $J \times J$ transition matrix. The production technology is then described by a function $f: \mathbf{R}_+ \times \Xi \to \mathbf{R}_+$. Parts (d) and (e) of Assumption 18.1 and the technology restriction in Assumption 18.2 can be modified in the obvious way to hold for each ξ_j. Then define $\bar{k} = \max\{\bar{k}_1, \ldots, \bar{k}_J\}$, where $\bar{k}_j$ is the maximum capital stock maintainable out of after-tax income when the shock takes on the value ξ_j, as defined in the modification of part (e) of Assumption 18.1. Let $K = [0, \bar{k}]$.

We retain the other features of the model above. In particular we maintain the assumption that the only tax is a flat-rate tax of θ on income from capital and assume that the proceeds of this tax are thrown away. Let $\psi(k, \xi_j) = f(k, \xi_j) - \theta k f'(k, \xi_j)$ be the function describing after-tax income.

By an argument exactly analogous to the one used in Section 18.1, we find that an equilibrium for this economy is described by a function $g: K \times \Xi \rightarrow K$ satisfying

(8) $\quad U'[\psi(k, \xi_i) - g(k, \xi_i)]$

$$= \beta (1 - \theta) \sum_{j=1}^{J} \pi_{ij} f'[g(k, \xi_i)] U'\{\psi[g(k, \xi_i)] - g[g(k, \xi_i), \xi_j]\}.$$

Equation (8) is the analogue of (1), modified to include the stochastic shocks. Now consider the problem of establishing the existence of a function g satisfying (8).

Let $C(K \times \Xi)$ be the space of bounded continuous functions on $K \times \Xi$, and consider the conditions in (2)–(6) used to define F in the deterministic case. It is reasonable to suppose that the analogues to (2) and (3) are conditions that hold for each $\xi_j \in J$. However, there does not seem to be any reason to suppose that anything like (4)–(6) hold in the stochastic case, at least in the absence of further restrictions on the transition matrix Π and the technology f. Thus, for the stochastic case, we take $F \subset C(K \times \Xi)$ to be the set of functions $h: K \times \Xi \rightarrow K$ satisfying the analogues of (2) and (3). Note that $K \times \Xi$ is a bounded subset of $\mathbf{R}^2$ and that F is nonempty, closed, bounded, and convex.

Next, define the analogue to the operator T defined in (7):

(9) $\quad U'[\psi(k, \xi_i) - (Th)(k, \xi_i)]$

$$= \beta (1 - \theta) \sum_{j=1}^{J} \pi_{ij} f'[(Th)(k, \xi_i)]$$

$$\times U'\{\psi[(Th)(k, \xi_i)] - h[(Th)(k, \xi_i), \xi_j]\}.$$

The following exercise then parallels Exercise 18.5.

Exercise 18.8   Show that the operator T in (9) is well defined and that $T: F \to F$.

The proof that F is an equicontinuous family then parallels exactly the proof of Proposition 6, and the proof that T is continuous parallels the proof of Exercise 18.6. That T has a fixed point in F then follows from Schauder's Theorem. Moreover, the proof that T is monotone parallels exactly the proof of Exercise 18.7, and minimal and maximal elements of F can be constructed as there.

Exercise 18.9   How must the assumptions or arguments, or both, above be modified if Ξ is a closed, bounded interval?

18.4   Bibliographic Notes

For a more detailed description of the pseudo-economy approach described in Section 18.1, see R. Becker (1985).

Lucas and Stokey (1987) use arguments similar to those in Section 18.3 to study monetary policy in a model without capital in which money holding is motivated by a cash-in-advance constraint that applies to one class of consumption goods. Coleman (1987) uses a similar approach to study capital accumulation in a monetary model with a cash-in-advance constraint. Bizer and Judd (1989) use arguments of this type to study capital accumulation in a model with a tax on income from capital and an investment tax credit, in which it is the tax rates themselves that are random.

Blume (1982) and Duffie et al. (1988) contain results on the existence of stationary equilibria for models of the type discussed in this chapter.

References

Abreu, Dilip, David Pearce, and Ennio Stacchetti. 1986. Optimal cartel equilibria with imperfect monitoring. *Journal of Economic Theory* 39:251–269.

Aghion, Philippe, Patrick Bolton, and Bruno Jullien. 1988. Learning through price experimentation by a monopolist facing unknown demand. Unpublished manuscript. Massachusetts Institute of Technology, Cambridge, Mass.

Albrecht, James W., and Bo Axell. 1984. An equilibrium model of search unemployment. *Journal of Political Economy* 92:824–840.

Araujo, Aloisio, and José A. Scheinkman. 1977. Smoothness, comparative dynamics, and the turnpike property. *Econometrica* 45:601–620.

Arrow, Kenneth J. 1951. An extension of the basic theorems of classical welfare economics. In *Proceedings of the Second Berkeley Symposium on Mathematical Statistics and Probability*, ed. J. Neyman. Berkeley: University of California Press, pp. 507–532. Reprinted in Arrow (1983) 2:13–45.

——— 1953. Le rôle des valeurs boursieres pour la répartition la meilleure des risques. *Econometrie*. Paris: Centre National de la Recherche Scientifique, pp. 41–48. Translated as "The role of securities in the optimal allocation of risk bearing." *Review of Economic Studies* 31(1963–64):91–96. Reprinted in Arrow (1983) 2:46–57.

——— 1983. *Collected Papers of Kenneth J. Arrow*. Vol. 2, *General Equilibrium*. Cambridge, Mass.: Harvard University Press.

Arrow, Kenneth J., Samuel Karlin, and Herbert Scarf. 1958. *Studies in the Mathematical Theory of Inventory and Production*. Stanford, Calif.: Stanford University Press.

Arrow, Kenneth J., and Mordecai Kurz. 1970. *Public Investment, the Rate of Return, and Optimal Fiscal Policy*. Baltimore: Johns Hopkins University Press.

Back, Kerry. 1988. Structure of consumption sets and existence of equilibria in infinite-dimensional spaces. *Journal of Mathematical Economics* 17:89–99.

Bartle, Robert G. 1966. *The Elements of Integration*. New York: Wiley.

Beals, Richard, and Tjalling C. Koopmans. 1969. Maximizing stationary utility in a constant technology. *SIAM Journal of Applied Mathematics* 17:1009–15.

Becker, Gary S. 1962. Investment in human capital: a theoretical analysis. *Journal of Political Economy* 70:9–49.

Becker, Robert A. 1985. Capital income taxation and perfect foresight. *Journal of Public Economics* 26:147–167.

Behnke, Heinrich, et al. (eds.). 1974. *Fundamentals of Mathematics,* vol. 3. Cambridge, Mass.: MIT Press.

Bellman, Richard. 1957. *Dynamic Programming*. Princeton, N.J.: Princeton University Press.

Ben-Porath, Yoram. 1967. The production of human capital and the life cycle of earnings. *Journal of Political Economy* 75:352–365.

Benveniste, Lawrence M., and José A. Scheinkman. 1979. On the differentiability of the value function in dynamic models of economics. *Econometrica* 47:727–732.

Berge, Claude. 1963. *Topological Spaces*. New York: Macmillan.

Bertsekas, Dmitri P. 1976. *Dynamic Programming and Stochastic Control*. New York: Academic Press.

Bertsekas, Dmitri P., and Steven E. Shreve. 1978. *Stochastic Optimal Control*. New York: Academic Press.

Bewley, Truman F. 1972. Existence of equilibria in economies with infinitely many commodities. *Journal of Economic Theory* 4:514–540.

Billingsley, Patrick. 1968. *Convergence of Probability Measures*. New York: Wiley.

—— 1979. *Probability and Measure*. New York: Wiley.

Bizer, David, and Kenneth L. Judd. 1989. Taxation and uncertainty. *American Economic Review* 79:331–336.

Blackwell, David. 1965. Discounted dynamic programming. *Annals of Mathematical Statistics* 36:226–235.

Blume, Lawrence. 1982. New techniques for the study of stochastic equilibrium processes. *Journal of Mathematical Economics* 9:61–70.

Blume, Lawrence, David Easley, and Maureen O'Hara. 1982. Characterization of optimal plans for stochastic dynamic programs. *Journal of Economic Theory* 28:221–234.

Boldrin, Michele, and Luigi Montrucchio. 1984. The emergence of dynamic complexities in models of optimization over time: the role of impatience. Unpublished manuscript. University of Rochester, Rochester, N.Y.

—— 1986. On the indeterminacy of capital accumulation paths. *Journal of Economic Theory* 40:26–39.

Border, Kim C. 1985. *Fixed-Point Theorems with Applications to Economics and Game Theory.* Cambridge: Cambridge University Press.

Boyer, Marcel. 1975. An optimal growth model with stationary nonadditive utilities. *Canadian Journal of Economics* 8:216–237.

Breeden, Douglas T. 1979. An intertemporal asset pricing model with stochastic consumption and investment opportunities. *Journal of Financial Economics* 7:265–296.

Breiman, Leo. 1960. The strong law of large numbers for a class of Markov chains. *Annals of Mathematical Statistics* 31:801–803.

—— 1968. *Probability.* Reading, Mass.: Addison-Wesley.

Brock, William A. 1973. Some results on the uniqueness of steady states in multisector models of economic growth when future utilities are discounted. *International Economic Review* 14:535–559.

—— 1982. Asset prices in a production economy. In *The Economics of Information and Uncertainty,* ed. John J. McCall. Chicago: University of Chicago Press, pp. 1–43.

Brock, William A., and Edwin Burmeister. 1976. Regular economies and conditions for uniqueness of steady states in optimal multi-sector economic models. *International Economic Review* 17:105–120.

Brock, William A., and Leonard J. Mirman. 1972. Optimal economic growth and uncertainty: the discounted case. *Journal of Economic Theory* 4:479–513.

—— 1973. Optimal economic growth and uncertainty: the no discounting case. *International Economic Review* 14:497–513.

Brock, William A., Michael Rothschild, and Joseph E. Stiglitz. 1989. Stochastic capital theory. In *Joan Robinson and Modern Economic Theory,* ed. George R. Feiwel. New York: New York University Press, pp. 591–622.

Brock, William A., and José A. Scheinkman. 1976. Global asymptotic stability of optimal control systems with applications to the theory of economic growth. *Journal of Economic Theory* 12:164–190.

Brown, Donald J., and Lucinda M. Lewis. 1981. Myopic economic agents. *Econometrica* 49:359–368.

Burger, Ewald. 1963. *Introduction to the Theory of Games.* Trans. John E. Freund. Englewood Cliffs, N.J.: Prentice-Hall.

Burmeister, Edwin. 1980. *Capital Theory and Dynamics.* Cambridge: Cambridge University Press.

Burmeister, Edwin, and A. Rodney Dobell. 1970. *Mathematical Theories of Economic Growth.* New York: Macmillan.

Caplin, Andrew S. 1985. The variability of aggregate demand with (S, s) inventory policies. *Econometrica* 53:1395–1409.

Cass, David. 1965. Optimum growth in an aggregative model of capital accumulation. *Review of Economic Studies* 32:233–240.

Cass, David, and Karl Shell. 1976. The structure and stability of competitive dynamical systems. *Journal of Economic Theory* 12:31–70.

——— 1983. Do sunspots matter? *Journal of Political Economy* 91:193–227.

Chung, Kai Lai. 1967. *Markov Chains,* Second Edition. New York: Springer-Verlag.

——— 1974. *A Course in Probability Theory,* Second Edition. New York: Academic Press.

Clarke, Frank H., Masako N. Darrough, and John M. Heineke. 1982. Optimal pricing policy in the presence of experience effects. *Journal of Business* 53:51–67.

Coddington, Earl A., and Norman Levinson. 1955. *Theory of Ordinary Differential Equations.* New York: McGraw-Hill.

Coleman, Wilbur John II. 1987. Money, interest, and capital. Doctoral dissertation, University of Chicago, Chicago, Ill.

Cox, John C., Jonathon E. Ingersoll, and Stephen A. Ross. 1985. An intertemporal general equilibrium model of asset prices. *Econometrica* 53:363–384.

Dana, Rose-Anne, and Cuong Le Van. 1988. On the structure of Pareto-optima in an infinite horizon economy where agents have recursive preferences. Unpublished manuscript. University of Paris VI, Paris.

Danthine, Jean-Pierre. 1977. Martingale, market efficiency and commodity prices. *European Economic Review* 10:1–17.

Danthine, Jean-Pierre, and John B. Donaldson. 1981. Stochastic properties of fast vs. slow growing economies. *Econometrica* 49:1007–33.

Debreu, Gerard. 1954. Valuation equilibrium and Pareto optimum. *Proceedings of the National Academy of Sciences* 40:588–592. Reprinted in Debreu (1983), pp. 98–104.

——— 1959. *The Theory of Value.* New Haven, Conn.: Yale University Press.

——— 1983. *Mathematical Economics: Twenty Papers of Gerard Debreu.* Cambridge: Cambridge University Press.

Denardo, Eric V. 1967. Contraction mappings in the theory underlying dynamic programming. *SIAM Review* 9:165–177.

Donaldson, John B., and Rajnish Mehra. 1983. Stochastic growth with correlated production shocks. *Journal of Economic Theory* 29:282–312.

Doob, J. L. 1953. *Stochastic Processes.* New York: Wiley.

Duffie, Darrell, John Geanakoplos, Andreu Mas-Colell, and Andrew McLennan. 1988. Stationary Markov equilibria. Unpublished manuscript. Stanford University, Stanford, Calif.

Dynkin, E. B. 1965. *Markov Processes,* vol. 1. Berlin: Springer-Verlag.

Dynkin, E. B., and A. A. Yushkevich. 1979. *Controlled Markov Processes.* New York: Springer-Verlag.

Easley, David, and Daniel F. Spulber. 1981. Stochastic equilibrium and optimality with rolling plans. *International Economic Review* 22:79–103.

Eisner, Robert, and Robert Strotz. 1963. Determinants of business investment. Commission on Money and Credit. *Impacts of Monetary Policy.* Englewood Cliffs, N.J.: Prentice-Hall.

Ekeland, Ivar, and José A. Scheinkman. 1986. Transversality conditions for some infinite horizon discrete time optimization problems. *Mathematics of Operations Research* 11:216–229.

Epstein, Larry G. 1987. A simple dynamic general equilibrium model. *Journal of Economic Theory* 41:68–95.

Fama, Eugene F. 1965. The behavior of stock market prices. *Journal of Business* 38:34–105.

Feller, William. 1971. *An Introduction to Probability Theory and Its Applications,* vol. 2, Second Edition. New York: Wiley.

Foley, Duncan, and Martin Hellwig. 1975. Asset management with trading uncertainty. *Review of Economic Studies* 42:327–396.

Futia, Carl A. 1982. Invariant distributions and the limiting behavior of Markovian economic models. *Econometrica* 50:377–408.

Gihman, I. I., and A. V. Skorohod. 1974. *The Theory of Stochastic Processes I.* Trans. Samuel Kotz. New York: Springer-Verlag.

——— 1979. *Controlled Stochastic Processes.* Trans. Samuel Kotz. New York: Springer-Verlag.

Gilles, Christian, John M. Marshall, and Jon Sonstelie. 1987. An infinity of Arrow exceptional cases. Unpublished manuscript. University of California, Santa Barbara, Calif.

Gould, John P. 1968. Adjustment costs in the theory of investment of the firm. *Review of Economic Studies* 35:47–55.

Green, Edward J. 1976. An introduction to Markov processes. Unpublished manuscript. Carnegie-Mellon University, Pittsburgh, Penn.

Hall, Robert E. 1978. Stochastic implications of the life cycle-permanent income hypothesis: theory and evidence. *Journal of Political Economy* 86:971–988.

Halmos, Paul R. 1974. *Measure Theory.* New York: Springer-Verlag.

Hansen, Lars P. 1985. Results on existence, convergence, and stability for the quadratic control problem. Unpublished manuscript. University of Chicago, Chicago, Ill.

Hansen, Lars P., and Kenneth J. Singleton. 1983. Stochastic consumption, risk aversion, and the temporal behavior of asset returns. *Journal of Political Economy* 91:249–265.

Harris, Milton. 1987. *Dynamic Economic Analysis.* New York: Oxford University Press.

Hildenbrand, Werner. 1974. *Core and Equilibria of a Large Economy.* Princeton, N.J.: Princeton University Press.

Hirshleifer, Jack. 1966. Investment decision under uncertainty: applications of the state-preference approach. *Quarterly Journal of Economics* 80:252–277.

Hopenhayn, Hugo A., and Edward C. Prescott. 1987. Invariant distributions for monotone Markov processes. Federal Reserve Bank of Minneapolis Working Paper No. 299, Minneapolis, Minn.

Hotelling, Harold. 1931. The economics of exhaustible resources. *Journal of Political Economy* 39:137–175.

Hutson, V., and J. S. Pym. 1980. *Applications of Functional Analysis and Operator Theory.* London: Academic Press.

Iglehart, Donald S. 1963. Optimality of (s, S) policies in the infinite horizon dynamic inventory problem. *Management Science* 9:257–267.

Istratescu, Vasile I. 1981. *Fixed Point Theory: An Introduction.* Dordrecht-Boston: D. Reidel Publishing Corp.

Iwai, Katsuhito. 1972. Optimal economic growth and stationary ordinal utility. *Journal of Economic Theory* 5:121–151.

Jones, Larry E. 1984. A competitive model of commodity differentiation. *Econometrica* 52:507–530.

——— 1986. Special problems arising in the study of economies with infinitely many commodities. In *Models of Economic Dynamics,* ed. Hugo F. Sonnenschein. Berlin: Springer-Verlag, pp. 184–205.

Jones, Larry E., and Rodolfo E. Manuelli. 1987. A model of optimal equilibrium growth. Unpublished manuscript. Northwestern University, Evanston, Ill.

Jorgenson, Dale W. 1963. Capital theory and investment behavior. *American Economic Review* 53:247–259.

Jovanovic, Boyan. 1979. Job matching and the theory of turnover. *Journal of Political Economy* 87:972–990.

Kamien, Morton I., and Nancy L. Schwartz. 1981. *Dynamic Optimization.* New York: North Holland.

Karlin, Samuel. 1955. The structure of dynamic programming models. *Naval Research Logistics Quarterly* 2:285–294.

Kehoe, Timothy J., and David K. Levine. 1985. Comparative statics and perfect foresight. *Econometrica* 53:433–454.

Kemeny, John G., and J. Laurie Snell. 1960. *Finite Markov Chains.* Princeton, N.J.: D. Van Nostrand.

Kemeny, John G., J. Laurie Snell, and Anthony W. Knapp. 1976. *Denumerable Markov Chains,* Second Edition. New York: Springer-Verlag.

Kolmogorov, A. N., and S. V. Fomin. 1970. *Introductory Real Analysis.* Trans. Richard A. Silverman. Englewood Cliffs, N.J.: Prentice-Hall.

Koopmans, Tjalling C. 1960. Stationary ordinal utility and impatience. *Econometrica* 28:287–309.

—— 1965. On the concept of optimal growth. *The Econometric Approach to Development Planning.* Chicago: Rand McNally.

Koopmans, Tjalling C., Peter A. Diamond, and Richard E. Williamson. 1964. Stationary utility and time perspective. *Econometrica* 32:82–100.

Kurz, Mordecai. 1968. The general instability of a class of competitive growth processes. *Review of Economic Studies* 35:155–174.

Kydland, Finn, and Edward C. Prescott. 1982. Time to build and aggregate fluctuations. *Econometrica* 50:1345–70.

Labadie, Pamela. 1984. A test of risk premia behavior in an overlapping generations model. Unpublished manuscript. Columbia University, New York.

Lang, Serge. 1983. *Real Analysis,* Second Edition. Reading, Mass.: Addison-Wesley.

LeRoy, Stephen F. 1973. Risk aversion and the martingale property of stock prices. *International Economic Review* 14:436–446.

Levhari, David, and Nissan Liviatan. 1972. On stability in the saddle-point sense. *Journal of Economic Theory* 4:88–93.

Lippman, Steven A., and John J. McCall. 1976a. The economics of job search: a survey: part I. *Economic Inquiry* 14:155–189.

—— 1976b. The economics of job search: a survey. *Economic Inquiry* 14:347–368.

Loève, Michel. 1977. *Probability Theory I and II,* Fourth Edition. New York: Springer-Verlag.

Long, John B., Jr., and Charles I. Plosser. 1983. Real business cycles. *Journal of Political Economy* 91:39–69.

Lucas, Robert E., Jr. 1967a. Optimal investment policy and the flexible accelerator. *International Economic Review* 8:78–85.

—— 1967b. Adjustment costs and the theory of supply. *Journal of Political Economy* 75:321–334.

—— 1972. Expectations and the neutrality of money. *Journal of Economic Theory* 4:103–124.

———— 1978. Asset prices in an exchange economy. *Econometrica* 46:1429–45.

———— 1980. Equilibrium in a pure currency economy. *Economic Inquiry* 18:203–220.

———— 1988. On the mechanics of economic development. *Journal of Monetary Economics* 22:3–42.

Lucas, Robert E., Jr., and Edward C. Prescott. 1971. Investment under uncertainty. *Econometrica* 39:659–681.

———— 1974. Equilibrium search and unemployment. *Journal of Economic Theory* 7:188–209.

Lucas, Robert E., Jr., and Nancy L. Stokey. 1984. Optimal growth with many consumers. *Journal of Economic Theory* 32:139–171.

———— 1987. Money and interest in a cash-in-advance economy. *Econometrica* 55:491–513.

Luenberger, David G. 1969. *Optimization by Vector Space Methods*. New York: Wiley.

Majumdar, Mukul, and Roy Radner. 1983. Stationary optimal policies with discounting in a stochastic activity analysis model. *Econometrica* 51:1821–37.

Manuelli, Rodolfo E. 1985. A note on the behavior of the solutions to dynamic stochastic models. Unpublished manuscript. Stanford University, Stanford, Calif.

Manuelli, Rodolfo E., and Thomas J. Sargent. 1987. *Exercises in Dynamic Macroeconomic Theory*. Cambridge, Mass.: Harvard University Press.

Mas-Colell, Andreu. 1975. A model of equilibrium with differentiated commodities. *Journal of Mathematical Economics* 2:263–295.

———— 1986a. The price equilibrium existence problem in topological vector lattices. *Econometrica* 54:1039–53.

———— 1986b. Valuation equilibrium and Pareto optimum revisited. In *Contributions to Mathematical Economics,* ed. Werner Hildenbrand and Andreu Mas-Colell. Amsterdam: North-Holland, pp. 317–331.

McCall, John J. 1970. Economics of information and job search. *Quarterly Journal of Economics* 84:113–126.

McCallum, Bennett T. 1989. Real business cycle models. In *Modern Business Cycle Theory,* ed. Robert J. Barro. Cambridge, Mass.: Harvard University Press, pp. 16–50.

McKenzie, Lionel W. 1987. Turnpike theory. In *The New Palgrave: A Dictionary of Economics,* Vol. 4. ed. John Eatwell, Murray Milgate, and Peter Newman. New York: Stockton Press, pp. 712–720.

Mehra, Rajnish, and Edward C. Prescott. 1985. The equity premium: a puzzle. *Journal of Monetary Economics* 15:145–162.

Milnor, John W. 1965. *Topology from the Differentiable Viewpoint*. Charlottesville: University Press of Virginia.

Mirman, Leonard J., and Itzhak Zilcha. 1975. On optimal growth under uncertainty. *Journal of Economic Theory* 11:329–339.

Modigliani, Franco, and Merton H. Miller. 1958. The cost of capital, corporation finance and the theory of investment. *American Economic Review* 48:261–297.

Mortensen, Dale T. 1970. A theory of wage and employment dynamics. In Edmund S. Phelps et al. *Microeconomic Foundations of Employment and Inflation Theory*. New York: Norton, pp. 167–211.

―――― 1973. Generalized costs of adjustment and dynamic factor demand theory. *Econometrica* 41:657–665.

Muller, Walter J., and Michael Woodford. 1988. Determinacy of equilibrium in stationary economies. *Journal of Economic Theory* 46:255–290.

Muth, John F. 1961. Rational expectations and the theory of price movements. *Econometrica* 29:315–335.

Neveu, Jacques. 1965. *Mathematical Foundations of the Calculus of Probability*. Trans. Amiel Feinstein. San Francisco: Holden-Day.

Onicescu, Octav. 1969. *Calcolo delle Probabilitá ed Applicazioni*. Rome: Veschi Editori.

Peleg, Bezalel, and Harl E. Ryder. 1972. On optimal consumption plans in a multi-sector economy. *Review of Economic Studies* 39:159–170.

Pontryagin, L. S. 1962. *Ordinary Differential Equations*. Trans. Leonas Kacinskas and Walter B. Counts. Reading, Mass.: Addison-Wesley.

Pontryagin, L. S., et al. 1962. *The Mathematical Theory of Optimal Processes*. Trans. K. N. Trirogoff; ed. L. W. Neustadt. New York: Wiley-Interscience.

Prescott, Edward C. 1975. Notes on dynamic programming with unbounded loss. Unpublished manuscript. Carnegie-Mellon University, Pittsburgh, Penn.

Prescott, Edward C., and Robert E. Lucas, Jr. 1972. Price systems in infinite dimensional space. *International Economic Review* 13:416–422.

Prescott, Edward C., and Rajnish Mehra. 1980. Recursive competitive equilibrium: the case of homogeneous households. *Econometrica* 48:1365–79.

Prescott, Edward C., and José V. Rios-Rull. 1988. Classical competitive analysis in a growth economy with search. Federal Reserve Bank of Minneapolis Working Paper 329, Minneapolis, Minn.

Radner, Roy. 1961. Paths of economic growth that are optimal with regard only to final states. *Review of Economic Studies* 28:98–104.

—— 1972. Existence of equilibrium of plans, prices, and price expectations in a sequence of markets. *Econometrica* 40:289–303.

Ramsey, Frank P. 1928. A mathematical theory of saving. *Economic Journal* 38:543–559.

Razin, Assaf, and Joseph A. Yahav. 1979. On stochastic models of economic growth. *International Economic Review* 20:599–604.

Rebelo, Sergio. 1987. Long run policy analysis and long run growth. Unpublished manuscript. University of Rochester, Rochester, N.Y.

Rockafellar, R. Tyrrell. 1970. *Convex Analysis*. Princeton, N.J.: Princeton University Press.

—— 1976. Saddle points of Hamiltonian systems in convex Lagrange problems having a nonzero discount rate. *Journal of Economic Theory* 12:71–113.

Rosen, Sherwin. 1976. A theory of life earnings. *Journal of Political Economy* 84:545–567.

Rosenblatt, Murray. 1971. *Markov Processes: Structure and Asymptotic Behavior*. New York: Springer-Verlag.

Royden, H. L. 1968. *Real Analysis*. New York: Macmillan.

Samuelson, Paul A. 1965. Proof that properly anticipated prices fluctuate randomly. *Industrial Management Review* 6:41–49.

Sargent, Thomas J. 1979. *Macroeconomic Theory*. New York: Academic Press.

—— 1980. "Tobin's q" and the rate of investment in general equilibrium. *Carnegie-Rochester Conference Series on Public Policy* 12:107–154.

—— 1987. *Dynamic Macroeconomic Theory*. Cambridge, Mass.: Harvard University Press.

Scarf, Herbert E. 1959. The optimality of (S, s) policies in the dynamic inventory problem. In *Mathematical methods in the Social Sciences*, ed. K. J. Arrow, S. Karlin, and P. Suppes. Stanford, Calif.: Stanford University Press.

Scheinkman, José A. 1973. On optimal steady states of n-sector growth models when utility is discounted. Doctoral dissertation, University of Rochester, Rochester, N.Y.

—— 1976. On optimal steady states of n-sector growth models when utility is discounted. *Journal of Economic Theory* 12:11–30.

Scheinkman, José A., and Jack Schechtman. 1983. A simple competitive model with production and storage. *Review of Economic Studies* 50:427–441.

Shiryayev, A. N. 1984. *Probability*. Trans. R. P. Boas. New York: Springer-Verlag.

Solow, Robert M. 1956. A contribution to the theory of economic growth. *Quarterly Journal of Economics* 70:65–94.

Song, Byung Ho. 1986. Dynamic programming with constant-returns-to-scale return functions. Unpublished manuscript. University of Chicago, Chicago, Ill.

Stigler, George J. 1961. The economics of information. *Journal of Political Economy* 69:213–225.

Stokey, Nancy L. 1986. The dynamics of industrywide learning. In *Equilibrium Analysis: Essays in Honor of Kenneth J. Arrow*, vol. 2, ed. Walter P. Heller, Ross M. Starr, and David Starrett. Cambridge: Cambridge University Press, pp. 81–104.

Strauch, Ralph E. 1966. Negative dynamic programming. *Annals of Mathematical Statistics* 37:871–890.

Sutherland, W. R. S. 1970. On optimal development in a multi-sectorial economy. *Review of Economic Studies* 37:585–589.

Swan, Trevor W. 1956. Economic growth and capital accumulation. *Economic Record* 32:334–361.

Taub, Bart. 1988a. Efficiency in a pure currency economy with inflation. *Economic Inquiry* 26:567–583.

—— 1988b. The equivalence of optimal lending and monetary equilibria under asymmetric information. Unpublished manuscript. Virginia Polytechnic Institute, Blacksburg, Va.

Torres, Ricard. 1988. Stochastic dominance ordering in metric spaces. Unpublished manuscript. Northwestern University, Evanston, Ill.

Treadway, Arthur B. 1969. On rational entrepreneurial behavior and the demand for investment. *Review of Economic Studies* 36:227–239.

Tweedie, Richard L. 1975. Sufficient conditions for ergodicity and recurrence of Markov chains in a general state space. *Stochastic Processes and Their Applications* 3:385–403.

Uzawa, Hirofumi. 1964. Optimal growth in a two-sector model of capital accumulation. *Review of Economic Studies* 31:1–25.

—— 1965. Optimum technical change in an aggregative model of economic growth. *International Economic Review* 6:18–31.

—— 1968. Time preference, the consumption function, and optimum asset holdings. In *Value, Capital, and Growth: Papers in Honour of Sir John Hicks*, ed. J. N. Wolfe. Chicago: Aldine.

Weitzman, Martin. 1973. Duality theory for infinite horizon convex models. *Management Science* 19:783–789.

Yosida, Kosaku, and Edwin Hewitt. 1952. Finitely additive measures. *Transactions of the American Mathematical Society* 72:46–66.

Zeidler, Eberhard. 1986. *Nonlinear Functional Analysis and Its Applications.* New York: Springer-Verlag.

Index of Theorems

General Index